Extracts From Quarterly Letters [of Wesleyan Methodist Missionaries At Colombo].

Wesleyan Methodist missionary society

erection of the School House. So that I hope, by the end of the next quarter, I shall be able to inform my Brethren, that those Schools are in a very forward state. I hope soon to receive the supply of Books &c. which I wrote for a few days since.

I remain, my dear Brethren,
very affectionately yours,
JOHN McKENNY.

MATURA AND BELLIGAM STATION.
Midigam, September 29th, 1817.

My dear Brethren,

IN conformity to the Resolution of our late meeting, I now proceed to give a statement of a few matters connected with this station; but I am sorry that I can only spare about a quarter of an hour to set down the principal transactions of a quarter of a year. The circumstance of being frequently from home, and my other multiplied engagements, in addition, being unwell, I beg to mention as my present apology.

Through mercy we, in some degree, feel our ground, and are assured that we do not labour in vain. Those who have cast in their lot with us, and are desirous of adorning the doctrine of God our Saviour, give us much satisfaction, by continuing to walk by the same rule. Many, it should be recollected, were professed heathens before our arrival, but they have abandoned their ceremonies, temples, offerings, and idols! And though a great number manifest much indifference about divine things, we have to rejoice over several who hear the word with attention, and who, we believe have received divine impressions.

On Sundays I preach in the morning in the Fort Church. After service, Br. Lalmon visits the Jail and converses, exhorts, prays, or preaches among the prisoners, as occasion requires. At five in the evening, we have the children of our neighbouring Schools assembled in our virandah, where they have portions of Scripture read, and a Sermon preached. In future we intend catechising the most attentive boys. In the week we have one discourse in Portuguese, delivered alternately by Br. L. and myself, and one on another evening in Cingalese. Too Class-meetings are also held for the people who speak these two languags. The Cingalese class attends so regularly, and is now so large, that I believe it will be necessary, ere long, to divide it into two.

The present is rather an unfavourable part of the year for our Schools. Many of the children, are gone for a time into the country. It gives me pleasure, however, to notice the progress of many. For some time they suffered much inconvenience for want of suitable books in the native language, but this evil is now in some measure remedied.

This day we have employed in the formation of a new School. We had a congregation of several hundred men, women, and children; and, with the exception of a few individuals, *all heathens!*—47 girls, and 79 boys, were presented, by their relations, and

B

had their names set down immediately, to be instructed in reading, writing, and in the principles of Christianity.

I have arranged a plan, by which I hope to bestow much more attention to the Cingalese language than before. I have been long solicited to give some of the celebrated heathen writings an attentive perusal:—I do not intend passing them over altogether; but, at present, as I do not understand them, and having great difficulty to get them explained, I believe the New Translation of the Testament will render me the more essential Service.

Br Lahmon joins me in kind love to you and all the Brethren.

I remain,

Very affectionately, yours,

J. CALLAWAY.

NEGOMBO STATION.

October 16th, 1817.

Very Dear Brethren,

YOU will of course, expect but very limited, and that but imperfect, information from this station; seeing that it is quite new, and so, for the present, necessarily irregular, and also from the very short time I have been here. With regard to the School statement, I have only one in existence, but many embryo. When they are established, I will gladly give you any early intelligence: till then, it is only necessary to say that, if I can possibly find masters, and time to superintend them, I hope to have the one multiplied by ten.

At present my hands are fully occupied, being obliged to compose and write so much in Portuguese, and to attend much to the repairs and alterations on the premises. These two things, will I hope be done away together; and then, with much more delight and ability, I shall attend to the Schools, and the Cingalese language, to which you will easily conceive I could not yet have given any proper application. Such is the extreme prevalence of ignorance and superstition in this place that the prospects of success in winning souls would be by no means encouraging did we only look at this: but, notwithstanding, by depending upon God—by a degree of Faith—and by earnest Prayer, my mind is more than supported—it is animated—it is encouraged—and I do look for success in the glorious work of the Lord: because it is his work, and especially I look for this among the rising Generation. I have in contemplation, if I can effect it, several little exercices which may be useful, especially to them. I have preached hitherto three times on the Sabbath, in the three different languagess, and twice in the week. In future, one of the Sermons, (the Cingalese) will be in one of the Native Churches, near the Town, for the greater accommodation of the people. I am thankful to be enabled now to pray extempore in the Portuguese language, in the Family, only, as most of them understand this better than English. And I can also pretty well succeed in writing my Sermons in that language. I believe that God is with us. I am sometimes exceedingly blest in the exercise of Family prayer, in which I sometimes have a little

Congregation, with the workmen, coolies &c. and get an Interpreter when I can. On the whole, I have abundant cause for ceaseless gratitude to God, when, I view his mercy and goodness in bringing me across the mighty Ocean, and in conducting me, under every pleasing and providential circumstance, to the very scene of my labour in this Island; where I am surrounded with every temporal and spiritual blessing. It furnishes at once a strong motive for gratitude and exertion; and the present feeling of my heart, allow me to say, is, that by His grace I will se all my powers to his glory.

With my affectionate love to you all,
I remain, Dear Brethren, faithfully yours,
in the bonds of the Gospel.
ROBERT NEWSTEAD.

JAFFNA STATION.

October 7th, 1817.

My dear Brethren,

As I am very unwilling that we, who are in this part of the Island, should appear to disregard our discipline, I take up my pen (though after the appointed time) to write you. On the day that I should have written, I was on my journey from the Conference; and since my arrival circumstances have rendered it impossible for me to write sooner.

Our little Society is much the same as when I left. There is a good work upon many; and that which God has begun, he is deepening and widening. At our Class-Meeting the power of Divine Mercy is always felt. We never meet without sensibly feeling that God is with us.

At our English preaching, the Congregations, are but small. I have not resumed the Portuguese preaching, but intend to re-commence on Thursday Evening.

Br. Carver began to meet a few boys, Dutch, and Half-casts, on Wednesday last, and will continue to meet them every Wednesday Evening, for the purpose of instructing them in the knowledge of the Scriptures. They are fine boys, and regular in their attendunce, at our preaching, prayermeeting, and Sunday school; and I have no doubt that some of them will turn out well; though I think it best to say but little of them now, as our expectations have been so often blasted, &c.

Yours affectionately,
T. H. SQUANCE.

POINT PEDRO STATION.

No Communication from hence.

TRINCOMALEE STATION.

No Communication from hence.

MADRAS STATION.

No Communication from hence.

BOMBAY STATION.

Extract of a Letter to Brother Harvard.

"————I suppose that by the time you receive this, your Conference at Colombo will have been held: gladly would I have been there, if all circumstances had admitted of it; but the setting in of the rainy season necessarily confines me on my own station: however, I hope soon have some account of your proceedings.

I assure you, my dear Brother, it is from *a certain prospect, of eventual success,* that I derive at present, a great part of my satisfaction in the work of a Missionary. Were there room for only a suspicion that the preaching of the Gospel might be attended by no good effects, I should be half inclined to regret the blessed advantages, of a religious nature, which are so abundantly enjoyed in England; but, I thank God, I have no such suspicions nor regrets! the honour, as well as the love, of God is engaged to accomplish all his gracious promises, in behalf of the heathen nations of the world; and surely, if we are so honoured as to be employed in dispensing the word of salvation, we may safely leave the event of it to him whose word it is; not overvaluing any sacrifice, however costly, so we become workers together with God in building the New Jerusalem, which stands founded upon Christ, the Rock of ages.

I succeed as well as I had expected, for the time, being alone. I have great reason to be thankful for my advancement in learning the language, so much so as to converse with tolerable freedom in it. Have several times communicated with a few of the Hindoos, though not publickly, and find in them, in general, a strong attachment to their own creeds and forms of worship, and yet a deal of curiosity respecting ours; this latter I consider a good sign If they will but listen to us, and much more if they ask us questions, there is hope of their receiving good. I should have long before now preached to the people through an interpreter, but on my coming here and making enquiry among those who were best acquainted with the subject, I found it would be almost an impossiblity to meet with a person qualified to act in that capacity; and the expence of employing him would, according to the general rates of salaries in Bombay, be very heavy: under these impressions, therefore, I concluded that my duty would be to follow just the plan which I have adopted.

Am glad that you have begun to print something in the way of a periodical Missionary Correspondence, I have no doubt of its turning to advantage; whatever I can contribute from this quarter, shall be gladly given.————   I am, my dear Brother,

Yours, in the Gospel of Christ,
JOHN HORNER.

MISCELLANEOUS INTELLIGENCE.

1.

From " the Missionary Notices," for April, 1817.

AFRICA.

Letter from Rev. B. Shaw to the Committee, dated November 14, 1816.

Rev. and dear Sirs,

You have already had an account of my departure from Cape Town, and a few extracts from my journals towards this place. Since then I have written my father, some part of which, viz. the extracts, &c. will speedily be sent to the Committee. My remaining upon the Khamies mountain, among this people, is doubtless of the Lord, as I had not the most distant idea of it, when we began our journey. I think I mentioned in my last, that on our arrival at the Namacqua kraal, brother Schmellen preached from the words of the Apostle, " *This is a faithful saying,*" &c. when all were still as night, and some wept aloud. After service, we c:i'ed for the captain and his people, to ask some questions relative to ~ ipettling among them. Before our conversation begun, prayer was offered to the Lord for his assistance and direction; when the captain fell with his face to the ground sighing and weeping in such a manner, that we were constrained to wait a considerable time, after prayer, before we could begin our conversation. When he arose, his people surrounded him on every side, and the following questions were proposed, with the answers which were given.

Q. 1. (To the Captain.) What is your name? Ans. Haimoep is my, Namacqua name, and Jan. Wildschot my Holland's name.

Q. 2. Why did you not receive a teacher when one was before offered to you? A. Some had not a desire, and were against it, but now we have a greater desire to hear the word of God.

Q. 3. Have you a suitable place where a Missionary can settle, good gardenland, and plenty of water? A. Yes. We have good land, and many fountains.

Q. 4. Will you give a portion of land to your teacher, or to the Society to which he belongs, that he may have a garden, and sow corn for his own use? All of them answered, Yes. He may have land where he pleases.

Q. 5. Will you allow him to keep oxen for the yoke, and cows, sheep, or goats for his own use? A. Yes, as many as he pleases.

Q. 6. Should a Missionary remain with you, will you ever forsake him? A. No; never.

Q. 7. Will you keep your people in good order, not suffering disturbances; and punish those who will not live in peace? A. I shall forbid all disturbances.

Q. 8. Will you erect a chapel, or place wherein you may keep divine service, at your own expence? A. Yes: we will do so.

Q. 9. Will you assist the Missionary to build a house, wherein to dwell, and any other work which he may have to do? A. Yes; we will all assist him: and we have three houses built of stone and clay, any one of which he may dwell in, till the other is completed.

October 15, 1816.   Jan. Wildschot.

On the evening of the 16th. brother Schmellen took his departure from us, in hopes of reaching the place of his abode, in four or five weeks. We felt exceedingly sorry on being separated from so worthy a man; a man, I suppose, as well calculated for missionary work, as any one on the continent of Africa. O, how sweet is the word of God, in times of trial. Here we are left solitary, and our earthly friends afar off; while heathens surround us, speaking a language that we can scarcely under-

c

stand; yet that promise stands immoveable and sure, "*I will never leave thee, nor forsake thee.*"

The people with whom we now reside, have two places of abode; the one on the top of Khamies mountain, and the other at the bottom. As they are now about to remove to their summer's seat, we began our journey thither on the 20th, but did not arrive at the end thereof before the 23d. There is one way much nearer, but no waggon can go upon it: indeed we found it exceedingly difficult to climb the mountain with 14 oxen drawing together, the way on which we travelled. While going up the most steep part of the mountain, the rain began to descend in abundance, so that before we could reach a boor's place, we were both wet and cold. The family at the place where we halted, and remained a night, were as cold within, towards us, as we were without.

23d. About 3 P. M. we set out for the Hottentots' abode; and after having climbed one mountain after another, for about three hours, we reached it. Having made choice of one of the three houses, our waggon was brought up to it, and the oxen loosed to rest and recover their strength. In our house there is no chimney, no window, nor have we any door, save one that I have made of a few sticks and a little sacking. We have no chair, or stool, or bedstead; but when weary, we find no inconvenience in resting upon the ground. I have chosen a place where we intend to build a house, and a piece of land for a garden; so that in a few months we hope to make considerable progress in our work.

27th, Sunday, Endeavoured to preach to the people, Jesus and the resurrection, most of which they understood.

Nov. 2. During the week that is past, I have been engaged in digging in the ground, and sowing different sorts of garden seeds, believing that the Lord will bless us in our labour, and cause the earth to yield us its increase. The 3d, being the Sabbath of the Lord, after having spoken to the people from a portion of Scripture, I proceeded to ask them several questions; some of which they were able to answer, but others they said were *al te sware*, too difficult. 4th. This evening, after the labour of the day, I read the account given of the woman of Samaria; and spoke somewhat of the living waters, which are equally as free for Hottentots as for Europeans. The Lord, I believe, owned his word, by giving them to understand, and to feel its power. While engaged in prayer before the conclusion, some, I had reason to believe, were "groaning the sinner's only plea, God be merciful to me."

As the people returned to their houses, the few lines, or sentences of those hymns they could remember, were the subject of their song: and long after we had laid down to rest in our little hut, we heard them raising their voices on high. Previous to our service, I did not remember that it was the first Monday evening in the month; but, on seeing so peculiar an influence in our meeting, I began to recollect that our friends in England were pleading in our behalf. 5th. Last night we had much wind and rain, and this morning the poor Hottentots appeared half-starved to death. Before the evening, we had snow and hail in abundance, and the two following days were equally cold. It is said by a traveller of great respectability, that the huts of the Namacquas differ very materially from those erected by other Hottentots; or by the Bosjemans, or by the Kafters. They are perfect hemispheres, covered with matting made of sedges; and the frame work, or skeletons, are semicircular sticks, half of them diminishing from the centre, or upper part, and the other half crossing these at right angles; forming out a true representation of the parallels of latitude, and meridians on an artificial globe.

I have begun to dig a foundation, in order to build a house. When that is completed, we shall lose no time in beginning of the chapel. I am under the necessity of labouring, like the Apostle, with my own hands: for though the Hottentots are willing to work, yet they are generally so weak and so ignorant, respecting any kind of business, that if some one is not with them to give them instruction, they are good for little or nothing. I hope you will send me the Magazines, Missionary Register, Minutes of Conference, and Missionary Notices, that I may have them when I come to the Cape. The greatest disadvantage to our erecting a house, chapel, &c. is the want of wood. There is wood to be obtained about a day's journey from hence, but it is unfit for building; so that, before we can erect a chapel, we shall be under the necessity of making a journey, with two waggons, to the great or Prang river, which is about 12 days from this place. Two of the twelve oxen that I purchased in Cape Town, were left behind, the one died, and the other could travel no further. On account of the heavy sand, and difficult road, I was forced to purchase ten more, which makes the number under my care to be 20.   Yours, &c.

B. SHAW,

*** The Number of the Notices from which the above was extracted, was obligingly enclosed in a letter from the Rev. Joseph Cusworth, of the Rochester Circuit, to Br. Harvard,—in which he observes:—"I believe most of the other circuits in this District are doing well; and I hear from the north of England, there is a good work.—They have had a very great revival in the London West Circuit; and, upon the whole, God is graciously carrying on his good work in the whole Connexion.—I have sent you the April Notices, as it contains a very interesting document from Br. Shaw, in the Interior of South Africa.—I suppose 400 miles from the Cape.—Mr. Brown is gone to St Domingo.—We have had a very pressing invitation from the Governor of the Isle of France, for two Missionaries for the Island of *Madagascar*.—O, what is God doing!————"

2.

From the Rev. W. JENKINS, London, to Brother Harvard.

May 14, 1817.

HAVING a friend just about to embark for Ceylon, I cannot deny myself the pleasure of writing a line by his favour.

Your letters, and those of your Colleagues, I often heard and read, with great pleasure and thankfulness to God, for his great goodness in opening a wide and effectual door for you, to preach the unsearchable riches of Christ, to the heathen in Ceylon, and the Continent of India; and I pray that he may bless your labours more and more, until   "The earth is o'erflowed,
                        And the universe fill'd with the glory of God."

I am much pleased with your plan of Schools; and you will have heard, ere this, that we have voted you £300 per annum, to support them.

We held the Annual Missionary Meeting, for the London District, the week before last; and had several blessed opportunities, in the Preachings and two Public Meetings. During the Anniversary, the Collections amounted (bad as trade is) to near £600.—So mightily does the Lord influence the minds of the people, to promote his blessed cause!

The last and present week, we have had the annual Meetings, of the British and Foreign Bible Society, and also of the British and Foreign School Society—the Church Missionary Society, and the London Missionary Society, and of several other Institutions for spreading Divine Truth; all of which are encreasing and prospering in a surprising manner. So does the Lord condescend to make use of England, notwithstanding her many sins, to spread the knowledge of his name, and savour of his grace, all over the world.

The work of the Lord is still encreasing, among us, though but slowly. We are now erecting a very large Chapel, in Queen Street, which will be opened in July, or August, and another, at Oxford, which will be opened about Christmas: the second in Bath was opened last Summer, and succeeds well. Blessed be the Lord, for all his mercies! The first Methodist Chapel built in France is nearly ready for opening, and another in contemplation. What is too hard for God!

My kind love to your wife and Colleagues. And be assured that I am; &c. &c. &c.

W. JENKINS.

END OF OCTOBER EXTRACTS, &c.

₊ The Brethren are requested to forward to Colombo extracts of such of their Europe or other Letters, as may contain Information of general interest.

Printed at the Mission-Press, Colombo, for the Use of the Missionaries.

THE CASE OF PETRUS.

Mission House, Colombo, May 28, 1817.

ON Wednesday morning, the 14th inst. we, the undersigned, embraced an opportunity of stating to Petrus, the wishes of our Society in England relative to his joining more fully with us; and receiving his appointment at the hands of our Mission. At first, Petrus seemed reluctant to such a measure, urging that the Governor and Mr. Twisleton would look upon him as an unfaithful man, after all their kindnesses to him, were he so to unite with our Mission.—We reminded him of the claims which his conversion from heathenism gave us upon him; and assured him that if he were disposed to accept of our proposal, we were confident, his present Friends would give him up to us, most cheerfully. To which he replied, if they would, he should be most happy to come among us; and Br. Harvard told him he would write to Mr. Twisleton on the subject. We parted with Petrus desiring him to think seriously of our proposal, and to beg direction of God.

On the next morning (the 15th) Br. Clough received the following communication from the Hon. and Revd. T. J. Twisleton.

MY DEAR SIR,

Petrus Panditta came to me this morning, and asked me whether it was my wish that he should become a Missionary under the Wesleyans. My answer was that I had no wish of the sort: but I recommended him to act as he felt: he then decidedly told me that he wished to remain as he now is.

A

If you are in want of Native Missionaries, I wish you would take the two Abraham Peraras, recommended by yourself and Mr. Armour: for I am not very anxious to appoint Preachers on the part of Government, who cannot converse with me in English.

Yours faithfully,

15th May. T. J. Twisleton.

To which he returned the following answer, Br. Harvard being from home:

Hon. and Revd. Sir,

I am surprised you have not had a letter from Mr. Harvard on the subject of Petrus, as I know he wrote at some length this Morning.

It is far from our wish that Petrus should do any thing contrary to his most private feelings; and this I think Mr. Harvard's letter will fully explain.

I have the pleasure to remain, &c.

B. Clough.

In consequence of which he received as follows:

My Dear Sir,

As Petrus has personally informed me that he wishes to remain as he is, I think it would be useless for Mr. Harvard to address me on the subject; and I hope you will take Abraham Perara off our hands.

Your's Sincerely.

15th T. J. Twisleton.

In the afternoon Br. Harvard forwarded to Mr. Twisleton the following letter.

Mission House, May 15, 1817.

Hon. and Rev. Sir,

Having received by our newly arrived Brethren a verbal communication from our Committee respecting our Friend Petrus Panditta, in reference to our aproaching Conference, we yesterday opened the case to Petrus, and stated to him the expectation of our Society that he is at present engaged in the service of their Mission, as well receiving his support from our Funds, as labouring under our directions.

. At

At the Conference last year, you were so kind as bring us a message from His Excellency, requesting that we would appoint Petrus to one of our country stations, under the superintendance of one of our Brethren. And though from tenderness to the feelings of the late excellent Mr. Tolfrey, we did not wish to remove him from the Translation of the Cingalese New Testament, yet we forwarded to our Society in England information of the Governor's obliging desire; and contemplated taking him more fully among us, when that important work should be completed.

It is not necessary for me to recount the steps by which our Friend Petrus was converted from heathenism, introduced to the Government, and taken under its generous protection; you are so well acquainted with them; and the kindness of Government in allowing him the pay of a Native Preacher, while engaged in the work of the Translation, though it was done without any communication with our Mission, (and at a time when in fact we were in treaty with him to take a country station with one of our Brethren, on his own application, to which he had consented with thankfulness,) yet we felt the generosity which produced his appointment too strongly to intimate any apprehensions that such a circumstance would detach him from our Mission. We have ever indentified the object of the Bible Society with that of our own Mission; and this has regulated us in all our proceedings in relation to it.

But as we are happily advanced I trust to the eve of the accomplishment of the Translation; and having been so well furnished with the wishes of our Society in England on this point, we beg to express that it is our wish likewise, (should it not interfere with the views of Government,) to receive him into a closer connexion with ourselves, to relieve the Government from the pecuniary supply they have hitherto so liberally favoured him with, and to attach him to another sphere of labour, in a country station, with one of the Brethren of our Mission, with a view to his greater improvement in the knowledge of Christianity, and to introduce him more intimately into our itinerant method of labouring among his countrymen.

Trusting that such a measure, when properly submitted to you, would meet with your fullest concurrence, as well as that of his Excellency the Governor, (in case it were not to encounter some previous arrangement unknown to us;) we thought it our first business, as I have already observed, to ascertain the mind of Petrus himself, which we carefully endeavoured to do yesterday morning.

Petrus, we are happy to find possesses a strong sense of honour, and a powerful feeling of gratitude: and as he has been given to understand, by some persons, that his receiving the generous allowance from Government,

ment, has attached him to a cause distinct from our Mission, he fears that were he to comply with our desire, it would appear a breach of faith with the Government, and subject him to the disapprobation of the Governor and yourself.

It is due to Petrus, as well as to the generosities of his Excellency and yourself, to avow that he entertains the highest sense of gratitude to the Government and yourself, who have supported him from the commencement of his Christian life until now. He looks upon you as the friends who have disinterestedly kept him from want, shielded him from reproach, and preserved him from the malicious attempts of those who on hearing of his conversion even had the baseness to imagine his destruction: and I believe he would on no account embark in any cause, without the full and complete concurrence and approbation of the Governor and yourself. But I believe with such concurrence, he would esteem it a priviledge to comply with our desire. Indeed he has assured Mr. Armour, Mr. Fox, Mr. Clough, and myself, that *on that hinge he will allow the circumstance to turn.*

I feel pleasure in saying that the Communications which our Society have received from Petrus, and especially a copy of his First Sermon, which has been printed in our publications at home, have produced a strong bias in his favour, and a warm interest in his welfare and comfort; and you will easily conceive the unfavourable opinion which our leading characters and Friends in general would be induced to form, either of him or us, if we, who are on the spot, were to manifest a less degree of interest in the welfare of our worthy convert than themselves, to whom he is personally unknown.

It appears therefore to devolve upon us, to lay a candid statement of the case before you, and to request you will have the goodness to communicate it to His Excellency, with our humble and ardent request, united to the anxious wishes of our Connexion in Great Britain and Ireland, in whose hearts this mission is so peculiarly cherished, that (should it not interfere as I have already observed) that our Friend Petrus may be fully made acquainted with your wishes on this subject; and that should he be permitted to unite with us as a member of our Mission, he may still be honoured with the approbation and confidence of his present generous and Christian Friends.

I would not have troubled you and His Excellency the Governor with so long a Communication on the subject, but I am so fully aware that it is a delicate and difficult circumstance. It is so natural that you and Petrus's other honourable Friends, who have so steadily patronised him from the begining, should feel a strong attachment to him;—that a

sen

sense of his acquirments in literature, as well of his personal integrity—should induce you to wish that he would continue to ornament the character of a Government Preacher——I repeat, its so natural, that I could easily excuse, if not justify, an unwillingness on your part, to give him up to our Mission entirely——But this fact would only tend to encrease *our* desire.—For if the *Friends* feel an attachment so strong, what must be felt by the *Parents?*—And it is well known to you, Dear Sir, that Petrus Panditta is *the Child* of our Mission—I may say indeed, our First born!

It is a satisfaction to us, therefore, that this feeling of attachment is so mutual; because it will enable us to judge of the circumstances under which we are mutually propossessed in his favour, and will likewise, in *your* estimation, *"easily excuse if not justify"* our earnest wish to incorporate him more fully with ourselves.

Were we desirous of attaching him to a cause *in opposition* to the one in which he now feels himself enrolled, we should justly be ashamed to prefer our request; but labouring *in unison* in the same blessed work,—as we have ever continued to do,—we trust that we submit our wish to you with the utmost candour and uprightness; and hope, should it be complied with, it may tend to the more abundant acceleration of the great common object we all have in view.

Our only motive, as well as of our Society in England, is to follow up his conversion from heathenism, with all those instructions which would be helpful to his own final salvation, and to endeavour to give him all those views of vital piety, which would tend to encrease his usefulness among his countrymen, and make him our *"crown of rejoicing in the day of the Lord Jesus."*

We, however, would not press the subject, should it not meet with the fullest and most unreserved approbation of our honoured Governor and yourself, whom I hope we shall ever be allowed to claim as the Friends of our Mission, and whom we should be sorry to displease, in the least degree.

With our united best respects, I remain,

> Honble and Revd. Sir,
> Yours very sincerely,
> W. M. Harvard.

The next morning (the 16th) the following was received in consequence from Mr. Twisleton.

My Dear Sir,

According to your wish I had forwarded your letter to Mr. Bisset to be laid before the Governor; but as I forwarded, at

B   the

the same time the declaration of Petrus, Mr. Bisset suggests (as you will see by his enclosed letter) that it would be better for you first to see the said declaration.— You will also see some forcible observations of Mr. Bisset; and I cannot help thinking that as Government would neither turn out Petrus nor attempt to influence him, it will be unnecessary to trouble the Governor on the subject.

I am very faithfully yours.

T. J. Twisleton.

Be so good as to send back Mr. Bisset's observations as soon as possible, as the letter contains matters on other subjects.

Petrus' Statement &c. were likewise enclosed.

Copy of a letter to Petrus Panditta Sekara from Mr. Twisleton, accompanied with a copy of the Translation of Petrus' answer.

Colombo, May 14th, 1817.

To Petrus Panditta Sekera :—

As the Wesleyan Missionaries wish you to belong to their Mission, and as they seem to claim you as their Child, you are requested to write underneath, your own Sentiments and Feelings in your own Language. But I first most sincerely assure you that I am neither desirous of losing you, nor desirous of retaining you, nor will your decision to join the Mission, lower you, in the smallest degree in my Opinion; nor do I think it would, in the Opinion of the Governor.—I recommend you to act as you feel.

(Signed)   T. J. Twisleton.

The Letter of Mr. Harvard to the Honble and Revd. Mr. Twisleton has been explained to me. Following is my answer about the same.— I am by no means inclined to alter my present Situation.

The Situation wherein I am now employed by Government is a most convenient and a fit one for me, that I may preach to the World and for my own spiritual benefit. If I leave this, I will be considered by the world as a variable man, who had no fixed resolution for my changing my first Religion, and now this happy situation. Though I have learnt the Value of Christianity

from

from the Missionaries, there were many Obstacles that made me too feeble to form an Idea as to change the Religion I held.— Let me never be separated from the shadow of that Senior Chaplain who cleared me from those Obstacless and led me to Christianity, and protected me from the Dangers that were about to come upon me, and was instrumental to my present and next world's happiness. He has greater claims on me.— Tho' I cannot agree to alter my present Situation. I am always happy to remain a Friend to the Missionaries by performing what they bid me.

(Signed) P. Panditta Sekera.

An extract from the Rev. Mr. Bisset's letter enclosed.

Extract of a Letter from the Revd. G. Bisset to the Revd. T. J. Twisleton.

"I have just received your packet. It appears to me that Petrus' Answer has not been shewn to Mr. Harvard. Now I think it would be as well that he should see it before the Papers are shewn to the Governor. Surely Mr. Harvard don't mean to claim Petrus as a Wesleyan Missionary, against his will? Petrus seems to me very distinctly to prefer the regular service of Government

I do not pretend to enter into the rights which the Mission had to consider Petrus as their Child.—But they must recollect that Petrus was regularly baptized in the Church of the Fort, that he had rank given him by Government; and that he was finally appointed as regularly a Proponent under this Goverament as you and I were ordained by an English Bishop.

Now all this looks much like a deriletion of any original claim founded upon his first introduction to the consideration of Christianity —Petrus himself attributes his *Conversion* to *you*.—But surely Mr. Harvard will allow him to judge for himself.—I am unwilling to shew the Papers to the Governor, until Mr. Harvard has seen Petrus' reply. lest it should appear that Mr. Harvard presses Petrus against his inclinations, and it will only be so much time saved, as the Governor would of course desire that Mr. Harvard should see it.——Pray get his Answer.

(A Copy)   Your's truly,   G. Bisset."

The next morning (the 17th) Mr. Twisleton wrote as follows:

My Dear Sir,

Be so good as to return to me, Mr. Bisset's private letter which in confidence I lent, and which you are to consider a *dead letter.*

Yours faithfully

T. J. Twisleton.

To which Br. Harvard replied.

Hon. and Revd. Sir.

With much thankfulness I return you Mr. Bisset's letter— and am just now writing you the answer it requests and which shall be forwarded to you in about an hour or so

Believe me, Hon. and Revd. Sir, with much esteem.

Yours very sincerely,

W. M. Harvard.

To which was returned the following reply.

My Dear Sir,

I am sorry you should Contemplate writing to me another letter on the subject of Petrus, For I consider the declaration which he has made as precluding me or the Government from taking any measures in the business.—At all events, I beg not be addressed again on the subject: and if you wish to communicate any thing to Coverment in respect of Petrus, I beg you will do it through the Chief Secretary to Government

Sincerely yours,

T. J. Twisleton.

Br. Harvard then forwarded his second letter, enclosed in the following private note.

Hon and Revd Sir,

Having prepared my letter which seemed to be called for by Mr. Bisset's saying with respect to me *"Get his answer,"* I am sorry to send it you under circumstances which make it appear an intrusion.

My great respect for you would induce me almost to let the

matter

matter drop, did not Mr. Bisset suspend the matter till he has seen my answer.

And, as if the Governor does not get a proper view of the affair, he will have a garbled account, perhaps to our discredit I earnestly beg you will be so kind as let the whole be laid before him, that we may not be liable to any imputation on a future day; and with the assurance that we are so far satisfied with Petrus's own statement, as to forbear any intention of applying for him. or even of receiving him, only as a Friend.

I hope Petrus will ever consider us his Friends—We are so in reality.

Of course it will not be communicated to the Governor in an official form, *as the Government*, since now we make no application, and do not request any interference on the part of Government.—We only wish His Excellency to be satisfied that there has been nothing unbecoming in our application; and to satisfy our Friends at Home that we have not been regardless of their Instructions and wishes.

Hoping that our present measure will not lessen us in your estimation.

I remain, Honorable and Revd. Sir,
yours very sincerely,
W. M. Harvard.

Br. Harvard's Second Letter.

Mission House, May 17, 1817.

HON. AND REV. SIR,

I had yesterday the pleasure to receive your obliging letter, with its enclosures, on the subject of Petrus; and should have answered them immediately, but was prevented by an engagement for which I was preparing.

We were all much gratified with the manner in which you appear to have stated the matter to Petrus, and the readiness you manifested *on your part*, to give him up to our Mission in case he desired it.—I am sure it will satisfy our Friends completely to observe the candid manner in which you assured him of your own as well as the Governor's undiminished friendship and esteem, whether he continued in his present situation, or whether he attached himself to our Mission.—Had we not possessed a confidence on this head, we would not have preferred our request.

C

I

I need not repeat the result of our conversation on this subject, with Petrus, the other day, attested as it is in my letter of the 15th on the veracity of Mr. Armour, Mr. Fox, Mr. Clough, and myself.——And, that in a conversation with both you and Mr. Bisset, he should give "*a decided preference to the regular service of Government,*" I can easily account for without the least impeachment of the veracity of Petrus——The conclusion, however, to which we have felt authorised in coming, on seeing Petrus' declaration, &c. is not to press any further claim upon him; especially as we observe it is contemplated, that in the first place *we have no claim at all in reference to him:* and secondly, that we *manifested a derilection of all claims,* first by *offering him for baptism in the Fort Church,* and secondly, *by not objecting to his appointment as a Proponent or Government Preacher, last year.*

Not to tire you by too long a letter, I would just observe that Mr. Clough's offering Petrus for baptism in the Fort church, was merely intended as one of those respectful deferences to the Established Church, for which (and I do not repeat it notwithstanding) we have been so observable since we commenced this Mission; and which you have ever been so kind as favourably to appreciate.—And with respect to his appointment as a Proponent, I have, I trust, thrown some light on our relation to that fact, in my former letter, which few will have thought us capable of producing.

It is a fact—that at that time he applied to us to make him a Preacher; that he complained to us of his inaction—urged that he had always been accustomed to teach from his early days, and begged us to employ him as a Teacher of Christianity.——It is a fact—that we had engaged him; and that he had even made arrangements for the disposal of his household furniture, with a view to his taking a country station. —(If our avowal needed any confirmation it might easily be obtained by the testi mony of Samuel Perara, Catechist, a young man of probity, who interpreted on the occasion.) The next day or so we heard of his being made a Government Preacher.——The reason we did not remonstrate was the same *respectful deference,* united to the reason assigned in my former letter.

It was in this manner that Daniel Theophilus was taken from us last year. He had repeatedly told the Revd. Mr. Glenie, Colonial Chaplain at Jaffna, that he would not become a Government Preacher, (as Mr. Glenie has assured me) lest his conversion from Mahometism should be attributed to improper motives: he expressed *a decided perference for the regular service of* our Mission. Our Brother Mr. Lynch had supported him in his own house, for nearly two years, at Jaffna, at his own expence, in food and cloathing.—And, at the earnest request of Daniel, Mr. Lynch paid his expences, and brought him up to our Conference in
Colombo.

Colombo.—He was brought to Colombo, with Wesleyan Money, and was examined and approved of by the Conference. The Conference engaged to discharge some debts in which he was involved. And two days after he had solemnly in the name of the great Head of the Church, given himself into our hands, we heard of his appointment from Government.

We have too great a respect for the Christian candour of the parties concerned, to harbour the supposition that these facts were previously known (though they were subsequently communicated); and, as Daniel had thus disqualified himself for admission among us, though we had sent his name home to our Society, we did not make any official attempt to recover him.——This, however, will explain the appearance of his name on our Minutes, which we are daily expecting from Home.

We have ever made it our study not to manifest a spirit of rivalry with respect to other Christians. We have recommended to the Government service many valuable individuals*. We have never enticed one from it. Besides the personal labour we have ever continued to give to the same cause.—Knowing that those little circumstances are apt to produce a difference, where in reality there is none, and to separate in affection even individuals who have the highest esteem for each other.

Our good Friend, Mr. Bisset, in the midst of his very numerous engagements, seems not to have a very clear idea that Petrus' conversion was effected by the instrumentality of Mr. Clough; and seems to apprehend that it was effected by yourself. Never having heard you hint such an idea, I was surprised at seeing it: though we have heard that some persons in England have started something like it. We never knew on what foundation. We have, however, sufficient documents to set the matter at rest.

Your Sermon preached at the baptism of Petrus, as well as your invariable sentiments, expressed from time to time, will decide the point. The account which appeared in the Government Gazette, to which was prefixed a short introduction by an esteemed and respected Friend of our Mission, will go to the same purpose.—The Third Report of our Colombo Bible Society; and a letter which Petrus has sent to our Secretary, and which probably is by this time printed in England:—these will all remove any doubts on this head.

Besides—the fact that his change was effected at Galle, where none but Mr. Clough was;—That Mr. Clough was the person who introduced him to Mr. Bisset, stood as one of his sponsors, and at your kind request, wrote an account of his conversion;—all prove that Mr. Clough was the honoured instrument used in the conversion of Petrus to Christianity.——If Mr. Bisset refers to any conversion subsequent to his arrival in Colombo, I do not contend: but *his first conversion* was evidently through the instrumentality of our Missionary Br. Mr. Clough.

I am

* See lines 2, and 23, of page 2.

I am sure Mr. Bisset will generously allow my statement to be correct; and I only make it, because our Society would wonder, if, after the lapse of more than two years, the pleasing satisfaction of having produced the first public conversion from Budhism, were to be removed from the brow of its Ceylon Mission.

Not to enlarge; I beg to assure you we most completely give up our Friend Petrus; *not, however, on the ground that we had no claim upon him;* but from the *circumstances* of the case. And though, from the nature of his statement, we are necessarily prevented from being able to recommend him to our Society, as an assistant Missionary; yet, we shall ever personally respect and regard him: never mentioning the circumstance to him more. We will always maintain, on our part, an inviolable attachment to this *first-born* of our Mission; and will cheerfully give him (as we shall at all times be ready to do to any of the Government Preachers) every instruction and assistance in our power.

Though we wish to found no measure upon it, and do not wish it to be done in the form of an application; (the point being settled by Petrus, himself,) I have, however, Dear Sir, still to request that the whole correspondence on the subject may be laid before His Excellency the Governor. Since doubtless, the rumour of our application will reach his ears; and since, as we inexpressibly value His Excellency's favourable opinion of us and our conduct, and as an imperfect account of this transaction might deprive us of the great priviledge, we should wish him to know the whole of our proceedings on this occasion.

I am sure our openness on this peculiar affair will pleasingly satisfy both yourself and Mr. Bisset of our *real* character and principles; and additionally convince you with how much unalterable esteem and respect, I continue,

Honble and Revd. Sir,
Yours very sincerely,
W. M. Harvard.

Mr. Twisleton's reply to Br. H's. Private note.

My Dear Sir,

I have forwarded the whole to Mr. Bisset for the Governor.

My motive for wishing to avoid being the medium, is, that Petrus has started a new question, in which I am particularly alluded to; and I did not wish to enter into a matter of a collateral nature, when the main question was decided; fearing it might produce controversy, or at least protracted correspondence.

dence. The declaration to which I allude, is his conversion: and altho' he wavered when he arrived at Colombo, I conceived there was no real fear of the result before I took him in hand.—Yet, I certainly took great pains to settle him, and had him in my private room five hours, impressing upon his mind the Gospel Scheme, and the preparatives from the Old Testament.—I am glad you think I have behaved candidly; and it is truly the case.—Had I allowed myself to offer the smallest influence in Petrus's declaration, I should have tried to make him expunge the part about conversion; but to, my astonishment, he says he did not intend to be baptized when he visited Colmbo, and that Mr. Clough misunderstood him. It is evident, however, that he was strongly impressed with Christianity, and virtually educated, by Mr. Clough.   Yours sincerely,   T. J. Twisleton.

Br. H. wrote in reply to Mr. Twisleton as follows:—

HON AND REVD SIR,

Thank you for your kindness in forwarding the Papers &c. for the Governor's inspection.—I believe Petrus, in his letter to our Secretary, has mentioned with thankfulness your many kindnesses to him, as he has besides in his First Sermon, which has been printed in England.—We have likewise much to say of a similar nature; and with a grateful remembrance thereof, I remain,   Honble and Revd. Sir.

Yours very sincerely,   W. M. Harvard.

On Whit-Monday Mr. Bisset called at the Mission House, and conversed with us on the subject: and at our request promised to send us his sentiments on Paper, for the satisfaction of our Society.

On the 27th. Inst. Br. Harvard received the following letter from Mr. Bisset.

Colombo, 27th May, 1817.

DEAR SIR,

I was very sorry to see, in your late correspondence with Mr. Twisleton, that you had any doubts of my having a clear idea of the Origin of Petrus Panditas conversion.—I always attributed it to Mr. Clough: nor did I ever hear till lately, that Petrus himself considered his conviction of the truth of the

D   Gospel,

Gospel, and of the abominable absurdities of idolatry, to have been established on any other foundation, than Mr. Clough's admonitions and his own reflections.

The full Account published in our Bible Society's 3d Report of Petrus' Baptism, will show what my Sentiments were upon that occasion; for I need hardly tell you that those Reports are written entirely by myself, except where something is introduced avowedly the composition of another.

I will now also enclose an entry made in our Baptismal Register, in which you many see what were the Sentiments at that time, of Mr. Twisleton and myself.—The Entry is in Mr. Twisleton's hand writing, though the ceremony of the Baptism was performed by me.

Petrus was much agitated, and even alarmed for his personal safety,, when he came up from Galle, and the protection as well as conversation of Mr. Twisleton, who was very attentive to him, doubtless confirmed him in the resolution of embracing Christianity.—He has now been some time in the employment of Government, as a Proponent, which is in fact equivalent to a Native Clergymen of the Established Church.—But were he to chuse to leave that office, and to enter into your Connexion, it would give me no concern.—I should consider him as merely pursuing the same end, by a course somewhat different.—I should be far from scrutinizing his motives for such a change; but give him credit, for their being honest and sound.—On the other hand, you cannot be surprised that Petrus should attach himself to the permanent Service of Government. What ever reason he might have given you to induce a supposition that he would enter into closer bonds of union with your Society, he might, upon reflection, very naturally have considered that the Religion which you profess was the same with that of the regular Church, but that ever, as a zealous Preacher, a Native would stand upon surer ground in the public Service.—He must remain here with his friends and relations in the country of his birth.—In the unfortunate vicissitudes to which Colonial Governments are liable, there might come a Governor "who knew not Joseph".—Allowance should be made, on this ground, for Petrus's peculiar situation.—I hope, indeed, and trust, that no such change will

ever

ever take place.——Attached, as I am, to the Established Church, I must regard the Wesleyan Missionaries as by far the most efficient instruments in propagating the Gospel in Ceylon. As such, I cannot but rate them highly in point of utility: and, in regard to their individual Conduct, it has been always marked with a propriety and discretion, that entitle them to the personal esteem of the Clergy, as well as to the protection and favour of the Government of this Island.　Believe me to be,

Dear Sir, Your Faithful and Obedient Servant, G. BISSET.

BAPTISM. 1814.

Dec. 25—Petrus Panditta Sekera, a converted Priest of Budhu, who was induced to embrace the Christian Religion thro' the mild, clear, and persuasive arguments and exhortations of the Revd. Mr. Clough, a Missionary of the Wesleyan Persuasion, who had been residing at Galle, and had taken frequent opportunities of visiting the Idolatrous rites and ceremonies where the Convert was a leading Priest.——

This newly converted Christian had received from the Revd. Mr. Clough the valuable present of the New Testament, in Cingalese; which circumstance caused him not only repeatedly to read it throughout, with a mind bent on the search of truth, but induced him, at a numerous meeting of Priests of Budhu, to take with him the New Testament, and lecture them during a whole night in the Gospel of Matthew, which they heard with no less astonishment than attention.

A true Copy of the Colombo Baptismal Register. Witness my Hand, this 27th May, 1817.　　　　　　　G. BISSET.

Assistant Colonial Chaplain.

To which Br. H. replied:

REVD. SIR,　　　　　　　　　　　　　　*May 28, 1817.*

Your kind letter on the subject of Petrus goes to a much greater length than we had even desired, and calls for our thankful acknowledgments of the handsome compliment you have been so good as to pay our Mission here. I am sure it will much gratify our Friends; and compleately reconcile them to the disappointment which of course they will feel on first hearing of the case; but which they will soon fairly understand, as well as from a few candid observations which we shall feel happy to make to our Committee for that purpose.　Our wish was not to make it any thing like a bone of contention, but only clearly to satisfy the minds of our Committee, on a point which otherwise would have been unaccountable to them. I remain, &c.——W. M. H.

Thus

Thus the correspondence has closed. We have been thus particular in the detail, to render the greater satisfaction to those who will feel interested in it.—It is very natural, as Mr. Bisset observes, that Petrus, under Circumstances, should alter his Resolution of being with us; and give a decided preference to the Service of Government. We are far from suspecting Petrus's principle from such a change.—We still respect and regard him. He was, possibly, much influenced by his connections. He was married about six months since: his wife's family are all in the service of Government.—This, together with what may easily be gathered from the various parts of this Correspondence, will we have no doubt, in the eyes of our Friends, preserve the individual uprightness of our Convert unimpeached, and convince them that we have left no prudent means untried to have him under our nurture and guidance.—He will still, we trust, be an extensive benefit to the Christian Church: and though he has thus been taken from us, contrary to our desire, yet it is a satisfaction and cause of thankfulness to God, that, by the instrumentality of our Mission, he has been enlisted from the ranks of Budhism, to fight in Emmanuel's Cause; and that he is still prosecuting the Christian warfare, though not immediately under *our* banner.

But for the change that has been effected in him, he might have this day, been wandering about, in his yellow robe, an enemy to God, and directing the languid hopes of his Countrymen, to an endless succession of transmigrations after this life.—But, in his present state, he is daily employed in translating the word of life, for the benefit of his benighted countrymen; occasionally in preaching the Gospel to them; telling them of eternal blessedness, through the merits of the common Saviour; and constantly doing justice to his profession by an upright and unblamable life.—The Friends of our Mission, then, have no ground of discouragement.

—To the Lord be all the praise!

We have no doubt Petrus will gladly maintain a friendly intercourse with our Mission in this Country, and correspondence with our Society in England.

(Signed)

W. M. Harvard,
W. B. Fox,
B. Clough.

Extracts,

FROM

QUARTERLY LETTERS, &c.

No. II.   *JANUARY*, 1818.

THE COLOMBO STATION.

Colombo, Mission-House, January 7th, 1818.

VERY DEAR BRETHREN,

THE reception of your affectionate letters, both in the last and present quarter, has afforded us a gratification of a most superior kind, and produced in our hearts the warmest returns of affection towards you, and of thankfulness to God, for all your prosperities, prospects, and expectations. May it please God to continue opening our Providential way, making us all *workmen* that need not to be *ashamed*, and giving us to see that his work encreasingly prospers in our hands.

We have abundant reason for thankfulness to the Great Head of the Church, while we "rejoice with trembling," that some little good has been done in our Station in the preceding quarter. To the Lord be all the praise!

The hopeful circumstances attending the latter days of a poor man, late a private in H. M. 73d Regt. who was shot for mutinous conduct in this place, pursuant to the Sentence of a General Court Martial, will doubtless be read by you all with much interest. And as several of you have expressed a wish to become acquainted with them, we make no apology for inserting them as briefly as possible.

John Jenny was a Native of Nottingham; his parents poor, but honest and respectable. In his native land he displayed much addictedness to loose company and intoxication, which were the means of his entering the army, at a very early age; not being above sixteen years old at the time of his enlistment.

The same causes which operated to bring him into the army, continued to influence him afterwards, and procured him the character of an unsteady, dissolute man. These propensities often involved him in trouble; till at last, being one day brought before his Captain for some minor offence, he had the temerity, from the stupifying effects of late intoxication, to raise his arm against his officer, and to strike him an unprovoked blow on the face.

He was accordingly immediately ordered into confinement; and a Court Martial having been summoned, examined into the affair, and transmitted their verdict to His Excellency the Governor, in Kandy. Though their verdict had not transpired, it was the general conviction that the sentence of death would be executed upon him. Actuated by the most commendable impulse, our two dear Friends, Serjeant Busain and Corporal Frazer of the same Regiment, visited him in the Main Guard-Room, where he was confined in the stocks, to await the issue of the Governor's decision. They found him rather desirous than otherwise of Religious conversation; and the former sent us out a short note requesting that we would see him, which we regularly continued to do until the moment of his execution.

On our first visit, we felt it a painful duty to assure him, from our local knowledge, that there was not the least room for him to hope for a pardon from his earthly judges, which he seemed fully sensible of; and hence we exhorted him to use every precious moment of his short remaining life, that he might obtain mercy at the hands of God, and have a well-grounded hope of everlasting life, through faith in the Saviour.

We lent him two or three suitable books to read, with a Bible and Hymn book he had received from Corporal Frazer, and were in the habit, at our Evening visitations, of catechizing him on divine subjects, as well as expounding to him some portion of Gods word, which particularly related to experimental Religion; *that* being the only kind of Religion which his situation rendered him capable of. Ours was an awful task! he seemed to devour every word: and such was his desire for Salvation, that could it have been accomplished by manual labour, every nerve would have been gladly and strenuously brought into exercise. But still his mind appeared to be very dark, and his ideas confused on religious subjects. He always however manifested great thankfulness to us when we went to see him; and on parting would grasp our hands with much affectionate fervor, as though to acknowledge his obligations to us. While he continued in the Guard-Room he was visited likewise by Brothers Osborne and Newstead; by the latter during a short visit from his Station.

At the expected time, his sentence was read to him by the Judge Advocate. He was to suffer the dreadful sentence of the law on the 27th of October, and was accordingly removed to a condemned cell. The time of his residence in the cell was about a fortnight. On his being sent there, the Fort Adjutant, at his desire, politely wrote us an official request to attend him during his last days, which we assured him we should do with the utmost pleasure. And it was in this outwardly melancholy little room, that the Lord appeared to work more powerfully upon his soul. His views of himself and of religion rapidly improved; and his feelings likewise; for he seemed to be a man who had but *one business* to attend to:—the salvation of his soul!

As we intend to enter more into particulars, in a small tract, we shall not needlessly enlarge. We had the satisfaction of seeing that the Lord was very merciful to him. Mr. Griffiths, our Baptist Brother, accompanied us to see him, and was much satisfied with his state. Mr. Chater also expressed a wish to visit him, on which we were consulted, when of course we gave an assurance that it was our desire that the poor man should have every possible assistance in his great work! and Mr. Chater's wish was complied with.

The sincerity of his repentance was evidenced in his desire to make restitution, to the utmost of his power; for which purpose he made a free confession of several crimes he had committed, that the characters of others, who had lain under undeserved imputation on account thereof, might be cleared. In one case, especially, in which a Serjeant had been reduced on suspicion of a robbery, which he had committed, he voluntarily sent for the disgraced Serjeant. confessed his crime, and begged his forgiveness.

As his end approached, his spiritual improvement daily became more and more evident. He was truly a wonder to all who came to see him. When some superior Staff Officers visited him, and supposing, from his serenity, that he was buoying himself up with the hopes of pardon, he assured them, in the most modest manner, that that was not the case; and added, " *Gentlemen, this Cell has been more than a palace to me.—I bless God that ever I was brought in here!—I would rather take my sentence to-morrow, with the humble hopes I have, than have a pardon, and live to sin against God, as I have done, in my past life.*"

The day before his death, Mr. Twisleton visited him, as he expressed himself. " *to behold a man, who, at the close of a wicked life, has repentant feelings. and to congratulate him on his happy change of state,*" and was much struck with admiration at his case. He was not a man of many words; but what he said clearly displayed the state of his mind

Feeling a holy jealousy for him, we were careful to examine him, in the most scrutinizing manner, setting before him the awful danger of a miscarriage in a work which, in his situation, could only be done but once. He always answered our enquiries with the most childlike openness; and we are satisfied that he found peace with God, and experienced the renewing influences of the Holy Spirit.

On the Evening before his Execution, we administered the Holy Sacrament of the Lord's Supper to him. There were present, besides our two selves and the prisoner, Brother Griffiths, a pious Officer, and the pious Serjeant and Corporal already mentioned. That Cell never saw such a scene before. It was an awfully pleasing time!—Jehovah was present. The poor man appeared greatly refreshed; nor we believe will the season ever be forgotten by us who survive. Surely Jesus is present *wherever* two or three are met together in his name!

After the Sacrament, we sat and had a kind of Class meeting, each telling something of the goodness of God towards him; and about twelve o'Clock. we left poor Jenny, with his two Christian Friends, to take a little sleep, and thus be the better prepared for the solemn duty of the approaching Morning. On going to him again, between four and five o'clock, we were glad to find that he had slept almost the whole of the time of our absence, not appearing in the least agitated or discomposed, excepting, as our Friends observed, he had one sudden start during his short sleep; we suppose an involuntary effort of lingering humanity against the dreadful moment which was drawing so near.

Mr. Twisleton kindly accompanied us to the cell in the morning, and prayed with us. The prisoner had no fears; and when the gun fired, as a signal for the troops in the Garrison to assemble, he requested the Provost Marshal to be informed that he was ready, and did not wish any delay on his account. The Commandant, Colonel Young of the Royal Artillery, displayed much compassionate interest in the case of the condemned penitent, and generously acceded to any request which was made in his behalf.— It is remarkable, his two pious comrades had had no acquaintance with him prior to his imprisonment. His trouble was the foundation of their friendship, and the means of his Salvation. By the express permission of the Commandant, these two friends supported him to the awful spot, and performed the last offices for him after his execution! May the Lord ever remember them for good! Colonel O'Connell, likewise, considerately set them free from Regimental duty, for the same purpose.

Mr. Twisleton accompanied the solemn procession along with us, and was much pleased with his continued peace and serenity of mind. When he had got outside of the Fort, in view of the parade, he commenced, quite unexpectedly to us, repeating the 43rd Hymn: *And am I born to die?* &c. which he went completely through, without any mistake, repeating the last verse with the sweetest expression and emphasis imaginable:

"So shall I love my God
Because he first lov'd me,
And praise thee in thy bright abode
To all eternity."

and casting his eyes upward, with humble confidence, he added: "*Yes; Glory be to God: I shall.*"

At Mr. Twisleton's request he repeated the whole Hymn again in the same manner. This Hymn had been pointed out to him by Corporal Frazer, at the commencement of his confinement, and it had been rendered so useful to him, that he had it all off, most correctly.

When the procession approached the line, down which we were slowly to move, it was observed by some in the ranks that his countenance appeared to glisten with joy and composure! He retained his firmness; while we continued, on either side, to assist his remembrance by repeating several portions of Scripture to him, adapted to his circumstances; to which he two or three times returned the most pleasing and satisfactory replies. On reaching the end of the line, we marched to the centre of the army when his coffin was placed down. We kneeled round it, and commended him to God, in solemn prayer, and he was almost immediately dismissed from the body, into an eternal world. His last words were "*Farewell, Glory be to God! I am a happy man.* So died John Jenny, Octr. 27, 1817, aged about 26 years. "*Is not this a brand plucked out of the fire!* Zech. 3 2nd.

The peculiar circumstances of this poor man's case excited a very general interest. One of us preached on the occasion, on the Wednesday following, to an overflowing congregation in the Garrison, from Ezekiel xxxiii. 5th verse; and we have reason to believe that lasting serious impressions were made on the minds of some notorious characters by the blessing of God on the solemn services of that night.

The state of affairs in the Interior, has deprived us of several of our pious Friends in the 73d Regt. and the remainder are gone round, with the Staff, to fix Head Quarters at Trincomalee. While our numbers have thus been diminished at this station, we nevertheless rejoice that the hands of our Trincomalee Brethren will become the more strengthened thereby.

In the middle of this quarter, H. M. 83d Regiment arrived here from the Cape of Good Hope, commanded by Colonel Brunt. By this means we received an encrease in our European Society of about thirteen members, all of whom appear to be faithful followers of the Lord Jesus, and to have a good report of all men. One of them, Brother John Kelly, having acted as their Class leader while at the Cape, and being fully satisfied with him in all respects, so far as we could obtain any information, we have confirmed him in his office, and are happy to say that the good work of piety and holiness goes on well among them.

On the arrival of this Regiment, we felt it our duty to wait upon the Colonel, and state to him our mode of proceeding, and request his favourable sanction of our intercourse with the men under his command. Having mentioned our desire to Colonel Young, Commandant of the Garrison, he immediately proposed to go himself and introduce us to the Colonel; which, however, we declined with gratitude, not desiring to give him so much trouble. He then wrote us a note of introduction, and recommended us to the Colonel's attention in the most gratifying manner.

As we were proceeding to the house, we conceived Colonel Brunt to be engaged, and it occured to our minds to delay our visit a short time by waiting upon Colonel O'Connel, commanding the 73d Regiment. This respected Military Officer has always shown himself friendly to the labours of Missionaries among his men; and the religiously disposed have never been refused any reasonable application for Passes, to attend the preaching carried on in the Pettah. His maxim is, "*a good Christian is a good Soldier.*" Colonel O'Connel received us with great kindness, and most readily promised to recommend us in the warmest manner to Colonel Brunt and the newly arrived Officers in general. On our mentioning to him that some evil-disposed persons, at a certain Out-Station, had raised the report that poor Jenny had been a member of our Society, and that his mutinous conduct was the result of the doctrines we were in the habit of preaching, he displayed much displeasure at

No. II.   E

such an unworthy aspersion, and observed it must have been circulated either by very ill-designing persons, or else very ignorant of the general effects of our labours. He then proceeded to enumerate the names of several men in his Regiment, formerly of notoriously depraved characters, who had been reclaimed from their vicious habits through the influence of religion, and had been made Non-Commissioned officers in consequence of their exemplary conduct: and added, "I confess some men have taken a change, by attending your meetings, whom I never could expect would have changed; and if it should be in my power to give any assistance to your Mission, on my arrival in Trincomalee, I shall do it with the sincerest pleasure." It afforded us real satisfaction to hear the names of our Friends thus mentioned by their Commanding Officer, with such a testimony to the efficacy of religion upon them, and to the consistency of their general deportment. This will we hope stop the mouths of gainsayers, and put to silence the ignorance of foolish men.

On proceeding to Colonel Brunt, we were received with every kindness by that venerable officer. When he had read the note with which the Commandant had favoured us, he assured us that he would give his men every facility in attending our religious services, both in the Garrison and out of it. He spoke very highly of the religious soldiers under his command; and when we repeated the Names of those of them who belong to our Society, he said "*I know them all: they are all very good men, and very good soldiers. One of them I have, on account of his steadiness, recommended to a situation under Government, since my landing here: and when I was at the Cape, I procured Colonial situations for several, as a reward for their good character.*" You will, very dear Brethren, participate in the pleasure we experienced, on having our newly-arrived Friends recommended to us in such unexceptionable terms, and will unite with us in praying that all who believe in Christ may be careful to maintain good works; and that they may let their light so shine before men, that they, seeing their good works, may glorify our Father which is in heaven.

We were happy to hear the Colonel speak favourably of the labour of Mr. Thom the London Missionary at the Cape, who, he said, had been useful to several of the Soldiers at the Cape, and who had obtained deserved respect from his general mode of Proceeding.

On requesting a Pass, for our Friends to be allowed to come out of the Garrison for religious purposes, the Colonel replied, he would give it with much pleasure, and would always extend a similar favour to any whom we would recommend. We assured him we felt much indebted to him, and would avail ourselves of his kind offer whenever we had any to propose to him on whose steadiness we could depend: to which he added, "*I have had the most unsteady men turn. And I am sure the men you have mentioned will not recommend any of their comrades that they cannot well depend upon.*" We took our leave of the Colonel with mixed feelings of thankfulness and encouragement.

Notwithstanding our own Friends could so easily obtain a Pass to attend our services in the Pettah, yet, from a variety of considerations, we have thought it the most adviseable to have English Preaching in the Fort, on a Sunday evening. This though it has encreased our own labour we have cheerfully done; and many come to hear, who perhaps would not have taken the trouble to have applied for a pass, and who would have gone to no other place of worship.

By this means, we are both engaged at the same time, on a Sunday evening, as in fact we are through the whole Sabbath. And though we do not complain, we certainly think this Station should not be left to two Brethren. And to travel six or eight miles in the heat of the sun, and preach six times, besides superintending two small Sunday Schools, which we regularly do every Sunday, is the surest way to undermine the strongest constitution.

Our work in the Pettah goes on much as in the last quarter. We now conduct our Class in Portuguese, and have one or two more seriously disposed persons, who regularly attend. The souls of all our Friends appear to be in a good state, and we find the meetings to be indeed profitable seasons.

The Schools of this Station in the general promise well. They however require our ever-wakeful attention, and superintendence; and we are happy to say that in this laborious part of our duty we meet with many very lively sources of encouragement.

On a small scale, there is a good work of grace going on at Colpetty and one of our other Schools. Their Weekly Classes are well attended, and the conduct of the Children consistent. A pleasing instance occurred lately at Colpetty of a mother bringing her daughter, who was not a Scholar, and requesting that she might be permitted to meet in the Girl's Class for the good of her soul!

Our Schoolmasters regularly attend at the Mission House every Saturday morning at ten o'Clock, when they are met by one of us, in turn, and receive instructions on various points. All School business in the course of the week are referred to this meeting; at which every Master makes a report of any thing particular relating to his School. The names of all Children for admission into the Schools are brought on paper to this meeting, for our signature; and the names of no Scholars can be erased from the School-papers, on any pretence, without a similar authority. To this meeting all applications for new Schools are brought; and here all candidates are examined, before their appointments to the office of Schoolmaster. The meeting begins with singing and prayer, and concludes by the Masters reading, verse by verse, a Chapter out the Scriptures, in English and in Cingalese, after which one of them prays, and they are dismissed with the blessing. From experience we have found this arrangement to be attended with many advantages, and have hastily detailed the same for your information.

In the month of November, we commenced a new School at a village, about 6 miles north of Colombo, called *Mabola*, and have a very good prospect of a useful establishment there. It at pre-

sent consists of about 50 Children, and has enabled us to connect
this Station with the Negombo Station, the most southern of whose
Schools is within about three or four miles from *Mahola*.   Our
Schools on the other side of Colombo reach to within three or
four miles of Pantura, on the Caltura Station.   May the Lord give
us his grace, to cultivate this extended field, with that persevering diligence, which will ensure us an abundant harvest of success!

According to the directions of our last Colombo Conference, we
have prepared a Report of all our Mission Schools on the Island,
and which we hope you will all have received before the arrival
of this.   We regret the detached style in which it has been drawn
up, (which has arisen from its having been principally composed
at intervals, surrounded by pressing avocations of other kinds,) as
well as our inability, from the want of local knowledge on some
points, faithfully to represent the more distant branches of our
School economy.   But as we have made it our sincere aim, so we
trust all our dear Brethren will discover, that we have made the
best of our materials, though in some cases these were but scanty, in order to do justice to their several laudable endeavours in
this Department; and (we are persuaded our Brethren will pardon
the freedom) we beg to recommend them, as all such particulars
will of course be most interesting to our Committee in London,
and to those who may support our Schools in general, to adopt
something of the plan of a SCHOOL-JOURNAL, which might likewise be the Minute Book of their Masters' Meeting, into which
every interesting particular relative to their Schools may be entered, as it occurs, with the impressions made by it on their
minds at the time.   We shall, by this means, be the more habitually influenced by the encouraging circumstances which Providence may cast in our way, from time to time, and be enabled
regularly to provide an Annual recompence of encouragement to
those benevolent persons in our Native land, who may generously
second our exertions in the behalf of the rising generation of
this Country.

Amidst many other animating circumstances, which bear upon
our Schools, we cannot conceal the satisfaction which it has afforded us to behold how warmly and affectionately our revered
Fathers and Brethren, the Missionary Committee, have entered into
the subject.   In the spontaneous grant of £300 per annum, that
we were to begin with, we might have learnt sufficiently the bias
of their judgment that way.   But, in their last official Communication, dated June 8th 1817, we have counsel and direction added
to pecuniary support.   It will be a very gratifying circumstance
to our Committee, as it is to us, to find that, by following the
openings of Divine Providence, we have already anticipated their
valuable and important advise on this head.   And, so far as we have
been enabled so to do, their anticipated directions wear the aspect of a powerful ratification and commendation of our humble
attempts to extend the means of education to the Ceylonese youth
universally.   We therefore have the utmost pleasure in enriching
our letter with an extract from the valued communication we
have referred to:

Extract from the Committee's Circular Letter, dated June 8, 1817.

"The instruction of the rising generation is also of vast importance; and though there are some of the Missionary stations in which the formation of Schools would be impracticable, yet in others it might be accomplished, and would lay a foundation for extensive and everlasting good. The Committee have lately been considering more fully, the very great importance of the establishment of Schools in every station where it is practicable, and strongly recommend them to your attention. Sunday Schools may be established in most places, and in others, Day Schools may also be established. The Missionaries should, in each place, have them under their own direction and superintendance; and, as frequently as possible, speak to the children collectively, and also converse with them individually, respecting their spiritual and eternal interests. In all places, if possible, procure truly pious persons to teach in the Schools; persons who will undertake the work, not for fee or reward, but from a love to Jesus, and to the perishing souls of the children. Such persons are most likely to be useful to the rising generation, who will embrace every opportunity of leading the infant mind to God; for having experienced the salvation of God in their own souls, they will be anxious that all should be led to the same Saviour, who has opened the way of mercy and salvation, by the shedding of his own blood.

"In some places, where the Missionaries are labouring, it would at first be impossible to procure pious teachers; and the only way is, to select such persons as are the most suitable to assist, till it shall please God to raise up pious persons to fill up their places. By instructing the children in reading, they will become acquainted with the Sacred Scriptures, which are able to make them wise to salvation. They will also be induced to read the Bible to their parents; and in that way the light of Divine truth will beam upon many of the dark habitations of those who are only nominal Christians, and also of the avowed heathens. It is highly probable, that out of the large number of children who are brought under instruction, some who may be awakened, and truly converted, will also be raised up of God to become preachers of the Gospel.

"We are well aware that, in some places, Schools are already formed, and are in a state of prosperity; from several of our Brethren we have received pleasing accounts of their utility; but we wish them to become more general."

Such an unequivocal document, we are satisfied, will operate powerfully upon us all!—While, however, we are encouraged, by the above directions, to proceed in our plan of Native education, we are convinced, that *too much stress* should not be laid thereon, much less ought it to supercede in the least degree, the great work of preaching the Gospel, to which we have been most solemnly set apart by the Church. We therefore look upon Schools but as an auxiliary (though a very efficient one) to the grand duty of a Missionary; and hence, on this Station, we make it always subservient thereto; and we bless God, we have not a single School Room, where we cannot and do not erect the Gospel standard, and unfurl the royal banner of the adorable Emmanuel. And, we joyfully add, though with *but* a little, yet *still* a little degree of success.

By the great goodness of our God, we commenced the present year, with the memorable occurrence of two Budhist Priests, openly renouncing their idolatry, and casting off their yellow robes, in the presence of a large congregation, in our Chapel in this place.

Don Andries de Silva, and Don Adrian de Silva, were both born of parents who were nominally Christians, and who had them both baptised in their infancy. However, when they grew up to youth, they were placed under the care of two Budhist Priests, by whom they were educated, and initiated into all the rites and ceremonies of their idolatrous System. This faithless practice of their parents, which is too common among our nominal Christians, entirely estranged them from the religion into which they had been baptised; and hence they grew up as confirmed heathens as any in the dark jungles of the Interior.

At a proper age, they were regularly appointed to exercise the functions of the Budhist Priesthood, and were attached to a celebrated temple at *Tottegamma*, near *Amblangodde*. Here they continued to lead their deluded disciples, for several years; and perhaps would have remained in that situation till their days ended, had not the late revived attentions to Christianity, attracted their notice, and led to their serious reflection on the Faith from whence they had revolted.

Several months ago, they were brought to our house, by our Friend Petrus; and a conversation ensued relative to Christianity, which, under the Divine blessing, ultimately led to their final resolution to forsake their heathenish employment. With this determination, they entreated Petrus Panditta to introduce them to us a second time, when they requested that we would take them under our care, promising to submit to any discipline, and to perform any service, we might appoint them to.

Before we received them under our protection, we prescribed them a period of probation, which they accomplished, under the eye of our young friend Cornelius at Colpetty, to his, and consequently our, satisfaction; and, at the expiration thereof, they earnestly requested us to baptise them. In making this request to us they were not aware that they involved us in a difficulty; as, having been baptised in their infancy, it would have been contrary to the usages of our branch of the Christian Church to baptise them a second time. Notwithstanding which, having seriously deliberated on the subject, we concluded that some outward ceremony ought to be observed, in such a case, to mark their change, especially in the sight of the world; and as we had never heard of any provision on that head among the moderns, we though, it would be useful to borrow an idea from the expressive ablutions of the Sacred Scriptures; and accordingly appointed them religiously to wash their hands, in the presence of the congregation, to signify their total separation from the filth of heathenism, and their return to the pure and sacred Religion of the Lord Jesus Christ.

Accordingly, on New Year's day, a Cingalese congregation assembled in the Mission-House, when one of us expounded and preached from the story of Philip and the Eunuch, the two Priests, in the meanwhile, sitting in their robes before the pulpit; after which the other of us proposed the following questions to them, which they answered in a very modest and satisfactory manner:——

1. Do you here publickly profess the Falsehood of the Budhist

Religion, in denying one Supreme Creator and God, and attributing all things to Chance?

II. Do you hereby declare your conviction that the Budhist Religion is insufficient for salvation?

III. So far as you are acquainted with the Truths and Doctrines of the Christian Religion, do you profess your firm belief of it, as a true Religion, and as a Religion from God?

IV. In particular, do you believe, that after death there will be a Resurrection of the Body—A general Judgement—and Eternal Rewards and Punishments?

[A difficulty was here suggested to them, relative to the Resurrection of the same indentical Body, which they resolved with the utmost readiness and address]

V. Do you, then, before God and this Congregation, confess yourselves to be sinners, and the Lord Jesus Christ to be your only Saviour?

VI Do you fully rely on the merits of his atonement for salvation?

VII. And, Finally, do you hereby engage to receive his laws, as contained in the Holy Scriptures, as the constant rule of your life?

After their answers to these questions, they were conducted into a room to change their dress, which they appeared to do with much cheerful satisfaction; and returned, each dressed in white cloth, and with his yellow silk robe in his hand, which were laid on the table, as a trophy from heathenism. They then washed their hands, in the name of the Lord, and were publickly received within the pale of the Christian Church, and sealed their renunciation of Idolatry by solemn prayer to the sacred Trinity.

The Congregation, which was unusually large, appeared to feel deeply interested in the new method of beginning this New Year. May their impressions continue: and may these public renunciations of Pagan superstitions have an effect to raise the spiritual religion of the New Testament in the general estimation!

At the Class-meeting, in the evening of the same day, the reclaimed converts were present; and though they were by far, much meaner clothed, than when the disciples of Budhu, yet they seemed to derive no small degree of pleasure from that circumstance; and testified their happiness at being recognized as Christians. One of them said: "I have been like a man in darkness, until this day, but I am now both blessed with light; and likewise brought into the right way—a way in which I hope to obtain the mercy of God!" We are sure you will add, most devoutly! "*Amen.*"

They appear since to maintain every consistency; and are living at Colpetty, under the care of our two young Friends there.

The Printing department continues as usual. We have just completed a new edition of Two Thousand Copies of our First Part Spelling Book, from which we shall be happy to furnish you with any supply. "*Green's Principles,*" in Cingalese and English, a large Tract which we have printed for the Religious Treatise Society, is also just finished. The edition consists of 2,000 Copies. Our

Lord's Discourses, in Tamul and English, are now in the Press, with two or three elementary works, in the different languages of the Island.

The Sermon preached on the occasion of the execution of Private John Jenny, with a few particulars of his happy end, is in hand. It is designed principally for distribution among the Soldiers, and will, we humbly trust, accomplish good. When finished some Copies shall be transmitted to you.

We are about to print some extracts from the Old Testament, in Cingalese and English, for the Bible Society. The Book of Genesis is now translating, and will we hope be soon ready for the press. Having been favoured with the use of the Government Tamul Types, by the express permission of the Governor, we have it in contemplation to print an edition of the Old and New Testaments, in that language. We shall, however, wait the opinion of our Tamul Brethren on the subject; and will thank them to send us, as early as convenient, a probable estimate of the number of Tamul Scriptures which would meet with a good circulation in their several Stations. We expect the Bible Society will likewise take a number of Copies.

We rejoice in hearing of the success of the Gospel, in various parts of the world. O, that very plentiful effusions of the Holy Spirit may descend on us, in this Island; that we may rejoice, in the day of the Lord, that we have not run neither laboured in vain.

We shall have the pleasure to insert, in the *Miscellanea*, an interesting account of a Colony of Romish Christians, lately found, among the hills of the Interior of this Island.

With love to all our Sisters, and Families, We remain,

Very Dear Brethren, Yours affectionately,
W. M. HARVARD.
B. CLOUGH.

THE CALTURA STATION.

Caltura, January 3rd 1818.

MY DEAR BRETHREN,

With unfeigned gratitude to God, who has duily manifested his boundless mercy to me and mine, I sit down to discharge a grateful duty, to communicate to you some account of my proceedings in my new Station, and of what God has graciously done, and is doing for me. When I reached my appointment, I found that the Old Dutch Church, was totally gone to decay, and, there was no place substituted in its room.

When a Preacher came this way, (an unfrequent occurrence,) the people were accommodated with a part of the Government-House, in which they might occasionally hear the Word of God. When I came to this place the Honble John Rodney, favoured me with the use of this room, though at that time, this frequent occupation was far from being convenient to him.

Under those circumstances, I found a delicacy in going, and on my mentioning my feelings, to him he obligingly, answered "Be under no uneasiness; when you wish to occupy the room, drop me a line, two hours before, and the room shall be put in order, and I and my Family, will make a part of your Congregation." From that time I have regularly occupied this Place. It was one of my first labours to ascertain in what manner I could best fulfil my Ministry here, and most profit the people that Providence had put into my Hands. I found that I had people of five languages, in my Congregation; but too few understood English to render it a duty to preach in my native language. I ascertained that all understood the Portuguese or Cingalese language, or both, with the exception of two persons.

The People wished to have, according to their ancient usuage, three sermons a week, and these in the Portuguese language. I was not sufficiently versed in this Language to promise more than two sermons a week, in Portuguese, and this arrangement, with a Sermon by an Interpreter, in Cingalese, has been my plan since in Caltura. In all other parts of my Station, the Cingalese is the only Language that can be understood, except by a few.

I believe I have faithfully delivered the whole counsel, of God; and though it is not my pleasing task to tell you of sinners savingly converted to the living God, I have witnessed as great attention, and as great apparent concern as I have often seen in Europe. The tears (may I hope of true penitence) frequently flow down the faces of some of my hearers, especially, when I have endeavoured to shew, that if any Man have not the Spirit of Christ, he is none of his. You are, by experience, well acquainted with the difference, between a Christian Congregation, in Europe, and in this barren land; and I confess, that this difference would oftimes have sunk me down in discouragement, had not the Lord particularly refreshed my own soul, and filled my heart with tender compassion for souls ready to perish.

With some happy exceptions, I see little of Christianity but the name; and it is well known to be no reproach to say, that great multitudes consider Christianity to be nothing more than to be baptised; hence my Interpreters, generally use a word for baptism, which literally signifies, to make a Christian: and I firmly believe that there are thousands, that have just so much of Christianity as this, and no more.

Except in Caltura Town, and near the Romish Churches, I see very little appearance of a Christian Sabbath.

In a Sabbath Day's journey, it is needful to reprove one company of Christians, for building a House, on the Lord's Day; another company, for building a Boat, and others at various occupations; and it is not a little astonishing to see the surprise they manifest, that I should think that it is wrong so to do. This is a field for labour. Here poor immortals are born in ignorance, and brought up in ignorance, and they remain ignorant still. They generally possess soundness of intellect, and manifest great ingenuity in many of their proceedings; but they have

No. II. G

an inaptness almost bordering upon incapacity, to understand spiritual things. And it is scarcely to be wondered at, for they have been acquainted with nothing that could inspire a spiritual idea, beyond those rays of light which enlighten every man that cometh into the world: and those rays have been greatly obscured by the surrounding heathen darkness.

Yet I labour on with hope respecting these, believing that my labour will not, ultimately, be in vain in the Lord.

It is, however, very obvious to me that to secure the most extensive and lasting good, is to cultivate the minds of the rising generation. No children in the world are more tractable, and apt to learn, than the Children of the Cingalese; and "just as the twig is bent, the tree's inclin'd." These Children, in many cases, become more excellent Missionaries to their Parents, than we can be, and are not unfrequently the means of inducing their Parents to hear the word of God. Conformable to these views, my efforts have been directed since I came here. I have succeeded in establishing a School in Caltura, containing 62 Children; and the number would be much greater, if I had more room; but I am yet obliged to teach them in the viranda of my own House. The improvement and behaviour of the Children surpasses my expectation; and they seem to vie with each other to give me satisfaction.

I have four other schools in a state of preparation, the establishment of which I shall have the pleasure hereafter to communicate.

In my journeyings, and in my intercourse with the intelligent Natives, I have endeavoured to ascertain the state of every part of my district; and I find, that, in various places, Heathenism is overflowing nominal Christianity. To these places my mind has been particularly directed, as most suitable to try to establish Schools; but in the execution of my plan, I have hitherto been prevented by attending to *applications* from the Natives for Schools; though some of these are in the very places where I conceived Schools to be most necessary. In these efforts I shall not relax as long as I have power to move; and the prospect of a chain of Christian Churches, extending about 23 miles, is a sufficient compensation for every toil. I have, in many respects, laboured under the most favourable circumstances; as I have received from the chief authorities, both Native and European, every help in facilitating the execution of my plans: and while I duly appreciate every act of kindness from man, my gratitude is directed, in larger degree, to Him who has the hearts of all men in his hands.

With respect to my studies, I always act by a regular plan; and as I consider it an important circumstance that a Missionary should be able to speak, with his own mouth, consequently the acquirement of the Native languages has formed an important place in my course of study. I am now able to preach in the Portuguese language with nearly as much fluency as in the English, and for this I feel truly grateful to God. I have, at the same time, paid some attention to the Cingalese, but my attainments are yet small: and though I do not anticipate to preach very early in this language, I shall pay every attention to it that my other duties will allow.

With respect to myself, I have abundant cause for gratitude: for though it has pleased the Lord to try me severely, by family affliction, his fatherly chastisements have been graciously sanctified; and my soul has been raised higher in the enjoyment of that "peace of God which passeth understanding" than I have ever before experienced In my daily supplications to God I remember you, and pray that every blessing of the new covenant may be given to you abundantly, and that when God shall say to his worn-out Servants "come up hither," thousands of Indians saved, may hail you welcome to the shores of peace and eternal felicity.

I remain, in the best of bonds,

Your affectionate Brother,

Wm. BUCKLEY FOX.

P. S. Daniel Alexander, the converted Priest, is with me. He is the most laborious Cingalese I have seen. He labours almost Day and Night. I am much satisfied with him. I intend to place him in one of the New Schools; and the Inhabitants are very glad of the prospect of having him for a Teacher.

THE GALLE STATION.

Point de Galle, December 30th, 1817.

My Dear Brethren,

Another Quarter has elapsed since my last Quarterly communication. How very quickly do the Weeks and Months pass by! I feel thankful, indeed, to be able to say that I have been, properly speaking, employed in the work of a Missionary since that time; that is, in endeavouring to establish Schools for the Children of the Natives. I can say, with truth, that I feel this to be a most blessed work; and am fully convinced that the ever blessed God has been present to divinely assist and direct me All glory to his Holy Name! Though I have at present eight Schools in hand, I have only been able to open one, as yet; that is the School on the Circular Road, which stands about two English Miles from the Fort. The others are, however, in a good state of forwardness; and I trust they will all be opened in the course of another month.

The Circumstances attending the opening the second Wesleyan School on this Circuit were most encouraging indeed. The first day of this month was the appointed time. I repaired to the spot, at an early hour, to make the necessary preparations: and was much pleased to find the School beautifully adorned with the simple yet elegant ornaments, which you know are in use among the Cingalese. All anxiety, and expectation to see how this trial would succeed, I was much delighted to see the people flocking with their Children to be admitted into the new School. The Hon.ble Sir Alexander Johnston, Chief Justice, H. R. Sneyd, Esq. Provincial

Judge, M. J. Smyth, Esq. Collector of Galle, and The Revd. James Glenie, Colonial Chaplain, were so very kind as to encourage this Institution by their presence on this occasion. I delivered a short address to the parents of the Children, explaining the nature of the Institution, and pointing out the great advantages which their Children would derive from it; after which we united in solemn Prayer to Almighty God for his Blessing on the School.

It is with great joy that I say that this school is doing well. It contains about One Hundred and Fifty Children, 70 of whom are Girls. O that it may go on to prosper. Since its opening, I have commenced service in it, on Sunday Mornings, and no words would be sufficiently strong to express the happiness that I feel in this work. I do not preach one Sermon to them without feeling my Heart deeply affected; so that were I to give way to my feelings, I could stop speaking, and weep over them. Every Sunday the School is crowded with the Children: and many of the Parents, (both Fathers and Mothers,) come to hear the word of Life. Now I am blessed with the sight of what I long wished for: to see a Cingalese Congregation assemble of their own accord, without a *Government Order.* Well, glory be to God our Saviour; for he can and will work.

The other work of this Circuit goes on as usual. Our English and Portuguese Congregations are regular and attentive.

As all the men of the 73d Regt. are now removed from this, (with the exception of one,) we have lost our little English Class: however, I trust that some of the 83d Regiment will join us, to walk in the commandments of God. Our Portuguese Class, which was established since Conference, goes on well, and I doubt not but that in some time it will be a large one: at present we have ten members.

I must not forget to acknowledge the goodness and mercy of God in giving me such good health. It is true that I have been indisposed with colds, several times since the Conference; but I have not been obliged to give up one meeting upon that account. I must regret that there is only one Missionary at Galle, where there is at present ample work for three or four: however, I do not mean to reflect on the decision of the Conference, as to this: I know that it could not have been otherwise. But still I must feel to see the most promising openings, and not be able to take them up. Well, I trust to spend all the strength I have, in the blessed work of a Missionary; and then I can do no more.

This morning our good Friends and Wellwishers, the Honble Sir Alexander and Lady Johnston, embarked on board the Ship Alexander for England; and it is but just, that I should mention to my Brethren, his marked attention to us, during his stay at Galle. If it be the will of God, I hope he will return to this Island. But, however this may be, he will no doubt be a friend to our Mission, and to Missions in general, wherever he may be.

I remain, my dear Brethren,
Your very affectionate Brother,
JOHN McKENNY.

THE MATURA STATION.

Matura, 29th December, 1817.

My dear Brethren,

Our Quarterly correspondence will be rendered, I think, a great blessing. My colleague and I derived much satisfaction from the perusal of No. 1. and doubt not but it was equally encouraging to all.

During the last Quarter, our labours have been generally regulated by a plan similar to that of our circuits at home. This enables us to preach in some of our Schools on Sabbath mornings; and frequently to visit all of them on week days. These seasons are often refreshing. The progress of the Children is beyond what might be expected; and the appropriate manner in which several of them answer questions on doctrinal points, when proposed out of the ordinary way, shews their capacity, and assures us that in attending to their instruction our labour will not be in vain. We have had several openings lately for new Schools in various quarters; and we hope to be able to say, on a future occasion, that our efforts in these villages have been owned of God.

Several of the Scholars belonging to our Day-School having manifested a relish for divine things, and being particularly given to search the Scriptures, we formed them, and some others, into a kind of Class, a few weeks ago. Our Meetings are pleasing and profitable; and we indulge strong hopes of their future usefulness.

Our labours have not been confined to the rising generation. When we visit the Schools there are many who stand around, and hear the word of life;—and frequently in the bazars and other public places a great many hear with attention. Several pleasing proofs convince us, that on these occasions the word has been attended with power.

Though we have many difficulties in acquiring the Cingalese language, I feel great satisfaction in attending to it, not only on account of the necessity of acquiring it, in order to be extensively useful, but because of its intrinsic strength and beauty. I have begun to read sermons in it.

I remain, very affectionately yours,
JOHN CALLAWAY.

THE NEGOMBO STATION.

Negombo, Jonuary 2nd, 1818.

Very dear Brethren,

The real pleasure which the receipt of the *Quarterly Extracts* for October gave me, furnishes a very pleasant stimulus to write this quarter, independant of the evident benefit resulting from such a mode of periodical circular information.

Being *then* but newly arrived at this Station, of course I had but little to communicate to you; and even *since* that period little could be done here, in the *School* department especially.

owing to the almost incessant and very heavy rains. However I am glad to have been able to open three, and commence a fourth, in the villages of *Catoonnyaker*, *Radulonee*, *Zempellee*, and *Odepoo*, all within 8 miles of Negombo, though in different directions, in which there are at present about 200 Children, more or less, with expected increase.

The *Negombo School* goes on well. The Scholars are generally regular, their pronunciation of the English language improves; and the facility with which they commit to memory, and repeat their tasks is very pleasing. One boy, at the monthly examination, the other day, repeated to me 15 answers of a rather difficult Catechism, and the first 17 verses of the 13th Chapter of St John's Gospel, almost without an error. But they make by far the best progress in *Spelling* and *Writing*. Some *Christmas Pieces*, which the larger boys were allowed to write, by way of encouragement, were particularly neat and well written; and of several of the boys I have good hope in better things. Through the gracious providence of God, my health has been nearly uninterrupted, so that I have been able to attend regularly to the same plan of preaching, &c. which I mentioned last quarter. I am thankful also to add, that I have been enabled, this quarter, to lay aside the written helps which before were necessary to my preaching in Portuguese, (with the exception of translating the Scriptures, which I think best to continue,) and have thus been relieved from a heavy tax upon my time, which leaves me more at liberty to attend to the *Cingalese*; in this, however, my progress is rather slow, having no teacher at present; but I earnestly hope and intend to go on with steadiness and perseverance, having very little expectation of any success among the *Natives* without it.

Although I have met with some opposition, and many discouragements, yet, matter for *praise* greatly predominates. One circumstance in the last Quarter has given me much pleasure, and furnished at times cause for gratitude and devotedness: I have formed a small *Class*, which though but *very* small (consisting only of 5 Members,) is yet a blessing. I am happy to say that they evince the most undoubted sincerity, and give proof, by their deportment and conversation, that they are eagerly enquiring, " What must I do to be saved?" One has already received a happy answer to that all-important question, and rejoices in God.

I have to be thankful for the continuation of innumerable mercies by which I am surrounded, and want nothing but more Zeal for the glory of God, and love for the immortal souls for whom Christ died;—my heart goes out in fervent wishes and prayers for the happiness of all our dear Brethren, and for the universal diffusion of the Gospel throughout the world.

With love to Sister Harvard,

I remain, Dear Brethren.

Very affectionately yours,

ROBERT NEWSTEAD.

Revd. Messrs. Harvard and Clough,
Colombo.

THE JAFFNA STATION.

Jaffna December, 29. 1817.

VERY DEAR BRETHREN,

To give you an account of our present situation, and of the goodness of God to us, during the last Quarter, is a subject, as pleasing to us, as we know it will be gratifying to you. With humble dependance upon the Lord, we are proceeding onward, labouring for the Salvation of precious Souls sowing our seed in the Morning, and in the evening witholding not our hand.

Although not unacquainted with the temptations of the Wicked One, who rejoiceth only to do evil, yet we have abundant encouragement from God, who is able to subdue all things unto himself, and to reduce the rebel sons of men to the obedience of the Gospel. Great indifference to eternal things, marks the Character of the Natives of this part of the Island, who, by plunging themselves into awful superstitions, frequently quench the light which had dawned upon them.

The acquirement of the Native tongue, which we hope, by the blessing of God, to accomplish, will open to us a wide door of usefulness among the people; therefore we give ourselves to this part of our work, endeavouring, with all diligence to obtain it.

We have Service, every Morning, at half past seven o'Clock, when we collect our own Servants, and others who may be near, reading to them a portion of the Scriptures, and singing and praying in Tamul.

These exercises we hope will conduce to the good of the people, familiarize th· language to us, till, in the end, we shall be fully enabled to declare unto them the unsearchable riches of Christ.

Our European Class continues to prosper. Some have found peace with God, and can rejoice in Christ Jesus, while others are striving to enter in at the strait gate. Among the half cast young men, the Spirit of God appears working, convincing them of sin, and of righteousness, and of judgment. Several have begun to pray in publick, and one requested to be permitted to partake of the Holy Sacrament.

In Jaffna, our day School and Sunday School are upon the encrease; but in the Country, we have not been able to form Schools, as we desired partly; from the want of proper teachers, and partly, owing to the deep rooted prejudice, and almost invincible antipathy of the Hindus of these parts, to be taught any thing except their own fables. Few of them wish to learn English; and, as it respects their own language, they think themselves, not only best qualified to teach it, but also fully suppled with teachers, to whom Old Customs bind them to send their Children. To read and write a little is all they think needful; therefore when Schools are gratuitously offered, the reasons we have already mentioned, combined with the fear of being turned from heathenism, prevents their attendance.

Perhaps our disappointment in establishing Schools, here, at present, is intended, by a gracious and a wise Providence, to be over ruled, for the more abundaut diffusion of his Word, by the preaching of the blessed Gospel. And, although Schools can only be considered as secondary means, yet, when the word of God takes root among the people, they will become powerful auxiliaries in the general cause. While, therefore, we are thankful to God, for additional helps, we cannot but consider, with our Committee in England, (Letter, June 8, 1817,) "the preaching of the Gospel, under the influence of the Holy Ghost, as the most general method, by which a guilty and ruined world is to be brought to God." Faith cometh by hearing: and we have no doubt, when faithful Ministers are sent among the people, preaching the Lord Jesus, the hand of the Lord will be with them, and multitudes, will believe, and turn unto the Lord, as in the days of the Apostles. We have the same Word—the same Spirit—the same Promises, and we shall see the same *Effects*. "The world cannot withstand its ancient conqueror."

We are, very dear Brethren,
Your's affectionately,
T. H. SQUANCE.
R. CARVER.

P. S. Our place of worship has lately been fixed up in a plain and decent manner, and will be opened on the first day of the New year. In our next we hope to give you particulars.

Circumstances having rendered it necessary for our residence at Jaffna, no communications from Pt. Pedro can be expected.

~~~~~~

THE TRINCOMALIE AND BATTICALOA STATION.

Trincomalie, December 27th, 1817.

MY DEAR BRETHREN,

Multiplied, and various have been my trials, and painful the exercises of my mind, since my arrival at this Station. Yet I have not been left to bear my trials alone: my everlasting Friend, has been my light, my support, and my consolation. "The Lord is good, a strong hold in the day of trouble; and He knoweth them that trust in him." Since our last Conference, I have had a humiliating view of my great unfaithfulness, and unprofitableness, since my landing in India. I trust the discovery, though painful, has not been altogether in vain. It has tended to quicken me in the Divine way, and caused me to cleave to Christ, and long for *his* fulness of grace and mercy. Thank God, my health is tolerable; so that my life is crowned with mercy, and loving kindness. "Bless the Lord O my Soul." As to the work of God at this Station, it is yet in an infant state. However, even here, Jesus hath witnesses of his power to save from the guilt and defilement of sin.

I meet our little Class on Monday evenings, and our condescending God and Saviour, enables us to rejoice in the conscious

comforting manifestations of his precious love. Wednesday evening, we have preaching in English, Friday evening preaching in
Portuguese: the congregation in general small. Saturday evening
we have a well attended, and in general a very profitable, prayer
meeting. Sunday morning half past seven o'Clock, preaching in
English: few attend, but these few appear to hear for eternity!
Preaching, Sabbath evening at 7 o'Clock. The congregation large
and solemn. Ever since my arrival here, I have been in a constant bustle with Masons, Carpenters, Coolies, &c. to get the Bungaloe finished, &c. And, thank God, we have so far succeeded, as
to enter it on Christmas evening, and preach to the people Jesus and his power and willingness to save. The Bungaloe is very
large. I intend to have a partition in it. Divine worship in one
part, and our School in the other. Our School here is of importance: there are more than 30 Boys, nearly all Malabars. Great
I believe, will be the increase of Children, in consequence of having
a place suitable for the purpose of instruction. I have been making enquiries, in order to establish Schools amongst the Natives;
and, notwithstanding my offers, proposals, &c. the people are exceedingly backward; so that. as yet, I have seen no favourable
openings. Indeed, until Br. Osborn's arrival, I have abundance of
work on hands. And such have been the rains since his arrival
at Jaffna, that to come by land was impossible, on account of several
large rivers, and by sea is out of the question at this season.
And now, my dear Brethren, begging a place in your fervent and
constant prayers,

I remain,
Your affectionate Brother,
G. ERSKINE.

~~~~~~~

THE MADRAS STATION.

<div style="text-align:right">*Madras, December 24th, 1817.*</div>

My dear Brethren,

I enclose you my accompts up to this date. My Congregations
are encreasing. I preach on Thursdays, and twice on Sabbath Days;
and read and expound a Homily every Tuesday. And I sincerly
recommend the latter to all my Brethren. I still live in Black-
Town, and preach in my own hall. My health is very good, and
my soul cleaving to God. I trust I feel a humble and thankful
heart.

If Brother Harvard's health should permit his removal, I would
strongly urge his taking this place as his appointment, from many
reasons; and I fear we did wrong in not allowing him to come,
and leave all events to God. I was quite mistaken in the expensive living. Every article (House Rent excepted) is cheaper than
at Colombo or, at least as cheap.

I cannot be pleasantly nor usefully employed, till I have a separate and comfortable place to preach in. To rent a suitable
place would cost £70 per annum; and, besides, such a place can-

not be rented at Madras. My hall holds only about 50 persons. I could purchase a tolerably suitable place for (I think) 600 pagodas, 78 feet by 16 long; 8½ feet in the side wall. It is the judgment of several who have built in Madras, that for 2,000 pagodas, the whole premises might be made extremely suitable for our purpose. I am almost determined to make the purchase. I have 300 pagodas promised, as a Subscription, and have no doubt I could raise 300 or 400 more,

After next week, I intend to spend a month travelling through the country.   Your's &c.
                                        J. LYNCH.

P. S. One of the London Missionaries lately lost an excellent wife. She was only 23 years of age. She died in a strange land, far from any Missionaries: and left an infant of 10 months.

~~~~~~~~~~~~~~~~~

BOMBAY STATION.

No Communication received from Brother Horner.

From a Friend at Bombay, to Brother Harvard.

MY DEAR SIR,

I take this opportunity, to send you a few lines, by —————— who is going to Madras and Bengal. with ——————————for the benefit of his health. I sent an answer to your last, directed to Colombo, and I hope that you have received it. The Rev. Mr. Davies, who used to deliver Lectures at St. Thomas's Church, every Thursday evening, is returning to England, on account of his health; and either Mr. Hall or Mr. Newell deliver a Lecture, the same evening, at the house of Mr. Beck. Yesterday was the second Lecture. Mr. Horner will begin his preaching again next Tuesday, please God. Only a few attended in the rainy season, and it was discontinued a short time. Mr. and Mrs. Horner and Child are in good health, and I venture to give their sincere love to you, Mrs. Harvard, and Child: did he know of this opportunity, you would have received a letter from him. We hope that you are prospering in the vineyard of our Blessed Lord and Saviour, and that your soul is strengthened and refreshed, day by day, from the presence of the Lord.

O! may the Almighty own and bless your Ministry in the Gospel of his Son Jesus, and give you many souls for your hire; may him who walked among the Golden Candlesticks, be in the midst of your little Flock, and may his countenance, which is as the sun shining in his strength, rest on them, filling you with consolation, from the river that maketh glad the city of God.

I bless the Lord, that this leaves me and my Family well. I have four souls now committed to my charge, to train up for glory. Pray for us, my dear Friend. Mrs. —————— unites in kind love to you, Mrs. Harvard, and little boy. May the Lord bless you and keep you.   I am your affectionate Friend,

                              ————————

Bombay, August 22d, 1817.

Miscellaneous.

No. I.

Brother Clough's Account of the Oriental Library purchased from the Estate of the late W. Tolfrey. Esq.

Mission House, Colombo, Dec. 26, 1817.

VERY DEAR BRETHREN,

At our last Annual Meeting, you will recollect, we considered the propriety of our purchasing the oriental library of the late Mr. Tolfrey, for the use of our Mission in this Island. We felt however, at that time, considerable backwardness in making such a purchase, not having it in our power to ascertain the opinion of our Committee: and though Brother Harvard and I wrote to them, immediately when the idea occurred to us, yet we were aware that the matter must be settled before we could possibly receive their answer. Another circumstance made us hesitate considerably, in making immediate proposals; a fear that a larger sum of money would be required for it, than we should consider ourselves justified in advancing, on behalf of the Mission. But as you were kind enough to express your decided opinion that they would be peculiarly valuable to us, and that we ought, by all means, to possess them, we conceived it a kind of duty, if possible, to secure them.

We watched for the most favourable opportunity of making a proposal; and it was not till 4 months after our meeting, that we could do any thing; at which time we were informed, by an Official Note from the Supreme Court, that the Books would be put up to public Auction, unless we made some offer. We were aware that if the Books were sold in that way, the Library would be ruined, as they would be put up in separate parcels. Under these circumstances, we proposed to the Court to give one Thousand (1000) Rixdollars for the whole, according to the Catalogue which was shewed you at the Conference. The terms were accepted, and the whole library is now safely lodged in the Mission House.

I am sorry to say that I have found both the books, and manuscripts, in the greatest disorder and confusion. This had been occasioned, no doubt, by the sudden manner in which they were left by their late possessor. Much time has been given to them, for the last two months, endeavouring to get the whole into order, and to enter as much as possible into Mr. Tolfrey's plans. But I am sorry to say, that, by some accident or other, the Library has suffered essentially, and particularly the manuscript part of it, and I believe no man ever understood Mr. Tolfrey's plans besides himself.

But, perhaps, our Brethren will be desirous to know what the library contains. We would have had a Copy of the Catalogue printed and sent to each of you, but it is so extremely incorrect, that is, it was either made out in a hurry, or the person, who made it out, did not properly understand the nature of the Books. The first part consists of a few printed works, not very numerous. There are a Sanskrit Grammar, and Dictionary, both in the Old *Devanagare,* Character: the Dictionary, is Mr. Colebrooke's Translation, of the Celebrated *Amara Singa,* which will be explained, hereafter; likewise, a Grammar, and Dictionary in Bengalee, a Grammar and Dictionary, in Tamil, besides som other little works. Mr. Tolfrey's Manuscripts, form what we conceive the second part of the Library, I cannot possibly, at present, give you an adequate idea of them;

though perhaps in a future letter I shall, if spared, be able to give you something satisfactory. The first part are the Ola Books: these are peculiarly valuable, on many accounts: and we are really happy our Mission has been able to get them in so short a way. It would have been an extremely difficult thing, if not impossible, for any Missionary, at this time, to have secured such works. There are some of the great standard works of Budhism.

The Ola Books are in the *Sanskrit, Pali, Eloo,* and *Cingalese;* the four principal Languages of this Island.*

I am having the whole regularly numbered, and shall make out a correct Index, by which any book may be referred to at once. From number 1 to 14, is the celebrated work, called පන්සිය පනස් ජාතක පොත *Pansia panas jātaka potta.* This book, which comprises fourteen pretty large Volumes, contains the history of the Transmigrations of Budhu, from the time he became a candidate for that greatest of all Characters, and to which the unnumbered Millions of gods and goddesses bow with reverence, until he had completed his work, and enterred into නිර්වාණ *Nirewany.* From the Title of this book, (or rather history) it appears he was born 550 times, and transmigrated through the bodies of 550 living beings. The word පන්සිය පනස් *Pansia panas,* means 550, ජාතක *Jātaka,* is Birth, පොත *Potta,* is book; which words, when compounded as above, පන්සිය පනස් ජාතක පොත *Pansia panas jātaka potta,* signify the history of the 550 transmigrations of Budhu. This Book is written in very elegant Cingalese, and contains most of the beauties of this language. It is replete with the most extraordinary stories that surely the mind of man ever invented, all of which are in reference to Budhu. I hope shortly to have a little time to translate a few of them.

[*To be continued.*]

No. II.

From a Friend in England to Brother Harvard.

Southampton, April 1817.

"I have now before me a BULL of the Pope's, which is published expressly against THE BIBLE SOCIETY: in which he calls it:— *" An abominable device—a pestilence—a defilement of the faith—an imminent peril to souls—an impious machination of innovators—an abominable scheme.* That THE BIBLE, *printed by* HERETICKS, *is to be numbered among other prohibited books.* He says also that *the Holy Scriptures, when circulated in the vulgar tongue, have, through the temerity of men, been productive of more injury than advantage: that it is a snare prepared for the eternal destruction of souls.*"

---

* *The Tamul is much spoken in most parts of Ceylon, and is the only Native Language in the Northern, and Eastern Provinces. Yet it is generally considered a Foreign Language in Ceylon, being brought here by the Malabars, at a period subsequent to its being regularly inhabited by the Cingalese.*

No. III.

Statement of Portuguese Cambawadda, Jowan Mendoze, of the village of Wohakatto, *in the* Audagodde Corle, Matala District, *about eight miles N. West of* Nalande.

I am head of the Church, but not a Padri. I am called, in consequence, Saint Christian. There are about two hundred of us professing the Roman Catholic Religion. I have a Cingalese Testament written by a Portuguese Padri, (a native of Portugal) named Jacob Gonsalle, I have also several prayers written u on olas.

After the expulsion of the Portuguese from the Kandian country, by Raja Singa, some prisoners were captured, who were not permitted to quit the Interior, but had lands granted them: the following villages were appropriated for their residence, viz. *Waauda, Caloogalla,* and *Wahakotto*; about the same time a number of Malabar Christians established themselves at a place called *Galgamma,* in the Seven Corle, three days' march from Putlam, where there is now a fine large Church, with about two hundred people professing Christianity.

The village of *Waauda* is situated in the Seven Corles, and *Caloogalla* is in Toompany. The people of *Wahakotto* are the descendants of Portuguese, as were the former inhabitants of Waauda and Coloogalla, who were deprived of their lands, and driven out of the Country, in consequence of joining and assisting the Dutch in the invasion of the interior. Such of them as could not effect their escape were murdered; and there now remains no vestige of them or Christianity in those parts of the country, On the borders of the Lake at Candy, at a place called *Bogambera,* was the principal Church, and twelve Padries were attached to it, King Koondasala, who was third successor to Raja Singa, would not allow the Roman Catholic Religion to be exercised in his Dominions and caused the principal Church of Bogambera, as also the inferior ones throughout the country, to be destroyed, and ordered the Padries to quit it.

King Kierty succeeded Koondasala, and it was during his reign that the Christian inhabitants of Waauda and Caloogalla were expelled. Shortly after this event, a great famine and plague raged in the Interior. The King, attributing the cause of those calamities to the persecution of the inhabitants of the last named villages, ordered the images which had adorned the Church of Bogambera, and had on its destruction been deposited in his stores, to be given to the people of Wahakatto, with permission to rebuild their Church, and enjoy their religion.

The younger Brother of Kierty (name unknown) succeeded him, who allowed them the full enjoyment of their Religion, as did the late King; and they have not been interfered with since the reign of Kierty.

K

The Kandians call them Portuguese. They are considered on a footing with the Vellalas, and perform the same duties as people of that Class.

The above is a correct Copy of the original statement of *Portuguese Cambawadda*, obtained through the kindness of the Honble and Reverend T. J. Twesleton. A more particular account of this interesting Colony, of newly-discovered Christians, will, we expect be published by the Reverend G. Bisset, at present in the Interior.

No. IV.

The brig Hercules, Capt. King, arrived at Falmouth from St. Domingo, in 49 days. On the 20th spoke the brig Susannah & Grace, bound to Gibraltar. A short time before the Hercules sailed, advice had been received at Jacmel, which was generally credited, that Christophe had ordered his subjects to embrace the Protestant religion! and that the English language should in future, be spoken throughout his dominions!

END OF JANUARY EXTRACTS, &c.

** The Brethren are requested to forward to Colombo extracts of such of their Europe or other Letters, as may contain Information of general interest·

Printed at the Mission-Press, Colombo, for the Use of the Missionaries.

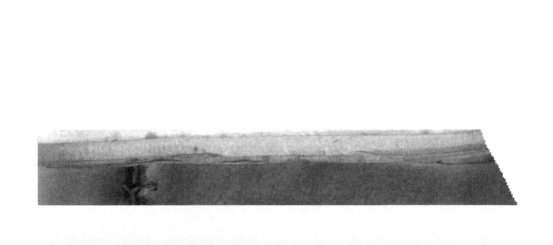

Extracts,

FROM

QUARTERLY LETTERS, &c.

No. III.   *APRIL*, 1818.

THE COLOMBO STATION.

Colombo, Mission-House, April 10th, 1818.

VERY DEAR BRETHREN,

WE have much pleasure in renewing our pledge of affectionate union with you in the great work of evangelizing the heathen. And having engaged therein "*by choice and conviction*," we are happy to assure you that neither has the latter been diminished, nor the former repented of, since our last communication. So far from that, we see, daily, more and more reason to redouble our exertions in behalf of a benighted people, whom God has committed to our charge; and by grace divine, we are resolved to continue ever faithful to the standard which has enlisted us from the ranks of Satan, until, either we have a goodly number of immortals ranged with us under the same banner, or else are raised to celebrate the victories of the Saviour, in the land where he reigns as King for evermore.

In a work so great and momentous, we are not surprised that difficulties present themselves. We had almost said *discouragements;* but Johnson's octavo dictionary being at hand, we observe it affixes such a meaning to that word, as renders it utterly unsuitable to our circumstances, as Christian Missionaries. We have, it is true, our moments of depression; but we have nothing "*to deprive us of confidence*," nothing "*to deter*," or "*to fright from* the *attempt*," of bringing, at least, some of the worshippers of idols to the knowledge and worship of the true God. Had we, indeed, seen no instances of divine grace, in conversion, since our arrival in this distant country, we might have some sanction for discouragement. But we know we *have* been made useful, both to Europeans and Natives, since the commencement of our Mission: and what the Lord *has* done by us, he is able to do again; and the change which has been produced in a few individuals, he is able to repeat in cases as numerous as the sands upon the sea shore. And certainly He who in infinite love, died to save sinners, and whose nature is ever unchangeable, cannot be ever unwilling to extend the glories of his saving grace.

No. [III.   L.

We have, no doubt, that, of the great Missionary family, scattered as it is all over the face of the earth, the majority, either have or once had, their feelings of depression, with respect to the progress of their work. This however may be accounted for without any reflection upon the work itself, and without drawing after it any forebodings of being finally unsuccessful. As it respects success, the lip of truth has said "*The earth shall be filled with the knowledge of the Lord as the waters cover the sea:*" and He has added, "*Prove me, now—saith the Lord of hosts, if I will not open you the winnows of heaven, and pour you out a blessing, that there shall not be room enough to receive it.*" We conclude, then, that in the general the depressions of a Christian Missionary proceed eminently from himself— from his own heart—though often encreased by the artifices of Satan; and that the nearer we live to God, in the acts of personal piety and faith in the Saviour, the more lively and animating will become our apprehensions relative to our grand work, and the more assured will be our expectations of success in the salvation of immortal souls. Therefore, beloved Brethren, let us be "*stedfast, unmovable, always abounding in the work of the Lord, forasmuch as we know that our labour is not in vain in the Lord.*" The seed sown shall take root in many blessed instances: and though some, falling by the way side, may be prevented from vegetating, and though others, from the peculiarity of the soil, may only encourage our hopes for a short time, and the growth of other may be counteracted by the effects of the cares of this world, and the evil tendencies of earthly temptations, yet, Dear Brethren, while we continue to sow the pure seed of the word of God, some shall be received into honest and good hearts, and shall bring forth fruit, "*some thirty fold, some sixty, and some an hundred fold.*"

In this Station, the last quarter has been a very painful one. We have been made to pass through deep waters of domestic affliction. But we have been graciously supported, and have, we trust, had our trials greatly sanctified to our advantage, both as public characters and private Christians. In the former sense, they have caused us to prize the present moment, as the only one we can secure, to improve every passing opportunity of usefulness, and to labour "*while it is called to-day;*" and, in respect to our individual experience, our afflictions have led us to a minute scrutiny of our doctrines and attainments, and a nearer and closer intercourse with our God, by faith, and prayer, and watchfulness. May the Lord grant that we may still lose much of our moral and spiritual dross in the furnace of affliction.

Mrs. Harvard and Brother Clough, (the latter of whom must be considered as jointly addressing you with myself, thus far,) having been so much reduced by illness, it was recommended by the physician that they each should take a short trip to sea, for the benefit of the air, &c. For both of us, now, to leave this station at once, was next to impossible. Brother Clough affectionately wished us to take the first change; but knowing that in the meanwhile he would be unequal to the Circuit-work, my dear Partner cheerfully resigned the opportunity to Brother Clough, with an eye to the necessities of our station. And we, yesterday evening, accompanied him on board the Ship Forbes, bound to Madras. He has doubtless a peculiar interest in all our prayers. We have calculated upon his being absent from us about two months; and should Mrs. H. not be better, we hope for a relaxation on his return, "*if the Lord will.*" This will likewise be of no small advantage to myself, who am greatly relaxed and ennervated by former exertions and illnesses.

Our dear Brethren will excuse my having said so much about ourselves. Our grateful acknowledgements are given to Brother Callaway, who very kindly left his station for our assistance, and has been already with us nearly a month. His presence with us, just now, is of peculiar importance; and I fear we shall be under the necessity of requesting him to remain with us for some time longer.

There is one point on which, I know, you will all feel with me, while I refer to it: and we shall be glad if you would severally refer to it in your correspondence with the Committee. Having now had the management of our Printing and Book-Concern, &c. more than three years, and during the greater part of that time, having paid a more laborious attention to the business than any of our workmen, I cannot forbear to express my conviction that it is no small evil, that, out of two Missionaries at this station, the time and constitution of one of them, should be so largely monopolized and trespassed upon by the drudgery of worldly business, as they have been. I do not make this observation from any selfish feeling; because, in the order of things, I can derive no advantage from it. Before its importance will have been felt in England, the burden will have devolved on some one else. But, painfully competent to give an opinion on the subject, I here record my sentiment, that unless some remedy be applied to this evil, either by the appointment of an additional Missionary, or by the sending out of a suitable person, as a local preacher, to manage our temporal matters, this station will never give us that satisfaction in spiritual things, which we derive from those stations, which are purely Missionary.

It does not, however, become us to complain. By the great goodness of God, we have been enabled to carry on our labour in the last quarter, not only without any diminution, but, on the contrary, with some small encrease. Our English services in the Fort have been regularly observed, excepting in one or two instances, when it was impossible, from my being alone, and obliged to preach in the Pettah. Among the Soldiers a very pleasing work is going on. Some of our pious friends are in the field, and we believe are supported and preserved by grace divine. In the Fort there are impressions on the minds of several of our hearers; and though the work is noiseless, it is real and progressive.

A poor woman from Ireland, who had been a member of Society there, passing our Mission-House, was melted to tears, on unexpectedly meeting with a Methodist Chapel in so distant a land. Seeing her stand in the road, we invited her and her husband into the house, and spake to them about the things of God, which they both seemed to feel greatly. She has since joined the Fort class, and we believe is a humble pious Christian. Her husband likewise regularly attends the preaching, though a member of the Romish Church.

In the Pettah, our number is as usual. Among the great body of the inhabitants we have to complain of a great want of the spirit of hearing. Our Congregations, however, either English, Portuguese, or Cingalese, have not decreased; though they have not increased, in proportion to our sanguine hopes. We will nevertheless persevere. The army of the god of this world must give way. Occasionally one and another comes in, and throws down the weapons of his rebellion. One Country-born person and a Cingalese young man have joined our Pettah class last quarter. Adrian and Andries, the two converted Priests, continue stedfast, and appear to be growing in the knowledge and experience of divine things; particularly the former. At the last Class Meeting, he said, *" My Prayer to God is, that no badness may ever come near my heart."*

We have this quarter established regular Sunday Morning preaching in a village called ඔලවත්තෙ *Wellawatte,* about 6 miles from the Mission-House, which at present promises well. We preach in our School Bungaloe, lately erected there. We have thus three Sunday morning services at the same hour. For our assistance in this increase of Sunday labour, we have begun to employ our young friend, Don Cornelius de Silva Wijasinga, of the Colpetty School, as a local Preacher, believing him to be called of God to the Ministry of his word among us. He underwent a regular examination, by Brothers Callaway, Clough, and myself, on the afternoon of Easter Day last, with respect to doctrine and experience, much to our satisfaction, and was publickly appointed to the work on the day following, when, being Easter Monday, he preached in the Mission-House (as in our custom at all the Festivals) to an overflowing congregation of children and young people. We felt a peculiar pleasure in hearing the first Native Cingalese Preacher with which God has honoured our Mission. May he be kept, humble, zealous, and faithful, and be made very useful to his benighted countrymen.

In our Schools we have been visited with a violent attack of the Measles, which has spread like a plague, and carried off great numbers of Children, and many adults. Of our Scholars about seven have died, and about 122 continue sick. It was very gratifying to hear of some of our pious children praying with, and reading the Scriptures to, their sick and dying schoolfellows. Some of whom have given hopes that they have profitted by our endeavours, and are reaping the blessed advantages of Religion in a glorious world, where sickness and sorrow cannot come. A pleasing instance of this was the death of Jesse Felsinger, a lad

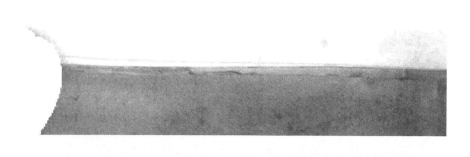

about 13 years of age, who died on the 2nd of February last. The following account of him was taken from his mother's mouth by one of our Country Friends. His style is preserved.

"Jesse was a boy who lived as wickedly as most of the young boys of his age, from his infancy; but since the establishment of the Mission School in the Slave Island, which is only four months, he made a wonderful alteration in his whole conduct, and at once became a very good boy, and loved his learning and his religion. He often spent his time in reading the New Testament, and never failed to attend to his morning and evening prayers, which he did with so much attention and strictness, that I could not help thanking God Almighty for the piety of my son, in so tender an age, which naturally is apt to turn to play more than to any thing else.

"But he was not long to be spared to his relations; the Almighty being pleased to call him to that eternally happy state in heaven. He was taken ill in a very sudden manner, and died in the course of six weeks. A few days before his death, seeing him very contented and patient in his lingering hours, and that he does not think so much of his life, as he does of heaven, I asked him "*Son are you not fear to die?* to which he readily answered, "*Why—why—Mother? Why must I be afraid to die? Did not our Saviour died for our sake?* I then spake to him of the death of a friend of mine; and he, turning towards me, observing that I was weeping, endeavoured to console and comfort me, saying, "*You should not be so sorry, mother; it is better to die, while one is young, than, being filled with all wickedness, to die in old age.*"

"He was, till his last moments, much attentive to his Bible, which he had received at School. His last reading was the eighth chapter of the Gospel according to St. Luke. He one day happening to see that his sister-in-law, took up the Bible, and put it aside in a careless manner, he appeared angry, and said to her: "*Mind, that you should pay more respect to that Book!*— As I found that there was no hopes of his recovering. I sent for Mr. Appellton, a friend of mine, who had the kindness to call a few days before his death, and prayed with him, speaking much with him about religious matters, and the long suffering and death of our Saviour. And on the day of his death, the same friend calling again, asked him if he recollected that conversation, what it was about: Jesse replied, "*Yes: it was a discourse about God.*" Mr. A. then asked him, if he liked to hear him pray; he said, "*O yes.*" He then prayed. When the prayers were over, appearing very happy, he called me to his bedside, and embraced and kissed me; and then he called his brothers, and did the same to them; next he called his little servant, and kissed him also. All this time, he was very thoughtful and sensible: and, in about three minutes afterwards, he died, to the greatest astonishment and sorrow of me, and his brothers, and all his relations, and the spectators."

No. III.   **M**

The above, which is a very faithful narrative, will, I am persuaded, be gratifying to you.—I have often noticed the appearance of the boy, on visiting the School to which he belonged;
and, from all I heard since his death, believing that he died in
a very safe state, I preached his funeral Sermon, before the Schools,
in the Mission-House, from 2 Timothy, iii. 15.—His death appears
to have made some good impressions, upon the mind of his mother,
who has, since that time, been admitted into the Pettah Class,
and seems to be seeking the salvation of God.

We have added one more School to our list since the last
quarter, which is the one at එවැල්වත්ත Wellawatte,
the place I have already mentioned, as having established Sunday
morning preaching therein. The ground on which the School,
Bungaloe is built, has been kindly granted us by Don Carolus,
a Mohandiram, who has sent his son and daughters to the School;
and appears much determined to assist and befriend, our exertions
in that village. The number of boys is at present 41, and of
girls 21, and promises to be greater.

According to our intention, expressed in our September letter,
we have inspected the Class of pious boys which had been formed at the Colpetty School. Thinking it would be a relief to
my dear wife, I took her with me; and, truly, human language
is utterly unable to express our emotions at what we then saw
and heard. It is surely a work of God. O that it may deepen
and widen! On looking at the Class-paper, we were struck with
the regularity of their attendance, which had very few exceptions;
and since the establishment of the Class, there appears to have
been but one exclusion; though it has continued for nearly a
year! On entering the room, what was our surprise to find it
completely lined with about thirty native Cingalese boys, who immediately rose to receive us. After feasting our eyes for a moment, I desired them to sit down, and began the meeting: but,
such a serious attention, and in so many boys, I never saw before. We seemed to be in the midst of a number of old men.
There was nothing affected or whining about them. They gave
simple reasonable answers to simple reasonable questions. Their
expressions were remarkably modest and diffident, and several of
them spoke of their innate sinfulness; in a manner, at which we
hardly know whether we were the most astonished or gratified.—
Some had just recovered from severe attacks of the measles, and
appeared to have been greatly profitted in the School of affliction. I asked one boy if he had had thoughts that he should
die, during his affliction; to which he replied that he had. I then
asked him, how he then felt— if he had any fears of dying. He
answered, that, *since God had given him power over temptation,
and taken away the love of sin from his heart, that he did not
fear to die!* To this effect several boys replied.

Upon the whole, I do not hesitate to say that there is a genuine work of grace upon all their souls, more or less. About
six of them seem to enjoy peace with God, a blessing which they

are all earnestly seeking after, and give a very rational and simple account of the change which has taken place within them. I closely pressed them on the score of conduct, and obtained every evidence, that not only their outward character, but that their general temper and spirit also is according to the Gospel. At the close of the meeting, a new boy was proposed as a member. I hesitated at receiving him; but all the boys united in recommending him as a steady boy. I then asked him a few questions. "*Well, my dear boy,*" said I, "*do you think you have been a sinner?*" "*O, yes, Sir,*" said he, "*a greater sinner than I express.*" "*Are you sorry, then, because of your sins?*" "*Always, Sir.*" "*Well: if we take you in to meet with these boys, which of your sins will you forsake?*" ඔක්කොම "*Ockomma,*" was the reply, or, in English, "*all of them.*" I was pleased with the simplicity of his answer, and admitted him on trial, according to his desire.

It is a considerable satisfaction to my mind, that Brother Callaway has since visited and examined this Class. There were several children absent, on his visit. But he found about twenty in whom he thinks the work is genuine. And in respect to those who profess to have found peace with God, he is fully inclined to receive their testimony.

I must here observe three things :—*First,* that this little Society has been formed by the pious, watchful care, and zealous attention, of our Friends Cornelius, and Mr. Coopman. *Secondly,* that for the first nine months, this Class was entirely conducted by them: never having been met by a Missionary. This we studiously avoided, from a settled principle, which we had well weighed. And hence, their meeting cannot be attributed to any servile principle, but appears to have been produced by a deep sense of divine things. *Thirdly,* that none of the Boys are more than 14 years of age, and the greatest part of them from 8 to 12 years. Glory, for ever glory, to the Triune God. "*Out of the mouth of babes and sucklings thou hast perfected praise.*"

Our Friend Cornelius mentions that he has found the visiting of his sick Scholars, a very interesting and profitable employment. On visiting one young man, and setting before him the necessity of giving himself up to God, in order to experience the witness of the Spirit, and peace with Him, the young man leaped from his seat, embraced him with great affection and many tears, and earnestly besought him to pray for him. They kneeled down and poured out their hearts together at a throne of grace!— Master and Scholar supplicating the mercy of God!

We have before us a great work to do. The ignorance of many is astonishing. A young man who offered himself for baptism, the other day, had not the least knowledge of Christ, even in the history. He however professed to believe in him!! A young woman, at the same time, on being 'asked how many Gods there are, answered "*Four!*" and on my asking her mother, who was present, the old woman replied she "*did not know any thing about it!*" Of course we have appointed them a course of instruction, before they can be admitted to the sacred ordinance of Christian

baptism. A short since, being on a journey in the country, I ask
a Cingalese man, if he was a Christian; බැහැ *Naha,*
"No!" said he. "What religion are you, then," I enquired.
ප්‍රතිපාදේ *Reppremado,* was the reply: or, "*I am
belonging to the Reformed Church!*"

Our temporal concerns go on much as usual. Most of the Books
sent us out by the Alexander are disposed of, and we have had
several orders sent us for others, in consequence of the proposals
issued from our Book Room, and advertised in the Government
Gazette, a copy of which shall be inserted with the other Missel-
laneous articles.

We have lately finished a new Printing Press, with the Iron-
work brought out by the Alexander, and have now four presses
at work. Indeed we have to acknowledge with gratitude, several
essentially useful articles which were sent out to us from our
esteemed Fathers the Committee by that Conveyance. The printing of the Scriptures in the new Type, has been retarded, by the
incomplete state in which we received the fount from Serampore,
owing to many types having been lost out of the box on the way
down. We have waited for some time in hopes of receiving a fresh
supply, which we suppose unavoidable business has prevented; and
have at last resolved to try our own resources. A Punch-Cutter and
Mould-Maker have been set at work. The *first Type* has been
cast, and shall be sent home as a curiosity to our Museum; and
we hope by our next communication to report, that a new, por-
table, edition of the Cingalese Testament, has been commenced,
agreable to the generous intentions of the British and Foreign
Bible Society, and the earnest desire of their Correspondents
in this place.

The Bible Committee of this place, has obligingly granted two
hundred Copies of the New Cingalese Translation, for the express purpose of supplying our Mission Schools. We shall faithfully send to all our Southern Brethren their share of this quantity, which will amount to forty copies for each Station; and for
any further number which may be wanted for the supply of the
Adult part of the Population, of their several stations, we
recommend them to apply separately to the Secretary of our
Colombo Bible Society. So small an edition as a thousand Copies, cannot be supposed to be equal to a very general circulation; we shall therefore remit no exertion on our part to expe-
dite the printing of the octavo edition.

The Translators meet regularly upon the Old Testament, in which
they have advanced as far as the 24th Chapter of the book of
Genesis. We are anxious to have several parts of the Old Testament in the hands of the Native Cingalese, and especially of our
Exhorters and School Masters. An acquaintance with that part of
the Scriptures will tend very greatly to enlarge their conceptions
of Christianity: and the chain of connection subsisting between
the Old and the New Testaments, will furnish them with an argu-
ment in defending the latter of which at present, they are not generally sensible.

Feeling the want of a Morning Service, and there not being any thing of that kind yet attempted, we have made a selection from the Liturgy of the Establishment, and translated it, for the use of our Native Cingalese Congregations. This Selection includes:—

1. Introductory Scripture.
2. Exhortation.
3. General Confession.
4. Absolution or Remission.
5. The Lord's Prayer, &c.
6. The Ninety-fifth Psalm.
7. A Space is left for the reading a Chapter out of the Holy Scriptures.
8. O, be joyful in the Lord, &c.
9. The Apostles' Creed.
10. The Litany.

[In the Litany, after the Prayer for the Nobility, is inserted the following:————"That it may please thee to bless His Excellency the Governor, the Supreme Court of Judicature, the Council, and all who are entrusted with any authority amongst us."]

11. The General Thanksgiving.
12. The Prayer of St. Chrysostom.
13. 2 Cor. xiii, 14.

It has been translated under the eye of Brother Clough; by whom it was finally corrected; and who is about to add thereto, a selection from the offices of Baptism, the Communion, the Burial of the Dead, and Matrimony, &c. We wait for his return from Madras to complete this and several other important works in Cingalese, which he has either begun or contemplated; especially a Cingalese and English Dictionary, upon a large scale, the materials for which he has been for some time too closely applying himself in collecting and aranging, and which will be an essential acquisition to the literature of this island.

We have just finished a Tract against Idolatry; being a selection of the principal Scriptures against it. It is printed in Cingalese and English, in parallel pages, under the direction of the Bible Society.

An Historical Scripture Catechism, in parallel columns of English and Cingalese, is just finished, and may be had at the Book-Room, price One Rixdollar. The manuscript of this work was given us by Hardinge Giffard, Esq His Majesty's Advocate Fiscal, who had previously had it in use in an excellent Native School, supported by himself, near his residence. It is calculated to give the Native youth a very interesting idea of Scripture History; especially, in relation to the truth of Christianity, of which it contains many striking proofs. This gentleman having lately left Colombo, on a visit to Europe, we gladly embrace this opportunity of expressing to our Brethren our grateful sense of the many kind attentions with which he has favoured us, both in his private and in his professional capacity. The last wishes he expressed to us were for the prosperity of our Mission.

We have in the Press, besides other smaller works, an excellent Vocabulary of Words and Phrases, in English, Portuguese, and Cingalese, compiled with much labour by Brother Callaway. It makes about 150 pages of demy octavo, and will be useful, not only in this country, but will enable our Friends at home to form a tolerable idea of these languages, even without the aid of a Native Teacher. The Price is Three Rix Dollars.—An Abridgement of Mr. Sutcliffe's Grammar, by Brother Callaway, is likewise in the Press.

The present delay in the Cingalese department of our Office, will enable us to turn our attention to the wants of our Brethren in the Tamul part of the island; whom we hope soon to furnish with a good supply of elementary Tamul works. Their reasons for delaying the reprinting of the Tamul Scriptures, appear to possess force and propriety: and of course the present state of the inhabitants of the Tamul districts, will render smaller works of more immediate use that large and voluminous ones. We shall however, in the meantime, not lose sight of a new edition of the Word of God in Tamul, as soon as we have the means of accomplishing it.

Among the Miscellaneous Articles, will be found a continuation of Br. Clough's account of Mr. Tolfrey's Library, which he wrote in pencil, on his couch, a day or two before his departure for Madras.

I have been favoured to receive a letter from the Honourable the Chief Justice, dated the Isle of France, February 4th last. Our Brethren will feel interested and thankful to learn that Lady Johnston bore the voyage to that place much better than was feared. And, in consequence of the pleasing amendment in her Ladyship's state of health, Sir Alexander had determined to proceed on to England. He and all the family were well. Our Honourable and kind Friends, retain the strongest wishes for our usefulness and prosperity, as a Mission, and expected to reach England early in May.

At the desire of one of our esteemed Secretaries, the Rev. George Marsden, I intend to add, at the end of this Quarterly, a copy of a valuable and truly interesting letter which I have lately received from him, dated London, Oct. 18, 1817.

Praying that we may be favoured to see an extensive revival of pure and undefiled religion in this distant Island, and that many of the poor heathen may become witnesses of the power and willingness of Jesus to save to the uttermost, all who come unto God by him,

I remain,

Very Dear Brethren,

Yours very affectionately,

W. M. HARVARD.

THE CALTURA STATION.

Caltura, April 3rd, 1818.

MY VERY DEAR BRETHREN,

IT is with more than ordinary pleasure that I avail myself of this, and similar opportunities to communicate to you circumstances relative to my present state, and that of the department of our Mission, which providence has committed to my charge. This pleasure would not have been diminished, if I could have described my Circuit and success as I could with truth have done of the spheres of my labour in England; this I cannot, nor did I ever expect to do, though I left England with the assurance that God would be with me in all the varieties I should meet with. I have had all kinds of feelings excited, except those that may *properly* be denominated discouragement; from this I have been preserved; sometimes, only by a clear conviction that God sent me here: this conviction remains with all its former clearness, and enables me to labour on with more than hope. I should be happy to see more immediate fruit, though I am preserved from the folly of expecting it, till I have sown the seed. My station is in, perhaps, not a few respects peculiar. I have found none, beyond my own Family, that could witness the power of Jesus to save. With only one exception, there is not a European resident within 19 miles of me. The consolations which, in many Stations, arise from, at least occasional, intercourse with pious European Soldiers, have never fallen to my lot; nevertheless the peace of God which passeth understanding has kept my mind in peace; and this has enabled me daily to say, from the heart, " No climes or regions differ; every place is home.". I have the testimony of my own conscience that nothing that I could do has been left undone.

I left England to minister to the Heathen, and, lo! here I have found them, truly without hope, and without God in the world, invelloped round with thickest darkness, and influenced by the most pernicious prejudices. If there is a place beneath the sun where misery extreme calls for Christian help, *it is here!* if there is a place in the world where it is more honourable and glorious to perish in administering the balm of life, than another, *it is here!* If there is a place where the Physician of souls is more needed than another, *it is here!* Some persons may, perhaps, say that I am on a Christian Station. It may be so: but, I have not yet been so happy as to find the Christians; though I have been unwearied in my search after them. There are some, it is true, called Christians; but I really cannot distinguish them from people *who are no Christians;* except by personal enquiry; and I have not yet been able to learn the difference between a Christian and others; except that *some* once learned three prayers, that they have now forgot, and have been baptized in the Name of the Holy Trinity: and some of these have even forgot their *Christian Names!* This is not a universal case, but the *Shadow* of such a Christian as is described in the New Testament, is as rare (I will not say as a Comet) as an Eclipse in the Solar System.

As for a Christian Sabbath, it is in vain you look for it. Corn is pounded—Casks are made—Houses are built—Boats are framed, Houses tiled—in the sight of the Minister's House—in sight of the Church—on the Lord's Day—by *Christians!* These things my Eyes have seen, and must yet see Yet you must not suppose that we make no distinction of seasons, or that our weeks are 356 days long, or rather the length of our lives. We have a *Seventh day;* and *we,* who are strangers in the place, discover it by this circumstance: viz. on the evening of the seventh day (which always falls on the same day with the Christian Sabbath) we hear, not far distant, the noise of Tom-toms and singing, which we are informed, is accompanied with dancing, and this generally lasts nearly the whole night. The people of the place also seem surprised, for we see them run in all directions toward the place whence the sound proceeds, and in all probability their surprise does not soon abate, as we seldom see them return. A few Sabbaths past the noise was so great, and so near to my house, that I supposed we had some Heathen ceremony; and, not being willing that a *Christian Town,* on the *Lord's Day,* should be made the scene of such abominations, I sent a person to make enquiries who they were that made such a disturbance; my Messenger returned and said, "*Sir, they are Christians!*" You will say this is a melancholy picture. So say I also; but it is accurate, unless the shades are too faint. But it is not enough to view the case as it stands, we must try to account for it, or leave it among the unaccountables.

What advantages have the people had? what means of instruction? For a long period previous to the time of our present excellent Governor, the people had no means of instruction at all, at least the number that had any, was always exceeding small compared with the whole population. The singularly kind patronage and encouragement which his Excellency the Governor and our other Honourable countrymen have invariably given to every effort to improve the moral condition of the British subjects under this Government, have been of too recent a date materially to alter the scene; yet, what has been done, will bring the blessing of many who were ready to perish, on the heads of the kind patrons of such efforts.

What has been done to improve the moral condition of the British Subjects in this Island?—An edition of the Cingalese New Testament has been distributed —But few are the people that can read. At the opening of one of my Schools, upwards of 80 Children were present, and only *one* of these *could read!* In other Schools the case has been similar. The greatest number of Children I have met with, who could read, were indebted to the *Budhist Priests* for their instruction, and you well know, from the nature of Cingalese elementary works, with what disposition such pupils would read the Word of God. Of preaching they have had little; and a majority of them never heard 10 Christian Sermons, of any kind, in their whole lives. I have taken great pains to ascertain their real state, if, peradventure, it might be possible to prescribe a remedy. It is easy to say, "*The word of God is the remedy—the balm of life;*" but how shall we administer it? The water of life itself will quench the thirst of none, but of those who drink it. What mind could ever be so sanguine as to suppose that human beings, like these, who know nothing of Christianity but what was contained in the three prayers they learned as their qualification for Baptism, (and these perhaps they never repeated after, and have now forgotten them,) that these would rush forth from their huts, to hear what they considered of no importance, or perhaps judged false? Should I, under present circumstances, see them crowd the hills and the villages, as in Yorkshire, Cornwall, &c. to hear the word of God, this would astonish me much more than their present apathy!

It is my settled conviction, that there is no mode of access to the natives of this country, but though the medium of Schools—well-conducted Schools; and that these will answer many valuable purposes. The supple minds of the Children have a right tendency given to them. They have line upon line precept upon precept. Without this the Scriptures are printed and diffused in vain. You well know the great unaptness of the minds of the adults to understand divine things. Schools will remove this, in the rising generation. Here congregations can be collected, (experience proves it,) the parents will attend with their Children to hear the word of God. In the vicinity of our Schools the Sabbath-day is respected; and people not connected with our Schools hang down their heads when we detect them breaking the Sabbath day, and manifest a consiousness of what we find not elsewhere—that they are doing wrong. Though some of my Brethren (not less desirous, nor less diligent,) have found great difficulties in the establishment of Schools, I have been differently circumstanced. —The People have applied. I have *selected* from their Petitions such as I judged from their situation, &c. promised most to promote the Christian Cause. The Schools I have established are as follows: 1st, පානදුර් or පණාතොත *Panedura* or *Panatota*, 10 miles North of Caltura: this School contains 60 Scholars. 2d, පින්වත්ත *Pinwatta*, 8 miles North of Caltura: this School contains 85 Scholars. 3rd, වස්කඩුව *Waskaduwa*, 3½ miles North of Caltura: this School contains 62 Scholars. 4th, කලුතොත or කලුතර *Kalutota* or *Kalutera*, the place of my residence: this School contains 62 Children. 5th, බේරුවල or බැර්බරීන් *Beruwela* or *Barbareen*, 8 miles South of Caltura: this School contains 50 Children. 6th, අළුත්ගම *Alutgama*, 12 miles South of Caltura: this School contains 57 Children. 7th, කොස්ගොඩ *Kosgoda*, 20 miles South of Caltura: this School contains 68 Children. Thus I have 444 Children under my care, and 7 Cingalese Congregations. I have already as much work as I can do; but it grieves me to have so many applications that I cannot attend to. Amongst the Petitions I have by me, 3 only, contain 363 names. To expect an extensive conversion of souls, without indefatigable labour, in this

No. III.　　O

opening way would be absurd. The Goliah with which we have to fight, is, Ignorance—the most awful Ignorance—Ignorance of all that is good. To remove it is not a work of a day: but it must fall before our weapons. I was greatly encouraged in a late visit to the Station of my Brother Missionary at Galle. In visiting his truly Christian Churches, his well-conducted Schools, his Cingalese Congregations, collected uncompelled, his excellent arrangement, &c. I was truly astonished: I saw, and laboured, and improved: and now "I follow, though not with equal step." Such means cannot be used in vain. It is labour, hard labour, but pleasing labour; and will be gloriously-successful labour. Praised be God, for what he has graciously wrought, my Missionary Brethren! Inspiration has said, your labour is not vain in the Lord. He will yet, having brought us through the Water and Fire, bring us into the wealthy place. If I am not permitted to see the *towering summits* of our Zion here, my bones will lay at the *Foundation* of a work that shall never end. With the most hearty Christian affection,

I remain, Dear Brethren,

Yours affectionately,

W. BUCKLEY FOX.

~~~~~~

THE GALLE STATION.

<div align="right">

Point de Galle, March 30th, 1818.

</div>

MY DEAR BRETHREN,

I am again called to the pleasing duty of giving you, and the rest of my Brethren, some further account of the work of God on this circuit. I rejoice to be able to say that the last three months have been the happiest of my life. With a heart overflowing with gratitude to God, the Fountain of blessing, I have marked the progress and prosperity of the work in general, as well as all its different parts. Glory for ever be to the name of God, that it has been pleasing in his sight to crown my labour with the most abundant success; and which I think it a duty I owe to him, whom I believe is the glorious Author of the work, to the Christian world, and to you my Companions in labour, to enter into a detail of circumstances. It is at the same time the feeling of my heart, that God should have the glory; and to this sentiment I know your hearts will say, Amen. The fact is, my way has been so opened, and my path made so plain, by the providence of God, that I have had only to walk it, and to attend to the calls of duty, so as to promote the prosperity of the work. However, I cannot say that I have had no difficulties or causes of depression; but when they have presented themselves, I have just endeavoured to follow the path of duty, leaving events in the Hands of Almighty Power and Infinite Wisdom.

During the last three months, I have opened five new Schools, which are in a state of gradual improvement, and exhibit the the most flattering prospects. They are established in the villages of Tottogamme, Hickodde, Gindurah, Minuangodde, and Unnewattene. The Tottogamme School (which stands about a mile and a half from Hickkodde, and half a mile from the Sea,) was opened on the 27th of January. It contains 65 Boys, who are in general regular in their attendance. To point out the necessity of a School in this place, I have only to mention that few of the boys knew even the Cingalese alphabet, on its commencement. On January the 21st the School of Hickkodde was opened. It contains 74 Boys and 10 Girls; I have been particularly favoured in getting a most suitable English Master for this School; I mean Mr. Henry Mattheys; who became an early member of the Galle Society, and has continued for about three years to walk consistently, and to adorn his Christian profession. Since his appointment to the School of Hickkodde, he has been active, zealous, and persevering; and the effect produced, is, that his School is in a very prosperous state, and all the Boys attend with great regularity. If the length prescribed for this communication would admit of it, I could enrich it, with several anecdotes which would fully demonstate the above statement; however, I cannot but notice one fact, that is, he has made himself well acquainted with all the houses of the boys of his School, so that when any are absent he goes himself, finds them out, and makes particular enquiry into the cause. The importance of Mr. Mattheys being placed at Hickkodde, is not to be viewed only in reference to the School of that village: he will be surrounded by Schools under Cingalese Masters, in the neighbouring villages: he will have seven, within six English miles of of him; these he will regularly visit, in my absence, and that without the least prejudice to his own School, as I have been able, out of the Galle School, to supply him with a Monitor, who is very attentive during his visits.

The School at Hickkode, has been built entirely at the expence of the Coral, or headman, of the place. And now I wish to take the opportunity of particularly mentioning to my Brethren, the conduct of this rich and respectable Modeliar. I have received kindness and attention from several of the headmen of this district, but nothing to equal *that*, which this man has manifested to our cause. He has not only given the ground for the School, and built it at his own expence; but he has done more; when the School was ready to be opened, there was no house to be had for the English Schoolmaster and Family to live in, and this appeared a formidable difficulty; but this man most generously gave up for the Master's use, a fine new house which he had just built for his own Family, and into which he was about to remove. Thus my way was made plain. This Modeliar regularly attends divine service in the School, and expresses great satisfaction and gratitude, at being so blessed with the means of Christian instruction. A little anecdote respecting this man will give you a proper idea of the purity of his principles. Some time ago he was very sick, and supposed to be dying; his friends used all their influence to prevail on him, to use charms and heathenish ceremonies, as affording the only hope of recovery; but he firmly answered. "No: *I am in the hands of God: for he only is able to save me: and I will not use your charms!*" This was firmness, in a *Cingalese* man, with death in view!

I shall be obliged to go to some expence at Hickkodde ; first to build a little dwelling house, for the English Master, and secondly, to erect a proper place for divine worship. The School is strong and well built; but it is only large enough to accommodate the boys of Hickkodde, leaving no room for the boys of the surrounding Schools, who are to assemble there, to attend divine service on Sundays. So that it is indispensably necessary to have a place large enough to accommodate at least four hundred. However I believe that the Brethren have the fullest confidence in me, that I will not go to any expence, which the interests of the work of God do not absolutely require. Therefore I shall cheerfully and confidently go on my way.

On the 2nd of February, I opened our new school at *Unniwallane*, about three English miles from the fort, on the Matura road. I have had more to encounter in the establishment of this School than any of the others. It contains about 60 boys; and as the master has been under the care of the Missionaries at Galle for three years, and is at present a member of the society, I have good hopes of its ultimate prosperity. The grand hindrance is the Government Master of the school of Talpy; who is a most determined enemy, though he has been brought forward and promoted through the interest of the Missionaries.

On February 3rd, I opened our school in the village of *Gindurah*, accompanied by our highly esteemed friend, R. H. Sneyd, Esq. Provincial Judge. This school contains 78 boys; and is doing well.

On the 16th of the same month, I opened our school in the village of *Minuangodde*, one mile from the fort. This School stands on the top of a Hill, in a very beautiful situation, and is near the House of our good friend Mr. Laneroll, the Head Catechist Master of the Galle Distrect, who has generously given me the ground for the School free of expence, and proposed to make it over to our Mission, so long as we shall keep a School in the Village. This School contains about 85 Boys, and 15 Girls. It is under the superintendance, of Don Nicholas Perera, my Interpreter, who is very diligent in his work. He has joined the Society, and in general gives me much satisfaction: his abilities are of a very superior kind. Our School on *the Circular Road* contains to prosper. I have made quite a little Settlement there, and have four Bungaloes built so as to form a Square. The first is appropriated to the use of the English School, the Second to the Cingalese department, the Third to the use of the Mahabadde Children, (who wished to have a Second Bungaloe being Fifty in number, which wish I deemed proper, all circumstances considered, to gratify,) and the Fourth is intended for the Girl's School, which I have not been able to organize, for want of a suitable Mistress. This Establishment is one of peculiar interest, and contains many fine and promising Boys. The English Master is a Portuguese young Man, a Member of our Society, and which is better, he is under the saving influence of the Grace of God. Our Fort School is on the increase. During the last Quarter, I have added 11 boys to it, and appointed three out of it, as English monitors to other Schools. The present master is a serious young man of excellent moral character: he regularly attends preaching, but has not yet joined the Society.

Thus I have given you some account of the seven Schools under my care, containing in all about 606 Children, 46 of whom are girls. In addition to this, I have Schools building in the following villages, which are all in a state of forwardness, so that I hope to have them all opened in the course of another Quarter: 1st Boepe; 2nd Dadala; 3rd Boesse; 4th Dodandoewe; 5th Wawelle; 6th Tilwatte; 7th Ditto; 8th Kahawe; 9th Weheregodde; 10th Akoerelle; 11th Madampe; 12th Amblangodde. The most of these twelve Schools would be finished in two weeks, were it not that the Cingalese New Year is so near, a time when no Cingalese man will work. Those twelve Schools when opened, will add at the least 600 more Children to my present number; so that by the divine blessing, in another Quarter I hope to be able to inform my Brethren, that I have, on this Circuit, Twelve Hundred Children under regular instruction, Moral and Religious.

Since my last communication I have commenced a weekly Meeting for my School-masters: however the object of it, is not so much the transaction of business, as the inculcating of Religious Doctrines and Christian principles. I find it to answer best, in the general, to conduct the business of each School within its own walls, there to receive, and there to expel, in the presence of all the other boys: this has a good effect. I intend to establish a similar meeting at Hickkode and Amblangodde, as it would be too far to bring all the School-masters every week to Galle.

From the nature and extent of my work, you my Brethren, will naturally wish to know something of my plan of labour, and how I get through it all. I endeavour to make the best of my means; and rejoice to inform you that I find in Br. Anthonisz, a most useful Assistant: so that by his zealous and faithful labours, I am able to be every other Sunday from home; as in my absence he takes my place in the Mission House, I mean in Portuguese, much to the satisfaction and profit of the people: he preaches every Sunday morning in Cingalese, in one or other of the schools, and is working hard at the study of the language: he is at present much embarrassed for time, however in a few weeks there will be such an alteration in his circumstances as will give him the whole of his time to devote to that work in which his soul delights: as I meditate taking him into closer union with me and the Mission: which I think I am fully entitled to do, from all that past in our last Conference in reference to him. I have also received very considerable help from Br. Griffiths, since his arrival at Galle: he kindly takes a School for me every Sunday, and is very ready to assist me whenever I find it necessary to apply to him: however I cannot expect to have his help long; as he no doubt will soon be able to cut out work for himself. The Catechist Master (of whose excellence you have all heard) is also very forward to give me all the help in his power; so that he takes a School on Sunday when I require it. Thus I endeavour to turn all the help I can obtain to the best account, and aim at securing the interests of all and every part of the work. The Sunday I am absent from Galle, I spend at Hickkode, and in general am able to complete my *present* work there, so as to return to Galle, on Monday or Tuesday; but when our other Schools are opened, I shall be much more from home.

Our School plan is evidently of God, and is to be viewed as a powerful auxiliary to our Mission; not only because it proposes to secure the education of the Children; but our Schools will evidently prove our key to the Natives, by which we shall be let into their confidence and affections; so that through the medium of Schools, the fair opportunity will be afforded to us of *Preaching the Gospel*, and of *Distributing the Scriptures*; which two things taken in conjunction with the Schools themselves, are considered the means, and, I believe the only means, of Evangelizing the Heathen Then let us,—let our dear Fathers and Brethren of the Committee,—let the body of our Ministers,—and let our whole Connexion, in union with all our dear Christian Friends of all denominations who rejoice in the prosperity of Zion,—hail the extensive establishment of Christian Schools in India, as the sure prelude of the most lasting, yea eternal advantages to its inhabitants.

The expence of our Schools will certainly be considerable; and I often think of this: but England is determined that the Inhabitants of Ceylon, as well as all other parts of India; shall have the Gospel, and will not England rejoice to hear of the fruits of her liberality being expended on a *Genuine work?* It is laudable to go to expence, even with the *anticipation of good*; but we have in some degree our expectations realized; and do we not already begin to gather the fruits of a most abundant harvest? Shall we then fear the want of of support? No, England will say, Go on, ye Christian Missionaries, in your blessed work; follow the openings of Providence and we shall support you in all your measures. For the light of Heavenly truth first beamed upon us, from the East; and we shall now send it back again!

But, my Brethren, I have far exceeded my bounds. However, I trust that the facts contained in this letter, will form a sufficient apology for its length.

With Christian love and affection,   I remain,
Your Brother in the best of Bonds,
JOHN McKENNY.

P. S. Lately we were favoured with a pleasing and profitable visit from Br. Fox, which was attended with good. We are deeply affected by the trying state of Br. Clough's health, and upon account of the afflictions which have existed in Br Harvard's family; but trust that God, in his great mercy, will restore them all to the enjoyment of health and strength. God has been particularly gracious to my family this past Quarter: my beloved partner with myself have enjoyed in general good health, though we have had a little affliction to suffer. We thought, we were about to sustain a heavy loss in the death of one of our dear little boys: he was so ill that I may say we gave up hope: it was our youngest: we were waiting for one of our Brethren to come and baptize him: however he was so ill that I thought it right to administer the ordinance privately to him; (his name is Robert Newton;) but God was pleased to spare him to us, and we trust to his cause. I should not forget, among other things, to mention, that for two months past I have been able to preach extempore in Portuguese; so that I now find it comparatively an easy task. My progress in Cingalese is but little. I do not forget it altogether; but attend to it when I can get a spare hour.

MATURA STATION.

Colombo, April 4th, 1818.

VERY DEAR BRETHREN,

I remember entering on the quarter just elapsed with a mind determined to continue on the Lord's side. Through mercy I have in general been enabled to proceed in the blessed work with satisfaction. I need not enlarge on the difficulties incident to Missionary exertions. In common with the Lord's faithful Servants, we must "endure affliction." But it is animating to reflect that the God we serve, extends his special providence over us;—he sees us humbly labouring, watching, praying; and if we are faithful unto death, he will remove us to that region of enjoyment, where the wicked cease from troubling and the weary are at rest

No very material alteration has of late taken place in our mode of proceeding. We find it of importance to adhere as closely as possible to our regular plan. A few have joined our little company during the Quarter; and a work of grace is evidently on many souls. Several desirable objects of minor importance may be accomplished by Missionary efforts; these naturally afford encouragement in their degree; but to be instrumental in the conversion of sinners is our primary object. Sometimes we have been led to suppose that our labours have not been attended with such success, as might have been anticipated. Yet when we turn our views to the superstition by which the people are deluded, and the evil habits in which they are established, we have much ground for thankfulness; and perhaps evidence of usefulness is sometimes concealed from the instrument, to accomplish the gracious designs of Infinite Wisdom.

On Sabbath mornings the Children belonging to our Schools in the neighbourhood are assembled to one place of worship, and form a pleasing congregation. They are addressed in a manner adapted to their understandings, and are generally serious and attentive. On other occasions, our congregations are subject to much variation. At times, as many attend as might be expected, from the limited population of the town; at other times a lamentable neglect of divine things seems to prevail.

You may form a pretty exact idea of our labours, when in the country places, by the following extract of a Letter from Br. Lalman, which I have just received. "In the evening I preached to great numbers of people at the market at *Angamme,* (a village about half way between Galle and Matura.) Many seemed very attentive, and tried to keep the noisy crowd as quiet as possible, in order to hear the better. I feel my soul much drawn to the work of the Lord, and to the souls for whom he shed his precious blood. I rested there that night at our Schoolmaster's house. We spent the evening by reading the Scriptures I prayed with the family and the neighbours who purposely came down to hear the word of God. The next day at *Marissia,* on my return home, I went to the market place and to the sea side, where was a great number of people standing idle, some gambling and others waiting till the return of the fishing boats. I spoke to them particularly of the goodness of God, and of their ingratitude for the blessings they enjoy, by living in their sins. They heard with silent attention—staring at one another. I believe they felt the power of the truth of God."————

In addition to the places where we have hitherto laboured it is gratifying to be requested by the people of other village, to visit them also with the everlasting Gospel. The field of our exertion is rather extensive; and our labours have sometimes exceeded the bounds of prudence: but who can witness the deplorable condition of the people without using every possible means of effecting their salvation?

You will remember the circumstances which led a Candian youth to request Christian instruction of our Brethren at Colombo, and to desire, if necessary, to become a servant: though of respectable connexion and then educating for the Budhist priesthood. He was placed under our care, at Matura, about 15 months ago. He had previously studied the best Cingalese writings, and had evidently made proficiency in the literature of the country. At all times his conduct was not so satisfactory as could be wished: but he would listen to good advice, paid much attention to his studies; and was generally in a promising way. I regret to inform you that he was removed to eternity on the 25th of January last. About six weeks before that period he caught cold, and not suspecting its dangerous tendency was not perhaps sufficiently careful of himself. Though he grew worse, and was strongly urged to take suitable medicine, he refused every thing but that which was administered by his medical countrymen. When he became sensible of his state, he expressed a wish that Europe medicine might be applied. Mr. Evers, I am thankful to say, was particularly attentive, and used every means to effect his recovery: and for several days we entertained strong hopes that he would be restored. His complaint, however, operated so fatally, that the best efforts were of no avail. Not long before he died he made, in my hearing, some good reflections on the shortness and uncertainty of life—the vanity of worldly pursuits—the happiness of the Christian—and the necessity of being prepared for the better world. It was evident from the solemnity with which he conversed on these subjects, that he felt their importance. Most of the Members of our little Society frequently called to see him, and he strongly advised them to attend regularly all the means of grace, and to be entirely devoted to God. One young man who had been under serious impressions and Christian instruction for some time, was much affected by hearing him say, - "Andries, you ought by this time to preach." On the morning of the day he died, he seemed quite resigned, and perfectly sensible. He often expressed his hope and confidence in God through Jesus Christ; and said he had rejected all trust in any refuge besides. I continued with him till Br L. had preached to the Cingalese congregation, and then I was compelled to leave him for the English service. I hardly expected to find him alive on my return, and as I was going to his room, I was meet by one of his juvenile companions, who is pathetic accents, which no expression can pourtray, said, "Joseph is dead, Sir!" He expired a few moments before, while Br. L. was commending his spirit into the hands of Jesus.————It would have been more gratifying to have witnessed a more joyful triumph of faith; but the fact of a superior young man leaving the system of religion in which he had been bred, and in which he had expected to be distinguished, on hearing the evidences in favour of the religion of God, and in sickness and death, resting his hopes of salvation on the redeemer of the world, demands our thankfulness. How different from what we frequently witness! Persons evidently or the margin of eternity, destitute of a rational hope of glory, acknowledging no moral offence but such as relate to accidental injury to insects or animals—anticipating nothing but a course of transmigration—happy or miserable, as their conduct in this life has been consistent or inconsistent with the Budhuist superstion.

Our attention has been partly directed to some little helps for the rising generation. The Cingalese Spelling Tables are printed, and already used, in many Schools. I have, by request of several of our Brethren last Conference, abridged Mr. Sutcliffe's very excellent Grammar. The Abridgement is now in the press, and I believe will be eagerly studied by the upper class of learners in our different Schools. Our principal effort in this department. has been to compose a Vocabulary in English, Portuguese, and Cingalese, to which is added a pretty copious collection of Phrases and Dialogues. I need not enlarge on its probable usefulness.

It is perhaps unnecessary for me to add the reasons which induced me to come to Colombo. Though the unfavourable weather, and my close attention to study, had injured my health, I should not have removed, if my place had not been in a great degree supplied. Since my arrival here I have been enabled to superintend the execution of the works mentioned above, and several others, and in other respects rendered timely assistance to the Brethren here; while the change, I am happy to state has been of great benefit to me. I believe I shall return with renewed resolutions, to live to God, and to be useful to men. I remain, Very Dear Brethren,

Affectionately yours,
JOHN CALLAWAY.

THE NEGOMBO STATION.

Negombo, 2nd April, 1818.

MY DEAR BRETHREN,

With much pleasure I communicate to you, several particulars relative to this Station, since our last Quarterly Report. And as it appears, to be rather first in importance, am happy to say that I have succeeded in adding *four* more Schools to the former number; two of them in Negombo, and entirely of *Females*, with the exception of a few of their very small brothers. The total Number of Schools on this Station now, is 9, containing, in all, about 455 Children, of whom 153 are females. They are generally going on well. I had another very promising School in a great state of forwardness, in a very populous neighbourhood, and which I should have opened this Quarter, but it was entirely dispersed, and broken up, through the strange prejudices and unprovoked persecution of a Roman Catholic Priest, who used coercive measures, both with the Parents, and the Children, to induce them to leave the School. And as he is resident on the spot, and has *twice* thus dispersed the School, while I am living at a distance, I thought it best altogether to give it up, as there could be no security, the Parents being absolutely afraid to send their Children, if refused Confession, &c.

In the course of the last Quarter, governed by existing circumstances, I have somewhat altered the plan of preaching, &c. and instead of going into the Country, (which I only do occasionally now,) I generally on the Sunday preach in the Bazar, and visit the prison between my own services. In these exercises, I have met with several, very pleasing circumstances, not the least of which is, that the Bazar, which before was open, and filled with noisy buyers and sellers; more than on other days, is now, through the Magistrate's kindly seconding my views, entirely shut up on the Lord's Day. I have stood as quietly on the Bridge to preach as in our own place, and had as attentive, and far more numerous, a congregation. On these occasions, I have distributed a great number of Malabar Scripture Tracts, furnished me by Mr. Twisleton from the Bible Society; which have been received with so much avidity, both by Roman Catholics and Heathens, that I have been followed home, by many at one time, to beg more tracts: and a few Sunday since, a man from *Manaar*, (a Merchant) having seen one of these tracts, came to me, earnestly begging to have one, while his goods were all on the water, ready to sail; he seemed quite delighted when I gave him two; and promised to read them to his family and neighbours.

On the third Sunday in March I baptized a Cingalese man, a convert from Heathenism, by the name of *Cornelius Robert*, before the congregation. He is an inhabitant of one of our School villages, and, (with all his family) was a professed Budhist. He gave a most interesting and satisfactory account of his views, and of the progress of his mind from darkness to light, (which began to take place under a Sermon by the Catechist Master,) and answered every question proposed to him, with almost Scriptural consistency. He is now one of our Schoolmasters in that village, *Tempeleo.*

This Quarter, I have been enabled, with the blessing of God, to complete the Translation of the New Testament, into the Ceylon or *Indian Portuguese,* just as the people commonly use it. I was led to this attempt partly by the great desire manifested by the people for it, who were frequently hearing me read from the Pulpit, parts which I had translated for that purpose, and partly by a conviction that I could not do better than furnish myself with a whole New Testament, in a language which the people understood, for my own use amongst them. It has at least tended greatly to enlarge my views of the Sacred Scriptures themselves, while it has also much aided me in speaking to the people. Several portions of it have been *lent,* while I have been going on with it, to sick persons, one of whom died with a chapter of St. John, I believe, under his pillow*.

I have been in no small degree, discouraged, through this Quarter, by the extreme apathy and carelessness of the people. Even those who used regularly to attend our meetings, with seeming delight, at first, are now kept away by the slightest thing: and through the time of *Easter* especially, the Preaching has been almost literally deserted. One who met with us in Class, and from whom I hoped much, has preferred the opinion of the world, and left us. His place, however, has been supplied by two more; and there are now 8, who meet pretty regularly. The *Schoolmaster* on this Station, (who has experienced a change,) at his own desire and request, meets a few of the elder School-boys, weekly, in a kind of Class, in which there is some promise. As to health, I have felt through the latter part of this Quarter, considerable weakness, induced, I believe, by violent perspirations, which, perhaps, have been occasioned by the increasingly warm weather. Through mercy I am a little better now, though not well.

My mind has been greatly raised by the cheering intelligence which we have received from home, as also by the kind communications of Private Friends. On these accounts my heart has often rejoiced with unspeakable joy, and I have been led to

* Several of the Brethren having translated detached portions of the Scriptures into the Country Portuese, which they are in the habit of reading to their several Congregations, it is requested that they would send to Colombo, as soon as they can, corrected copies of their Translations. Br. Harvard has proposed to compare these different parts with Br. Newstead's complete Version, and to examine and revise the whole for the press.

To the present time, we have never heard of any Translation of the Sacred Scriptures, in a style which can be read and understood, by the thousands in India who speak the Portuguese language. We know, from experience, that the edition printed in London, of which we were favoured with a good number, by the kindness of the BRITISH AND FOREIGN BIBLE SOCIETY, though eagerly received from us, both in Bombay and in this Island, could nevertheless be understood, but by a very small proportion of the Portuguese descendants, to whom they were given.

The importance, therefore, of such a Version of the Scriptures as is now proposed, it will need no animadversion to prove. Our Brethren will cheerfully enable us to make it as vernacular as possible, by furnishing their various contributions; and the Bible Society will doubtless give us assistance, in a pecuniary way, if needful.

dore the infinite goodness of God. I do not know that I have ever been more blessedly supported with the cheering presence of God, and the consolations of the Holy Spirit, than through the past Quarter, which has thrown a ray of peaceful enjoyment over my most solitary hours, and enabled me abundantly to rejoice in the Lord as my *Portion*, and my exceeding great reward.

.Very affectionately yours,

ROBERT NEWSTEAD.

THE JAFFNA STATION.

Jaffna, March 30th, 1818.

VERY DEAR BRETHREN,

We feel more than ordinary pleasure in writing to you on the present occasion; as our intelligence is of a more pleasing nature than any thing we have ever before been able to communicate. During the past quarter the arm of the Lord has been made bare: Sinners have been awakened; Sinners have been comforted; and believers have been stirred up to "press toward the mark for the prize of the high calling of God in Christ Jesus."

According to the intimation in our last quarterly letter, we re-opened our Chapel on the first day of the present year. It had undergone many repairs, which involved us in considerable expences, amounting to 600 Rds. This sum, we fear, would mostly fall upon our Fund; but the liberality of our friends disappointed our mentioned fears the Collections, Subscriptions, &c. in the end, exceeding, by a few Rix Dollars, the whole of the expences. Thus the Lord again laid us under fresh obligation to be grateful.

The morning service was conducted in English, and that of the evening in Portuguese. In the morning Br Carver read the Prayers, and Br. Squance preached from "*O Lord, I beseech thee, send now prosperity.*" Psalm 118, 25. and Br Osborne preached in Portuguese in the evening. It was a day that will long be remembered. Many had their convictions deepened, and several were stirred up to cleave to God with purpose of heart. Collections were made after each of the services. It is a circumstance worthy of being noticed, that the four Artillery men of the Garrison, (all the English Soldiers we have here,) sent by one of their number 4 Rix Dollars "to support," (as he expressed himself,) "the cause of God." An acknowledged reformation has taken place among these men, since they began to attend our preaching; and one of them has begun to meet in Class.

Several little circumstances occurred, which manifested a willingness among the people to do what they could to help forward the blessed work of God. One we may just mention. A little Malabar Girl had been disappointed of casting in her mite, owing to our passing over some of the Children. After the sermon, she watched an opportunity, came forward, and with mingled emotions of Fear, Diffidence, and Desire, put a Rix Dollar on the plate, and retired with a countenance beaming with satisfaction.

In the middle of January the Spirit of God was gloriously poured out upon us. Our religious services were greatly owned of God; and our Class Meetings especially, were seasons in which the Lord made known his power and willingness to save. In the course of four days, four were set at liberty; and in the short space of a fortnight, six were enabled to testify that God had blotted out their sins. This, in an Heathen land, is a matter which calls for our warmest gratitude. Some found peace with God while wrestling and praying in their own homes; others in the Chapel, and the Class; while every heart overflowed with gratitude and love. Great simplicity of spirit was manifested by those who had found Jesus, connected with an ardent desire for a deeper work of grace. But those who were still crying out for mercy, seemed to be oppressed with a burden intolerable, and too heavy for them to bear. Some of those afterwards experienced the goodness of God, and had their sorrow turned into joy.

Several of our Members have been providentially called to other parts of the Island. By the accounts from some of them, we believe they are resolved to cleave unto God with purpose of heart. May Jesus, that great Shepherd of the sheep, lead them unto fountains of living waters!

In an early part of this quarter we formed a class of young men, of whom in a former letter we had entertained hopes. They all understand the English language; have long been noticed for their uniform good moral conduct; and lately have been more or less convinced of their sinful state by nature, and of the necessity of a change of heart. In introducing them into our excellent discipline they were informed of its foundation in the Scriptures; the spiritual advantage resulting from meeting together, and praying with and for each other; and the impossibility of any one continuing among us, should he not walk by the Scripture rule. We then gave them notes on trial; seven met the first time: they have now increased to ten. The Serjeant Major of Artillery has begun to seek salvation by Jesus; he has been admitted to the Sacrament, and also meets in the young men's class. Several of these young men possess very promising abilities; and, as most of them are well acquainted with Malabar, we are not without hopes of seeing them become very useful.

Our attention, as usual, has been directed to our main object, the language of the country, as introductory to more extensive usefulness. Br. Squance has made some little attempts extempore; but has not yet ventured to preach without his book. Br. Carver will be able to preach soon: he is now writing his second sermon.

Our Schools are becoming encouraging; about 50 is the average attendance of the Jaffna Day school, and 60 or 70 that of the Sunday School. But it is not the numbers that attend, but the great improvement of the Scholars, that gives us encouragement. They make great progress in learning, are much improved in their morals, and many who attend the Sunday School are under very serious impressions. We have secured a piece of ground, and built a School, in the Village of எல்லாளர் என்னும் *Van-*

narpannay, or the Washermen's Village. It is so called from having been originally the residence of Washermen. It is now inhabited by all descriptions of Natives; and is the most populous village near Jaffna. It is situated about two English miles from the Pettah. We have a promise of many Scholars. We intend opening it on Monday the 26th April, and hope in our next to be able to tell you of a flourishing School there.

We have considered the subject of printing the Tamul Scriptures; and are of opinion that it would be adviseable to defer it at present. The old Translation is replete with errors; and before it be put to the press, we think it should be revised and corrected. We think it would be adviseable, also, to prepare the minds of the people to receive the Scriptures, by dispersing among them a number of short and suitable Tracts. The Bible is so voluminous a book that the size of it deters the Natives from reading it. This we have often witnessed. But if a small tract be put into their hands they will read it with avidity; and, deriving benefit from it, they will naturally enquire for the Book to which the Tract refers them. We have some Tracts ready; and as soon as our Colombo Brethren inform us that the press is at liberty, we shall forward them. We wish also to have a selection of Hymns, printed in Tamul, for the use of our Schools and for Public Worship. This will be ready immediately. In the mean time we shall be very thankful for Wood's Catechism, which has been at Colombo for some time.

It is with much concern that we have heard of the afflictions of several of our Brothers and Sisters. We have sympathized with them in all their sufferings, and have always borne them on our minds when approaching the Throne of Grace. May every dispensation of God be sanctified to us: and O! that all our afflictions may " work out for us a far more exceeding and eternal weight of Glory." We, too, have had our trials; and trials of the most painful nature; but they have had this one good effect—of driving us more frequently to the God of all grace, when we have had our souls refreshed with divine consolations. Our determinations to lay ourselves out for God become increasingly strong every day. We have, of late, had enlarged views of the power and willingness of God to save unto the very utmost; and this has made us thirst for a full baptism of the Holy Ghost. In public, in private, and in our family devotions, the chief language of our hearts has been

> " O that the perfect grace were given,
> " The love diffus'd abroad:
> " O that our hearts were all in heaven,
> " For ever fill'd with God!"

We bless God that he is fulfilling our desires; he is deepening and widening his work in our souls; and we feel ourselves growing up into Christ our living head, in all things. Commending you, dear Brethren, to God, and to the word of his grace,

We are, your very Affectionate Brethren,

T. H. SQUANCE.
R. CARVER.

P. S. All the books sent from Colombo are distributed, except a Magazine or two, a few Tracts, and one or two Hymn-books. Young men, &c. &c. have begun to buy English books; a thing in Jaffna, before unknown. One boy this evening bought to the amount of 10 Rds. and another immediately after him to the amount of 12. Many copies of the useful ones I have been obliged to keep back, lest one young man should get them, and the rest not, so readily, have an opportunity of reading them. Thus with about 12 little vols. I have established a kind of little circulating library for the benefit of all.

About 20 of the Gospel Warning remain. Jenny's penitential case, and glorious last moments have been read with great interest. Many have expressed their satisfaction on having had an opportunity to obtain a copy. This teaches the propriety of improving every fleeting circumstance.

R. CARVER.

THE TRINCOMALIE AND BATTICOLOA STATION.

Trincomalie, 24th March, 1818.

Very Dear Brethren,

Spared and preserved by Infinite mercy, to see the end of another Quarter, we avail ourselves of the opportunity of mutual communication. Thank God we have much cause for gratitude and praise. Our souls make advances in the divine life, and we do taste and see that the Lord is gracious. With respect to the work of God at this Station, it is pretty uniform. Our English congregations are not very large, owing in a great degree to the Kandyan affairs. But those who do attend, seem very attentive. Our Portuguese congregation in general continues small. Our Class is rather in a prosperous state; though our number has not been much encreased by the removal of the Head-Quarters of the 73rd Regiment to this Station; only having received one additional member, with a few seriously disposed, who attend our preaching. Our greatest prospect of usefulness among the Natives here, centred in the Caffre village; but just as we were about to erect a Bungaloe, to serve as a place of worship and to answer the end of a School-house, the Caffres were suddenly called to take arms, and are now in a state of readiness for Kandy. So, with respect to this apparent field of usefulness, our hopes for the present are blasted. However we must persevere in the paths of prayer, faith, and holiness; and by doing so, we shall doubtless see the openings of Providence leading to usefulness. Sister Osborne joins in kindest love to all the Brethren and Sisters.

We remain,

Very Dear Brethren,

Yours affectionately,

G. ERSKINE,

THOS. OSBORNE.

THE MADRAS STATION.

Madras, March 26th, 1818.

MY DEAR BRETHREN,

During the last Quarter I have had very little change in my Station. On the 2nd day of last month, I set out on an excursion with the Rev Mr. Rhenius, Church Missionary. His chief object was to visit and establish Schools. All his Schools (that I saw) are under Heathen Masters, who profess to teach the Children out of the Scriptures, and books of heathen morality, at their Schools. Mr. Rhenius had an opportunity of preaching Christ to the people. This is all the good that I look for from these Schools. The people always heard with apparent interest, and always denied worshiping an Idol as God.

At a Place called Conjevaram (the street nearly 2 miles long) there are two temples. One is 12 stories high, and near it what is called a Montepam of 72 by 65 yards on the roof, which is flat, and composed of long flat stones from 10 to 20 feet long. This roof is supported by 1000 stone pillars, each pillar one stone. In this is kept the articles belonging to the great car and the temple. Here, for the first time in my life, I saw men and women fall flat on their faces before their idol. We spent two days at this place, and most of the time, Mr. Rhenius was preaching to the people.

We spent one Sunday at Arcot (73 miles from Madras) with the Revd. Mr. Smith, a pious zealous man. We then proceeded to Vellore (87) and stopped two days with another Chaplain, the Rev. Mr. Jackson, who has established a *Christian School*, and determined to have such, or none. I had a long conversation with him on the extraordinary conversions which took place amongst us in England. I believe many of his prejudices were removed. He gave me a horse for 20 pagodas, which several judges say is worth 50.

We spent our 2nd Sabbath at Chittoor, (99) with the Revd. Mr. Horper, a very lively zealous man. Here I met a Mr. Daker, a Judge As Mr Horper and Mr. Daker are both pious Calvinists, we had much conversation, chiefly on the doctrines of imputed righteousness and holiness. I trust much of the prejudices of both are removed. Mr. Daker, evidenced as much Christian temper and candour as any man I ever conversed with. He was completely astonished, when I (in private) explained to him our views and feelings of Christian perfection, and that thousands amongst us not only enjoy the witness of the Spirit, but likewise the perfect love of God.

On my journey I met 3 poor backsliders, soldiers. They acknowledge their awful state, and promised very faithfully to turn again to God. I trust, on the whole, my excursion was not useless. Several I believe, sincerely thanked God for it. Especially one poor woman, a member of the Class in Madras, who with her husband had removed to Chittoor She had heard I was to be at Velloer; and determined to walk the 20 miles to see me. She is truly a child of God. I would go 20 miles again to make another of his children so happy, as she was when she saw me at Chittoor. Here you cannot go more than 15 miles from Madras without a passport. The face of the whole country far exceeds Ceylon in cultivation.

At Madras, I have been several times requested, in little parties, *to pray and give* some Religious instructions. The present ————, who is rather a pious man, has had a little party for that purpose. I always endeavour to set before them, the plain truths of the Gospel; and I now believe I can preach better, sitting at a table, than standing in a pulpit, or behind a chair. The last evening, after explaining 1 John iii, 1—3. when at supper, we had a very free conversation on the real principles of Christianity; and I believe God directed us by his Spirit. But I feel that I am alone. I sincerely praise God for that light, and love which I possess. I feel an increase of both: and am surprised that God continues either with me. I am resolved, God being my helper, to dwell more on the subject of experimental religion, than I ever yet have done. A Major in the Army, who has been one of the little society, lately called on me; with whom I had an hour's very serious conversation; and shed tears when we came to converse on the love of the Lord Jesus. I gave him Mr. Wesley's 13 Discourses on our Lord's Sermon, and am to give him Mr. Benson's Apology in a few days. ———— is now reading it.

My present labours are divided betwixt where I live, 2½ miles from town, and the town. I have lately felt very happy in my own soul while preaching to others. But, alas, I either do not preach in faith, or the people do not hear in faith: I believe the former is the cause of my unfruitfulness. Your last Quarterly Report was truly profitable to me: every Brother evidently happy in his soul, and in his place and work: this always rejoices me: and my mind would be much grieved were I to learn that any Brother regrets his coming to India. I left a place and work in which I was happy. I have met with disappointment, and trials since then. I left England under deep exercises of mind. But, since I first offered myself for the Indian Mission, to this moment, if one deliberate wish could have placed me again in an Irish Circuit, I dare not make it.

Farewell, Your's in love,

JAMES LYNCH.

~~~~~~~

THE BOMBAY STATION.

No Communication from Brother Horner. We hear that he and Sister Horner are well: and that they have lately had a second child added to their family.

Extract of a Letter from a much respected Friend. ————, to Sister Harvard; dated March 21, 1818.

I heartily rejoice to find the great cause to which you and so many others are voluntarily devoting yourselves, prospering and spreading. Surely, Missionaries have encouragement to hope that their labours are owned and blessed of God; and that by their means, the Gospel may soon be expected to reach to "all the ends of the earth!" We know that man can only sow the seed. God must give the increase. And I pray that he may abundantly bless you in the harvest.

I find one of your party, Mr. Ault, has been taken; we will hope to receive his reward. The field of your labours must have been enlarged. Have you a proportionate increase of Missionaries to fill it up? I see that two or three have been appointed in addition.

It is very interesting for those who live in India, to mark events, as they pass here, to converse with the people, and to know the exact state of all things; and then to turn and contemplate all which our own dear country is planning and doing for the good of these benighted ones. We cannot but be led to hope for, and expect much, good to result from such endeavoures. A heavenly spark seems to be kindled in the breasts of many, which will not, I believe, be allowed to rest, till its light and influence have extended to bless and cheer these dark regions. Such at least it appears to me: and such, I trust, will be the will of God.

With every wish and prayer that God may bless and prosper you,   I remain, &c. &c.

N. B. I want to know how you get on with your Schools; and, indeed, I hope to hear that you all prosper and are happy.

Miscellaneous.

No. I.

Brother's Clough's Account of the Oriental Library purchased from the Estate of the late W. Tolfrey, Esq.

[*Continued from page 36.*]

From No. 14 to 19, inclusive, are the book called මිලිඳුප්‍රශ්න *Milindaprashné*, from මිලිඳු *Milinda*, the name of a King, and ප්‍රශ්න *prashné*, questions.—This book is held in the highest estimation among the priests, and others of the learned Natives, as it contains a complete triumph of *Budhism.*—මිලිඳු *Milinda* was one of the Kings of the යවනරට *Yawanas*, and he appears to have been a kind of Infidel, or one who affected to disbelieve all Religions. He however adopted a plan either to find a Religion that could be defended, or to refute them all. He consequently determined to investigate the following systems. පූරණකාශ්‍යප *Poorunakashyape*, කකුඩකාත්‍යයන *Kakoodakatheyana*, සඤ්ජයබලරිත් *Sunjayabalarte*, අජිතකේසකම්බෙලි *Ajitekesekambeli*, මක්ඛලිගොසාල *Makkhetigosala*, නිග්ගණ්ඨනාත්‍යපුත්‍ර *Nignantenatepootra*.

He summoned the chief priests of these respective religions, to his Court, under a pretence that he wished to become acquainted with them. This he did, successively refuting every one of them, by proposing such questions as they were unable to answer. He finally sent for the priests of the Budhist religion, and was equally triumphant over them. Hearing however of one celebrated නායක *Nanyaka*, called නාගසේන *Nagasene*, in a country where Budhism was professed, he sent for him, to his court. The නායක *Naayaka* went attended by a vast number of his disciples and inferior priests, and offered to answer any question the king might propose. මිලිඳු *Milinda* put the same questions to him which he had done to the other priests, who had left his court confounded; but this නායක *Naayaka* answered the whole in so satisfactory a way, that the king was convinced of the truth of Budhism, and immediately became a convert to it. This book contains the account of the whole controversy, which lasted a considerable time, and gives a most interesting picture of the wit and good humour which both the king and the priest displayed on the occasion.

As for the truth of this story, I conceive it rests on the same foundation as most of the oriental histories. That there was such a kingdom as the යවනරට *Yawanas*, is very probable. It frequently appears in their histories. Some European writers have placed them near the Kashmirs, others make them an independent state, in the Southern Decan; and others, without the least hesitation, call them the ancient Greeks. From this book it appears, මිලිඳු *Milinda* was a

Moor, and that his kingdom, යවනරට *Yawanaratta*, was on the borders of Persia. But we shall always labour under considerable difficulties in tracing out *Cingalese history*, as they have no regular work on Geography, (at least I can find none); which is not the case with the Hindus. The only Geography which I can find is in the travels of Budhu; and a considerable part of this is, as yet, beyond my investigation. It is a little remarkable, that one of the most celebrated Astronomers and Philosophers in ancient Hindū history, is called යවන ආචිවය *Yawana acharga*: he is supposed to have been cotemporary with Pythagorus, and to have travelled in ancient Greece; and that these two great characters had much intercourse. The works of යවනා ආචවය *Yawana Acharga*, are in Sanskrit and are now studied by the Priests of Ceylon.

Nos. 20, 21, 22, To the ධණ්පදයහි අර්ථකතාව *Dharmapadayehi arte kathawa*, ධණ *Dharma*, Sacred, පදයහි *Padayehi*, Verses, අර්ථකතාව *Artekathawa*, Commentary. The same work is sometimes called the බුධඝස සආවා ඊකරාන්සේ *Budhaghosa acharinwahansa*, or the harmonious voice of Budhu. The three volumes, which are pretty large, contain the 423 ගාතාවල් *Gatawal*, or Songs of Budhu, with a copious Commentary, said to be written by one බුධගය *Budhagaya*, a learned priest.

No. 23 and 24. This work is incomplete. It is part of the work called සූත්‍රනිපාත *Sootranipata*. This would be a valuable book could it be completed. It is said to have been written by the united council of 60,000 priests, and gives an account of the different countres into which Budhu travelled, while in this world, and the various encounters he had, from all classes of People, Kings, Bramins, Priests, &c. &c. with their questions respecting himself, his authority, his religion, &c. &c. with all his answers. In all his travels he was attended by the priests who after his death wrote the book and called it සූත්‍රනිපාත *Sootranipata*, part of the whole.

25 and 26. Are the book called පදීපිකාව *Perdipikawa*, literally a candlestick: but the priests when they speak of it call it සධණ්පදීපිකාව *Sadharmaperdipikawa* the sacred candlestick. This book is much read by the priests, and is an excellent work, written by a Cingalese priest, in Pali, Elu, and Cingalese. The language is very pure. The work is an exposition of the 4 following subjects: බුධභාසිතය *Budhabhasetaya*, or the Exhortations of Budhu, දෙවභාසිතය *Dewabhasitaya*, the Exhortations of God, පහභාසිතය *Pahabhasetaya*, the Exhortations of his Prophets, සුවකභාසිතය *Srawakbhasitaya*, the Exhortations of wise men.

27 and 28. Are the book called සාරසංඟ්‍රහ *Sarasangraha*; සාර *Sara* good, සංඟ්‍රහ *Sangrahe*, a collection. This work is in Pali, and generally considered a religious book: but it treats of various subjects, in both Religion and History.

29.

No. 30, විමානවඃයනව *Wimanawastoa,* විමාන *Wima-na* is palaces, වඃයනව *Wastoa* is history. This book is in Pali and its proper title is the History of the Heavens, or the future abodes of those who have merited reward in this world. The origin of this work is a little singular. One of the Disciples of Budhu, on a certain occasion, made an excursion into the abodes of the blessed. He remained there for a length of time, and examined as far as possible the different states of the inhabitants; many of whom he had known in this world, and many others of his acquaintances came while he remained there. As he had a perfect knowledge of their different characters, and saw what kinds of situation and degrees of happiness were allotted to each he was enabled, on his return into this world, (according to the account,) to write a complete history of future rewards and punishments, publishing to mankind, that, if while they were in this world, they practiced such and such virtues, they would receive such and such rewards in a future state.

31. පාලිනිඝඬසඞනෙ *Palinihandasanne,* a Pali Dictionary, or an explanation of the Pali language.

32. එළුවිමානවඃයනව *Eluwimanawastoo,* This is a work similar to No. 30 in the Elu language.

33. බාලපඬිතසඞ *Balapanditasootra,* this book is in Pali and Cingalese, a kind of novel or fictitious history of the dunce and wise man: බාල *Bala* is dunce, and පඬිත *Pandita* is wise.

34. සඞඝසඞ *Subhasootra:* සඞ *Subha* the name of a Bramin, සඞ *Sootra,* heard. When Budhu was in this world this Bramin came to him, and asked him 14 important questions respecting the religion which he was teaching. This සඞ *Sootra,* contains, in full, Budhu's answers. This work is both in Pali and Cingalese.

35. සාලෙයසඞ *Saleyasootra,* සඞලයඞ *Saleeya,* the name of a village in ඞසරට *Kusaratta.* In one of Budhus journeys, an inhabitant of that village came to him and proposed many questions to him, all of a religious nature: and this සඞ *Sootra* contains the whole of Budhu's answers to this enquirer after truth.

36. උපාසඞඃනාලඞනඃාඞ *Upasakajanalankare:* literally, the beauty or ornaments of true believers: from උඞ සඞ *Upasake,* faithful, or true faith, උඞ *jana* people, ලඞඞඃඞඃ *Lankare* beauty, (one of the names of Ceylon). This book was written in Pali, by an eminent Budhist Priest on the commands and ordinances of Budhism. It is held in great repute by the priests, and a copy of it is in all the Temples.

37. රසවාහිනඃ *Rasawahene:* from රස *Rasa* savour,

චාබිනි *wahene*, to shed or shedding. This book is thus denoted, from its peculiar nature. It contains a striking description of the beauties or excellencies of Budhism.

38. බාලවතාරසන්න *Balawatarasanne.* This book is a help to the study of Pali; and is an instance of the singular names the Cingalese give to their books. Its title is, literally the dunce turned over. Thus බාල *Bala* is dunce, වතාර *Wotara* is over, සන්න *Sannee* is explained.

39. දම්පියාදපදාර්ථ *Dampeyadapadartha.* Another commentary on the Songs of Budhu.

[*To be continued*]

~~~~~~~

No II.

Character of Mr Wesley.

"On a review of the Character of this extraordinary man, it appears, that, though he was endowed with eminent talents, he was more distinguished by their use than even by their possession. Though his taste was classic, and his manners elegant, he sacrificed that society in which he was particularly calculated to shine: gave up those preferments which his abilities must have obtained; and devoted a long life, in practising and enforcing the plainest duties. Instead of being, "an ornament to literature."[*] he was a blessing to his fellow Creatures. "Instead of the genius of his age," he was the "*Servant of God.*"

Vide " *Literary Anecdotes of the Eighteenth Century.*" Vol 5. Page 2.7.

━━━━━

[*] Our Brethren will, probably, very justly think that in this excellent and comprehensive character of Mr. Wesley, the writer has sacrificed something to secure the beauty of a rounded period: for no one that knows Mr. Wesley's writings, can any more doubt that he *was* "an ornament to literature," than that he was a "blessing to his fellow Creatures;" since it is allowed on all hands that his writings are a prefect *model* of simple elegance: his style being at once remarkable for perspicuity and strength, for purity and *precision.* Besides, the great number and acknowledged utility of his works secure to him no ordinary share of that excellence which stamps the writings of all truly *Christian Authors;* and which the wise and the liberal minded, are now by no means disposed to withhold from him: to which likewise the above well-written extract bears ample *testimony.*

R, N.

No. III.

Extract from a Poem called "ADIEU TO CEYLON" by Captain Anderson, of H. M. 19th Regiment.

Dedicated to H. R. H. the DUKE OF YORK.

" FAREWELL, ye churches, newly built,
" Where saints may pray for sinners' guilt!
" Farewell ye Missionary crew:
" Though ye a heavenly call pursue,
" Ye hold self-interest still in view:
" I deem you all a whining tribe
" Nor to your creed or fund subscribe."

We understand that Dadee, the Persee Merchant, has a few Copies of the work to sell, from whence the above extract is made. But, as the price is 12 Rix Dollars, we suppose our Brethren will "*hold self-interest*" too much "*in view,*" to interrupt, at so dear a rate, the oriental repose of these undisturbed volumes.

With respect to the Work itself, the author tells us, in his Preface, that it has had a very untoward origin; and it is rather an unfortunate evidence thereof, that "IN SPITE," are literally the two first words with which he introduces himself to the public notice.

The author having opened such a vein, we are prepared to anticipate the nature of the flowing current. "THE ADIEU" is printed at the end of the book, in company with some other Miscellaneous Poems.—It contains some "*spite*"ful reflections on individuals, who are better able to defend themselves than we should be to defend them. From these characters the author supposes he has received either some negative or positive injury. This, though we do not presume to assign it as his justification, is doubtless the reason with which he justifies himself.

But, also "*in spite*," he cannot forbear an adieu to the "*Churches newly built.*" Captain Anderson, then, it should seem, is no Friend to *Churches*, or, at all events, to *newly built* ones. We were at a loss for a moment to conceive the reason of this dislike to the new Churches of Ceylon; but we find it explained in the last line we have quoted. They were built by *subscription!*—It is a sad misfortune to be obliged to subscribe to the building of a new Church, in a heathen land! And, where not to subscribe would be considered singular, an excuse was certainly necessary; and one "*in spite,*" however untenable, was considered as better than none at all.

Another reason it should seem, is that the Missionaries are a *selfish, whining, crew,* or *tribe.* At least, this is what Captain Anderson "*deems*" us to be. We must thank his Captainship for so freely telling us his opinion of us: and we can assure him, that we, in our turn, have formed an opinion of him likewise. And though should he say that he is regardless, as to what ours may be of him, he may be assured, we are no less so, as to any he may conceive of us.

The only "*Churches*" which have been "*newly built*" by *subscription,* at Colombo, are the *Wesleyan Mission House,* and the *Portu-*

guese Episcopal Church. As the Captain would wish the world to suppose that his being unable to subscribe to *our Missionary "Creed,"* was the reason of his not subscribing to *our "Fund,"* we have made enquiries, hoping, for the sake of our Author's generosity, that we should find his name among the Subscribers to *the Government Church!* But, alas! we are informed, from authority, that *"Captain Anderson was not a Subscriber."*

This is a misfortune certainly. As it might lead some unfriendly persons to *"deem"* that our Poet's lack of subscription, did not proceed from any tenderness of feel, on the score of *"creed,"* as his rhyme would insinuate. The aforesaid might *"deem"* it to be the result of some supposed contraction in the regions of *the left shoulder.* If so the following couplet of delicate affectation, would likewise be *"deem"ed,* as the school-boys say, *"a complete come-off!"*

> " I deem you all a whining tribe
> Nor to your creed nor fund subscribe."

The poet may believe us, there is not one in this said *"whining tribe;"* but who, had he been in his unfortunate circumstances, would have had too much modesty thus to have referred to a Ceylon subscription, in which he had taken no share. We expect to find in a Soldier and a Poet, conjoined in one person, a little, at least, of that noble generosity, which, by common consent, is attributed to each profession. It is for our Brethren to judge how far the Captain or the Poet shines resplendantly in the present case.

In reference to the *"whining tribe,"* we have to observe, that this *tribe* were imported from England, under the express sanction of the British Government; and that, on this point if the Captain has any doubts on his mind, he may have them fully resolved, by applying at the Office of Secretary of State for the Colonial Department, in London; where he will find the whole *"crew"* are all regularly registered.

This POLITE work is dedicated to His Royal Highness the Duke of York, we conclude *" With our "Permission."* We have other reasons for this conclusion, besides the silence of the dedication on this Point. We have too high an opinion and reverence of the judgment and religious feeling, *not to say British liberality,* of that Illustrious Personage, a true-born Son of the revered and beloved George the Third! to whom this author has ventured to dedicate his work, to apprehend that His Royal Highness will view with complacency, so unprovoked an attack upon a body of men, who have not yet forfeited the reputation which they had when they were favoured with the Sanction of His Majesty's Ministers in England.

Captain Anderson was, for some time, Commandant of Batticaloa, until it was *"deem"ed* proper for him to join his Regiment. He must there have heard a great deal of our late revered Brother Ault. We owe it to the memory of a man, whose character will not lose by competition with that of him who affects to despise his *"tribe,"* to make the following remark. Brother Ault was well known at Batticaloa, as was also our disconcerted poet. And, on the ground of *reputation* and *disinterestedness,* were all classes of inhabitants to give their opinion, from the Collector, down to the lowest menial, the *"Missionary crew"* are so well acquainted with circumstances, as not to shrink from the result of such a comparison.

Upon the whole; on the supposition that our ruling men select their attendants and companions, according to *their* estimate of their respective deservings, our Brethren will not be surprised at finding the author (UNWITTINGLY, they will think,) making the following *dolorous* complaint:

" FAREWELL ye Staff, with formal face,
" In all the pomp and " *pride of place!*"
" Of you I have not much to say;
" I never touch'd your double pay:—
" But ever was a luckless sinner,
" Who *seldom* shared *a King's House dinner!!*"

~~~~~~~~

No. IV.

Extract of a Letter from the Rev. G. Marsden, to Brother Harvard, Dated London, October 18, 1817.

DEAR BROTHER,

Immediately after the Conference we sent you a copy of the Stations, and a few weeks ago a copy of the Minutes of the Conference, the Magazines, the Missionary Notices, and the Missionary Register. We hope by the time you receive this, that they will all have been received safe. From them you will see how the good work of God has been going on; and that notwithstanding the general distress of the people during the last year, the Lord has graciously supported his own cause. Through mercy trade is reviving, and we hope that while the hearts of many are raised in gratitude to God for the favourable change which is taking place, the cause of true religion will more powerfully prevail, and that our Nation will more fully be visited with the mercy of God.

We hope the Lord is also graciously visiting you in Ceylon, and that you have the pleasure of seeing your labours crowned with much success. The accounts which have been transmitted to us from several of the Brethren encourage us to hope that your way has been preparing for extensive usefulness, and that the seed which is sown will produce a plentiful and a glorious harvest. The Committee rejoice with you in the prospect of good, and trust that they shall have to rejoice with you in the conversion of multitudes of souls to God. They are fully aware of the peculiar situation in which you are placed, with respect to administering the ordinance of Baptism, especially to Adults; and that while on the one hand you would not refuse it to a person who from his heart renounces Idolatry, and believes on the Lord Jesus Christ as the only Saviour of the lost; so on the other, that you would not administer that blessed ordinance to any person, merely that he may inherit property, or for any secular purpose whatever. The Committee have maturely considered the subject, and the following is the Minute which was made at the time, and which we think it necessary to transmit to you.

That on the subject of the administration of Baptism by our Mis-

No. III.   U

sionaries to the natives of Ceylon, the Committee approve of the care taken in the examination of Candidates for that ordinance, as expressed in the letter signed by Brothers Erskine and McKenny, dated Point De Galle, February 11, 1817, and wish to fortify them in this practice, by expressing it as their deliberate and most serious opinion:—

I. That Baptism ought not, under any pretence, or for any reason, to be administered to any Adults unless they are first instructed in the first principles of the Christian Religion. Nor without sufficient evidence of their having sincerely renounced Idolatry; and unless they confess their sins, and promise to renounce them, and also engage to attend Christian worship.

II. That in the case of Children, baptism ought not to be administered unless the parents have either themselves renounced Idolatry, or that by introducing them into the Schools, and placing them under the superintendance of Christians, they can be assured that the Children so baptized shall be brought up in the Christian religion, and in an attendance on Christian worship.

As I understand that a Packet sails for Ceylon tomorrow, I am anxious to send you this letter, and shall be obliged to you to send a copy of it to each preacher on the Island immediately; though I hope to have an opportunity of writing again, in a little time, to each Brother. We have been waiting with some anxiety to receive letters from Ceylon, for two or three months past, but have been disappointed. We wish to hear from you all frequently; and wish you to write in the most full and free manner.

With kind love to all our very dear Brethren, I am, Dear Brother,

Yours affectionately,

GEORGE MARSDEN.

No. V.

[From the Nottingham Review.]

A very numerous and respectable meeting of the *Wesleyan Methodists*, was held in the New Chapel, *Lincoln*, on the 23rd ultimo, it being the first Anniversary of an *Auxiliary Methodist Missionary Society for the Lincoln District*:—the Rev. R. Newton, in the Chair. It appeared from the Report, that upwards of £500 had been collected in the course of the past year; and that Collections on the occasion amounted to upwards of £80.

The eleventh anniversary of the opening of the *Methodist Chapel, Derby*, was held on Sunday the 3rd instant. For five years successively the religious services on these occasions have been most ably and satisfactorily conducted by the Rev. Robert Newton; and at no period more so than this last. The great and important doctrines of the Gospel of God our Saviour, with the privileges and duties of real Christian believers, were, in the three sermons delivered, illustrated, defended and enforced, with peculiar ability and energy. Without doubt the season will be reflected upon with singular pleasure and profit after many days.—The collections amounted to about seventy pounds.

No VI.

From the Rev. G. Dermott, Kingswood, to Brother Callaway.

On Tuesday, Aug. 26, was opened our very large Chapel in Bristol, being our fourth in that City. At half past 10, Mr Watson, of London, commenced from Col i. 26. *The Mystery*, and *Christ in you*. At half past 2, Mr. Bunting, from London, from Ps. lxxxix. 7. on *Religious Worship*. In the Evening, Mr. Robert Newton, of Wakefield, from Gal. vi. 14 *Glory in the Cross of Christ*. Very large is the house, and very large was the congregation. The Chapel itself only cost £3000, but the houses and Premises £8.700. There had been privately collected previous to the opening of the Chapel, £3,400. That day the Collections amounted to more than £250.

No. VII.

THE FITZWILLIAM FAMILY.

The amiable founder of the present Noble Family of Fitzwilliam, was Alderman of Bread-street Ward, in the year 1506. Before his death he forgave all his debtors, and wrote upon the erased accounts of each, "*Amore Dei remitto!*" Cardinal Wolsey was the chief means of this worthy Citizen acquiring his large fortune. After the disgrace of the Cardinal, Mr. Fitzwilliam very hospitably entertained him at Milton, in Northamptonshire, one of the fine seats of the present Earl. Henry VIII. was so enraged at this, that he sent for Mr. Fitzwilliam to Court, and said, " Ha, Ha! how comes it, ha! that you dare entertain a traitor?" Fitzwilliam modestly replied, " Please your Highness, I did it not from disloyalty, but gratitude." The angry Monarch here interrupted him by, ' Ha, ha!" (the usual interjection of his rage). Mr. Fitzwilliam, with the tear of gratitude in his eye, and the burst of loyalty in his bosom, continued, " From gratitude, as he was my old master, and the means of my greatest fortunes." Impetuous Harry was so pleased with the answer, that he took him by the hand, and said, " Such gratitude, ha! shall never want a master. Come into my service, worthy man, and teach my servants, *gratitude*, for few of them have any." He then knighted him on the spot, and Mr. F. was immediately sworn in a Privy Counsellor.

END OF APRIL EXTRACTS, &c.

---

*⁂ The Brethren are requested to forward to Colombo extracts of such of their European or other Letters, as may contain Information of general interest.

☞ It is hoped that the present Circumstances of the Colombo Station, will be allowed as a sufficient reason for this Quarterly not having been ready for the Tappal, till this day, May 20th.

Printed at the Mission-Press, Colombo, for the Use of the Missionaries.

Extracts

FROM

QUARTERLY LETTERS, &c.

No. VI.　　　*JANUARY*, 1819.

THE COLOMBO STATION.

Mission House, 11 *January,* 1819.

GREATLY ESTEEMED BRETHREN,

SEVERAL of you understand so well the circumstances of this Station, that I am almost sure you would excuse me were I to pass over in silence the present season for communicating our Missionary labours: my situation is certainly a laborious one at present, both for body and mind. I had almost said my days and nights are occupied, which if I had, it would not have been far from the truth, However, I bless God that he has so far engaged my whole soul and affections in his blessed and important work, that I never feel, however exercised, any thing like a murmuring thought, or a disposition to repine. I think I can say without hesitation, and without any thing like boasting, I have made an offering of myself to God and his cause; my days, my strength, my all are His, and the constant and ardent prayer of my heart is, that I may be enabled to do a little in his cause, prove by happy experience his full salvation, and when the warfare is past, be admitted to some humble station at the foot of his throne in heaven.

The work of God, my dear Brethren, daily presents so great a variety of incidents, that we never need be silent. I am not prepared to say that all those occurrences are such as we should wish to see, or make choice of, were we left to our choice; but yet, as we are labourers, and soldiers in the same great cause, and united under the same head, we shall find a pleasure in enumerating even our labours and conflicts; and when it pleases God to bless our efforts, we may dwell on this part of our work with increased feelings of joy. I never hear, without pain of mind, the insinuation, that because it pleases God to carry on his work in this country not quite so rapidly and triumphantly as in some other parts of the world, that therefore we have just cause of relaxing in some of our efforts, and ought to say little respecting it. Such thoughts, such insinuations, are by no means decorous in any Christian, but are infinitely unbe-

coming a Christian Missionary. You will kindly pardon me, my dear
brethren, I had no intention to make these observations when I began
scribbling at the heat of this sheet of paper; they are thoughts that
strike me as I go over the paper. and having the pen in my hand I let
them go. But when God brings me in full view of his work, and says
by his Word, his Spirit. and his Providence, this must be done, and I
must take part in it, I have no idea of demurring as to the exact manner in which it shall be accomplished : no, it is my place to say, "Here
am I," ready to enter into the work of the Lord ; ready to do it in any
way thy Providence and Grace may point out. And if, when we are
engaged with such feelings as these it should please God to display his
saving power, as in the days of Peter, and Paul, and Barnabas, &c,
and save souls by thousands in a day, we will join our hallelujahs to
theirs, in singing praise to God and the Lamb. But if the work is to
go on in our days as the seed which is cast into the ground, and which
in due season furnishes a glorious crop, let us never forget our place,
the station we occupy, the feelings of mind we should cultivate, the
hopes we should cherish, the promises we have, the master we serve,
the God who will prove faithful to every part of his covenant with man,
and who has most explicitly promised his servants that they shall reap
if they faint not. This, by the bye, furnishes me with a good idea in
beginning my present report. We are God's husbandry, the world
is the field, but the heathen world that part of it into which the Lord
of the harvest hath sent us. Now the world of nature presents us with
a vast variety of scenes, with regard to agricultural prospects ; some
places being more barren than others require more at the hands of the
husbandman, yet by persevering diligence he succeeds. And there can
be little doubt but Divine Providence has fixed us in a place where
the moral and spiritual state of the inhabitants is deplorable, yet it
must be cultivated. A spiritual harvest must be produced ; God must
have fruit from this part of the world : immortal souls must rise up in
these barren regions to the praise of the Lord of all ; and though we
may meet with difficulties, the encouragements are so great, and so
numerous, as leave us no room for complaint. We live in the anticipation of glorious days.

Though I have deeply to lament the loss of my dear colleague
Brother Harvard, yet I am happy to inform you that not a department of our work has failed, nor so far as I know, any one *branch*
of our operations. This has been very happily prevented by the
assistance which has been most providentially sent to this Station.
Our printed plan will furnish you with information respecting the places
and hours at which we have regular preaching in the three languages.

You will see how God is raising us up help, on the very spot where
we have been labouring together. Who could have thought a short
time since, that we should have had on this Station several active
local preachers? God does indeed take care of his own work, and it
has so happened that now when our congregations have so multiplied
that it would have been impossible for us to have supplied them,
we have got three or four fine young men, of the *most promising*
abilities ; and having imbibed in their religious progress a zeal

for the cause of God, they have imbibed at the same time (praise God for it) the real spirit of Methodism, and of Methodist preachers. And I feel a pleasure in stating to you, that in our Native Congregations, though we go as often as we can, and shall ever do it while God gives us strength, they really begin to take the precedency of us, being Natives, and as Natives perfectly familiar with their own languages; it is no small gratification to the Native congregations to hear the things of God faithfully and zealously delivered by their own Countrymen, and in their own style of language; indeed they have access to persons and places that we cannot get at. We have one or two more coming forward, who appear actuated by the same spirit but we thought it best to try them another six months before we enter their names on the plan. The Lord be praised for them, and the Lord bless them. Brethren, pray for them: I am almost sure they will be an eternal honour to the cause of the Methodist Mission in Ceylon.

Our young Friend Cornelius I think should be taken out to travel this Conference. Last Sunday I met, and gave tickets to two of his Native Classes, I think nearly 30 in number; it was an affecting time.

When I had finished he brought me a third Class paper of another Native Class, which he had raised himself, and which no European Missionary ever saw. Said he, " Now Sir, we must go to Wellewatte, about two miles farther, and meet the Class there." I told him I was so circumstanced that it was morally impossible for me to go that day. " O Sir" said he, " I wish you could go, there are two or three that have been lately set at liberty and are very happy, and rejoicing in a sense of the pardoning love of God, and you would be much pleased to see them." Thus religion is finding its way into the jungle of Ceylon. Our Schools are daily opening our way into every village and hamlet. Every School-house is a church, and always sacredly set apart for divine worship on the Sabbath-days. It is certainly one of the most important considerations at present connected with the concerns of our Mission, that knowledge of every kind is rapidly spreading in all directions by the means of the Schools, and wherever they are established, they carry with them a blessed leavening influence. The Schoolmaster of our New-Bazar intimated to me, at our last general monthly visitation, that he had about 25 heathen boys and girls ready for baptism. But before I gave consent to their being baptized I ascertained that they had been many months in the way of training for the solemn ordinance; indeed some of the boys I found met in Class, and this was quite enough. It was appointed for them to be baptized in the Mission House in the presence of the Cingalese congregation. The scene was really an interesting one. The congregation was large: the children of five Schools were present, as were also many of their parents and neighbours. When the candidates for Christian baptism were formed in a semi-circle round the font, I saw one boy that had something remarkable in his appearance, and after all was over and we were rising from our knees from prayer, I enquired strictly about him, and found he was the son of a Persee, who had been

given up to the teacher of the New Bazar school to be instructed in
the principles of Christianity and to be baptized. His Father, the Persee, was present and witnessed the whole ceremony; he appeared greatly interested, and even affected; for when the congregation kneeled for
prayer he likewise went upon his knees on the stone floor of the
Mission House, and I can assure you I considered this a pleasing triumph, and which was the first time I had ever seen one of those con-
ceited worshippers of Fire prostrate before the Lord Jesus Christ in
a Christian Temple After prayer I spoke with him at considerable
length upon the solemnity of the service, and the eventful circumstance
of his having thus voluntarily given up his son to the Lord Jesus
Christ, and I hoped he felt satisfied in his own mind that what he had
done was right, and consistent with his own most private convictions
and feelings. When I had thus spoken, the poor man, with his eyes
and hands lifted up to heaven, exclaimed, standing close to the font,
and before all the congregation, I feel satisfied in my conscience that
I have acted right in giving my son to be baptised by a Christian Minister. And I have no other wish in this, than that my son may
become an acceptable worshipper of the true God. This was certainly an honest and fair confession. I may be mistaken, but I think
this is among the first instances of a Persee having been baptized;
may it be productive of lasting good to thousands of his countrymen!
He is himself a fine interesting young lad, about 13 or 14 years of
age: appears passionately fond of his schoolmaster, of the Missionaries, and the means of grace. I hope God has great and glori
ous designs of mercy towards that most numerous and interesting
race of men, the Persees, in the baptism of this youth. It perhaps
would have been a far more difficult thing for such a circumstance
to have taken place had that class been equally numerous in Ceylon, as in other places, such as Bombay. However, it is done, and
if it should please God to bring him to the enjoyment of real religion,
and qualify him for his own work, we will most gladly give him up
to some station, where we know that class of people are vastly numerous.

On Christmas-day we kept up our usual custom of assembling
all the Schools in this station at the Mission-House, and giving them
a suitable Sermon. This season exceeded in interest by far any previous commemoration of any of the Christian festivals. I suppose
it is a long time since Ceylon witnessed such a scene before. At an
early period of the morning of Christmas-day the Mission-House was
crowded by people from all parts of the country, as far as from 10
to 12 miles, many were carried out sick occasioned by the crowding
and heat, before the service began. About 10 o'Clock we began
worship; Cornelius read the Liturgy in Cingalese; Br. Newstead then
gave out an hymn, and prayed by an Interpreter; I then preached from
Isaiah, chap. 11. 9. After which Br. Harvard came up, spoke a few
words and dismissed the congregation. But there is one circumstance
which I must not omit to mention, which though of minor importance was indeed really pleasing, and affecting. Our greatly esteemed Secretary, Mr. Watson, had sent us out a box (which had arrived

only a few days before), containing a number of valuable little
presents from many of our dear friends in London, Bristol &c. &c.
and we so arranged these little memorials of the affection of our
dear people for us on a large table in the Mission dwelling house,
that as all the children and the people left the Church they might
have a look at them. When I went in to the pulpit again, and published
what we had to show them, it was delightful to see hundreds of eyes
sparkling, and how anxious they were to have a sight of them.
However, they were regularly called out, one School after another,
and allowed to pass out at the side door of the Mission Chapel
into the front room of the dwelling house, and to walk round the
table, and then to pass forward into the street. This, in some places,
even in England itself, would have been attended with considerable noise and confusion. Yet it was done on the present occasion with the utmost quiet and regularity: for though the poor
Children were exceedingly desirous from the time they heard the
first report of the articles to indulge themselves in viewing them;
and though they walked out of the Mission House on their toes
and did their utmost to stretch their necks to look over their fellows, yet all was gone through with the utmost order and decorum.
I had the gratifying part to stand the whole time at the head of
the table, and as the children and their parents, and others of the
natives, from the country, passed round, to point out, to lift up,
and describe to them the various presents which laid on the table,
and informed them from whence they came, and why the good
Christian people of England had sent them; and I can assure you,
it was a high day indeed to hundreds of the children, and ourselves were gratified in no small degree. I had an opportunity of
witnessing the effects which this novel exhibition had upon their
minds. And when they came in sight of the table, which was
covered with the presents. I could not but observe with great
pleasure the movements in their black faces: they looked, they
smiled, they appeared surprised and charmed. They turned their
heads; smiled at their companions: they talked, and chatted to
each other, and really wondered what kind of people it was who
had showed so much kindness to the poor children in the Island
of Ceylon. The street in front of the Mission House was crowded
for an hour or two by all sorts of people coming in to witness
this novel scene, and the report spread so rapidly that we were
after all forced to lock up every door in the Mission House.
However, it all added to the general interest of the day. And I
can easily imagine how very pleasing it would be to see the
people retiring to their huts in the jungle, for 10 or 12 miles
round the country, talking about the benevolence of English
Christians. A noble subject indeed! Well, I could easily pardon
any little extra feeling of joy which the children and their parents might express on the occasion; for I must assure you, my
dear Brethren, that when we opened the trunk containing this
deposit of the unexpected kindness of our people, I was really
surprised. We could hardly credit our own eyes, yet the articles

B

Were before us—yes and they of all things were just what we wanted. Well, thought I, O England "*who is like unto thee?*" The Lord reward them all.

On New Years day we had another general assembly of the Schools, principally for the purpose of Br. Harvard's preaching his farewell Sermon to them. The Mission House was almost equally crowded as on Christmas day, only I observed a greater proportion of adults. This also was an affecting season. The late converted Priest, *Adrian*, read the Liturgy in Cingalese. Br. Harvard preached, and afterwards I baptized a young man who was brought to us by one of the most respectable of the Ceylon Priests: indeed he is one of the *three Nuayekas*. This boy has been under our instruction for more than two years, and during the whole time has been labouring daily in the printing office. O that it may please the Lord savingly to convert his Soul.

As it is natural to suppose, Br. Harvard's last Sermon to the Schools was really an affecting scene to us all. Many, yea very many things we could not prevent rushing into our thoughts at this time. And I believe these feelings were general, and without an exception. Both Parents, Children, and Schoolmasters, have been in the habit of looking up to Br. Harvard, not only as their attentive Missionary and benefactor, but as their Father and Protector. And let it never be forgotten, either by ourselves or our friends in every part of the globe, that whatever good may result to the poor Natives in Ceylon from our School system, Br. Harvard was among the first movers of it. And to the moment of his being laid aside by the dispensations of Providence, which appears to have deprived our Mission of his labour, he gave his most unwearied, unabating, ever active, and persevering attention to the Schools. Indeed it would be an exceedingly difficult thing for any one, even one the best acquainted with him, and the most constant witness of his incessant labours, to give any thing like an adequate idea of the extent of his exertions in this department.

But the Lord has mysteriously called him away from us: had he been continued we should have rejoiced and laboured together, yet our place is submission and our prayers and affectionate regards will ever accompany him.

I shall have need to say very little respecting the state of our Schools. The Report which is now in hand, and which we shall begin to print in a few days, will furnish you with particular information. It is matter for thankfulness and encouragement, that in all our Schools the children are getting on remarkably well in their learning; and the principal part of the scholars on our station are learning English. I see much, very much depends on our pious Schoolmasters; for this is a department so uninteresting to a man born in this country, that he really never will do his duty in a Christian School unless he is under the influence of Religion. I am happy to say that most of our Schoolmasters meet in class, and labour as much for the salvation of the souls of all the children they have to do with, as for their improvement in learning. In addition to this it calls their talents into exercise. We much want about 20 or 30 faithful, zealous, local preachers, to be continually itinerating about Colombo and its neighbourhood: men truly converted to God, and conversant with the languages which are spoken.—When we have their strength, men of God going from door to door, we may then say the heathen, and the heathen Christians of Ceylon, will have a fair chance. And I think by the blessing of our good Master this shall be given to us. The time is coming.

Our Schools it is true require much attention, and those in Colombo must have suffered when Brother Harvard was forced to lay bye, but for the timely aid of our dear Br. Newstead. After the district meeting removed him from Negombo to Colombo to our help, he was exceedingly kind and attentive, entering most heartily into all our plans, and to the utmost of his power exerted himself in this department to keep things going on. Indeed, I feel truly thankful to the Brother for the great interest he has taken in the concerns of this circuit; and as I hardly know what I should have done, had I not had his help. Should the Conference appoint him as my colleague, either to this or any other station, I am sure we shall get on well together.

It affords me sincere pleasure to assure you that the Lord continues to bless our labours: we have had, during the last three months, several pleasing evidences that his work is prospering. I never forget, I think, that our principal object is the salvation of souls, and though I am variously engaged and occupied from day to day, I endeavour daily to summon up all my unworthy efforts to this point. *Are immortal Souls coming to the knowledge and enjoyment of the Gospel Salvation.* And it is gratifying to my feelings that I shall be able, at our approaching Conference, to report upwards of 80 Members in Society. A number of these, as I have already observed, are Scholars in our native Schools; or Children who were under our instructions but are old enough to labour, and have left the School, but continue to meet in class. We have endeavoured to act with the utmost caution in giving them tickets, and receiving them as members of the Society, but the principal part of them have met more than a year; and, in addition to their giving the clearest evidences of a work of grace on their mind, they have conducted themselves in a way consistent with the word of God we could hardly ever have expected youths to have done in their situation. A few nights ago I happened to be walking out about 2 miles in the country, and on coming near a native hut, just at sun-set, I heard a noise, something like singing; on a nearer approach I found some children within were singing, in the best way they could, a Singalese Hymn, to the tune which is usually sung to the Evening Hymn, on enquiring the cause of this, I was informed it was one of the religious boys, belonging to the Colpetty School, who was performing evening worship with the family before they went to rest. The people that stood by told me, he always performed this service in the evenings and mornings. Among the European soldiers we have nearly 30 members in Society, several of whom are lately gone into the Interior. It is, however, satisfactory to learn, that they continue stead fast in the faith and hope of the Gospel. We have had several interesting letters from some of them, from which I intend to make a few extracts for our Miscellany. From a number of circumstances which our pious soldiers are in the habit of communicating respecting the poor heathen inhabitants of Kandy, I should by no means think them an unpromising people to carry the Gospel to; the late war, or rather revolution, has brought them exceedingly low in a political view, and has made the triumph of the English over them complete.

Though our numbers will not allow of our sending them Missionaries at the present time, yet I consider it, my dear Brethren, no trifling circumstance we can send books of various kinds, in their own language among them. We have not put many new things in hand to be printed this last quarter. the presses are principally employed, and will be I expect for several months, in the second edition of the New Testament in Singalese, and the Liturgy in the same language. The book of Geneses is finished and the Psalms will be begun upon immediately. Our Printing concern goes on now without any interruption since the arrival of Mr. Gogerly. His arrival was indeed most providential, and besides securing regularity in our printing establishment, affords a great relief to the missionary on the station, and the prospects in this department of our work are extending in importance and interest.

Upon the whole, I think our circumstances on this station will warrant me in saying, that we are going on exceedingly well, many things of a painful kind do occur. these I always expect. We frequently meet with things that grieve. and almost distress one's feelings. but these are lost when we see how the work in general is going on. I have still to lament my own great unworthiness and unfitness for the work. my want of faith, of love. of patience, and other graces particularly necessary for a Missionary; yet I bless God for the happiness of mind I in general do enjoy. I am happy, yea very happy in my work; I should not like to be in any other part of the world just now: my soul as well as my body are in Ceylon: my heart and affections are in the mission. I am favoured with many displays of the divine favour in my soul: hence I frequently think I am just where I ought to be, and employed as I ought to be.

I am, your affectionate Brother,

B. CLOUGH.

THE CALTURA STATION.

Point de Galle.

VERY DEAR BRETHREN,

IT is with great difficulty I write to you my present Quarterly communication, from the peculiar trials with which it has pleased the Lord to afflict me. I have now lost my most valuable earthly stay, counsellor and friend. My dear Wife has been removed from me, and though once doubtful the race, she has gained the haven of rest before me. I could not murmur at this painful dispensation of Him who cannot err; but I submitted with a broken heart. While she was with me I fainted under nothing, and scarcely any thing but her affliction filled my heart with sorrow. She lamented that she could personally do so little, comparatively, in the great work; but she encouraged me in all my labours and difficulties, though she sometimes told me I was frustrating the end I designed, by attempting labours beyond my power to accomplish.

Wherever the cause of God demanded my presence, she not only gave me up, but urged me to go, with only one caution, do not mistake murder for sacrifice. Indeed she was so associated with all my plans, that I find it yet too much for my feelings, to attempt to finish works begun while she was with me. There is, however, one consolation that mingles itself with all my sorrows, I shall soon meet her again, in climes where death and parting are no more. I was but ill prepared for this afflictive stroke, though I had had the most painful fears for some time, yet having succeeded before in raising her up, I trusted, aided by a milder clime, Providence would again graciously turn aside the stroke. The complaint which brought her to the grave was of a long standing, a consumption.

When she reached this Island she was stronger than she had ever been since I had the happiness to be acquainted with her; and this continued till she was far advanced in a state of pregnancy. During this period I was very careful of her diet, and as some slight symptoms of her old cough returned, I laboured, by proper lenieuts, to counteract it. In this success crowned my efforts in a good degree, and as soon as my duties in Colombo would allow, we went to our appointment at Caltura. Here for a season the cough left her, and my heart was gladdened with the pleasing prospect that she would enjoy many years of health. In the latter end of the year 1817, her cough returned, and my mind was distressed beyond measure; but medical aid again moderated it. On the 18th January 1818, my little girl pulled a table over, and my Katharine was much frightened; I ran into the room, and found her vomiting a small quantity of blood, (a circumstance of a similar kind occure in her former pregnancy) I immediately gave her about two drops of Vitriolic Acid in a tumbler of water, and the blood stayed at once. The day following it returned, but was again stopped, and the day following she was safely confined. She recovered far beyond our most sanguine expectation; but was occasionally troubled with the cough;

No. vi.   C

this was again greatly moderated by using a prescription that eminent physician Jas. Scratchly, M. D. sent us. She had in general a good appetite, and complained of no inconvenience, but the cough. In March she said, My Dear William, it is in vain for us to expect that this cough will be removed, I know it will carry me to the grave. I said nothing is too hard for the Lord, and burst into tears. She was much moved, and wiping the tears from my face said, Come, never mind, all will be well: I shall have my wish, you will be spared to take care of the children, which you are much better qualified for than I am.

I said, no my Katharine, I cannot live without you. Perhaps the Lord will graciously accept of me in your stead, and prolong your life. No, she replied, you are of use in the Church; but the Lord knows I can do but little. At this time her language was.

> "I the chief of Sinners am;
> "But Jesus died for me.

She often repeated her favourite Hymn, begining with "Shrinking from the cold hand of death;" and so partial was she to that Hymn, that she got an old Hymn Book bound and clasped with silver, because, in that edition, the Hymn was uuabridged, and her favourite verse was there.

> "Walk with me through the dreadful shade,
> "And certified that thou art mine,
> "My Spirit calm and undismayed,
> "I shall into thy hands resign."

On giving the ground of her hope she repeated the lines,

> "Because thou didst for Sinners die,
> "Jesus in death remember me."

From this time her complaint was variable, sometimes she was but little affected by her cough, her appetite remained, and she complained but little of a decrease of strength. In July, the lamented Sir William Coke, on his last journey, kindly called to see us, and on his departure she remarked how well he looked; observing, that health however was no security against death. At this time her mind was quite calm and composed, and the adversary who had fiercely assaulted her, was not permitted to afflict her soul. She was very urgent with me to send our dear little girl to England, considering this one of the worst places in the world to bring up girls, where an afflicted mother could not attend to them. I was not very willing to part with my children; but thinking it would lessen her anxiety I consented to do it, when we had a good opportunity. Our dear little boy, she added, I hope will ever be with his father, where he will be well educated, and brought up in the fear of the Lord. You cannot conceive how difficult it was to command my feelings under such conversations, which seemed like the language of one ready to die, and one for whom, had Heaven permitted, I could gladly have given my life to save. She was particularly gratified with the Psalms, according to the Version in the Book of Common Prayer, these I read to her in the order they are appointed to be read in Churches.

We then occupied a wing of the Government House, and at first the air appeared to be of great advantage. From J. Atkinson, Esq. and his most excellent Lady, we received every comfort which could be found in the four Quarters of the Globe. Their kindness and attention to my dear Katharine, exceeds all that can be written, but it is written on my heart, and time nor eternity can erase it. For many months I rarely undressed to sleep; but was in readiness at any hour to prepare any thing that she wished for, and for the little one also, which at the age of 10 weeks I put in a small cot beside the bed. But all our efforts seemed to be in vain. After a few weeks her cough was worse than before, and I was recommended, from all quarters, to try another air. The sympathizing affection of my Brethren and Friends, was a consolation to us under these trying circumstances. Having by the help of Br. M'Kenny made due arrangements, we set out for Point de Galle, where we arrived without the usual inconveniences in travelling. For a fortnight she seemed to receive no advantage from the change; but afterwards symptoms were more favourable, and in the beginning of November I had little doubt of her recovery. As it was necessary for us to hold a District Meeting, I said to her; My dear, I will write to the Brethren to meet at Galle, as it will make but little difference to them, at all events my presence is not particularly necessary at this Meeting. She answered, No, my dear, you may leave me very safely, it is proper for you to go, you can see how your circuit fares, and as Brother Harvard is going home you will be able to make some arrangments for his taking Katharine home. I hesitated and she wept, saying she was the cause of my neglecting a duty. I wept, and said I do not feel happy to leave you, since I can do my duty in some degree without it. But as she continued to improve in health I at length set out: I was far from being well when I left Galle, and when I had been in Colombo three days, I was seized with so obstinate a bowel complaint, that it was not till I was given up, that medical skill, a load of medicine and copious bleeding had power to arrest it My Brethren, with broken hearts, told me the doctor's opinion, which I heard unmoved, and my soul, within a few hours (apparently) of the eternal world, stood unmoved on the Rock of ages. My dear wife and little ones were on my heart, but I had confidence in him who said, "leave thy fatherless children, and let thy widows trust in me." When the disorder turned, as soon as I could use a pen, fearing my dear partner would be afflicted greatly on hearing that I was sick, I wrote as follows.

MY DEAREST KATHARINE,

My first degree of returning strength, I devote to the welcome duty of writing to you a few lines: you will have heard that it pleased our good Lord to bring me within a few steps of the grave; but he never forsook me, and I heard without the slightest emotion that my dissolution was near. I did not forget you; but I felt that he in whom I had an unshaken confidence, would never leave you nor forsake you. I am yet weak, but recover strength faster than could be expected. To day I have walked out, and eaten tolerable heartily. My soul is happy in my Saviour's love. I think about Thursday next, I shall be strong enough to venture to return in a palanquin. I firmly believe, had not the Lord sent me to Colombo at this time, I should have lost your company till death had brought us together again. O my dear wife, bless the Lord with me; distrust him no more, do not say he has forgotten you, he has mercifully remembered you and will never forget you. With my affectionate love to you and my dear little Babes.

I am

Your Affectionate, Husband.
W. BUCKLEY FOX,

I was then seized with a severe relapse, but fearing if I did not write, she would fear the worst, I wrote in a deathlike faintness.

MY DEAR KATHARINE,

I am slowly recovering. I have taken a slight cold, and am a little griped to day; but it will not much interrupt my recovery. Tomorrow I hope to be able to say when Br. M'Kenny, shall send the coolies. I am very anxious to be with you, but I dare not sacrifice myself on the road. I find it hard work to write. I have just received a letter from Br. M'Kenny, giving me the pleasing intelligence that my little family are doing full as well as when I left Galle. The inclosed Letter will give you the doctor's opinion; I am compelled to be of a different one. My soul is stayed on the Lord; but the Enemy thrusts harder at my soul in a state of weakness, than when severely afflicted. My cause I leave in the hands of my Saviour and my God.

> "I the chief of Sinners am;
> "But *Jesus died for me.*"

The Lord keep you, my dearest, and fill you with the love which is stronger than death; so prays.

Your poor, but Affectionate Husband.
W. BUCKLEY FOX,

Kiss my; dear Babes for me accept my love. Adieu.

I then received a Letter from my dear Partner it was the last she ever wrote.

Galle, November 21st

MY VERY DEAR HUSBAND,

I forbear mentioning the agitation of my mind during your illness, and thankfully acknowledge the kindness of the Lord in sparing you to me and the Church a little longer. I hope my dear Love, you will not make too free with yourself: do not hasten home before you are quite capable for the journey. I have done exceeding well since you have been gone, with the Children; as appoo is very attentive. William thrives apace. Have you said any thing to Mrs. Harvard about taking Katharine to England, do not omit it. I have been about the same as when you left. I must leave off. I write this on my knees, as I sit on the couch, and my eye sight is almost gone: my love to all. The Lord bless you, and send you safe back to

Your Affectionate Wife,
KATHARINE FOX.

22d. I had not long finished this when I received your welcome letter. Welcome indeed. Although I long to see you, I think Thursday will be too soon to commence so long a journey, Adieu my dear love, I can write no more.

Your Affectionate Wife,
KATHARINE FOX.

On receiving this, my mind was much dejected, and I was so low weak and ill, that I could scarcely leave my room. My heart was at Galle, though my body was confined at Colombo. As soon as the coolies came, I set out filled with a thousand pleasing ideas of seeing my dear Katharine, but a few hours before I could reach, she had, without even a sigh, entered into the rest that remains for the people of God. When the breathless messenger met me with the news, I was overwhelmed with sorrow that could not relieve itself by tears, and I came only to see the remains of all that was dear to me, on whose countenance death had fixed the most placid smile. I looked on my little ones and wept: but for them perhaps I had murmured to be brought back from the grave, when to live was to be separated from her I loved. She did not apprehend herself to be so near death till the day before, and then, in giving an account of her hope to her affectionate friend Mrs. Griffiths, she repeated two lines of her favourite Hymn.

> "Because thou didst for Sinners die
> "Jesus in death remember me."

For several months she was often severely tried by the grand adversary, and often tempted to think that even boundless mercy could not make her meet for Heaven. Often have I wept with her, and often has the snare been broken; but her weak state of body often pressed down the mind and made her a mourner indeed. O may I labour more diligently in that cause, which, above all others she loved, till the great Head of the Church shall say, Well done good and faithful Servant, enter and share with thy Partner, the joy of your Lord.

I am grateful for the sympathies of my Brethren, and the kindness of my numerous friends, The Rev. Mr. Mayor and his kind Partner took my little girl to their own house some weeks before my Katharine, died; and Sister M'Kenny, has kindly and voluntarily taken charge of my little Boy. My little Katharine will return to Europe under charge of Brother Harvard, and thus my dear little girl, if all be well, will twice have crossed the Atlantic and Indian Oceans before she will have completed the third year of her age. I can scarcely support myself under the prospect of losing my little girl. though I know the Lord will take care of her, and she will never want a friend.   A few months ago I was surrounded by my little family, a happier family lived not; now I am stripped, and left alone; but it is the Lord's hand that hath done this, I must not murmur, he knows what is best.

> "Good when he gives, supremely good,
> "Nor less when he denies,
> "Even trials from his blessed hand,
> "Are blessings in disguise."

I am happy to say that my station prospers greatly, under the indefatigable labours of Mr. Anthoniesz; the congregations greatly increase, and the schools are in a very prosperous state.   On these I shall not enlarge, as the particular details will be found in our School Report, now in the Press. With my grateful acknow, ledgments of your sympathy in the trying Hour I remain

Very Dear Brethren,

Yours Affectionately,

W. BUCKLEY FOX,

THE GALLE STATION.

Galle, January 6th, 1818.

MY DEAR BRETHREN,

It is with peculiar pleasure that I receive every returning opportunity of renewing the pledge of my affection for your all. On contemplating the strength and closeness of that union which exists between us, I am inclined to think that I feel something of that satisfaction and pleasure which must have filled the mind of the Royal Psalmist, when he said, " *Behold how good and how pleasant it is for Brethren to dwell together in unity.*" Well, glory be to God who makes us one, and will not les us part. The last quarter has been a time of great trial and affliction. I am sure you will all have heard of the very alarming illness of our dear Brother Fox, at Colombo, during our District meeting. There we were obliged to see him brought near to death by a most obstinate and dangerous complaint: our hope respecting his recovery, was like an exhausted lamp, near to expire, when the Lord was graciously pleased to sanctify the use of the means, and raise him up again, to continue to be useful in his Church. You have also heard the mournful tidings of our dear Sister Fox's death! It is true that this was an event which my dear partner and myself had reason to anticipate, yet it was more sudden than we expected, and attended with one circumstance peculiarly trying, which was the absence of Brother

Fox, at the distressing moment of our Sister's dissolution ; for he had not returned from Colombo, where he had been detained by his own illness. Our dear Sister's mind had been harassed by the grand enemy until within a few days of her death : but when her weakness became extreme, and when we might have conceived her most exposed to the onsets of the adversary, her glorious Saviour was mercifully pleased to appear in her behalf, and gave her a good degree of comfort and confidence. The night before she died I was with her until it was late, and found great liberty in pouring out my soul with her in prayer, when she was much strengthend and comforted, and spoke in a very satisfactory manner : her last words to me were, " Well, I believe I shall be saved, though as at the eleventh hour. I rest upon the Blood of Jesus Christ, and I have given myself into the hands of God." Thus I left her with faith in exercise, resigned to the Divine will, and much comforted: and the next morning, Dec. 3d, between six and seven o'clock, she sunk, without a struggle, into the sleep of death.

My own health has not been so good as usual during the past quarter. I have suffered from bilious affections, head aches, &c, however, I trust I can safely say, that these afflictions have all been sanctified to the good of my soul ; and have tended to increase my spiritual blessings generally, but more particularly those of deadness to the world and resignation to the will of God. My soul is still more fully given up to the work of the Mission, and the language of my heart is, let me live and die to the glory of my Divine Lord and Master.

I am happy to say that the good work on this station continues to prosper, and to justify the expectation of a considerable increase if it can be afforded additional help.

In some of the Schools there has been a falling off, but in others so great an increase as fully to make up the loss. The good effects of our Schools begin evidently to appear; and I have no doubt but that they will be the medium through which the blessed truths of the Gospel will be communicated, in a general way, to the inhabitants of this Island.

Praying that the best blessings of grace and mercy may descend upon your all,

I remain, My Dear Brethren,
Very affectionately yours,
J. M'KENNY.

THE MATURA STATION,

Matura, December 29, 1818.

VERY DEAR BRETHREN,

The various afflictions of the members of the mission for many months past have doubtless protracted our anticipated prosperity; and have suffered me to bestow a limited attention only to the concerns of this Station. It is but three weeks since my return but I have endeavoured to get an accurate knowledge, by personal examination, of every part of the work under our care. Little more could reasonably be expected than to keep our ground, but I am thankful to say the Lord has been pleased to enlarge our borders.

Our Portuguese preaching on Sunday evening is well attended. I believe there are few families who do not avail themselves of this means of grace, statedly or occasionally: several aged persons at present attend regularly who went seldom to any place of worship. We are often much pleased with the serious attention of the people, and have good reason to believe they do not hear in vain. We have at different times attempted to institute a Portuguese Class, and had on one occasion about eight individuals who attended well. Although we have done all in our power to promote their edification, I have been pained to observe some degree of prejudice against that part of our economy; arising, I believe, partly from its apparent novelty among Protestants, and because it is supposed to have some affinity to a Romish confession. But though several, whom we are confident derive profit from the word do not see at present the necessity of being in close communion with us, they are glad to be visited at their houses, and to converse on religious subjects; and Br. Lalman frequently spends an evening among the people in that profitable way. We intend, if possible, to hold Prayer Meetings in different parts of the town, so as to accommodate the various classes of people, and excite attention to that sacred duty.

The Singhalese population require the largest share of our exertion, and nothing is more gratifying than the assurance of usefulness among that people. It is in vain for us to expect to reap that on which we have bestowed no labour. Patient perseverance must have its perfect work. My mind has been sometimes discouraged by the apathy of those who surround us; and the smallness of our apparent success has been to me a source of considerable uneasiness. I want to see many turn from dumb idols to the living God. I want to see a wide display of Jehovah's saving grace. Early converts have certainly many more difficulties than those who become serious when their numbers are considerable. In the present stage of the work all who depart from iniquity are constantly exposed to powerful temptation, the contagion of bad example, and suffer persecution with little aid from experience, or the example and encouragement of Christian Brethren. An accurate view of the situation of those under our care, should prevent a hasty comparison between their profession, and what we should expect in a country where heathen systems and heathen ceremonies are passed away for ever: and where the essential doctrines of Christianity are known and believed from the days of infancy.

Though we have not had equal cause of rejoicing in every individual brought under our instruction, we know none who have relapsed into heathenism. Our little Cingalese female class continues much the same, without increase or dimunition, but divine knowledge and Christian experience appears to be deepening; and from the attention of others to the Word, we hope for some additions to the number. We continue weekly to meet those of our School boys who are serious in a kind of class meeting, but to render it the more suitable and interesting it often borders on the catechetical mode. It is truly pleasing to notice their experience of Divine things, and observe their advancement in useful knowledge. Several of them pray in a very sensible and humble manner.

It was our custom some time ago to hold a weekly meeting for the instruction of the more advanced boys in the evidence of Revelation, and Fleming's Great Things in Religion, an admirable tract, republished a few years since by R. C. Brachenbury Esq. appeared the best summary in a condensed form I had ever seen, and served as a text Book. I required each to write down what I delivered, and it was highly gratifying to witness their attention to the subjects, though it was a task of no ordinary difficulty, as they had to clothe the ideas in their own style. I am sorry my absence interrupted those lectures, but I fully intend resuming them.

To accommodate as many of our Schools as possible with instruction on the Lord's day, we have lately sent two of our best informed pupils to different Schools to read the Scriptures, give short exhortations, and pray with the people. We point out appropriate chapters, and shew them where it is necessary to make a remark. Their labours appear to be approved; and by this means they have been excited to study the Scriptures with renewed attention.

Andris, who though of parents professing Christianity, and had been baptized in his infancy, was for many years a Priest of Budhu, is now a faithful Schoolmaster at a village altogether heathen, about half way between this place and Galle. He is an active, and truly pious young man, of good talents, has given us invariable satisfaction, appears to be much respected in the neighbourhood, has a promising School of 60 boys, and will, I hope, be rendered a blessing to the people.

One of our hearers, a serious active man, desirous of improving himself by usefulness, wished to assist us for a small consideration in conducting our day School. His presence leaves us more at liberty to attend to other work of importance, and under his unremitting care the number of children has increased. The Cingalese is taught principally by Don Daniel, a man of respectable acquirements. He studied for some years under the same tutors, and in the same College, with Petrus Panditta Sekarra, and Petrus and he were ordained Tirananseys the same day. The late king of Kandy was present at the ceremony. His attention was first excited to the subject of Christianity by the Dialogue between a Priest and a Missionary, which he got from a Cooley, and which had been distributed in the Morwa Corle with other tracts. He studied the Dialogue so often as to be able to repeat it without book; and says, he concluded *that* religion to be confused and imperfect which a Priest, after studying 20 years, was unable to defend. A more

diligent reader of the New Testament I have seldom seen; and
that his soul is under the teaching of the Divine Spirit I have
no doubt. As I am anxious this School should excel, I have just
engaged an eminent Cingalese Painter to copy a Map of the
World on an unusually large scale, to be fixed at the end of the
room, so as to give the children an outline of Geography, and
think of placing the Solar System on one side, and a Map of
Ceylon on the other.

A particular account of our Schools I am preparing for the Annual Report. From their limited superintendence of late I scarce
expected to find them doing so well. The one at Belligam, though
not opened above three months ago, has got on charmingly. Mr.
Kemps resides there as English Master, a young man of this place,
of whose conversion I believe most of our Brethren have heard.
I have seen few country born young men display a better judgment, or a more accurate knowledge of English.

I know nothing that has gratified me more for some time past
than a School of about 40 Girls I visited the other day, begun in
my absence. The Mistress is the wife of a Native headman, and
teaches them lace-making. The machinery was of a very indifferent kind, the pins were of Cingalese manufacture, and for scissars
the mistress used a razor; yet she had in hand a piece of lace
of rather a splendid pattern. Nearly all the girls have learnt the
whole of W. Fox's Catechism, the Lord's Prayer, Creed, and Ten
Commandments, and a few could read a little. What was surprising, they
had learnt this by the daily visits of an interesting little boy, a
son of the mistress. This lad belongs to a School at a short distance, and can read English.

A no less pleasing fact is the formation of a small Girl's School
at Pamburende, a small village about two miles on the Galle road.
Soon after my appointment here, I was induced to take a Cingalese boy, about 10 years old, under my care, who had five younger
sisters and a brother, depending for support on his mother and
aunt, who procured a livelihood chiefly by making lace. The
father is still alive, but has lived in another district, in total neglect of his truly interesting family for several past years. Cornelius paid much attention to every thing he was taught, and a
few months ago, his Sisters, observing his improvement, requested
him to give them some instruction at their home. He attended
them daily, and to this little company two of his cousins were
added, and lately 15 girls belonging to different families in the neighbourhood. It is truly animating to see the improvement they
have made. Seven can repeat some Sections of the Instructions
for Children in Cingalese, Portuguese and English, with the Lord's
Prayer, &c. and can spell almost any monosyllable. Five can make
lace, and nine are learning to sew. The two elder girls can read
the New Testament in Cingalese and English, can write a tolerable hand, and have learnt several pages of English Grammar.

I remain, Dear Brethren,
Very Affectionately Yours,
J. CALLAWAY,

THE NEGOMBO STATION.

Negombo, January 4, 1819.

V<small>ERY</small> D<small>EAR</small> B<small>RETHREN</small>,

HAVING been called to Colombo, very soon after writing my last Quarterly letter, by the district Meeting assembled to arrange about the departure of Brother Harvard; I have only been on my Station at intervals since that period. But I rejoice to say that from the arrangements which we were enabled to make, I believe that nothing has suffered materially in my absence.

I confess that I felt considerable reluctance at leaving the Station on the first intimation of it; but it instantly gave way to the conviction of the imperious necessity of *first* securing the interests of the Colombo Station, and all hesitation was removed when I found that while I might be of some service there, I could also (by a Providential help,) keep all things on the usual footing at Negombo, and by occasional visits, &c. superintend the rising interests of our Mission here.

The Station has had the advantage of one circumstance by my absence, which it would not otherwise have had, i. e. the benefit of *various* labourers, and a diversity of talent. Among those who were sent to supply on the Sabbath I am pleased to hear that our young friend *Cornelius* was not the least successful, having the double advantage of all the languages, and of that zeal which seldom fails. Our dear young Friend also, who has been with me through the year, has used every effort to fill up any little unexpected vacancy, and to keep all things in order and regularity on the Station. I feel truly thankful therefore, that in this we may say, "*Hitherto the Lord hath helped us.*"

I cannot but be grateful to God for the *peace* I have felt in my mind while at Colombo, in the experience of his love, and the sense of his approval: as well as for the great blessedness I have enjoyed in preaching the everlasting gospel there. Nor ought I to be less grateful for the harmoney and affection which has subsisted, (I trust mutually,) between myself and our dear Brother Clough, with whom, I have felt it truly a happiness to labour. On the *cause* of my removal thither I cannot express my feelings. The final departure of our dear Brother Harvard from the Island, I doubt not, has an affecting voice to us all. I deeply feel, what is doubtless a general sentiment, that the Lord is calling us, by these awful visitations of *Affliction* and *Death*, to closer union and intercourse with himself, and each other, while thus our numbers are decreasing, and our hands consequently weakening. The removal of our dear Sister Fox, however, to a better world, we could scarcely regret on her own account, were it not for the relative situation in which she stood.—But we are not the best judges in such cases; while the Lord is exercising *His* divine prerogative in calling whom he will fit to the enjoyment of heaven, may *we* be "also ready, for in such an hour *as we think not* the Son of Man cometh."

Our little classes here have been each regularly met every week, and their great stedfastness is truly pleasing. I trust that many of them will be our "crown of rejoicing" in the day of the Lord Jesus, even as they are here truly the *soul* of our Missionary system. It is delightful to hear their artless but forcible expressions, even the lads who assemble on these occasions, make our hearts glad : one of them at their last meeting observed to me, that "though he former- ly prayed from *custom*, yet now he always felt that the prayer of the lips was in vain, if the *heart* did not feel." "For," said he, "Our Lord Jesus in his *Sermon on the Mount*, has commanded us, when we pray not to use *vain repetitions*."

The Schoolmasters continue to grow in knowledge, and in experi- ence of Divine things, one of them after long probation with a view to it, is become a communicant; a second has made an application, to whom I have recommended yet more seriously to consider the im- portant subject, for I am pained to observe, if not in this instance, yet generally, an eager desire in the people around, to press to the Table of the Lord, who never dream of attending to any other religious ordinance! except indeed in a very common place way. I have been obliged conscientiously to deny four of those kind of presumed Chris- tians, who conceive that *all* is well, if they occasionally receive the Sacrament; and of whom I felt assured that they had no proper idea of *any other Saviour!* It is with the utmost difficulty, however, that I can prevail upon them to submit to a previous course of instruc- tion and preparation, for they generally answer every proposal of this kind, however delicately urged, by stating that they *have* been, at some indefinite period past, *accepted communicants*, and therefore they see no need of begining again. It is often very painful to deal with them, for they generally receive the impression that we are needless- ly scrupulous, if not cruel. But I trust that in this our views are all in unison, that no person so obviously unprepared and unfit should be admitted to the Holy Sacrament. I wish some of the Brethren would mention it in our next Quarterly communication, for the case is no doubt, pretty general. My soul rejoices in the recollection of two of the most blessed seasons of refreshing I ever remember to have any where enjoyed, at our two last Sacraments. The Lord was indeed, *very* gracious unto us. The Schools, I am happy to say are gaining strength, both by experience, and by increasing numbers. I trust the *hearts* of some of the Masters are in the work. The *Akelle* School is increased to 100 Boys, and when I think of *this* little army in the very heart of Heathenism, I rejoice over it with exceeding great joy ; for here the gospel of Christ, ("which is the power of God,") is sounded every week, although by a feeble tongue, and some eter- nal good will surely succeed! "*Not by might, nor by power, but by my Spirit saith the Lord of Hosts.*" Already the strong holds of Satan begin to shake for the *name of Jesus* is sounded constantly around the walls.—It is delightful to hear that even the *Females* of the most respectable family in the village now seldom meet the Priests of Budhu who resort thither, but they enter into arguments against them to prove a *Supreme cause*, and that consequently the deity of their former worship and adoration was a *creature* and as a creat- ed being is unworthy of divine homage! This is certainly a victory of the Cross, though a very silent one; for it is scarcely heard or known beyond the family, except in a whisper. But a circumstance occurred lately in the same family, which will more strongly illustrate the idea. The last time I preached there, while all the family were attentively hearing the Gospel, an enemy came, and poisoned the water in their well! the unconscious family, as usual, making use of the water, were all soon thrown into the utmost consternation and affright, by the alarming symptoms that followed; they were all affected more or less, and some of them even anticipated death;—The Priests of Budhu were at hand, (their former refuge,) but now, having heard of the only way of Salvation, they preferred to send for the *Mission Schoolmaster*, who they knew was a *Christian*, to pray with them, and *to entreat the Lord for them*, and in this office he was busily engaged for some time from couch to couch! He wrote me a joyful account of the pleasing circumstance, and how the Lord had brought good out of threatened evil, for all the family, by the use of means were preserved, and added, "Indeed there appears quite a change in all the country round."

Another pleasing anecdote connected with our Schools, shall close my already very long letter. Our School-boy's Class at Negombo is regularly attended by five boys from the School of *Calvonuake*, about five miles from the Station; who, though at first they only came once a fortnight owing to the distance, now come always every week. The origin of their serious desires marks the progress of *Divine Light*. Under the blessing of God, the Catechisms, Preaching and instructions of various kinds which they were constantly hearing and receiving at School, had a good effect on their minds in leading them to *think* about *Christianity*; (for they were generally heathens,) and they carried home with them from time to time such convictions, as would not let them join with, or approve the heathen customs and ceremonies usual in their families. One boy in particular was very conscientious; his father was taken ill, and, as is common with them, sent for the usual persons who perform the *Devil dance*, who assured the man that he would recover if he followed his directions, and made the customary offerings; the boy knowing this, was resolved, as he could not prevent it, that he would not *witness* it; and to avoid it, he fled on the appointed evening into the jungle, and continued there all night, praying, he says, at intervals. The family were alarmed at his absence, being aware of the cause and especially as he did not return home in the morning; but went straight to the School. On his return the parents were angry and expostulated with him, but he was inflexible in his determination to be a Christian, and to avoid such abominations: his continuing always to pray and read the word of God regularly before them, at length became such an annoyance to them that they gave him leave to build himself a little *Ola house*, at the end of their own, where he might pursue his devotions unmolested. Of course, he gladly embraced the offer, and as soon as it came to the knowledge of his School fellows, which was not till some time after, *four* others followed his example, and all begged to be permitted to meet in the Negombo School Class: and now I believe they have each their little *House of Prayer* in the jungle, and endeavour to serve God to the best of their power.

Entreating an interest in your prayers, I continue,
Very dear Brethren,
Most affectionately your's,
ROBERT NEWSTEAD.

THE JAFFNA STATION.

Jaffna December 29, 1818.

VERY DEAR BRETHREN,

IT is with much satisfacton and delight that I sit down to give you a short account of the progress of the work of God on this Station in the last Quarter, as the prospect is becoming increasingly promising.

In the first place our English congregations are larger than ever I saw them before. At Portuguese preaching we have generally more than can get into the Chapel. We have had two more young men added to our Portuguese class. One of the former I believe has considered our discipline too strict for him and is gone back. Our English class is doing well.

At the commencement of the quarter we set on foot a *Benevolent Society*, which I am happy to say promises to be a very successful medium of access to the huts of the poor, sick, and ignorant inhabitants of Jaffna. We have been led through this institution to discover such scenes of distress as cannot well be described, and what makes it still more distressing, many who have been in good circumstances under the Dutch Government, but are now in their advanced years wanting the common necessaries of life. I have found many who were not ignoraut of the way of salvation, and some who actually enjoyed it, and were waiting with a joyful anticipation for death to relieve them from their present distress. Jaffnapatam abounds with descendants of Dutch and Portuguese who are now far, *very far*, beneath the Natives in almost every sense of the word. Their poverty makes them ashamed to make themselves known, and they seem to study to hide themselves from the eye of the world. But the discipline of our Benevolent Society finds them out, and by giving them a little for the relief of their bodily wants we can say something to them concerning their souls. This Society has also another happy tendency in bringing our young men forward who are appointed visitors. They euter into the work with spirit, and attend strictly to our rules. Though they appear a little diffident and backward, when we are with them, they speak boldly we find when alone. I believe our Benevolent Fund will supply us pretty well with money to carry on our purpose to considerable extent, as our friends enter into it tolerably well, and I have no doubt will more so when they understand it better and see more of its effects. Mr. Mooyaart fills the office of Treasurer, and the Revd. Mr.

Knight that of Secretary. We found many cases to which we could administer little or no relief, from not knowing the use of Medicine. The greater part of those visited by us are so poor that they cannot get Medical advice. This we have remedied by employing a Portuguese Doctor to visit the sick under the direction of the Committee, and to be supplied with Medicine from the Treasurer, who is now providing a proper stock. This will I trust prove of important good to the poor of Jaffna.

I am sorry that in the Quarter past I have been so little favoured with the society and help of our dear Br. Squance, and still more so that severe affliction has been the cause of it. Having been accustomed to so much spiritual help from him I feel it sometimes difficult to be warm alone. However, I find the great Head of the Church is still with me, and being constantly engaged in the very extensive work of this Station, my mind is generally employed. I have not been able to visit any country-place since Br. S. left, the work of the Town being as much as I can possibly attend to; indeed it is too much, as it leaves me no time for the *study of Tamul*; or if I could find a few hours in a day for this, I find my health would not allow me to fill them up with close study, were I to do this I should soon be unable to attend to what I now do. I regret this *much*, as I know that a knowledge of the Native tongue, and an acquaintance with the Natives to gain their confidence, &c. &c. are of the first importance. I hope before long we shall have *much* more help in the Jaffna district.

Though I have not been able to visit our country-places, they have not been entirely neglected, for the young man we mentioned in our last, goes his weekly round to all the Schools which are accessible during the wet season, and brings his report every Friday. I hope by this time Br. Squance is safely arrived at Colombo, and in better health than when he left Jaffna.

I am, very dear Brethren,
Your's Affectionately,
THOS. OSBORNE.

THE TRINCOMALIE STATION.

Trincomalie, December 29th, 1818.

VERY DEAR BRETHREN.

To lay before your the principal circumstances that have marked my path, since the last Extracts, will not occupy much of my paper nor of your time.

Out of the way as I have been of more abundant usefulness by the advantage of a more intimate acquaintance with the natives of this part of the Island, I lament that I cannot secure to you and myself the gratification of more progress among them; I am not, however, without sufficient encouragements to hope for success, as well as louder calls to stimulate me to greater exertion. Sad necessity, arising from the value and danger of immortal souls, daily admonishes me " To cry behold the Lamb."

With common care, and a temperate use of things needful to subsistence, I have enjoyed, with thankfulness, uninterrupted health, during the last three months: and I trust, have made some advances in the Divine life.

To some discouragements, glimmerings of hope have not been denied; so that regret has not found access, and despair has been a stranger: indeed, my trials, privations, or sufferings, are not worthy to be named where those of the first servants of Christ are remembered. A sense of the presence of the Lord with me, and the recollection of the *promised glory* of his Church, have left me little room for despondency of mind, and given stability to my confidence in the Royal Psalmist's declaration, "The Lord reigneth."

It is my delight to "*Shew forth his salvation from day to day, to declare his glory among the heathen. His wonders among all people:*" And to cry aloud, "*Give unto the Lord, O ye kindreds of the people, give unto the Lord glory and strength. Give unto the Lord the glory due unto his name: bring an offering, and come into his courts.*" Labouring in so blessed a cause, and for so gracious a Master, I see it my duty and privilege, to be able daily to deny myself, and take up my cross and to follow him: whose smile is felicity and whose favour peace.

By the rains and uncertain weather, together with the distance from the Mission House of many of our hearers, our congregations lately have been much interrupted: many females have sometimes come out from the Fort, in very uncertain weather, which has convinced me of their love to the Word and worship of God.

Notwithstanding, we have had many blessed and refreshing seasons from the presence of the Lord, proving that "*They that wait upon the Lord shall renew their strength: they shall mount up with wings as eagles; they shall run, and not be weary; and they shall walk and not faint.* Some, also, who had been mercifully raised from beds of sickness, and whom I had visited in their distresses, remembered their obligations to God, and came to pay their *vows* unto the Lord in the midst of the great congregation

The Holy Sacrament, as usual on the first Sabbath of every month, has been observed by us, with increasing interest in Him who said, "*Do this in remembrance of me.*" On these occasions we have had generally 14 or 16 communicants, but lately fewer, for the reasons before mentioned. Our class meeting likewise has felt the same inconveniences, and has been as frequently interrupted as every other service; but we are recovering a little, and hope to regain our wonted strength.

The uncertainty of my remaining here has prevented me from making any attemps at forming more Schools among the natives; nor, indeed, could I have done so with any propriety, from so very slight an acquaintance with the people. Great ignorance and great wickedness is very apparent among them; and it is lamentable indeed to have daily to contemplate so awful a scene as human nature here presents.—Yet, how to gain their atten-

Yet, how to gain their attention, how to excite their desires, how to shew them the necessity of fleeing to the Saviour, requires all the wisdom, all the patience, and all the perseverance, we can collect, But, if insensibility to danger, if bewildered imaginations, if perverted judgments and depraved hear's be objects of pity, these poor heathens demand our commisseration and our help. And that Missionary who separates himself from his father's house;—foregoes the comforts of civilized society, and submits to behold the barbarous spectacles of savage life, though he cannot escape the pains which they inflict,—endures to be deprived of the opportunity of cultivating his own mind in useful knowledge, and tasting the sweets of intellectual pleasures, and at the same time plunges himself among comparative intellectual darkness, with the heaven-born desire of shedding forth some rays of borrowed light; I say, such an one surely is offering no unacceptable sacrifice to God: and the sacrifice of his country, his friends, his comforts, yea, his own feelings, shall not be forgotten of the Lord.   Brethren, though utterly unworthy, I rejoice to be counted with you, and with those men of God, who have not counted their lives dear unto themselves so that they might win Christ.   While the military man unsheaths the sword, to carry the sovereignty of his Prince into regions where it was not before acknowledged, let us unfurl the bloody banner of the Cross, *and say among the heathens the Lord reigneth.*

While the skilful minister bends all his powers to successful negociation in the service of his sovereign, let us continue to assert the right of our Divine Master, and join the Apostle while he declares, "Now then we are ambassadors for Christ; as though God did beseech you by us: we pray you in Christ's stead, be ye reconciled to God."   But I need not tresspass upon you further: these, and a thousand more encouraging passages of God's word, may occur to you, for the Spirit has promised to bring all things to our remembrance, to cheer you in your work of mercy and labour of love.   I sometimes think, if the present reviving prospect of the work of the Lord on earth be too big for utterance, and stretch beyond the expression of our scanty language, what shall be the glorious happiness of the overwhelming felicities of heaven?   What shall be our feelings when we see the four and twenty Elders fall down before the Lamb saying, "Amen, Alleluia;" and hear a voice saying, "praise our God, all ye his servants, and ye that fear him, both small and great." "Alleluia: for the Lord God Omnipotent reigneth"?

You may, perhaps, be led to suppose that thoughts of our departed Sister Fox were with me, and I confess to you her premature death has not been forgotten: she has finished her weary pilgrimage, fledged her wings before us, and escaped to glory, to claim, of our party, the third Missionary Crown: where I hope to see her for the first time.   Our dear bereaved Brother will deeply feel her loss, but still, there is refuge and consolation in the Lord, and a glorious satisfaction when we can confidently believe our departed friends are among the happy number, which the poet describes:

No. VI.   G

Lift your eyes of faith and see
Saints and Angels join'd in one;
What a countless company
Stand before you dazzling throne;
Each before his Saviour stands,
All in milk-white robes array'd;
Palms they carry in their hands
Crowns of glory on their head.

Angel-powers the throne surround,
Next the saints in glory they;
Lull'd with the transporting sound,
They their silent homage pay;
Prostrate on their face, before
God and his Messiah fall;
Then in hymns of praise adore,
Shout the Lamb that died for all.

The work of mortality has relaxed little of its terrific power with us; death has been busily engaged from couch to couch, and many have embraced the dust, who were as young and seemed fitter far to live than we, but death as it respecteth them, individually, hath deprived disease of an object, and sorrow of its prey—One is so fresh upon my memory, and yet so visionary, Captain Fleck, that the remembrance of his arrival with Brother and Sister Gogerly, and his subsequent sudden death, seem equally to solicit belief. Unceasingly pursuing, death suffers none of his victims to escape, and sometimes marks his footsteps with both public and private prey. A few days ago we lost a very worthy, useful man of the former description, Dr. Hannay; and many of the latter have sunk beneath the hand of death whose names have perished with them.

With an increasing desire to hear of your welfare and success
I remain, my dear Brethren,
Your's very affectionately.
ROBERT CARVER.

THE BATTICALOA STATION.

[The following Letter having been mislaid during the Printing of the last Quarterly, being happily found is here inserted, in order, before the Letter received from that Station, for the present Quarter.]

Batticaloa, September 29, 1818.

MY DEAR BRETHREN,

THROUGH the kind care of my heavenly Father, I am spared and favoured with an opportunity of again addressing you. Since my arrival at this place my health has greatly improved, but what is of still more importance, I have to bless God for a more intimate union with Jesus at present, than at any time since my departure from England. Indeed, God was always disposed to bless, comfort, and save me, but by my unbelieving fears, doubts, and reasoning with the common adversary, instead of believing, loving, and obeying, I sustained loss in my soul, and prevented the descending blessing from lighting on my feeble labours! Happy the man who believes, loves and obeys; to him, "wisdom's ways are ways of pleasantness," and in every sense he shall see the salvation of God.

Much of my time and labour through the last Quarter have been confined to the sick and dying Soldiers. And while I felt this the path of duty, it was not without some fatigue. Besides my stated visits to the Hospital, I have been called for by the dying both by day and night. Sometimes there were 80 sick in the hospital, divided between four apartments, and independent of giving a general exhortation, I have frequently spoken almost to every individual. This was unavoidable in order to satisfy them, and to ascertain their real state and spiritual progress. Often, if I seemed to pass by some, *the heart melting look of a dying fellow creature has nailed me to his side, to point him to the Soul-healing blood of Jesus.* The mortality among them has been great, having read the funeral service over 80 men and one Lieut. Some were truly penitent, and I trust found that mercy they so much desired.

While much of my time was necessarily given to the sick soldiers, others were not forgotten. I have, in the course of the last Quarter, generally preached 3 times every Sunday. At eight o'Clock in the morning to the Malabars by an interpreter. At half past ten o'Clock in English, and at 5 o'Clock in the evening in Portuguese. I have visited (Pedeatorry) a village about four miles distant, containing about 100 nominal Christians three times: here there is a Govt. School containing 20 boys; I always spent the day examining the children, preaching, &c. There are other villages of nominal Christians equally contiguous, where the Missionary may visit and very probably raise Schools productive of real good. But while the Kandian war continues, and the sick come to Batticaloa, *God, humanity*, and the *blood* of Jesus, loudly call to rescue souls from sin and hell. So that one Missionary must in a great degree devote his labour to this work of mercy.

My attention to the sick has had a pleasing effect on some minds; a gentleman, who was more than shy towards me when I arrived here, is now become friendly, and told me, " I believe your coming here when you did was providential;" he now comes to hear the word of life. ——— took hold of my hand lately and exclaimed, "I love and respect your Society, and my seeming opposition at Colombo had nothing of evil in it to any of your body." There is an officer of the 73rd Regt. here, Lieut. Lidwell, ill of fever.* At his own request I have to visit him two or three times every day, and a more humble and sincere seeker of Jesus the Crucified, I have seldom seen: the Doctor thinks he will not recover. I have not yet many Scholars in our School, but believe it will increase. I bless God for love to his cause, and ways: love to all my dear Brethren, yea to all who love the name of Jesus, and a real wish for the conversion of sinners.

I remain, My dear Brethren,
Affectionately your's,
G. ERSKINE.

* See an interesting account of this Gentleman's conversion and happy death by Br. Erskine, inserted in the Miscellanea of the September Quarterly.

Batticaloa, January 4, 1819.

MY DEAR BRETHREN,

WITH unfeigned gratitude to God for the exercise of his boundless mercy towards me, in that I am spared to see the beginning of the new year, and with an humble determination that my added days shall be spent in his delightful service; with these sentiments, and I trust correspondent feelings, I take up my pen to hold pleasing communication with my beloved Brethren. "Jesus and his people for ever be my choice." Through the course of the last quarter we have had much rain, and just now it pours. Thanks be to the Giver of all good, my health has been much better through the wet monsoon, than I had expected. My congregations are pretty uniform and constant, They are, however, rather on the increase since the arrival of Mr. Pennell the present Collector. He attends the Church constantly, and example, generally, has a good effect, and this I am happy to say is the case in the present instance. My week evening congregations are pleasing and interesting, and the people attend with becoming solemnity. If labourers are continued *here*, I think we may reckon on yet seeing good days, at Batticaloa.

I continue to visit the sick in Hospital, some I find to care for divine things, and some do not; I have buried more than one hundred soldiers since I have been at this place! And besides my regular visits two or three times a week, I have never once omitted a call to attend, whether required by day or night. Of several I had hope: they are known to God, and to his Name be all the glory.

In consequence of the heavy rain my School has sustained some little detriment, yet on the whole it prospers. I attempted our Missionary Collection on Christmas-day. The sitting Magistrate; Mr. B. ————, kindly carried round the plate; never did I witness more apparent joy in the countenances of people giving to a collection, than upon that occasion. It amounted to Rds. 124. which for Batticaloa was very well.

I have felt much on hearing of our worthy Brother Fox's, bereavement, the death of his amiable partner. She, however, is safely lodged in the bosom of eternal love, and God I doubt not will be his refuge and portion. I am much concerned at the near approach of our beloved Brother and Sister Harvard's departure from us, and this is heightened by the consideration that I am not likely to see them before they leave Ceylon. Well, what a delightful place will Heaven be, when all God's children meet together! And the LAMB that sitteth on the throne shall dwell among them." This is enough!

I remain

Your Very Affectionate Brother,
GEORGE ERSKINE.

THE MADRAS STATION.

Madras, January 4, 1819.

MY DEAR BRETHREN,

SINCE my last Quarterly letter my labour and circumstances have varied very little, only that for several weeks I was closely confined, and suffered much by the country sore eyes; but at present, blessed be God, I am in the enjoyment of my usual state of good health, and I trust my soul feels as fully engaged in my work as ever it was, and I am happy to inform you that the society is in a more prosperous state than at any past period since I knew it: we have now 24 regular members, and I believe they are growing in grace, and I feel unusual happiness in preaching to them: we have also a few Natives who meet at our place once or twice a week to whom the two young men who live with me read the Scripture, and a plain sermon, and sing and pray in their own language; these have expressed a desire to be formed into a Society or Church by us, that they may have the Sacrament and Baptism administered to them; this I intend to do in a few weeks. One circumstance I cannot but mention with gratitude to God; nearly the first concern of Native Christians is a place to bury their dead, and they particularly inquired where they would be buryed if they joined our society; the utility of having a burying ground never struck me when I made the purchase; and on it there is ground for one. The Chapel is nearly finished, and I hope to open it this month. I believe it is generally allowed to be a very neat one, and I have no doubt but God will sanction the building of it. I have lately had several interesting letters from several regiments in the Madras establishment, several of the the pious soldiers have died very happy in God. The number who are formed into regular classes is about 50, one young man of the Artillery on the mount 8 miles, from Madras, has begun to preach. The two young men who live with me are I hope doing well, so that upon the whole I have cause to be thankful. I never was so firmly established on the great doctrine of the universality of the atonement, the witness of the Spirit, and holiness, as at present. I have lately been led to an impartial investigation whether they are Scriptural, and have felt it profitable. I have had to vindicate these doctrines, and the divinity of the Scripture and of Christ, against pious and sensible Calvinists, and against sincere Deists and Socinians, with the former I could live and die, but with the latter my soul can have no union. One of the latter (a Socinian) was much hurt because I would not acknowledge him to be a Christian. I find that much of my Ministerial duty is in public and private statements of the Gospel, and being able to give a reason for the hope within me. I feel myself as an " Epistle of Methodism read and known of all." I felt the commencement of the New year a solemn and profitable time. I trust to be more faithful than I have been during the past year.

I remain, in Gospel love,

yours, &c.

J. LYNCH.

Miscellaneous.

No. I.

ON THE DEATH OF MRS. FOX,

Beloved Sister, O *farewell!*
(A word how painful, who can tell
  Where kindred hearts unite?)
We dwell upon the mournful theme
Thy flight from earth, in our esteem
So like a short uneasy dream,—
  The phantom of a night!

But, 'tis a *real* heartfelt woe,
That wrings the heart with misery's throe,
  The heart of those bereft;
Thy stricken Spouse, thy Infants dear,
Thy Friends, who bathe with many a tear
Thy memory, with a love sincere,
  The Circle thou hast left.—

From our endear'd, our native land,
We came together, hand in hand,
  To serve our Jesus here;
And Jesus first hath call'd *thee* home,
Thy Spirit beckons us to come,—
And we shall follow to the tomb,
  When Jesu's voice we hear.

We bid thee tenderly farewell,
Thy virtues we forbear to tell,
  They're written in the skies:
Awhile we trace thy upward flight,
And follow on in Jesu's might;
To yonder blissful world of light;—
  To meet in paradise.

Colombo, December 21, 1818.   ROBERT NEWSTEAD,

HUM DESEIJO.

POR NOSSA AMADO IRMAÕ HARVARD.

JESUS, per tua servidor,
Da tua graça e favor;
E enchi sua coraçaõ,
Com preçioso salvaçaõ:
Per outra bande de O Mar
Com misericordia, O manda!
Dia per dia O benze!
Com amor e santidade;
Com segurançe O guarda,
E tambem sua *Familia*,
E elle desse asserta,
Ne sua mesmo bom terra
Felizidade bastanto,
Ate te irgui per çeo.

Colombo January, 7, 1819.   ROBERT NEWSTEAD,

No. II.

Definition of Methodism, *by* DR. STYLES,

"IN the *Senate*, Methodism is another term for the benevolent disposition which would abolish slavery. Mr. Wilberforce and his coadjutors are stigmatized there, as a set of Methodists, who dare to believe that all human Beings have human rights; and that it is a crime to make those slaves, whom God has created men. In the *Church*, Methodism signifies an honest and conscientious subscription to doctrinal articles, in the sense in which they are imposed by those who drew them up, and a deportment conformable to this sincerity, and the legitimate influence of the doctrine believed.

Among Mankind in general, he is a Methodist who worships God in his family, who refuses to violate any of the precepts of the Decalogue, and who imbibes the benevolent, amiable, condescending, and holy Spirit of the Christian Lawgiver. The world determines who are Methodists, not by their opinions, but by their dispositions and conduct: and the more entirely an individual resembles Jesus Christ, in that exact proportion he is considered and condemned as being guilty of Methodism."

No. III.

The following *Extracts* from several letters of a pious soldier of our Society now in the interior of the Island, to his friend in Colombo, afford the most pleasing illustration of the *leavening* influence of DIVINE TRUTH, which makes its way under the most inauspicious circumstances, and frequently by channels and instruments which escape the notice and the calculation of man, that the excellency of the power may the more evidently appear to be of God. It is delightful to reflect upon the numbers of pious men which are scattered through our Army and Navy, and who are the very best defenders of their Country; combining the force of both worlds in their warfare, because they also know the use of those weapons which are *"not carnal but mighty through God, to the pulling down of strong holds."*

A military Gentleman lately mentioned to us a pleasing circumstance of about 20 pious soldiers who, in the same ship in which he was sailing from Ceylon to Bengal, kept up regular morning and evening worship on the Forecastle of the ship all the way: singing Hymns, praying and reading sermons; and, to the great honour of the Commanding Officer, it was added, that he gave the strictest orders that none should molest them, though all were permitted to join them that were disposed. The pious soldiers on the coast of India are greatly assisted by the numbers of Bibles, &c. furnished to them by that excellent institution, the Naval and Military Bible Society.

No. I.

Kornegalle, 1st December, 1818.

DEAR BROTHER,

Through the interposition of Divine Providence I am arrived at my destination, in company with my Christian friends on the 28th November.—Glory be to our heavenly Father! he has blessed my going out and my coming in. O that he may "compass my weakness round about, and keep me safe from sin!" It is justly remarked by an author, that "soldiers who carry their lives in their hands, should above all others carry grace in their hearts, that so having made peace with God, we may be more fit to encounter with our enemies, and by faith in Christ, having disarmed the grand enemy death, we may be ready to undergo with contentment whatever may be the dispensations of God towards us." The following is the way we carried on during our journey, after we came to our ground, P. N. F. and myself got as close together as possible, and after refreshing our frail tabernacles we withdrew for the purpose of returning God thanks for his boundless mercies towards such unworthy creatures; and, pleasing to relate, we were always directed to a convenient place; so that we met twice every day. All the way we were greatly annoyed with *Leeches* in the morning. I walked out in the afternoon to seek for a more convenient place for evening worship,

and was led to a small vista where were two or three small huts;
there I walked with comfort, calling to mind the mercies of God
towards me with sensations of gratitude and joy; thither we went
in the evening, and to my surprize the woman of the house brought
a large mat sufficient for us all to kneel upon, and then retired with
the greatest caution; my heart felt for the woman, and I made her
a small present. I pray that God may reward this "cup of cold
water,"—to her, and bring her to receive the truth in the love of
it, that her soul may be saved! The next day we were greatly distressed by leeches in the morning. I again went out to find a "thresh-
ing floor" to pray on, as we could not build temples, and God led
me to another grove of trees, where I had sweet communion with my
God and his Son Jesus Christ! O the tongue that can tell the privilege of a Christian; even in the wilderness, must be more than human. This was a sweet season to my soul. C. came to me, and told
me he had found a *Swammy house* where we might meet out of
the rain. I was determined that that night the *true God* should be
praised in the house of Dagon, but we had only the outer courts,
and if ever I prayed that Satan's kingdom might be destroyed, and
the mustard seed of the Gospel never cease to spread its beneficent
branches till the whole earth was covered with the righteousness
of the Lord as the waters cover the abyss of the mighty deep, this
was the night—for I found God, in his pleading spirit, animating my
whole soul, and all my powers! O for more of that humble, meek
and patient love which was in my Redeemer! that I may feel
an affectionate concern for the souls of my fellow creatures; and
O that every one that has drank of the waters of salvation, may
be swayed to cast in their mite to help to roll the stone from the
well's mouth, that others may drink without money and without
price. We came in here on Saturday, and on Sunday morning I found
a hut built upon a rock, that I was determined to convert into
a Chapel if nobody lived in it I went up and found it empty,
to my great satisfaction; there we began the Sabbath with a Prayer-
meeting. I mounted guard this morning, notwithstanding I performed public worship in the forenoon, and found it good to wait
on the Lord. Our meeting being near the barracks, as you know
I like the wicked to hear, they made many remarks; one was, "I
think these fellows might go a little further from the barracks to
make a noise:" again, (three men having been executed and left
hanging on a tree,) they said, "One of those fellows is coming back
to disturb us." When I was told of it by a friend who was on
guard, I said, "Though one rose from the dead, they would not
believe." We are surrounded with rocks, and the country is a complete emblem of the minds of the people.

I am at this moment obliged to move my things off the old cot
I have, but before I could do it, they were all wet; but what signifies this, I never was more resigned to the will of God in all my
life; for what are all my troubles, when compared with our dear
Redeemer's? Why, like the small drop of the bucket; and, blessed

be God, I hope I have learned in all afflictions and deprivations to be thankful for past mercies. I pray God, we may be more so. While we enjoy the comforts of life, we are generally too insensible of our obligations to Providence, it is the *removal* of our comforts that makes us feel the value of them. Thus, in a state of banishment from Zion, David learned to think and speak with peculiar fervour of its privileges, and particularly of the preciousness of the Divine word. Yea, and though I am now deprived of the ordinances of my Father's House, yet, I bless his holy Name, I enjoy those blessings which the world can neither give nor take away. I thank God, that I heard that Sermon from Mr. Newstead, from *Peter,* "Be ye holy, for I am holy." I pray God it may follow every one that heard as it has done me, I cannot say to strange *Cities,* but to strange deserts, and never let them rest till,—"Behold he prayeth!"

No. II.

"There is not a single Post but the worship of God is set up and meets with no opposition, excepting that they pulled down one hut that was built upon the rock, because their cards were torn up: the men of the world were more concerned about it than us, for they said, they might as well have pulled down a Church, as our hut! Thus you see how Satan is divided against himself, and of course it is impossible that his kingdom should stand. But, the kingdom of Emmanuel shall flourish in contempt of, and in opposition to, the world, the flesh, and the devil:

"The world, sin death oppose in vain,
Thou by thy dying, death hast slain;
My great Deliverer and my God.
In vain does the old dragon rage,
In vain all hell its powers engage;
None can withstand thy conquering blood"!—

"I was touched with affectionate concern for poor—'s case, what need have we all, when the flesh tempts, to *flee* and pray; when the world tempts, to *watch* and pray; and when the Devil tempts to *resist* and pray!

"I might send you a description of the country, but however, I believe they will feel the calamities of the war for a considerable time. They put me in mind of the Gibeonites that submitted to any terms proposed by Joshua, as it is in the 9th. Chapter of Joshua. But, my Brother, how is it with you and me? will we submit to the terms of Christ? Are *we* willing to be hewers of wood and drawers of water to the house of God? so that we may but belong to his blessed household."

"There is a very large temple where J. is, but Dagon is dethroned, and the worship of the true God is set up there: there are many monstrous images a little distance from this, one in particular, which the men call Sampson, because of its magnitude; they have begun to hinder our people from going into his place, without taking off their shoes, but cannot stand that."

No. III.

"We have a fine place for public worship and private prayer; may the Lord give us sincere hearts to improve this opportunity, lest there be a heavy charge against us for neglecting the care of our souls, as there was against *Eli* the Priest for not restraining his sons when they made themselves vile. It is a large temple, full of heathen images, but I trust God's true worshippers do now assemble here: at first we were only four in number, but now we are seven."

No. IV.

Some account of Captain JOHN FLECK, of the Store Ship Cyrus, who died at Trincomalie, November 12th, 1818.

BY ROBERT CARVER.

Captain Fleck was, I believe, a native of Seymour, a Village in the north Riding of the County of York. He left England, for this Post, with stores; and accompanied by several passengers; among whom, were our dear Brother and Sister Gogerly.

After a favourable passage, they arrived at Trincomalie in September last, and no symptoms of indisposition were experienced by the Captain for some time. Fresh and healthy, together with the consciousness of having been exposed in warm climates, in the West Indies, he often walked much in the sun, after his necessary business.

Of the danger of exposing himself so, even in discharge of a lawful calling, I one day took occasion to gently warn him: after which he remained on board during the heat of the day, except when absolute necessity required his attendance on shore.

The first notice that I had of any tendency to indisposition, in time, was on the 20th of October, at the Mission House, after dinner, when he was suddenly seized with a tremulous shivering, which is, generally, a forerunner of fever. He was alarmed, but it shortly left him. Not seeing him for upwards of a fortnight, I began, therefore, to be very anxious to hear of his welfare, and upon enquiry was told, he had been tolerably well till within a few days, when he had some attack of sickness.

On Saturday, September 7th, I was called out before day break by the Second Officer of the Cyrus, saying Captain Fleck was taken very ill, and most anxiously desired to see me. Having hastily slipped on a few cloaths and got into the boat, in a quarter of an hour we were alongside the vessel, when I found the Captain considerably alarmed at his situation. The Doctor came in during my stay and bled him a second time, and he then found himself more easy; he was advised to keep himself as quiet as possible; therefore I promised to see him again soon. - About mid-day, the boat came for me and I found him worse:

He had just been bled a third time that day, to try, if possible, to check the very complicated disease.

A strong conviction seemed to rest upon his mind that he should not recover; and he remarked, that conviction had been much deepened last night, during which he had called up the Carpenter, who it appears is a serious man, to kneel down with him, while the Captain himself read aloud part of the service, out of the Prayer Book.

He earnestly enquired into the nature of the plan of salvation by our Lord Jesus Christ, and seemed deeply convinced of the depravity of the human heart, and of the utter helplessness of fallen man to deliver himself, without the grace of God. I was endeavouring to set before him the efficacious, and cleansing power of the blood of Christ, when he interrupted me suddenly, and looking full in my face with most enquiring anxiety, asked, "But may we not *know* that our sins are pardoned?" I replied, such mercy is promised to us; we may *receive the Spirit of adoption, whereby we cry, Abba Father. The Spirit itself beareth witness with our Spirit, that we are the Children of God."* He added, "May the Lord grant me his Holy Spirit, and prepare me."

The thoughts of his dissolution where too firmly rooted in his mind to be removed; and he therefore earnestly enquired about his funeral, wished to be informed where Europeans were interred, and what steps were necessary to be taken. On attempting to divert his mind from these subjects to give, if possible, every opportunity to the operation of medicine in his favour, he replied, he was quite certain he should not recover, therefore he made these enquiries; and added, Who will perform the funeral service? Is there any Chaplain, or are you the only Minister at this place? I told him we had a Chaplain and a proper burial ground for Europeans; on which he began to pray in a loud voice, and soon after begged I would read to him some parts of the Scriptures, to which he paid great attention. He readily agreed to my proposal to pray with him, but begged the carpenter, to whom he seemed much attached, might be allowed to come into the cabin. After prayer his mind appeared quite easy, and he told the carpenter to sit down near him, and took hold of his hand, and said to him, when he said he was much affected; Well, carpenter, if I die here, Mr. Carver will tell you what to do as it respects my funeral; you see we must all die.—Carpenter, you and I have long known each other, but we are going to be parted. The poor carpenter, who could no longer contain himself, burst into tears, which rolled plenteously down his furrowed cheeks, and his heaving bosom swelled with grief at the thoughts of loosing his master; while I could not remain unmoved amid so tender a scene. The Captain looked at me and said, "Poor fellow, he is afraid I shall die."

He then began to converse about his parents, and seemed to dwell with pleasure upon circumstance of their taking in, and accommodating our ministers at the village where they dwelt; and what pleasure he had in his youth, in reading and singing our hymns; and especially this, said he, repeating it:

Thou God of glorious majesty,
To thee, against myself, to thee
    A worm of earth, I cry;
An half awakened child of man:
An heir of endless bliss or pain;
    A sinner born to die!

Lo! on a narrow neck of land,
'Twixt two unbounded seas I stand,
    Secure, insensible.
A point of time, a moment's space,
Removes me to that heavenly place
    Or shuts me up in hell.

O God, mine inmost soul convert!
And deeply on my thoughtful heart
    Eternal things impress;
Give me to feel their solemn weight,
And tremble on the brink of fate,
    And wake to righteousness.

He paused a moment and said, Oh, that is a fine prayer, and then continued:—

Before me place in dread array
The pomp of that tremendous day,
    When thou with clouds shalt come
To judge the nations at thy bar;
And tell me, Lord, shall I be there
    To meet a joyful doom?

Again he paused, and then began to repeat:

Pass a few swiftly fleeting years,
And all that now in bodies live,
Shall quit, like me, this vale of tears,
Their righteous sentence to receive.

But all, before they hence remove,
May mansions for themselves prepare
In that eternal house above!
And, O my God, shall I be there?

The last line seemed to dwell upon his lips, and he raised his eyes, saying,

            And, O my God, shall I be there?

During the visit he had a very bad fainting fit, but a little sleep overcame his wearied frame, and I left the ship; no more to have any rational conversation with him.

Occupied on Sunday, it was Monday morning before I went on board, and I was a little surprised to be kept in waiting; but he had got up and dressed himself in an entire suit of clean cloaths, and received me with a smile; yet accompanied by a wildness in his countenance, which too fatally evinced that *reason had given up her charge.*

No. VI.   K

Though in that lamentable state his first enquiry was, if his ship's company had attended our place of worship, as he had told them.

He was bled a fourth time, but still the distemper gained upon him; and on Monday evening I sat up with him. Restless with disease, and sometimes burning with its heat, he wanted to get up and go out a thousand times, but after moistening his parched lips, and telling him it was better to remain, docile as a child, he sought for rest, though it fled far from him.

Being prevented from seeing him on Wednesday, by necessary engagements, early on Thursday morning the chief officer announced to me the death of the Captain, which happened a little after midnight on the morning of the 12th. The complicated nature of his case baffled the power of medicine; and though young, and of a fresh and healthy appearance, and a stout, strong man, yet death is not to be resisted by strength.

I attended his funeral, and his ship's company mournfully surrounded the grave, while the service was repeated, and the unaccustomed tear, stole silently down many a manly cheek:
"Sad was each heart, uncover'd ev'ry head."
Passing by his grave, a few weeks after, I saw, raised over it, this humble tablet:

IN
Memory
of
JOHN FLECK,
Captain of the Ship *Cyrus*,
who
Died the 12th November, 1818:
Aged 31 years and 4 Months.

At *Anchor laid remote from home
† Toiling I cried sweet Spirit come;
Celestial breeze no longer stay,
But swell my sails and speed my way.

~~~~~~~

No. V.

A short account of the Death of Elizabeth Kearns, who died in the full triumph of faith, at Jaffna, on the 10th of December, 1818. By Thos. Osborne, in a letter to his Brethren.

MY DEAR BRETHREN,

AS it is a source of much satisfaction and delight to us to see sinners turned to God and made partakers of his favour and salvation, through the preaching of his word, it must be still more so to see them continue faithful unto death, to witness a good

~~~~~

* The ship was at anchor, in the harbour, at Trincomalie.
† Incessant restlessness marked the last day or two of his life.

confession before the world, and gratefully to give their dying testimony to the power of Christ to save. This Elizabeth Kearns has done, and it will be particularly gratifying to our Brs. Erskine and M'Kenny, as she received her first religious impressions under their preaching.

From my first arrival at Ceylon, I have been acquainted with Mrs. Kearns as a member of our society; I met with her in class many times at Point de Galle. About the time of my appointment to Trincomalie the Regiment to which her husband belonged was removed to that station, (her husband was at this time engaged in the war in the Interior,) here she regularly attended our preaching and class meeting. After a few months I was under the necessity of leaving my station (because of affliction) for Jaffna. A short time after this her husband returned from Kandy, having lost the use of his limbs by the jungle fever, and was with many others in similar circumstances appointed to proceed to Colombo by way of Jaffna. From the smallness of the vessel in which they sailed a few families were left at Jaffna till another conveyance offered itself. Here I have had an opportunity again of meeting Mrs. Kearns in our class. A few weeks after her arrival the wet season commenced, upon the setting in of the N. E. monsoon, which is generally very unhealthy. Mrs. Kearns (with several others in the Fort,) was attached with a Dysentery and liver complaint, of which two have died and others are still sick. During my acquaintance with Mrs. Kearns as a member of our society, I have always found her to be of rather a fearful and doubting turn of mind, and very seldom dare venture to express her confidence in the divine favour; but still made religion the business of her life, and the love of God the object of her ardent desire. She felt no disposition to turn back again from the ways of God, being persuaded he would hear her and that she should one day know his great salvation. She had very humble views of herself, and thought she could not expect that she could enjoy the degree of grace and comfort which others did. In the early part of her affliction I visited her, and found her trusting in the Lord, but not deriving that comfort nor filled with that peace which she desired. As her affliction increased she became more anxious after the testimony of the Spirit of God, to bear a more indubitable witness with her spirit that she was born of God. From not being able to lay hold on this Divine promise she frequently had her mind much tried. She had a strong presentiment of her death from the commencement of her affliction, and often told us she should not recover. At first her mind was exercised about her children, she sent for Mrs. Osborne and requested she would take her daughter after her decease, and her husband, who is about to return to England, would take the boy with him. Mrs. O. promised to do this; to take care of the girl as if she were her own, after this she left her mind more easy: within a few days of her death I spent as much time with her as I could, conversed much with her on the promises of God, the necessity of having faith in *them;* urged her to believe *them all*—endeavoured to help her to believe by speaking largely on the faithfulness of God, that he was not man that he should lie, that we believe a good man if he promised us any thing, how much more should we believe God: that God had promised to save us for his *own* sake, that our sinfulness and nothingness was a proper recommendation to him who came *not* to call the *righteous* but sinners to repentance, that we should not look so much to our own unworthiness as at the meritorious sacrifice of Christ. That God justified the ungodly, and him that worked not but *believed* &c. &c. After praying with her she said she felt more assured than ever that God would not suffer her to die till she had seen his full salvation. About two days before her death she had a particular change; which apprized us of the near approach of death *her faith increased* In the evening I called on her, and while talking with her several of our members in society came in till we had nearly all our Class with her. She seemed to have more than ordinary strength, and spoke particularly of the preciousness of Christ, and her hope of being soon with him. She said she could now rest her soul on the promises of God in Christ Jesus, expressed her hope of seeing us all again in glory: we then sung part of the 537 Hymn from the 9th verse to the end. Her looks were expressive of the happiness of her soul. She seemed to join us though silent, till we sung the 2 last lines of the Hymn when she shouted aloud Amen! Amen! I am happy! happy! We commended her to God: she cheerfully took her leave of us, saying, she should soon see us again, either there or at her Father's house. I said, though we must leave you, you have better company to stay with you. She with a smile answered *yes I have.* The next morning I visited her at six o'clock, accompanied by Mr. and Mrs. Mooyaart, upon seeing us she said, *I am still in the flesh waiting the Lord's time.* I asked her if she felt patience to suffer the will of God. She said "*O yes! though I never suffered so much before.*" It will soon be over I said, and you will find rest more delightful. She said *yes, blessed rest!* I asked her if she had any doubt or fears, *then* she said "*none.*" I then repeated a verse from Dr. Watt's Hymns,

"Jesus can make the dying bed
"Soft as the downy pillows are
: While on his breast I lean my head
"And breathe my soul out sweetly there."

She said *yes I feel he can.* I then read the 1st Chapter of the 1st Epistle of St. Peter, making some remarks as I proceeded, after this we sung the 74th Hymn, prayed with her, and left her rejoicing in the Lord. The next morning I found her very low, her hands and feet cold: I told her I thought she was very near her end, she said *I think so, but I will wait the Lord's time that is best, I have no fears or cares now.* Before I left (I stopped but a short time) she looked very earnestly at me and said, *you must take a part of my care.* Upon her saying I did not exactly understand her, she said, "*my Child, and wept.* I was too much affect-e'd to answer her. I left her, desiring her husband to let me know if any change took place before I should come in the evening. About 12 o'clock he sent to me in haste; I and Mrs. O. went immediately: well, I said, it is nearly over now. She said, *yes, it is.* I immediately prayed with her, she joined with us with her loud Amen. I asked her now of her hope (for it was visible she would speak but little more,) she answered in broken accents, "I the chief of sinners am," here she paused for want of breath and then proceeded, "but— Jesus—died for me." I told her that was enough. She said, *I shall soon drink of the streams of eternal bliss.* I asked if she experienced that Christ was with her; she said, *yes, he is here,* laying her hand on her breast. She called Mrs. O. and said she must speak with her: when Mrs. O. came near, she said, *do not neg-lect:* paused, and said again do not neg lect, but could say no more. Mrs O. seeing this, said do not neglect what? your child? she made no reply. Mrs. O. finding this was not her meaning, said, do not neglect to be prepared to die? She answered *yes.* She made signs for me to come near but could not speak: she attempted it several times but could not be heard. She now looked much frightened, pulling at every thing she could touch, reaching to her husband she said, My dear! my dear! my sight is going! I cannot see you! I can see nothing! all my senses are going! what is this? I am suddenly—so suddenly—she could say no more. I said, do not let your spirit be hurried, Jesus is here and he is the conqueror of death! He will help you to die—He will soon now give you the victory. She seemed a little composed now and whispering to Mrs. O. said *my spirit is so hurried.* After laying still a few minutes I said, is Jesus precious to you *now,* she said *yes:* I asked again, was he ever so precious before? she said *never.* When we expected she would speak no more, she with a loud voice said *Betsy* (i. e. her daughter) *loves me.* Finding she could hear us, I continued to talk to her though she could not answer. At last she said with a very low voice, *come Redeemer;* and a something more which we could not understand. After this she spoke no more, but in a few minutes after breathed her soul into the arms of her Saviour, and entered into her rest. Thus died one, who till she heard the Gospel of Christ preached by Missionaries in a foreign land, was a stranger, yea an enemy to God. But through the preaching of God's word she was convinced of sin, and proved *in time* that the blood of Christ cleanseth from all sin. This one soul gone to God through this Mission is worth infinitely more than all that has been expended in it. But thanks be to God this is not the only one (see last Quarterly). Many more are still on the way, and we trust will also finish their course with joy.

The affliction and death of Elizabeth Kearns, I trust have been very profitable to us all, to our Society, especially; as they had never before seen a Christian die in the full triumph of faith. Death has lost its terrors to several of them since they saw how much our departed Sister was his conqueror, through faith in Christ.

The next morning at six o'clock the corpse was brought into our Chapel, when I endeavoured to improve the occasion to a full Chapel, from Numbers 23rd chap. and 10th verse, "Let me die the death of the Righteous, and let my last end be like his."

T. Q.

 END OF JANUARY EXTRACTS, &c.

Printed at the Mission-Press, Colombo, for the Use of the Missionaries.

Extracts

FROM

QUARTERLY LETTERS, &c.

THE COLOMBO STATION.

Mission House, 5th April, 1819.

VERY DEAR BRETHREN,

WE feel truly thankful to the God of all our mercies, who still continues to shine upon our souls with the refreshing influences of his grace, and upon our work with his merciful help and approval. Had we been more faithful no doubt we should have witnessed greater, and more glorious displays of his saving power both in our own experience and the souls of others. O the mercy of God that has been graciously exercised over us. We do it is true meet with many hindrances in our work and in our efforts to obtain more inward piety and devotedness to God. Yet praise the Lord our feet are still in the narrow way, and our hearts are more than ever desirous to know and enjoy more of his sanctifying love.

We have lately met with several things of an encouraging nature which tend to keep our hearts above our trials. These we think are sent us as tokens that better days are hastening, but little good can be done in any station unless the people hear the word of God, and in order to this, they must be assembled and preached to.

On this station we now preach to about 13 or 14 congregations every week. And for some time past they have been greatly on the increase. All our congregations in the Mission House are improving in a ve y pleasing manner. On Sunday morning at seven o'clock in English, we never could anticipate a large number; in fact, the service was designed chiefly for the benefit of our own family. However we have now a very pretty company that regularly attend. Our Singhalese congregation at 10 o'clock in the forenoon continues large and attentive. O that we could cast away our Interpreters and written Sermons, we might surely augur that great such things would be done in this congregation. However it is pleasing to discover that many minds are under serious impressions, and are beginning to enquire what they must do to be saved. During the last quarter we have opened several new places for preaching, which promise well. There are large and attentive Native congregations. Indeed we have not very sanguine hopes of ever doing much, even on

M

this station, in English, and on this account we endeavour to bend our whole attention to Singhalese, and partly to Portuguese. In the former of these we are greatly assisted by the young men whom God has mercifully raised up to our help, and who are labouring (on the Sundays principally) with all their might. And our country congregations some of which are seven, eight and nine miles from Colombo, are as regularly supplied by preaching as any circuit in England. Their efforts are collecting people from all quarters to, the regular worship of God; and our Schools furnish us with charming little chapels. We are now witnessing on this station what perhaps 5 years before would have been considered an impossibility, large and attentive congregations of Natives assembling in the evenings for the purpose of hearing the word of life, and this not in the town of Colombo, but in the country, and from among the jungle, and such as an Apostle would have rejoiced to see. We visit these places as often as we can, but the principal part of the preaching is done by our young men, and we feel our mind the less uneasy at this, knowing what spirit they are of, knowing they live in the enjoyment of the life and power of Religion. God appears to own and bless their labours in many places in a remarkable manner. We will just copy a note which our young friend Cornelius, sent the other day, having occasion to write on some Mission business:

REV SIR,

I am happy to say while I cried out at Wellewatte (on Friday night) "*There is therefore now no condemnation to them who are in Christ Jesus who walk not after the flesh but after the Spirit,*" the Lord was pleased to wound and cure the souls of two old woman who now sometimes ago was awakened and regularly attended to Class. And after the service, when I spoke to them, they with, out of ardent and pure love to God embraced me, and said with tears of joy, yea full of joy, " There is now not any condemnation to *us*, for Christ Jesus has made us free." "We now feel peace of God and all mankind."

The whole congregation was astonished. Perhaps they might have thought while they with wounded spirit cried out in the middle of the Sermon they are mad. It is the Lord's doing and is marvellous in our eyes. O when shall the earth be covered with the knowledge of the Lord as the waters cover the sea.

Sir, your's &c &c.

To   C. D. Z. Wijisingha.

The Rev. B. Clough.

Such are the little fruits that are springing forth in this worst of deserts. The Class at this village, about 6 miles from the Mission House, and which Cornelius referred to is in a blessed state. It is met every Friday night by the preacher who goes there after preaching.

We have lately had a considerable removal among the Soldiers in the Fort. The congregations are crowded, and would be if the preaching house were larger. Several have been truly awakened, and have begun to meet in Class, and are seeking with many prayers and tears the liberty of the Gospel, the pardon of their sins. They suffer many inconveniences from their being in the Barracks, where scarcely any thing but the works of darkness abound, but this they endeavour to remedy by retiring for prayer into the preaching room, and frequently when it would not be prudent to continue in the room they retire for hours together upon the batteries, and in the silent hours of darkness unitedly pour out their souls to God.

Two members of our society have died last quarter, one of them John Sharp, of H. M. 83rd Regt. of foot, in the city of Kandy. From the accounts which have come to us we understand his death was very happy and triumphant. He had met in Class for a considerable time, and had conducted himself every way worthy of his profession, giving consistent evidence of his living in the enjoyment of inward religion. On his removal to Kandy he continued to watch and pray, and the Lord was pleased graciously to support his mind; his companions in Colombo received from time to time very pleasing accounts of his religious experience. Indeed it is most gratifying to learn that almost every one of the members of our society, who have been called to serve in the interior, have maintained their peace of mind and continued to encrease in the life of God. The temptations to sin are fewer in the interior to men situated as soldiers generally are than on the coast; and though on leaving this part they have been removed from many of the outward means of grace, they have been driven closer to God in prayer, and have watched over themselves with greater care, under a lively apprehension of the danger they were in of leaving the fountain of living water.

Our dear departed Friend, when on his dying bed, was frequently visited by the Rev. Samuel Lambric, Church Missionary, who is now doing duty in Kandy. This Gentleman was exceedingly kind to him, and attentive to his spiritual wants, and continued to watch over him until his happy spirit took its flight to the Paradise of God. When our Friend Sharp was called to leave the world, he possessed a little money which he had by great frugality saved out of his pay as a private soldier; part of this money he gave to the Bible Society, and the rest, which amounted to 30 Dollars, he gave to our Missionary Society. Thus the city of Kandy, the rendezvous of Heathenism and Idolatry, has been honored by the death of one of the Saints of the most high God, who from that mountain took possession of the kingdom for ever.

Our other dear Friend died only a few days ago of the Epidemic Cholera in the Fort. We have not yet had the particulars of his death, only were informed by the Doctor of the Regiment that he had bequeathed the little property he possessed to the Wesleyan Missionary Society. We hope to insert something interesting about him in the Miscellanea.

It gives us pleasure to inform you that our Schools, without almost a single exception, continue to prosper. In several of them however the daily attendance has been affected by the Epidemic Cholera, which continues to make awful work among us. Its ravages extend to all classes of inhabitants, the old and the young are taken off by their dreadful visitation of providence

Our printing concerns under the management of Mr. Gogerly, are going on well indeed. He has succeeded in bringing almost every person in the office to do their work by the piece, and this has made a most astonishing difference in the quantity of work done. The book of Psalms in Singhalese is nearly finished. The 2nd Edition of the New Testament in Singhalese is advanced as far as the Acts of the Apostles. And the quarto Edition of the book of Common Prayer, which is printing on behalf of his Lordship the Bishop of Calcutta, and the Archdeacon of Colombo is advanced as far as the service for the week before Easter. Several little things have been completed last month, such as Mr. Fox's Dictionary, in the Portuguese, Singhalese, and English languages; his Primeiro Ensinos in Portuguese. The Gospel of St. Matthew in Portuguese as far as the 12th Chapter.

Thus dear Brethren, by the united efforts of our presses, our various translations, our Sermons, and attendance upon the Schools, is the great work of God going on in this Island, and we have no more doubt of seeing glorious days among us than we have that Divine Providence first sent us here While the God of heaven is raising us as his humble instruments in this land, O let us pray, believe and love each other, and help each other and the glory of our God shall be upon us, and the ends of earth shall see it—Amen, Amen.

We remain, yours ever Affectionately,

B. CLOUGH,
G. ERSKINE.

THE NEGOMBO STATION.

Negombo, March 31, 1819.

My Dear Brethren,

It is with increasing pleasure every quarter that I attend to our plan of general correspondence, and wait in return for your interesting communications, because I have continued to find it, from the commencement, a most agreeable source both of pleasure and profit, and trust we shall all feel an increasing interest in what is so well calculated for the general benefit of our cause, and the improvement of our Mission.

Never has my mind been more pleasingly influenced in my work since on the Island, than at our last Conference meeting, where we mutually pledged ourselves afresh to renew all our energies in the the great cause in which we are engaged, and to lay out every faculty for the glory of God, in publishing among the Heathen " the unsearchable riches of Christ." I returned from that Meeting with stronger views than ever of the vast importance of our work on this Island, and a feeling which I believe was common to us all—

a most grateful sense of obligation to our God, for the extending
and encouraging prospects of our Mission, yet a determination to
count nothing done while so much remained undone; but to redouble every effort to rebuild again the waste places of Zion, and to
proclaim among the Heathen the adorable name of the Lord Jesus.

Our Brethren who were present at the Conference will remember,
that we engaged to use every prudent and practical effort to extend
the blessings of Christianity to the Kandian territories, as the way appeared to be opening which had been so long desired : accordingly, on
my return to Negombo, this was one of the first things which claimed
my attention, and being, perhaps, rather more favorably situated, as
to distance, than most of the Stations, I resolved, with the help of
God, to make the attempt ; and, after two days journey of some difficulties and many mercies, I arrived at a very pleasant village in Kandy,
called Rellegalla, where the inhabitants received me very hospitably
in their way, though evidently with much suspicion. Most of the
villagers had fled into the jungle on account of the late war; we
sought some of them out, and next morning I first preached to the
people, and afterwards proposed a Christian school to them. I believe they were pleasingly surprised, but their fears made them backward ; however, I offered to send a Schoolmaster I had then with me
to live with them some time, that they might use their own judgment,
and act accordingly ; not desiring them to receive even a blessing by
force. To this they most readily assented, and I hired a little place
for him to teach in for six months. I am happy to add that the master has been well received, is gaining the confidence of the poor scattered and frightened people, and has already received, in the first
month, 17 children under his care, who are now learning the alphabet and the Lord's Prayer in their own languages. He is promised
many more children after the Singhalese new year is over, though in
all probability they will increase slowly, owing to the causes alluded
to above.

Although I cannot but rejoice in this event as a favorable opening
to the vast Heathen population of Kandy, and believe my Brethren
will rejoice in it too, yet I am by no means sanguine about it, as it
may possibly be interrupted by many events, to which it is unnecessary to allude here : but I shall feel a peculiar interest in labouring, as
circumstances shall direct, to make it a permanent Missionary School ;
for it would form a most delightful residence, from which a chain of
Schools might extend, in a direct line, to Jaille : the most flourishing
school we have on this Station making one of them, I mean Akelle,
which is three miles from Jaille, in that direction, and a Brother
might reside at either end of his circuit, or occasionally at both by
turns, and so be in fact a Kandian Missionary. I shall feel no hesitation, if the Brethren think proper to send another to fill up the Negombo Station, immediately to enter upon this plan myself. I could
easily enter into many weighty reasons for it, but will only suggest it
now; it may perhaps be worth a thought upon the arrival of our expected Brethren. At all events, I very earnestly entreat your fervent
prayers, dear Brethren, for this infant undertaking.

No. VII.   N

This place has very much improved in its trading concerns since the Kandian war, which is very evident from the appearance of the bazars, &c. but lately it has been visited by the alarming voice of the Cholera Morbus, which has removed about 100 persons, I believe, into eternity, in the short period of a fortnight. Many of them forsook their own habitations and came and laid around the Mission Bungaloe, as they said it was the only place not infected. Several times about 30 of them have attended our preaching, but I suppose it is at present unknown to the priest. Negombo would undoubtedly be one of the finest fields of usefulness in Ceylon, were it not for the unnatural opposition experienced to our work from those who call themselves Christians. A young gentleman, a Roman Catholic, was lately awakened under the preaching, but when he requested leave to attend our class meeting, he soon ceased to be allowed to attend our preaching. I am sorry to be obliged so frequently to advert to the systematic hostility of my Roman Catholic neighbours here, but as it so insinuates itself into the concerns of our Mission on this Station, as to be unquestionably the greatest obstacle to our work; it is of necessity that I recognize the hindrance. In the course of the last quarter their indefatigable industry has been employed in decoying away, during my absence at the Conference, even one of the domestics of the Mission-House, whose weak mind has been seduced by the attractive bribes of baubles, and ornaments of dress, to forget the more than ordinary obligations he was under to our Mission for his support, and a course of instruction under which he professed to experience a change of heart. They have received this boy into their houses while he was yet the servant of the Mission, and turned away his mind from the proper object of his duty, baptized him with a pompous name into the holy Catholic faith, and are now using him as an instrument against the interests of our Mission, to go about the village from house to house, decoying our children from our schools, I suppose to teach them for his own support. I anticipate a serious declension in our schools about the town from these mean and despicable proceedings, for efforts are even made to make the children swear, when taken to confession, that they will not attend our instruction.

But blessed be God our schools in the jungle go on well, and at my last visitation I was more than ever encouraged by the numbers and deep attention of the people, chiefly the parents of the children. At one of our village schools (Seidera) there are 40 females in a school consisting of 80 children; here I have lately placed a respectable mistress, and intend to distribute some of our very seasonable English presents. It is truly delightful to observe their cleanliness and order on the day of visitation. A large class of girls here read the New Testament in Singhalese, and another class read elementary works, and write on sand.

Soon after returning from Conference I endeavoured to purchase a little piece of ground on which to erect a small chapel, according to the recommendation of the Brethren, believing that it will be an instrument in raising our cause here, and having a clear prospect of building it without any expence to our Mission; this I have not yet got through, having applied also to Government for an old premises which would much assist us, and yet waiting an answer to that application.

The little Portuguese Hymn Book, I wish to inform the Brethren, is now quite ready, and will be forwarded from the Book Room by an early opportunity. Of the Portuguese Gospel, which was ordered by the Conference, 48 pages are already through the press, and the whole will probably be finished as soon as we can secure another opportunity of meeting at Colombo.

I remain, very dear Brethren,

Yours, with much affection,

ROBERT NEWSTEAD.

THE CALTURA STATION.

Caltura, April 7, 1819.

VERY DEAR BRETHREN,

While the rapidly revolving periods continually remind us of the proper seasons for the performance of various duties, it is highly consolatory that, through the blessing of the Lord upon the work of our hands, we can always record events bringing glory to God, salvation to mankind.

I have thankfully beheld what God hath wrought for us and by us, and have concluded, if ever any Missionaries to the Heathen had cause to triumph in God, we more. The ground he has given us is ample, and the waters begin to overflow it, and give us the most favourable prospect of an increasingly abundant harvest of precious fruit. It is a delight to my heart, when retracing the events which have marked the different stages of our work, and comparing them with God's gracious declarations in his word, and what he has done for his Church in different ages of the world, to observe that the various paths by which he has led us have uniformly tended to that point which we have principally aimed, to extend and establish that pure religion, which illumines the mind and savingly converts the soul ; and converts in that eminent sense which makes it meet to partake of the inheritance with the saints in light.

I have reviewed our difficulties, at least so far as they have reached my notice, and applying them to the whole history of our labours, and the successive steps of our progress, cannot but view them as heavenly teachings and divine interferences, stopping up ways at least less excellent, and directing to where our field would be more extensive, our labours more solid, and our operations more combined : and while we walk by the same rule, and mind the same thing, keeping a single eye, and believing according to the Scriptures. that *all things* WORK TOGETHER for good to them that love him, our disappointments will be estimated success, and our difficulties an abundant source of future triumph. The sun does not shine equally on every part of the earth at the same time, yet even the poles are visited in their season, and we are taught to believe what no astronomy would have taught us, that there will be a day when the sun shall rise to set no more. Haste happy day !

What has been taught me by reviewing our Mission generally, has not been less taught by attentively considering the part of it in which I labour particularly. I consider my part of the field the whole in miniature, and several parts of it seem to have the peculiarities of some of the general Stations.

In the early part of my labours here I met with a common circumstance, a variety of difficulties, but I considered my field, and was not astonished, and was chiefly supported by a firm assurance that my labours would not ultimately be vain in the Lord. I saw no immediate fruit, but the land was untilled. I sowed light and it spread: light in darkness, and was assured that the operations of light and darkness would differ. The event justifies such anticipation! what must I do to be saved is now an enquiry, and we have now in Caltura a little company of 15, who give us reason to believe they are earnestly fleeing from the wrath to come. Our Portuguese congregation, which assembles at the Government House, increases, and the place is too strait for us, and the abundance of the bread of life has not been bestowed upon them in vain. Our second congregation is Caltura, which is of later date and assembles in one of our schools, about three quarters of a mile from the former place, and the service is in the Singhalese language. The congregation is pleasingly attentive and increases in number; and here too we have proof that our labour will not be in vain.

Our school at Caltura, in the Mission Garden, is one of the most interesting kind, and will doubtless send into the world children that love and fear God. It contains now about 70 children, Protestants, Roman Catholics, Mohammedans, and Heathens. My active Colleague has taught them to sing our Portuguese hymns, which they do several times a day, and with greater harmony than I expected to hear in this country. Arnold's Gabriel, Clarke's Cranbrook, and Amsterdam, are tunes they sing with considerable accuracy. A very good impression is made on the minds of many of the children, and every attention is paid to them. The following circumstance will shew you the children's attachment to singing. Two days ago a little interesting boy, 25 months old, the son of a worthy and respectable man, a Roman Catholic, came to me, and sung the hymn beginning " Canta per nosso Deos," to Clarke's Cranbrook, in a manner that would have surprised any one, and brought into action the most latent feelings of the heart.

Lately Brother Lalmon found a person in a deep consumption; he made some enquiries about him, in addition to his labours to mitigate what could not be cured: at first he did not admire the subject, but after some visits he was alarmed about his state, and was glad to hear how a sinner could find mercy, and manifested the power of an awakened mind in every possible way: he appeared to look back upon his sins with distress of mind, and as he had lived with a woman to whom he had not been married, he made what reparation he could by obtaining a licence to be married to her, and he was married accordingly. When I visited him I was satisfied that he was in the sure way of mercy, and as he had an earnest desire to commemorate the dying love of that Saviour who was his only hope, he received the Lord's Supper the following evening. He may hold out a little longer if the rains should not set in, but I trust the Lord will give him a clearer manifestation of his mercy, and cause him to triumph in our Lord Jesus Christ. O how precious is that Saviour who can save to the uttermost, and that Gospel which offers light to all.

The Schools are in general in a promising state, and their good effects begin to appear in all places. By an accession of native help I hope during the next quarter to see great things, and when I can accomplish my plan of having a sermon in each of them almost every Sabbath day, I hope to be able to collect together in more intimate communion the few who fear God in the different places.

The almost constant presence of a Missionary if not absolutely necessary is highly desirable; yet useful young men raised up in our Societies will, as exhorters and local Preachers, in a pleasing degree answer the same end. My Colleague, besides our regular congregations, has found several itinerant ones. Once, on passing the river, he observed that the ferry boat crossing our river, with seldom less than fifty persons in it, was from 12 to 20 minutes in passing to the other side; hence he began to preach to a congregation which could not run away, and no sooner was the boat discharged than it was again immediately filled with a new congregation, to which he preached on his return: this he does frequently, and has very attentive congregations: thus the bread is cast upon the waters, and will I trust be found again though after many days. He does not slight the temples, nor visit them without the word of God. In one of these විහාරය wihāraya excusions a young priest, a most interesting lad, left all and followed him. This youth is with me, and has, I believe, left the idols in his heart

How deep the work of extending light is we have no conception. I think we are most in danger of underating it. In my own heart, amidst my joys of triumph, I have mingled sorrows, which the recollection of a year past cannot fail to produce. A year ago I was in this place, surrounded by a wife and two children, I am now stripped of all. Those days cannot return, but more glorious shall come, and every passing moment brings that period nearer. I believe my only desire and aim is to spend all I have and all I am, in spreading the light of heavenly truth, and thus enjoy a heaven below, till I am called to enjoy one more noble above. I remain,

> Very Dear Brethren,
> Your's most affectionately,
> WM. BUCKLEY FOX.

~~~~~~~~

THE GALLE STATION.

Galle, April 1, 1819.

My Dear Brethren,

I am fully convinced that nothing under heaven is so dear to me as the prosperity of the divine work in which we are engaged, consequently. nothing can be more joyful to me, than to hear of its success; nor can any thing more deeply depress me, than the appearance of any thing that would hinder this blessed work ; I know that much depends upon each member of our Mission as well as upon the whole; I have, since our meeting, been particularly led to look into my heart, and to examine well my principles; and this examination has been attended with real advantages to my soul. As I have looked at myself in the Gospel glass, I have more clearly seen and deeply felt, that our work is altogether holy and spiritual; in fact, that it is immediately the work of Jesus Christ, and that to accomplish this work holy and spiritual means alone can succeed; that every principle and every motion, must be such as HE by whom we are sent can approve of. I have been brought more forcibly to feel the necessity of having self destroyed, so as always to aim at exhibiting the Saviour of Sinners to the view of a lost world; and so as to abhor myself, and to delight in dwelling upon the glories of the Redeemer's grace. Indeed I believe I have even thought, that these are the qualities of mind which alone can prepare the Christian minister and missionary for the proper discharge of every duty to which he is called by his sacred office And, if there be no impropriety in the sentiment, I would say, that in this country the holiness, the purity, the humility, and the whole spirit of the Gospel is more required, if possible, than in Europe: because I cannot help thinking, that here we are more exposed than at home to think of *ourselves* as well as of Jesus Christ. In India, the active, laborious, studious, laborious Christian Missionary, is raised to the view of the world, and is in danger of looking for his reward, or at least *part* of it, in this life—of this I am persuaded: and if none of my Brethren have ever felt the remains of unrenewed nature willing to lean towards these things, they have not hearts like mine; but thank God for his divine illumination, which points out the evil, and for his grace which gives power to resist it.

My views on this subject are such, that if I could believe it consistent with duty, I should silently go on in my work, knowing that my reward is with the Lord. But we must communicate with our Society, our friends, and through them to the Christian world: therefore the Spirit of grace says within my heart, Attend to your duty—give all the information you can, to encourage the friends of Christianity to support the work of God—but state plain facts, such as you could wish to be examined by those whose good opinion you most value, and such as your heart, before God, tells you will stand the test of the last day. In all your communications make it your study to conceal yourself, and let the Lord Jesus and his work appear, that he may have all the glory ; and only estimate any thing in proportion as it is the genuine work of God, or leads to the conversion of souls ; and only glory in the cross of Christ, by which you are crucified to the world, and the world to you. I praise God that I desire to walk in the light, to be faithful to my convictions, and to aspire after all the mind that was in Christ, my Divine Master.

During the past quarter I have had many deep exercises of mind, particularly from the peculiar circumstances of the Station, but God is my refuge, and I have consolation in being able to give up his cause into his own hand, knowing that he can and will bring light out of darkness. For some time past my health has rather been in a precarious state, and no doubt the exercises of my mind have not tended to improve it, but my times are in the hand of Him who cannot err, and he is graciously pleased to save me from anxiety respecting the termination of my earthly career, for I know that God does all things well.

The prospects of usefulness upon this station continue bright, if it only had the Missionary strength which it requires　Just at this time the attendance of the children is but indifferent, and this is to be accounted for on the ground of this being a very unhealthy time among the poor natives; their new year being at hand, and but a partial superintendency, which of all other things must be considered most to operate against our native schools, but I hope to see them better taken care of

On the 16th of last month our new school, in the village of Dadala, was opened. The importance of this village is well known. which is so celebrated for its famous temple and Budhist establishment. The Christian church and school which were built in the Dutch time had been allowed to fall into decay, so that while Budhism was flourishing Christianity was sinking into obscurity; this our Mission could not behold with indifference, or without an attempt to maintain the honour and glory of the Cross; hence you know that the attention of the different Brethren who have been at Galle has been much directed to this place, and now we have got a little work begun, which I trust will go on until idolatry falls before it, and until the village becomes as much noted for the extent and purity of its Christianity, as it is now for the splendor of its heathenism. Our good Governor has given us the old church; the modeliar of the village has repaired it in a respectable and permanent manner entirely at his own expence; a young man of the Mahabada caste from Mr. Armour's Seminary is appointed master, and between thirty and forty children are admitted to commence their Christian education. O that God may cause this school to be an eternal blessing to the people of this benighted village. Here I would acknowledge the kindness and friendship of R. H. Sneyd, Esq. Provincial Judge, and E. Boyd, Esq. Collector, who were pleased to attend the opening, and to give the institution their warm sanction, which you all know is a matter of great importance, as the natives look so much to the powers that be.

In my observations respecting sickness among the natives of this place I particularly refer to the Spasmodic Cholera. This disease, which has raged with so much fury in other parts of the island has reached this station, and from its already destructive influence, has given strength to the voice of mourning, lamentation, and woe, which is to be heard from many quarters. O that this formidable affliction, which has already carried hundreds from the island into eternity, may be sanctified to the good of the inhabitants.

Our little Society has been much reduced by the removal of some of its members; however, I trust that God will raise up more to praise his name. Don Nicholas, who has been my interpreter since my first arrival at this station, is doing well, and I have hope of his being eminently useful in the Church of God. I do not think that he is yet fully converted, but that a blessed change has taken place in him I am sure of; however, to speak with the greatest safety respecting him, he has the fear of God before his eyes, and he is convinced of the necessity of knowing that his sins are pardoned, and of having an entire change of heart, and I am much mistaken if he is not pressing after this great salvation in good earnest. Since our meeting I have thought it right to give him an appointment to the schools in turn, and I find that his addresses are most acceptable to the people; at Hickkode the modeliar told our English master there, that he never heard a man who could speak as Don Nicholas, and that if there were such preachers as him sent among the people, they would soon all leave their temples and become Christians; and I cannot question the sincerity of these remarks, as I am not aware that the modeliar could have any improper motive in making them: I trust to watch over this young man with the utmost care, and hope that the Lord will soon bring him into the full liberty of his children: and when I am satisfied that this is the case, I shall have no reluctance to bring him forward as a fit candidate for the office of the Gospel ministry, for I am persuaded that he has very superior talents.

Adrian, the converted priest whom I have received from the Colombo Station, is diligent in his work, and upright in his conduct, though I cannot say he knows very much yet about the real nature of the religion of Jesus, as a living, renewing principle in the heart, but notwithstanding I do not despair of his doing well, and of his being brought to feel the soul changing power of the grace of God.

On the 18th of February the Lord was pleased to bless us with the addition to our little family of a daughter, and in this case, as in former ones of the same kind, the Divine goodness and mercy were great indeed; my dear partner's recovery was regular and safe, and our sweet little girl is doing well. On the evening of the 19th of last month, after English preaching, she was baptized (Mary Smyth) by Brother Squance, and we trust that in faith we were enabled to give her up to God. O that she may be baptized with the Holy Ghost, and be the Lord's for ever. Intreating an interest in all your addresses to the throne of Grace, and praying that you may richly enjoy every nenecessary temporal and spiritual blessing, I remain,

My Dear Brethren,
Most affectionately yours,
JOHN M'KENNY.

~~~~~~~~~~

THE MATURA STATION.

Matura, March 29, 1819.

VERY DEAR BRETHREN,

This quarter has been distinguished by events of unusual interest to the Mission, of a pleasant and painful nature: and which future experience will not soon obliterate. With the affairs of our Conference you are fully acquainted and, though our afflictions have been various, and the Divine Providence has in some instances been mysterious, nothing is wanting to convince us that almighty goodness, wisdom, power and love continue in active operation. The best men experimentally know that clouds and darkness are round about the Lord, but that righteousness and judgment are the habitation of his throne.

With regard to the concerns of this Station, I am thankful for uninterrupted good health, and unabated resolution of mind to persevere in the good work. I have been incessantly engaged; and even the little time I usually allot to my own improvement has often been trespassed on in order to discharge the various duties devolving on me. My different employments, however, are not of an extraordinary complexion, and in my view cut so little figure that I should not enter into detail were I not well assured of the interest you feel in the feeblest as well as the most splendid endeavours to promote the knowledge and love of God

Our School-Report is, I suppose, almost ready for delivery, and will contain an accurate statement of what we have been enabled to do in that department here. I need only observe that the Schools are in general doing well, and that some anticipations noticed in the Report are likely to be soon realized. The School at Karawe in particular is rebuilding, and is likely to prosper. I have just received the names of a number of girls of this place desirous of being formed into a school, and no time I hope will be lost in making a beginning. I had no intention, at present, of enlarging the number of our schools, but as the native women generally introduce their daughters to idolatry and are not often disposed to have them instructed in divine things at all, it is well to afford a counteracting influence wherever it is practicable. I could wish our assortment of elementary works and religious tracts were more plentiful, for few things pain me more than being cramped in this respect. Something has been done; but I suppose the best of our Schools are not near so well furnished as the Sunday Schools at home. On the end of one School Room here, I have drawn a map of the world on two circles, each six feet diameter. I thought it would be difficult to draw the meridians and parallels of latitude, as I had no suitable instruments; but, by a very simple process, I succeeded in laying them down with the utmost accuracy.

To ascertain the extent of the knowledge of divine truth possessed by our Schoolmasters, I lately required each of them to write me a short epitome of Christianity. Several expressed themselves beyond my expectation, and I do not remember an error of consequence in one of the productions. Several added a prayer at the end of their discourse

Our plan is so made as to visit each School once a fortnight at least. This has been sometimes difficult to accomplish, as we have scarce any means of conveyance, and walking in the sun is dangerous, this extremely hot weather. I have some acceptable exhorters who assist me in various ways, and do their work cheerfully. Besides meeting them in class, I gladly embrace opportunities of giving them a view of the evidences of Christianity, and the nature and importance of true religion. Brother Anthoniez about a fortnight since was at Ahangam, and saw about 50 women going to the temple. He spoke to them on the wickedness of worshiping idols, and told them he intended preaching that af-

No. VII.   P

ternoon in the School there. They came, and many adults besides,
and with the children he had such a congregation as is seldom
seen in the station

. We paid Tangalle a visit a few weeks ago, and preached in
Portuguese and Singhalese. I was exceeding glad to see a good
woman there who did not seem a stranger to Christian experience,
and had good hope of a happy immortality. I believe that place
never had a Christian Minister of any denomination, but I do not
think it a spot of equal importance to many within our reach.
There is an extensive and romantic prospect from a small fort there.
It has but one European soldier, a north Briton, who I was glad
to learn fills up his spare time by reading the Bible and other good
books. I gave him a few odd numbers of the Magazine for which
he was very thankful. The road from this place is extremely bad,
the village itself is small, and the surrounding neighbourhood has
a barren appearance-

In noticing these little events I am sure you will not suppose
I am neglecting what appears to me the surest foundation for
usefulness, a knowledge of the Native language. Different opinions
may be formed of the means I adopt to acquire it, and the progress I have made. This I can safely affirm that my assistance
has been scanty, and my absence from this station at various times
has been to my disadvantage, but I have endeavoured to improve
as my means and opportunities have allowed. If any of my Brethren
have superior advantages, and proceed more rapidly, it will afford
me the sincerest pleasure. Either to pray or preach extempore in
a language having no affinity with our own, must be allowed a
serious step, and should not be taken without adequate qualifica-
tions. I am thankful to say the Catechist of this province has been
particularly attentive of late, and has kindly assisted me in translating, so that I hope to have in a short time a few good sermons in Singhalese. On subjects relating to the mind, every man
must be sensible of the frequent difficulty of expressing ideas which
he clearly conceives, and how must the difficulty be increased in
another tongue among people unaccustomed to reflect on any
thing but objects of external sense. To learn merely by the ear
is, in my view, a most hazardous project, and to make every individual with whom you converse a sort of Dictionary, as to establish an endless variety of standards. To trust entirely to memory would be like a silversmith giving all the tools in his work-
shop to his apprentices at night, with orders to hide them in every
hole and corner of the city, and employing the next day in finding them again.

From the begining I have seen the great importance of having
at least the primitive words of the language in writing. To accomplish this, I have laboured hard, and during the last eight
weeks have made considerable progress towards it. The printing
of a Dictionary of Singhalese, modestly called a Vocabulary, was begun some years ago at the Government Press, and carried on to
the close of the vowels. That part contains upwards of 2000 words.
It does not appear to have had the encouragement it deserved, as

it was printed on dismal paper of various sorts, and I believe the work was long ago dropt. If it had been completed it would have saved a Missionary at least two years time. I have been endeavouring to complete the work principally for my own use, and in this I was assisted by a collection of Singhalese words drawn up or copied by George Nadoris, and lent me by our kind friend the Collector of Tangalle. This I have copied out, and added to it, all the words I had previously collected, and put the sets as I finished them into the hands of some good Singhalese scholars, requesting them to revise the whole, and add such words, as were deficient. This they have accomplished in a manner that does them much credit, and I have arranged every word alphabetically and had the whole copied out in the form of a Dictionary, and am spending some part of every day in rendering it into English.

At intervals I have translated part of a judicious abridgment of Entick's English Dictionary; and had I a few people about me who would enter into my plans with a little laudable enthusiasm it would be soon done.

It would, I believe, be an increase of my happiness to be employed in a way more congenial to my feelings: but I have no wish for every newly arrived Missionary to wade through the same difficulties; I am rather desirous of abridging this tedious labour. My mind is often refreshed by reading the lives of Brainerd, Elliot, Schwartz, and others, and I dare say a frequent perusal of the life of the venerable Father of our Mission, Dr. Coke, so highly spoken of in the Magazine, would be equally profitable could I possibly get a copy of it. I perceive in these blessed men a generous disregard to what would deter most people, a hearty, habitual devotedness to God, and a judicious adaptation of their talents to their situation and circumstances.

                    I remain, very dear Brethren
                              Affectionately yours,
                              JOHN CALLAWAY.

~~~~~~~~~~~

THE JAFFNA STATION.

Jaffna, March 9, 1819.

DEAR BRETHREN,

I have but little to communicate this quarter, as my labours, (in consequence of being alone) have been chiefly confined to the Town of Jaffna. The work of grace among the English and Portuguese I believe is going on. The congregations are large and attentive.

The dreadful ravages of the Spasmodic Cholera has increased the earnestness of our members in Society, and it has been peculiarly gratifying to me to see them not only raised above the fear of death but rejoicing (almost with impatience) in the hope of

Glory. I have often noticed among professors, that their religion has not been sensibly enough connected with eternity; but I am thankful to say this appears to be the constant and decided object of most in connection with us in Jaffna, "To glorify their God below, and find their way to Heaven."

Though I *see* and rejoice in the importance of the little good which has been done, and is still doing, among the Europeans of this place, I do not feel satisfied in giving all my time to them. But anxiously look forward to a time, which I trust is not very distant, when I shall be more immediately given to the Heathen, *Our work in the Lord.* I oftentimes feel sorry that I still remain such a stranger to them. How *very, very* little are they the better for me as a Missionary sent *to them*. The more I know of the Native Character the more I am convinced that our success, (next to the divine assistance) depends greatly upon a familiar acquaintance with them. They often observe that they do *not know* us; that we are so frequently changing our places: this part of our discipline, however excellent in other places, does not appear to be at all suited to this side of the Island at present, whatever it may *be* when the Missionaries are well acquainted with the Native languages. I hope, before *long*, to see some of the many excellent Native Stations, in the province of Jaffna, occupied by Missionaries who will give themselves entirely to the study of Tamul, and *live* among the people; which will not only facilitate their acquiring the language, but will be the best way to find out their many prejudices, and prepare them to answer such in the most successful manner.

Little or nothing has been done in our Schools during the last quarter on account of the prevailing sickness; the parents were afraid to send their children from home, as it was no uncommon thing to hear of those who left their houses in the morning (in good health) to return no more: several of our most promising Schools have been entirely laid aside; but, as the sickness has now nearly disappeared, the Schools will be recommenced on the beginning of the next month

We have been a little tried during the last quarter by family affliction, but I am thankful to say that at this time we are all tolerably well. Our souls have been in health, and we experience they are growing in conformity to him who has called us to his kingdom and glory. Mrs. O. feels herself willing (as much as in her is, and as much as she can spare from family concerns) to give herself to the work of the Lord in Missionary labours.

Praying that the great head of the Church may be with us and crown us with prosperity.

I remain,

Dear Brethren,

Yours Affectionately,

THOMAS OSBORNE,

THE TRINCOMALIE STATION.

Trincomalie, March 29, 1819.

BELOVED BRETHREN,

SO interesting was the perusal of the last communications to me, and so great the need of the helps of affectionate concurrence in the service of God, that I am led to desire and hope for a renewal of the same kind of pleasure. This desire may be raised higher, and my feelings more interested and strong, from the circumstance which has providentially befallen me, of being deprived of the happiness of meeting my colleagues, more than any other Brother. Some I have not seen, and some of our Sisters I shall not now see, till we appear together before the unveiled Majesty of God.

It was fully my intention to be at the meeting held at Point de Galle, and I was making arrangements accordingly; when I was informed by the Chairman the time for holding the meeting was altered. Though cut off from a land journey through Kandy, my hopes of being with the Brethren did not quite expire on being told H. M Frigate the Liverpool, commanded by Captain Collyer, was going round to Colombo.

The Admiral Sir Richard King condescendingly spoke to the Captain to give me a passage, to which he kindly assented. But the vessel being unavoidably detained for provisions, put it altogether out of my power to attend.

With increasing veneration for that adorable Being, by whose help I have been graciously assisted, to trace my way with safety, through the last three months, I again commit myself unto him, casting my care upon him knowing he careth for me.

My labours during this quarter, whatever good they may have done to others, have never been satisfactory to myself. Though I might sometimes be led to think the talent has not been hid with design, yet on a review of the work, the little fruit of my labours causes me to lament not being more industriously zealous, and more resolutely faithful in the name of the Lord Jesus.

In secret however, my prayer has been to the God of my life; and in public, that he would arise and maintain his own cause.

The seed, from time to time has been scattered, with what weakness, God knoweth. Most part seems to have fallen by the way-side, among thorns, or upon hearts harder than marble. Yet if any grain has taken root in good ground, may the gentle dews of heaven distil upon it, and may the first and latter rains facilitate its perfection. Something toward establishing our form of discipline with more uniformity has been attempted.

A public collection was made, which happened on one of those evenings when few were present. Our Class money has increased a little, but many of our small number of members are subject to be called off by the necessary duties of their stations. The Sacramental seasons have been very profitable. The whole of this first attempt quarterly is as follows : Public Collection 70, Class 30, Sacrament 16, Total 116 Rix Dollars; Members 12. Also from the

Q

Government for Schools 120 Rds. besides a present of 50 Dollars from Commissioner Upton, of the Naval Department, most generously sent unsolicited

Our congregations have been generally better than last quarter, and would no doubt be much increased, if we had a more convenient place of worship. On this subject I have expressed my opinion to several of my Brethren whose judgment I hope will so far agree with mine, as to see the necessity of having a *decent place of worship* on such a station as this; especially where the foundation of one is already laid.

I have been happy lately to see greater numbers of the military attend preaching on Sunday and Wednesday evening, and hope many will be benefited thereby. Nevertheless there appears great reluctance among the remnants of European families to acquire instruction or the knowledge of God.

The Epidemic which has made its appearance chiefly among the Natives, now occupies their attention. Not how it is caused, or for what purpose permitted or sent, but how to avoid the calamities it threatens by terminating their prospects in death. Deities without number have been propitiated, and schemes used, to avoid what is considered the angry visitation, as various as their confused views figure to them the existence of predominating powers. A Malabar youth who has been sometime in the School, came to me one day with strong marks of concern in his countenance, and with an almost breathless awe observed, " Sir, the pestilence is in the land, certainly God must be angry with the wicked people."

Yet this place has been visited but in mercy; not very many have felt attacks and few have fallen victims to their effects.

I may close this short letter with putting you and myself in mind that the work in which we are engaged is the Lord's; the vineyard, the trees, the fruits are his; the water of life that nourishes every plant. flows at his command; the allotment to any part of it, the abilities to perform the work. the measure to be accomplished, and the time allowed to remain in the vineyard are at his disposal; therefore, Brethren. let us strengthen each others hands in the Lord.

Desiring to see Zion in prosperity, and immortal souls saved by grace

I remain, My dear Brethren,
Your's affectionately,
ROBERT CARVER.

THE MADRAS STATION.

The following extracts of letters from Br. Lynch, to Br. Clough, will be read with interest.

Madras, January 22, 1819.

My Dear Brother,

I embrace this opportunity of writing by a Mr. Taylor, who I believe is a truly pious young man though I have but a slight acquaintance with him. He I believe was of Mr. Loveless's church, and is now on his way to England.

Mr. Richards is here on his way back to Ceylon, just alive; Br. Warren, died most gloriously at the Cape; I invited Mr. Richards to come to our place, but he prefered the invitation from a respectable family near town where he could have such attention as would be impossible for me to give. he is truly happy and resigned, and is just going home to die with his wife and friends.

Another Br. is come out to Mr. Loveless; there are now five of them at Madras. three of the church Brethren, and one to Mr. Rotler. I am still alone. The Chapel will be opened the next month. I have gotten about 200 Pagodas, subscription, exclusive of Mr. Malkin and Mr. Thompson's. The School is beginning to thrive, and the Class is in a good state.

My health is *very* good, and my soul very happy. O what would I give for a Br. and Sister to be with me at Madras.

On the first Monday of next month we are to attempt the formation of a Wesleyan Auxiliary Missionary Society. This is Mr. Durnford's doing.

Theodorus, and Joseph Williamson, are doing well. We have a congregation of from 10 to 15 Natives every Sunday, and have established weekly prayer meetings in Native houses—Joseph is now on a Missionary excursion of about 200 miles; two coolies and the little Poney are his whole retinue. I fear your Conference will be very small this year. My mind is much exercised about going; a few days ago I had made up my mind to remain at Madras, but now I am half determined to trust the Society to God and the leaders, for six or eight weeks, as I may never see my Brethren again. May God direct me, I am almost half determined to accompany Mr. Richards.   Yours in Gospel love,
JAMES LYNCH.

Madras, March 17, 1819]

My Dear Brother,

Yesterday I received your agreeable letter of the 4th instant, and am truly glad to hear that you are so happy. Give my best love to Mr. Knill, it is more than 16 months since I urged him to visit Ceylon, but his friends here are not satisfied that he should preach so much.

On Sunday the 7th, we opened our Chapel at half past nine A. M. Mr. Rhenius performed in Tamul to a good congregation, at half past six P. M. we sung the 3 first verses of Hymn 526, tune Hermit; we then read Prayers in English, and sung 4 verses of Hymn 37, Cornish tune: Mr. Ward then prayed and sung 1, 2, & 7 verses of Hymn 34, old Trumpet, I preached on Mark xvi. 15, 16, and took the collection about 40 pagodas. Mr. Loveless, sung 3 verses of Hymn 535 and prayed, then sung the dismission and pronounced the blessing. The house was pretty well filled, and looked well, our friends sung well. I believe we shall soon have a place in black town. The place I pointed out to *you*, but what am I to do with two places I have received the stations, but have little hopes of Missionaries either for Ceylon or Madras.

Yours in Gospel love,
JAMES LYNCH.

THE BOMBAY STATION.

Bombay, **25** *March,* 1819.

MY DEAR BRETHREN,

I embrace with much pleasure the opportunity of contributing my *mite* to our common stock of religious information. A short letter of mine to Br. Harvard, dated 30th December. 1818, I observe was not noticed in the January No. of Quarterly Letters, probably it did not come to hand. The death of Sister Fox, the departure of Brother Harvard, and other still more painful circumstances of an older date, but of which I have but recently heard by way of England, unitedly call upon us all to redoubled diligence and the most scrupulous circumspection. May God mercifully grant that our weapons of war may never "perish"! may our watch word and our motion be still "Onward"; and unless disabled in the field, let the sword of conflict be never laid aside, until it be exchanged for the crown of victory! Here, how many things rush into our minds, and stimulate to the faithful performance of our duty. Certain success, if we persevere; inevitable disgrace, if we recede; The promises of God for our consolation if faithful; his curse, if we do his "work deceitfully;" the glory of God, the happiness of millions, the honour of Methodism, and our own souls at stake! How awful is our responsibility! and what reasons appear for "fear and trembling"! You will not suppose, Brethren, that I am assuming the office of a dictator; I am only mentioning my own views of the importance of the Missionary work; but which are doubtless common to us all.

No doubt we all wish to learn, if possible, the best way of conveying religious instruction to the minds of the Heathen. Our hopes of success will in a great measure depend on the strength of the Evidence which we are enabled to bring forward in support of our assertions. The question has of late occupied a great proportion of my thoughts, "*How can we prove to the satisfaction of the Heathen that the Bible is the only true Revelation from God, and that the Religion it contains is the only true Religion*"? I heard, indeed, some time since a proposal made to translate Paley's Evidences into several of the vernacular tongues of India, and circulate it among the people; a proposal that carries folly in the face of it. In dealing with persons whose minds are enlightened by science, and who are in any degree accustomed to patient investigation of moral evidence, there are advantages which it is evident *we have not*. Such persons will rationally admit, as satisfactory and conclusive, deductions fairly drawn from well attested grounds. But Hindoos and I suppose Bouddhists also, are quite a different sort of materials: they are not used to examine into the real merits of a thing: what the Shasters say is sufficient; and to enquire farther is presumption and impiety. Impatient of listening to a series of argumentation however simple, and incapable of drawing the most obvious inferences; to apply to them certain kinds of testimony would be a waste of time, and an unnecessary exercise of patience. I humbly conceive therefore, that evidences in favour of the Bible drawn from Prophecy, Miracles and the

moral character of the sacred writers, are likely to be deemed by
the Asiatics as very inconclusive, at least in their present comparatively uninformed state. On each of these grounds they will
meet us: *They* have their prophecies, and miracles, and many of
their ancient sages and religious instructors were men of severe
and unimpeachable morals. To rest then much weight on *these*,
would be to give them an advantage which we might not find
it very easy to deprive them of. The inherent purity of the
doctrines and precepts of the Bible, their perfect consistency, and
freedom from all *real* contradiction of each other, give us an infinite advantage over them. Here we need fear no opposition in
whatever shape. It cannot be denied that their religious books
sometimes inculcate the sublimest parts of even Christian morality;
such as the supreme love of God, and an equal regard to the
wants of all men with our own: but then they palpably contra-
dict themselves, so that what at one time is Religion, at another
is weakness; and the practice of certain moral virtues in one
caste of men, is most unbecoming in another, and so on. Here I
conceive lies our *principal* advantage; as we can make it evident
that the Religion of the Bible is not a partial and heterogeneous
thing; but universal, and binding equally upon all men, and at
all times; being infinitely more worthy of an unchangeable God of
truth than their distorted, contradictory and unintelligible systems.
Added to this, the evidence of a *holy and consistent life* will become still more convincing; by which, being the living epistles of
Christ, we shall be known and read and believed by many.

I trust you will forgive the freedom and prolixity of these remarks. They are not offered as containing any thing new; but
merely in the hope of leading us to the shortest and simplest way
of giving to the Heathen a satisfactory reason why we do, and
why they should, believe the Bible in preference to their own
writings.

Last month I received a printed Circular letter from the Committee, dated 21st September, 1818, on which, as you have all
doubtless seen it, I shall not make any remarks. I was particularly
gratified at reading the following Resolution passed by the Committee on the 11th September, 1818.

" That a sum, not exceeding one Hundred Pounds, be allowed to
Mr. Horuer, Bombay, for the ensuing year, in order to the establishment of Schools for the Native Children; and that if his
hopes as to their success be realized, and further encouragement
is afforded for increasing the number of Native Schoos the Committee will determine from the Reports of these Institutions
transmitted to them from time to time, as to the exeusion of
this grant for such purposes."

Accordingly I have added two Schools to my former ones, having now 4, containing 180 boys: the teachers are Brahmuns;
indeed no others are considered eligible to the office of Schoolmaster. I hope to open more Schools when my long expected
colleague arrives.

A change is soon about to take place in the administration of public affairs here. Sir Evan Nepean, the present Governor. is expected to resign in a few months, and return to Europe; when he will be succeeded by Mr. Elphinstone, Resident at Poona. I waited on His Excellency a few days ago, and, (knowing I might safely make use of your names) in your name and in my own " presented our most grateful acknowledgments for the favourable notice His Excellency had taken of our Indian Mission at its commencement, and for the protection which I had since enjoyed, &c. &c." To which His Excellency replied in terms of the highest respect and cordiality. " That it was his opinion that we deserved to be countenanced and protected; he highly approved of our proceedings; he had not heard a single charge of impropriety alledged against us from the commencement of the Mission. He felt a very high regard for the Missionaries in Ceylon who first landed at Bombay; and most cordially wished us success in our undertakings." I assured His Excellency that " We should all consider ourselves honoured and obliged by so explicit and favourable an expression of His Excellency's sentiments, and should consider ourselves in duty bound to remember his attentions with gratitude."

Sir Evan Nepean has invariably shewn himself to be a steady friend to Christianity and Truth.

The weather at present is very hot, and trying to the constitution. The Cholera Morbus is pretty will gone. In general my dear partner and myself have reason to be thankful for good health.

Wishing you prosperity in all your endeavours to advance the interests of the Redeemer's kingdom, and requesting an interest in your prayers,

Remain,
Very dear Brethren,
Your's in the Gospel of Christ.
J. HORNER.

Miscellaneous.

No. I.

Mission House Colombo, April 20, 1819.

My Dear Brethren,

I am really sorry I have not been able to continue the catalogue of the Mission Oriental Library according to my original plan. Two or three Quarterlies having come out and no mention being made of it, may perhaps have led some of you to think I had forgotten the matter altogether. However, I have kept it in mind, and that has been all I was able to do respecting it

My time has been so occupied, both with the concerns of the Mission in general, and likewise of this fatiguing station, that I have not been able to give any attention, either to the library, or to other things of importance which I have in hand.

The catalogue, however, will be finished on the same principle as it was begun and continued, through the two Quarterlies of January and April of last year.

A Translation of a very interesting book from high Singhalese on the History and Religion of Budhu which I began about 2 years ago, has now been at a stand for the last 15 Months. This first stood when I was taken ill and forced to go to Madras. Since my return I have not been able so much as to translate a line, or even to correct any part of what I had previously done. I am now forced to say the same of the Dictionary; several of you have made very kind enquiries how this work is going on; I really could not answer you, in a satisfastory way: but, as this is a kind of circular, I will just give you the state in which the work is, and the interruptions I have met with.

My plan, as some of you are already aware, is to publish the English and Singhalese part first. My reason for doing this I only need inform you was, because it was the most convenient; There were other reasons which led to this determination, but they need not be stated. I have carried this part to the end of the Dictionary, giving the Singhalese for the most plain and common words; the other must be filled up as it is printed off. The work has been *sadly* detained for want of Type; we really had it not; and now we are forced to begin the work in a size and type which are very far from meeting my wishes. However we have no alternative. If nothing serious interfere again, I hope, in another Quarter, the first part will be printed off. It appears the most advisable way to publish it in parts, of about 48 or 56 pages each. It ocurred to me that it would be well to abridge this work as we go on, and to include only as many words as is contained in a very small School Dictionary, and to leave out all the examples and illustrations, and simply give the Singhalese word for the English. This would be very useful for the larger boys in our Schools, and also for those of the Natives who could not afford to purchase the larger work. I would propose also, when we begin to print the second part, which will be in Singhalese and English, that an abridgement of it also be made for a similar purpose. For, according to the plan I have laid down for this part of the Dictionary, and the great number of materials which I have collected, and which still remain to be collected, the Singhalese part of the Dictionary will be rather voluminous. This will be unavoidable when it is recollected that the language is so very copious, and to bring the whole fairly into English will require much explanation. For the vast number of words in this language is not the only difficulty, but the same words are so variously used, and made to convey meanings so very different from each other. This is the case in most languages, but particularly so in the languages of the East, and perhaps in none is it more frequent than in Singhalese.

In forming, therefore, a Dictionary of Singhalese and English, it will be necessary not only to give the English interpretation as it occurs in daily conversation among the people, but to exhibit the word as it is used in the books, and to enable a person to understand, not only when he *hears* the language, but also when he reads it. It will be indispensably necessary not only to interpret the word according to its popular use, but to give as far as possible the interpretation of all the meanings which the same word is used to convey in the books and writings of the Natives.

To show the force of this observation we need only select one of the most common words, and which is in daily use among the people, and is found in most languages derived from the Sanskrit. I mean the word කල් *kal*, which is almost invariably translated *time*. This is strictly correct. But in tracing the use of this word in the classical writings of the Singhalese we find it used to convey meanings very different. For instance, in history this word කල් *kal* is used as a discriptive or characteristic epithet of යාමරාජ *yama Raja*; it sometimes means also *a Husband* or *Protector*, a *Decease* or *Demise*. At other times it means *Good, excellent*, &c. &c. and a person unacquainted with these differences, would be liable to endless mistake and blunders both in reading and translating.

There is another difficulty which appears at the very head of such an undertaking which is, the very great care and caution which must be observed in fixing the boundaries of the Singhalese language. I believe this was never attempted either by Native or European writers. We have three popular dialects which

are mixed into each other. both in the books and daily intercourse.
The *Pali*, *Elee*, and Singhalese, so called.   There is scarely a y
such a thing to be found as a regular dictionary in either of these
dialects. or perhaps more properly langu ges.   There are books which
contain large collections of words; and which, from their arrangement, are looked upon by the Natives as Dictionaries. Some are
alphabetically arranged, others are arranged in the same form as
our popular English vocabularies. one of which I have now by
me. completely translated, principally in Pali, or high Singhalese,
which makes 204 pages in China folio paper.   It is in fact a literal
translation of a popular vocabulary called the අන්තාසංවැරුදිස්සා
and which will be exceedingly useful hereafter,

But such a thing as a book, with all the Singhalese words properly arranged, and those words again explained by other Singhalese words. after the manner of our English Dictionaries does
not, I believe exist in the language: this is a part of Native
cassical labor that must be effected by Europeans, and which
perhaps may be attempted in the projected work.

                    I remain,
                    My dear Brethren
                              Your's Affectionately,
                                        B. CLOUGH.

~~~~~~

No II.

Extract of a Letter from a Soldier in the Interior.

                              Kornegalle, March 2, 1819.

DEAR AND BELOVED BROTHER IN CHRIST,

Grace be with you and all the little flock in Colombo: I now
sit down to write you a few lines, in answer to my part of the
letter you sent to Brother Jones; you have got a very easy way
of answering letters.— you can answer three at once.   My dear
Brother, you tell me that I must go to preach again.   I have
gone once—I dare not go again.   I have used the means, and
leave it in the hands of the Lord to do according to his will.
Be content. my Brother, where you are. and the Lord will bless
you.   All are very well here:– the Lord is amongst us, and he
will not let us want for any good thing.   We have a Sepoy drummer that has attended with us for some time; he is one that can
both read and write English: he says there is a great many Sepoys asking, What must I do to be saved? After he began to attend our meeting. he was forced to flee for safety among the Sepoys, as he was counted not worthy to live among the drummers.
When he begins for to sing a hymn, the Sepoys flock round him
and desires him to tell them the meaning of what he is singing;
he then begins to tell. as far as he knows. and when he tells
them about Jesus Christ they begin to shed tears, and says, O
that I could get somebody to open my eyes, for I do not know
what I worship; you must learn me to read.   One of them says,

If you will learn me to read, I will go, and take my book with me, and live in the woods, and I will never come home only when I am for duty. Another says, that, as soon as his time is out, he will go and live in the woods, and he will always cry, Lord Jesus save me. One of them, he says, will not let him go to bed till 12 o'clock; he says, let us sit a little longer, and try if we can do a little good before we go to bed, we do not know what may happen the night A Bramhun came to him one day, and heard him gladly; after some time he took the string in his hand for to break it; and he told him, if he would instruct him in the way that he was to go, that he would break it. There was two more came up to him, and began to talk to him, and he went away for that time, but I think he will come again. Two days ago I was on guard, along with the drummer, and a few Sepoys; I had Baxter on Conversion with me; he took it out of my hand and began to read to the Sepoys. He would read a few words, and then explain it to them. They were very attentive:—one of them I saw begin to weep; I could hardly forbear weeping myself. O! my dear Brother, how gladly would they receive the Gospel! Pray that the Lord may bring them to the light; perhaps I may be able to give you a further account in my next.

"Our number here in Kornegalle is 16, including a Sepoy drummer; we should be glad to see a Missionary coming up here; he is much wanted."

No. III.

A short account of————*Malborough, Sergeant 73 Regt. who died at Trincomalie, February 4, 1819.*

Extracted from Br. Carver's Journal.

I was called upon to visit this man by one of our Members, who had been induced to go and see him, upon hearing he was very ill.

It appears he was brought up under the influence of Roman Catholic principles, and consequently possessed those exclusive notions natural to that Church, but how agreeable soever such views may be to the possesser, in health, it appears from what follows, they sometimes give way at the test of death; teaching us, that there is but one God, and one Mediator between God and man the man Christ Jesus "Who will have all men to be saved, and to come to the knowledge of the truth." 1 Tim. 2. 4.

"This is the God we adore," "Man's Author! End! Restorer! Law! and Judge!"

When this friend first went to him, knowing his principles, he felt a little reluctance to speak on religious subjects, because he supposed they must have so widely different views; but Malborough, as if anticipating such an idea, suddenly remarked:

"There was a time, when I would not have submitted to talk

to you, but now I find, there is one true religion only, that can make a man die happy; pressing his hand at the same time with the fervency of truth.

This declaration, though at that time unknown to me, was fully confirmed by my conversations with him.

On January 26, after reading the funeral service over a poor sailor. I went to visit the sick sergeant, according to his own request. Malborough, poor man, had tasted of the cup of sorrow, but was soon about to prove, that in acting towards each other, the best disposed may err.

When troops, I am told, were much wanted against the rebels of the Interior, strict scrutiny was necessarily made among the sick, that no loss might accrue to the service, and it was thought Malborough wanted to skulk, that is, be excused from duty, on pretended sickness: and he was therefore, reduced to the ranks. Forbearing, however, to imagine what might be the feelings of an innocent man, as it may be supposed he was, who could not make that innocence appear; it ought to be observed, that it was afterwards thought proper to restore him to his rank: a circumstance which, no doubt, softened his dying pillow, at the close of his life

During his sickness, he was not in the Hospital, but occupied a house raised by a party of Freemasons of some Regiment which had once been there. This house was his own. He was aware of my visit, and received me with seeming satisfaction. He appeared more fallen and reduced; but his soul was in a better state. Another invalid, who sat on his bed side, made way for me to speak to him, while his wife drew near also, that she might not miss the words spoken to her sick husband. I enquired of his state, but scarcely waiting for my questions, he expressed his dependence solely on Christ for salvation; said he had more comfort and clearer views of heaven. I wished him to preserve a thankful remembrance of God's great mercy to him, and to seek a still deeper work of grace, that he might be fully ready. He observed, he was sometimes oppressed with doubts. These I endeavoured to remove, by saying, the adversary will do his utmost to rob you of your present measure of happiness and your future felicity; but resist him. Doubt not the work of God. Our blessed Saviour promised to send the Spirit, the Comforter, who should convince the world of sin, of righteousness, and of judgment. The work within you is not of man but of God. He, the Spirit, hath convinced you of sin:—you are now convinced of your utter depravity and shewn the necessity of being made righteous;—and you have an aweful belief of the approaching judgment of God, when Christ shall be revealed from Heaven, with his mighty angels, taking vengeance on his adversaries and rewarding his saints; and if these things are wrought in you they have been done by the Spirit of the living God, therefore hold fast whereunto you have attained. His eyes had been fixed on mine, all the time I spake, and when I had done, he raised himself a little with both hands, and with tears which would not be restrained said, "I thank God I have experienced these things which you have mentioned. And I bless my Saviour that I am spared a few days longer to know these precious things."

I had great liberty at prayer with him, and could not check the tears of sympathy which sometimes nearly interrupted me, and I left him exceedingly thankful to me for my visit; a visit, which again proved to me, that it is better to go to the house of mourning than to the house of feasting.

This was the last visit I had an opportunity of making, I am told he continued ripening for glory, where now, no wave of trouble rolls across his peaceful breast.

No. IV.

Extract of a Letter from a Friend at Madras, to Br. Clough.

April 12, 1819.

The Sunday School is indeed flourishing,—all our rules drawn out,—officers appointed,—meetings arranged.—and the effect is, *more Scholars* (164 on the Books,) plenty of Teachers, enough Books. A Sunday School Library is established;—have sent home to England for One Hundred and Fifty Pagodas worth of Books, to the privelege of which we admit *all* who will subscribe half a Rupee per month, so that none need be without. I am engaged four days of the week in prayer meetings and preaching, some at my own House, and might be at more. Yes, Madras is an altered place, truly the harvest is rich but the labourers are few.

Our Madras Wesleyan Methodist Missionary Society, will at the end of the quarter be able to send home above One Hundred Pagodas, besides a regular supscription of nearly 20 Pagodas per Month.

A piece of ground is about to be purchased for a Chapel in Black Town in Popham's Broadway very cheap—Pagodas 760.

Printed at the Mission-Press, Colombo, for the Use of the Missionaries.

Extracts

FROM

QUARTERLY LETTERS &c.

THE COLOMBO STATION.

Colombo, July 8th, 1819.

VERY DEAR BRETHREN,

With every sentiment of sincere affection we again avail ourselves of the privilege of mutual communication—We unite to
praise our God for his great goodness towards us through the
last quarter. It has been a time of grace, mercy, and divine love
to our souls, both in our private and public approaches to the
throne of our heavenly Father; to the praise of infinite mercy
we testify what the Lord is doing for our own souls: we do feel
an inexpressible sweetness in Jesus, and His ways, and set to our
seal that to those who believe He is precious! yes, Brethren,

> "This Jesus shall be all our theme,
> "While in this world we stay,
> "We'll sing our Jesu's lovely name,
> "When all things else decay!"

We have cause not only to be grateful for what the Lord is
doing for us, but in addition, for the displays of his grace and
mercy towards those among whom we speak in his glorious name.
Our Sabbath morning congregations, at the Mission House, are
rather on the increase, and these are generally times of refreshing.
The Singhalese congregation, at half past 10 o'clock, is well attended. To see so many native children and adults brought under
the blessed word of the merciful Saviour, is at once a pleasing and
an interesting sight, to every lover of *Him* who came to seek and
to save that which was lost. Our Sabbath evening congregation is
pretty much as usual, and even with respect to this we have
abundant cause to hope that we do not labour in vain. Our Portuguese congregations, in general, are large; and, at least, external
decency, order, and deep seriousness, is apparent among them. The
29th ultimo being the Anniversary of the first Wesleyan Missiona-

ries landing on Ceylon, in gratitude to our Heavenly Father whose
hand of mercy has been with us for good for 5 years, we
agreed to dedicate the day, and its sacred services, to the glory of
His worthy name. The printing office was shut up, and all appeared with interesting solemnity upon the premises. We had service
in our chapel at 7 in the morning, a love-feast at 10, on which
occasion we delightfully enjoyed all the sweetness of nearness to
Jesus; tears of gratitude flowed from our eyes, and we believe
every heart felt the heart consoling power of bleeding love. Indeed it was such a season as shall not be soon forgotten by those
who were constrained to exclaim, surely God is in this place. At
half past 6 o'clock commenced our watch night. Brother Chater
opened the meeting by giving out an appropriate hymn, composed by our respected Br. Ault, (see Miscellany,) then called his
hearer's attention, by a very interesting and occasional exhortation,
impressing on their minds gratitude to the Father of Lights, for
his favours, among which blessings he reckoned the landing, and
continuance, of Missionaries on Ceylon. Br. Armour preached in
Portuguese from that most encouraging Missionary text, Isaiah. 55.
11, a sermon calculated to be a lasting source of encouragement to the Missionary, and a faithful warning to the people to
receive the word of reconciliation. Br. Newstead sung and prayed, and was succeeded by Br. Lalmon, who preached with his
usual tenderness for the souls of sinners, and becoming warmth
in the best of causes. Br. Clough concluded the spiritual exercises
of the day by singing and prayer. Never have you witnessed more
appearance of solemnity, and personal interest, and seeming concern, than was evidenced upon this important occasion, when the
Trumpet gave a certain sound, both in the English and Portuguese languages. We believe the feelings of every Missionary, at
our watch night, to be well expressed as follows:

"O that my Jesu's heavenly charms,
    Might every bosom move,
    Fly, sinner, fly into those arms,
    Of everlasting love!"

Monday evening, the 5th inst. we held our Missionary prayer
meeting; it was truly encouraging to see men of God, of different
religious denominations, with united hearts and voices, crying to
the prayer hearing Jehovah, in behalf of the benighted heathen.
Brother Newstead, from Negombo, gave us a most animating and
suitable exhortation on the occasion. Our congregation is so
much increased in the Fort, that we may exclaim, "the place is
too straight." Here we preach with pleasing delight, and are heard
with mingled joy and gratitude. Our class here grows in grace
and marked conformity to that Saviour whom their believing
souls adore. Our schools flourish, by the frequent visitations; and
we mark their every progress in learning, and regularly shew them
the way of salvation by faith in Jesus. To see more than 700
native children on one station, in the way of instruction, industry,

and above all, in the way of *Him* who said, " Suffer little children to come unto me:" is no little pleasure to us, and must afford every encouragement to those generous souls from whose bounty the poor and the needy reap such advantages. But ah! who can explore the advantages eternity is left to explain!

Thus, Dear Brethren, have we given you some imperfect account of our labors and prospects, and we do feel determined to live and die in his service, who is our refuge in trouble, and our portion in the land of the living. Our dear Brother Newstead is here with us at present, going forward with printing the Gospel of St. Matthew in Portuguese. We feel united in heart, in design, and in determination to spread the Saviour's name abroad. And now, commending you to God, and to the word of his grace, we remain,

Very Dear Brethren,
Sincerely and affectionately yours,
B. CLOUGH.
G. ERSKINE.

THE NEGOMBO STATION.

Negombo, June 26, 1819.

VERY DEAR BRETHREN,

Although but little variety occurs in the concerns of a country station in the course of a quarter, yet as that little is a part of an interesting whole, in which we are deeply concerned in common, our smallest movements to promote the glory of God in our different little spheres, can never, under any circumstances, be wholly devoid of interest to each other.

Considering the great preponderance of influence against the interests of *our* cause here, there is, on the whole, matter for rejoicing, that though the enemies of the Cross do not fail to put forth all their strength in their unrighteous opposition to the spread of truth, yet the God of Heaven, who graciously watches over the interests of his own blessed work, has not suffered any injury to result to the *vital* part of our system.

I have yet to lament, that on this Station, the spirit of the world, blended with a strange mixture of superstition and heathenism, continues to produce a total indifference to spiritual things, and an awful deadness to the concerns of salvation; hence, but very few attend the preaching of the Word, which we are accustomed to look upon as the principal instrument of the Most High in turning the hearts of men to himself. There are here a sufficient number of persons, who understand the English language tolerably, to form a pleasing little congregation, but such is their complete indifference to religion, and almost contempt of the Gospel, that they are chiefly known by their bitter invectives against the Ministers of the Word, and sad perversion of the

Word itself: hence, for the last three months, I have only preached once in English here. However, not one of our services has been given up. I preach in Portuguese, Singhalese, or Tamul with an interpreter, as occasion calls for; and not unfrequently the service is a complete mixture of all, just as I observe persons to come in who understand either: for, where there are so few, it is needful to give every one a portion as far as practicable.

I am thankful to have been able, through the chief of the past quarter, to read the Singhalese Liturgy in public, and the Scriptures, with some prayer, in family worship. this has much assisted me in the reading department which is not unimportant, and I am encouraged to hope I may soon be enabled to get a step farther: for, though I agree in the main, with the judicious remarks in the last quarterly of one of our dear Brethren, who has laboured much in this part of our work, yet I cannot conceive it *essential* to some degree of usefulness in it, to be a critic in the language before we begin: we rather find that the active use of the little we have increases the stock. We must not neglect the "five barley loaves and the *few* small fishes," because they are but little among so many; use will increase them, and that little degree we have already gained will be of some service to those around us, while we are labouring continually for more.

I am led to hope, that, under the blessing of the Lord, the erection of a small place of worship here will certainly promote the interests of our Mission, and essentially serve our cause, and am glad therefore, that the piece of ground, purchased for that purpose, is in a more eligible situation by far than our own Bungaloe, being more in the town, and near the church-yard (for they attach a great reverence to certain places.) Though I have not yet been able to begin laying the foundation, almost every thing is now ready for it, and I hope the next quarter will see it in progressive forwardness. It is a pleasing circumstance that the most costly part of the materials are now nearly ready, at a very small expence, having procured a *Sannas* from the Collector of the Chilaw district, J. Walbeoff, Esq. to cut down all the timber required in the neighbouring forest of Otterpalate: accompanied by the following obliging note, which will no doubt give pleasure to our Brethren.

Chilaw, May 10, 1819.

DEAR SIR,

I have the pleasure to enclose you a Sannas to enable you to fell in the forest of Otterpalate the timber you sent me a list of I send you also an order, addressed to the *Headman* Don Bastiar Perera, relative to cutting it for you; however, it will be necessary to advance him about 25 Rix Dollars to pay the labourer he employs. If I can be of further service to you pray let m know,   Believe me, Dear Sir,

Your's faithfully,

J. WALBEOFF

Several of our Brethren are aware of the circumstance of our having a lease of the old Dutch Church, on the Fort Green here, though it has never been used. The stones, &c. of that church have been very kindly granted by the Government, in order to build our new little place, on the following application being made; which I insert, with the answer, &c. because they illustrate at once the circumstances relating to the church, not before explained, and the sentiments of the Governor towards us.

To His Excellency Lieut. General Sir Robert Brownrigg,
&c.   &c.   &c.

Sir,

May I beg permission to lay the following statement before your Excellency. When the Wesleyan Mission was first established at Negombo, in 1817, your Excellency was pleased to allow to the Mission the use of the church there, on a lease of 7 years; but, from several circumstances, your Excellency's kindness in that instance could never be enjoyed by the Mission to the extent designed. From the very commencement of our efforts at Negombo it appeared evident, that the Roman Catholic interest had attained to such a preponderance, that the Protestant faith was nearly extinct there, and it was therefore utterly discouraging, as well as useless, to enter upon using so extensive a building; added to which, it was found that the walls were in so dilapidated a state that they would not have supported the roof we intended to put over it: but, that in the event of our using it, it must be entirely rebuilt. Under these circumstances the design was given up, though we have continued from the first to make use of the church-yard as a Christian burying place, and for this purpose had it cleared and fenced in. We have continued, till now, to occupy a part of the Mission dwelling house as a place of worship, but this has ever been very inconvenient, as well as less separate and sacred than a place of worship should be; and, hoping that it might induce a more regular attendance in the few remaining Protestant Christians, as well as in any also who, under the blessing of God, may be raised up from Heathenism in future, the Mission has lately been endeavouring to purchase a small piece of ground contiguous to the church-yard, on which it is proposed to erect a small place, to answer the double purpose of a place for public worship, and a school occasionally. But, feeling with gratitude your Excellency's kindness in allowing us the use of the church, and our consequent obligations, it is a pleasing part of our duty to lay our little plan before your Excellency, and trust the design will excuse the liberty we thus presume to take. Your Excellency's high regard for our Holy Religion, and uniform patronage of every well directed effort to spread the influence of Protestant Christianity, leaves us no room to doubt of your Excellency's kind approval: but as the Mission has been so constantly accustomed to experience your Excellency's fostering care, we presume, on this occasion, at once to express our gratitude for past,

favours, and to evince our entire wish to continue to direct all
our Missionary proceedings under your Excellency's condescending
approbation. I had intended to have solicited your Excellency's
kind assistance, in this our little design, by allowing us permission
to purchase an old house, belonging to the Government, near the
church-yard, which we might alter for our use; but, from a circumstance with which I will not trouble your Excellency, I have
declined to press that point, but should it meet your Excellency's
approval, it will greatly assist us to be allowed to use some of the
falling stones around the old church, to assist in laying the foundation, as nothing of that kind can be procured nearer than Colombo.

I beg your Excellency kindly to excuse the liberty I have taken
in thus addressing you, and to allow me the honor to remain,

Your Excellency's obliged, obedient, and
very humble Servant,
ROBERT NEWSTEAD.

Negombo, April 14, 1819.

Answer to the above, through His Excellency's Private Secretary.

Colombo, April 22, 1819.

DEAR SIR,

I have this day received His Excellency's direction to write to
you, in answer to your letter of the 14th instant. The Governor
did not receive your letter until yesterday, and he desires me
particularly to mention that circumstance, lest you should think
the reply to your application had been delayed or neglected. His
Excellency has given directions that your request, to have the stones
of the old building, should be complied with. I am sure His Excellency has the strongest disposition to second the efforts of your
Mission, in every way that the encouragement and countenance of
Government can be shewn. I will only add my own wishes for
your prosperity and success in your praiseworthy undertaking, and
am,   Your faithful and obliged Servant,

G. BISSET, P. S.

To this very handsome manner of conferring so great a favour
I felt obliged to return the subjoined note of thanks.

Negombo, April 23, 1819.

REV. SIR,

I have the honor to acknowledge your letter of the 22d inst.
conveying the kind expression of His Excellency the Governor's
pleasure, in allowing me the favor which I requested on behalf
of our Mission; allow me now the favour, Sir, to return through
you my very grateful thanks to His Excellency, for the kind permission he has granted, and for the very condescending manner
in which he is pleased to regard us.

I beg also to offer my most sincere acknowledgements for the encouraging remarks, and kind wishes, which your obliging letter includes, relative both to our Mission in general, and to this little undertaking in particular, and have the honor to remain,

Reverend Sir,

Your much obliged and obedient Servant,

ROBERT NEWSTEAD.

The Rev. G. Bisset,
&c. &c. &c.

Thus, the ground, and the timber, and the stones, are all *providentially* ready: may the same indulgent Providence, superintend the erection of the little temple, to the honour of the name of Jesus Christ!

I am happy to say that, though some interruptions have occurred to the regularity of our schools, from the serious illness of three of the best of the masters, (one of whom is obliged to go to Galle for his health, and two others are come to Negombo, who are not yet recovered,) yet on the whole they have gone on encouragingly; at *Seidua,* where we have an excellent school of nearly 100 children, a piece of ground has been given, by our schoolmaster's father, to build two schools for the boys and girls, and a native church between them, in a beautiful situation on the banks of the Dandugam river, the wood for which is already cut. At one of the monthly visitations in the last quarter, I had the gratifying task of distributing among the females of this interesting school a number of our English presents; and it would have delighted any beholder to view the animation and emulation displayed by them, and their joy on being allowed, according to their various degrees of merit, to choose their own reward: those who read the Singhalese New Testament, learn Catechism, and work Sampler, being privileged with the first choice. I was not forgetful to remind them of their obligations to our excellent female friends in England, to whom it will be a pleasing reflection, that their liberality and kindness have occasioned thanksgivings to God among those who are emerging out of the darkness of heathenism and ignorance into the proper sphere of the female character, and beginning to estimate the value of learning and industry.

The Kandian school continues, and has 20 boys in it. It is much hindered, at present, from the sickness prevailing there; two masters have returned sick, but several have volunteered to fill up their places. Blessed be God! these men, who were once wholly ignorant about their own salvation, thus begin to desire and seek the salvation of others! The Budhist priests in Kandy are so good humoured with us, that they have been entreating the use of our School-room to read the Banna in, to avert the present sickness! of course, their request was not complied with. The schoolmaster's meetings continue to be very profitable: I hope to themselves as well as to me. The lad's class is increased to twenty. It is generally led by our dear young friend who is

with me, and I believe much to their mutual profit,* as I am
thankful to say he is making advances in spiritual things, and frequently visits the prison in turn, to give an exhortation to the
prisoners. Our Brethren are of course aware, from the Gazette,
of the unexpected death of Mr. Sutherland, his respected father:
by which event of unerring Providence he becomes more immediately connected with us, as it was his father's express and particular wish that he should be, at all events. It gives me much
pleasure to say, that his mind seems bent on the great object,
first to secure his own salvation, and then to devote his life to
the service of God as a Christian Missionary among us, to which,
I trust, it will eventually appear that God has called him.

I have cause to be truly thankful to the God of all grace,
that though, through almost all the quarter, I have felt very
unwell, yet never so as to prevent my giving the necessary attention to the duties of the station; and, through infinite mercy
I am now much better, and do *above all* feel grateful that I
have never passed three months in my whole life of more solid
spiritual enjoyment, and blessed conscious sense of the presence
and favour of God. Frequently, in my solitude, my heart has
overflowed with the rich enjoyment of Jesu's love; and the delightful anticipation of eternal glory has been as heaven begun below.
I feel myself highly favoured of a merciful God, and only want
to be more conformed to his Divine image and blessed will in
all things. Praying that the Lord may graciously succeed the
work of our hands on every station,

I remain, very Dear Brethren,
Affectionately yours,
ROBERT NEWSTEAD.

---

* Brother Newstead received a very pleasing note, while with us, from
our young friend at Negombo, of which the following is an extract.

" I have this evening met the class: I was indeed very much com-
" forted among them; *Bartholemus* I really believe has experienced a
" *saving change*, he expressed himself very strongly in saying, he had
" no fear *of death*; he says he does not want to live but to serve God
" and to do good. These are his own expressions. The Mohandiram's
" son (the candidate for Baptism,) after I had been telling him that he
" must pray to God to pardon him more than any thing else, and that if
" he would seek it sincerely he would find it! as I was going to prayer,
" stood up, and asked with great warmth, *Can I be pardoned before I*
" *am baptized?* To hear the several boys state what they feel often
" quickens myself, and to night I felt very happy. I really think our
" own *Bastian* also has a good work on his soul. He says he has experi-
" enced that God has forgiven him for *Jesus' sake*. I set before him the
" danger of being deceived on such an important point, especially if he
" were to remain in such an error till the day of death, and advised him
" to examine himself much: as for myself, I feel an increase of the grace
" of God, I see every day occasion to be more sincere, for the heart is
" deceitful. I feel at this time much peace of mind, and satisfaction
" within me: I would not exchange *for the world*. Praised be the Lord! I
" really believe that the sickness of *Adrianus* has been a great blessing
" to his soul. He says, he feels *now* in his heart that God has par-
" doned him; and that he sensibly felt the change take place from so
" great grief that he could hardly speak, to joy that he cannot describe,
" because he felt God had taken away his sins. I am myself seeking to ex-
" perience the same peace and joy, *O may the Lord grant it me!* I could
" now burst out in praises to God and to Jesus for such love to me, &c."

THE CALTURA STATION.

Caltura, July 16, 1819.

VERY DEAR BRETHREN,

IT is needless for me to inform you concerning my late in-disposition, or of the kind interposition of a gracious Providence, which has enabled me to resume my usual labours, in a better state of health than I have enjoyed since I came to the Island. These things you are already acquainted with, and have, with me, been grateful to the giver of all good: the idea of a temporary absence from you, at a time when our work was heavy upon us, had almost the force of a sentence of death, and my resignation to a circumstance, apparently unnecessary, was very imperfect.

I feel very thankful to Brothers Erskine, and Clough, who kindly took upon them the care of my station, when all their strength was measured by the labours of their own.

I was most highly gratified on my return, to find prosperity in all my borders, and the prospect of being shortly able to furnish two additional places with a sermon on the Lord's day. Our congregations at Caltura, both Singhalese and Portuguese, are uni-formly large and attentive, and still increase: so that though J. Atkin-son, Esq. Collecter of Caltura, had kindly enlarged our place of worship, it is still too small. The prayer meeting is well attended, and the classes meet so regularly that there is seldom an ab-sentee.

Daniel Alexander has been laid up for 8 or 9 months, by a severe affliction which left no hope of his recovery, but he is now fully restored and able to resume his labours. In one particular his affliction has been overuled for good. In the early part of his affliction he went to a relation's house, about 3½ miles from Caltu-ra, and was, I believe, useful to his countrymen. They have now petitioned to have a school, which they will build themselves, and secure the regular attendance of their children, exceeding 100. This will give me five places of worship in the space of 4 miles; which, I believe, I shall soon be able to supply uniformly on the Lord's Day, consistent with due attention to the others. I hope shortly to have two local preachers, who, with visitors, will enable me to visit weekly every part of my circuit with the word of life. A few day ago I was much affected, and much pleased, to see the blooming effects of Missionary labours: when I first came here the land was covered with one unbroken cloud of darkness: no person of feeling and observation could pass along the road without commiserating the unhappy state of a neglected people, humanised, but buried in superstition, and destitute of the know-ledge of God's mercy to mankind through a Redeemer: but the scene is already changed—I view the progress of light with tears of joy, while my mind prophetically, in a new view, applies "It rolls, it rolls, and shall for ever roll." Wherever I go I am saluted by a host of little coloured beings, which are immortal as myself, and who, I trust, we are leading in the way to a blissful immortality. A few days ago, I took a walk out into the country alone, about 6 miles. On returning home, being about 4 miles distant, 3 little boys came running out of the jungle and made their *salam*. I asked them who they were. They replied Mission children belonging to the schools of Kudā and Mahapayagilla; I made inquiry into their progress in learning, and was much pleased with their answers; while we walked on, a little boy, about 5 years of age, darted out of the jungle like an arrow, with an ⊙ഀൠ in his hand, and made his *salam*, and informed me he was a Mission child also. I then caused the boys to give me a specimen of their pillam powers, which they did successively, as did others who every few minutes joined our company. The people we met seemed astonished, and could not tell what these things meant, nor whereunto they would grow. In this mode I marched on till near Caltura, and could not forbear saying to myself as I marched along, Surely I am engaged in Missionary work. I have hitherto done the best I could, but I anticipate, from increasing ability and the benefit of experience, to be hereafter more extensively useful. My love to the work increases with my years, and my assurance of success is measured by it. I greatly rejoice to see that our united labours tend to preserve our Mission from perpetual infancy, that every labour tends to make a successor's path more easy, and that our uniformity of plans and designs, executed with equal zeal and prudence, tend to consolidate and establish the great work which, in the name of the Lord, we have engaged to do.

The seasonable help which it has pleased the Lord to send us is a happy circumstance, and will, I am sure, be gratefully acknowledged by us all: it is seasonable, because we have work ready, and work which could not long have been sustained by our former number.

I am a little anxious to hear of the Brethren who sailed in the Bristol, whose passage has been a long one at this season of the year.

The sick person mentioned in my last is since dead, and left behind him a satisfactory testimony that he is now mixed with that company, which no man can number, who have washed their robes and made them white through the blood of the Lamb. None, who know the value of an immortal spirit, will esteem this as a small thing. I should mention, in addition to the satisfaction I feel in the general improvement of my school masters, an instance to shew that their increasing knowledge of Christian truth leads them to examine the absurd system of absurd atheism called Budhuism. One of my school masters, from the interior, has brought me a paper which he entitles, "The ten follies of Budhuism." This paper contains one of the ten, and is to be followed by nine others. It displays a good degree of genius, and what we may call natural logic. The plan is as follows: He first relates an unbroken story from the Capuas books; then he points out, first, the absurdities contained in the story; secondly, points out the contradictions; and lastly, in the true spirit of a reviewer, makes general remarks on the absurdity of the whole. As I consider that there is something both novel and amusing, I shall send translations of them. Did they possess no great interest in themselves, I believe all who know this people, and feel interested in their welfare, will consider it no small thing that we have brought them to *think.*

> I remain
> Very dear Brethren,
> - Your's very affectionately,
> WILLIAM BUCKLEY FOX.

··

THE GALLE STATION.

Galle; June 30th, 1819.

MY DEAR BRETHREN,

THE innumerable blessings which an infinitely good God has bestowed upon myself and family since my last letter, require that our hearts should be filled with gratitude, and that all the powers of our minds should unite to praise his holy name. We have, however, during the last three months, been several times called to feel that we are *mortal*; but I trust that every intimation of this kind, will lead us to seek a more perfect preparation for a glorious and happy immortality, and that we may be more established in the humble confidence, *that when our hearts and flesh fail, that God will be the strength of our hearts and our portion for ever.* Since my last communication the concerns of the station have gone on as usual: our English congregation is now very small, as there are few soldiers here, and only one who has the fear of God, or that has any wish to hear his word: our Portuguese congregation is much the same, and the people hear the word of God, in their own language, with much attention, and I hope not in vain. As we have now as many schools as I suppose our present means will justify us in establishing, it will not he expected that we shall have much to communicate respecting enlargement relative to this part of our work; however, I have the pleasure to notice the very pleasing addition to our school on the Circular Road, of thirty two girls; this was what I had long desired, but never could carry it into effect, for want of a suitable woman to employ as mistress; however, this difficulty is now obviated, and the above mentioned number of poor female children have commenced attending divine worship, to learn the alphabet of their own language, Wesley's Instructions, and needle work. The other schools, with a few exceptions, are doing well; but the attendance of the children is by no means as good as it was at first. At the outset curiosity brought many, as indeed might be naturally expected; and now, that the thing is no longer new, some prefer to stay at home. I have lately

felt great satisfaction in examining the children, and marking
their progress in the knowledge of Christianity. Oh! that it may please
the Lord to bless, to their eternal salvation, the instruction which
they receive. In my last letter I noticed the opening of our
school in Dadala, but I am sorry now to say that the children
do not attend; however, there must be a cause, which I hope to
find out and remove, if possible. The hand of death has removed from us our school-master of Kahawa; he was an upright
and steady man, who was much respected by his countrymen.
The circumstance of his death has caused a short interruption
of the school; however, I hope to find, in the son of the Aratchey
of the village, a suitable candidate for the situation. I have been
supplied with a number of copies of the Book of Genesis in Singhalese, and find them a great acquisition: the school-masters have
commenced the diligent study of it, and at our weekly meeting
I examine them, one by one, as to the progress they have made
during the week, in acquiring a knowledge of the contents of
the chapter for the week; and to me it is wonderful with what
exactness they go through it, and notice almost every particular
it contains. We are making preparatory arrangements to carry
into effect our proposed place of travelling by bullocks, so that
we shall be able to travel with more regularity and less expence
than formerly. It will be remembered by the Brethren who were
present at our last Conference, that I mentioned my desire of endeavouring to build a regular Mission Chapel for this station,
and that my proposal met your views, though you could not
consent to its being built at the expence of our Mission Fund,
but promised to give me all the help in your power. At that
time I thought of building it outside the Fort, that all our
schools near Galle might meet on the Sabbath, however, upon
very particular enquiry, I found that they had not yet acquired that maturity which would have justified the attempt to bring
them from their villages, and require them to walk one, two, and
three miles to Christian worship, when they could have it in their
own schools; and yet this is a most desirable object, but the time
to accomplish it is not yet come. So, after very mature consideration, I came to the conclusion that it would be most for the
glory of God, and the good of his cause, to build the chapel in
the Fort, and having been encouraged by many very favourable
circumstances, I have thought it my duty to proceed with the
work; having first, however, secured three fourths of the expence,
and having a good hope of being able to raise the whole, so as,
in the end, to bring no charge against the Fund, at least nothing
of any consequence: you all know that in our dwelling house we
have a very neat apartment for our religious services; but the
circumstance of its being in a private house is an immoveable
obection to it, if it could be avoided; and this I have long felt.
In every country where people meet together to worship God, it
is very desirable to have a place entirely set apart for the purpose,
but how much more so, in a place like this, where there are so,

many Heathen temples, and Mohammedan mosques, which are held so profoundly sacred by their superstitious attendants. It is true, *we know* that "*the hour is come and now is, when the true worshippers* (in every place) *worship the Father in spirit and in truth;*" yet, without any thing chargeable with superstition, we can, and ought, to do all in our power to produce the impression upon the minds of Heathens and Mohammedans, that the blessed religion of Jesus Christ is not a *common thing*, and there cannot be a doubt but that the establishment of regular places of worship will have this immediate tendency.

As I have already so much to do in the immediate and indispensable calls of the station, I should not have engaged just now in the erection of the chapel, only that I thought it likely that I may be removed at our next meeting; and I know, that the knowledge of the place and people which I have acquired, by a residence of nearly three years, would be necessary to enable any of my Brethren to build it under as favourable circumstances.

On the 8th of this month, the foundation stone was laid by our friend, W. C. Gibson, Esq. and Brother Fox then declared the intention of the building, and offered up the dedicating prayer. The work is going rapidly forward, and I hope, by the beginning of the new year, to have it completed. I must not forget to mention the encouragement which His Excellency the Governor has been pleased to afford us, in giving *Five Hundred Rix Dollars* towards this good work. I feel thankful to God for that divine goodness which continues to be manifested to all my Brethren on the Island, and am cheered by the prospect of perhaps soon having the privilege of welcoming five more to this extensive field of Missionary labour.

remain, my Dear Brethren,
In the best and strongest bonds,
Very affectionately your's,
J. M'KENNY.

THE MATURA STATION.

Matura, 29th June, 1819.

VERY DEAR BRETHREN,

The present is an afflictive period to the inhabitants of this neighbourhood. The epidemic cholera very generally prevails, and has already swept away upwards of 150 of the people. In some cases not one of a family has been spared to relate the mournful story; and several instances have occurred of persons seized, in apparently perfect health, and have quickly expired. I am happy, however, to hear, that timely aid has frequently proved successful.

The advocates of error have not been backward in improving this calamity to their own advantage. In every quarter offerings to imaginary or infernal beings have been made, and a night seldom passes but the sound of drums, used in the ceremonies, assails the ear. The professors of the Romish worship have vied with the heathen in splendid and noisy performances, and proved how fatally the god of this world, and the things which are abolished, has blinded the minds of them that believe not. However diversified the people may be in rank and occupation, they vigorously unite in promoting the works of darkness. As in the ancient days, "the carpenter encourageth the goldsmith," "they helped every one his neighbour, and every one said to his brother, be of good courage" Two temporary places of worship have been lately erected here. One is large enough to contain some hundreds of people, and a tent connected with it stands on a spot where I am told a Christian church stood about a century ago. The other is in a village where the sickness has fatally prevailed, and as room is scarce, it is built across the highway. Unenlightened by revelation how awfully dark is the mind of man! The judgments of the Lord are not followed by the practice of righteousness, but man resorts to lying vanities in the most precarious period of life.

It is, however, pleasing to observe, that few of the children belonging to the schools have been afflicted, and that the attendance is not much lessened. I am sorry I have been so circumstanced as to be unable to pay them, of late, the attention they deserve, as my colleague, and those who occasionally assist me, have been more or less unwell. All things considered, I by no means think the state of the schools discouraging. It is in times like the present that we perceive their utility, and the attachment of the masters to their work. By my request several of them have brought me an outline of their life. They display some judgment in the selection, and simplicity in the statement of facts. One, by an interesting little boy, the son of a school mistress, pleased me more than ordinary, and I intended to have made an extract from it, but I find it would be rather long, and things of this kind are not unusual to our Brethren. I will, however, send a copy of it to the Committee.

Our Portuguese congregation has been favoured with plain and faithful preaching. I am thankful for the occasional services of my Brethren, and believe they have not laboured in vain. But the unfavourable circumstances and habits of most of the people who speak this language leads us, from past experience, to rejoice with trembling, till we have some satisfactory evidence that they are gone to Abraham's bosom. They profess and call themselves Christians, but as they have no part of the scriptures, and no religious books in their own tongue, they are often deplorably ignorant of the plainest Christian doctrines. Perhaps this imaginary Christianity, connected with practical Antinomianism, is the most unfavourable soil for the word of life. The religion of the ancient Jews was often a fancied imputation of the holiness of their law, their patriarchs, their priests, or their temple; and hence the most thundering of their prophets was unto them as one that had a pleasant voice, and could play well on an instrument, while they heard his words but performed them not.

My mind has been sometimes deeply exercised on various accounts, but I have not been destitute of consolation and encouragement. The work is of superlative importance; and I, in general, feel happy in doing what I can to promote its prosperity. The most eminent men have been sometimes circumscribed when there has been a pressing call for their public labours. Though they have been compelled, as one observes, for a time, "to throw the plough by the hedge," their writings, produced in these intervals, have been blest to thousands, whose attention they could command by no other means. You will excuse my transcribing a passage I lately read, which afforded me much satisfaction. "If the Lord was to shew us the whole before hand, who that has a due sense of his own insufficiency and weakness, would venture to engage? But he first draws us by a constraining sense of his love, and by giving us an impression of the worth of souls, and leaves us to acquire a knowledge of what is difficult and disagreeable by a gradual experience. The ministry of the Gospel, like the book which the Apostle John ate, is a bitter sweet; but the sweetness is tasted first, the bitterness is usually known afterwards, when we are so far engaged that there is no going back."

I have laboured as incessantly, I may say, as my personal safety would allow, and the little works which I have been so happy as to bring to a close I shall briefly notice.

In revising the Vocabulary I am pleased to find so few mistakes in the Singhalese. The phrases are considerably curtailed, and I think, in their present form, they are strictly conformable to the vernacular standard. In the Portuguese part I was sorry to find so many words unknown to the people; and it is now newly done throughout, and drawn up in a separate and improved form. I resolved to be unfettered by precedent, and never once consulted any book in the High Portuguese for orthography, or any thing else.

I mentioned in my last that I had arranged, in the form of a Dictionary, an extensive collection of Singhalese words. The present state of that work far exceeds my former expectations. The English rendering has been some time complete. I have marked every word which appears to be primitive, and intend drawing them out in a detached form; and by that means have formed the groundwork of an inquiry into their derivation. I have succeeded also in getting the whole work explained by correspondent words in Singhalese, just like our common dictionaries. This is the first thing of the kind I have ever seen. There are indeed some poetical dictionaries in use, one of which I had transcribed about a year ago, and took the trouble to translate it into English. It surprises me that so little affinity appears between the popular and poetical dialect. The copiousness of the Singhalese language appears to arise from its frequently having several words to express the same thing, rather than from any great variety of ideas. The anxious and toilsome nature of a work like this, arising partly from the prejudices and indolence of assistants, must be obvious to every man of reflection. One instance of adherence to the work is worth relating. A Mohandarim, who often transcribes for me, knowing I was anxious for the finish of a part, sat up two whole nights to complete it.

Our Mission is much in want of a fount of Singhalese types. We have reason to be grateful for the occasional use of those belonging to the Colombo Bible Society; but, on several accounts, the two founts now used would but badly serve our purpose, supposing we had them entirely.—The former founts have been exceedingly uneven and defective; and I have endeavoured to remedy this inconvenience by ascertaining the average number of times each character occurs in a sheet of demy. I made choice of pages differing as much as possible in style, or rather in the subject of writing. I should, perhaps, have been for the present deterred from the attempt, if one of our Brethren had not been here who was pleased with the plan, and was so kind as to give me some assistance.—Having ascertained the relative proportion of each sort, and knowing the old plan of the cases to be extremely injudicious and inconvenient, I drew up one on a plan which seems to me to unite simplicity and convenience with dispatch. A more particular account I hope to draw up shortly for the Book Committee.

> I remain,
> Very affectionately Your's.
> JOHN CALLAWAY.

THE AMBLANGODDE STATION.

The following letter from Brother Broadbent, who is labouring on the station, to one of the Brethren, will give an interesting view of the manner in which he is getting on there.

Amblangodde, July 28, 1819.

MY DEAR BROTHER,

I beg to return you my sincere thanks for the affectionate letter I last received from you, and in return I give you a short account of my station and labours.

I removed from Galle to this place on Saturday the 22d of May. Mr Frazer the English-schoolmaster arrived on the 24th of the same month. On the 25th we re-opened the school, but I am sorry to say that we have not yet been able to raise more than 20 boys, and not above 13 regular attendants. On Sunday, 30th, we assembled the scholars in the morning, and read part of the liturgy of the Church of England in Singhalese, and catechised the children. In the evening I preached to 25 people, in Portuguese, on Luke xxiv. 46, 47. In a neat little room, prepared and lighted up by the magistrate: this is the way in which I have spent my Sabbaths to the present. My congregation in Portuguese sometimes amounts to 30. I thank God I have been favoured with many refreshing seasons while engaged in his work, and I believe the word preached has not, and shall not be in vain to the hearers.

In consequence of Brother Fox's illness the schools at Bentotte were delivered to my charge. On Monday the 7th, I went to visit them; there are two schools of boys and one of girls. Tuesday 8th, I spent in catechising the children, and the teachers: on Wednesday 9th, I collected a small congregation consisting of 15 persons, to whom I preached in Portuguese, on 1 John i. 9. who said they not only understood every word, but every idea. I have visited this place once a fortnight ever since, and proceeded as above stated. There are several populous villages between this and Bentotte where they want schools, particularly, Galmougodde, Ballipitty, Wellitoty, Kosgoddy and Hindurra. I have had applications from these villages to open schools in them: there was one in Kosgoddy. but it has been discontinued some time, because the master was found guilty of putting down false numbers in his class papers.

Monday 14, I walked to Zelwatte, where there are two schools; at one of them I appointed a new master, the former had been dismissed for bad behaviour. Monday 28, I went to Hickodde and met the schoolmasters. Tuesday 29, passing by the celebrated rocks at Cenegamma, having heard that 100 priests breakfasted there a few days before, and that people are frequently sent there from courts of justice to be sworn, I stepped aside to see them; at the same time an elderly man, who was travelling, lay down his burden and large straw hat, and went to the seaside and washed his hands, and with both hands put a pice into a hole in the rock, made black with oil, &c. I asked him what he had done that for, he said, that I may have a safe and prosperous journey. I said, I think you had better have bought something to eat with your money: he said *appé ngama*, it is *our religion*, and would not hear another word, but walked off: this was an offering to the devil: I am told there are several rix-dollars offered some days, particularly on full-moon days. There are some Capuas who remain at a short distance and take away the money; however, I took the devil's pice this time, and gave it to a poor sick man whom I met on the road a few miles distant. I visited the two schools at Telwatte, and then went to Kahawa, where I appointed a new schoolmaster, the former having died a few weeks before. There were 30 children present and a number of adults, the parents and relatives of the children, come to give them up to the school to be educated. I preached to them by an interpreter, and then received the children. I preached twice at Hickodde in Portuguese, before I came to Amblangodde, and intend to visit that station once a fortnight and preach: so that, according to the above statement, I shall have to spend every Sunday in Amblangodde, and go out one week into the circuit to the north, and the other one to the south.

This place is very populous, but wholly given to idolatry and superstition; there are several Budhist temples, but Dewalles are in every direction; there are some rocks on the sea side, a few hundred yards from my house, where the devil is supposed to reside, and near which there is a temple for his service, and no

other purpose whatever: people also come here to be sworn from
courts of justice. I am often grieved at heart to see the poor
deluded people pass my house to make offerings to the adversary of God and man. Mr. Frazer and I followed a number of
women, one day, to see how they proceeded. The dark looking
fellow of a Capua arrived at the same instant: he had spread some
handkerchiefs on the rock on which the offerings were placed.
he made some light, on which he sprinkled some resin, and bowed
to them, muttering something unintelligible to every body: the
women made him some presents, and then began to light a great
number of wicks, and placed them on the rock, and an old woman poured oil on them: they bowed several times, and taught
their little children to do the same. I asked them what they
meant by that; they said, when they had been sick they promised
the devil, if they recovered, they would take an offering to him.
I began to talk to them on the folly and sin of what they had done.
The Capua said, it was their religion, and the religion of their
forefathers, and ordered the women to go away and hear no
more, so they went: there was a short painted stick that I was
taking away with me, and a man said, that a painter once went
there and took some oil which had been offered, and he was
immediately seized with a vomiting of blood and died. Thus the
poor wretches are kept in fear, and dreadful slavery! I am told
that the women of this town, when pregnant, go to that place and
offer to the devil their unborn children, and also after they are
born, that he make take care of them and keep them from sickness. I requested the magistrate to inform me how many applications he had, in the course of a month, for permision to have
a devil dance; he said, some days there will be none, again others
two or three, that on an average there are 30 devil dances in a
month. The other evening I had the mortification to see and
hear one very near my house: one evening I saw them making
one just under the walls of the Government church, and last
evening I stepped aside from the road, with the magistrate and our
English schoolmaster, and I saw some women sat on the ground,
with a little child about 6 weeks old, that was sick, exposed to
the night air, and the smoke and horrid noise of a devil dance,
enough to kill a healthy child. I have lived near twelve months
among the natives in these parts, and I know the sentiments of
the more intelligent class of them on the subject of devil dances,
and I have heard them repeatedly wish that Government would
prohibit them altogether. I know, from my own personal observations, and from the accounts I have heard from the natives, that
the devil dances are a great evil to them in many respects, which
I could specify; and that an order from Government, prohibiting
them, would be *generally* received as a great blessing: they origi-
nate with the infamous Capuas, who are mean low cast people;
by these the poor, ignorant, weak women are frightened on the
most trifling occasion or appearance of sickness, and apply to
their husbands for a dance; sometimes he refuses, then they beg,

and cry, and threaten to force him to compliance: if he is firm against this, sometimes she will go out, crying he hates her, and her children, and wants them to die, &c. until, for the sake of quietness, he is obliged to call the devil dancer. This I know to be the fact, and many husbands would be glad to tell their wives that it was prohibited, and the poor creatures would not say another word about it, and many lives would be spared, and much expence, and the poor natives in many respects improved. May the Lord, who took our nature upon him that through death he might destroy him who had power over death, that is the devil, and deliver them who through fear of death were all their life time subject to bondage, speedily send the glorious deliverance to these captivated creatures, that his praises may be heard in the place of those awful yells which so often annoy my ears, and pain my heart.

I have not time to enlarge, only to express how sensible I am of my very great obligations to God and his people, and my desire to glorify his adorable name.

Wishing you success in all your labours of love, and all happiness,

I am, Dear Brother,
Your's very affectionately,
S. BROADBENT.

JAFFNA STATION.

We have not received any intelligence from this Station this quarter.

THE TRINCOMALIE STATION.

Trincomalie, June 29, 1819.

MY DEAR BRETHREN,

I began these remarks at the usual date, but was obliged quickly to lay aside my pen; to give attendance to other things. For several days more, an inflammation in the face, by sleeping in a damp bed, prevented me from preaching or writing, and I may now perhaps be too late. However, I could not write sooner by reason of the things mentioned, and the necessity of looking after the work-people, who are repairing the roof of the house, and making some addition towards preventing a like occurrence, and preserving, at least, one room dry to sleep in.

Returning seasons bring strongly to my mind, *whatsoever thy hand findeth to do, do it with all thy might.* I desire to listen to the admonition, knowing that to do good and to communicate are sacrifices with which God is well pleased. Therefore, what might appear unnecessary and irksome to many, whose actions are regulated by other principles than general benevolence, is accounted useful and pleasant by those, who desire the salvation of the world. Principles, rectified by the Spirit of God. I am more than persuaded stimulate my companions to action; and cause many of them to leave me toiling behind at a great distance, but without any diminution of desire to hasten onward, though with little hope of coming up with them.

My path, in general, has been strewed with so many things the reverse of prosperity, and my success so seldom marked with incidents *very* worthy of notice, that, had not obligations, superior to the gratification of my own feelings, compelled me to speak, I should often have been silent: but seeing our friends participate our joys and share our sorrows, I cannot withhold my mite of information, if even of the most inferior description.

During the last quarter I have enjoyed good health, and have been in a measure thankful to him, "*in whom we live, and move, and have our beings.*" Our congregations have been described in former letters, from which little deviation has taken place: they are in short, neither so large as to elate, nor so small as to depress us.

The Society fluctuates, I mean the military part of it: several have gone into the Interior, of some of whom, I am thankful to say, I have heard a good account. One or two fresh members have been added, who evidence their sincerity by pleasing marks of humility and dependence upon God. But others, alas! of whom we hoped better things, have caused our hearts to bleed: nevertheless the voice of God, with trembling has been obeyed— "So thou, O Son of man, I have set thee a watchman unto the house of Israel; therefore thou shalt hear the word at my mouth, and warn them from me."—"If thou warn the wicked—thou hast delivered thy soul."

Circumstances, however, of a pleasing nature have not been wanting this quarter: of which I will speak, in the order in which they took place.

During the months of April and May, I was much called out to visit the sick. Those months are considered here as the most trying to European constitutions. Notwithstanding, I was not altogether prevented from pursuing that, which I have ever had at heart, benefiting the natives. For a long time I humbly commended my cause to God, and exercised that measure of wisdom and prudence bestowed upon me, looking this way and that, to secure steps, the most permanent and useful.

A way appeared opening to establish native schools among the people, which I immediately entered, and formed in the Bazar, near the Moor's Street, a school for the education of the numerous children in that neighbourhood. Very providentially a middle aged and respectable master, who had been a teacher for nine years, offered himself, to manage the school. His deportment and conversation much prepossessed me in his favour, and his subsequent conduct hitherto has justified my expectations. In answer to some remarks made to him in a private conversation, he declined naming a salary, and spoke with such feeling that I could not refrain from sympathizing in those tears which appeared to flow from sincerity and truth. "God," said he, "hath fed me all my days, and has not suffered me to want a covering, and I know this (the school) is for the good of my people."—"I want nothing," he continued, "but a little to support me with food and clothing: you may give me what you please." I assured him, so long as he retained these sentiments he would find in the Missionary a faithful friend A temporary school is built, and 80 children entered on the list: among whom are about 20 Mohammedans.

I have been several times to visit them; and my first school master proceeded to arrange them into a little order. Few conceptions will reach the low and humiliating state of ignorance in which we found the poor children: and much labour, and many disappointments, ought to be provided for, before they reach a desirable state of social and intellectual improvement. Rough, however, as the diamond may be, let us endeavour to take it from the rubbish where it is in danger of being for ever buried.

The third school is attended with circumstances still more pleasing, and which will be grateful to every one of you, as well as the friends of humanity and advocates for the melioration of mankind. An aged and venerable man, named Don Philip, who had formerly been the native Protestant priest at this place, but had resigned the situation through infirmities, had set apart, by his will, a house for charitable purposes; and it being my intention to raise a school in that part of the Bazar, therefore, I communicated my intentions to him. No sooner was my design mentioned to him than he most generously came forward, and voluntarily made an offering and free gift of the house for the purpose of a native school and church.

To prevent all misunderstanding after his death, a legal instrument was prepared and executed, which conveyed the premises over to the Mission for ever. One of his sons wished, and I had no objections, to insert a clause that the ground might revert back again to the family in case the Mission, at any time, should be discontinued; but to this the old man would not consent, saying, "I have given it the Lord, a whole offering, for ever, for charitable purposes, and it shall be so according to my original intention." The house is built of stone, in a good situation, will contain about 200 people, and may be worth 1500 Rds.

Thus the Lord sometimes opens our way in a manner which our minds never suggested, and attended by circumstances the least of all expected. To him be all the praise. For this school also a master has been appointed, and about 45 scholars admitted: so that at present we have 3 schools in Trincomalie; two purely native, in the midst of the people, and one at the Mission House; which last embraces all descriptions of children, who are taught chiefly English.—It appears, also, that the Roman priest, lately sent here, has established schools among the natives; and, from what I hear of him, he seems a man of more liberal views than some of his predecessors—From these Schools, and that of the Government, some good may be anticipated to the rising generation, the hopes of succeeding years. And, Oh! that the voice of God may be heard, while he so loudly calleth, *" Assemble yourselves, and come all ye heathen, and gather yourselves together round about."* Joel. iii. 11. *I am the Lord; that is my name, and my glory will I not give to another, neither my praise to graven images "* (Isai. 42.)

It is my pleasing duty, on this occasion, to express my gratitude to God, and several kind friends, for those marks of favour which I have received from some gentlemen, at present resident here: one or two of which I may be allowed to mention. In my last communication I noticed the unsolicited generosity of Commissioner Upton, of the Royal Navy; a bounty which, at that time, I little apprehended would be followed so soon by a stronger expression of benevolence, and which was accompanied by the following very kind note.

DEAR SIR,

I return the Report of the Wesleyan Mission to which I have given my first attention, of the two Books you were so kind to send me; I have read it with attention, and with deep interest, and I trust and sincerely believe the Mission will ultimately be of high importance and benefit to this wretched place.

In furtherance of the views of the Mission immediately under your care, I beg leave to transmit to you Fifty Madras Rupees, with the assurance of an annual payment of that sum, so long as it may please God to spare me, and continue me at Ceylon.— And I beg leave to add, that wherever my fate hereafter may lead me, I shall be happy in availing myself of the resident Missionary, to give my aid in support of a Mission, which I see such ample reason to appreciate,

Believe me, &c.
Dear Sir,

Royal Naval Yard,   Very faithfully your's,
15 *April,* 1819.   C. UPTON.

Being worn out by fatigue with attending upon some sick people, after a little sleep, I returned the following reply.

SIR,

A little indisposition, caused by waiting all the night at a sick bed, prevented me, this morning, from answering your letter immediately.

Unable to express my feelings of gratitude for your present of 50 Madras Rupees to the Mission; and your intimation of a gift of that sum annually, I beg you will accept my thanks for these spontaneous acts of goodness.

That your life may be long spared to discharge those important and useful duties your station confers upon you, and which feelings of charity prompt, is, the earnest wish of one, who has a high sense of its value.

Britain, I use her name with love and reverence, appears clothed with Majesty and Honour; at her feet lie the laurels she has achieved by actions unparalleled—and, before her, are extended others, more glorious, which now she stretcheth forth her hand to gather; and when I see her Naval Sons press forward, I am ready to exclaim— May they embalm their memories with deeds of benevolence as illustrious as their victories!

Most thankfully,
I am your Obedient Servant.
ROBERT CARVER.

To Commissioner Upton,
15 *April,* 1819.

The Commandant, Lieutenant Colonel O'Connell, also very kindly sent a subscription to the Mission, in the same voluntary and unsolicited manner; a circumstance, which, together with his liberality in giving encouragement to the men under his command to attend our place of worship, reflects upon his character much honour.

Another very pleasing event will close my letter, which is the establishment of " *The Trincomalie Branch Bible Society,*" which was set in motion, *at this time,* by the following letter to the chaplain, Mr Ireland.

MY DEAR SIR,

I address this to you, to communicate only my earnest desire to see established at Trincomalie, a Branch or Auxiliary Bible Society, to co-operate with the Society at Colombo, in the manner of the Societies at Galle and Jaffna. This has long occupied my thoughts, and I have mentioned it here also to gentlemen, whose readiness to unite in so laudable and praise worthy a design, gave me great satisfaction.

That some may think it unnecessary, because partial subscriptions are already made, ought not to be matter of surprise; but that a Society on the spot will be more permanent and effective every one will allow.—Where we are agreed on the propriety of an object which ought to be pursued, and in the pursuit of which many are already engaged, I flatter myself we shall be surprised in the sequel only, that we did not unite to accomplish this object sooner. As I am but seldom in the Fort, and your acquaintance there is extensive, you can form a better judgment than myself, how far the gentlemen who reside in it may be disposed to unite in so benevolent a plan.

Support, or opposition, however, I allow, are minor considerations to those who feel it to be an imperious duty to their fellow creatures, and to God; and though I anticipate not the latter, yet, should it be unavoidable, the Sacred Volume teacheth the faithful Christian to adhere to his duty.

While the Society I propose will not interfere with those liberal donations made annually to the Society at Colombo, any farther than turning them into a regular channel, it will secure many smaller sums, withheld by motives of delicacy, or the want of the knowledge that the widow's mite is not despised.

Should these remarks meet your approbation, it is my intention to have the pleasure of a personal interview with you on this subject, when next I visit the Fort; and should it appear proper to establish such a Society, I can assure you it will ever be a satisfactory reflection to me, to know that it was formed during our residence here; and that the ground was opened to those who followed us.

I am, my Dear Sir,
Your Obedient Servant,
ROBERT CARVER.

To the Rev. T. Ireland,
April, 20. 1819.

To this letter I received the following answer.

"MY DEAR SIR,

I thank you for your letter, and shall be very glad to see you, when you come into the Fort. Suppose we say tomorrow, and if convenient, come and dine with me at 3 ½ o'Clock.

And oblige,
Your's truly,
THOS. IRELAND.

A meeting of gentlemen was called on the 9th May, and afterwards the General Meeting was held on the first Sunday in June, after Divine Service. Lieutenant Colonel O'Connell was chosen President, and the Rev. T. Ireland, Secretary.

The Subscriptions have been liberal.

Your's affectionately,
ROBERT CARVER.

THE MADRAS STATION.

Madras, April 3rd, 1819.

MY DEAR BRETHREN,

In great mercy I am spared to write again at the end of the first quarter of 1819, and during the three months which are past I have had several happy seasons, and enjoyed many mercies; but I have had a few painful trials to pass through, yet their number and nature are very trifling when compared with my mercies; so that, though I feel them, and feel that they are not joyous but grievous, I do not allow them to distress my mind or rob me of my peace of mind. I trust I can, in a good degree, adopt the language of the poet, and say, "No changes of season or place, do work any change on my mind." Leaving therefore "my light afflictions, which are but for a moment," between God and myself, I shall state a few of my causes of thanksgiving and rejoicing.

The first which I shall mention is the opening of our little chapel, which took place on the 7th of last month. I doubt not but a brief history of the origin of our Mission establishment here, till the present, will be acceptable to you and the rest of my Brethren, and to do this I shall just copy the address which I drew out for the public, in order to obtain subscriptions for the institution. The following is a copy of the address:

WESLEYAN MISSION,

ROYAPPETTAH,

MADRAS.

ORIGIN OF THE MISSION.

"After repeated solicitation from several of the inhabitants of Madras, the Conference of the Wesleyan Methodists held in England in the month of August, 1815, appointed one of their Missionaries, then in Ceylon, to this station, under which appointment Mr. James Lynch came to Madras in the year 1817.

"As great inconvenience had arisen to the ROYAPPETTAH FREE SCHOOL from the want of a suitable school room, and Mr. Lynch having been requested, in June 1818, to take that institution under his superintendence, he was solicited by the managers thereof, and several other regular attendants on his ministry, (and who generously engaged to assist him with their subscriptions,) to purchase a place, which would at once answer the purpose of a School-room, and afford convenience for Divine worship. Thus encouraged Mr. Lynch made a purchase of a house and ground, as a MISSIONARY STATION, situated on the road leading from Royappettah to St. Thome, on which he has erected a building, which he trusts will prove suitable as a SCHOOL ROOM AND CHAPEL: under these considerations Mr. Lynch avails himself of the advice, and takes encouragement from the liberal example of some of his friends, to apply most respectfully to the residents of the Presidency for any assistance they may obligingly afford, towards defraying the expences of the purchase and building; feeling confident that what may be contributed to such an institution will not lose its reward; an institution where it is hoped the rising generation will receive a useful and religious education, and both Heathen and Christian inhabitants have the Gospel preached to them."

On the first of January last a friend put a paper into my hand, stating the propriety of forming a Methodist Missionary Society at Madras. I was rather apprehensive that it was premature, but fearing to discourage such zeal and good will, I agreed to hold a meeting for that purpose on the first Monday of February, when a tolerable congregation assembled. I copy the statement as now in circulation:

Formation of the Wesleyan Methodist Missionary Society in Madras,
February 1st, 1819

GENERAL STATEMENT,

BY THE REV. JAMES LYNCH.

" In the year 1735, the Revere d John Wesley, A. M. late Fellow
of Lincoln College, Oxford, went as a Missionary and Chaplain to
Georgia, in America; at which time he was the only Protestant
native in Great Britain engaged in any foreign Mission, so that he
may be considered the first Protestant English Missionary to foreign
parts: on his return from America the churches were too small to
contain the congregations which came to hear him; and, not being
allowed to preach in some, he began to preach in fields and private houses, and formed into societies such as were awakened by
his ministry and felt a desire to flee from the wrath to come.
(See the Rules of the Methodist Society.) As these societies frequently met for prayer and reading the Scriptures, several individuals
not only grew in grace but in divine knowledge, and began to explain the word of God to those around them: of these Mr. Wesley chose such as he judged most capable of instructing others,
and sent them occasionally to visit other societies, and thus Itinerant Methodist Preachers were raised up and sent into the world.

" In 1770, at the earnest request of several of the inhabitants of
America, two Methodist Preachers were sent by Mr. Wesley to
that part of the world, and such abundant success has attended the
labours of Methodist Preachers in America that, at present, there
are more then 322,500 members in the societies, and of them
44,000 are blacks and people of colour.

" In the year 1786, the late Reverend Thomas Coke, of the Uni-
versity of Oxford, under the direction of Mr. Wesley, sailed from
England to America with three preachers; but, by adverse winds
and stress of weather, was driven to the Island of Antigua in the
West Indies; and, at the urgent request of the inhabitants, the three
Missionaries were left in the West Indies, where there are at present about 80 Missionaries, and more then 22,800 members in the
societies, of which number 20,000 are blacks and people of
colour.

" In Africa there are 4 Missionaries and 160 in society.

" In New South Wales there are 2 Missionaries and 50 in society.

" In Gibraltor one Missionary, and in France two.

" In the year 1814 the above mentioned Dr. Coke sailed from
England, for Ceylon and the East, with Six Missionaries: there are
at present 12 Missionaries employed in India, and the total number of Missionaries now under the direction of the Conference is
about 120, and who occupy 80 Stations; and the number in the
several societies under these Missionaries is 25,000. These are exclusive of the preachers and societies in Great Britain and Ireland
and America.

" Since the year 1786 about two hundred Missionaries have

been sent to foreign parts, and about 30 have died in the work; and it may be hoped that more then 10,000 slaves and Negroes, in different parts of the world, after having heard the Gospel by the Methodist Missionaries, have died with a comfortable hope of everlasting life; and that the Wesleyan Missions, throughout the world, are supported by the voluntary donations and subscriptions of the Christian community at large." After the above statement (but more at large) was given, the following Resolutions were proposed and agreed to unanimously.

1st RESOLUTION. That this meeting most heartily approve of the Wesleyan Methodist Missions in this, and in every part of the world.

2nd RESOLUTION. That this meeting ackowledge, with gratitude to God, its obligation to the Methodist Conference in England for having appointed a Missionary to Madras.

3rd RESOLUTION. That on account of the increasing extent and expenditure of the said Mission, we consider it expedient to form a Society for the express purpose of assisting its funds; by the benevolence of which the glad tidings of salvation is made known in this and in other distant parts of the world, and that it be denominated the Madras Wesleyan Methodist Missionary Society.

4th. RESOLUTION. That all the Subscribers of 3 fanams per week, and all Benefactors of 15 Pagodas, shall be deemed members of the Society.

5th RESOLUTION. That there shall be a meeting annually at the Wesleyan Mission House, Royappettah; the time to be fixed by the Committee.

6th RESOLUTION. That Fredrick Orme, Esquire, be requested to accept of the office of Secretary for this Society for the present year.

7th RESOLUTION. That Mr. B. Durnford be requested to accept of the office of Treasurer to this Society for the present year.

8th RESOLUTION. That the following persons compose the Committee. PRESIDENT. Reverend James Lynch. MEMBERS. Messrs. E. Robam, J. Hartly, T Ritchy, W. Graham, J. H. Williamson, J. Lambert, J. Gore, T. Rodrigoes, H. Hart, W. Gay, J Aylward.

9th RESOLUTION. That a Subscription Book be opened this evening, and be kept open for all who wish to contribute; and that the money received be transmitted to the General Treasurer of the Wesleyan Methodist Missions, in London.

N. B. Subscriptions and Donations to be received by the President, Treasurer, Secretary and any Member of the Committee.

On the 17th Instant we held our first monthly meeting, and found nearly 70 Pagodas were in the Treasurer's hands, including donations and subscriptions, and that already we have subscriptions to the amount of 20 Pagodas per month, 8l 15s. at the present rate of exchange, and now that we shall not have house rent to pay, this sum will considerably lighten our expences. The chapel was opened on Sunday, the 7th Instant, at ½ past 9. A. M. the Reverend Mr. Rhenius performed service in Tamul to a good con-

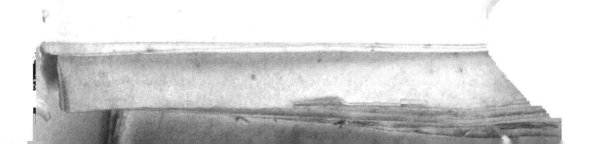

gregation, many of whom were heathens, and all seemed deeply
interested. At ¾ past 6. P. M. our English Service commenced; Mr.
Rhenius read and sung the 3 first verses of the 526th hymn, Hermit
tune, then read the Evening service according to the Established
Church. He then gave out the 4 first verses of the 37th hymn,
Cornish or Weston Flavel, and the Reverend Mr. Hands of the
London Mission, prayed: after prayer he gave out the 1st, 2nd and 7th.
verses of the 34th hymn, Trumpet, or Portsmouth new tune.
I then preached on Mark the xv. 15, 16. after which we took up
a collection. The Reverend Mr. Loveless then read the 3 first verses
of the 535th hymn, Bolster or Shirland tune, and prayed: and after
the people arose from their knees he sung the dismission hymn,
and pronounced the blessing. Besides these brethren, who most kindly assisted, there were also present the Reverend Mr. Flemming, of
the London Society; the Revd. Messrs. Schmydd and Borenbruck,
of the Church Mission, and also a Brother of the Baptist Society
who that very evening arrived at Madras; so that there were in
all 8 Missionaries present. Our Brethren and Sisters sung exceedingly well, and the whole of the service appeared to be solemn and
interesting. The collection amounted to about 40 Pagodas. Thus
at last we have erected a small chapel at Madras; and, however it
may succeed, I shall have the satisfaction of having simplicity and
godly sincerity in all I have done. My schools are also pros per-
ing; both the English and native school at the Mission place
are doing pretty well, and I have another native school at a place
called the Mount, about 5 miles distant; this school is in the centre
of Heathen and Roman Catholics. I could establish many more
but dare not do it until I can procure Christian Masters, and here,
as well as in Ceylon, hope to raise up Christian Masters and Missionaries out of our schools.

On the 26th last month, at the request of an English gentleman,
I paid a visit to Sadras (41 miles.) On Sabbath morning I preached to a congregation of 25, and at 5 again to a congregation of
30; with this journey I was much pleased, and the Governor of
Sadras, and his Lady, and several others, express the warmest gratitude, and were very urgent for me to repeat my visit as soon as possible, which I hope to do in 4 or 5 weeks. It will be exceedingly gratifying for you to learn, that with the ready and warm
consent of our London Missionary Brethren, one of them (Mr.
Traveller) supplied my place on Sabbath evening, and I doubt not
but they would continue to do so were I to repeat my visits. It
will also give you pleasure to hear, that I have again taken to
my preaching to the natives by an interpreter, my own boy, Theodorus, has now obtained such a knowledge of divinity, and of
the Tamul and English, that he feels very little difficulty in in-
terpreting a Sermon, besides he holds 4 meetings every week a-
mongst the natives. Br. Robam has also begun to preach in Portuguese in the suburbs of the town. A young man who was a
member of our Society in England, and left it in the Lady Cas-

tlereagh, for New South Wales, and came in her to Madras from thence; and who is now employed in one of the Government Offices, is now an acquisition to us; he is teachable, and humble, and active, he meets the soldier's class, and also preaches to them once a week, so that I trust God is raising up help to me. Indeed a more cheerful and willing people to help the work of God, both temporally and spiritually, I have not met in any part of the world; and it will be next to the parting with my Irish friends when I come to part with them. You may publish just as much or as little as you please of the above,

Your's in Gospel love,
JAMES LYNCH.

P. S. The following little circumstance will be gratifying to you: two days after the formation of the Missionary Society, a young Lady took her Bandy or Carriage, and went to several of her young acquaintances and others, and raised I believe nearly two Pagodas per month subscription. One of our Brethren, who writes in a Government office, took the liberty of presenting the Missionary Subscription paper to a Gentleman, I believe of the office, who exclaimed against the Methodists as a bad and most dangerous people. Our Brother prevailed upon him to read the paper, after which he was so far changed as to give a donation of 10 Pagodas, and seemed to think that too small a sum. At the opening of the chapel, both morning and evening, several natives brought money to give, but by some means they were passed by, which seemed to grieve them very much; but they were fully reconciled when Theodorus called at their houses with the subscription Paper, and took what little they could give.

THE BOMBAY STATION.

Bombay, July 1, 1819.

My Dear Brethren,

Although the state of affairs here is not such as to enable me to give a long and detailed account of interesting particulars, yet I consider it a duty, as well as feel it a privilege, to communicate with you in the manner established among us. If I cannot rejoice in much fruit of my labours here, yet it affords me joy to hear of the prosperity of the work of God in other parts of the great vineyard, which are more highly favoured, and though frequently cast down, still I live in hope of seeing better days.

Since my last letter I have been engaged in my usual work, at home and abroad, viz. study, inspecting schools, instructing the natives, &c. but nothing particularly noticeable has taken place, to deserve being mentioned. The offence of the cross has not ceased; and the cause of Bruhma seems to be very little on the decline: I still am convinced of the supreme importance and necessity of attending to the rising generation. By instilling Christian

principles and religious truths into their minds while they continue
under our tuition, we shall have the way prepared to their more
readily receiving the Gospel when they come to an age to judge
and decide for themselves. To stand up and preach to the people in their own language is certainly a very necessary and desirable part of a Missionary's work: but as yet it is impracticable
here. I have, through the divine blessing on my endeavours,
acquired a sufficient degree of readiness in both the Mahratta,
and Hindoostahanee languages, to deliver my thoughts in them
without any trouble or hesitation;—but whenever I have attempted
any thing like a public address, I have been opposed and interrupted, either by ridiculous questions, or downright denial of what
I was saying. The pride of " the gods of the world" as the
Brahmuns arrogantly call themselves, is hurt at the idea of a
European Shoodree's attempting to teach *them!*

Mr. Mault, from the London Missionary Society, with Mrs. M.
arrived here in May. They are to proceed to Travancore, to join
Mr. Mead who is on that station. As they cannot leave Bombay
till after the present monsoon, they have accepted of lodgings in
our house: and we are glad to give each other mutual assurances
that we have but " one Lord, one faith, one baptism, one God
and Father of all, who is above all, and through all, and in us
all."

Mr. Bardwell, one of the American Brethren, has lately buried
his second child, a fine girl of 20 months. They appear to be
graciously strengthened under the bereavement.

My long looked for colleague is not yet arrived. I am doubtful whether he has yet even set sail; for my last letters from
the Committee mentioned nothing of the kind.

And now, Brethren, commending myself to your prayers, and
the work we are all engaged in to the blessing of God, I subscribe
myself,

Your's in the Gospel of Christ,
J. HORNER,

Miscellaneous.

No. I.

VERSES TO BE SUNG

AT THE

WESLEYAN MISSION-HOUSE COLOMBO,

ON TUESDAY EVENING THE 29th JUNE, 1819;

BEING THE 5th ANNIVERSARY OF THE ARRIVAL OF THE

MISSIONARIES ON THE ISLAND OF CEYLON,

*Composed by the late Rev. W. AULT, a short time before
he departed this life.*

1 WELCOME! ye Messengers of peace,
   Sent to proclaim the way to bliss,
      And point us to the sky!
   Oh! come ye blessed of the Lord,
   Publish to all the Sacred Word
      Who now in darkness lie.

2 The Isles exulting hail the Day!
   Blessing the bright refulgent ray
      They pluck their Idols down;
   Rev'rent adore the Great Supreme,
   And humbly join each hallowed theme,
      And Christ their Saviour own.

3 Behold we see from British Land,
   To India's coast, at Heavens command,
      The sacred Heralds fly!
   O'ercome the charms of wealth and ease,
   Surmount the dangers of the Seas!
      To bring Salvation nigh.

4 Oh! labour on ye chosen few,
   Heaven has a Sacred work for you
      Designed in Heathen Lands;

Faithful to Death secure the prize,
Then join your leader in the skies
    Amid the Angelic bands.

5 As the great Angel from the Lord
Convey'd the everlasting word
    Thro' the expanse of Heaven.,
So flies the Missionary band
From shore to shore, by Sea and Land
    The bread of life is given.

6 Asia salutes the rising day,
And glad to own Messiah's sway,
    Spreads forth her hands to God;
Welcomes the Gospel to her shores,
The Saviour CHRIST as God adores,
    And treads the heavenly road.

7 Each Herald clad in armour bright,
Before the word of Sacred light,
    Idolatry retires.
The wondering Heathen flock around,
To hear the Trumpet's joyful sound
    And join the heavenly choirs.

8 Glory to God who rules on high,
Glory to God the Indians cry!
    Angels and Men unite
To spread abroad the sacred Name,
Ascribing honors to the Lamb
    In purest realms of light.

No. II.

HYMN,

SUNG AT LAYING THE FOUNDATION STONE OF
NEGOMBO CHAPEL,
August 9th, 1819.

———

1 JEHOVAH, Lord of Earth and Heaven,
    The triune God whom we adore;
To thee be endless praises given
    By all thy works for evermore.

2 Thy word went forth,—Creation 'rose,
    And all things fair around thee smil'd;
But Man rebell'd, and hence our woes,
    Yet Man is still thy *Mercy's* child.

3 *Redemption's* gracious plan unfolds,
    Thy milder glories, God of love,
The wondrous cross a *world* beholds,
    Which points us to a crown above.

4 Diffused around the spacious earth,
    The tidings of a Saviour's grace,
Hath given a *new* creation birth;
    And brought Salvation *to this* Place.

5 Hence, to *thy Name* an altar rear'd;
    O God of Jacob hear our pray'r,
Here let accepted Praise be heard,
    And sinners find redemption here.

6 Here let the *Heathen tribes* ascend,
    And throng thy *House of prayer* around:
Here let the showers of grace descend,
    And mercy sanctify the ground.

7 Here O thou "High and lofty One,"
    Dwell in the lowly contrite heart;
And *here* erect thy mercy's throne,
    And never from this place depart.

ROBERT NEWSTEAD.

No. III.

Fort Macdonald June 7, 1819.

REV. AND DEAR SIR,

I gladly embrace the liberty which you so kindly gave me before I left Trincomalie, in sending these few and imperfect lines to you, humbly praying Almighty God, that they may find

you in perfect health of body and peace of mind, and going on
your way rejoicing in the might of God your Saviour. Dear Sir,
I may surely say I have experienced much of the goodness of
God since I left you: for I have been in the midst of sickness
and death, and yet, O wondrous mercy! I have been still preserved in good health and strength, whilst many have been cut
off, both on the right hand and on the left. Sickness first made
its appearance amongst us on the second day's march from
Mandoor, and the same day one was called into eternity and
two more were sent back to Batticaloe; one of them is since
dead, 6 more of the party have died in Badulla, and the most
of the remainder are either in hospital or sick in quarters. I
brought nineteen to this post, out of which, 2 have died, 4
are in hospital, and only three but have been sick; and yet
alas! they lay not these things much to heart. O! that they may
not be lost to me; but while I see my comrades falling around
me, may it teach me to hold the things of the world with a
loose hand, and cleave closer and closer to the adorable Saviour;
and ever keep eternity in view, that should it please Almighty
God in his infinite wisdom to call me hence, I may find acceptance in his sight through the alone merits and mediation of
Jesus Christ our Lord, to whom with the Father and Holy
Spirit be praise and glory ever more, Amen. I shall endeavour
to give you a faint description of the country, as far as I have
been about this place; and, I think, it is the most delightful
part in the whole Island. The country is open and clear from
the jungle that so much infests the sea coast; and beautifully
diversified with lofty mountains, and small hills covered with
fine grass or lofty trees; while the vales are cultivated for the
growth of paddy; and in each of them a small village full of
people. It must have been plentiful before the war; but it bears
the sad marks of devastation at present; and the inhabitants must
have perished, had they not been employed by Government, for
which they receive 2 fanams and ¾ of a seer of rice per day.
But I trust things will soon wear a brighter prospect. The sickness with which we have been visited we brought from the low
country, where it was raging as we passed through, for this part
must be healthful. as the country is open, the air is cool and
pleasant, and it is seldom so hot by day as to be the least annoyance to an European, and by night we find a blanket little
enough for covering. And now, Sir, I will inform you how I
pass my time here: I read the Psalms for the day, morning and
evening, and a chapter of the Old or New Testament: when I am
at leisure through the day, I read part of Young's Night Thoughts,
or, Doddridge's Rise and Progress of Religion in the Soul; or, a
tract or two, of which I have about 20 of the best I could get
before I left Trincomalie: after eight at night, I read to the men,
who generally hear me with attention; and I have some hopes
this little labour will not be lost. I hope, Dear Sir, you continue
to remember me in your prayers, (and it is an idle wish but in

sincerity of heart,) and I trust you are enabled to labour joyfully in the Lord's Vineyard; and that in some measure, you see the fruit of your labour, that your soul may rejoice therein. I conclude with praying that the Lord may continue you in health of body, to declare his great salvation here to lost sinners, and benighted heathens; and then take you to himself, to rejoice in his presence for evermore.

I remain Rev. Sir.
Your's with humility,
ROBERT NICOLL, Sergt 73rd,

To Rev. R. Carver.
    Trincomalie,

END OF JULY EXTRACTS, &c.

Printed at the Mission-Press, Colombo, for the Use of the Missionaries

Extracts

FROM

QUARTERLY LETTERS &c.

No. IX.   OCTOBER 1819.

THE COLOMBO STATION.

Mission House, 29th September, 1819.

MY VERY DEAR BRETHREN,

In the absence of my dear Colleague, I shall be under the necessity of addressing you singly on the present occasion; a circumstance which, though painful, appeared necessary. Brother Erskine has been on the Caltura station nearly two months, supplying in the absence of Brother Fox, who has been in the North of the Island, attending the district meeting which was lately held in Jaffna. The concerns of this station would certainly have suffered very seriously in the absence of Brother Erskine, had not help been at hand. But a kind Providence, ever watchful over the concerns of our Mission, I believe, in a very peculiar manner sent us help, apparently at the time it was needed. I am happy to say that Brother Hume has been with me since the latter end of July, supplying the place of Brother Erskine, and from him I have received very essential help. It may naturally be expected. that as a stranger on the Mission almost, and having not much acquaintance with the nature of our work, in some of its departments, he could hardly supply the place of a Brother possessing much acquaintance and experience in the work; yet it gives me pleasure to assure you, my dear Brethren, that I have found in Brother Hume an active, willing, laborious, persevering assistant. A Brother, ready on all occasions to do every thing which laid in his power to ease the burden which necessarily lays upon me. And I feel thankful to God, that we have been enabled to keep the whole work going on in its usual course. I only regret my want of a fair opportunity of entering minutely into our situation and labours, that you may feel with us, and rejoice with us.

I have now been nearly five years on this station, but do not recollect that my mind has ever had to undergo, and endure so great a variety and mixture of painful and pleasing sensations as since we had last an opportunity of writing you. Sometimes we have been in the very furnace of affliction, and very frequently have we been rejoicing with our blessed Lord on the mount. One of the principal sources of our painful feelings is, to witness the ravages the small pox is making among our Schools. This most distressing affliction has got among the inhabitants of this whole station, and it is most deplorable to see its effects. Such a visitation of divine Providence I do not recollect ever to have witnessed before. The spasmodic cholera made awful work among the people in this part, but when at the worst it bore no comparison with the present affliction. The inhabitants of colder regions can form but an imperfect idea of the havoc which this complaint makes in a climate like this. It seizes alike the old and the young, though I suppose not more than one half of those recover who take the decease, who are passed the meridian of life. During the last two months many hundreds have died, both of children and adults, in Colombo and the neighbourhood and at this moment it appears to get worse than ever; hardly an hour of the day passes that we do not witness either funeral processions, or coffins pass our door, or else hear the affecting howling of those who have lost a child, a parent, a husband, a wife, a brother, or sister. In several instances, even in the very neighbourhood of the Mission House, in our street, out of very large families, only one or two have been left to weep over those taken away. It was affecting this morning to see two coffins carried out of the same house, not 100 yards from our chapel, and scarcely had the procession left the door, when the news of a third death was heard by the heart rending cries of the same afflicted family.

The natives are, as is natural to suppose, horrified at the thoughts of taking the small pox, and I am really fearful that scores of the poor creatures perish for want of proper help. I have just received the accompanying note from one of our schoolmasters, which I insert to show you how this sickness affects the natives, and consequently our schools.

     REV. SIR,

I beg to inform your Reverend that one person was seized with the small pox, who living in a house near the School, and this day the people are going to another part, leaving the said House, and remaining only in the house he who has the small pox, with 2 or 3 persons to nourish him, and the carpenter's family is going to the house of his father in law, and other all people are going to other part, who live near to the house of now in small pox.

Therefore the school boys says they cannot attend to the school till that place get well, and concerning that I informed you as soon as I known. And in this country any one never will go to such places where is the small pox, because the Singhalese people is very afright of the same.

           I am, your most humble Servant,
                  ELIAS PERERA.

To the Rev. B. Clough.

I have visited several, and should consider it my duty to go more among them, could I see the least probability of rendering them any help. But, as it respects the little children, they must be left principally in the hands of God, and among the adults the complaint is generally so rapid, and so awful, that it admits of very little opportunity. I went this evening at 5 o'clock to bury one of our School girls, about 14 years of age, who though she died only 3 hours before she was put in the earth, the smell of the body was insufferable. The English teacher told me he saw her about 3 hours before her death, and said that her whole body was one complete mass of corruption. She was covered with the small pox which had united, and literally fell from off her body, carrying the skin from head to foot.

About a month ago I got a priest, of the rank of *Terenunsy*, out of the country, to assist me a little in the translation of some Sanscrit and Pali books. The poor old man was taken ill as he sat at my side. I advised him to go immediately to his lodgings, which I had previously provided, but the people of the place seeing he was unwell refused to admit him; he came back to me, and fearing the consequence, he began to weep like a child, and begged me to allow him to put off his robes and to be baptised immediately. He then told me, that for a week or two past his mind had been greatly affected while he had attended the translating room, and particularly at the idea of our beginning our translating work with singing and prayer. The poor man assured me, as he stood in my room, with the tears tumbling down his cheeks, "That though (said he) I have worn this robe, and been in the priesthood almost from a child, I am now convinced, that I have lived all my days without any God." He begged I would baptise him, but it was a point of such delicacy that I advised him to go to the hospital and see how his present indisposition turned out, and I would think of his proposal. I gave him such advice as I thought was suited to his situation. Thus I gave him into the charge of the doctor of the Hospital, begging him to let me hear of the progress of his disorder. I was exceedingly unwell at the time, and could not get out to see him, however the Doctor came two mornings after to say that it proved the small pox of a bad kind, and that he had just expired. I could not but feel this, for though I had from particular reasons refused to baptise him, and reasons which I think justifiable at the time. I am now sorry I did not. However, I believe he died a penitent believer in Jesus Christ, and notwithstanding his time of more serious reflection was short, I have some hope of meeting him in Heaven.

One would suppose that such a visitation of divine Providence as the present affliction would create much concern among the people, upon the great enquiry what they might do to be saved, but it is really distressing to see that none of God's efforts to save the inhabitants of this place will move them. I know not how to account for it, but all Heaven's dispensations appear to be re-

ceived in the same indifferent manner. I fear with regard to a
very great proportion of the people of this country, who have
now an opportunity of hearing the word of God, and of being
instructed in the way of salvation, that nothing will rouse them
from that strange unaccountable apathy respecting the things of
God which rests upon them, but the pains of hell. I have often
been surprised that we do not hear of more frequent miserable
deaths among them. People who have the Gospel may live quietly
in sin, but how they can generally leave the world in the same
unconcerned manner is somewhat singular. and the only way to
account for it, I think, is, that they are given over to the wickedness of their own hearts, and that the blessed Spirit of God has
forsaken them. I do not say this is an invariable case, but a
common one. That God has thoughts of mercy towards the people of this part is very evident, first from his word and his ministers being among them, and secondly from the frequent evidences we
have of a work of grace on the minds of many.

On Thursday, the 2d of this month, we held our quarter day,
for the purpose of ascertaining the exact state of our Society, and
of making a number of arrangements which the increasing state
of the Society required. It was very pleasing to see in this meeting with the two Missionaries, Brother Hume and myself, 5 leaders
and 4 local preachers, including Cornelius. Our first business was
to enquire into the state of the classes, which appeared from the
Class-papers which were laid on the table as follows:

1st Mission House class - - - -	14
2nd Mr. Gogerly's Portuguese class - -	6
3rd Fort class - - - - -	23
4th Colpetty male class - - - -	27
5th do. female class - - -	14
6th New-Bazar class - - - -	16
7th Wellewatta class - - - -	9
Total	**109**

At our Conference held in Galle the numbers returned were
92, giving us an increase of 21, which, when every thing is taken
into the account, was cause of sincere rejoicing to our souls,
and we felt greatly encouraged: since then 15 have joined our
class in the Fort, and a most blessed work is going on among
them still. This makes our number in Society on the Colombo
station 124, and though this, in English circuits, would be looked
upon as a small number, you my dear Brethren. who know the
nature of the soil we have to work upon, will unite in opinion
with me, that God has done much for us. I believe two or
three of our Singhalese members have since been carried off by
the small pox, concerning *two* of whom I had the most pleasing.
accounts, one at Colpetty and the other at New-Bazar. They gave
the most satisfactory evidence of their dying happy in the love
of God. A second subject of enquiry at our leader's meeting was,
whether sufficient care had been taken to make the members of

our Society acquainted with the whole economy of Methodism. It was found that many of the Singhalese members, in particular, had never yet seen our Society rules. It was immediately agreed upon to have them translated and printed, both in Singhalese and Portuguese, and that every member be furnished with a copy as soon as possible. Brother Armour, who knew very well how much my time is taken up, kindly engaged to translate them into both these languages, and is now pushing them on as fast as possible. We also found it necessary to make more permanent arrangements about class leaders; when, after some deliberation, the following was the result:

1. That Br. Armour take charge of the English class at the Mission House. 2 That Mr. Gogerly continue to have the charge of the Portuguese class which is held in his own house. 3 That Br. Kelly be continued the leader of the class in the Fort. 4 That Cornelius be continued the leader of the Colpetty male class; but 5 that Mr. Coopman take the charge of the female class. 6 That Mr. Appelton continue the leader of the New Bazar class. 7 That Cornelius be continued the nominal leader of the Wellewatte class, but that, on account of the distance, the Preacher who preaches there on the Friday evening shall always meet the class after preaching. Another subject brought before the Leaders' Meeting was, whether the leaders had pressed upon the members the necessity of paying class money; it was most heartily agreed upon that this plan be more than ever attended to, and that every member be given to see the necessity of doing it weekly, no matter how trifling the sum. Brother Gogerly was appointed Circuit Steward, and this I doubt not will give greater regularity to our Society money concerns. Finally, it was agreed upon that a more particular attention be given, to see that all who are now united with us, as members of Society, do most sacredly attend to the rules of the Society, and that in addition to every member having a copy of the rules, that they be read at least once a quarter in the class by the leader. Our Local Preachers Meeting was rendered a little trying, by the examination of one of them whose name we had been obliged to omit when the last Plan was printed, though we had not had an opportunity of considering his case in a regular way. However, it gives me pleasure to say that the young man has entered again most heartily into his work; and is, if all be well, to be restored as on trial again in our next Plan. The young man was not charged with any thing sinful, or even with any impropriety which implied guilt, hence there will be no difficulty in his being taken on the plan. I should have felt greatly distressed, had matters in the end turned out unfavourable, as he is, without any exception, the most laborous active young man I have seen in this country.

Many of the members in our Singhalese classes are the elder scholars in our schools, and it may perhaps turn out that some of them may not prove so stable as one could wish; yet I say it with pleasure, I see no actual reason for indulging this fear, but rather the contrary, as many of them have braved difficulties and trials, on the score of religion, which would have done credit to older Christians. The little class at Wellewatte are all adults, and principally females. They have lately undergone a trial of their faith worthy of the apostles' days. When the present distressing affliction threatened that village, the Heathen-Christian inhabitants, as was the case in most other villages, sent for the Cappuas, those most of all devout servants of the Devil. They began making the grandest preparations to offer sacrifices to the Devil.

Unhappily for the Devil, he built his Fortress a little too near our School in that village, in fact within the range of our artillery. The whole village almost, both old and young, flocked round his standard. Great preparations were made; these I saw myself, and when the ceremonies began, I believe several thousands on different occasions came and made offerings to කරුවෙ ඇදා, the goddess of the small pox, to ward off the threatened affliction. Some of the parents of the children in our school compelled their children, with threats and punishments, to offer on this occasion, and I understand in some cases the children resisted so far as caused a good deal of confusion. And be it known to all men, that these old sinners, who thus forced their sons, who had got better instructions in our school, these I say were some of the " Ceylon Christians," so called. Our little Society in the village could not endure these things; they made a complaint to me on the subject, which was my signal for coming forward; I went first to the place; I saw the preparations which had been made; the Cappuas came forward with all the impudence and wickedness their master could inspire them with, but what was still a little more, they told me they were Christians. I had soon the mortification to find that all reasoning and advice on the subject was spurned at by them, we therefore lost no time, but took down the names of all the Christians concerned in the business. The only person I could get to help on the occasion was the 2nd headman of the village. The day after, being Monday, I drew up a statement of the whole to Mr. Bisset, the Principal of Schools, and begged him to lay it before Government. And I am happy to say, that in 24 hours an order of the most peremptory kind was sent by the Collector to the headman, of the place to see the whole demolished. Mr. Bisset also gave orders for the names of the Cappuas to be brought to him, and he would have them put out of the Thombo. (The parish register.) But when the headman gave out his orders to the people to destroy these infernal preparations, not a person could be compelled to touch them, after much to do the headman set to work himself, and with the help of some of his own servants (for some of them positively refused to help) soon brought the whole to the ground. The Cappuas now set to work with their pretended divinations and enchantments, and gave it out to the inhabitants

that the headman would die in 24 hours. Hundreds of people, at different times during that period, came to witness his awful death. The 24 hours passed away; all was still well with the headman. The Cappuas then said he would die in 8 days of the hydrophobia, and it was singular enough to see, that during the whole of these 8 days the headman's house was surrounded with people, at a distance, to witness the fulfilment of the prediction of the Cappuas. In the course of the 8 days the headman came to the Mission House, and telling me the whole story, smilingly said, "At this moment, Sir, the people are in all corners about my house, expecting to see me siezed by the *Hydrophobia*." When the whole enchantment failed, then the torrent turned against our little Society in the village, who were looked upon as the movers of the order that had produced the overthrow, but I am happy to say they all stood their ground well. Our young friend Cornelius was pelted out of the jungle, when on a journey through the village, with stones and dirt, and it was next to a miracle he was not killed; but through mercy he was not hurt. Many of the inhabitants vowed vengeance on the School on account of this triumph over these devilish ceremonies, and annoyed us a good deal for some weeks, but the steady activity of the Master, and the attention which we have paid it, is now smoothing every thing, and many begin to be ashamed of their conduct.

Our Schools are kept up exceedingly well, considering the present affliction, but this may be attributed in a good degree to the persevering system of attention which we bestow upon them. During the last two months every School on the station, with the exception of the two distant ones, has been visited once a week by a Missionary. The class papers and weekly returns are examined with the strictest scrutiny at the weekly meetings of the teachers, and on no account is any teacher allowed to be absent from this meeting, unless in cases of sickness. In addition to this, every School, without any exception, has a sermon a week either from a Missionary or a Local Preacher. This kind of attention, and regularity, both encourages the children and parents, and acts as a stimulus to attention. And not a scholar hardly thinks of being absent from school, unless absolutely necessary.

We have opened two new Schools this quarter, the one at Nagalgam, in a populous neighbourhood close on the banks of the Calany River. There are about 50 boys in it. The School is close to a large bazar, were there are generally several hundreds of people from the interior, who come down the river in the boats on mercantile speculations. The situation will be a good one to establish preaching in, which we shall do as soon as the new School-house is built. It will also afford us great facilities of sending Tracts into the interior. A second school has been opened on the Colombo road, between Wellewatte and Morotto, which is greatly encouraged by the headmen of the village. We have a third school almost ready for opening in the neighbourhood of Lepers Hospital, which is situated nearly at the mouth of the Calany river, in a retired part of the country, and surrounded by several interesting villages. The inhabitants are building the School-house by subscription, and they have made it sufficiently large and substantial to answer the purpose of a Church. We have at present a room fitted up in the Lepers Hospital complete, with Pulpit, Forms, and a Bell, all entirely at the expense of the people. There are about 30 Lepers, poor creatures, quite outcasts from the society of men. They get a sermon once a week, with others who attend with them, and which makes up a very good and regular congregation. And some of our young men who have *lately* preached to them, gave us the pleasing information of a good work of grace among some of them.

Respecting the cause of God in the Town of Colombo, I wish it were in my power to give you a more encouraging account. The people have the means of grace in abundance, and they are now as regular as in most places. There appears a disposition to hear the word of God, and this so far affords satisfaction; but we wish to see the Gospel of Christ effectual in the conversion of multitudes. Our various sermons are pretty well attended. In the English congregation we can hardly look for much alteration, since comparatively so few of the mass of the people understand the language so well as to understand us, and be interested by the sermons. I have long entertained this opinion, and am now by daily experience convinced of it. Our Portuguese congregation is large and serious, particularly so of late; and many regularly attend on these occasions who, though they understand English, yet never come to hear a sermon in that language; the reason is plain—they cannot enter fully into it. They know enough of English to transact the common business of life, but a sermon in English is in a great measure uninteresting to them, from a want of sufficient acquaintance with the idioms of the language as to enable them to keep the thread of a discourse. This however is a circumstance which in a short time will be done away.

The case is very different in the Fort. Here we can speak freely, and we are well understood: our Meeting house is crowded every time we preach, with an attentive congregation, eager to understand and profit by what they hear, and could we get a place in the Fort twice the size of our present one, I have no doubt of its being always crowded; many scores are kept back at present for want of room.

The Society among the soldiers has sustained a great loss in the death of our dear Brother Kelly. I had intended drawing up a short account of him for the Miscellany this Quarter, but my time has been so much taken up with the labours of the station, that would not allow any abatement of attention on my part, that it was impossible for me to get at the work.

The death of our dear friend Kelly was an event most unexpected, he being in general so very healthy. The affliction which finished his earthly course was but short, and he left the world when apparently he bade fair to be extensively useful. In the beginning of this month his duty required him to be up the whole night in rather painful circumstances. Before he went to bed he found himself very unwell, but after an hour's sleep thought himself a little better, and came down to the Mission House to attend the Quarterly meeting, but while we sat in the Chapel he was taken so ill again that he was forced to lay down on bed. After the business of the day was finished I sent Kelly home in a bandy, being too unwell to walk. Two days after he went to the Hospital where I visited him a few times before his death. The attack proved an inflammation in the head, which, from the beginning was so distressingly painful as almost entirely to deprive him of all recollection. His mind however continued in a very happy frame. He was only about ten days in the Hospital. I was with him several hours the day he died. The principal part of the time he was quite delirious, though it was very satisfactory to find that his whole conversation, in these painful moments, was upon the things of God. About an hour or so, before he died, God gave him a lucid moment, of which I availed myself to find how his mind was affected at the prospect of his approaching dissolution, when he bore a blessed testimony of the power of saving grace, and expressed a happy resignation to the will of God, and a blessed anticipation of future glory. The last words the good Brother ever spoke were while I was talking with him in this season of mental recollection, " The will of the Lord be done." The Sunday evening after his death I endeavoured to improve the event, by preaching from Philp. i. 21. "*For me to live is Christ, but to die is gain.*" The congregation was exceedingly large and solemn, and I hope good was done—about 18 have since joined the class; most, if not all of whom, are truly awakened and seeking the salvation of their souls with great earnestness. One fine young man belonging to the band engaged the night in which the funeral sermon was preached to come and lead the singing, being a good singer, and good musician, and knowing that Kelly had always led the singing in our place of worship in the Fort. I do not recollect ever to have seen the young man in the meeting house. However he got that night a serious concern for his soul, came to class the following night, and appeared in great distress of mind. But from what I have heard of him since, I hope the Lord has put a *new* song into his mouth, of praise and thanksgiving. Who can tell but this same young man may in time fill up Kelly's place. Two or three others of the band, fine young lads, and very promising, have joined the class, and I have great hopes of them all. The work of God is going on so blessedly

among them in the Fort, that it is really next to visiting heaven
to go and preach to them. There is so much of the power of
God among them, that it is impossible not to feel among them.

For the last few months our printing concerns have suffered
most grievously for want of paper. The Bible Society's paper
fell off in the most unexpected manner. We had no stock on
hand that would enable us to supply their works until they could
have a fresh supply from England. The consequence was that
our office made an immediate stand. To keep a press or two
going, and prevent the whole from standing, we have printed some
of our School books in long numbers in China paper of which
we had a pretty good stock. But this has fallen off also, and
there has not been much going forward, as we could not procure
a Ream of China paper in Colombo. I wrote about 3 months
ago to Madras to beg a friend to purchase 200 Reams for us, which
was done immediately, but there being no ships from thence at this
season of the year, we could not get it sent to us. But what was
still the most unfortunate business in this crisis, our Committee
in London, sent us out a supply of paper and books in a ship
bound to Madras, where of course she landed them. So that the
Europe paper which would have kept the office in full employ
until the Bible Society could recruit their stock, has been laying
about in the Madras Custom house. Such grievious circumstances
as these ought to be guarded against, and prevented by those
whose place it is to manage them. You dear Brethren can but ill
conceive the sufferings of my mind for the last 3 or 4 months
to see so large a printing office almost standing still, and a good
deal of this occasioned by a want of a little thought. The articles sent out by our Committee were sent in three ships. That
which had the paper and books in was the *Sappho*, bound to Madras. The *Hayton* had the types &c. on board, according to the
Bill of lading the Captain engaged to land them in *Ceylon*, so he
did: for though he called at Galle, yet being quite at liberty to
land them where he pleased in Ceylon, he took them to Trincomalie.
This is about 4 months ago. The boxes are not yet arrived. I
wrote to Br. Carver, when I could make out where that ship had
left the boxes, and found they were laid in the Custom house of
Trincomalie. Br. Carver kindly sent them off in a brig when he
knew of them, but where the brig has taken them to I know
not, yet I hope she has not taken them to the bottom.

The third ship was the *Eclipse*, she had only one box on board
of which I received a Bill of lading, and as I supposed a copy
of the invoice of what the box contained, copied apparently by
the Committee's clerk. In order to free the boxes from the Custom house, I took the invoice and swore to it before a Magistrate,
which is always the case unless we wish to have things dragged
about the floors of the Custom house by the ignorant impudent
Peons. When we got this box home we found that it contained

about one sixth of the articles I had sworn it did contain, and that the said copy of an invoice must be the invoice of the whole. This, however, was the conjecture which the Custom Master and I were forced to make to adjust things, so that how it will prove in the end I know not. I wish for my own comfort, and for the comfort of any one who may come after me here, as well as for the credit of the Mission generally, we could get our little concerns into a more business like train. I have been the more particular in detailing these facts to you, my Brethren, to enable you to see how we have been situated the last quarter. Several of you have written for School books of various kinds, I am sorry I could not send you the supplies, nor would my circumstance allow me to write you each a particular statement of what stood in our way, as my whole attention is taken up with the engagements of my stations, that long letters it has been impossible for me to write.

We have several large editions of School books which only want a sheet or two each of being finished, but cannot get paper to complete them, they have laid in this state some time. I need not say as soon as it is in our power the works shall be got out of hand that your various applications for books may be attended to. But when this will be is partly uncertain.

But while however the printing office has had to encounter these interruptions in its more enlarged branches of operations, we have not lost the opportunity of supplying the Book room with large Editions of smaller works, principally for the use of schools, and which will prevent the necessity of our stopping the printing of the Scriptures of the Old and New Testament when we get the English printing paper.

These editions of the small works will all be finally sent out of the printing office the first thing after the arrival of the China paper from Madras.

I am happy also to inform you that we have been enabled to put our binding room upon a very respectable footing. We have engaged a young man from Madras, who binds excellently in every kind of work; and you will do well to make this known on your respective Stations to your different friends, and perhaps a supply of work might be got which would make the binding room a more profitable concern. The Committee have sent out by an order from Br. Harward a considerable quantity of materials, both for the Binding room and Type foundery, which will materially assist these departments.

We have been going on much the same in the translating department as before. The book of Psalms is quite finished, Proverbs is also finished. We have now gone back to the books of Moses, and have nearly finished the book of Exodus, This brings us a good way a head of the printing. I have also been labouring pretty hard to get on the Dictionary; but this work has also stood some time for paper.   Upwards of 100 pages are printed off. I have finally corrected for the press as much manuscript as will make 100 pages more, and which would be printed in less than a month had we paper.   But this I find laborious work, having to go three times over the manuscript before it goes to press.   I am also now going on with the translation of a course of short sermons into Singhalese which I hope to complete in the course of the ensuing quarter. These I am persuaded will be of use. I have completed the occasional services in the Liturgy, which are printed off. It has since occurred to me that it would be well to translate a number of forms of prayer adopted for other occasions, such as for Evening and Morning worship for every day in week; also for visiting the sick &c. and to let these be bound up at the end of the Liturgy. I can with a few little alterations according to the circumstances of the people find all that is necessary I think in Mr. Wesley's Forms of Prayer.

I have also nearly finished the Catalogue of Mr. Tolfrey's Library which I hope to put in the Miscellany.

Previous to the death of my old *Terranancy*, I had begun an Index to the Library, which would have given a complete insight into the Singhalese books, but after getting through two volumes, the poor old man died, and I lost my assistant, and my hands being so full of other works I have not yet had time to look out for another assistant.

The various works which at present occupy my mind and attention some times try me a good deal, and call for the exercise of patience. However I endeavour to ease my mind by attending to my other duties of a Christian Missionary, and which I find particularly useful to my soul. I regularly take my plan in my appointment of preaching both on Sundays and week days, visiting the Schools, and meeting the school masters regularly, giving them all the help, advice, and encouragement I can. Laying out plans of labour for our young men, the local preachers, receiving their Reports, and giving them hints &c. and in fact doing what lays in my power daily to keep the Machine at work. I bless God for a continuance of a tolerable state of health, but more abundantly can I praise the Lord for a lively assurance daily of his favor and that my soul is growing in grace. I remain,

        Very Dear Brethren,

                Sincerely and affectionately yours,

                        B. CLOUGH.

THE NEGOMBO STATION.

Negombo, 7th October, 1819.

VERY DEAR BRETHREN,

Various and almost incessant occupations have kept me beyond
the usual time of writing the Quarterly communication from hence;
I hope, however, it will yet be in time for insertion, because I am
persuaded it will give pleasure to you to be made acquainted
with several little particulars which it contains. We need every
help in our arduous work that will tend to our encouragement,
and assist us to persevere in the name of the Lord; and such an
auxiliary, I am sure, our Quarterly Letters have been, tending at
once to keep alive brotherly union, affectionate emulation, and
a spirit of prayer for each other in our different stations: each
of which dispositions must essentially promote that "*same care
one for another*," which the apostle recommends, that, "*whether
one member suffer all the members should suffer with it, or one
member be honoured all the members should rejoice with it.*" 1 Co-
rinth. xii. 25, 26. In my last letter, a large portion of which
related to the building of our chapel here, I anticipated having
the happiness to state in this that it would be in a considerable state of forwardness; I am thankful to say that expectation
has been realised, the foundation is laid with much strength and
the walls raised nearly to the windows. I trust the blessing of
God is upon the work, and hence I have been thus far carried
through a course of difficulties and trials attending it, which none
can calculate upon but those who have been similarly engaged:
not that I consider any difficulty attending the work worthy to
be at all compared with the probable benefits which will result
from it, as connected with our blessed cause in this Island, nor
in the least degree regret the trouble incurred; but, on the contrary, rejoice in it every day, having already seen many remarkable instances of *Providential* interposition in its erection. It
would be wrong for me to omit mentioning the encouragement
and help I derived from our dear Brethren, who favoured me
with their counsel, their assistance, and their prayers at the time
of commencing the work. On the 9th of August the first stone
was laid by our Brother Hume, newly arrived from England, and
myself, on which interesting occasion we had a very profitable
religious service on the spot. A temporary Bungaloe was erected
near, which the zeal of our school-boys had tastefully ornamented
with flowers and olas, and in which a respectable little congregation assembled, and were most attentive through the following
service. Brother Clough gave out an occasional hymn, and prayed
with peculiar spirit and energy, and evidently attended with a divine blessing. Br. Chater read most impressively the 132 *Psalm*,
and afterwards prayed. Br. Hume then gave a very animated address, from 72 *Psalm*, 19 *verse*, which I believe made us all feel;
and, after giving out an appropriate hymn, "Except the Lord con-

duct the plan," &c. I concluded with prayer, humbly rejoicing that the God of Jacob had conducted his glorious cause so far, that we had witnessed the first stone laid of a building on which we were all ready, on that joyful occasion, with one consent to inscribe BETH-EL! *Gen* xxviii. 18, 19.

A circumstance which has given me no inconsiderable pleasure this quarter has been the completion of the printing of the Portuguese Gospel, a pleasure which has been enhanced by the kindly expressed opinions of most of our dear Brethren, as to its general correctness and clearness. I am well aware, however, that there are many imperfections and errors in it, which all my care could not prevent in its going through the press; nevertheless, as they are principally orthographical, they may be corrected with the utmost ease on a future occasion. Meanwhile I am truly thankful to have heard, from several quarters, the most pleasing testimonies of its being generally *understood*, which is certainly of the last importance. In a note which I had lately from J. Deane, Esq. Collector of Colombo, a gentleman well able to judge on this subject, the following passage occurs relative to it. "For your Portuguese translation of the Gospel of St Matthew I beg you to accept my best thanks. I trust it will prove beneficial to a numerous class of inhabitants of Colombo and other towns, and I may mention as a satisfactory evidence of its clearness and correctness, that a child of eleven years of age to whom I shewed it perfectly understood its contents." At Negombo it has been much applied for, and I am not without hope, will be very useful; particularly as it is principally among the Roman Catholics, who will thus become acquainted with divine Truth though they may not hear it. I consider it a Providential circumstance that the Book-Committee pressed its being finished as they did, when I was last at Colombo. although Br. Fox was prevented from attending by his severe illness: because it was by that circumstance ready for his active distribution on his late visit to the Northern side of the Island, and will probably reach a little beyond where our personal instructions are likely to go at present, as appears from a letter which I had from him while in Trincomalie, in which he says, "Providence brought me to *Ramisseram*, where I distributed some of the Portuguese Gospels to such as were able to read them. Some I have sent by a Military Officer to the continent, some I have left at Jaffna, and some I have brought here. I am happy to say they are quite easy to *read* and to be *understood*. On my return I mean to send a few to Bombay, as the Portuguese are numerous there, and their dialect differs little from ours. May the Spirit of the Lord accompany them!"

Considering it to be a mark of respect which we owed to the Colombo Bible Society, I took an early opportunity of sending under cover to the Rev. G. Bisset, the Secretary, 6 copies of the Gospel to present to the Committee. I am induced to insert the whole of Mr. Bisset's obliging answer here, not only as it is a gratifying instance of liberal feeling, but as it convincingly touches

on a point which even some of ourselves have differed on, the expediency or inexpediency of keeping up the Portuguese language; about which, however, I believe we have now but *one* opinion:

Colombo, July 31, 1819.

DEAR SIR,

I received your letter yesterday with 6 copies of the Portuguese translation of St. Matthew, and am very much obliged to you for your attention. The constant occupation that has taken up my time lately must be my excuse for not answering your former note. I am sorry that your letter did not happen to come an hour or two earlier yesterday, as in that case I should have had the pleasure of laying it, with the Gospel, before the special Committee which met to hear the Report. I think your Portuguese translation may be a very useful work : many people say " why do any thing to encourage or continue the use of such a barbarous jargon, why not endeavour to bring the people to a better language." That is all very just, and I hope the schools, numerous as they are, will do much towards this desirable end, but in the mean time, unless something is published in Portuguese, there must be great numbers left *in total ignorance of their Religion*, so that your work is, in my opinion, very beneficial and deserving of much praise. I should be glad to know whether the priests suffer their flocks to read it !

Believe me to be,

Your's faithfully,

G. BISSET.

On the subject of our general work on this station, I have through the quarter been alternately elevated and depressed, but although, to be candid, I must acknowledge I am generally under depression to observe the total indifference of the people to every exertion made for their salvation; yet this quarter has furnished many pleasing circumstances of an opposite tendency, among which, independent of what has been mentioned, I may include our *Love feast* which was held on the 19*th September*, of course for the first time in Negombo. I thought after 2 years instruction and initiation in Christian doctrines and duties, our little scattered flock on this circuit were sufficiently ripened in judgment and experience to participate in the enjoyment, as well as to assist in the conduct of such an ordinance, and I was not disappointed. With great thankfulness to God I must observe, that I have never witnessed a more orderly and animated and profitable Love-feast, even where the people are favored with the constant use of such ordinances. Being, however, so familiar with class meetings and sacramental opportunities for a long time past, our friends entered on the engagement in the true spirit of it, and a few words explanatory of its object and design at the opening was sufficient to preserve the most perfect regularity and consistency, although each spake in his own language; so that we held it in

all the four languages spoken here. Having arranged for the
absence of our Schoolmasters from their respective villages 29
members were present, the rest were only prevented by sickness,
or dread of the epidemic. A good number of them spoke, and
drew tears of unfeigned gratitude from my eyes to hear their
simple yet striking relations of experience and to observe their
eagerness to bear a testimony for Jesus; several times two were
rising at the same instant, and I believe about 6 of them gave a
clear account of their justification and their sweet enjoyment of
the *love of God*, deliverance from the fear of death, &c. I preached
to them 3 times in the course of the day, and administered the
sacrament in the evening, at which 10 were present besides the
Gracious Master of assemblies, who has promised to be " WHEREVER
two or *three are met together in his name*." I designed those spiritual ordinances in one day, not only to accommodate our friends
from the country, but also as a little celebration of the second
Anniversary of our Mission here. as it was two years on the 17th
September since my arrival at Negombo; and nothing could be
more congenial with the feelings of my heart on such an occasion than thus to assemble our little forces, and concentrate our
spiritual strength that " *with one accord in one place*," we might
return our humble acknowledgements to the " God of the spirits of
all flesh," to whom be glory for ever! It is a delightful and
consolatory reflection, amidst the general apathy and indifference
of the multitude around us, that here and there a solitary individual believes our report, joins our Society, and rises up a decided witness for Jesus. Such evidences of the power of Divine
grace, under the most uninviting appearances, are not wanting
(Praise the Lord) on all our stations, and I exceedingly rejoice
are found even here. I did not so fully know, till our Love-feast,
what the Lord was graciously doing for us, nor would my unbelieving apprehensions and anxieties have calculated upon such clear
and unequivocal proof of his regenerating grace on this unfriendly
soil; but, in the past quarter, I have been favored to behold another instance, even under my own roof, which has changed my
prayers into praises, and added to those of whose real conversion
I have no doubt, the name of our dear young friend James
Sutherland.

I believe that for a year and a half he has been seeking. "*peace
with God through our Lord Jesus Christ*" in the conscious sense
of sin forgiven, lately with increased earnestness, and recently
with entire success:—so that he now rejoices in the precious love
of God, and seems "*determined to know nothing among men but
Jesus Christ and him crucified*." His language at the Love feast
was highly decisive and animating, and, I am happy indeed to add,
that his general conduct is ornamental to his profession. and his
progress in the languages very satisfactory. He uses the Portuguese
extempore in prayer, or in occasional exhortation, and reads the
Scriptures and the Liturgy in the native language with tolerable
fluency.

Of the Schoolmasters generally I can speak most encouragingly; their growth in Christian knowledge and experience is evident, and their conduct, as far as I am capable of judging, unimpeachable: two of them are communicants, and all meet in class. Our School Boys class has had to encounter hindrances from the Providential visitations of epidemic sicknesses, of which it is well known the people are afraid even to superstition, and indeed not now without reason. No sooner had the *Cholera Morbus* ceased to stalk through our streets devouring its hundreds, but the small pox followed and has taken many into an untried eternity, and confined every person to their houses from fear, who was not absolutely obliged to be out on his business. In many instances this has been abandoned, and their houses together; especially near our Bungaloe. What a mercy would it be would they "*take the warning and deliver their souls*," but alas! to this they seem dead, the majority of them offering idle vows to the images of their saints, and conceiving when they have made a feast for the Virgin they are wholly exonerated! such fetters are stronger than those of Heathenism! Is is, however, pleasing to observe, that our youthful class has struggled against these difficulties, and continue to assemble every week, some of them coming from a distance of 7 miles, and returning the same evening: this zeal, there is no doubt, is promoted and encouraged by the piety of their masters. Our *Schools* also, I am very thankful to state, go on prosperously; the old ones are receiving additions, as some are of course leaving. Last month I had an account of 24 new boys in 3 neighbouring schools: in two schools, not far from each other, we have nearly 100 children respectively, and I have just succeeded in properly organizing one, which I have long had in hand, in the most populous, and I may add, most ignorant, part of Negombo, which I every Sunday visit myself, and am charmed with their progress: we have had 4 able masters raised from our School here, who are now in active employment in different situations. I have also this quarter fully opened and established our little *Kandyan School*, which I hope will be the first step to many there, under the direction of Heaven; the Master is a zealous and useful man, and I have just directed him to try and extend his borders a little as a favourable opening appears. A very pleasing circumstance took place there a few days ago; the Governor, Lady Brownrigg, and their suite, accompanied by Lieut. Colonel Hook, who commands at Kornegalle and extensively round, including the district of our School, all passed the School, which the Schoolmaster had ornamented with olas, &c. as well as the road before it, which attracted the Governor to notice and enquire about the School, which he did most minutely; asking, When and by whom it was instituted? Who supported it? How often, and by whom it was visited? What was taught &c. &c. &c. to all of which the master gave him a satisfactory answer, and he was pleased to express the highest approbation of the whole; said, he was glad to see a Christian school there, and would recommend the matter to me. Colonel Hook, on his return from escorting His Excellency to the boundaries, called at the School and seemed much interested, examined the books, &c. but having no interpreter could only say " *Bohoma honda*," very good. I have written to Colonel Hook to allow, and to sanction, our future endeavours, and have hope that this little unexpected incident will have a happy effect on our Kandyan School, and our further exertion in that idolarous region, as the known approbation of Government will do much more for us than many exertions on our part unassisted, and as Col. Hook has so unlimited an influence over all that part of the Kandian territory. On my last journey to Kandy I visited two very large Budhist temples, and had some interesting conversation with the priests, who do not seem much opposed to us, except from a kind of traditionary prejudice, than which nothing is more natural; but there is dead inertness about them and their system which would never stand against the energetic exertions of a Christian Missionary, attended with the blessing of his Divine Master. I fully believe, that, *unsupported by the arm of secular power*, they would fall before us like dew before the sun! The lower orders of the people, so far from appearing to defend their priest and their temples, seem rather disposed to laugh at their absurdities when they hear them rationally exposed in their own language; and, though a Missionary would of course calculate upon difficulties, (for when was a Mission ever established without them?) I am persuaded, that with ability on the one hand to preach the Gospel to them in their own tongue, and on the other to avail himself of the silent, but sure operation of Christian schools, he would in a few years see Dagon fall before the ark of the Lord all around him! It is a glorious prospect, may a "*great door and effectual*" be immediately opened unto these Gentiles although there are so many adversaries. Our dear Brothers Clough, and Hume (my first visitors since I have been here) on their return from Negombo very kindly assisted at the anniversary of our *Akelle school*, which forms the boundary of my circuit that way, and I am happy to know were delighted to see the change which one year's Christian instruction has made on nearly a hundred fine heathen youths. It was indeed truly pleasing to see the order and progress of the school, scarcely a child of the smallest class but could repeat the Lord's Prayer, Creed, and Ten Commandments, many of them already, much to the credit of the masters, learning Mr. Wesley's Catechism in both language. Br. Clough read with them the translated Liturgy, and Br. Hume preached, after the examination, to a very large and respectable congregation, who were deeply attentive and highly gratified. I rejoice much that the Lord has been pleased to send us so large an accession of Missionary strength, and very heartily congratulate our dear Brethren and Sister on their arrival. May they never have cause to regret the hour when they set foot

on this Island, but have eternal cause to remember it among the high and peculiar favours conferred upon them by Him who fixeth the bounds of our habitation! I am anticipating the return of Br. Hume to assist me a little, which has been long delayed by Br. Fox's detention on the North of the Island, and I trust my expectation will now be soon realized, for I have in view an extension of the boundaries of this station northward as far as to Chilaw, and am on the eve of setting out for that purpose, waiting only the Collector's appointment The intention of occupying Chilaw has long existed, as its importance has always been apparent, but hitherto I have been entirely prevented from obvious circumstances. Recent occurrences, however, have repeated the call on one hand, and on the other led me to expect help on the station soon. But as I am sure it must be pleasing to the Brethren to see the favourable disposition of Mr. Walbeoff, the Collector towards us, I will insert the following correspondence which has taken place on the subject, and which will develope the whole:

Negombo, September 13, 1819.

DEAR SIR,

It has given me the most sincere pleasure to hear, through my interpreter, that you continue still so strongly to wish for a Missionary and a Native Church and School at Chilaw. Ever since I conversed with you on the subject at Negombo it has continued to occupy my mind at intervals, and although the circumstance of my being alone, with a constant round of missionary engagements in this immediate neighbourhood, has hitherto precluded almost the possibility of my meeting your benevolent wishes for those more directly under your notice and care, yet I assure you I have never once lost sight of it. I cannot but be aware of the importance of Chilaw as a Missionary station, and of the crying necessity of some kind of religious instruction in a district where no class of the inhabitants enjoy the benefit of a Christian ministry, either Native or European, nor can I be insensible to the kind and liberal offers which you then made in the event of my being able to occupy the place, and the repetition of those kind offers now through Perera. Indeed, the consideration of this has afresh awakened my very ardent wishes to see the place occupied by, at least a Christian School, and as frequent visits as I can pay to preach to the people until a more efficient step can be taken. The arrival of two more of our Brethren on the Island, and the expectation of two others in a short time, induces a hope that at our next Conference in January 1820, I shall be able to obtain help on this station so as to permanently occupy Chilaw, if not immediately as a distinct station, yet as the occasional residence of those who may be stationed here alternately. This, with the constant residence and care of one or two steady Christian Schoolmasters, favoured with your kind sanction and protection, will I am persuaded render incal-

culable benefit to the inhabitants who are so happy as to be
under the government of one who cares for their moral and spiritual welfare. If, therefore, dear Sir, you will kindly raise a place
for us to preach in and to instruct the children, (who I am
sure, though your extensive influence will readily attend) I pledge
myself, with the blessing of God, to come prepared to form such
an establishment, and to take it under the constant care of our
Mission. I shall, of course, most gladly hearken to any suggestion
which your extensive local knowledge and long acquaintance with
the inhabitants, as well as superior wisdom may dictate, either by
letters previously, or verbally when I have the pleasure to visit
Chilaw, for I infer that a previous visit would be almost indispensable. May I beg you to present Mrs. Walbeoff with the accompanying volume, a little more worthy her acceptance than
the last, with best compliments and allow me the happiness to
remain,

Dear Sir, your much
Obliged and Obedient Servt.

To J. Walbeoff, Esq.   ROBERT NEWSTEAD.

Answer to the above.

Chilaw, 16th September, 1819.

MY DEAR SIR,

I had the pleasure of receiving your kind letter yesterday, with
the book, for which Mrs. Walbeoff begs you will accept her best
thanks. Be assured I will have much pleasure in doing my utmost towards erecting a building of the description you mention,
but previous to commencing it I am of opinion it would be advisable for you pay us a visit, when you could fix on the spot
as well as arrange matters more satisfactory than by correspondence. Believe me that nothing would give me greater pleasure
than to see one of the Gentlemen of your Society stationed here,
being convinced in my own mind, from my long residence, that
great good might be done in this district, as the inhabitants in it
are well disposed, and by no means of so troublesome a disposition as those amongst whom you reside. Schools would be of a
great importance here; it is true we have one, but like the rest
of them no attention is paid, and as long as that is the case no
good can be derived from such an Establishment. I am obliged
to quit this about the end of the week for Putlam, where my
stay will not be more than 7 or 8 days, and if you could make
it convenient to come up on my return we could finally arrange
matters. Mrs. Walbeoff offers her best compliments to you. Pray
are you getting the timber from Otterpalatte? I have just
written to the Corale on the subject, desiring him to be expedious.

Believe me,
Very truly yours,
J. WALBEOFF.

Thus, very dear Brethren, you see. here is an opening before us which it would be a sin to neglect, and which, when entered upon, will of course involve much additional labour on this station, as it will extend the limits of the circuit 40 miles along the coast, and at. least 30 into the Interior. All this, however, I may leave with perfect confidence to the consideration of our next Conference, and the Providence of God.

I am truly thankful that my last quarter has abounded in spiritual consolation, and though I have frequently been depressed I have ever been supported, having experienced the fulfilment of the Divine promise in having strength exactly proportioned to my day. One object, I hope I may say, governs my life, i. e. to be *Holy* and *useful*; and, while I am very sensible of daily deficiencies in both, I yet would despair of neither, but "*forgetting those things which are behind reach forward to them which are before, and press towards the mark for the prize of the high calling of God in Christ Jesus.*"

I remain, very dear Brethren,
Most affectionately your's,
ROBERT NEWSTEAD.

P. S. By letters lately received from our dear Brother Osborne, I am happy to learn that he is safely arrived at Batticaloa, through many distressing dangers in landing, &c. He would be unable, he hinted, to write any Quarterly Letter this time, from his yet unsettled state; but expressed himself very happy in his new station, and anticipated much success in his future labours, feeling a persuasion that he was in his Providential way. His situation, however, recommends itself to our prayers, being alone, in much difficulty, with his little family, &c.

R. N.

THE CALTURA STATION.

Colombo, October 15, 1819

VERY DEAR BRETHREN,

Unavoidable absence, for a considerable period, from Caltura, renders me incapable of giving you many particulars relative to my Station. I have, however, the pleasure to inform you, that it continues to prosper. The prospect of being absent from a place which, for many reasons. will ever be dear to me, formed what may be justly called a trial; but hesitation is scarcely lawful where duty calls. Brother Erskine, as on a former occasion, kindly engaged to supply Caltura during my absence, as far as possible, since Brother Hume was providentially at hand to supply his place in Colombo: to Br. Erskine I am under peculiar obligations for his labour of love. From him I have lately received

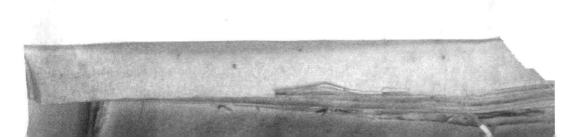

very gratifying accounts of the prosperity of the station, and
of the satisfaction he has had in his labours there. He has opened
a new school in a village, favourable in every respect in a Missionary point of view, a people of great simplicity of manners.
desirous of instruction, and well disposed to attend the house of
GOD. Its situation is favourable for frequent visitations, and is
properly under continual pastoral care. I have never been very
forward in establishing schools, though none can conceive them of
more importance than I do, but they are only important
when they are well conducted, and to have schools of this
description several things are necessary, which are not always
under our control: 1st. a people interested in the improvement
of their children, without which it is not easy to secure regular attendance; 2d. a suitable person as a teacher, in whom we
can place confidence, who has himself the confidence and good
will of the people; 3d. so situated that it may be often visited,
and, if possible, within such a distance of another school that, not
only they may be check upon each other, or move laudable e-
mulation, but also that two or more may be visited in the same
journey.

Acting from these views I have had applications from different
places for many months, and many journeys have been made by
those interested, before I have considered the people to feel sufficient interest in it to secure a regular attendance of their children at school, and their own with their children at public
worship. There are yet many important villages, quite unoccu-
pied, from which I have had petitions, but we have not strength to
attend to them, from their number, situation, and the excessive
difficulty of travelling in this fervid climate. It was my intention, had I not been called away, to have travelled for a fortnight into the interior, by means of the rivers, creeks, &c. as
I am told the country is, in one direction, very populous, even
to the Kandyan mountains. There is a situation, about 20 miles
up the Kalu Ganga, on an elevated country, in the neighbourhood
of populous villages, probably no bad situation for a Missionary;
from whence, in case of sickness, he might come down the river
to Caltura in 3 or 4 hours. There are a few nominal Christians
in that part of the country, but the great majority of the people are Budhuists. Brother Erskine represents both the schools and
congregations as in a prosperous state; the following extract from
a letter, dated October 10, will give a brief account of the state
of the circuit. " The congregations are large and many hear with
seemingly profound attention, and this evinced occasionally by
the falling tear! The largest Singhalese congregations I have seen
on the Island are those of Caltura, I mean regular and constant
hearers; at other places I have seen, now and again, large congregations; but here we have commonly from one to more than
two hundred men, women, and children. Let God be magnified!

The Portuguese and Singhalese classes are regular in their meet-

ings, and in their attendance; and I trust in this tried and blessed way, they will learn to know themselves as sinners, and that that knowledge will conduct them to the saving knowledge of God, their Saviour.

The schools, during the last quarter, have been all regularly and usefully visited: Brother Lalmont has visited them all, and many of them I have also seen, and had cause to rejoice in their order and in the progress of the children. The new school, in the village of Pallatotta, contains about 40 scholars, males and females. I have been there two Sabbaths, and preached to a tolerable large congregation of both adults and children. The 3d inst. Brother Lalmont preached at Kuca Payagilla school, and was quite delighted and encouraged with his prosperous excursion. Let us then be encouraged to look up and go forward, for our Jesus shall soon have the Heathen for his inheritance, and the uttermost parts of the earth for his possession. Hallelujah! You recollect the *promising Kandyan boy*, of your English school; you only can conceive how I was affected by his reply to me, a few a few days since, I was asking him some questions relative to God, &c. The poor boy said, "While in Kandy I did not know that there was a God." Ah! how such instances cry aloud for pity and for help in every possible way." The little Kandyan boy is the son of one of the late Kandyan chiefs, who was actively engaged in the disturbances which lately affected the interior. He is an affectionate little boy, to whom I am very much attached, in whose welfare I am much interested, and have a pleasing hope that he will live to experience the unspeakable blessings which the CHRISTIAN's GOD abundantly bestows on them that fear him. The English school referred to has been a blessing and will still be so: few things I have seen give me higher gratification than that school. It may with great propriety be called a church: many times a day are the praises of God, in various languages, sung in it, and several times a day fervent supplications ascend from it before the Throne of Grace. All the scholars in it learn English, while they cultivate, at the same time, their own languages. During the period the Singhalese is taught, the children who learn it retire to a little bungaloe, at the bottom of the garden, that there may be no confusion; and, having completed their task, they return to those who read English, Portuguese, and Dutch, in the English school. I had only a few copies of the *Tokens for Children*, which I gave to several of the children, they were so interested with that judicious work, that I could not forbear weeping that I had not more copies to give.

With respect to myself, I can truly say I never loved the work more; I have not been without a disposition to mourn that, for the least 12 months, I have been so peculiarly circumstanced, as to be so little settled in my regular work, the work which is the delight of my soul. Yet I do not murmur, I dare not chuse; let me live to serve my GOD below, and find my way to Heaven.

On the evening of July 31st I sailed from Colombo, bound for Trincomalie; but, from stress of weather, we were obliged to run to the northward, and after the most perilous and uncomfortable voyage I ever made, arrived at Jaffna, August 10th.

I have not often, even in my own station, been more gratified than I was in visiting the schools of Jaffna and Trincomalie: there are two of the Jaffna schools particularly, that possess every thing that can excite interest, and inspire pleasing anticipation. Brother Carver's native schools especially, considering peculiar difficulties, are very interesting. I shall not soon forget the feelings excited on entering one of them, wholly composed of Hindoo and Moor children. When Br. Carver left the school, the childrens' eyes were turned upon him with such expression as touched my heart most sensibly. Blessed are the angels of mercy engaged in so glorious a work! The work in Trincomalie labours under inconceivable disadvantages from want of a proper place of worship, without which, I conceive we cannot from the most zealous and prudent Missionary efforts anticipate any very extensive work there.

Being obliged to return by land, I went through that lonesome wilderness extending from Poneryn to Putlam, upwards of 120 miles, travelling in some instances for more than 26 miles without seeing a cottage. Near Putlam little villages appear, but no part appears populous till near Chilaw, which district J. Walbeoff, Esq. Collector, informed me, contained above 30,000 souls, as appeared by a late census. He observed, that the villages, in many places were so situated as to be very favourable for the establishment of schools, and he was particularly desirous that a Missionary should be stationed there; he added he had just received a Note from Brother Newstead, and should feel himself happy to render us all the help in his power. It appears a very important place, and is almost the extent of population northward on this side of the Island. It will probably appear a place worthy of attention as far as our means will allow.

> I am, very dear Brethren,
> Your's affectionately.
> W. BUCKLEY FOX.

~~~~~~~~~~~~~~~~~~~~~~~~~

THE GALLE STATION.

Galle, October 6th, 1819.

My dear Brethren,

I need not tell you that the revolving periods of time continue to increase our obligation to gratitude, I feel that every days exerience calls for yet louder songs of praise. O that my eyes may ever be open to behold, and my heart to feel the divine goodness!

At different times during the past quarter we have been visited by our Heavenly Father's chastising hand; first my dear partner was ill, then our little girl was much indisposed, and afterwards I was laid up; however, we see *mercy* through all our little afflictions, and believe that they are intended to answer the most valuable end. O that we may fully enjoy the sanctified use of them!

I am happy that our schools in general are in a prosperous state, all circumstances considered, for of late several things have operated against them, but particularly the different diseases which have so much prevailed throughout the country. While I was out on the circuit the last time, I was obliged to witness a most heart rending sight, having been called to see a poor little boy, belonging to our school at Hickody, dying of hydrophobia: when I went to the cottage of his mother, (for his father was dead,) I found him lying with his face to the ground; his mother spoke to him and informed him who had come to see him, and on hearing that the *Padré* was there, he made an effort to sit up, which he was able to do with his mother's assistance, when she took him on her lap, and with much affection endeavoured to comfort him; his head and face were much swollen, and he appeared greatly agitated, though quite sensible, for he knew every one about him. I felt so deeply affected that I couldnot remain long with him; however, after I left the garden, while I stood in the road speaking to the people on the great impropriety of allowing so many half starved dogs, having no owners, to run about the country, the poor little boy made his mother help him as far as the garden fence, that he might see me once more. I think he had some idea that I could do something towards saving his life, for he said, that if he only could be made well he would never be a day absent from the school, but alas! poor child, his case was far beyond the power of human skill! O how much I felt, no language can explain! after I left the place, he went into the house, lay down again with his face to the ground, and in less than an hour expired!

I sent his poor mother a little help, and paid the expences of his funeral, at which the boys of the school attended. This boy was an attentive, diligent scholar, and had made a considerable proficiency in English; and I know, from every thing that I have heard of him, that he did not receive Christian instruction in vain—when he was taken ill, his ignorant friends, according to their customs, brought their chains to tie upon him; but he expressed his disapprobation of them, by taking hold of them and throwing them from him: may not this be considered as an additional evidence of the good effects of our Schools. This boy took ill just thirty days after he was bitten, and died in twenty eight hours from the time of his becoming ill; it is wonderful that his brother who was bitten at the same time has escaped. The natives say that only the person whom the dog first bites will die! but this is certainly not according to reason.

During the greater part of the last quarter I have been highly fa-

voured with the acquaintance and society of Lieut. Col. Penson, of the
Bengal service, a gentleman of a most liberal mind and very enlightened views respecting the nature, necessity, and importance of Christian
Missions. He very kindly visited several of my schools, and was
greatly pleased to find that we had so many heathen children under
our care. Col. Penson met Br. Harvard at the Cape, and heard him
preach there; he is also acquainted with Brs. Shaw and Edwards,
and gives an interesting account of their Mission; a few days
ago he left the Island for Calcutta, before his departure he presented me with the liberal donation of *one hundred and fifty*
Rix Dollars towards the support of our Mission, and left the same
sum with me for the Church Missionary Society, Mr. Mayor
being in the country. Surely the Lord will bless such friends to
his cause among the poor Heathen.

How strange it is that so many of the *Pagans* of Ceylon should
be called *Christians!* a few weeks ago I was called to witness
a devil dance near this Cutcherry, in the garden of one of those
Christian pagans! being informed of the circumstance, I went to
the spot, and found the devil dancers hard at work in behalf
of a young man, who was laid on the ground, and near death.
I went over to him, but he could not speak; so as I saw plainly
that the poor fellow was just expiring, I talked to them on the
folly and wickedness of their conduct, in thus distressing the lad
who was just about to leave the world, but they would go on,
and the miserable sufferer died just when they had ended the ceremony! I called one of the capuas, or devil dancers, and asked
him if he and his companions had engaged to cure the man,
they said no. I then asked them why they attempt to deceive
the people, and so greatly to disturb the dying man? to this they
replied, that they were only doing as they had been desired by
his relations! The next morning the uncle of the deceased called
upon me, to express his sorrow for having had the ceremony,
and to tell me how the matter ended, when I endeavoured to
improve the circumstances of the case for his good.

I feel happy at having the society and help of Br. Allen; he
enters upon his Missionary work with all his heart, and has already made so great a progress in Portuguese, that on last Sunday night he read his first sermon in that language, with great
correctness, and with much satisfaction to the people; he appears
to have a good talent for languages, which is one of infinite
value to a Missionary in this country; he is young and possessed of
an excellent constitution, which appears to take well with the
climate; may he be spared long to be the messenger of light,
holiness, and peace, to the inhabitants of this land of *spiritual
desolation!* The building work of our Chapel is now nearly done,
and all the timbers for the roof will be ready in a few days, so
that it will be covered in before the end of this month, if the
weather be fine.

I bless God for the continued comforts of his grace, for without this how difficult would be the way; but with his favour,

the renewing influences of his Spirit, and an increasing hope of
eternal life through the Gospel, all is well; and that you may
all richly enjoy these blessings is the very ardent desire of, my
dear Brethren,

Your affectionate Brother,
JOHN M'KENNY.

THE MATURA STATION.

Matura, 29th September, 1819.

VERY DEAR BRETHREN,

I review the events of the past quarter with sentiments of fervent gratitude to the Father of Mercies. My health, I am thankful to say, has not been very materially affected; though, in this
neighbourhood, affliction and mortality continue to prevail, yet the
necessity of caution and the nearness of eternity have often been
suggested by the unfavourable season, and the attention I have
bestowed on the work before us.

We are not without instances of the power of God to change
and renew the heart; divine truth is gradually extending its influence, and a deeper attention to divine things is perceptible. I
lately asked one of our Singhalese school masters if he expected
to know his sins forgiven. His reply was as gratifying as it was
unexpected. I have received that blessing, said he; I prayed and
prayed till I felt my sin go away, and I was made happy. Our
Portuguese congregation was never more regular and attentive.
We find St. Matthew's Gospel and the little Hymn Book a considerable help, and the greater part can join in singing a few of
our plain tunes. Four or five of the Dutch and Portuguese youths
have met in class some time, and give every evidence of being
in earnest.

Our country-schools have been visited on the week-days, and
on the Sabbath have been supplied pretty regularly with preaching. As I do not preach in English now, six or eight services are
held in the forenoon. The adult attendance is casual, but from
the deep attention of some I trust the word is not forgotten.
Though there is seldom that sweetness in speaking by interpretation to a thoughtless people, that one enjoys in preaching to
a sensible, serious congregation in English, I frequently feel considerable pleasure and enlargement.

On the anniversary of the Colombo Bible Society we re-opened
the school of Karawe, which for some time had been discontinued.
I preached on 2 Tim. iii. 15, and also noticed what is doing to
spread the knowledge of God throughout the world. I shall not
soon forget the following. As I was preaching there stood in the
door-way a little Singhalese boy, his attention appeared to be
strongly fixed. His father with a child in his arms stood near
him, and going away told the boy to follow him. He looked

round as if very unwilling to go, and stood gazing some minutes longer, when he ran off to overtake his father. In this village the Cholera has been fatal to so many, as to induce part of the people to abandon their dwellings. A company of Budhuist priests, at present residing there, are active in enticing the boys to learn of them; so that the number will not be great, I fear, while there causes operate. Six girls are taught by the master's wife to make lace.

Since I begun this letter I have opened a second school at Dounder. The Modeliar of the corle may be considered its patron: and it is gratifying to see a chief of his influence and intelligence so ready to promote the welfare of the people under his jurisdiction. We took down the names of about 70 fine boys, few of whom bear the Christian name, and scarce any of them can read; but the master had previously taught the alphabet to about 20. About 50 adults were present, and I have seldom seen a Singhalese congregation so very attentive.

There is no people in whose welfare I feel a deeper interest than in that of the elder school boys, who for some time past have been able to read and write, and whose understandings are somewhat cultivated. One of them having drawn on the back of a school-class-paper the signs of the Zodiac, as laid down by the Singhalese astronomers, I requested him to draw a fair one, which I promised to send to England. In a few days he brought me the picture. The figures are in general proportioned, and neatly coloured. Another boy belonging to a school near Belligam pointed out a passage in Mr. Wood's Catechism, relating to the doctrine of the Trinity, which he could not fully comprehend. I am always pleased with enquiries after truth; and I felt much pleasure in satisfying him.

Principally for the improvement of the elder boys I have coloured and finished the map of the world on the school-wall, which I mentioned on a former occasion. Every body knows that the fabric of heathenism is chiefly supported by a false philosophy; and to complete the outline of geography, I have had a frame made for a globe, nine inches diameter, which was turned for the purpose long since, and though I cannot spare time at present to map it, I find it of great use in explaining, among other points of importance the true shape of the earth, and the cause of day and night. The map is drawn on a scale of six feet diamete, and does not look amiss; and I find it has excited some notice among the people. I told a Singhalese whom I observed looking on it very earnestly, that it was a picture of the world, that the painted part represented land, and the rest water; and requested him to try if he could find Ceylon. He first pitched on New Holland, and then the whole continent of Asia. Some small boys who can hardly reach higher than Ceylon, have obscured it repeatedly by pointing it out with their finger, I have been frequently amazed by enquiries and observations on this subject. As I was drawing the Islands of the South Sea, an ingenuous Portuguese boy asked me if they were meant for houses!

On finding himself wrong he conjectured they were stars!
The ignorance of remote descendants of Europeans is sometimes
surprising. I have been asked, for example, such questions as
"Which is the larger place, London, or Europe." To our schoolmasters also I give, by this means, some instructions on several
subjects; and I am glad to hear them enquire for Britain, Holland, and Portugal, and the way to sail or travel to Europe; and
for the marvelous whirlpools which are talked of among the people! It will be very easy to sketch the Solar System, and a few
of the plainer problems of Geometry.

This quarter I have been able to complete the translation into
Singhalese of an Abridgment of Entick's Dictionary. I have been
zealously assisted, particularly by Don Nicolas, whose services
have been afforded me by an arrangement with Br. M'Kenny.
The interesting and indefatigable labour of this young man has
formed a contract to the indolence, rapacity and ingratitude which
is so common; generally from seven in the morning till ten at
night he adhered to the work till it was finished. I hope no
apology is necessary for varying a little from the worthy author
and his reverend abridger, in rendering a few words of a certain
class: for what is the use of building error on error, and publishing false definition beyond the seas, where they are not likely
to be corrected? For example, the word *fanatic* is rendered by
my author, a wild pretender to religion, a *Methodist*. The first
term and the last convey ideas diametrically opposite. *Heresy*
is called a *fundamental error* in religion! *Conventicle, or Meeting-
house*, a secret assembly. In rendering words of this stamp, which
are purposely perverted to convey scorn or reprobation by the
lump, without any precise idea, it is better to be guided by their
true meaning. And as candour and good sense have not so far
operated as to keep such terms within their lawful boundary, I
would, by the way, recommend with Mr. Foster, in his excellent
Essay on the Romantic, that when a person employs an epithet
of this sort by way of reproach, he be requested to define its
meaning before any discussion be allowed to go on. Perhaps in
nine cases out of ten those who use them most would be in the
situation of the Athenian Sophists, when desired by Socrates to
explain themselves; since under the ambiguity of common language they had long sheltered their absurdities.

I have been at a loss for the reason of perpetuating so absurd
a practice as mixing the words beginning with I, and J, and also
those beginning with U and V. It certainly creates a good deal
of inconvenience, and I do not know that it has a single advantage. I believe I am singular in placing them in separate
lists.

From the counterpart of this work I have extracted the Singhalese primitive words, and arranged them by the parts of speech.
The first list contains animate nouns, the language in use just
after the creation—the second inanimate, the third abstract, their
adjectives and the other classes. They are parallelled by synony-

mous words and by English. By this plan the language is exhibited in a narrow compass.

My assistants have translatnd into Portuguese that admirable compendium of the Verites of Revelation, the Scripture Extracts, and have made a beginning with the Parables and Miracles. So far as the former is revised and copied, it conveys the meaning with perspicuity and force.

[I am pleased with literary efforts however humble. But this is not the time of day to expect, in these regions, much elevation of thought or richness of fancy. Illustrations are not uncommon of the propriety of the observations in the 60th and following numbers of the Spectator, relative to the efforts of industry to supply the wants genius. The fancy of doing without a particular letter in composing a set of rhymes has, I understand, prevailed among the Eastern poets of repute. It was mentioned to me lately, as a memorable display of talents, that a priest, remarkable for his learning, had composed a poem which could be read, I know not how many ways without changing the meaning. The following is a copy of a paper sent me some time ago. The original is written in an unusual manner, and embellished with stars, crosses, and figures, capital and italic letters, having a symbolical meaning, which is explained at large in notes. The whole must have cost the writer incredible labour.

Lamentation.

Oh woful day for birth the seventh day of January,
Goddess Charlott' departed in youth: old deer loiters depress'd in flurry.

Prayer.

Fall in but soon on me, oh Charlotte human last humane event,
Look pious at, I am also one of January the seventh.

Axiom.

Come soon to me thou gracious death—Ay it is but surely better,
The soul goes upward body beneath- mind the former not the latter.

Conclusion.

Happy tune { God bless and save the King, Defender of the Faith, Whole world and every thing Depending of his aid. } of Triumph

The whole is indorsed—*a couple of Arithmetical Poems, the first product of that science in Ceylon.*

I may just observe in conclusion, that the writer is an ecclesiastic, and in sense above mediocrity. We may learn at least what a figure tolerable abilities is apt to make in versification in a language which to the writer is not vernacular.]

I remain,

Very affectionately yours,
JOHN CALLAWAY.

THE JAFFNA STATION.

Jaffna, September 29th, 1819.

My dear Brethren,

Every thing which relates to the establishment and extension of the Redeemer's kingdom, must at all times be peculiarly interesting to us. To extend the knowledge of salvation, we have forsaken our fathers' house and left our native land, and when we hear that our labours are not in vain, it fills our heart with joy and gladness. How pleasing is it to observe with what rapidity light is spreading! Our eyes have already seen, and our ears have heard, what at the commencement of our Mission could not have been rationally anticipated in double the time. Let us, then, thank God and take courage

On this Station the hand of the Lord has been with us, he has crowned our labours with success, and many have been turned unto God.

A few months ago our schools were almost wholly destroyed in consequence of the dreadful ravages occasioned by the Spasmodic Cholera; most of them, however, have begun to lift up their heads, and some are in a more flourishing condition than ever. With four that are nearly ready to be opened we have now fifteen in this Circuit. Our labour in every department of our work is increasing; but God is with us, and he makes our consolations to abound. I was much gratified to hear lately that at the Tettar-teru School, several of the boys began talking to a Caffre man about his soul. They told him he must worship the true God or he could not be saved. He asked them who was the true God, whether they called those things which they worshipped, which were made of gold, and brass, &c. Gods? The boys said no:—these things cannot save us. We go to the temples because our parents make us go: but since we have been taught in this school we worship only the true God who made all things, &c. &c. The Caffre is now a constant attendant on our preaching, and I believe there is a work of grace upon his heart. He has requested me to baptise him; but I have thought it better for him to remain a little longer under Christian instruction; he appears to me to be seeking God with the utmost earnestness, and I have no doubt but he will become an ornament to the Christian cause.

Another circumstance of a very gratifying nature occurred lately. A little girl, twelve years of age, who has always regularly attended our preaching, was taken ill. She began to be apprehensive that she should not recover, and thought she was not prepared to die, this fear increased, till she became greatly distressed. In her agony she cried unto God, until he turned her sorrow into joy, and she was filled with peace and joy through believing. I visited her, in her illness and found her exceedingly happy in God. She has since recovered, and now meets very regularly in class. There are several other children in the house where she lives, and they frequently have prayer meetings together.

The following is part of a conversation I lately had with a Native young man:

Do you ever pray? Yes.

What do you pray for? To have my heart ful'y renewed and to be make like Jesus Christ.

Do you know that you are a sinner? Yes, I know that my heart is sinful, and that I have been sinful also in my actions.

Do you think that God is willing to pardon your sins? Yes, I believe he has pardoned me.

What makes you think so? Sometime ago I was in great distress, and was afraid that I should go to hell; I prayed very earnestly to God to have mercy upon me, and while I was praying I was made very happy, and now whenever I pray I always find great delight in it. He said many things more which was equally gratifying, and that with such feeling as fully convinced me that he was truly converted to God. He is now in our place as an exhorter, and is very active and zealous.

Our congregations in Jaffna are uniformly large, but are neither on the increase nor decrease. In the country more adults begin to attend our preaching, and what is rather a novel circumstance among the Malabars, women come to hear. It would, I am sure, be gratifying to any of our Brethren to go though this extensive Circuit, and see the pleasing openings which are before us. God be praised.

In one of my late tours, I got to a place where it appeared no Missionary, either Protestant or Roman Catholic, had ever been before. The natives looked at me with the utmost surprise, and when I began to address them in their own language their astonishment increased. While speaking to them I was repeatedly interrupted by such questions as these, Where is God? How can we know that he hears us if we pray to him? How can we find him out? &c. &c. I answered most of their questions, and they appeared to be highly gratified.

We are truly thankful for the accession we have received to our strength. We shall now be able to attend to our work better, but we have not yet sufficient strength to enlarge our borders. Br. Bott has entered into his work with all his heart and soul. He labours, preaches, and studies like a man, and I think he will in a very little time be able to do something at the languages. Br. Roberts has not yet entered on his labours. The Bungaloe at Point Pedro is repairing, and I suppose in another week will be ready to receive him. In the mean time he, and his excellent wife, are remaining with us at Jaffna.

We have been much delighted by a visit from our dear Br Fox. He remained with us a short time, and had an opportunity of rejoicing to see what God was doing among us. I believe he will not regret coming to see us, when he knows that his visit has been the means of strengthening our hands, and of encouraging us in our work.

You have heard of our District Meeting. We shall not soon forget it. The utmost harmony and love prevailed from the be-

ginning to the end, so that there was not a single (I shall not say disputed) but to my remembrance not a contradictory word spoken. We were united as the heart of one man. "Behold how good and pleasant it is for Brethren to dwell together in unity."

Our young man's class begins now to be rather small, as many of them are dispersed abroad. But it is matter of rejoicing that from all of them we hear the best tidings. Br. Lynch has one at Madras, (Theodorus) who appears to be very useful. Two are with Br. Carver, and one of them is likely to become an assistant Missionary; two are at Batticaloa, one went with Br. Osborne and of the other Br. O. writes very favourably. Thus are our young men scattering abroad, and I trust that in every place they will cause their light to shine, and by their example and conversation spread the knowledge of truth to all around.

I am, very dear Brethren,
Most affectionately yours,
T. H. SQUANCE.

THE TRINCOMALIE STATION.

Trincomalie, October 15, 1819.

VERY DEAR BRETHREN,

Nothing but absence from the Station would have prevented me from communicating in due time the little which we have to say concerning the work here: but perhaps I may be in time to occupy a page in the Miscellanea.

The arrival at this port of three of our dear Brethren, and Sister Roberts, has enlivened this quarter to us; as well with their encouraging presence, as the numerous tokens of *undiminished* regard, which they brought with them from our beloved friends in England. The Brethren, Roberts, Stead and Bott, landed in good health on the 10th of July, but our dear Sister Roberts had suffered greatly during the voyage, and came on shore much reduced and very weak. However, by a few days' refreshment on shore, after so long a confinement on ship board, and the blessing of Him, who crowned their voyage with tender mercies, she found herself much recovered. The Mission House being small, and undergoing repair, and partly without roof, laid us under the necessity of troubling our friends for accommodations for, at least, our Brother and Sister; while the young men put up with what we could provide for them. It is a work of respect and gratitude, which ought to be paid, to say, that the Lady, at whose house they remained, left her own bed to accommodate our dear Sister in her very weak condition, and when we are not at liberty to record the names of our friends who manifest hospitality towards us, we wish to remember our obligations.

I may also take the liberty, at this time, to mention the great pleasure which I had in observing the generosity and kind disposition of Captain Buckham, on several occasions after he had

2 L

landed our Brethren from the Bristol, at this place. And although I was prevented, during his stay here, from making a suitable ac-acknowledgement for some particular acts of kindness, yet I think it my duty to mention my sentiments of esteem and gratitude, that, should he touch at any port on this Island, on his return to England, the Brother resident there may oblige me by conveying these sentiments to him.

Our congregations, in English, which are not very large, were benefited by the spiritual and earnest discourses delivered by the Brethren before their departure to Jaffna: where the District Meeting was held, and is it to be hoped their labours, during the short time they were here, will appear not to have been in vain. Of that meeting and the appointment of the Brethren you are acquainted. Let us unite in prayer to the *God of Missions*, that the seasonable help afforded us, may enable us to accomplish a greater measure of good among the poor perishing heathen—perishing awfully for lack of knowledge.

Brother Stead being appointed to assist on this Station, where thousands are living without the true knowledge of God, we hope together to go forth, according to the example given us, to endeavour to seek, and bring to the knowledge of salvation, those that are lost. May the Lord help us!—in weakness become our strength —give to us the spirit of wisdom and grace—and lead us into paths of useful devotion to his cause!

We were favoured also with a visit by Br Fox, which we hope was mutually beneficial. He preached in English and Portuguese to attentive congregations: and had an opportunity of seeing some of our first efforts at Native Schools, at which he expressed delight and satisfaction. The two Native Schools appear very encouraging, and we trust by the blessing of God they will increase in number and value: already, we have nearly one hundred in the larger, and between 60 and 70 in the smaller: and the school at the Mission House becomes daily more and more pleasing.

Our Preaching, Class Meeting, &c. have been much as last quarter, except, towards the latter end of this, when we have had a declension. We hope, however, by a steady adherence to our duty, to discipline and order, to build up, by the blessing of God, our waste places.

A Missionary life, you are well acquainted, is a life of devotion to an *object* without a parallel; and though the cup is mixed with sweets and bitters, joys and sorrows, pleasures and pains, yet, thanks be unto God! the first infinitely outweigh the last. And whenever our peculiar situation becomes such, as that we can better understand what the Apostle meant by being "killed all the day long," for Christ's sake, yet will the Lord encourage us by his word of promise, "*as thy days so shall thy strength be.*"

Aware of the danger of being so late with these brief remarks I must conclude. Br. Stead joins me in affectionate regards to every one of you.

I am, dear Brethren,
Most affectionately,
ROBERT CARVER.

Miscellaneous.

No. I.

(Continued from page 72.)

40. පදවිතිහාරජාතක, *Padaveetihaarajaataka*, this book is in the Singhalese language in one large volume, but I think it is contained in the පන්සියපනාජ්ජතකපොත *Panseeyapa-naajaatukapota*, as given in the beginning of the Catalogue, in which case there are two copies of *this* ජාතක *jaatnka*. It would would be out of place to give any explanation of this book here, as it would be necessary at the same time to explain the whole of the jaatakas.

The design of the writer appears to have been to convince men that sin is culpable, whether outwardly committed in the life or only conceived in the mind, at the same time to give a regular system of laws for the proper control of both the thoughts and actions of men; පද *pada* feet, විතිහාර *veetehaara* steps, ජාතක *jaataka* birth. For instance, this book observes that if a man form an idea of robbing another, and move his *foot*, and take one *step* with that design, it is the same as committing the robbery and constitues the man a thief. Such is the spirit and design of this work.

41. මහඅනාගතවංසය *Maha-anaagatawansaya*, this book comprises one large volume, and is also in the Singhalese language. It is composed throughout in the style of prophecy, and is supposed to give an exact history of the Transmigrations of the Budhus who are yet expected to be born in this world. That is to say, at the end of the කලියුග *kaleeyooga*, or the sinful age. The nature of the work is seen in its title, මහ *maha*, great or chief, අනාගත *anaagata*, future or futurity, වංස *seed*, race, *decent* or *lineage*, which words, when compounded gives the meaning as above.

42. දහමිසරණපොත *Dahamsaranapota*, දහම් *daham* Scripture, (commonly called, both by the Natives and Europeans *Bana*,) සරණ *sarana*, help, favour, or happiness, පොත *pota*, book; literally the happiness of those who read, and study the Scriptures or Bana of Budhu. The volume is large, and contains a great deal of interesting matter, consisting principally of proverbs and parables, which are given in that peculiarly insinuating style for which the Singhalese books are so remarkable. It was writ-

ten in the Singhalese language by a learned priest, named ⓔⓣⓞⓖⓐⓜⓤⓦ *tolagamoowa*, who lived in the Galle district about the time, or a little before the Portuguese visited this Island.

43. බ්‍රහ්මජාලසූත්‍රසන්නේ   *Brahmajaalasootrasanne*, from බ්‍රහ්ම *brahma*, divine illumination, (commonly rendered faith) ජාල *jaala*, net, සූත්‍ර *sootra*, things heard, සන්නේ *sanne*, translation. This is a large volume which was originally written in Pali, afterwards translated into Singhalese, and a commentary added to it by a learned Priest of this Island, and which gives the history of 73 different Religions, or modes of faith as they existed at the time in which *Goutama* made his appearance in the මනුෂ්‍යලෝකය *manusyalokaya*, or world of men.

44 පූජාවලිය *Poojaawaleya*, offerings. This book was published by a Singhalese Priest not more than 4 or 500 years ago. It is a compilation from a number of Pali and Singhalese books. The subject upon which it principally treats is, a description of the various kinds of offerings made to Budhu by the people while he was in the world, with their consequent blessings. The style of the language being so modern, it is of consequence properly adapted to the capacities of the lowest classes of the people; yet it is authorized and read in the temples. It is sometimes called by the Priests මෝඩයාපනීපොත *modegayneepolu*, literally the foolish, or simple woman's book.

45. සංස්කෘතඅක්‍ෂරාදිය *Sangaskrita aksaraadeya*, a Sangscrit Dictionary parallelled with Singhalese words.

46. සාලෙය්‍යසූත්‍රසන්න *Saaleysyasootrasanne*, සාලෙය්‍ය *saaleysya*, villagers, සූත්‍ර *sootra*, things heard, සන්නේ *sanne*, translation. When *Goutama* was in this world, and travelling in that part of *Jambuddweepa* near Benares, the people flocked from all quarters to hear his sermons, and to get instructions on religious subjects. One of Budhu's usual ways of instructing the people was, to answer every kind of question which he allowed the people to ask him, and while in these parts the people put to him questions of all kinds, pertaining to religious devotion, and this book contains Budhu's answers. The work is in the Pali language, and consists of a considerable number of large volumes, but how many I can hardly say. In the original work there are not less than 17,575 of *Goutamas declarations*, but the volume in our library has only *one* of these සූත්‍ර *sootra* or *declarations* in it, and which fills 100 pages of the පුස්කොල *puskola* or talipot. It is generally supposed that there is not a difficulty in the whole circle of the science of divinity which is not satisfactorily solved in this voluminous book.

47. එලුඅක්‍ෂරාදිය *Eloonksaraadeya*, an Eloo Dictionary with Singhalese parallelled; a good work which I always keep on my table and make use of. It is not very large. There are 3 copies of this work in the Library.

48. ගෙබින්ශාය්‍රය *Gaybinsāstraya*, from ගෙ *gay* house, බින් *bin* ground, ශාය්‍රය *sās!raya*, science; an interesting little work on eastern architecture.

49. සිඟාලොවාදසූත්‍රසන්නෙ *Singālowādasootrasanne*, සිඟාල *singāla*, a person of that name, ඔවාද *owādu* advice, සූත්‍ර *sootra* heard, සන්නේ *sanne* interpreted. In one of Gautama's journeys in රාජගෘහපූරප්‍රවරය *Rājagrahapoorapra-waraya* in මධ්‍යදෙසය *madhadeseya*, he fell in with a certain rich husbandman at a river, bathing and performing his නමස්කාර *namaskāra*, or salutation to the four quarters of the heavens. Budhu, when he came up, asked him what he was doing; the man replied, he was performing his religious devotions. Budhu again asked why he did this; because, said the man, my parents commanded me to do it before their death. Said Budhu again, did they order you to worship in that form? Yes, replied the man. No, said Budhu, they did not, and then began and told him all that his parents had ordered him to do, and instead of making only four නමස්කාර *namaskāra* he was to make six, which Budhu then explained, but impressed particularly on his mind, that right religion was not so much a mere outward performance, but it was the cleansing of the heart; and the ideas which the man had formed of bathing, as a religious rite, were altogether erroneous; that bathing was not the washing of the body only, but was designed to purify the heart. After a multitude of instructions to this purport Gautama gave the man 14 commands, 10 of which concerned all men, but 4 were to be of a more private interpretation, and these 10 commandments are the same which are taught to this day by the Priests of Budhu in Ceylon. I have been a little more particular in mentioning this book, as it contains the legislation of the Budhuist, and gives an history of its origin. The Book was originally written in Pali, but afterwards translated into Singhalese.

50. ස(.සඃකෘතඅක්ෂරාඃදිය *Sangiskreta-akksarādeya*, another Sangiskrit Dictionary, with a Singhalese interpretation.

The books that now follow contain the system of instruction as given to the youths in Ceylon in the පන්ශල් *punsal*, or native schools, the whole of which I have collected myself, and have had a fair copy made out and most elegantly written. I put them in this part of the library to fill up a place out of which a number of Mr. Tolfrey's books had been taken, before I purchased it.

51. Contains several smaller books; the first of which is, the නම්පොත *nampota* or book of names, and is put into the hands of Scholars after they have properly learned the alphabet.

2 M

The names in this book are the names of a number of the ෙව ෙතර *wehera*, or places of worship in Ceylon. Secondly මගුල් ලකුණ *magoollakoona*, that is the marks in the soles of the feet of Budhu. This book contains an account of those significant marks which are exclusively confined to Budhu's feet, they are in the whole 116. Thirdly ගනෙදවිහාෙල්ල *Ganadevehélla* or the history of the birth, &c. of the God of that name. Fourthly ෙදන්කවිෙපාත *wadankawipota*, literally the book of poems, which are songs of thanksgiving to Budhu, from වදන් *wadan* words, කවි *kawe* poem, ෙපාත *pota* book. Fifth බුඩහගජ්ජය *budhagarjaya*, this book is in Sangskrit. The title of the book means the voice of praise to Budhu. Sixth සකස්කෘඩ *sakaskaoa*, this is also a Sangskrit book, and contains orations in prose, in honor of Budhu. Seventh නාමාෂ්ටකය *namastakaya*, the eight names, a title given by way of eminence to eight poems, composed on a particular occasion in honor of Budhu. This book is both in Sangskrit and Singhalese.

52. This book is in two parts, the first is, නවරත්නය *nawaratnaya*, literally the nine excellent or precious things; from නව *nawa*, nine, රත්නය *ratnaya*, any precious thing. This is perhaps one of the best moral books we can find in Ceylon. It is written in Sangskrit, but a Singhalese translation and commentary accompanies it. The history of the book is this: a certain king named විකුමාදිත්ය *wikramādilya*, one of the eastern monarchs who reigned about 800 years ago, had attached to his court nine wise men named, ධන්වන්තෙරෙ *dhanwanteree*, කෂපනක *kshapanaka*, අමරසින්හ *amarasingha*, ෙවතාල *waylāla*, භෂ්ලඝට *bhashlughata*, කප්පර *karpparu*, කාෙලදැව *kāledāwa*, ඛ්යාෙතා *khyāto*, වරහමිෙර *warahamehera*. These names will be known as persons who have distinguished themselves in oriental literature. It would be out of order to give their history in this place. The king in question commanded them each to make choice of some moral subject, as a kind of theme, and at a set time to submit to him nine poems written on these subjects. This they accomplished to the great satisfaction of the king, and this book contains these nine celebrated poems which are put into the hands of the Singhalese youth. The second book in this volume is ව්යාසකාරය *wyāsakāraya*, ව්යාෙසන *wyāsena*, the name of a celebrated Sangskrit author. who wrote this book, and which also is in the highest repute among the eastern literati. The book bears marks of great antiquity, at least 2000 years. The original work is in Sangskrit, and con-

tains about 1000 poems on various moral subjects, but only about 100 have been translated into Singhalese, which are in this volume.

53. අනුරුධසතකය *Anuroodhasatakaya*, අනුරුධ *Anu-roodha* appears to have been a Brahmin and probably lived in Ceylon, though it is uncertain. He became, however, a convert to the faith of Budhu, and afterwards wrote this සතකය *Satakaya* which is also a classical work of great merit, and contains 100 poems of praise and thanksgivings, addressed to Budhu.

54. බෞධසතකය *Bawdhasatakaya*, also a converted Brahmin, who wrote this book of poems in honor of the ත්‍රිවිධ රත්නය *Treewedharatnaya*, the excellent Trinity, namely Budhu, his Sermons, and the Priests; it is much in the same style as the former.

55. වෘත්තමාලේ *Werttamāle*, this book is in pure Pali, and is, I believe, almost the only book of poems in that language that is used in the course of education. The design of it, as far as I can learn is to initiate the pupils into the complete art of making poems. Such as adjusting the length of feet, and managing the cadence of the voice, &c. There are a number of books of the same kind in Sangskrit.

56. වෘත්තමාලඛ්‍යාව *Wertthamāla - ākheyāwa*, This is a book much in the same style as the former, only it is in Sangskrit, with a Singhalese translation accompanying it.

57. සූර්‍යසතකය *Sooryasatakaya*, this is a celebrated poetical work, which was written originally in Sangskrit by one පාඨසෝධන *Pāthasodhana*, but has since been translated into Singhalese, and also a commentary added. The poems appear to have been addressed to the Sun, in which, by the highest figurative language, he is compared to Budhu, who has always been considered as the friend and enlightener of men. The title of the book is from සූර්‍ය *sooryu* sun, සතකය *satakaya*, an hundred: that is, 100 poems addressed to the sun.

58. අමරසිංහය *Amarasinghaya*, one of the most celebrated *Sangiskrit* Lexicographers, that ever lived. There is something remarkable in the name of this oriental sage. අමර *amara*, immortal, සිංහය *sinhaya* lion, his family name, literally the *immortal lion*. This celebrated author was, as we have noticed under No. 52, attached to the court of වික්‍රමාදිත්‍ය *Vekramāditya*, and is generally acknowledged, I believe, to have been a follower of the sect of Budhu, and this opinion seems strengthened by the circumstance of his prefixing to his work two *slokas*, or poems, in praise of the greatness and excellence of Budhu. *Amara's* Dictionary has been translated into almost every language in the east that has the least connection with Sangskrit, and is generally esteemed, both by the Natives and Europeans, as

the most correct standard of the Sangskrit language. It was the custom with all ancient oriental writers to write on every subjects in metre, hence *Amarasingha* is in poetry, and contains about 1500 *slokas* or poems. We have, in the library, two copies of this work. The No. 58 is the dictionary only in Sangskrit, and is a pretty large volume of about 120 pages. In this form it is first put into the hands of Singhalese pupils in the temples. But in Nos. 59 and 60, is the same work with a Singhalese commentary, written by one of the literati of this island. This commentary is so copious, as to increase the size of the work to two large volumes of 330 pages each, of the largest kind of *puskola*. The language of this Singhalese commentary is so very high, as to be intelligible to a very few of the readers of the work. The copy in question I have had it copied by a Singhalese man from one which was in Mr. Tolfrey's library, but of which we were not quite certain whether it was not the property of Government. This book copying cost me nearly 100 Rds. or 7 £. this will give an idea what it would have cost the Mission, in *money* only, to collect such a Library as we now possess.

This class of books, from No. 50. ends the course of reading as taught in the Singhalese temples; and it is indispensably necessary for a youth, previous to his entering upon the regular study of the scientific works, to make himself well acquainted with these books. For before he can make much proficiency in the sciences he must have a pretty good knowledge of Sangskrit, Pali, and Eloo, besides his mother tongue, as all their regular classic works are in the three former languages.

61. එළුඅකුරාදය *Elooaksaradaya,* an Eloo Dictionary, with a Singhalese interpratation.

62. ජනවංසය *Janawansaya,* ජන *jana* people, වංසය *wangsaya,* families or tribes. That is the history of all the tribes or kinds of people in this world. This is estimated among the learned in Ceylon as an excellent work. The language is a very pure Singhalese.

63. වෛද්‍යඅකුරාදෙය *Waidheya aksaradeya,* that is a dictionary of the names of *trees, plants,* and *medicine.* The work is in Sangskrit and Singhalese, and could any one bestow time sufficient to translate it into English it would be doing a good work indeed. It is a task which I have certainly assigned to myself, should no one undertake it before, when I have a little time to spare.

64. ආඛ්‍යාතපදය *Aakhyatapadaya,* a Pali grammar with a Singhalese explanation, I am sorry to see the work is imperfect.

65. ආඛ්‍යාතපදය *Aakhyatapadaya,* this is another grammar of the same kind as the last number, only by a different author.

66. අඛ්‍යාතපදය *Akhyatapadaya,* the same by another author.

67. එළුඅක්ෂරාදිය *Elooaksarādeya,* an Eloo dictionary with a Singhalese explanation.

68. ලොකඋපකාරය *Lokaūpakāraya,* that is the world's help, from ලොක *loka* world, උපකාරය *ūpakāraya,* help. This work is in Singhalese, and is said to describe the good and evil qualities of men, and offers a variety of advices and warnings to each class of people, in the forms of proverbs.

69. ගිරාසන්දෙසය *Geerāsandesaya,* that is, the fable of the Parrot. ගිරා *geerä* parrot, සන්දෙසය *sandesaya* fable, a certain priest called තොටගමුව *totagamuwa,* who has been mentioned before, as the author of the පුජාවලිය *poojawaleya,* wrote a letter, containing a poem, to a distant temple, and sent this parrot to the person to whom it was directed. The parrot executed this charge faithfully, returned to his master, and gave an account of his whole adventure, upon which his master published it.

70. නාමවරනැගිල්ල *Nāmawaranegilla,* a work on the declension of Pali nouns.

71. රුවන්මල්නිසඬව *Roowanmalneghandowa,* the golden flower vocabulary, from රුවන් *roowan* gold, මල් *mal* flower, නිසඬව *neghandoowa* vocabulary, I have not had time to look much into this book, but should suppose, from its title, it is good work. The vocabulary is in Eloo, the explanation in Singhalese.

72. ලොවැඩසඟ්රහය *Lowedesanggrahaya,* a very good Singhalese book; it contains, as is seen in the title, advice published to the world. It is said to have been written by one of the disciples of the famed තොටගමුව *totagamoowa,* called විදාගමතෙරුනාන්සේ *veeägamateroonnänse.*

73. සිදත්සඟරාව *Sedatsangarāwa,* instructions in the Eloo language, and written in Singhalese. I have a good translation of this book into English.

74. 75. නැකැත්පොත *Neketpota,* both these books are on astrological subjects, and are carefully studied by all the common fortune-tellers who swarm in this country, and who are consulted on every occasion in life by all classes of natives. Every Missionary should read these books for the purpose of refuting that most pernicious principle, that the stars have an influence on the most minute, as well as the most important events in life, for with the Singhalese නක්ෂාස්ත්‍ර *naksästre,* or the influence of the stars, is Providence.

76. සුභසූත්‍රය *Subasootraya,* සුභ *Suba* the name of a certain Brahmin, සූත්‍ර *sootra* heard, a book containing some particular discoveries which Budhu made to this *subhu.*

77. සොළොස්ස්වප්නයන් *Solosswapnayan,* සොලොස් *solos* sixteen, ස්වප්නයන් *swapnayan* dreams, namely the sixteen dreams of a certain king called කොසල් *kosul.* This king dreamed 16 dreams which had an extraordinary effect upon his mind; and when the wise men of his court came to him to enquire after his welfare they found him in great fear and distress concerning them. This book therefore, gives an account of the discoveries he made to his Brahmins, with their interpretations, and directions with reference thereto, the whole of which proved abortive, but upon the king waiting upon Budhu, he received from him a faithful interpretation of the whole, with suitable advice on the subjects.

78. නැකත්පොත *Neketpota,* another work on Astrology in Singhalese.

79. දසරාජධර්ම්මය *Dasarājadharmmaya,* namely ten directions on advices addressed to kings by *Budhu Goutama.* Apparently an interesting work.

80. ලීත *Leeta,* Almanack, a Singhalese Almanack.

81. යාදින්න *Yādinna,* that is prayer, a collection of prayers, principally for the use of the Cappoas, and addressed to the gods, goddesses, and demons whom they are accustomed to invoke in their diabolical ceremonies.

82. දෛවඥමුඛමණ්ඩනය *Daiwangyamokhamandanaya* a very excellent work on Astronomy, as studied in the East; it is in the Sangskrit language.

83. සසනවන්සය *Sesanawansaya,* a work in Pali, giving the history of the government of the city of අමරපුර *amarapoora,* which is equivalent to the reign of Budhuism in that country, properly *the happy reign.*

84. ධාතුපාඨය *Dhātoopāthaya,* a very excellent little work on the derivation of Pali words, from ධාතු *thāto* root, පාඨය *pāthaya,* verse or section.

85 සුභාසිතය *Soobāsateya,* from සු *soo* good, භාසිතය *bhāseteya* speech, good speech, a collection of striking and appropriate proverbs and short instructions in the Eloo language.

This ends the account of the ola books, contained in Mr. Tolfrey's library. I had intended giving some account of the manuscript works which that Gentleman left behind him, but after looking over them all, carefully I think it would be an unnecessary task. Not one of the plans which Mr. Tolfrey commenced had been finished. The principal work in manuscript, is one in 9 thick volumes of china folio paper, in which Mr. Tolfrey had made some progress in the collection of Singhalese words, which he had parallelled with other words in the same language, and

added a translation into English, no doubt with a view ultimately to form a Singhalese and English Dictionary. but which has not the least appearance of any thing like a finish. I can say but little of this work, not having yet particularly examined it; it does not as yet fall in with my plans of labour. But there is an index to the words which have been collected, and I shall no doubt find it useful when I begin the second part of the Dictionary. Another manuscript, in 3 volumes folio, is a beginning of an English and Singhalese Dictionary, and which, when I first saw it made me think of a Dictionary, or rather to complete what Mr. Tolfrey had begun. But when I entered upon the work I found it so deficient, in all respects, that I was forced to abandon it entirely. This work must have been begun when Mr. Tolfrey was but young in his knowledge of Singhalese. I have consulted Mr. Chater about this manuscript, who was likely to give me the most information, and he assures me that it was Mr. T's. own attempt at a dictionary, in rather an early stage of his studies, but still mentions it as the best attempt that had ever yet been made in that language. However this may be I know not, I can only say I have laid aside Mr. T's. plan, and not only so, but have found it necessary to reject almost the whole of his translations. A third manuscript work is in 22 quarto volumes, in which Mr. Tolfrey proposed to himself the task of making a Concordance to his Singhalese library. Noble project indeed, but which would have been work enough for him had his life been spared 20 years longer. The plan of this concordance is excellent, and so far as it has been completed, is Mr. T's. best performance. The fourth work worthy of notice is a beginning of a Pali Dictionary, the plan is laid out to the end of the vowels, but only an inconsiderable part of it completed. A fifth work is a translation of Mr. Colebrook's Index, to the celebrated

අමරසිංහකෝෂ * *Amarasinghakosha.* Mr. Colebrooke first gives the Text of Amarasingha with interpretations and annotations. In a second volume he has arranged the words in Alphabetical order, with an Index to the interpretations, as given in the first volume. Mr. Tolfrey has interleaved the volume, and has given the various interpretations and acceptations of every word as they stands this alphabetical order. This must have cost Mr. Tolfrey incredible labour, and will be exceedingly useful to me hereafter.

The remaining part of the library, which is not of equal importance, consists generally of a number of smaller manuscript works, such as short vocabularies in Singhalese and English, scraps of various kinds of translations which have been made by Mr. Tolfrey, as exercises in the languages; and other little works of a similar kind: such works as the above no doubt Mr. T.

---

* කෝෂ *kosha,* which is added to Amarasingha, is a Sangskrit word which means a purse, a pocket, or bag,—but here it means a Dictionary, or collection of words.

would find useful in his first attempts, at Singhalese and they would indeed be the same to any one similarly situated; but with the works already in the press, and those which have been completed, with such also as are likely soon to be published by the Mission, with a direct reference to afford assistance to those who are desirous of learning the languages of this country, they cease to be of importance.

I think it will be seen that such a library of the standard books of this country is a great acquisition to our Mission. It would have been a laborious and extensive undertaking for the Missionaries to have attempted to make such a Collection, and I doubt, all things considered, whether in any reasonable time they could have accomplished this. But still I regret much the absence of many of their scientific works, which I know are studied in the temples. These will be come at, by a persevering attention to the languages of the country, and cultivating an acquaintance with the best informed of the Priests. At the same time we cannot expect to get from among the Natives those regular and distinct systems of the sciences with which we are furnished in Europe. There can, however, be little doubt but the literature of the East has fallen from what it was in past ages. When the spirit of authorship existed among those Nations they wrote separately and largely on every branch of science, according to the light they had. The principal part of these books are lost, and nothing but the names of a few remain. Indolence and depravity were the natural consequences of war and conquests, which made slaves of a fine people, and brought their minds to a state below even that of their civil situations. And had not the cunning and rapacity of the Priests kept alive some of their former energies, and which have preserved some of their religious books, we should at this moment have had but few traces of their former character to have reminded us what they really were. It is, therefore, on this account that their sacred books are predominant, yet, their divinity, jurisprudence, their generally history, and the little knowledge they have of philosophy; in its various branches, are all mixed together, at least this is in a great degree the case in Ceylon, and it is somewhat difficult for an European to make so rapid progress in his literary researches among them.

At the same time it would be desirable that those of our brethren, who have made it a principal part of their business to study the languages of this country, to use the talent thus given them, not only in the direct way of preaching the Word of Life, and of translating various little works connected with it into them, but also to turn their attention to translating into English the books we now possess, as this would be one direct means of exposing the consummate folly of their idolatry.

The books which the Singhalese now possess are for the most part in a style of language which not one among a thousand of the mass of population can understand. The consequence is, they know nothing of them but what they hear from Priests, and these men, who are not the most sacredly devoted to the intrests of the people only, make known such of them as will turn to their own advantage. I have myself put books, written in pure Singhalese, into the hands of clever and learned Natives, and they have declared to me that they did not understand a word in them. This ignorance I can easily believe to exist among a people so deplorably ignorant of their own language, and fallen from what they undoubtedly were in past days. So that it appears, that to put translations of the Singhalese books into the hands of the rising generation, in a cautious way, will be the most effectual way of proving their insufficiency to the native mind. Besides, there is the greater encouragement in such attempts when it is recollected what efforts are now making to bring the native youth to an acquaintance with the English language.

The work requires all of us to use our utmost endeavours, and to do what lays in our power to turn men from the darkness of heathenism to the light of the Gospel of the blessed God.

B. CLOUGH.

Mission House, Colombo,
1819.

No. II.

The Brethren of the Mission will bear in mind, that the approaching Annual Meeting will be held in Colombo, and will commence, according to the Minutes of the last Ceylon Conference, on the first Wednesday in February, 1820. The Brethren, whose presence at the Meeting will be absolutely necessary, will please to have the subjects connected with their Stations arranged as far as possible against that time.

(*Signed*)   W. B. FOX.

No. III.

We are under the necessity of omitting this quarter a number of interesting articles which ought to have been inserted in the Miscellany, having already detained the Quarterly much beyond the regular time of publication. This delay has been occasioned by several unavoidable circumstances.

2 O

No. IV.

WORKS IN THE PRESS.

FROM THE TAMUL DISTRICT,

A Selection from the Liturgy, translated into Tamul: 1000 Copies to be printed.

FROM THE SINGHALESE DISTRICT,

Short Sermons in Singhalese: 1000 Copies to be printed.

END OF OCTOBER EXTRACTS.

Printed at the Mission-Press, Colombo, for the Use of the Missionaries.

Extracts

FROM

QUARTERLY LETTERS, &c.

No. X.   **JANUARY, 1820.**

THE COLOMBO STATION.

Mission House, Colombo, 29th January, 1820,

VERY DEAR BRETHREN,

We wrote you a letter at the usual time of addressing you, but by some accident the copy got mislaid, and being so situated at this time, and the season being arrived when our Quarterly must go out, it will be out of our power to furnish a regular letter. I beg therefore to put in place of our regular letter the following letter to His Excellency our late greatly esteemed Governor, with His Excellency's reply which I am sure must be interesting to you all. I do sincerely regret the circumstance of being unable to write, as I feel a pleasure in being able to state that our labours on this station for the last three months have been upon the whole more interesting, more promising, and more encouraging, than we recollect them to have been,

I remain, my dear Brethren.
Your ever affectionate Brother,
B. CLOUGH.

To His Excellency General Sir ROBERT BROWNRIGG, *Bt. & G. C. B.*
Governor of the Island of Ceylon, &c. &c. &c.

MAY IT PLEASE YOUR EXCELLENCY,

We have learned, with the most sincere concern, that this favored colony is likely very soon to be deprived of your Excellency's residence and paternal government; an event which, we beg leave to assure your Excellency, will be very sensibly felt, not only by ourselves, but by every member of our Mission family resident in the island. Previous to your Excellency's departure we feel particularly desirous of communicating to your Excellency some additional testimony and assurance, that every respectful feeling of esteem and gratitude, which we have had the honor and happiness to cherish in our hearts towards your Excellency, from our first arrival in the Island, continues

No. X.   A

unalterably the same, unless in the one instance, that succeeding occurrences have tended very greatly to increase and strengthen them, and we earnestly intreat your Excellency will favorably receive this as our humble apology for troubling you on this trying occasion.

We are indeed sorry, that in consequence of our numbers being so widely dispersed over the colony most of them will necessarily be deprived of the happiness of uniting with us at this time, yet such is our union and oneness of feeling, especially in the grateful, respectful esteem we ever feel for your Excellency, that we beg, as an additional favor, your Excellency will kindly allow us to include all their names with those of our own.

As this may be the last opportunity we shall ever be favored with of addressing ourselves to your Excellency in this country, we wish to record, in the most lasting manner possible, that your Excellency's condecending, kind, and friendly demeanour towards us, during the whole of our residence in this Island, has invariably been such as to render your Excellency's name and government ever dear to us all; and we feel assured, that neither time nor circumstances will ever erase from our hearts those grateful feelings which have been created by unnumbered acts of voluntary kindness. It would be exceedingly difficult for us to retrace minutely the many pleasing occurrences to which we now refer, and which, by your Excellency's kind influence, have continued to accompany our efforts from the commencement of our Mission; yet we frequently recur to them with pleasure and delight, and the recollection of so many past favors, received from your Excellency, fills our hearts with the sincerest gratitude, and naturally excites in our minds very anxious feelings at the prospect of your Excellency's approaching departure. Notwithstanding, however, we shall to the latest period feel a gratifying pleasure in associating your Excellency's name with the success which has hitherto blessed our labours in Ceylon. We must beg your Excellency's condecending indulgence for the freedom we take in expressing our sentiments in so familiar a manner, but almost every thing connected with present circumstances gives rise to reflections in our minds which are exceedingly difficult to repress.

Before we conclude our present communication we cannot deny ourselves the pleasure of presenting your Excellency our sincerest congratulations, upon the great and lasting satisfaction it must afford your Excellency, when retiring from this colony, to leave it in so tranquil and improving a state: not but that your Excellency has had difficulties to contend with, and difficulties of the most trying and painful nature, yet by the continued smile of a kind Providence upon your Excellency's great and persevering exertions the disquietude that threatened us is completely calmed, and we not only enjoy peace and quiet in all our borders, but, so far as our knowledge of the state of the colony extends, the cheering countenance of prosperity smiles upon all its departments— upon its civil and commercial interests, and not less favorably

upon its moral and religious improvement. But here we can speak with more confidence, and from our peculiar situation reserve would ill become us.

From the most correct accounts we have been able to collect it appears, that even the nominal profession of Christianity was but in a languid state among the natives on your Excellency's arrival in this Island. The opportunities of improvement, and the means of instruction for the native population were exceedingly inadequate, and by no means answerable to the claims they had upon the attention of the Christian world, circumstances which, where ever they exist, will be lamented by reflecting minds. But the period to which we now refer was a happy era to the native inhabitants of Ceylon. The first great and effectual attempt that was made in their behalf was the establishment of the Auxiliary Bible Society, under your Excellency's immediate patronage and support, for the purpose of publishing the sacred Scriptures in their own languages. This Society has been enabled to extend its active and spirited operations into almost every part of the Island. It has already sent abroad about 3000 copies of the New Testament, and 3500 more will shortly be ready for publication. In addition to this it has printed about 22,000 copies of smaller works, extracted from the Scriptures, which have been every where distributed; hence not a town, not a village, and in some districts scarcely a family, but has experienced its good effects. Such efforts, when viewed in connection with other benevolent and Christian exertions, such as the repairing and erection of large and convenient schools, in the most populous neighbourhoods, for the instruction of the native youth; together with the erection of a number of commodious places of worship for the accommodation of the native Christians, to excite and encourage among them an increased attention to the visible forms of Christian devotion, must place in a very pleasing light your Excellency's ever watchful care, and anxious concern, for the moral and religious improvement of the inhabitants of this large Island, and we cannot but add our sincerest wishes that those plans, so well laid down and prosperously begun, may be fully accomplished; and this we are confident will call forth the thanksgivings of generations yet unborn.

But we must again beg your Excellency's kind indulgence while we mention another interesting fact, closely connected with the improvements, moral and religious, which for several years have been going on under your Excellency's government. We now refer to the liberal sanction, and extensive countenance which the cause of Christian Missions has invariably met with from your Excellency: and it is only from a fear of being tedious that we deny ourselves the pleasure of taking such a view of this subject as we conceive it highly deserves. When our Mission arrived in this Island we laboured under some of the most painful disadvantages. The loss of our venerable leader, the Rev. Dr. Coke, was an event of itself almost sufficient to have discouraged us from proceeding in our work, considering its ardous nature, and our great want of experience for such an undertaking; and, not having anticipated such an event, we were necessarily unprepared to meet it. Thus situated we landed in Ceylon, and though strangers, with little to recommend us except the goodness of the cause in which we had embarked, your Excellency honored us with the most condescending welcome in the colony; pointed out to us our respective spheres of labour, and at the same time favored us with many other encouragements which we cannot now enumerate, but which will ever live in our grateful remembrances. After a trial of several years, under such favourable circumstances, it is very natural to expect that considerable success would have resulted from our attempts:—on this head we have met with several things which have been cause of regret, and which, perhaps, had it been in our power we should have ordered otherwise; notwithstanding, it is with pleasure we can state, that we have had to encounter nothing hitherto in any of our operations that has amounted to a discouragement, but on the contrary we can assure your Excellency, that we have met with many things to encourage us and quite satisfy our minds that our undertaking is approved of by the great head of the church; hence we feel as much encouraged to prosecute our work as we ever did. We have now 14 Missionaries resident on the Island, besides several interesting young men, both native and country-born, who promise to be very useful. Several of our Brethren have attained a competent knowledge of the native languages, and are devoting almost their whole attention to the improvement of the natives by preaching to them and instructing them, both in public and from house to house; they also spend much of their time in making useful and necessary translations, either of the sacred Scriptures or of little works of a religious kind. We hope also the literature of the Island will ere long be considerably advanced by their publications, both of dictionaries and grammars of the language, as well also as of some translations of the native books which are in a state of forwardness, but which have never yet appeared in any European language. As our great object is to instruct the natives in the principles of Christianity we endeavour to make all our other pursuits subserve this desirable end, and as our holy religion can only be properly embraced by the natives of India from the clearest convictions of its great superiority over every other religious system, we are sensible that these changes can only be accomplished, under a Divine direction, by the regular diffusion of instruction among them. This persuasion led us some time back to resolve upon the establishment of Christian schools, to bring forward the children in the knowledge of their own language: in a considerable number of these schools the English language is taught with the most flattering success. But while we endeavour to make the rising generation acquainted with the first rudiments of learning, we study at the same time to accompany these instructions, with such others of a Religious kind as we are convinced ¡will answer the designs of our Mission; and on your Excellency's leaving the colony it may not be uninteresting to be informed, that we have so far succeeded in these attempts, that we have now established in different parts of the Island about 72 schools, which include 4591 children, all under daily instructions; and every child thus instructed is seen and examined by a Missionary at least once a month. From this system of schools, conducted on such plans, the most moderate calculations will be in favor of their proving greatly beneficial especially to the rising generation. And though it becomes us to speak with diffidence when we pronounce an opinion on what is still future, we cannot but entertain the most pleasing anticipations of the result of such a combination of effort as is now displayed in this Island, by the Bible Society, Tract Societies and Missionary Societies, all of which are actively employed in dispersing abroad the light of Divine Truth, and helping forward the great attempt which contemplates nothing less than the complete triumph of our holy religion over every prevailing system of heathenism. This is an effort which is not confined to the Island of Ceylon. The spirit and disposition is predominant in almost the whole Christian world; and it will, we have no doubt, be a soothing reflection to your Excellency in a future day, that during your Excellency's residence and government in a heathen country, you had an opportunity of taking so public, so honorable, so christian a part in this great work. May it please a merciful Providence to prolong your Excellency's continuance in this life for many years, and may your Excellency be favoured to hear from these distant shores, that every hope, every wish your Excellency may have formed with respect to the moral and religious improvement of the native Singhalese, has been very abundantly accomplished.

We shall not cease to recommend your Excellency and amiable family to the continued protection of a kind Providence, when on the great deep; and shall constantly implore him who has the uncontrolled command of winds and seas, graciously to vouchsafe every blessing and protection necessary, both for a safe and pleasant voyage; and assure your Excellency that the most grateful respectful esteem of our whole Mission will ever continue to accompany your Excellency's name, Repeating our entreaty that your Excellency will excuse our troubling you at so great a length, We have the honor to remain, with the greatest respect and esteem,

Your Excellency's greatly obliged and ever thankful
humble Servants,

Signed in behalf of all the Wesleyan Missionaries in Ceylon.

B. CLOUGH,
G. ERSKINE.

ANSWER OF HIS EXCELLENCY THE GOVERNOR.

To the Brethren of the Wesleyan-Mission.

GENTLEMEN,

IT is with a lively sense of satisfaction that I have received your respectful and affectionate address.

From the first moment of my entering upon the government of this Island, I considered the religious improvement of the people to be of paramount importance. It is therefore most gratifying to me to hear you, Gentlemen, who have devoted your lives to the promotion of Christianity, speak in high terms of my cooperation, and to know that the measures of my government, in aid of your missionary labours, have been sanctioned by the testimony of your warm approbation.

On this ground nothing can be more acceptable to my feelings than your strong expressions of gratitude, however they may attribute to me a degree of merit which I am not entitled to claim. The chief ends that I have had in view, were the happiness of the people confided to my care, and the honour of my own country to which I was responsible for the sacred trust.

It was therefore my bounden duty to foster and encourage the attemps of those who came forward with their voluntary assistance towards both at once of these great objects, by communicating that which it is our glory to spread as well as to enjoy, and labouring to enlighten the people of this foreign land, by a diffusion of that religious knowledge, with which Providence has blessed our own.

That I was influenced by motives of another kind, that I felt the full obligation of propogating, for its own sake, the divine truth of that Religion, which has been throughout life the source of my consolation and hope, I would rather choose to be collected from my conduct, than received upon any assurance of my own professions.

But it is unnecessary to dwell upon my sincere zeal for a wide extension of the Christian faith, as if it were independant of other motives, because it is in fact inseparably connected with the duties of my political office: it is the surest foundation upon which I could hope to build the permanent welfare and happiness of the people, whom I have been deputed to govern.

It would be to me a subject of most afflicting regret if I were to leave this Island, after presiding over it in the name of my king for almost 8 years, without a conviction that some durable improvement had been commenced under my temporary rule. I hope and trust that I may take my leave of Ceylon without any cause for such a mortifying reflection; whatever may have been the progress hitherto I confide in the goodness of Providence for producing hereafter effects corresponding with my laborious and persevering exertions for the public good.

If I were to quit my Government without some public expression of my respect and esteem for the Brethren of the Wesleyan Mission, I should be insensible alike to the general claims of

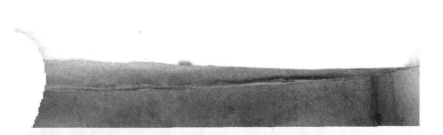

their meritorious conduct, and to the gratitude which I owe them
for their zealous aid in promoting those objects which I had so
much at heart.

From the beginning, Gentlemen, of your settlement with a few
Missionaries in this Island until the present moment, when the
number of your Brethren is augmented to 14, your exertions have
been principally directed in that course which is, I think, for the
attainment of your Christian purpose, the most secure and direct.

The numerous schools established under the vigilant superintendence of your Mission, forming a most extensive system of
public education, cannot fail to produce a most beneficial effect
upon the morals and habits of the rising generation. There can
be no doubt that even among the native people who call themselves Christians, the earliest application of religious instruction
will be most likely to make a deep impression upon the youthful mind, which has not been hardened by the prejudices and cor-
ruptions of a maturer age, and to convert a nominal profession
into a sincere reception of the Christian faith. But when our
observation is turned to that large part of the native population
which yet wanders in heathen darkness, the superior advantages
of early education are still more striking and apparent.

The native adult, who professes Christianity, is not unwilling to
hear, thought little disposed to retain, lessons of religious and
moral instruction.

But avowed heathens are averse even from listening to the
teacher who would convince them of their errors. The strong
hold of superstitious idolatry is then only accessible by a preoc-
cupation of the children's minds with a better knowledge, and it
is remarkable, that however the Budhist or Hindoo may themselves revolt from the pious attempts of Missionary conversion,
so desirous are they of improving their young families, that they
gladly send them to the Wesleyan Schools, and freely permit them
to learn the first rudiments of Christianity. The prevailing wish
also to have their sons aquire the English language as a means
of advancement, stimulates this general disposition with the powerful excitement of personal interest. This favourable state of opinion upon the subject of education gives among all castes of natives a fair opening, of which the Wesleyan Mission has taken
full advantage, and from their numerous schools it is but reasonable to expect the most beneficial results.

The great influence of the press is exercised with more or less
effect over every civilized country in Europe, but here, where it
was so much wanted, it was utterly unknown. It was rare that
any publication ever appeared in a language intelligible to the
people, except a Regulation of Government; the children had nothing
to learn, their parents had nothing to read: but the Wesleyan
Missionaries have established a press, from which there is such a
continual issue of elementary works of devotion, morality, and
science, that the native population is at length gradually admitted to a participation in the riches of European knowledge.

The first and last object of human learning is the kno wldge of salvation, attainable through the Holy Scriptures, and to that it is natural for a Missionary union to turn their chief attention and apply their most strenuous efforts supported by the Funds, and encouraged by the Patronage of the Colombo Auxiliary Bible Society, it is from the Wesleyan Press that the Scriptures are now given to the Singhalese, and will ere long, there is reason to hope, be supplied in abundance to every native of Ceylon.

Thus much I have said to shew the grounds for my belief, that this Island is already much indebted to the Wesleyan Mission: it will be still more indebted when their system of education is completed, when a sufficient number of scholars have been trained up to superintend the pious work, and the Missionaries themselves can settle and live among the natives, converse freely with them in their own language, and give them all the benefit of present example, enforcing the pure doctrines and precepts of the gospel.

Now Gentlemen I take my leave of you, thanking you for your kind assurance of esteem as well as for your prayers for my safety, in return I wish you most sincerely an ample share of prosperity and happiness, with the fullest success in the great object of your Mission.

That your efforts may be guided by Providence to a joyful termination is indeed a wish that I shall always cherish with a warmth in proportion to the fervent interest which I feel in whatever may contribute to the security, comfort, and blessing of the Island of Ceylon.

(Signed,) ROBT. BROWNRIGG.

Kings House, Colombo,
30th January, 1820.

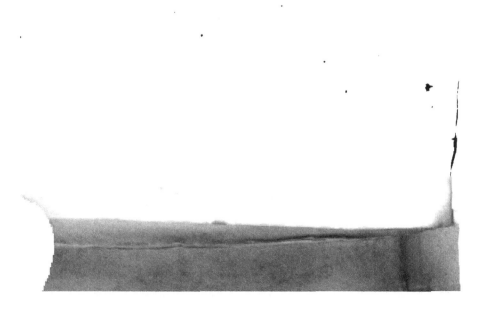

THE NEGOMBO STATION.

Negombo, January 3, 1820.

Very Dear Brethren,

The rapid flight of another quarter brings with it not only a forcible illustration of the brevity of life, but also a renewed admonition to review the concerns of our great work for that period, and record the mercies of God.

Our work on this Station has this quarter been a little diversified and enlivened by the occasional residence here of a part of the Bengal troops, including 6 English officers, some of whom have been most exemplary in their attendance on public worship, and, encouraged by their presence, a few others who understand English; so that we have been favoured with a novel treat of preaching in our own language to very attentive little congregations, before our usual services in the native languages; this, I need not say, has had a tendency to strengthen our hands, as it opened another door of usefulness which there is every reason to believe was not in vain. Br. Hume, being with me a little while previous to our meeting, has enjoyed several opportunities of preaching to them, and they have departed from Negombo with, at least, an increase of knowledge concerning the way of salvation, and with many copies of the Holy Scriptures, with which they were furnished at their own request. One little circumstance in relation to them I cannot but gratefully record. One of the lieutenants, a young officer of the most amiable manners and agreeable deportment, soon after I had waited on them to proffer them any service during their stay, came to the Bungaloe in the most friendly manner, and ingenuously opened his mind to me on the subject of religious experience: being the son of a very respectable English clergyman he had been brought up in the strictest habits of morality, although it was evident he did not apprehend the nature of spiritual religion; but, a more teachable, humble spirit I have never seen, and hence he listened with the most pleasing attention to every little instruction that was offered him, from time to time, on the necessity of a change of heart, faith in a Saviour's blood, &c. seeing the probability of his receiving good, I soon gave him a general invitation to the Bungaloe, which he mostly made use of to come at the hour of morning or evening family worship, and having access to my Book-case, he read many volumes of our most valuable writers, and declared himself much profited, particularly by Mr. Sutcliffe's Introduction to Christianity, part of which I believe he transcribed. Being particularly fond of singing he was with us at all opportunities of religious engagement, and several times came to the class-meeting: I had the happiness to present him with a few books, among which were a Pocket Testament, Doddridge's Rise, &c. and a volume of our large Magazines, which he received with every expression of gratitude, and owned to me that a change had passed upon his mind and experience which had rendered his two months re-

No. x.   C

sidence here the happiest of his life; our separation was with regret on all sides, for he began to grow a most profitable and interesting associate, and although I do not think he was truly converted, yet I believe he was become a sincere seeker of salvation, and consequently on the verge of it. I feel a hope that it will please the Lord to raise him up to some sphere of usefulness in Bengal: for with God all things are possible, and I own I was not a little agreeably surprised to meet with so much humility, simplicity, and amiable sincerity, in a young military officer in this country.

I am happy to say that our congregations among the native people have manifestly increased; both their numbers and their *seriousness* have been far more encouraging to our labours than usual, and I do believe that some are sincerely enquiring " What must I do to be saved ?" From among the aged woman who have constantly attended our preaching I have lately begun to form a class, and meet them after Sunday evening preaching, as it is inconvenient for them to come out more than one evening in the week; our other classes are very regularly attended, and their numbers this quarter present a total of 38, for which blessed be the God of all grace! I have divided our school-boys' class, as those in the country could not attend so regularly as they wished; and am rejoiced to have a very pious young man, a native schoolmaster, who I have the best confidence will be a most suitable leader for them: there are now 5 little classes attached to the station, and 3 leaders independent of myself: I hope some eternal good from these small beginnings.

The schools go on well, except from the opposition of the Roman Catholics, who diminish their numbers whenever they can, and continue to maintain the consistency of their character by every possible attempt to frustrate our rising cause: however the hand of the Lord is yet with us for good. I am sorry to say the building of the little chapel is greatly delayed by the unprincipled dealings of those employed. I am using every effort to get it up, assured that it will be a great instrument in raising our cause here; the people are already calculating on that very circumstance, the certainty of our continuing here, which before, it was industriously propagated, would be of very short duration; and hence many were hindered from coming among us. A young man, whose heart I believe the Lord has changed, has declared his intention of joining us from among the Catholics; they are much enraged against him, and it is not a little amusing to hear the idle trash which they advance to deter him from his resolution; he was prepared to receive the sacrament with us, but was deterred on the evening appointed by the unprincipled opposition of his own relations; however, being very desirous of joining us, he came at another opportunity, and several of us joined him in celebrating the memorials of the Saviour's dying love, at which he wept abundantly, with deep sensibility of so great a mercy. I believe him quite sincere, and acting from spiritual motives; for I am particularly careful to avoid drawing him by secular ones.

The extension of our cause to Chilaw has not yet been effected, owing to some necessary delays on the part of the Collector, whose appointment I am still waiting, and have just written again.* Our little School in Kandy continues, but has not increased to more than 20: I hope, however, that the clearly expressed approbation of the Governor, and the friendly views of Sir Edward Barnes, with whom I had some conversation relative to it, will eventually succeed it: I shall be glad if the little school be allowed to remain, though only a solitary witness for Jesus in a territory of heathenism, but I am striving to push our conquests yet farther, and in this I am greatly encouraged by some remarks of the Governor on this subject, when the other day I went to take leave of him. He was assured, he said, of the friendly disposition of Sir Edward Barnes towards it, and thought I might go on further towards Kornegalle, as the people there were both very numerous and very friendly. I expressed my sincere thankfulness at such an intimation, and informed him I was already making the attempt he had so kindly recommended: he appeared much pleased, and adverted to the pleasure he derived from seeing the little school I had already formed, on his return from Kandy, as mentioned in the last quarterly letter. I heartily wish I could recal every part of the conversation, for I am sure it would delight our Brethren to hear the kind, and I had almost said, affectionate concern which His Excellency expressed towards our Mission. On my thanking him for his uniform kindness to our cause at Negombo, especially in reference to his giving me the old Dutch Church to build our chapel, I shall not soon forget the great feeling with which he said, " Be assured I shall ever bear the warmest regard for your Mission, and those con-

---

* Since writing the above, I have visited Chilaw, and was most kindly received by the Collector, J. Walbeoff, Esq. who made every arrangement to meet my convenience in preaching to the people, &c. I preached in the morning in English, in the afternoon in the native language (through Mr. W's. interpreter) and in the evening in Portuguese, at the former and the latter services there were of course but few hearers, but not so in the other. Mr. W. had ordered a place to be prepared across the street near the Bazar, with an awning, and here a large company assembled, though many feared to come in, being nominally Roman Catholics; they heard very attentively, and seemed well pleased with the prospect of a Mission School amongst them. Mr. W. has kindly promised to build us a large school room immediately, to be ready in 6 weeks, according to a plan on which we had previously consulted, he took me to select a proper situation for it and will enclose a piece of Government ground entirely for our service. His house is very kindly open to any Missionary, and he is extremely anxious to have one resident at Chilaw, and has promised to assist him in every possible way in attempting to form a station, build a house, &c. Mr. W. has been resident on the station for 7 years and has were extensive knowledge of—and influence over the people; there is a population of nearly 20,000 in the district, and he believes a circle of Schools might be formed around the station, which a Missionary might visit even walking, if he chose. On the whole, it appears a most desirable opening, and at all events, with the blessing of God, if no Brother can be sent, I shall go and open a School there as soon as the room is finished.

nected with it, and most sincerely wish them every success; especially
in the schools, which are so excellently calculated to teach the people
of this country the nature of Christianity. I shall not fail to impress
their value and importance upon the minds of the people on my
return to England: I regret much that I cannot visit Negombo and
see your chapel, which it was my full intention to have done had it
been possible. I am glad to have been of any assistance to you
in the pious labours in which you are engaged." Both the Governor
and Lady Brownrigg took a very kind leave also of our dear young
friend who was with me, and adverted to the services of Mr. Sutherland, his late father, with the highest respect. I should also mention,
that on the same day I waited on the Honble Robert Boyd, who
has hitherto been the Guardian of our young friend, in connection
with the Mission, and received him fully into our entire care, as his
own decided wish and intention is to spend his future life among
us devoted to the service of God as a Missionary to the Heathen. Mr.
Boyd entirely approves of his choice, after having so long and so
maturely deliberated on the important point: and assured our young
friend, as his father had done before, that he accounted him happy
to have become associated with those whom he was perfectly convinced would be his kind and permanent protectors, and was pleased that
he had directed his views to a profession at once so honourable and so
useful Our dear young friend, therefore, will be proposed to travel
among us at our approaching meeting, and I am very thankful to add,
that I believe him from two years experience, to be every way
worthy of our kindest regards. May Jehovah be his guide!

On Christmas-day as many of the children of our neighbouring
country schools as could assemble were present at public service in
the Bungaloe, when Br. Hume preached to them, after prayers and the
second chapter of St. Luke had been read in the Native language;
their appearance was highly interesting, some of them wearing very
neat handkerchiefs wrought by their own hands in the school, and
the whole were very clean and orderly: a considerable number of the
parents attended with them, with their masters and mistresses; after
Divine service they all walked in order, two and two, past the new
chapel now erecting, down to the interpreter's house, where a good
dinner was provided for them in very nice order; after partaking
of which in the long school-room they returned to their villages
much gratified. The habits and feeling they are thus acquiring will
give a new tone to the next generation in the neighbourhoods where
they dwell, and surely from amongst them, many will rise up to adorn
the gospel of our Lord Jesus Christ.

On the first Sabbath of the new year we had our quarterly *love-
feast* and *sacrament*, at the former of which nearly 30 were present
and at the latter 13. I believe there was not one who did not bear a
testimony for Jesus, or at least declared that "*Wisdom's ways are
ways of pleasantness and all her paths are peace*," particularly I was
gratified with the no less novel than interesting circumstance of five
Portuguese females publicly declaring their joy in the service of God,

(these are they whom I mentioned as being formed lately into a class) and their bold testimony added greatly to our joy in the Lord, they were all present in the evening at the sacrament, with two additional communicants. Br. Hume preached in the middle of the day to a large congregation at our school-room, and our morning congregation exceeded 90, which for this place, where Roman Catholic influence so much prevails, is very large, praise the Lord! O may it go on! Blessed be the Lord I feel my soul much encouraged and strengthened, and hope to be enabled to bring forth fruit to the glory of his holy Name. I cannot speak enough of the goodness of God. My cup has frequently run over, and my spiritual enjoyments of this quarter have been of an increasingly delightful kind. "*Blessed be God even the Father of our Lord Jesus Christ, the Father of mercies and the God of all comfort, who comforteth us in all our tribulation, that we may be able to comfort them which are in any trouble by the comfort wherewith we ourselves are comforted of God.*"

I remain, very dear Brethren,
Most affectionately yours,
in the Gospel of our Lord Jesus,
ROBERT NEWSTEAD.

THE CALTURA STATION,

Caltura, January 4th, 1820.

VERY DEAR BRETHREN,

The nature of my present engagements forbids my writing largely this quarter. The Work on this Station is now tolerably uniform, and produces nothing that is particulary novel or interesting. On my return to Caltura I could not without considerable satisfaction notice the improvements made by Br. Erskine during my absence. He had, besides rendering essential service to the places I had established, opened some new ones, which promise much. Two of them are in every point of view as important as any previously established, except in Caltura itself. Since that period I have opened three places in the interior, places of great promise, and two other places have petitioned help through the medium of the chief modeliar in the district, and a third through one of the magistrates. My present schools, with the number of children belonging to each is as follows.

	Boys	Girls	Total.		Boys	Girls	Total.
Caltura	58	4	62	Brt. for.	522	55	577
Pantura	57	2	59	Rambucana	100		100
Pinwatta	74		74	Do. Female School		41	41
Goldsmith Street	67	22	89	Calamulla	23		23
Berbereen	36		36	Paredua	50		50
Alutgama	34	1	35	Palatotta	37	17	54
Bentotte	42	26	68	Disastra Caltura	57	5	62
Kuda Payagilla	62		62	Bandaragama	78	26	104
Maha Payagila,	42		42	Kehelinava	54	2	56
Horeluda	50		50	Anguratra	57		57
	522	55	577		978	146	1124

No. X.   D

During the past quarter I have had the pleasure to observe a greater attendance of adults than I have been accustomed to see, in places quite in the country. At Caltura the attendance is uniformly good, and I have reason to hope that the word is not preached in vain. One circumstance is very gratifying. Nearly a year ago an elderly man, who I believe had never in the gross sense been an idolater, came to me and desired to be baptised; he was placed under a course of instruction, and in due time he, his wife, and five children were baptized, and since that the remaining child. One thing worthy of remark is, that they are rarely absent from public worship, (or the little ones from school,) except for reasons which are fully satisfactory. I do not notice real decline in any respect, but in almost every place there is very visible progress; and, as the least consolation, such light is extensively spread as produces a very visible alteration both in the views and manners of the people. I fear we are sometimes in danger of giving conscience too extensive a province; it is a power of the mind, it is a witness, but it must have a discriminating rule, and I fear the original law written on the mind is in many instances very faint, and perhaps only very gross enormities are legible in this country, and my Brethren well know that in these regions ඥෝඨ෯ and *tem customado*, have generally more authority than the laws of God or man. It may be a libel but it is a *truth*, which can never be successfully controverted, that little or no regard is paid either to truth or even an oath. A good Christian was lately brought as a witness before a Court, and as usual before giving evidence the oath was administered. But before it was administered the worthy magistrate, as is his general custom, explained the nature of an oath. The magistrate then asked the witness what she thought would happen if she testified falsely. She answered by a word that signifies " ill luck would happen." He asked "of what kind." She replied "she had been told that the Magistrate would be angry." So that, as far as I have yet learned, there is but little fear in the minds of the people except of Man and *the Devil*. The former they endeavour to conciliate by presents, the later by offerings. I can pledge myself for the majority of the rising generation under my care that they have overcome this folly and wickedness. I expect of these growing plants to gather fruit, but the abundance thereof must be gathered by successors. As it respects the elementary part of education much has been done, and I have tried to do more; but the native mode of education, altered in Europe and called there the improved system, gives little opportunity except of furnishing proper books; and possibly in a few instances of being polished. We have, however, throughout the Singhalese schools introduced spelling, which will doubtless introduce more regularity in writing, but I dare not yet venture to say that it will greatly facilitate the progress in learning to read for by their own mode a child generally learns to read in less time than children usually learn their alphabet in Europe. I have, however, tried to give every facility to the plan in my power, and have divided upwards of 3000 Singhalese words into syllables. In the first general division of two syllables are four classes, all the syllables of which are pure, i. e. ending with a vowel. The first are both short, the second both long; the third, the first only short, the fourth the last only short. In the second general division one syllable ends with a consonant, and this division forms various classes from the sanguiaca letters, the benno letters, those having the inherent vowel suppressed, &c. The three syllables form a much greater variety. In dividing them into syllables I have not regarded the number of characters by which they are expressed, but attended only to the number of sounds and their quantity, which principally distinguishes it from the native system. It is highly approved of by the intelligent natives, but what are its merits experience must determine. To save as much in the expence of books as usefulness will allow, particularly with respect to the lower classes in the Singhalese schools, I have judged it advisable that the books should be copied on olas, which are far more durable than paper, and when a boy is perfectly acquainted with his book to give him a printed one as a reward. My plan is but in its infancy, but I am encouraged thus far. This is important in my Station, as in the 19 schools under my care in four only is English taught, in two schools by regular masters, in one by the missionary and an assistant, and in another by a monitor. I should be happy to introduce it into more, but the expence forms a mighty objection. I think, however, we might in some stations do more in this way by making a general rule that none should be received as English teachers, or assistant teachers, who had not previously been on the list of assistant monitors, labouring gratuitously until a vacancy offered, when a trial might be made of the different monitors on any station and the place be adjudged to the most competent. I sometimes mingle tears from different sources together. I mourn when I behold what a work is yet to accomplish, and rejoice with tears when I look upon what is done. Their power of committing any thing to memory may be judged of when I state, that several youths have committed the whole of my little Dictionary to memory, and several a great part of Brother Callaway's Vocabulary to memory. Many, who speak Portuguese, have gone quite through the Primero Ensinos, the Elements of Geography, and have made good progress in the Abridgement of Sutcliffe's Grammar. Some can repeat the whole of the Conversation of the Solar System, and I believe the children are well acquainted with Brother Clough's Singhalese Translation of the Liturgy, as I find the children join in the responses wherever I go. We yet want many things, but one thing very important is a well written tract in Singhalese on the sacredness of the Sabbath Day. I could mention more, but we must only go on according to our strength. In conclusion I must say, that every day unites me closer to the great work, and my most earnest request to the Father of Mercies is, that my life and labours in this work may cease together.

I am, Very Dear Brethren,

With the highest respect, Your Affectionate Brother,

W. BUCKLEY FOX.

THE GALLE STATION.

Galle, 12th January, 1820.

MY DEAR BRETHREN,

I sit down to address you this quarter with a heart filled with gratitude to my Heavenly Father upon account of that rich display of goodness and mercy which has been made to myself, my family, and our Mission, during the year that is past. I find it particularly profitable often to take a retrospective view of the operations of that gracious Providence, by which we have been directed, and which has crowned us with so many blessings, and while thus engaged I feel that the debt of gratitude, which I owe to God, can only be computed by that manifestation of infinite benevolence through which it has been created: of course then, the debt is infinite, and never can be discharged, but to all eternity the obligation must remain to be grateful; and this is a pleasing thought, as there is so much of heaven in this divine principle. The great and highly important concerns of our Mission continue to produce the same interest in my mind, and I think I never had a purer desire to work for the glory of God and the salvation of the inhabitants of this island; and I can truly say, that the more I know of them the more I see their need of the glorious Gospel of God our Saviour.

I am sorry, however, to be obliged to say, that my increasing knowledge of the Singhalese people leads me to still greater degrees of regret respecting the means which have been adopted, in former times, to bring them over to Christianity: these are known to you all, and the effects you have an exhibition of daily. As a further illustration of a painful subject, I shall give you an account of a case which lately came to my own knowledge, which may be considered as giving a just view of the deceiving nature of the Singhalese character, particularly on the subject of Christianity. In the month of November last, while out on the circuit, I was much disappointed in a village, about twelve miles from Galle, on finding the most of the children absent from the school, and on making enquiry respecting the cause, I was informed that it was in consequence of a great Budhist festival which was about to be celebrated in the neighbourhood at much expence, and at which a most singular ceremony was to take place, even that of manufacturing, and entirely completing a new robe for a priest, which in the estimation of the followers of Budhu is a work of great merit. As it is a matter of much consequence for a Missionary to collect all the information he can respecting the manners and customs of the people among whom he labours, and as he can be most certain as to the accuracy of the things which he beholds, I went to the spot of general festivity, and though it was in a very retired situation, yet there was not much danger of losing my way, if I had even been without a guide, for the road was distinctly marked out by the numbers of men, women, and children, all hurrying to this place of heathen worship. On my arrival I was surprised to see the large Bannamandowe which they had built, (not far distant from our school) and the expensive preparations which they had made in a very short

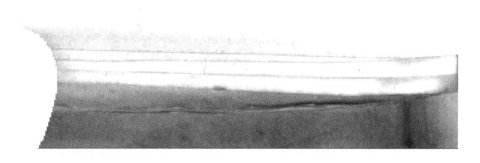

time, and without any authority. The inside of the mandowe was filled with women, who were all sitting upon the ground, and busily employed; some opening out the cotton, just taken from the tree, and preparing it for the spinners, who were diligently engaged making it into yarn, which as fast as it was spun was handed over to the weavers, who were waiting outside, with their simple looms, to make it into cloth. Having viewed the whole concern, and made as many enquiries as I wished, I returned to my quarters, intending in the evening to visit the place again, to see this garment which was to be entirely finished from the *raw material* in one day, even to putting on the yellow die, and to witness the ceremony of presenting it to the priest. Accordingly I paid my second visit about eight o'clock at night, and was just in time to see the robe drying over a fire of kajans, after having been died, and of course it was natural for me to expect that my curiosity would soon be gratified; however, I was now to be led into the secret, that I could not see the ceremony of the offering of the new robe, and that because the whole business had been conducted and completed under the direction and influence of the *Head man* of the village! and because the new robe was mostly at the expence of his family, who, when it was offered, must be present and have a hold of it with their hands, or else lose the blessing promised to so charitable an act, but this they would not do while I was there. I was told, they would not even make their appearance: however, notwithstanding this statement, I was not willing to give up my object, and told the head priest that I came for the express purpose of seeing the ceremony, and that I was determined to wait. He is a man of about fifty, a fine person, of most polite address, which he made use of in the most insinuating way to put me off, telling me that the ceremony would be unavoidably late; but if I would retire to rest, and not expose myself to the night air, he would have me called at the proper time; however, I understood him too well to be so easily deceived: I thanked him for his solicitude respecting my safety, but said that as the night was fine I could remain out, without much danger, and hoped that he would not detain the ceremony any longer than necessary; so I called for a chair and sat down, with much composure, to all appearance. I evidently saw that my conduct embarrassed them much, and I thought to oblige myself and relieve them, by sending for the head man, and informing him that I understood how matters were, and begged that they would go on with the ceremony, but he assured me that he knew nothing of the business, and pretended to be quite displeased with the people on account of their proceedings, but this was too glaring, as the mandowe was built upon his own ground, and not five minutes walk from his house! however, to humour the business, and keep up the farce, a junior priest came up, and addressed himself to us, saying they were engaged in the duties of their religion, and hoped that we would not be offended with them but grant them leave to go forward; the headman submitted this question to me, wishing me to believe that he was ready to suppress the whole affairs; when in fact, there was nothing that he

No. x. E

would have dreaded more than such a decision; but I told him
that I came not to disturb them, but only as a spectator; he then
replied, that as it was their religion they were at liberty to go on
with their ceremonies. I had now a hope that my point was gained,
but found afterwards that all they did while I was present was a
mere shame to deceive me; for they only brought the robe, with
the other things, which were to be offered, and after showing them
all to me, laid them on the ground before the priest; when the oldest
explained to the people the purpose for which they were designed,
and expressed his hope that they were all satisfied with the offering, and immediately there was a general shout of applause, the
priest then informed me, that the ceremony was over. I perceived,
however, how the matter was, but saw that there was no use in
waiting longer, as they would not go through the ceremony in my
presence. The next morning I was informed that as soon as I left
the place the proper ceremonies were commenced, when the headman and his family all came forward and made their offerings. Now
if it should be asked why do those *pure Heathens* wish to us believe
that they are Christians? The answer is at hand, because it serves
their temporal interests. Thus by attempting to make them Christians, by holding out improper inducements, and without the use
of the essential means of true conviction and conversion, the Singhalese people have been taught a system of the worst kind of
hypocrisy and deceit. Surely there is not in the world a similar case
of a nation sentimentally and practically Heathen, and at the same
time professing Christianity! During the past quarter my mind has
been exposed to painful exercises respecting our schools, seeing
that they were likely to suffer so much from the diseases which
have prevailed among the people, but particularly the small pox;
for though it is matter of thankfulness that this dreadful disease
has not raged in this district with that violence which it has in
others, yet it found its way into every village where we have schools,
and consequently more or less affected them all: however, I am
happy to be able to say that there is now little of the disease in
this part of the country; and the last time I went through the schools
I found them in a much better state than I expected. May the Lord
protect these infant Christian institutions, and make them the means
of destroying the very roots of idolatry.

On Sunday last our new chapel was opened in the Fort, and it was
a very interesting day indeed. At eleven in the forenoon the Chapel
was filled with all the respectable Singhalese inhabitants of the place,
and numbers of the lower classes were standing on the veranda, as
there was no accomodation for them inside. The service was entirely conducted by our young assistant Cornelius, from Colombo; he
addressed the people with much life and feeling, and told them all
the good things that he could muster; and I trust impressions were
made which will never be lost. About five in the afternoon we had
the pleasure of seeing a fine Portuguese congregation assembled, when
I endeavoured to improve Acts. 7. 48. *Mascomtudo altissimo Deos
nunca mora no templos concertado com maõs.* At seven in the even-

ing we had a fine assembly, to hear the word of life in English; Brother Callaway read the evening service, and Brother Fox preached from Pro. 11. 20. *He that winneth souls is wise*, with all that strength of reason and depth of thought which is so characteristic of his public addresses. The different collections amounted to Two Hundred and Eighty-five Rixdollars, which is not an inconsiderable sum, when it is considered how very few English residents there are in this station at present. The Chapel has cost about £250, of which sum £70 only will have to come from our friends The building is commodious, neat, and strong, being built of the very best materials that the Island can produce, and I believe it will be found just to suit the place. If its erection should prove the means of glorifying God and doing good, then I shall have gained my object

I look forward with pleasure to our approaching meeting, anticipating much happiness in the society of my Brethren, some of whom I have not seen for a long time, and praying that we may be brought together in the fulness of the blessing of the Lord,

I remain, Dear Brethren,
Your very affectionate Brother,
JOHN M'KENNY.

THE MATURA STATION.

Matura, January, 4, 1820.

VERY DEAR BRETHREN,

On this occasion I have little to relate of particular importance. We have proceeded in our usual course, and have had some pleasing proofs of the extending influence of divine knowledge; but the profanation of the Sabbath and excess of riot, at this season especially, among many who call themselves Christians, occasions very painful feelings.—Nor can I inform you of much improvement in the attention of the professed heathen, when addressed on the most interesting subjects that can engage the attention of man. In a few places there is an encouraging disposition to hear. Last Sabbath, in a school about 15 miles from this place, I had, I suppose, threescore adults, besides their children, and this number usually attend. As I was preaching I noticed a Budhist priest strolling through the village, but finding few people at home, he walked away.—We have sometimes preached occasionally under the shade of trees, and by that means addressed many who are not likely to attend elsewhere; but the adults who are present at the beginning, are sometimes all gone or their places filled by others, before we have ended. I have frequently felt much fredom in speaking and a deep concern for the salvation of those who are without God and without hope; and though it is impossible not to feel very sensibly the general inattention to divine things, I have no desire to relax in my efforts. The handful of corn though on a mountain, is in the earth. And though the ancient inquiry were made, who hath believed our report?

we should possess the ancient consolation, my judgment is with the Lord, and my work with my God.

An investigation of the circumstances which facilitate the reception of revelation by one heathen nation, or which issue in its rejection by another, merits the attention of the moral philosopher and the divine; and it is somewhat surprising that so little has been written on the subject. The best efforts on behalf of some places seem for a time altogether in vain, while occurrences apparently accidental lead in other places to the happiest results. A discussion of the subject in any way would be obtrusive in a letter expected to contain a mere statement of facts, but it is certainly an interesting subject for reflexion. Probation of some kind is the present state of every man; and the history of the world may be considered a comment on what we find in the Scriptures on the moral government of God.

St. Paul's speaking ten words which could be understood rather than a thousand which could not, has often stimulated me to express myself as well as I am able in the native languages; and had I not been previously under the necessity of collecting the very words, my progress would no doubt have been more considerable; and any assistance others may derive from my labours will yield me sincere satisfaction.

I have often thought we should see more fruit of our labours if we had a greater variety of interesting publications in circulation. They powerfully assist recollection, and several of our Catechisms and other works have been and are likely to be of eminent service. I mentioned in my last having got the Scripture Extracts put into Portuguese,— we have lately been turning that work into vernacular Singhalese. The passages for the most part are from the New Testament, so that little more is necessary besides exchanging the words, confessedly unknown, for those in use.—It is moreover desirable that some little treatises should be drawn up in a familiar way to give the intelligent youths the outline of some sciences. Observations on nature and common life are sure to excite their curiosity. I fully agree with the following observations in a pamphlet on schools published at Serampore. There is perhaps scarcely a more interesting object than a sensible Hindoo boy. Possessing all that precociousness of mind which arises from the accelerating operations of nature on the young in India, without that duplicity which is so common in riper years, and scarcely as yet affected by their wretched system of religion, they are often lively, ingenuous, and amiable in a peculiar degree, and in quickness of perception, and activity yield to scarcely any nation on earth." Our friend Mr. Chater has illustrated his grammatical rules by homely sentences. These I lately shewed to a Singhalese boy of some intelligence, and I never saw a lad more diverted.

In perambulating one frequently hears a man chaunting some fable or legend which he has got by heart, and the diligence of many in applying themselves to the native books is remarkable: but, not to mention the pernicious principles and bad examples with which they abound, from the obscurity of their style and disregard of nature and fact, they cannot be calculated to expand and strengthen the mental powers, nor perfect the students in their own language.

One of the happiest hours I have passed in this country was a few weeks ago, in holding our first love feast at this place. Nearly all present spoke with simplicity and freedom, and the occasion, I believe, will not be soon forgotten.

In meeting our schoolmasters I have frequently encouraged them to ask questions on points which to their minds are not satisfactory, or which they have known to be urged by heathens against Christianity. Many of their inquiries have been indicative of an ingenuous state of mind, and have related to difficulties which have engaged the attention of the wisest men. Others seem suggested by curiosity; but none by pertness. The following are a specimen: Is the account of the creation in the book of Genesis figurative or literal? Why did Christ object to be called good Master? Is the Budhuist religion the most ancient? Of what religion was Pontius Pilate? Was he a Budhuist?—— As an instance of the little intercourse between one Indian nation and another, not one of our schoolmasters had ever heard of the Hindoo custom of immolating widows till I mentioned it.

I do not think it is common in this neighbourhood to carry the sick and dying to the woods to be left to perish; for the ceremonies employed to restore them are frequent, and however shocking, shew a wish to save them; and deserted houses may be often seen in which some one has expired; but our schoolmasters say, they have in former days seen the poor creatures violently carried from their houses to be left to perish, and have heard them cry out, " Don't carry me away —I shall not yet die! The custom, however, is far from abolished, especially in such regions as are least civilized.

I was somewhat struck with the following account related by one of our schoolmasters and which I have no reason to disbelieve. A short time before the English possessed the Island a woman in his neighbourhood was attacked by the Cholera Morbis, and her friends supposing she would soon expire, prepared her grave, and wrapped her up in a mat, and laid her at the bottom of it alive; but retaining a spark of humanity, they waited for her to breathe her last, before filling the grave. While they stood around, she unexpectedly revived, and lived afterwards several years, in the family of the person who gave me the anecdote. It is scarce necessary to add, that cruelties analagous to this, and usages little better than murder, must blunt every feeling of humanity by rendering the heart insensible to every moral and religious claim.

Let us duly estimate and be unceasingly grateful for our privileges, and pity and improve the deplorable condition of those who are seeking death in the error of their ways. May we pray for an abundant increase of divine influence, and hail the period when Satan shall be dethroned, the rights of Jehovah acknowledged, and Christ shall reign for ever and ever.

　　　　　　　　　I remain,
　　　　　　　　　　Very affectionately yours,
　　　　　　　　　　　J. CALLAWAY.

No x.　　　　　　　　　P

THE JAFFNA STATION.

Jaffna, January 7, 1820.

My Dear Brethren,

It cannot be expected that I should have much to communicate, on account of the limited time which I have been at my station. My dear Brethren preceding had done what they could, but on account of their distance of abode, and numerous other duties, they were much contracted in their sphere of usefulness. On the 19th of October, we arrived at Pt. Pedro, our cottage could not be occupied for upwards of a month after, the repairs not being finished; in the mean time we were accommodated at another Bungalo, and when the rains came we found an asylum at the house of J. J. Kriekenbeek Esq. Not long after I arrived several people came, who (wishing to do me a favour) told me I might build schools, pay schoolmasters wages, &c. for some time I endeavoured to persuade them they were favoured not me, but it was without effect. I must confess I felt unwilling to build schools under such circumstances, so I told them the subject would receive due consideration, and they might call again the next week; in the mean time some people from the village of Alvoy had the condescension to inform me I might build a school for them also. After some conversation I told them to erect a school, and then they should have all proper assistance; at this they seemed quite astonished, and asked the question again: upon receiving a similar answer they started many objections, but at last they agreed to my proposal, and promised to make the place as fine as gold! the land and the school are now settled upon the British Conference. Two other places have been given, one of them is of considerable value, and there are five more building on the same principle; this I think calls for gratitude, not merely on account of the money saved, but on account of the change it must produce on the native mind; at the first I felt unwilling to state these facts, lest my Brethren should be led to think too highly of the work; but I hope this will not be the case, as all of you know it is but a small point gained in comparison with the great object we have in view; yet surely we may indulge a reasonable hope, that these schools will be powerful auxiliaries in our great work. It is true the native mind, although previously neglected, has shewn itself in many instances to be under the influence of God's Spirit, but we cannot expect any thing extensive and at the same time permanent without "line upon line and precept upon precept." As yet (in my station at least) I see the day of small and feeble things, neither do I expect great things without much labour and the blessing of God. The population is immense and the way is open, but what am I "amongst so many". On the 30th of December Mrs. R. and myself arrived at Jaffna, hoping to be cheered by the advice and prayers of our friends, but our feelings received a severe shock to see our dear Br. Squance so emaciated with his old complaint.

At Jaffna I know from observation the work is growing deeper. Our dear Sister Squance and Mrs. Ward (the wife of the Rev. Mr Ward) have, in conjunction with the other ladies of our Society, formed themselves into a Committee for the purpose of visiting the abodes of the poor and wretched, this I think is no small proof that the Lord is carrying on his work. Perhaps I may be allowed to state that they have already seen some fruit of their labour. A poor Malabar woman 80 years of age, apparently near death, could not understand who this Jesus was, (be it remembered she is a Roman Catholic) she could not see of what use the Lord's Christ was to sinners, but after they had given her many instructions and prayed with her several times, seemed quite changed and was continually desiring to go to this Jesus and to see his glory. It is only doing justice to our dear Br. Osborne to say, that this poor woman expressed herself as having received considerable light from his kind visitation, although it appears in the first instance she did not appreciate its value nor apply it to any useful purpose. How judicious is the advice of the wise man, "In the morning sow thy seed and in the evening withhold not thine hand." In conclusion allow me to say. I feel united with my Brethren and perhaps there is no vanity in saying I hope they feel the same disposition towards me: in the course of a few days we shall retire to our station to speak and work for our Heavenly Master. May the blessing of Almighty God be upon you at the coming Conference, and may all your measures be according to his will.

So prays yours affectionately,
JOSEPH ROBERTS.

THE TRINCOMALIE STATION,

Trincomalie, January, 1 1820.

HONOURED BRETHREN,

Objects seldom appear of more importance to man, than when he solemnly reflects on the pittance of time allowed him to secure an eternity of happiness. This reflection brings home every thing to his heart. And the terrors which are announced as the wages of iniquity discover sin to be exceedingly sinful. No object, therefore, connected with his own, or the salvation of others, can be accounted indifferent by the man whose views penetrate beyond the grave.

Enlightened by grace the Christian believer discovers the hole of the pit whence he was dug; and touched by the compassion exercised towards himself, he longs to stretch forth his hand to his sinking fellow mortals, that they also may partake the salvation of God. Thus Christian principles operate, and their effects extend themselves; and thus will they continue to widen till *the*

Redeemer "*shall stand and feed in the strength of the Lord, in the majesty of the name of the Lord his God: and they shall abide: for now shall he be great unto the ends of the earth.*" Micah 5. 4. Wherever this spirit of benevolence is breathed into the hearts of men, and accompanied by faith in the power and promises of God, there cheerful obedience will promote active exertion, and a suitable measure of success precede the happy era, when it shall be said unto the Heathen, "*Thou shalt no more worship the work of thine hands.*"

Humbled beneath a sense of undeserved favours from the Most High, yet desirous of acknowledging extended mercy, we at this time, Dear Brethren, feel pleasure in addressing you, and confessing also that we are "*not ashamed of the Gospel of Christ.*"

In the last Extracts Br Carver briefly made you acquainted with the general condition of the station; which admits, perhaps, of less variety than circuits more extensive. During the past quarter our intercourse with the natives, though much more frequent, has admitted of less opportunity than formerly to give them spiritual instruction We have indeed been busily engaged in that which to a Missionary is *labour extraordinary*, that is to say, building and forming somewhat of an establishment, without which no man in India ought to dream of success Undoubtedly many, through want of information, may think differently, and consider such things necessary only in a very limited degree. But we are almost tempted to ask, where shall the rising generation and others receive instructions? and how shall we convince a Heathen population of the permanency of our cause? is not instability constantly charged upon the natives? and does not every thing in civil, judicial, and military matters among them change. To expect, therefore, much success among a people, whose welfare you wish them to understand you desire to promote, and yet neglect to form places of worship among them, is a folly to be cured by time.

In our work we have been happy, but much interrupted by continual calls to look after work people, which break up all order and regularity of study. The congregations have been irregular, occasioned by the violence of the monsoon; and some of the class have removed to other parts of the Island.

The three schools have not been less interesting than usual, and reading the scriptures in them, catechising, and occasional preaching, has given the adults, who attended, an opportunity of hearing and understanding the redemption that is in Jesus Our first schoolmaster, Mr. Hunter, whom we might previously have mentioned with credit to himself, has been very useful in the arrangement of our schools here, and to be deprived of him would be a loss we could not for a long time repair. He speaks, reads, and writes Tamul fluently, and has lately begun to preach in that language He is familiar with Portuguese, and is our first Teacher in English. Br. Carver began, on his first entrance into his Mission work, to draw together the young men within his reach, and while several have been introduced into Government offices, and others have forgotten their obligations by manifestations of ingratitude; some have caused him much satisfaction, to behold in them a promising work of grace, among whom is this young man. His steady conduct during a residence of a year and a half on this station hath gained for himself the approbation of the Missionary under whose direction he has acted, and secured a measure of respect among the natives unknown before. The children look up to him with a measure of confidence, which is repaid with advantage by the care exercised over them; and, even while writing this, Br. Carver is called off to seek for a book in Tamul to help a Mohammedan boy, who has just applied to Mr. Hunter to contend by strong arguments with the head of that sect. The circumstance arose thus, the boy having made great progress lately in his learning began to find pleasure in singing praises to God and in prayer, and his parents wishing him one day to read the Koran he began to read to them, in their own language, some useful tracts which he had just received. This so astonished them, that they resolved to take him to the chief priest to have him, as they expressed it, "converted" to the true Musselman faith. He was furnished for the controversy with a dialogue between a Mohammedan and a Christian, and we have not yet heard the result.

Another circumstance took place previously, which will shew, in some measure, that the hindrances to Christianity in the East are widely different to what is experienced in Europe. In the nations of Europe the general tone of feeling is in favour of Christianity; but in India, the tone of feeling is against it. On the 23d November, 1819, the government schoolmaster, Gabriel, called at the Mission House, to say that Ferdinando, the old native Protestant priest was dead; Gabriel had taken much trouble to go here and there, but it was no one's business to bury him; he was told by one and another, they had nothing to do with it. The Heathens would not come near the place where he lay. The Roman Catholics could not be expected to look upon, or, according to their principles, afford funeral rites to one denominated by them a heretic: and thus,

"Deny'd the charity of dust to spread,
"O'er dust! a charity their dogs enjoy,"

it followed, that his bones must whiten upon the surface of the earth or be thrust into a hole without a coffin. Conscious what pernicious effects might follow from deserting a native Christian, and especially one among them accounted a minister, we immediately gave orders to our work people to make him a decent coffin, which they speedily executed; and coloured black as a great mark of respect. Our young man was ready to go and read the service over him at the burial ground, when a fresh difficulty started in our way; *no one could be found that would defile themselves by carrying him to the grave!* At last, on speaking to our coolies, eight of them bore the aged padre to the "*peaceful chamber*" where all *distinctions cease.*

No. x. G

Dear Brethren, your reflections on this subject may be as ours. Here we behold a case which shews heathenism only creditable and Christianity disgraceful and not to be desired. Here we have a circumstance, which *in India* may not be uncommon, though perhaps often unknown to the bulk of the followers of Christ, and by this we ought to receive instruction. Mankind, unenlightened by the grace of God, perceive not the duty. independant of opinions, man owes to man: or if they can perceive it, they are base enough to neglect that duty. Had we also thought a want of acquaintance with the poor man, or a difference of country, sufficient excuse to avoid paying the last sad ceremonies to the dead, it is probable his bones might have remained unsepulchred to this day.

In the beginning of December three married Missionaries from America landed here, bound direct to the province of Jaffnapatam, to reinforce the party of three, who were in that district before. One of them remained a few days at the Mission House, and then set out by land to Jaffna; the other two went round in the vessel by way of Colombo.

The conclusion of the year brought together, for the first time, in this place, the children of our native schools, to be examined and rewarded. On Christmas day a great number of them were waiting with presents at the door when our English congregation retired, which caused the greater surprise, because they were not expected to come before the time appointed, which was two days after—The circumstance, however, seemed greatly to affect some of our English hearers, and indeed many of the little innocent looking creatures were very interesting. We were the more glad, inasmuch as the smallest concessions in favour of our holy religion, in a place like this, ought not to be despised.

Monday, December 27th, our scholars collected themselves, though the rains every half hour came down in torrents; and at ten o'clock our place of worship was filled with children. So many sable, yet sparkling countenances, fixed upon us at our entrance, rewarded in a measure the Missionary for the hours of labour, anxiety, and toil, experienced in gathering them out of the hovels of heathenism. And be accepted it as a sign for good, that even any, in this place, were induced to enter the house of God. Our English scholars were also present, and seemed to gather consequence from the circumstance, that they had *now* to sit at the head of a greater number!

In examining the boys, one of the head class was called upon to question, from the catechism, the others on their progress therein. This he did in a confidential and masterly manner, proceeding through several sections of Wood's Catechism in Tamul, till he had two boys only left, the others being unable to keep up with them. Those two were rewarded with more distinguished honour. When the little presents, were distributing expectation sat sparkling in every eye: which, on the possession of the gift, gave place to satisfaction. A

few of the higher class boys sang a Malabar hymn much better
than we expected. They then sat down, and our English scholars
sang in English, equal to what we have often heard in our native land, we then dismissed them with prayer.

Thus, dear Brethren, have we briefly laid before you what we conceived chiefly worth notice. during the last three months ; with the
exception of one thing, which you may perhaps think it was our
duty to mention, especially as it gives an encouraging prospect
into public life, and shews that there these principles sometimes powerfully operate. Br Carver having no prospect of reaching the Conference at Colombo, without attempting to penetrate the dreary
jungles of Kandy, and passing across the island through the capital,
was obliged to look out for some means of conveyance by the
only mode of travelling by land used here. He therefore addressed the
accompanying note to Commissioner Upton, which produced the reply he thought it his duty to insert.

Mission House, Trincomalie, December 23, 1819.

Dear Sir,

The rains prevented me from having the pleasure to see you this
morning :—being called upon to attend our yearly meeting at Colombo I shall have to proceed by land. Hearing that you have
two palanquins, and believing you would pardon the trouble I am
giving by the enquiry, I should be exceedingly obliged, if without
any inconvenience to yourself, you could part with one for a month
or two, or altogether the one purchased from Mr. A. of the En-
gineer Department ; as I would very gladly replace the price given
to him. The difficulty of getting such a thing at Trincomalie, and
my confidence in your readiness to oblige, are my reasons and
apology for causing you this trouble which I hope you will forgive.

I am, Dear Sir,

To

Your most Obedient Servant,

Commissioner Upton.

R. CARVER.

To this request Br. Carver immediately received a very handsome and condescending reply, of which the following is an extract :

Trincomalie, December 23, 1819.

"It affords me very sincere pleasure, my dear Sir, having the
means of meeting your wishes ; the palanquin is much at your
service in any way you please, either by loan or purchase, my only
object in procuring it was to serve a friend, and I am happy in
the opportunity of doing so : it will be delivered at any moment
you may send for it, and is a light and comfortable one. I wish
you as pleasant a journey as the nature of this country will permit, and a speedy return to Trincomalie, believe me,

My dear Sir,

Very faithfully your's,

C. UPTON.

If, by *purchase*, you can procure me about a dozen of such parts of the Scripture as are translated into the Malabar, I think I could so distribute them among my household as to have some effect; also the same number of any publications as tend to explain to these people the nature of the Christian religion."

Too much occupied with a multitude of pressing concerns, there was not a moment of time on that and the following day to look over the books for the things mentioned, but on the 25th, a parcel was sent with the note which follows:

Trincomalie, December 25, 1819.

Dear Sir,

Would incessant engagements have permitted, a reply to your very pleasing answer to my enquiry would sooner have been sent. Allow me to offer my sincere thanks for that readiness to oblige me manifested in your letter: with no small pleasure I hasten to comply with that part of it, which requests useful publications in the Malabar language, seeing so great a number of that people are under your inspection, I beg leave to send, therefore, a copy of the New Testament in Tamul, expressly for the purpose of being referred to, at any time when you may have leisure to call a native to do so, accompanied by several parts of the Holy Scriptures printed at Colombo, and also, six different descriptions of tracts lately had from Madras, six copies of each; likewise one copy of our School Report. Some of the tracts are particularly intended to become as warnings on account of the dreadful visitations of disease among the natives; many have been distributed, which were well understood, and natives have come to the Mission House for one or two kinds, which I am sorry to say I was unable to supply, all my small stock being exhausted. However, we expect a fresh assortment in a short time.

I will not attempt to describe the pleasure I feel on the request being made which led to this reply; and equally unable am I to express that, which I have often previously experienced, when beholding persons busily engaged in necessary duties, secure also moments of time to do good to mankind. I may conclusively observe, that such indications of liberal feeling go not unrewarded, and prove a great cause of encouragement to faithful ministers, whose hearts, touched by the stream of generous benevolence, leads them first to forsake all for Christ, and then satisfactorily to contemplate the effects of that benevolence in others.

I am, dear Sir,

Your very Obedt. Servant,

To

Commissioner Upton.   R. CARVER.

Pleasing indeed is the work of gratitude when unlooked for help in the important controversy of light against darkness, calls for our acknowledgements. And we ought to observe, that the congenial feelings of satisfaction, arising from doing good, are not confined to the agents themselves, but impart a measure of happiness to all to whom they are made known, and not unfrequently excite emulation of Christian deeds: perhaps, even now, it may be the design of unbounded mercy to peculiarly turn the hearts of many in favour of his cause: for

"Man's heart the Almighty to the future sets

"By secret and inviolable springs" Young.

This sentiment may be considered perhaps as encouragingly illustrated by a short extract of a letter from England, lately received by Br Carver from a friend.

MY DEAR SIR,

"I hasten to give you some account of those things which I think will be most interesting to you. First then, as it respects the cause of Missions, which I can assure you has taken fast hold of many hearts and minds of men and women, especially the young, on this side the ocean. Among the rest your friend——— who has done what he could to help forward the great and good cause. Missionary meetings are now held, and societies formed, in nearly all the principal towns in this kingdom, and in some of them Juvenile Missionary Meetings also. Our (Huddersfield) J. M. S. was formed on the 12th May, 1816, by a few young people among themselves. Our second meeting far surpassed the first by more than double success. But our greatest undertaking is a new chapel. The ground was purchased in December 1817, for £ 2800 and the foundation stone laid on April 8th, 1818. The ground occupied by this chapel, including the walls, is 34 yards long by 24 yards wide; besides two wings of 3 yards each, so that it will appear 30 yards in front, which is by far the largest chapel in the kingdom, of any description. I expect the concern will cost (10,000) Ten Thousand pounds.

It is so much spoken of that a great many passengers, passing through the town, call to look at it. We expect to open it in July, 1819. And when that time arrives, may the great Head of the Church fill it with his presence and blessing." We are involuntarily led to say, Amen. For, *as truly as I live*, saith our God, *all the earth shall be fill'ed with the glory of the Lord*" Num. 14. 21.

But we are exceeding the general limits of a letter, and would conclude with an ascription of praise and thanksgiving to God, for his distinguished mercies during the past year: journeying by sea and by land hath he preserved us from danger. But above all, we thank him for communications of spiritual grace; for blessing us with a desire to enjoy more of the unction from above: giving us clear and comprehensive views of the state of man by nature: the redemption by Christ: the willingness of the Saviour to save unto the uttermost them that come unto him, and an enlarged knowledge of the general *benevolence* of God to mankind.

Dear Brethren, though sometimes faint yet pursuing, we are

Most affectionately yours,

R. CARVER,

A. STEAD.

No x.   H

THE BATTICALOA STATION.

Batticaloa, December 29, 1819.

MY DEAR BRETHREN,

From a postscript in Br. Newstead's last Quarterly you have been informed that I omitted writing my quarterly communications in consequence of my unsetled circumstances, and being then so little acquainted with Batticaloa I had nothing to write relative to that station. I could have filled a large sheet with an account of my voyage from Jaffna to Batticaloa, particularly with the danger and fatigue I experienced in landing, but the God of my mercies brought me with my little family in safety to this place.

The boat with which I attempted to make the vessel (anchored at the mouth of the river) to bring Mrs O. and the child on shore, was driven on shore by the violence of the sea, and in a few hours after broken to pieces. I escaped with the soldiers who managed the boat by jumping on shore while the boat was fast in a sand bank Had Mrs. O. and the little ones been in the boat there would have been little hope of their being saved. The surge at the entrance of this river is at times as heavy and dangerous as the surge at Madras.

I was very fortunate upon my arrival at Batticaloa to find a house empty, which had been the case I believe but for a few weeks. This I found in a miserable condition scarcely fit for a stable, large holes through the roof, the walls decorated with white ants' nests, rooms without doors, and where there were doors, without locks or hinges. But I am happy to say I have now a very comfortable house and premises, but had but just time to make the house good before the heavy rains began to fall.

I need scarcely inform you that much of my time has been occupied in the very unpleasant business of superintending repairs, &c. &c. most of you know what it is to build or repair houses in Ceylon, and Batticaloa I am persuaded is the worst part of Ceylon for such work: I have had a little trouble with the owner of the house about the expence of the repairs, he was not willing to pay for them, though he promised me if I would do the repairs he would take no rent till all was paid me again. But the sum being much greater than he expected (339 Rds. 2 Fs.) he objected to pay it unless I would pay 30 Rds. per Month instead of 20 Rds. I have agreed to pay him 25 Rds. and finding him an uncertain changeable sort of man I have drawn up an agreement, which he has signed in the presence of Mr. Pennell, that he shall pay for the repairs upon condition that I pay him 25 Rds. per Month, to commence with January 1820. Last week the rebuilding of the wrecked boat was accomplished; this has also been a troublesome and expensive business, and would have been much more so had I not been assisted by Messrs Pennell and Bagnett: (the Collector and Magistrate) the boat when completed will cost nearly 800 Rds. in consequence of having to pay Doctor Martin 450 Rds. for the wreck After all it is considered by those who understand the value of boats to be worth all it costs. It is sufficiently large to sail round Ceylon, and the lake at Batticaloa is deep enough for such a boat to sail to any of the neighbouring villages. A horse or palanquin would be of little or no use here, as the Island of Batticaloa is but 3 miles in circumference This boat is the one that Mr. Jackson began building before he left Batticaloa. In consequence of the heavy rains which have been falling here for many weeks I have not been able to itinerate much, however I have visited several places, and hope from what I could see of the disposition of the people that I shall be able to do something among them as soon as the weather is favorable. It is a little singular that in visiting two villages, whle waiting for the Headman, I stood on the very spot on which our Br. Ault had schools. I believe I might have established one or two schools in the country before the commencement of the monsoon, but I purposely declined it, as I could not have visited them; and feared that for want of proper discipline at first the schools might have got into such disorder that it would be difficult, if not impossible, to recover them from it. I had also another reason, I could not meet with proper schoolmasters: those who offered themselves were Heathens. I hope this difficulty will be removed by the time of the change of the monsoon, as I have two fine young men under instruction for that office, they are about 18 years of age, know a little English, are very steady, and I believe not entire strangers to religion. One of them will meet in class next Tuesday (if all be well) for the first time. Also a son of the Cutchery Modeliar, about 20 years of age, will meet for the first time. He is a well informed young man and has an excellent character. His father is a Protestant, but not like the generality of native Protestants. He studies his Bible as well as reads it, and can converse feelingly upon the vitals of Religion. He often visits me, and will come as often as he can with his son to class. He speaks Portuguese pretty well, and is about 60 years of age. I hope the young man will become very useful here. He is willing to go with me as often as he can to visit the country places—he speaks a little English.

There are three or four villages within about eight or nine miles of Batticaloa called Protestant villages, but I understand that the name is all they have of what we call Protestanism. They go to the Heathen temple, keep their feast days, &c. &c. Not being able to go I sent for a schoolmaster from one of them and had some conversation with him: I soon found he knew nothing of Christianity. I asked him if he had no Bible or Testament? He answered he had a Testament for the use of a small school but he did not read it himself. I asked why? He said it was not given for *him* to read, it was a book to teach the children to *read*. It appears he thought it of the same nature with a spelling book. I explained to him the nature of that book, desired him to read it much, and that when I should come I should question him upon what is written in that book and hoped he would be

prepared to answer, since then I have not seen him. The English
congregation here is generally tolerably large, having regularly 40
or 50 soldiers, besides most of the people who understand English
in the place. The greater part of the soldiers are very attentive,
and lately I have seen many of them in tears during Divine service. From a conversation with the sick in the Hospital a few
days since, I found that there were many of the men who had
become more steady since they had heard preaching and read the
tracts and old magazines which I distributed among them. The
Portuguese congregation is pretty large considering the population of the place, together with the number of Roman Catholics,
who will not come near us or allow their children to come. We
have had Portuguese preaching but once for five weeks in consequence of the inclemency of the weather, which has the appearance
here of a regular winter; we are now so insulated that had we
not, as the ants, laid up our store in the summer we must have
starved. At this time I believe I could not purchase a measure of
rice in Batticaloa. I have a small school which we keep in the
viranda of the church, the number of scholars generally under 20,
and their attendance very irregular; nor do I expect this school
will ever grow to much importance as the number of children
eligible for schools are but few, and that few divided into Heathen, Catholics, and Protestants, but at present it has not had a
fair trial.

I was very much encouraged, my dear Brethren, in reading the
last quarterly extracts. Every station seems to be prospering, and
our Messiah's kingdom gaining strength against the powers of
darkness, even in the strong hold of the Devil, *ignorance and superstition*. I know we can all join in one consent to supplicate
the great head of the Church in the language of one of our excellent hymns, and sing

On all the earth thy spirit shower
The earth in righteousness renew;
Thy Kingdom come and hell's o'erpower,
And to thy sceptre *all* subdue.

I hope next quarter, under the Divine aid and benediction of
our God, to have some thing pleasing to tell you from this p'ace.
Oh! that the Lord may pour upon us all a more enlarged portion
of true Missionary zeal, kindled by the same spirit which led our
Lord to die on Calvary for the sins of the world, and which influenced the holy army of Martyrs to shed their blood cheerfully
as faithful witnesses of the truth.

I thank God I feel an increase of this zeal. willing to spend
and be spent in the cause of the Gospel. I feel more deadness
to the world than ever, and a peculiar and inexpressible delight
of soul in the pleasing anticipation of eternal life. I feel as if
I could consider nothing important which is not eternal. Mrs.
Osborne, and the little ones, are tolerably well; our sickly little girl
has suffered a little from the cold damp weather. The Portuguese

young man I brought from the Jaffna class continues to do
well. He attends to the school and studies very closely. I hope he
will be of great service to me and our cause here after a little
time. I am sorry to say that a very promising young man, who
left Jaffna for Batticaloa about 12 months since, has now entirely
left us, so that our class at present is made up of only Mrs. Osborne, Mr. Heslic and myself. Next week I hope to muster five.
The Lord does not despise the day of small things. Farewell.

I am, dear Brethren,

Yours very affectionately,

T. OSBORNE.

Miscellaneous.

No. I.

Extract of a letter from Br. Carver on his visit to Batticaloa, in October, 1819.

Had time permitted, in the last Extracts I might have detailed to you a few incidents of my visit to Batticaloa to see Br. Osborne.

Not that any peculiar traits of character are exhibited by the natives, different to other parts of the northern side of the Island ; but because that place admonishes us, that there lie the ashes of a Brother whose memory yet lives. Every thing, therefore, connected with his work becomes interesting, and though premature death seems to cast a solemn gloom over the place where he lies interred, yet, the contemplation of his worth and excellence may not be unprofitable.

"Come, contemplation, from thy much lov'd shades,
"Which scarce a ray of Summer's noon pervades !
"Quit for a while thy consecrated cave,
"And pay with me a visit to the grave !"

On the 2d of October, after a short and pleasant voyage of two nights and one day, we reached the mouth of the Batticaloa river, and proceeded up gently towards the fort. On my first visit in 1816 I had not time for more than a hasty glance at the surrounding scenery; and several objects had passed unnoticed. The country near the shore is flat, and beautifully diversified by the lake, which gives the beholder continually fresh pleasure by introducing him to little basons, winding shores, and small islands, more or less covered with trees and shrubs. This is a peculiarity which renders the appearance of the shores of Ceylon superior to the low fatiguing prospects of naked barren sands, on approaching the continent. Immediately behind Batticaloa the country assumes a bold and majestic appearance: hills surmounted by mountains, stretch themselves into the Kandian country, till the sight is obstructed by clouds.

Whilst passing a Roman Church our sailors were busied with lowering the top sail, which informed me our vessel belonged to a Catholic; upon enquiry I found it so, he also being on board, and careful to observe this universal mark of respect to his church. On landing I found Brother and Sister Osborne had got a decent house in an open situation; and were regulating their affairs so as to turn their attention to Missionary work. On Sunday, Oct. 3d, Br. Osborne read the service in the Government Church, and I preached from Ezek. 11. 16. *Thus saith the Lord GOD; Although*

B

I have cast them far off among the heathen, and although I have scattered them among the countries, yet will I be to them as a little sanctuary in the countries where they shall come. The Collector, Magistrate, and the small Garrison were present.

On Monday we opened a new school for boys of all descriptions, to be taught, in the viranda of the Church. Dr. Martins was also present; twenty-one boys, chiefly Dutch and Portuguese, were admitted. As many as could read a little we directed to sing a verse of a hymn to the tune of New-Cambridge, which they managed but poorly at first, but after trying a few times they got hold of it a little. Let us not however despise the day of small things. Their numbers increased daily during my stay, and I hope the attempt will be crowned with success.

In the afternoon Dr. Martins accompanied us across the water to a village where once Br. Ault began a school. The prospect of a large sheet of water, skirted by trees, and fringed with low bushes, beguiled my attention, and fixed my thoughts on some parts of England, where pleasure had often been raised to delight. By this comparison I need not be afraid you will imagine I mean, that the prospects of the places are equally rich : for, however the torid zone may be represented by colouring writers, with all its advantages it is much less pleasant, and far less favourable to the comforts of man than the temperate. After some pulling against the tide and current we drew near to a very singular tree, whose beautiful green foilage attracted our notice at a distance : we landed under its shade, and found it composed of one large spreading tree in the middle, among whose branches a running plant, something like our ivy, had insinuated itself, completely covering the whole, and hanging down to the waters' edge, forming a cool retreat from the sun and a shelter from the rain. Near to it grew large quantities of a common kind of cane, very prickly on the outer rind: and running up 30 and 40 feet high.

Passing along the groves of Cocoa-nut trees, which had a rather singular appearance, two trees generally growing from one root, we came to an open plot of ground about 70 yards square, on which we plainly discovered a house of wood had formerly been built. I began to enquire the name of the village, and found that on the very spot where we stood Br. Ault had caused a native school to be erected ; but now not a relict of it remained : the places only where the posts had stood were marked. We walked forward into an enclosure, when it appeared the man of the house, which stood in it, was a worker in brass, and when their surprise at seeing such strangers was a little abated, the following conversation took place, begun by myself in their own language : சேலாம் Salām (peace) Answer

சேலாம் அய்யா Salām aiyāh, peace Sir.

Q. How many houses have you in this village?
A. About fifty Sir.
Q. How many people?

A. Perhaps two or three hundred.

Q. Have you any schools in the village?

A. No.

Q. Had you ever any?

A. Yes, we had once.

Q. How long since, and how was it established?

A. Alas! now a long time ago one Padrie came from Batticaloa and made the schools, but alas! he is dead!

Q. How long since?

A. More than three years.

Q. Do you remember what kind of a person he was—stout, tall?

A. No, No, he was a little man; a good man, but (they added) he is dead and we have no school.

Q. Do you wish to have one, and will you send your children if one is made?

A. (Two or three together) we will, we will.

After informing them Br Osborne was another Padrie like the one they had lost, we went away, but not before they had many times looked upon each other and expressed considerable astonishment that a European was able to converse in their own language. I asked them, as we passed through the garden, the names of several trees and plants, of their growth, and fruits, all of which they answered with no small delight. We then directed our steps to the beach followed by many both young and old; when recollecting that I had in my hand a Malabar book, part of the Gospel, which was taken by me to read in the boat, I gave it to one who stood near us, to take to the old man who had answered our enquiries. The others immediately surrounded him to know what he had got, and we lost sight of them winding through the trees as they wandered back reading the book towards the old man's house. May the Lord himself accompany with his blessing, even detached parts of his holy word! May he remove the darkness from their understanding, and may these Heathen worship no longer "*The unknown God.*" We returned home in our boat, much satisfied with our excursion, and encreasingly thankful to the Lord that we had been nourished under so great advantages compared to the poor inhabitants of these climes.

The first visit, paid in 1816, to the place where our Dear Brother's remains are deposited, filled me with that solemn awe and reverence which may be conceived to prevail over the minds of those who are exposed to a like fate: and whose dust also might perhaps be visited by another, when time had measured out the same space. I sought out the church with trembling anxiety; the more so perhaps, because I was charged to him, by his living friends, with messages of affection and tender regard:—but I was too late, the servant of God had finished his work; the opening flower had closed at noon; and death, untimely, death had laid his cold hand upon the fervour of his zeal. A stone in the church was all the remembrance of him I could behold, which bore the

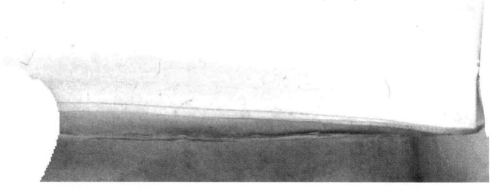

inscription of his name. A melancholy silence prevailed around, while occasional glances on the walls informed me that the tender husband also had here been robbed of his endeared wife;† which made death in this place appear to me terribly triumphant.

> "*Death*—King of Terrors, whose despotic sway
> "The mortal race reluctantly obey,
> "Distinction levels, when his bow he bends,
> "And all the noble with the ignoble blends;
> "With hand impartial strikes the fatal blow,
> "And lays mankind in common ruin low:
>
> . . . .
>
> "Yet calm reflection bids my hopes revive,
> "For Truth asserts, "The tree cut down shall live."

For many hours I sat alone in the church, ruminating on the spoils of death, and felt a kind of reluctance to leave the spot to mingle with the living. On this visit, also, my thoughts were often directed to the place where our Brother's dust awaits the glorious resurrection

The evening before my departure to Trincomalie Br. Osborne and I were walking along one of the roads which led past a Modeliar's house, who happened to be in the gateway, and invited us to go in. He shewed us his garden, trees, and plants, and we returned into the house, which was very tastefully arranged in native style, the rooms being bordered and painted divers colours. On the table lay, accidentally, a Tamul Testament, which I carelessly turned over, and began to read, when he opened his eyes upon us with no small surprise, and with haste sought out a passage, for he was a Roman Catholic, which he wanted us to explain. Having found it, he read out of Revelations, "*Let him that hath understanding count the number of the beast; for it is the number of a man: and his number is six hundred and three score and six.*" Rev. 13. 18. As he spake Portuguese fluently Br. Osborne endeavoured to satisfy his inquiries by a conversation of some length. He then shewed us his ornaments and pictures; one of the latter he wished us particularly to notice: it was about 18 inches square. In one corner our Saviour is represented on the judgment seat; on the other, opposite, an accusing infernal spirit is reading to him a long black catalogue of the offender's crimes, and beneath is a man just expiring, with a hideous demon ready to snatch him off.

Our visit seemed pleasing to the man, and we were glad to find the Gospel in the house of a Catholic: he spoke also of going to hear Br. Osborne preach in Portuguese, which I hope he has done.

Indifferent as to what particular instruments the Almighty is pleased to use for the conversion of men, we rejoice as over great spoil when we behold good done. We know "The Lord by wisdom hath founded the earth; by understanding hath he established the heavens. By his knowledge the depths are broken up, and the clouds drop down the dew." Prov. 19: 20.

---

† Mrs. Sawyers the amiable wife of the Collector, whose great kindness to our dear Br. during his illness, will long be remembered. R. C.

"For from the rising of the sun even unto the going down of the same my name shall be great among the Gentiles: and in every place incense shall be offered unto my name, and a pure offering: for my name shall be great among the heathen, saith the Lord of Hosts." Mal. 1. 11.

I left Batticaloa on Friday at 7 A. M. and reached Trincomalie in safety on Sunday; and landed just as the morning gun fired over our heads.

R. CARVER.

December 29, 1819.
Trincomalie.

No. II.

Trincomalie, December 31, 1819.

By the date of the following letter you will perceive it is upwards of one hundred and thirteen years since it was written. It is upon a subject closely connected with that which occupies the pages of the Extracts: and I think interesting in itself independent of that relation. Of the pious and zealous writer I need say nothing. Ziegenbalgh's name needs not my praise His praise is in all the churches; and of the fruits of his labours the Missionaries taste who occupy the ground he once trod. I have beheld marks of his worth, and seen vestiges of the good deeds he accomplished, and I am led therefore to venerate the man whose equal it may never be my lot to look upon.

Should the insertion of this be deemed proper the description given in a plain and homely dress, which it was thought best to retain, as well as the subjects on which the writer treats, may perhaps be acceptable.

I am, dear Brethren,
Affectionately yours,
R. CARVER.

Of the gross and blind Idolatry of the Malabarians. And an Account of their several Idols. Their Notion of the Sun and of other Celestial Bodies

Having made some Enquiry into the Principles both of the *Divinity* and *Philosophy* now in vogue among these heathens, and finding a vast Difference betwixt their Divinity, and that which God has conferred upon us in *Europe*, I could not forbear to impart to you some Account thereof; to the End that by comparing One with the Other, we might learn the better to set a right Value upon the Grace vouchsafed to us by the Goodness of God

First then, as for the *Divinity* of the *Malabarians*; (the name whereby they are commonly known throughout the whole Tract of this Country) I have observed, that the same is interlaced with a world of Fables and idolatro s Fictions. They have many Hundreds of Gods, but own nevertheless but *one* Divine Being to be the Spring and original Source of all other Gods and Things. It is called by them *Isparella*, which, in their Language, imports as much as a Deity. This *Isparella*, they say, before any thing was created, transformed himself into an *Egg*: out of which the whole system of Heaven and Earth, and all that is contained therein, was afterwards produced.

From this Divinity, as their Tradi ion runs, did originally spring forth something, which they call *Kuvelinga* and which they worship in their Temples for God. From this Kuvelinga, they say further, Three other great Gods took their Rise; viz. *Bramma*, *Wischnum*, and *Ispara*. *Bramma* is said to create and make all things; *Wischnum*, to rule over things created; and *Ispara* to destroy all again. They are all Three set up here in large *Pagodas* or Temples. Perhaps this poor People have heard heretofore that there is one divine Being only, but made manifest in Three Persons; for they ascribe in many things such characters to *Bramma*, as we appropriate to JESUS CHRIST. They say, he has a human nature, but four Heads, and that he has given to Mankind four Books. The *first* of these did treat of Divinity, and of the first original Principle of all things. The *Second* of Powers, and the various Metamorphoses or Transmutations of all things. The *third* they say contains good morals: and the *fourth*, the Duties to be observed in their idolatrous Worship.

I was some Days ago with an Old Teacher of theirs, and desired him to transcribe for my use the Three last of these Books in their own Language, offering him ready Money for his Labour: but I could not prevail with him; he pretending it to be contrary to their Laws, to communicate them to a Christian. However, he promised to copy out for me such Morals and Customs, as were usually observed among them. *Ispara* is the chief of all the *Malabarian* Gods, and worshipped accordingly. He is erected in a large *Pagoda* or Temple having Three Eyes; one of which is fixed in the Forehead, and by them believed to burn up all whatsoever it looks: on each side he has Eight Hands, making Sixteen in all. In each of these he holdeth something particular; but I have not been able as yet to learn all the Mysteries figur'd out by these things. On his Neck hangeth a little Bell, such as the Cows use to wear in our country. On his Forehead is seen a Half Moon, and he is arrayed besides with Serpents and Tygers. His Bigness, they say, encompasses all the Seven Heavens above, and all the Seven Worlds beneath.

There goes a Story among them that this *Ispara* making once merry with his heavenly Spirits, and looking on his Bigness, fancied he had none like to himself. *Bramma* and *Wischnum*, much nettled at the excessive Pride of their fellow God picked a quarrel with him, which at last arose to such a Heat that *Bramma* lost one of his Heads by *Ispara's* valour. The latter being soon after convinced of the false step he had taken in this, fell a repenting for his disorderly conduct, and rambled about begging for twelve years together. What strange Adventures he did meet with during that Interval. would be too tedious to relate here at large. *Wischtnum* seeing his poor Brother God wander about in such a beggarly condition, attempts to rescue him; and for that Purpose metamorphosed himself into a beautiful Virgin. But this Account is attended again with a long Train of Tales and Fictions, too prolix to be rehearsed here. However, these and many other impertinent Stories are set out by the *Malabarians* in so fine Flourishes of Wit, and adorn'd with such a poetical Air, as may make it pleasant enough to read them; though they refuse to impart them at large to any Christian, let there be never so much Money bid for them. I keep at present a particular Schoolmaster in my House, whom I hope to prevail with to transcribe for me the Stories and Transactions of their several Gods, in the Knowledge whereof he is extraordinarily well versed.

Ispara has got Three Sons; all which are worshipped here as Gods, in Three Temples. He has also one Daughter, whom they give out to be a great Princess among the Heavenly Virgins: she is as black as a coal, with three huge sow tushes in her Mouth. Our Governor lending me a Horse one Day to take the Diversion of riding a little about in the Country, I had the good hap to see this Dame, set out in all her Fineries, and riding in a handsome Chariot.

The Third God. who is greatly esteem'd among the *Malabarians*, is WISCHTNUM; whom they report to be quite black, with one Head and four Hands. They will tell you a world of Stories of his Life and Actions. Among other Fictions, they pretend that he is subject to a tenfold transmutation, the last of which is still to come. And this perhaps may be the chief Cause that hath given Birth to the notion of the *Soul's Transmigration* after Death, now generally believed among these Heathens. The *First* transmutation of this God was into a Fish; the *Second*, into a Tortoise; the *Third*, into a Hog; the *Fourth*, half into a Lion, and half into a Man; the *Fifth*, into a Bramin; the *Sixth*, into a fair comely Child; the *Seventh*, into a Ram. They tell us, that this God, in the Twelfth year of his Age, understood all the secrets and mysteries of things. That afterwards he wrought a great many Wonders up and down in the World; purchasing his Bride from a Powerful King, by the Means of many surprizing Exploits and Atchievements; soon after he had the Misfortune to be bereav'd of his Bride by a crafty and valiant *Giant*, who having secretly conveyed her away, put *Wischtnum* to a deal of Grief and Vexation. However he rescued her at last from her captivity, after a long and tedious combat, wherein he defeated Thousands of Giants. And from these and other Tales of that Nature, we may rationally infer, that this deluded People have heard some imperfect Rumour of Christ, but taking it in all in a huddle, have interlaced it with a world of Fables and Fictions.

As to the *Eighth* Transmutation, the Heathens do not pretend to any certainty themselves. The *Ninth*, according to their Tradition, ended in the shape of a Man, whom they represent as one sitting in a doleful Posture and imploring the great God, day and night, with Eyes turned downwards. And they give out, he is to do so still these many Thousand Years, before he can be set at liberty. And this, they say, was the time, wherein they now lived. It may be, that this is a shadow of the Intercession of Christ; which they seem to point at in their Narration. His last and *Tenth* Transmutation, (and here we may guess, that they have likewise some imperfect Notion of the Day of *Judgment*,) is to be into a *flying Horse*. About that time, they say, the sins of men would increase to a prodigious height; insomuch that this Horse would set down his Foot, now lifted up for the Punishment of Men, to the Ground, with so extraordinary an Impression, that the great Serpent which bears the Earth, trembling thereat, would let fall the World, and this would be the final period of this World and the beginning of another.

This short Draught may serve to give you a smack of their ridiculous Theology. One might add a great deal more concerning their *Philosophical* Principles; but for the present I will only tell you, that they hold there are seven Heavens and seven Worlds, altogether born up by a swinging Serpent. In *Physical* and *Mathematical* Affairs they don't seem to have any great knowledge; though otherwise they be quick enough of Apprehension. To the *Sun*, *Moon*, and other *Stars*, they attribute human Souls. And particularly concerning the Sun, they tell us, that he has Seven Eyes, whereof only one is open at this present time: should the remaining Six be opened too, no Body would be able to endure the Heat thereof. *Thunder* is called by them the *Talk of the Clouds*. They believe that there are many Angels, and that every one of them has a peculiar office to attend. They own no Resurrection of Bodies, but a *Transmigration* of the Soul into other Men, Dogs, Serpents, &c. From this springs up another Notion, viz. that, whoso any way abuseth a Man in this Life, shall after his Death become a Slave to the injured Person. They fancy the world has been already thrice destroyed by water, and would perish once more by the same Element. They hold that the Length of a Man had been in the beginning *Four Hundred Cubits*, but was afterwards gradually diminished, and would continue so to do, till he was reduced to a span. The years from the creation of the world exceeds already many thousands of thousands, after their calculation.

But I am tired with rehearsing to you so much of this useless Trash. May the Lord commiserate the Fate of these poor deluded Souls, and enlighten the Eyes of the Christians, to see how far

they are obliged, to improve the Light of the Gospel, now so
gloriously shining upon them, and walk as Children of the Light
whilst they have it!

I remain, yours,

B. ZIEGENBALGH.

Tranquebar, September the 2nd, 1706.

~~~~~~~~~~~~~~~~~

No. III.

*A List of Subscriptions toward the erection of the Wes-
leyan Mission Chapel at Galle.*

———

</div>

HIS EXCELLENCY SIR, ROBT. BROWNRIGG, BART.

K. C. B.	500
R. H. Sneyd, Esq. Provincial Judge of Galle	75
R. M. Sneyd, Esq. Provincial Judge of Matura	50
General Shuldham	21
E. D. Boyd, Esq. Collector of Galle	20
J. Atkinson, Esq. Collector of Caltura	25
J. N. Mooyaart, Esq. Sitting Magistrate of Jaffna	50
F. Dickson, Esq. Master Attendant of Galle	25
Captain Driberg, Commandant of Hambantotte	50
Mrs. Driberg	25
Rev. G. Bisset, Sen. Col. Chap.	50
A. Armour,	50
J. Chater	25
R. Knill	7
James Lynch	100
G. Erskine,	25
W. B. Fox,	50
J. H. Squance	50
B. Clough,	25
J. Callaway,	25
R. Newstead	25
R. Carver	25
A. Stead	15
J. Bott	15
A. Hume	20
S. Allen	20
J. M'Kenny	50
Mrs. M'Kenny	50
Mr. J. Anthonisz, Assistant Missionary	10
Mrs. Robinal	30
J. H. Robinal, Esq.	25
G. Brook, Esq.	20
Mrs. Brook,	20

Mr. Gogerly,	.		.	25
Rev. Mr. Broadbent	.		:	50
P. Rosmalecocq, Esq. Sitting Magistrate of Hambantotte				20
H. Rosmalecocq, Esq. Sitting Magistrate of Babareen				20
H. Van Hek, Esq.	.		.	25
J. Lembrughen, Esq. Sitting Magistrate of Amblangodde				10
Mrs Lembrughen			.	5
J. Breckman, Esq. Sittting Magistrate of Pantura			,	5
Mr. Gowder	.		.	20
Mr. Loret,	.	.	:	20
Mr. Rose .	.	.	.	25
Mr. Epherins	.	.	.	10
Mrs. Stroff' .	.	.	-	10
Mr. Faber	.	:	.	10
Mr. Ludovice	.	.	.	10
Mr. Zybrands,	.	.	.	10
Mr. Boggars	.	.	. .	10
Mr. Balkhuysen	.	.	.	10
Mr. Keller	.	.	.	5
Mr. Hingart	.	.	.	5
Mr. H. Mattheys,	.	.	.	10
Mr. Van Alkin	.	.	:	5
Mr. Jantsz,	. .	.	.	10
Mr. P. Jantsz,	.	.	.	10
Guard Modeliar			:	10
Sundry small sums per. Guard Modeliar			:	39
Wesleyan Mission Schoolmasters of Galle			.	40
Serjeant Major Grant,	.	.	.	5
Serjeant Smyth, H. M. 19th Regt.		(:		10
Mrs. Smyth,	.	.	.	10
Serjeant Nichol, H. M. 73rd Regt.			(	10
Corporal M'Nee H. M. 73rd Regt.			.	10
Corporal Black, R, A.	.	.	.	10
A. Friend,	.	.	.	14
Sundry small sums per Mr. Appelton, Colombo				33
Mr. Frazer,	.	.	.	10
Collections at the Opening.			:	280

No, IV,

Madras, February, 1820.

MY DEAR BRETHREN,

Previous to my leaving Madras for our Annual Meeting at Colombo, our prospects were more cheering than at any past period since my removal to it. During the last quarter several souls have been converted to God. I had the pleasure of seeing 14 native Christians at the Sacrament. Our congregations are nearly doubled, and we have a fair prospect of raising money to build a chapel in town. Our Missionary Society has raised more money than I

expected; it may be gratifying for you and the rest of the Bre~
thren to have the names of our generous subscribers. The case
of the 17 soldiers of the Royal Scots is singular. In that regt.
there had been a class of 8 or 10, but 4 or 5 of them died
truly happy in God, all the rest (except one man,) fell into sin.
The former leader, W. Ellis, previous to his death, had collected a
small sum to send to me at Madras; but by some means the
whole was lost. At the time the soldiers received their prize money and were spending it in wickedness, our good Br. who remained faithful, proposed to one or two well-wishers to take up
a subscription for the Wesleyan Mission at Madras, and 16 beside
himself contributed the 33 Pag. 6 fs.

The Br. of the 34 Regt. at Bangalou have expended I believe
more then 40 Pagodas in erecting a little place of worship. It
may be gratifying to learn that in the course of the last year of
8 members of our several classes who died; every one died truly
happy in God. My body and soul are as able and willing to labour for God and the salvation of souls as at any past period
of my life.

Yours in Gospel love,
J. LYNCH.

Subscription to the Madras Wesleyan Missionary Society.

No. of Months paid		Subscriptions.			Donations			Total		
		Pag.	Fs.	C.	Pag.	Fs.	C.	Pag.	Fs.	C.
11	T. Orme, Esq.	11	0	0	15	0	0	26	0	0
12	T. Thomas, Esq.	17	6	0	0	0	0	17	6	0
2	H. Mortlock, Esq.	2	0	0	0	0	0	2	0	0
11	A Friend, by Mr. Lynch	11	0	0	0	0	0	11	0	0
11	B. Durnford	22	0	0	10	0	0	32	0	0
11	Mrs B. Durnford	5	22	40	1	0	0	6	22	40
2	Mr J. Gore.	1	0	0	2	0	0	3	0	0
11	Mr J Corner	3	11	20	0	0	0	3	11	20
11	Mr W. Gay	3	6	30	1	0	0	4	6	30
5	A Friend, by do.	1	11	20	0	0	0	1	11	20
11	do. do.	3	6	30	0	0	0	3	6	30
3	do. do.	0	33	60	0	0	0	0	33	60
11	Mr W. Graham	2	33	60	0	0	0	2	33	60
11	Mrs Graham	2	33	60	0	0	0	2	33	60
2	Miss Wiliamson	0	24	0	0	0	0	0	24	0
3	Mr. J Williamson	0	22	40	0	0	0	0	22	40
11	Mr. J. Hartley	3	6	30	2	0	0	5	6	30
11	Mr. W. Aylward	7	42	60	0	0	0	7	42	60
11	Mr J. Harkness	3	6	30	0	0	0	3	6	30
11	Mr. T. Richey	1	25	40	0	0	0	1	25	40
11	Mr. J. Rodrigoe	2	25	40	0	0	0	2	25	40
11	Mr. Zhesple	11	0	0	0	0	0	11	0	0
11	Narsoo	0	22	0	0	0	0	0	22	0

No. of Months paid		Subscriptions.			Donations.			Total		
		Pag.	Fs.	C.	Pag.	Fs.	C.	Pag.	Fs.	C.
8	Mrs. Barr	2	0	0	0	0	0	2	0	0
8	Miss Bell	2	0	0	0	0	0	2	0	0
11	Mrs. Streng	2	33	60	4	0	0	6	33	60
11	Mr. Price	2	33	60	0	0	0	2	33	60
11	Mr. W. Lambert	1	21	0	0	0	0	1	21	0
11	Mr. J. Lambert	1	21	0	0	0	0	1	21	0
7	Mr. W. Richey	1	0	0	0	0	0	1	0	0
7	Mr. W. Frazier	7	0	0	0	0	0	7	0	0
2	Mr. Brady	0	12	0	0	0	0	0	12	0
4	Mr. J. Woolfe	1	0	0	1	0	0	2	0	0
4	Mrs. A. Woolfe	1	0	0	1	0	0	2	0	0
11	Mrs. Hartley	2	23	60	1	0	0	3	33	60
11	Mrs. Perriman	2	33	60	1	0	0	3	33	60
11	Mrs. Gregory	1	5	0	0	0	0	1	5	0
11	Mr. Hogg	2	33	60	0	0	0	2	33	60
11	Rev. J. Lynch	2	33	60	0	0	0	2	33	60
7	Mr. A. Smith	4	12	60	0	0	0	4	12	60
11	Mr. J. Vandergucht	1	35	40	0	0	0	1	35	40
11	Mr. Carraput	1	25	40	0	0	0	1	25	40
4	A Friend, by Mr. Lynch	1	22	40	0	0	0	1	22	40
3	do. do.	2	0	0	0	0	0	2	0	0
5	Mr. E. Robam	0	30	0	0	0	0	0	30	0
3	J. D. Shiphy	0	19	10	0	0	0	0	19	10
2	J. Wint	0	12	60	0	0	0	0	12	60
	Mr. Dighton	0	0	0	5	0	0	5	0	0
	Mr. D. Castilio	0	0	0	3	0	0	3	0	0
	Mr. J. Grant	0	0	0	1	0	0	1	0	0
	Mr. J. Anderson	0	0	0	1	0	0	1	0	0
	Mr. J. D. Shippy	0	0	0	1	0	0	1	0	0
	Mr. J. Bacon	0	0	0	0	22	40	0	22	40
	Mr. J. Richey	0	0	0	0	12	60	0	12	60
	A Friend	0	0	0	0	38	20	0	38	20
	G. Osborn	0	0	0	0	12	60	0	12	60
	Appavoo	0	0	0	0	11	20	0	11	90
	A Friend	0	0	0	0	25	40	0	25	40
	ditto	0	0	0	0	22	40	0	22	40
	ditto	0	0	0	0	38	20	0	38	20
	Several sums	19	0	0	0	0	0	19	0	0

Juvenile Subscribers, &c.

No. of Months paid		Pag.	Fs.	C.	Pag.	Fs.	C.	Pag.	Fs.	C.
11	Colebrook Durnford	5	22	40	1	0	0	6	22	40
11	Gilbert Durnford	5	22	40	1	0	0	6	22	40
11	Henry Durnford	5	22	40	1	0	0	6	22	40
7	R. J. Perremon	1	0	0	0	0	0	1	0	0
7	J. Rodrigoes	0	14	0	0	0	0	0	14	0
7	Rachel Lambert	0	7	0	0	0	0	0	7	0
7	Charlotte Lambert	0	7	0	0	0	0	0	7	0

No. X. M

No. of Months paid		Subscriptions.			Donations			Total		
		Pag.	Fs.	C.	Pag.	Fs.	C.	Pag.	Fs.	C.
7	Georgeanna Lambert	0	7	0	0	0	0	0	7	0
7	Hellen Lambert	0	7	0	0	0	0	0	7	0
7	Alex. Richey	0	14	0	0	0	0	0	14	0
7	Robert and Thomas Richey	0	28	0	0	0	0	0	28	0
5	Harriet M'Kae	0	10	0	0	0	0	0	10	0
1	Matthew Caldaira	0	1	0	0	0	0	0	1	0
1	Charles Caldaira	0	1	0	0	0	0	0	1	0

Total for 11 Month   307 38 60

No. IV.

The following article is contained in a Letter from one of our Preachers, to Brother Callaway, dated Manchester, January 11, 1819.

At the beginning of this year we held our first Annual *Juvenile* Missionary Meeting in our second Chapel. A number of young persons of both sexes a few months ago began to raise subscriptions among their friends on behalf of the poor benighted heathen. They had been so successful as to pay into the Treasurer's hands £110, and they now met to make collections, which together made about £150. Several young men came forward on the occasion, and made most admirable speeches, while a few of us with more years over our heads lent our assistance, and the whole was important and highly interesting to all present.— One common feeling ran through the whole assembly for the missionary cause, and all appeared desirous that the word of the Lord might have free course through the whole world, and that the name of the Lord Jesus might be universally magnified. I have no doubt that the period is arrived when the knowledge of God will spread itself through all lands, and in our missionary meetings I gave them my reasons for it. The principal one I mentioned was this. At the Civil War in this kingdom neither the Episcopalians nor the Presbyterians understood the nature of religious liberty. The Independents who principally composed the Parliamentary army had embraced it, but their number was comparatively small. The Officers, therefore, offered themselves first to the Episcopalians to strengthen their cause if a Toleration might be granted. They refused it with indignation. They then offered their services to the Presbyterians with no better success; and then they formed the desperate resolution to seize the reins of Government, and succeeded. Then, politics apart, every man worshipped God, as he thought in the most scriptural way.

Now mark the progress of things. This was about the year 1647, and in that year the Society for Propagating the Gospel in Foreign Parts was formed. In 1698, the Society for Propagating Christian Knowledge,—1706, the Danish Mission,—1709, the Scottish Society for spreading Christian Knowledge,—1732, the Moravian Mission,—1786, the Methodist Mission.—1792, the Baptist Mission,—1795, the London Missionary Society,—1796, the Edinburgh,—1801, the Church,—1809, the American Missionary Society.——Thus the way has been opened for Missions, and other benevolent Institutions, till it is difficult to number them, and as they increase, the principle which God has thus honoured has been strengthened and acted upon more and more; and no doubt but it will proceed till all nations bow to the Redeemer's name, and submit to his authority.———

No. V.

A friend has obliged Brother Callaway with a copy of the following advertisement.

GENERAL POST OFFICE, July 13, 1819.

THE Statute of 55 Geo. III. cap. 153, *so far as relates* to the postage and conveyance of Letters, Newspapers, Printed Prices Currents, and Printed Papers, to and from the Cape of Good Hope, Ceylon, the Mauritius, and the East Indies is repealed; and in consequence of which, no more Packet Mails will be forwarded between Great Britain and those parts. By an Act of this Session, all Letters brought into Great Britain by ships and vessels *from* the above parts, are liable to a Sea Postage of 4d. each, if not exceeding 3oz. and 1d. per oz. above that weight, in addition to the Inland Postage rates.— And all Letters *to* the above places, which may be sent through the Post Office are liable to a Sea Postage of 2d. each, under the weight of 3oz. and 1s. per oz. if above that weight, in addition to the inland rates. Newspapers, Printed Prices Current, and Printed Papers, duly stamped, may be conveyed to the above places, at 1d. each packet, not exceeding 1oz. and 1d. per oz. above that weight. The postage of all such Letters, Packets, and Printed Papers must be paid at the time they are put into the Post Office. The Act allows Letters and Newspapers to be sent to the East Indies, "otherwise than through the Post Office."

By command of the Postmaster General,

FRANCIS FREELING, Secretary.

No. VI.

The following specimen of the Madagascar Language is copied from a small Catechism kindly presented to Mr. Carver at the Isle of France, by C. Telfair, Esq. a Gentleman who had visited the Island of Madagascar, and obtained considerable information concerning it. The Catechism is in Latin, French, and Madagascaree, published in virtue of a Decree made by the Society for the propapagation of the Christian Faith, dated, 1785. The place of the Latin version of the Lord's Prayer is supplied by a literal translation in English, as the Madagascaree words do not correspond with the common version of the Lord's Prayer. The Madagascaree is written according the French alphabet, though there can be no doubt but the Arabic is much better adapted to it, as it is evidently a dialect of that language.

OUR Father in the Heavens; Thy name be magnified;
Răīt-sĭcă   an danghitsi   ăngăre ănŏ-hō fīssă tife

Thy kingdom come to us; the pleasure of thy heart be
i fănăsq-ăuō āvĭ āmĭnaĭe;   ămŏrōmpŏ ănō   hŏ-

done, in earth as in heaven: Give us for this days
ēfă, ĭz ān tănne, oūdoŭă āu dănghītsĭ; Măhoŭmé ănaĭe (or)

subsistence all bread; forgive us, O God! all our evil
ānāhĕnaĭ moūfe ābi; tăne ĭoŭ zāhāĭe ŏ zānhăr! gni

dispositions,   as we forgive the iniquities of our
fănnăhĕ-năĭe rātsĭ ābi; toŭă zaĭe mĭvăle, ĭ fānnăhĕ răts ĭ ă gnĭ

enemies;   And lead us not to evil conceptions, but
răfi năĭe;   ăĭă mănălītse ănāĭe rătsĭ   vēlsĕ-vētse fĕă

deliver thou us from all evil.   Amen.
nomīttĕnēză ănāĭe tăbīn rātsi ābĭ.   Hŏēfă.

No. VII.

TABLE I.

*For calculating the Prices of English Books in Ceylon Currency,
at the rate of 10 Fanams for the Shilling.*

s.	d.	Rds.	fs.	s.	d.	Rds.	fs.	£	s.	d.	Rds.	fs.
1	0	0	10	9	0	7	6	0	18	0	15	0
1	6	1	3	10	0	8	4	0	19	0	15	10
2	0	1	8	10	6	8	9	0	20	0	16	8
2	6	2	1	11	0	9	2	1	5	0	20	10
3	0	2	6	12	0	10	0	1	10	0	25	0
4	0	3	4	13	0	10	10	1	15	0	29	2
5	0	4	2	14	0	11	8	2	0	0	33	4
6	0	5	0	15	0	12	6	2	10	0	41	8
7	0	5	10	16	0	13	4	5	0	0	83	4
8	0	6	8	17	0	14	2					

TABLE II.

*The value of English Currency in the Currency of Ceylon, at the
rate of 14 Rix-dollars per Pound Sterling.*

£	s.	d.	Rds.	fs.	£	s.	d.	Rds.	fs.	£	s.	d.	Rds.	fs.
0	0	6	0	4½	0	9	0	6	3½	1	0	0	14	0
0	1	0	0	8½	0	10	0	7	0	1	10	0	21	0
0	2	0	1	5	0	11	0	7	8½	1	15	0	24	6
0	2	6	1	9	0	12	0	8	5	2	0	0	28	0
0	3	0	2	2	0	13	0	9	1½	2	10	0	35	0
0	4	0	2	9½	0	14	0	9	9½	3	0	0	42	0
0	5	0	3	6	0	15	0	10	6	3	10	0	49	0
0	6	0	4	2	0	16	0	11	2½	4	0	0	56	0
0	7	0	4	11	0	17	0	11	11	4	10	0	63	0
0	8	0	5	9½	0	18	0	12	7½	5	0	0	70	0
					0	19	0	13	3½					

END OF JANUARY EXTRACTS.

Colombo:——Printed at the Wesleyan Mission Press, for the Missionaries.

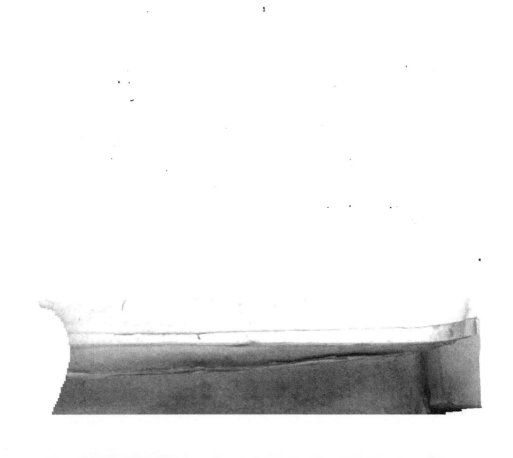

Extracts

FROM

QUARTERLY LETTERS, &c.

No. XI.   *APRIL*, 1820.

THE COLOMBO AND COLPETTY STATION.

COLOMBO.

Colombo, April 14, 1820.

VERY DEAR BRETHREN,

Since we had the pleasure of seeing most of you at our general meeting, few events out of the ordinary course, worthy of record, have occurred. Former letters from this station have made you acquainted with the nature and progress of our work here ; and we were happy to find on entering on the labours of our predecessors, *their* labours had not been in vain.

In a circuit extensive as this, embracing various descriptions of people, it may easily be supposed that the work will have its varieties and peculiaries, and will occasionally furnish room for trials and exercise of mind; yet we are happy to say that the prosperity of this circuit is not only general, but we have but few places which do not offer encouraging prospects.

We are justified in expecting fruit of our labours, and success in our work. The faithful promises of God cannot fail—we labour on with confidence, assured that though the kingdom of God do not come with observation, with any peculiar outward shew, the seed of the word shall not perish. We look with thankfulness to Almighty God on the many precious souls here, who through the tender mercy of God have been rescued from sin, and walk as becometh the Gospel of Christ ;—and we are not unfrequently gladdened to see the insuppressable tear start in the eyes of those who attentively hear the word of life.

Our congregations are various, and collectively are encouraging. Our English congregations, except in the fort, are small ; but they are attentive, and we have reason to believe, that most who attend are persons in some degree desirous to know and enjoy the power of religion. Our Portuguese congregation in the pettah gives us much encouragement. It consists of a considerable number of regular and attentive hearers, who understand and generally feel the power of what they hear.

No. xi.   O

The English congregation in the fort is formed chiefly from the military Most of those who attend are serious persons, and more than half of them members of our society, who form two classes, containing nearly 50 persons. Our other places of worship are out in the country, in schools or private houses, and in these, excepting in one instance, our public worship is conducted in the Singhalese language. In some of these places the congregations are good; in most, encouraging.

On Easter-monday, we had the children of the various schools assembled at the Mission-house, and Brother Clough preached to them the annual sermon in Singhalese. It was a most gratifying sight, especially on calling to mind the circumstance that this is a work of yesterday. A considerable number of children had come not less than 12 miles, and seemed to enjoy the scene with feelings as capable of being touched as our own. Fruits of these well-directed efforts appear in a particular manner in two Singhalese and Portuguese classes, raised up in one of the schools As far as human penetration can reach, a doubt cannot be started as to the reality of the work in their minds; and several give every evidence which can be demanded, that they know him in whom they have believed.

Brother Clough resides at Colpetty, where we trust he will in a good degree recruit his strength.—The various other concerns of the station proceed much as usual,—receiving all the improvement we are able to give them. Our Local Preachers are very laborious, zealous, prudent and useful, and give us the highest satisfaction, and are most important helps to us in forming and supplying congregations; which though generally small in the beginning, may perhaps be more durable than temples, and shine forth in splendour, when idolatry and idols are no more.

In our labours, we have in common with you, our trials and difficulties; but the present state of our work, under all circumstances, is of an highly encouraging nature; and if it be lawful to judge of the future by the past, we will anticipate to see at no very distant period, little societies in every place, walking in the fear of the Lord, and in the comforts of the Holy Ghost.

We have in compliance with the wishes of the Brethren and the desire of our Committee, at length completed the Catalogue of the Books in the Mission Library; and to furnish each of the Brethren with a Copy, we have inserted it in the Miscellanea.

We have used our utmost efforts in some measure to supply the deficiency of Books complained of in our Schools, and are happy to say we have several works in a state of forwardness, which, when complete, will we doubt not be acceptable.

With unceasing prayers for you, we are dear Brethren,

very affectionately yours,

W. BUCKLEY FOX,
JOHN CALLAWAY.

COLPETTY.

Colpetty, 20th April, 1820.

MY DEAR BRETHREN,

According to the arrangements which were kindly agreed upon at our last meeting for me to be allowed to reside at Colpetty, I lost no time in getting here as soon as I possibly could. I felt assured that the air and the little retirement of this place, would not only be more agreeable to my indifferent state of health, but I was anxiously solicitous to be in this part of the Circuit, that I might have an opportunity of giving it a little more attention than we had been able during the preceeding year.

Soon after I came here I and my colleagues consulted together on the best mode of dividing the labours of the Circuit; when it was agreed, that the side of the circuit south of the Fort of Colombo, should be placed under my care, but that our Sunday labors should be arranged according to our usual plan. One great advantage arising from this arrangement, which is *indeed such* in this country, it will save much laborious travelling without the least detriment to our work. Most of you know that our principal Schools extend northward and southward of Colombo; and with respect to the situation of the Pettah and Colpetty, naturally divide themselves into two branches; and as we visit them often, this arrangement will prevent unnecessary travelling.

According to this plan, the following Schools will fall under my immediate inspection, viz. 1. The School of Colpetty. which is near my door. 2, Welliwatta about 3½ miles distant. 3, Kallubowella, distant about 4½ miles. 4, Ratmalaney, distant about 6½ miles. 5, Morotto, about 10 miles 6 Huratudua distant about 13 miles. This last School situated on the south bank of the Pantura river, was transferred from the Caltura circuit, it being very inconveniently situated for regular visitation from that circuit. Since I came to reside at Colpetty, I have had opportunities of visiting *all* these Schools in a way I was not able before. Some of them are in a pleasing state, and are doing much good, but I am quite certain, that were I to give every moment of the time which I find it necessary to redeem from sleep, it would scarcely be sufficient to make these efficient, in that particular way which we must strive to make our native schools or they will not answer the great end proposed by them. What indeed can we expect from a native school consisting of from 50 to 100 children, provided it have only one visit from a Missionary every month? The Missionary goes to the school, he sees perhaps the children are there—that they are making improvement in reading, writing, &c. but what are they doing, or how do the conduct themselves during the 29 days the Missionary is absent from them? I say it is impossible for the Missionary to know, for I would hardly credit the Reports or weekly-returns of *any native master*, unless I were convinced he had the fear of God before his eyes.

Several, nay almost all our schools in this part of the circuit, are I believe, visited by one or another every week, and even this is not enough unless one could depend on the piety of the Master.

The conviction is daily strengthened in my mind, that our duty as

Missionaries in heathen lands, is by no means done when we have attended to the improvement of the children, in their books, and preached to them and their parents and neighbours. The principal part of the work will be done by going from house to house, and having personal intercourse with the people. In this respect the Roman Catholic Missionaries are an honour to their character. I do not wish my Brethren to understand, that I am an admirer of *all* the plans of missionary labour adopted by them. On the contrary, I am still of the opinion, that many of them are exceedingly absurd, if not contrary to every plan the God of heaven would have us make use of for the conversion of the unenlightened heathen, and mention them only in reference to their presevering plan of itinerating among the people. They go from house to house, as well as from village to village; and whoever little I might be disposed to admire their proceedings in other respects, I certainly do in this; and I would not deny, that this is *one* reason why they carry all before them almost in this country.

My situation at present has afforded me several opportunities of this kind. I have gone among our little native classes, which were raised principally by our young friend Cornelius, with some gratification. They have, I am sorry to say, suffered most grievously since his removal from Colpetty; but the knowledge which many of them possess of divine things is most gratifying. The other night I met the adult class at Wellewatta; and though I was sorry to hear the poor things grieve over their spiritual losses, I felt at the same time truly thankful to see so much of the power of divine grace among the natives. When I look at this village, our school there, and the little cause of God which is in it, I must think if ever the devil vowed vengeance against a little cause, he has done it against this school and this little society. I have been a good deal tried also with our little cause in Colpetty. Since Cornelius left, it has been subjected to several vicissitudes, which, when I came up here, had nearly expirpated the school. A considerable number of the elder scholars, and who also met regularly in class, had left the school entirely. Not that they were lost, but some had gone into service, others had begun trades, and this had greatly thinned the school.† Their places not having been filled up, I saw a very serious vacuum. I have done all in my power to raise the little cause. I have gone into the school *daily*, and am glad to see a little improvement. But still the circumstances of the school furnish us with another proof of the often-told fact, that it is an exceedingly difficult to make effectual impression on the minds and hearts of people in heathen countries. Yet how soon it wears off, unless watched with the most scrupulous attention.

It has often been a source of regret, that for the last two or three years, so much of my time should have been occupied in other work than that which is truly dear to me. For I can indeed assure you, that

---

† I have lately received two letters from the Lady of Colonel S ———, late Brigadier-General in this Island, now at Penang, one of which was accompanied by her subscription of 50 sicca rupees: and she speaks in the most pleasing manner of the two lads she took as servants out of our Colpetty school. She being decidedly a pious lady, and the youths both of the same mind, she says they are real treasures to her in that part of the country, where so little of God is known.

those are the happiest moments I spend, when I have opportunities of
travelling among the natives, and of personally recommending to
them Jesus the Saviour of men. Yet I am not conscious of being at
all out of my providential way. On the contrary, as I never forced
myself into any of the works I have in hand, and which confine me a
good deal to my room, I take it as *one* proof, that providence has
opened my way before me;—and it would have been, I conceive, a di-
reliction of duty to have withdrawn or returned from what appeared
to me to be an urgent call from God. And, on this account, I cannot
consider my time entirely thrown away which I spend in the part I
take in translating the word of God. This work, I am happy to say,
is going on well, and it often cheers a drooping feeling to reflect, that
in a short time the natives of Ceylon will have the whole of the word
of life in their own language. After completing the Book of Genesis,
the Psalms, and the Book of Proverbs, which was the order pointed
out by the Bible Society, we began the Book of Exodus, which is now
finished; and we have finished about half the Book of *Leviticus*. In
this work, I find my old friend Petrus Pauditta a most able and useful
co-adjutor; and I am truly thankful that a wise and gracious providence placed such a man under the influence of our Mission. The
other converted priest, George Nadoris, continues faithful to his work,
and renders an essential service in the translating-room. I wish we
had a few more such persons; men of established character; well
known, and universally admired for their learning, their abilities, and
general respectability. They would be of incalculable advantage in
our schools as Singhalese teachers. I find an objection very frequently
started by the natives against putting their children under the care of
young men. Their girls they never will; nor could it be expected unless in very rare cases. But even this difficulty, I hope time and experience will help us to overcome.

In my intercourse with schools, I have often remarked their great
want of a reading-book in their own language. We have hitherto
gone on the principle of introducing into our native schools nothing
but the New Testament in Singhalese, and a few little things which fall
much below that in point of classical reading. Now I observe, that
one great stimulus in the youths attending our schools, is in the first
instance, to become so far acquainted with the art of reading, as to enable them, if they like, to read their own *ola* books. But in the helps
necessary for this there is in our schools a great desideratum. The
language of the New Translation has generally been represented (by
those who know no better), to be generally too high. The truth is,
there is not a book on *olas* (and there are hundreds of different kinds),
as used by the natives, either in their common routine of instruction
in the *pansaleys*, or other places, or on the general topics of religion,
history, or science, so low as that translation. Of course, I omit the
alphabet, and the native spelling book, usually called the ඔ ව ඳඋඉනඹ.
And I have lately ascertained, that though many of the more respectable natives send their children to our schools for instruction, which
they do out of respect to them as Christian institutions, yet they have
men who come regularly to their houses, and in many instances, I fear
heathen priests, to teach their children to read the higher degrees of

No. xi.   P

Singhalese reading. Now, it may be, that you, my dear Brethren in the north, are provided with suitable books of this kind. If not, would it not be well to devise a plan of a good standard book , which would introduce a fine boy into all the peculiarities of the pronunciation of his own language?—Respecting the south, I would gladly see to it did my situation allow it. The Baptist Missionaries at Serampore have published a book for their schools, which I know only by the name; I think it is, *dhig dhershana*, but which, I doubt not, is of the kind I now have in view, and answers well, I dare say ;—and I wish we could follow up the idea of one in Singhalese and Tamul for our schools. At present my hands are pretty full with the Dictionary, which I find both tedious and laborious. But even to this work my mind is quite reconciled, when I consider the circumstances under which I engaged in it, and the great probability that it will, when completed, afford facilities to those desirous of learning Singhalese, which no other work hitherto devised can possibly do. Another circumstance which reconciles my mind to the work, is the idea, that I never forced myself into the undertaking—events regularly opened my way to it; even insomuch that I was about to say I was not even a volunteer in it at all. However, I hope to *linger* on, to finish the work. A hope which is the more anxiously indulged, in my present state of health, from a knowledge, that were I forced to give it up, I could not expect a successor in it for some time to come. But whatever individuals may think on such matters, I think also, and my sincere thoughts are, that such undertakings are weighty embargoes on the *precious* time and strength of a Missionary sent into the *torrid zone*, to fly as the *angel*, with the gospel of Christ among the untaught heathens.

It gives me great pleasure to hear from you, very dear Brethren, by letters from your various stations, that you are generally getting on so well. I would most gladly communicate with you more frequently, but both a want of time and strength prevents me. I was pleased when the time came round, that I could write you all at the same time by the Quarterly; and it may perhaps be one reason why I am so long and tedious in my letters of this kind. You must pardon me, but I dare say I err in this respect, if an error it be, by a feeling which I can never rid myself of, to know exactly what you are all doing; for when I begin to write, I wish to tell you all I am doing and engaged in ; and so strong is this feeling, that I suppose, could I do nothing but lay on my couch and count the tiles, you would hear at some time or other how many tiles I have on the roof of my house.

I have experienced, I am sorry to say, but little alteration for the better since I came to Colpetty, in the state of my health. I am carried on from day to day, by a hope, that perhaps things will take a favourable turn by and by. But this I must leave with my Master. I think I have not lost ground with respect to my experience of divine things. My little retirement here has afforded me many precious opportunities of renewing my covenant with the Lord, and my approaches to the throne of grace, have frequently been accompanied by the most pleasing manifestations of his love to my soul. During the last quarter, my mind has been much more led out in prayer to God for you all; and seldom indeed have I gone to the throne of grace, and more particularly when my soul has been happy, but my thoughts, my affections, and prayers have gone round from one station to another, and God has frequently made this a blessing to my own soul. We need the prayers of each other. The world will love its own.—Yes, my dear Brethren, let us love each other. And, may the God of peace sanctify our union with each other, and sanctify our labours;—and let us be more than ever in earnest with the Lord, that he would mercifully honour our labours with the conversion of many to himself. 　　　　I remain, as ever, your sincerely affectionate,

　　　　　　　　　　　　　　　　　　B. CLOUGH.

~~~~~~~~~~~~~

THE NEGOMBO STATION.

Negombo, April 10, 1820.

VERY DEAR BRETHREN,

My letter, this quarter, has necessarily been a little delayed by my journey to attend the Book-Committee; but as I trust it will yet be in time. I do not regret the circumstance, as I have, since my return obtained a piece of information relative to our work, which I can now communicate, and for which I had waited with much anxiety. I allude to the occupation of Chilaw as a part of the Negombo Circuit, about which I had been anxious on many accounts, but particularly as it was one of the acknowledged reasons for the additional help afforded to this station. Not that the occupation of Chilaw was *essential* to our *full* employment, seeing that the circuit already extends as far into the interior of the country as Chilaw would extend it on the coast: but my hopes were very sanguine relative to that place, as you very well know, dear Brethren, from what I stated at the Conference. I am, therefore, sorry to add, that for *the present*, we are quite prevented in the execution of our intended arrangements respecting Chilaw, by the awful visitation of the small-pox, which rages there, as it has not ceased to do also at Negombo for some time with uncommon violence. Our kind friend there, however, does not forget our engagement, nor intend to relax his efforts in the cause, when divine Providence shall please to remove the existing obstacle; than which we can hardly conceive one more powerful, from the trembling alarm of the poor people in every direction. The very kind note subjoined on the subject, will at once shew the reason of this unexpected delay, and also the condescending and friendly manner in which our kind friend regards us.

MY DEAR SIR,

Mrs. Walbeoff and myself propose leaving this to-morrow for Columbo, and as you were so extremely kind as to say you would give us a room at your house, we will avail ourselves of your polite invitation. We hope to be at Negombo early on Friday morning, and go on board a boat in the evening. The small-pox still prevails, and has put an entire stop to the erection of the little school-house, *only for the present I hope.* Mrs. Walbeoff offers her best compliments, and

I remain, my dear Sir, your's very faithfully,

Chilaw, 5th April, 1820.   J. WALBEOFF.

I have also had since I wrote last, many anxious fears relative to our important little station in the Kandian provinces. After the very condescending manner in which Governor Brownrigg was pleased to notice that little effort, I could scarcely have looked for a hindrance of the kind to which I advert; but I am sorry to state, that the Commandant of that quarter was not so friendly to Missionary exertions as the Governor, and hence it was not so much encouraged as the people were led to believe it would be from the Governor's approval. However, I strove according to the Governor's recommendation, as related in my last, to go on further. In this I have been prevented under circumstances which the following correspondence will best explain.

To His Excellency General Sir Robt. Brownrigg, Bart.
        &c. &c. &c.

SIR,

May I beg permission to trouble your Excellency for a moment with a little circumstance, which, however I feel reluctant to intrude on your most valuable time now, I am persuaded your Excellency will not think wholly unimportant. When I had the honour lately to converse with your Excellency about our first attempts to introduce Christianity into the Kandian territories by means of schools, your Excellency was pleased most kindly to suggest the idea of following up our plan to Kornegalle, which I then stated, was already attempted. I have this day received intelligence from our schoolmaster there, that the people in that direction are most willing to send their children for instruction but fearing to offend the Commandant, they waited for his sanction; without which I also directed them not to proceed, and had written to Colonel Hook to that effect. The schoolmaster had waited on the Colonel, who declined giving his sanction unless he brought that of your Excellency. I have therefore taken the liberty thus to presume upon your Excellency's condescension and kindness (in which I beg to be excused,) humbly trusting that you Excellency would give directions that I should be favoured with some document expressive of those sentiments with which you are pleased to regard our efforts among the Kandians, for Colonel Hook's satisfaction, previous to an event, which did we only consult our own private feelings, we could wish were yet long delayed; or that it may please your Excellency to advise the Colonel of your condescending sanction to our native mission-schools in the Kandian territories, in all proper subjection to the existing authorities.

Should your Excellency be pleased to accede to this humble request, so intimately connected with the welfare of the Kandian people, it must greatly add to those obligations under which I have the honour to subscribe myself,   Your Excellency's much obliged,

and very humble Servant,

Negombo, Jan. 13, 1820.   R. NEWSTEAD.

As the time of his Excellency's departure drew very near, and I received no answer for a week or so, I wrote the following short note to the Private Secretary, in order, if possible, to remove the suspense induced by such circumstances.

REV. SIR,   *Negombo, Jan* 20, 1820.

Will you pardon my again troubling you to beg the favour of a line, informing me if his Excellency the Governor was pleased to signify to Colonel Hook his kind approbation of our efforts in the Seven Corles. I have heard that his Excellency has been pleased so to do, but as I had not heard though you, I feared that the multiplicity of present engagements had entirely prevented my little request from meeting the usual kind attention both from his Excellency and yourself.

Do me the favour, Rev. Sir, to excuse this intrusion, and believe me,   Your much obliged and obedient Servant,
The Rev. G. Bisset.   R. NEWSTEAD.

After a short time. I received the following official notification; which, however, while it prohibits our further advance, by no means forbids the existence of our present little work.

SIR,   *Kandyan Office, Colombo,* 28*th Jan.* 1820.

I am directed by his Excellency the Governor to inform you in reply to your Letter addressed to him requesting permission to establish a School in the Seven Corles, that it is not deemed, under existing circumstances, politically advisable to sanction the measure for the present.   I have the honour to be, Sir,
                     your most obedt servt.   G. LUSIGNAN,
The Rev. R. Newstead.   *Sec. Kandian Provinces.*

. I am happy to perceive the words " at present" in the above document, and fully believe that it was not intended to restrict our prudent exertions if sanctioned by the *Local* Authorities. It may be proper to observe, that the late Commandant is removed, in order to return to Europe, and a Gentlemen of the Civil Service appointed, who is known to our Mission. Our Assistant visited the school the other day, and found it as encouraging as we had any reason to expect; and thinks with me that it ought to be continued. Our schools have all suffered more or less from the dreadful prevalence of the small pox, and two of them, I regret to say were obliged to be discontinued for a season, on that account. One of them is re-opened, but the other continues under its melancholy circumstances, for no one will come near them for fear of the contagion, as the sickness is all round it, and we have had the misfortune to lose the head-master by that fatal disease. This is the man whose public baptism is recorded in the Negombo Letter. (Quarterly Extracts, April 1818) Of his final salvation I cannot speak positively, but I *hope* very fervently, though when I heard of his illness I was told he was carried to a dewalla, and offerings were made for his recovery, I hasted to see him and ascertain the truth, which he assured me with death fully before him, was as follows: that he was taken there by ignorant and heathen relatives in a delirium, in which he continued a long time. When he recovered and found where he was,

No. xi.   Q

he insisted on being brought back, which was complied with, and declared to me that his only hope and reliance was on Jesus Christ the Saviour of the world   He suffered dreadfully from the disorder, to which he was a complete martyr, and died two days after I had seen and conversed and prayed with him.   His last words were, මාගේ දෙවියන්වහන්සේ ළඟට දැන් මම යනවාය. *Magey Dewiyanwahansey langa'a dan mama yanawaya.* Now I am going to my God.   My young colleague, I am happy to say, contines to grow, I hope, both in knowledge and grace; and to secure my best regards by a deportment every way worthy of his holy vocation; embracing every opportunity either of acquiring or of communicating instruction with a zeal which will, I trust, make him instrumental of much good.   Our Assistant Brother and his wife are also comfortably situated, and, I hope, will be very useful, conducting their little household in the fear of the Lord.

I am happy to add that the chapel is now just finished, and is both an honour to the workmen who have built it, and an ornament to the town, as the house of the Lord should be.   It is pleasing to observe, by the way, that Sir Edward Barnes, our Lieut.-Governor, and Sir Hardinge Giffard our Chief Justice, together with Mr. Justice Bryne, visited the chapel as they lately passed through Negombo, and expressed their high satisfaction at the erection of such a building in this place, and at its handsome appearance.   The latter gentlemen with whom we were invited to dine, came up to the bungaloe, and took some refreshment.   After inspecting our school, which I had appointed to meet them there, they declared themselves surprised and delighted with the proficiency to which the boys had arrived in the different departments of education.

Our little missionary prayer meetings have continued to be a source of real present enjoyment to us, and I doubt not will be also of lasting benefit.   We have been greatly assisted in them since my return from Conference, by the pious soldiers who are occasionally here, and who with about 60 others are marched to preaching every sabbath.   Their Officers also all attend.   At our last sacrament opportunity, our number was increased to 23, including the Commandant and six of the pious soldiers.   Their short residence here has enlarged our sphere of exertion, and we hope not without success.   Most of the serious men are now gone, but several more fill up their places, who begin to inquire the way to heaven.   At the last renewal of the quarterly tickets, our numbers were (including the seven non-residents), 50, and 15 on trial,—for which the Lord be praised!   They meet in general very regularly, and encourage our exertions by a deportment becoming the Gospel.

A recent very kind letter from our respected Secretary, Mr. Taylor, has afresh reminded me of our high privileges in being cared for by so many of the excellent of the earth.   Every temporal and spiritual blessing has mercifully abounded towards me this quarter, and I cannot better express the language of my heart than in the sweet words of David, " *Because thy loving-kindness is better than life, therefore my lips shall praise thee.   Thus will I bless thee while I live: I will lift*

up my hands in thy name: because thou hast been my help, therefore in
the shadow of thy wings will I rejoice."　　　I remain,

very dear Brethren, most affectionately yours,

ROBERT NEWSTEAD.

THE CALTURA STATION.

Caltura, April 16, 1820.

MY DEAR BRETHREN,

In consequence of my numerous engagements, I am later than
usual in making my periodical communication this quarter, but I
hope it will not be too late to have its place in the Quarterly Extracts.
Since my arrival at this very important station, my time has been
busily employed with its various duties. The school department has
engaged much of my attention, and this I have found the more necessary as it has suffered much by Brother Fox's necessary absence. However, I have no doubt, but that I shall be able to bring them into proper order by devoting to them all the time and care that I have in my
power. I have greatly to lament the want of books, but hope in some
time to be better provided than at present; as independent of those
which our mission can supply, J. Deane. esq. Secretary to the Colombo
Auxiliary Bible Society has kindly promised to afford me all the aid
in his power in this respect. Last week this gentleman was here in
his capacity as Collector; and during his stay was pleased to evidence
a decided wish to assist me, and promote the interest of the Mission.
For this I feel very thankful.

On my first coming this place after my appointment, I felt most
sensibly the necessity of our mission endeavouring to get a place of
worship; and yet I knew not how to think of any thing like a regular
chapel, because of the expense that such a building would involve.
However, I submitted the subject to Brs. Lynch, Fox, and Clough;
and after considering all things with much care, we came to the conclusion, that the best plan would be to build a place that would not
rise above the denomination of a school of the best quality; but at
the same time, such a place as would well answer for Christian worship
until such time as we may see our way plain to build in a more permanent manner; and towards this present building, it was agreed, that
500 Rds. should be expended from the mission fund, independent of
any little subscriptions that I might be able to collect on my circuit.
Now with this arrangement, and that made at the Conference respecting a house, I hope, in some months, to add much to the comfort of
this station.

I hope, very soon, to have a regular plan of the circuit arranged.
However, before this is done, it is necessary that I should have a tolerable knowledge of the different places where we have schools, so as to
fix upon those as regular preaching places, where we can procure the
best congregations. This perhaps, I should have been able to have accomplished before this time, but for two things; first, the Singhalese
new year; and secondly, the indisposition of Br. Anthonisz, who has
been confined for these eight days past with what is called here, the

...ter-pox. However, the complaint thongh troublesome, is not at all dangerous, and as he is now nearly recovered, and the new year of the Singhalese over, 1 hope in a few days, to get regularly at work, so as to organize my proposed plan.

I cannot perceive any remarkable difference between the natives of this Disrict and those of the other places which I have seen I can discover nothing but the same indifference to the religion of the bible. There is one circumstance which tends to illustrate this, and which is peculiarly worthy of remark, that is, since the departure of J. Atkinson, Esq. Collecter of this District, not a Headman is to be seen at public worship, whereas in his time they were generally present, and why?—because they thought it would please him. It is a good thing for the people to hear the word of life in any way, but O for the time when we shall see the natives coming to the house of God to worship him and waiting to hear the Gospel from a conviction of its own intrinsic worth. Well, before we can reasonably expect this we must be sure that the natives understand it in some good degree; so here is work for a Christian Missionary to find out people, and try to bring them to feel an interest in that which at present they consider of no value.

I remain, my dear Brethren, very affectionately, yours,
                                        JOHN M'KENNY.

THE GALLE STATION.

Point de Galle, April, 4th, 1820.

VERY DEAR BRETHREN.

We embrace the opportunity of mutual communication; and although we have little new or any way remarkable, yet each revolving quarter is accompanied with blessings innumerable.—therefore, "bless the Lord, O our souls!" Our congregations both in English and Portuguese are pretty large; and from their apparent attention to the divine word preached, we venture to say, promising. Our class is not large, but we believe earnestness of soul prevails among them;—and hope is the balm of life! Brother Allen is now at Amblamgodde, spending a few weeks there, knowing that we are debtors to the villages of Amlamgodde, and also to Galle.

Our schools are regularly and profitably visited; and while we thus move forward in the path of duty, it is in dependence on infinite goodness and mercy, "looking unto Jesus," whose grace is sufficient *for Missionaries!* and whose power is made perfect in our weakness. To him be all glory now and evermore.

Our health is tolerable; our souls are filled with a present heaven of love; and we look up and sing:—
                "There is our house and portion fair,
                "Our treasure and our heart is there,
                    "And our abiding home!"
Actuated by these feelings, and under the influence of a graciou hope, we remain, very dear Wesleyans, your affectionate Brethren,
                                        GEORGE ERSKINE,
                                        SAMUEL ALLEN.

N. B. From frequent and satisfactory accounts, we learn that Brother Hume is well, and heartily engaged in the great work at Matura.

~~~~~~~~~~~~~

THE MATURA STATION.

MY DEAR BRETHREN,

Matura, April 5, 1820.

After travelling about for six months in various Circuits, I have at length reached the place to which I was appointed at our general meeting I arrived at Matura on the 1st of March, and began my labours by putting my dwelling in order After my arrival, I took the earliest opportunity of waiting upon the Collector, Provincial Judge, and Commandant, and of calling upon the other respectable inhabitants, by all of whom I was very politely received.

After these introductory visits, it next became necessary to ascertain the nature and extent of my work, and to adopt those plans which appeared most adapted for promoting the object of my coming to this place.   For this purpose, it was expedient to visit as soon as possible every place where we had any establishment.   From this tour, which employed the greater part of my first fortnight, I found it would be necessary to make some little alterations in our school-bungaloes, most of which are of old construction, which though cheap, frequently require renewal.   Several of these were so far gone with age as to be incapable of properly sheltering the children from the slightest shower. To have these repaired in a permanent manner, (viz. with mud walls, hard floors, new roofs, and a few seats to each) and at as little expense to the mission as possible, I thought to try to interest the parents of the children, and the schoolmasters, in the work.   In this I have in a measure succeeded.   The second Doundra school, the Kadawidea school, and Madhea boys' school, are now done in this way with a very trifling allowance, and others will shortly follow the example, without any expense to us

As it would have been very inconvenient and unnecessarily troublesome to meet the schoolmasters at various periods, I have ordered them all to appear with their Reports at the same hour every Saturday.

As it is requisite to teaching that the teacher should understand something of what he professes to teach, and as the better acquainted he is with what he professes to teach, the better is he qualified to teach, and the more likelihood is there is of his succeeding in his work, I thought it would not be lost labour if the masters should read over through the week a given chapter, and on the Saturdays make their remarks upon it to me, and propose those difficulties which in reading might occur to them, and which they themselves could not solve.   At any rate if they should derive no advantage from the plan, I knew it would enable me to form an estimate of what I might expect from each in his work.—In this work, I proposed to spend one hour every Saturday after our other affairs were settled.

NO. XI.   R

From repeated and urgent petitions, and from the importance of the place, as well as the probability of its being occupied as a missionary station, I have been induced to open two new schools in the neighbourhood of Belligam. The school bungaloes have been built by the unaided efforts of the children's parents, and are by far the best on this station, except the Matura school, to which they are equal. The old school at Belligam is about to be modelled after the same manner. At this place there is an interesting girls' school, under the care of the master's wife. At Midigam we once had a school, and the place was considered important. I think of again opening a school there, especially as there have been requests made for it. At Pittecottua, we have re-opened a school, which for a time had necessarily been discontinued. A young man is appointed to superintend it, who, I think, will do well in the situation.

In my journeys among the schools, I have often been sorry at the scanty supply of *suitable* books. Fully to remove this inconvenience will be a work of labour and time. In the instruction of youth, and particularly of those who have passed a number of years without thinking for a moment upon any thing beyond the common requirements of nature, as it is of great importance to keep alive those feelings which the novelty of education generally kindles, and which, if properly directed may render essential service to the grand design, it is certainly necessary occasionally to gratify them by the introduction of entertaining and instructive books. Novelty excites curiosity, and curiosity prompts to enquiry, and enquiry opens the way for the communication of information. In the business of education, the feelings must be kept interested, or the work lags, and is perhaps entirely given up;—and therefore, as well to keep alive the desire of information as to excite and improve it in the children under our care, their curiosity must be kept up by a little diversity. But in these remarks, I am, perhaps, out of my way.

On the Sabbath mornings, I have English service, in the Dutch church, and have a congregation of between 20 and 30. On the Sabbath evenings, I have Portuguese preaching in the viranda of our our house. Here we have a congregation of between 50 and 60. On Easter-day, I think there were almost 100 in the evening. I cannot yet speak so fluently to them as I could in my own language, but a little more practice will render it more easy.

The assistance with which I am favoured, enables me to supply with regular Sabbath preaching the whole of the schools on the station. At Doundra, two schools meet for service every sabbath. At Neupe, four schools meet for the same purpose, and at Madhea, three; at Belligam all the four schools there can now meet in one place for preaching. At our old school in Belligam, I preached on the Sabbath before Easter, and was much pleased with the attention of about 30 adults who were present: unlike the common practice of some of their countrymen, they waited till I had said, amen.

From former communications you are aware, that there is a class of young men here. The number is small, but it is a begining, and I think they have some piety among them. I feel it good to meet them,

although I cannot get them to communicate with me so freely as Europeans would do. There is also a small class of Cingalese women that meet regularly every Tuesday. I think them serious, and two of them in particular, speak with more openness than is generally to be found among the natives.

I have made a begining with one or two of the boys to teach them a little singing; but they seem not very fond of it,—or perhaps they feel abashed in attempting to modulate their voices to music.

On the Tuesday evenings I meet the women's class, on Wednesday evenings we have preaching in Portuguese; and on the Friday evenings the men's class meet. Upon the whole, although there are many painful and unpleasant things through which I have had to make my way, I feel not only contented, but happy, being resolved to bear the inconveniences I cannot redress.

Thus Brethren, I have told you some of my doings; if your patience would endure my prolixity, I would now tell you some of my thinkings. The importance of Matura as a missionary station appears to be evident to you, by your appointing one of your number to reside here in preference to other places where he might be stationed. It has for some time been viewed in this light, and favoured with a resident missionary I know not but from the commencement of our mission in this island. Yet, notwithstanding this acknowledgment of the importance of the place, and when places perhaps of less importance have been furnished with a missionary and with a house belonging to the mission, and which in such cases were considered as necessary for giving stability to our work there, Matura to the present moment remains without the shadow of any thing permanent, except the residence for the time being of the missionary. With the reasons of the case I have nothing to do. They have probably arisen out of its impracticability under existing circumstances. But the same circumstances will not last always. It is true, we cannot evade the force of the objection, that it will be accompanied with expense. But is not the expense incurred in this place for house-rent sure to amount ere long to as much as would be necessary to purchase a place? From these observations my brethren will easily gather my wish, and I have made them with the hope that you will favour me with your sentiments upon the subject. I have already the offer of subscriptions to the amount of upwards of 1000 Rds. This will help, but I know that unless my Brn. sanction the design, and also grant some pecuniary assistance, it will be out of my power to effect my design. I would have saved you and myself the trouble of attending to these remarks, had it not been for the decisions of our last meeting on the subject.

The house in which I now reside, being for many reasons unsuitable, I have found it necessary to take another into which I intend to remove on the beginning of May; and as the house I intend to occupy is on the south bank of the Matura river, I intend to have a boat for occasional excursions up the river, which extends a good way into the interior.

I hope my Brethren will pardon the freedom of these remarks, and believe me to be in the sincerest manner, their brother and fellow-labourer,

           A. HUME.

THE JAFFNA AND POINT PEDRO STATION.

No communication from hence.

~~~~~~~~~~~~~~~~~~

THE TRINCOMALIE STATION.

Trincomalie, March 31, 1820.

MY DEAR BRETHREN,

We entered the year with a renewed dedication of ourselves to God and his most blessed cause; and found an increasing pleasure in discharging the duties of our mission work.

The necessity for one brother to attend the Conference in Colombo, required me to undertake a long and tedious journey by land through Kandy, which, after overcoming many dangers and fatigues, I was enabled safely to accomplish.

During my absence, Brother Stead managed the concerns of the station; applying himself also to the study of the Tamul language. The difficulties of going to Colombo and returning again at the season the journey was undertaken, were so many, that much precious time was irretrievably lost, much expense unavoidably occurred, and more than two months elapsed before I could resume my labours. Nevertheless, Brother Stead conducted every part of the work in a manner highly creditable to himself: and was able also to make advances in the language, which he now reads with tolerable ease. In this place, I should be wanting to my Brethren and to myself, were I to neglect to acknowledge how much my hands have been strengthened by the appointment of my colleague to this station: a brother whose views so much harmonize with my own.

The congregations, during the quarter, have been rather better; and we hope good has been done among them: a serious attention is paid to the word of life when preached; and our prayer is, that the sun of righteousness may arise upon us with healing in his wings. Some of the members of our class have been confined by sickness, but the rest have not forgotten to assemble themselves together, and they have frequently received tokens for good from the hands of him who giveth liberally and upbraideth not.

Since I had the pleasure of seeing my Brethren at the late meeting, my mind has been much encouraged, and fresh confidence will, I hope, excite me to greater exertions, in my work. I was especially gratified by the appearance of those schools which I had an opportunity of seeing in Colombo. I have ever been an advocate for the instruction of the rising generation, and its importance appears greater as I see its beneficial effects. If one thing more than another can afford pleasure to a benevolent mind, surely that sight must be the most delightful, where native children and youth, up to manhood, are beheld assembling around a throne of grace, and lifting up their voices to God in praise and prayer.

Our school-superintendent Mr. Hunter, has gone on as usual regularly among the natives, reading and expounding the Scriptures, declaring to them that Christ has power upon earth to forgive sin. And this we purpose to do more than ever, for it is our chief delight to preach Christ and him crucified.

May the richest blessing of grace be with you, and with the whole Church of God: and may it be said unto her, *" Then shalt thou see and flow together, and thine heart shall fear, and be enlarged; because the abundance of the sea shall be converted to thee, the forces of the gentiles shall come unto thee*   Affectionately yours,

                                        R. CARVER.

THE BATTICALOA STATION.

Batticaloa, March 29, 1820.

MY DEAR BRETHREN,

I sit down to write you on the present occasion with much more satisfaction and comfort than I did last quarter, as I have been able to enter more fully into my work, and can give you a more particular account of this station. The district of Batticaloa is very extensive and populous; and most of the villages are very conveniently situated for missionary exertions. The inhabitants are mostly husbandmen, and are a remarkably simple and industrious people. In this respect they differ much from the general native character: you will seldom see in any of their villages an *idle man*. This saves them from that want and misery which is so common among the inhabitants of other districts.

Most of the last quarter I have spent in travelling from place to place, but have not yet visited any place more than 10 miles distance, as I found it would be impracticable for me to attend to a larger circuit than I have at present marked out, till *this* is so far established as not to need my constant attendance.

I have not found the people so favourably disposed towards my coming among them as I at first anticipated; nor have I been able to collect any number together without sending previously an order from the Collector for the people to meet me. The reason they assigned was, that they must attend their fields and their cattle. They altogether, at first, objected to send their children to school; saying they must work for their living, and they did not know that it would be any advantage for poor children to learn to read and write. However, after several visits and conversations, four villages have *consented* to build themselves school rooms, and to send their children. Two of these are the protestant villages I mentioned in my last. But there has always been some particular difficulty in the way to prevent them from commencing this work till last week, when the sitting-magistrate, Mr. Bagnet, wrote officially in the absence of the Collector, that he would visit the villages himself on the 10th of April, and expected that he should find the school-rooms built according to their promise. So

I think it very probable that next month I shall have a place to *preach* in at least, if no scholars to teach; and as the Collector and Magistrate will often accompany me, I shall in all probability have a considerable congregation

In the protestant villages there is but one heathen temple, and that a very small one; and the headmen informed me there were but four heathen men in the place. In a small school kept by a poor man in one of the villages, I saw a little fellow with ashes upon his forehead, and inquired if he were a heathen boy. While I turned to speak with the master, the youngster had contrived to rub off the ashes, so that I could scarcely recognize him. From many little things of a similar nature, it appears plain enough that their *prejudice* is in favour of what they call *Reformados*. I inquired into the origin of these protestants, and was informed, that during the Dutch government a few protestants were sent from Jaffna to colonize there; and that from them, these three villages were formed. They promise, if I can preach to them on the Sabbath day, they will all attend. At present, my Sabbath-days are taken up in English and Portuguese preaching.

One of the principle objections which the natives advance against sending their children to our schools, or to admit us among them, is, that we are *always changing our* Missionaries. They think Mr. Ault would have continued with them if he had lived; but since him no one has stayed more than a year; and notwithstanding my having assured them, if I have my health, I shall continue with them a long time, I often hear them inquiring about it, as they appear to doubt the truth of it. The school which was held in the viranda of the Government church, notwithstanding all possible attention, has dwindled away to the small number of 10 boys, and these by no means constant in their attendance. I have lately made particular inquiry into the cause of this, and find it is this, they will not send their children to a place where the dead are buried; but that if I would establish a school, and and build a place for public worship more among them, they would not only send their children, but attend themselves. Thinking this exceedingly probable, and being convinced that neither the school nor native preaching would ever produce much good in the Government church, I commenced the erection of a place on a very eligible spot, just in the centre of the island, having obtained a lease of it for ten years, at the rent of one fanam for annum. I had no sooner commenced this plan but the people came forward, and requested me to allow their children to come to school, and to assure me of their constant attendance at divine service; and to *confirm* this, many of them have sent wood for the building; so that I shall have little more than workmen's wages to pay. The place when finished will be very neat and commodious. It will be an open bungaloe, with a wall round it, about three feet high. I proposed a partition for the purpose of a school for girls; but upon mentioning this, I was led into a very long and warm controversy. Such an innovation upon the custom of their forefathers was as unexpected to them as ridiculous; and could not possibly be encouraged. I stated to them plainly the folly of such a custom; and argued that they who had so far forsaken the custom of

their fathers so far as to forsake heathenism and embrace Christianity,
ought to lay aside a custom so contrary to the religion of the bible.
But it appeared, that though they and all the inhabitants of Batticaloa
are nominally Christians, either Roman Catholics or protestants, they
were altogether ignorant of the Christian religion—After having, I
believe, convinced them that the custom was a bad one, they drew this
conclusion, that though it were a bad custom, yet if their forefathers
practiced it, they must not depart from it; and if their forefathers are
punished for it, they must be punished with them. I asked them if
my father were a thief, and were hanged for his misconduct, must I
follow his example, and share his fate? They said they could not answer, but begged I would not request them to send their daughters to
school or to church: any thing else I requested they would do, but
this they could not. I begged them to consider of it before they determined. They have done so, and I find many are inclined to send their
girls, and I think it likely that upwards of 20 may now be formed into
a school. A respectable Portuguese woman, who can read a little and
sew well, has engaged to take charge of them, and a little place will be
immediately erected near her house. This I was forced to accede to,
for they would not let the girls come to the same school with the boys.
Mrs. Osborne will be able to superintend the school every day, as the
distance from our house is but short. I hope the time is not very distant, when this very injurious custom will be entirely banished from
the east, where it has reigned so long; and also that custom will no
longer be considered as a sufficient reason for every species of inconsistency and wrong. I assure you, my dear Brethren, that dame Custom has more worshippers here than any deity in Batticaloa.

Both these schools would have been ready for opening next week,
were it not that the workmen are losing this week, and I fear will also
lose the next week in celebrating *Good Friday*, *Easter*, and other Roman Catholic nonsense. The *superstitious* institutions of the dark ages
are inviolably maintained, but the ordinances of DIVINE appointment
are little regarded. Tis encouraging to be assured, that primitive
Christianity shall revive and flourish, when God will be again worshipped in the spirit, and not in dead and idolatrous formality. But before
this be accomplished, there must be much missionary labour, and much
of the " help of the Lord against the mighty "

My soul has often been led out in earnest prayer for the preservation
of my dear native country, which at present appears to be sorely rent
by public broils. I believe the Lord will overrule every event for ultimate good; and that England will continue to be a medium of Gospel
light to the whole world.

During the last quarter, I have formed two societies, which I trust
will be productive of much good in Batticaloa. The one is a *Bible
Society*, and the other a *Benevolent Society*. The first we have denominated a *Twig* of the Trincomalee Branch Bible Society, as it is in immediate connexion with *that*, and through that to the Colombo Auxiliary Society. Both these societies have met with much support. A
copy of the resolutions and a list of the subscribers to each I enclose
for insertion in the Miscellaneous. The Benevolent Society has opened

many doors for me; and I trust the seed sown may spring up, and become fruitful unto eternal life. I find it is also a means of bringing the respectable inhitants of Batticaloa into a train of doing good; in which I have always found them willing, and sometimes beforehand with me in matters of this nature.

My little class is doing well. The two native young men I mentioned in my last, go on charmingly; and I believe there is a deep work of grace in both of them. I have my eye on several more, who I hope will soon be ripe for class-meeting. I am sorry to find I am likely to lose my English congregation, as the English troops are under orders to remove. and a detachment of Caffres are just arrived, and it is reported they are to be stationed here. They all speak Portuguese;—therefore, if they are marched to church, I must read the service and preach in Portuguese in the morning, and in English in the evening.

The young man I brought from the Jaffna class, who has been of great use to me, was taken ill a few days since of a complaint he was subject to when a child (namely fits) and will sail to morrow for Jaffna to put himself into the hands of a Medical man, who partially cured him when a child. I have no hope of his returning to me again. This will prove a great loss unless another can come from Jaffna to supply his place, indeed I cannot go on without some one to attend the English and Tamul school I have laboured the last quarter to the very extent of my strength, and sometimes beyond it, so that I have been compelled to take more than ordinary rest: I have necessarily been much exposed to sun and rain and have walked through jungles surrounded by Elephants and wild Buffaloes; still I never felt more disposed to give myself entirely to the cause of God among the Heathen, neither desiring or anticipating rest till I end my life and labour together. But I rejoice in the prospect of one day wearing a Missionary Crown. May the Lord preserve and bless us all and finally give us life for ever more.

I am, dear Brethren, ever affectionately yours,
THOMAS OSBORNE.

THE MADRAS STATION.

No communication from hence.

THE BOMBAY STATION.

No communications from hence.

Miscellaneous.

No. I.

𝕭𝖔𝖔𝖐𝖘,

IN THE WESLEYAN MISSION LIBRARY, COLOMBO,

(Chiefly furnished by the late Rev. Thomas Coke, LL. D.) as taken
March 27, 1820, and compared with former lists.

In Folio.

Ambrose's Works, 1 volume
Beveridge's Works, 2 volumes
Chambers's Dictionary, 5 vols.
Diadoti's Annotations, 1 volume
Fox's (George) Journal
Goodwin's Redemption Redeemed
Haak on the Testament, 2 copies
Hammond's Commentary, 1 volume
Haweis's Expositor, 2 volumes
Henry's Commentary, 3 volumes
Holy Bible, vellum paper, fine black
 print, presented by W. B. Fox.
Hopkins's Sermons, 2 copies
Howe's Works, 1 volume
Malbranche's Search after Truth, 1 v.
Middleton's Geography, 2 volumes
Old and New Testament, 1 volume
Owen's Sermons and Tracts, 1 vol.
Pearson on the Creed, 1 volume
Pocock's Works, 1 volume
Poole's Commentary, 2 volumes
Rapin's History of England, 2 vols.
Rider's Bible, 3 volumes
Saurin's Dissertations, 1 volume
Whitby on the New Testament, 2 v.

LATIN.

Leigh's Critica Sacra

GREEK.

ΤΗΣ ΘΕΙΑΣ ΓΡΑΦΗΣ ΠΑΛ
ΑΙΑΣ ΔΙΑΘΔΗ ΚΑΙ ΝΕΑΣ
ΔΙΑΘΗΚΗΣ, ΑΠΑΝΤΑ·

FRANCAIS.

La Sainte Bible avec argumens et
 les Reflexions, par J. F. Ostervald
La Sainte Bible, par David Martin,
 *Pasteur de l'Eglise Wallone, d'Eu-
 trech.*

In Quarto.

Ainsworth's Latin Dictionary, 2 vols.
Ashley Sykes's Paraphr. and Notes
 on the Epistle to the Hebrews
Benson on the Epistles, 2 volumes
——— on Christianity, 1 volume
Brown's Bible, 1st volume only
Bryan's Natural Philosophy, 1 vol.
Chandler on Galatians, &c. 1 vol.
Cordiner's History of Ceylon, 2 vol.
Cruttwell's Concordance of the New
 Testament, presented by the Rev.
 George Marsden.
Dodd's Common Place Book, 1 vol.
Dubois's Account of India. Pre-
 sented by the Committee
Fleetwood's Life of Christ, 1 volume
Goodwin on the Spirit, 1 volume
Guyse's Paraphrase, 3 volumes
Henderick's Lexicon, 1 volume
Heylyn's Theological Lect. 1 vol.
Holy Bible, 1676
Jones's Persian Grammar
Littleton's Latin & Eng. Dictionary
Locke on the Epistles, 2 volumes
Macknight's Harmony, 1 volume
Missionary Voyage, 1 volume
Moore's Hindoo Pantheon, present-
 ed by Mr. John Somerville Wood.
Parker's Commentary, 2 volumes
Pearce's Commentary, 2 volumes
Simon on the New Test. 2 volumes
View of Hindoostan, 2 volumes
Webster on the Testament, 1 volume
Wesley's Notes on the Old Testa-
 ment, 2d and 3d volumes
——— Notes on the New Test. 1 vol.

LATIN.

Friderici Hoffmani Medicinæ Ra-
 tionalis Systematicæ 9 tomi,—presented by W. B. Fox.

Lexicon Linguæ Arabicæ, Wilmet,
one volume
Sexti Aurelii Victoris Historia Ro-
mana curante Joanne Arntzenio

FRANCAIS.

Le Nouveau Testament de Notre
Seigneur Jesus Christ, traduction
de Geneve de 1726, 1 tome.
Le Sainte Bible avec un Com-
mentaire Litteral par M. Charles Chais. 6 tomes.
Sainte Bible en Latin et en François avec des notes litterales,
critiques et histo.ique, en 17
tomes.

In Octavo.

Antiquities of Great Britain
Arminian, or Methodist Magazine,
from 1778, to 1812.
Arminian Magazine, 2d of America
Asiatic Researches, 11 volumes
Beeyan on Family Worship, 1 vol.
Beveridge's Private Thoughts.
Beveridge's Thesaurus, 4 volumes
Blair's Lectures, 3 vols.
Bohem on True Christianity, 1 vol.
Brown's Dictionary, 2 vol.
Buffon's Natural History, 2 volumes
Cavallo's Elements of Natural or
Experimental Philosophy, 4 vols
Chillingworth's Works, 2 volumes
Christian Penitent, 2 vols.
Christian Perfection, 1 volume
Clarke's (Mr. Rd.) Gospel, 1 volume
Clarke's Body of Divinity, 1 odd v.
Clarke's Jewish Gospel, 2 volumes
Coke's West Indies, 2 vols.
Cole's Dictionary, 1 volume
Conybeare's Sermons, 2 volumes
Derham's Physico Theology, 2 vol.
De Pauw on the Egyptians, 2 vols.
Dodd on the Parables, 4 volumes
Doddridge's Family Expositor, six
volumes, 2d wanting
Durham on Prophecies, 1 odd vol.
Edwards's West Indies, 2 volumes
Ferguson's Astronomy, 1 volume
Ferguson's Lectures, by D. Brew-
ster, 3 vols. the 3d containing the
plates, 4to.
Fleetwood on Relative Duties, 1 vol.
Fleming's Apocalyptical Key 1 vol.
Goodwin's Moses and Aaron.
Gospel Tracts
Grove's Philosophy, 2 volumes

Gurnell's Complete Armour, 1st and
4th volumes
Guthrie's Geographical Grammar
Hall's Contemplations, 3 volumes
Hardy on the Prophecies, 1 vol.
Harmer's Observations, 4 volumes
Horæ Solitariæ 2 vols.
Horne on the Psalms, 2 volumes
Hutton's Recreations in Mathemat-
ics and Natural Philosophy, 4 vols.
Imison's Elements of Science and
Art, 2 volumes
Indian Antiquities, 7 volumes
Israel, a Poem, in 2 Parts.
Jenkins on the reasonableness of
Christianity, 1st vol.
Johnson's Dictionary, 2 volumes
Key to the Revelations, 1 volume
Latimer's Sermons, 2 volumes
Law's Appeal, 1 volume
Law's various Works, 6 volumes
Leighton's Theological Lect. 1 vol.
Leighton's Works, 2 copies, imperf.
Leland's Deistical Writers, 2 vols.
Leslie's Tracts, 1 volume
Milher's Church History, 3 volumes
Min. of the Conference, 1st & 2d vol.
Moral Reflections, 2 volumes
Newton on the Messiah, 2 volumes
Natural Religion
Original Poems
Paraphrase on the Gospels, 2 vols.
Pilgrim's Progress
Piries's Posthumous Works, 2 vols.
Reader on the Revelations
Redemption Redeemed, 1 volume
Rolin's Ancient History 16 vols.
Romaine's Life
Roman History, vol. 7th only
Simeon's Helps, 3 volumes, defective
Simpson's Sermons, 1 vol,
Simpson's Sacred Literature, 4 vols.
Smith's Longinus
Spooner on Matthew and Mark, and
the Epistles, 2 volumes
Stanhope's Epistles, 2 volumes
Sufferings of the Son of God, 1st vol.
Titles of Christ, 1 volume only
Taprell's Lectures, one volume
Wakefield's Testament, 2 volumes
Warlaw's New Testament, 1 volume
Walker's Sermons, 4 vols.
Webster's Natural Philosophy, 1 v.
White's Sermons, 1 volume
Whitfield's Life, 1 volume
Wood's Dictionary, 2 volumes
Worsley's Translation of the New
Testament, 1 vol.

LATIN.

Davidson's Virgil, 2 volumes
Lexicon Mannale Græco-Latinum et Latino-Græcum a C. Schrevelio
Virgilii Opera.

GREEK.

ΠΛΑΤΩΝΟΣ ΔΙΑΛΟΓΟΙ Ε-ΘΕΟΚΡΙΟΥ ΤΑ ΕΥΡΙΣΚΟ-ΜΕΝΑ·

FRANCAIS.

Careme de Messire par Jean Louis de Fromentieres Eveque D'Aire. 2d tome.
Discours Historiques, Critiques, Theologiques et Moreaux, sur les evenemens les plus memorables du Vieux du Nouveau Testament par M. Saurin. en 11 tomes.
Essais de Sermons pour tous le jours du Careme, par Feu M. L'Abbé de Bretteville. 4 tomes.
Le Même. 2d et 3me tomes.
Le Même. 2d tome.
Le Missionaire de L'Oratoire, par Jean la Placet.
Le Nouveau Testament de Notre Seigneur Jesus Christ, traduit sur l'ancienne Edition Latine. 1er et 3me tomes.
La Parabole de noces expliquee em cinque Sermons par Jean Claude. 1 tome.
Le Predicateur Evangelique, par Jean Frederic Nardin. 5 tomes.
Le Saint Evangile selon Saint Jean avec une explication. 4me tome.
Le Temoins de resurection de Jesus Christ par A Le Moine.
Pseaumes de David mis en vers François. 1 tome.
Recreations Mathematiques et Physiques, par M. Ozanam 3me tomes.
Sermons de Feu Monsieur de Beausobre. 1er et 2d tomes.
Sermons pour tous le jours de Careme per M. Jaques Biroat. 2d tome.
Sermons sur divers sujets par Jean Mestrezat, en 3 tomes.
Sermons sur Divers Sujets, par M. Basnage. 2 tomes.
Sermons sur divers Textes de Escriture Sainte, par Feu M. Charles Chais.
Sermons sur divers textes de Escriture Sainte, par Mr. J. Colas de la Treille. 2d tome.

Shakespere traduit de l'Anglois 2 t
Tableau Politique, Religieux et Moral de Rome et des Etats Ecclesiastique, par Maurice Le Vesque. 1 tome.

ITALIAN.

Quaresimale di Paolo Segneri della Compagnia di Giesu. 1 tome.

PORTUGUESE

Memorias Economicas da Academia Real das Sciencias de Lisboa pelo O. Duque de Alfoes

In Duodecimo.

Account of two Danish Missionaries
Addison's Poems
Alleine's Letters
American Methodist Book of Discipline
American Hymn Book
American Minutes of Conference from 79 to 91
Antidote to Deism, 2 volumes
Beauties of Homer
Beauties of Watts
Bible, 1628. Another small Bible
Blackmore's Poem on the Creation
Botterell's French, Italian, and English Dictionary
Boyle on the Scripture Style
Bunyan's Visions
Burnet's Pastoral Care
Centaur not Fabulous
Chambaud's French Grammar
Chariar's Pocket French Dictionary
Christian Companion
Christian Triumph
Coke's Answer to Horne
———— Life of Christ
———— Life of Smith. – On Europe
Craddock's Gospel liberty
Duties of Religion
Dyer's Poems
Drew on the Soul
Earl of Moreland
Edwards on the Existence of God
Elizabeth Berry's Life and Death
Flavel's Mystery of Providence
Fletcher's Appeal
Fletcher's Letters
———— Posthumous Works
Gay's Fables
Gospel Sonnets
Gouge's Grammar
Harris's Life
Hervey's Sermons
History of Alexander the Great
History of England, 2 volumes

History of Guinea
Hopkins's Sermons
Horace, Francis's, 4 volumes
Introduction to Scripture
Irish sermons
Italian Grammar
Junius's Letters
Lacy on Prophetic Writings
Milton's Works, 2 volumes
Minutes of Conference from 05 to 12
Murray's Grammar
Nature Delineated, 4 volumes
Odyssey of Homer
Origin of Divine Revelation
Oxford Guide
Paradise Lost
Parkhurst's Treatises
Perrin's Conversations
Perrin's French Syntax
Petitpierre on Divine Goodness
Philips's Poems
Physician's Library
Pious Thoughts
Pope's Works, 4 volumes
Porteous's Evidences
Primitive Church
Principles of the Christian Faith
Propagation of the Soul
Review of Christian Evidences
Romaine's Triumph of Faith
Roman History
Scotch Confession of Faith
Scott's Introduction to Reading
Scott's Vindication
Shaftesbury's Characteristics, 1st vol.
Shakspeare, 9 volumes
Sing's Works, 1 odd volume
Socinianism unscriptural
Spiritual Combat
Sunday Service of the Methodists
Synonymous French Words
Telemachus
Tracts, 1 volume
Tutor's Guide
Waller's Works.
Warton's Virgil, 4 volumes
Watt's Lyric Poems
Welsh Dictionary
Wesley's Sermons, 9 volumes
———— Journal, 5 vols. 1 wanting
———— Notes on the Test. 3 vols
———— Philosophy, 4 volumes
Wesley's short Hymns
Whitfield's 15 sermons
Wonders of the Microscope
Wonders of the Telescope

LATIN.

Cornelii Nepotis 1 tomus.

Vita Catulli, Tibulli, Propertii, et Cornelii Galli 1 tomus.
M. Tulli Ciceronis de Officiis
C Julii Cæsaris Commentarii.
Opera Virgilii
Artheri Jonstoni Psalmi Davidici 1 tomus.
Gradum ad Parnassum.
Salamonis Van Til Homiliæ.

GREEK.

Compendium Græcum Novum Testamenti 1 tomus.
ΤΗΣ ΚΑΙΝΗΣ ΔΙΑΘΗΚΗΣ ΑΠΑΝΤΑ· Γ
Η ΠΑΛΙΑ ΔΙΑΘΗΚΗ ΚΑΤΑ ΤΟΥΣ ΕΒΔΟΜΗΚΟΝΤΑ· Β

FRANÇOIS.

Pere Le Jeune. 4 tomes.
Sermons du Pere de la Rüe 4 tom.
Abrege de morale de L'Evangile 2 tomes.
Nouveau Voyage du Pere Labat aux Isles de L'Amerique. 6 tom.
Le Paradis Perdu de Milton. 3 tom.
Divers Traites sur des Matiers de Conscience. 1 tome. Par Le Mr. Jean La Placet.
Traite de la Foi Divine. 1 tome. Par le même Auteur.
Essai sur L'Origine et L'Antiquite des Langues. 1 tome.
Le Nouveau Testament, avec Notes et Reflexions, 1 tome. Par M.André Pralard.
Lettres du B. Pere Saint Francis Xavier. 1 gros tome.
Sermons divers sujets. 5 tomes. Par Jean Mastrezat.
Pratique de la Perfection Crétienne 2 tomes. Par R. P.A. Rodirguez.
Instruction Pastorale de Monseineur L'Archevesque, Duc de Cambray. 3 tomes.
Les Aventures de Telemaque, 1 tome
Pensees sur differents sujets. 1 tome. Par M. Massillon.
Reflexions sur L'Histoire des Juifs. 2 tomes. Par Massillon.
L'Harmonie de Monde. 1 tome.
La Vie du Venble. Pere Bernard. 1 tome. Par P. Lemprenr.
Gonnelieu sur la Presence de Dieu. 1 tome.

La Religion Un Poëme 1 tome.
Par Monsieur Racine.

Le Cantique de Cantiques 1 tome

Le meme un autre copie

L'Histoire de Vieux et Nouveau
Testament, 1 tome

Le Voyages de Cyrus. Ramsay 1 t

Meditations sur les Evangiles, 1 tm.

Traite de la Religion, 1 tome

Les Pseaumes de David, mis en
vers François, 1 tome

Nouveaux Memoires de Mr. No-
dot, 1 tome

Point de Croix, Point de Cou-
ronne, 1 tome, par G. Penn

Historie Morale des Isles Antilles
de L'Amerique, 2 tomes, par
Christofle Fourmy.

De la Recherche de la Verite, 2
tomes, par Malbranche

Le même complet

L'Imitation de Jesus Christ, tra-
duite et paraphrasée en vers
François, 1 tome, par Pierre
Corneille

Sonnets Chretienne sur divers
sujets, par Mr. Drelincourt

Le Nouveau Testament en la
langue François avec reflexions morales, 6 tomes, 3 me
et 5 me tomes besoin

Meditations sur la Passion de Jesus Christ nôtre Seigneur, 1 er
et 3 me tomes, par M l'Abbé
Clement

Les Aventures de Télémaque, 2
tomes

Homelies sur les Evangiles de
tous les Dimanches de l'année,
6 tomes, par M. L'Abbé de
Monmorel.

Exposition de la Religion Cre-
tienne, 1 tome, par C. Pegorier

Reflexions, Sentences et Maxi-
mes Morales par Mr. Amelot
de la Houssaye

Essai Philosophique sur Le Plai-
sir, par M. E. Bertand

Abregé de la Theologie et de la
Morale Chrétienne, par Jaques
Saurin

Le Messie, Poëme, 4 tomes, par
Klopstock

Grammaire Recueil de Pieces
Choises, 1 tome, par Arthur
Masson

Discours sur L'Historie Univer-
selle. 1 tome, par Mr. J. B.
Bossuet

Essais de morales 1er et 3 me
tomes, par Jean la Placet

L'Art de bien employer le temps
en toute sorte de conditions, 1 t

Pensées et Reflexions sur les
egaremens des hommes dans
le voye du salut, 1er tome

De la Recherche de la Verité,
1er tome

Pratique de la Perfection Chrétienne, et le meme, 1er tome

Religieuse 3me tome, du R. P.
Alphonze Rodriguez

Poesias et Cantiques Spiritual,
3me tome, par J. M. B. de la
Mothe Guion

La Theologie de la Croix de Jesus Christ, 1 tome

La Liturgie ou Formulaire des
Prieres Publique selon l'usage
de L'Eglise Anglicane, avec
L'Nouveau Testament, 1 tome

Sermons et Instructions Chreti-
ennes sur divers natures, 2
tomes, par P. D'Orleans

Memoires sur L'Education des
vers a soie, 1 tome, par Mr. L'
Abbé Boissier de Sauvages

Sur L'Existence de Dieu, par M.
Fenelon

Preservatif contre L'Irreligion

Grammaire de la Langue François par Mr Jean Perrin

ITALIENNE.

Novelle Morali di Francesco So-
ave, 2 tomos

Guida alla pronunzia e all' in-
telligenza dell' Italiane, 1 tomo, di Vimenzo Peretti

Triompho della Croce de Christo,
di Padre Saunarola Ferrara

B

PORTUGUESE.

Testamento Velho traducido em Portuguez por Antonio Pereira 17 tom
Novo Testamento 6 tomas.
Hystoria de Portugal por Antonio de Moraes da Silva e continnado por Hyppolyto José da Costa 3 tm.
Rimas de Mantel Maria de Barbora du Bucage 3 tomes
Viagens de aenrieue Wantonas a' Terras Austraes e ao paiz das Monas 5 tomos.
Obras Luis de Camões, 4 tomos.
Deducção Chronologica e Analitiia pelo José de Seabra 3 tomos.
Provas da Deducção Chronologica e Analitica pelo Mesmo autor. 2 tomos
Sermons pelo Luis Sam. Franciscus de Borja 1 tomo.
Vida de Dom Jeaõ de Castro 1 tm
Cantigas de Trangambar.

TAMUL.

தாவிதராசாவும மற
ற அறிசெய லீட்ட
வாசகுமபாடிளகுசள
சசங்கீதங்கள குாள
உப லெகசதிறுடைய
குறிபபிடம
இதிலெ

SINGHALESE.

සකල ජනයන්මගේ ගැල
විම පිනිස ප්‍රකාශකරන
ලද අපගේ ස්වාමිවූ ගැල
වූන්කාර යේසුස් ක්‍රිස්තුස්
වහන්සේගේ අභිනාව ගි
විසුමය.
මහේන්ද්‍රන් නොනොත්
සහ ඔවුගේ ශෙලුවා ස
මාන සිඩවූනාවූ කථාවන්
ය. ආගමෙහි මූලකාරණා
යෝගී

Other Books belonging to the Mission.

1 Sanscrit Dictionary
1 ditto Grammar
1 ditto New Testament
1 Hindustani Grammar
1 Bengalee Dictionary
The Scriptures in Bengalee

Books in Dr. Coke's original Catalogue, but which appear never to have landed in Ceylon.

FOLIO.

Clarke's Mirror.
Wilson's Christian Dictionary.

QUARTO

Guthrie's Geographical Gram.
Calmet's Dictionary.
Field's Bible

OCTAVO.

Chandler on Revelation.
Ray on the Creation.
Pilgrim's Progress, 2 copies, one of which is in verse.
Social Religion
Marshal on Sanctification
Cooper's Recreations, 4 volumes
History of England, 5 volumes
Kett on the Prophecies, 2 vols.
Drew on the Body
Missionary Sermons *in French*, 11 volumes. *Query?*
Sermons par M J Saurin, 7 toms

DUODECIMO.

Songs in the Night
Heart delineated
Life of Philip Henry
Lives of the Martyrs
Beak's (probably Buck's) Anecd.
Williams's 20 Sermons
Watson on a Future State
Knight's Prayers
Importance of a Religious Life
Watts's Death and Heaven

Atmore's Family Altar
Bigland's Natural History
Circle of the Sciences
Addison's Evidences.
Pope and Blackmore, 2 volumes
Lowth's English Grammar
Owen on Spiritual Mindedness
Spelling Book. Life of Silas Told
Pindar ———

BOOKS MISSING.

QUARTO.

Bryan's Natural Philosophy, 1v.
Dodd's Common-place Book
Goodwin on the Spirit
Parker's Commentary, 1st vol
Cordiner's Ceylon, 1st volume
Webster on the Testament, 2 v.
Wesley's Notes on the Old Test.
　2d and 3d volumes
Wesley on the New Testament

OCTAVO.

Beevan on Family Worship
Blair's Lectures, 3 volumes
Clarke's Divinity, 1 odd volume
Coke's West Indies, 1 odd vol.
Cole's Dictionary
Conybeare's Sermons, 2 volumes
Dodd on the Parables, 4 vols
Durham's Prophecies
Gurnell's Complete Armour, 1st
　and 4th volumes
Nugent's Pocket Dictionary
Hanley on the Prophecies
Harmer's Observations, 4 vols
Horne on the Psalms
Johnson's Dictionary, 1st vol.
Key to the Revelations

Redemption Redeemed
Sibb's Light from Heaven
Simpson's Sacred Literature
Taylor's Holy Living and Dying
Smith's Longinus
Davies's Virgil
Stanhope on the Epistles
Wesley's Life. Whitfield's Life
Titles of Christ.　Wood's Dict.
Atmore's Methodist Memorial
Warlaw's Testament
Mason's Pilgrim's Progress
Derham's Theology, 1 vol.

DUODECIMO.

Beauties of Watts
Wesley's Sermons, 7th and 8th v.
Bunyan's Visions
Dhariar's or Nugent's Dictionary
Coke's Life of Christ. On Europe
Collins's Voyages
Cave's Primitive Christianity
Duties of Religion
Pomfret's Poems
Thomson's Seasons
Christian Library, 1st and 2d vs.
Earl of Moreland
Fletcher's Appeal
History of England
Junius's Letters
Origin of Revelation
Paradise Lost. Murray's Gram.
Oxford Guide. Pious Thoughts
Pope's Works, 1st and 2d vols.
Review of Christian Evidences
Scott's Introduction to Reading
Sunday Service of the Methodists
Tutor's Guide.　Tracts

☞ *Many of the above works are old, and in bad condition ; especially the French works. Several of the theological works are sadly mutilated, some having many leaves cut out. Of the few scientific works in the Library, several are very imperfect, many of the plates of reference being in whole or in part cut out. No labour has been spared to make the list as perfect as possible, though it may be capable of improvement. The books which are missing are, probably, for the most part in the hands of the different Brethren.*

No II.

The following account of Madagascar will doubtless be read with interest by those who feel solicitous for the introduction of Christianity among a numerous people hitherto much neglected. It is extracted from a work, originally published in French, by the Abbé Rochon, a character of great celebrity in France, who had attained high academical honours and filled important places of trust. Perhaps his views in some cases were a little mistaken, but the work, generally, contains important information. EDIT.

Description of the Island of Madagascar.

The Island of Madagascar was discovered in the year 1506, by Laurence Almeyda; it was however known to the Persians and Arabs from time immemorial. Alphonso Albukerque ordered Ruy Pereira da Conthintho to visit its interior parts. This general dispatched Tristan d'Acunba to make a tour round the island and to take the soundings of the principal capes. It is divided into 28 provinces, viz. Anossy, Manapani, the valley of Amboul, Vohitzban, Watte Manahou, Ycondra, Etomampo, Adchimoussi, Erengdranes, Vohitz Anghombes, Manacarongha, Mantalana, Antaveres, Ghalemboul, Tamatava, Sahaveh, Voolou Voolou, Andafoutchy, Manghabey, Adcimoutchy, Mandrarey, Ampatra, Caremboul, Mahafalley, Houlouveh, Sivah, Yvaudrhou, Mashicores.

When the Portuguese first discovered Madagascar they gave it the name of St. Lawrence. The French, in the reign of Henry IV. called it Isle Dauphine. Though its real name is Madecassa, it is more generally known by that of Madagascar. This great island, according to several learned geographers, is the ancient Cernea of Pliny and the Menuthiasde of Ptolemy. Its situation is pretty near NNE and SSW. Its limits of latitude are the 12th and 26th degs. The surface of this isle may be estimated at 800,000,000 acres of good and arable ground, celebrated for the fertility and variety of its productions. All the different parts of Madagascar are watered by torrents and large rivers, and above all by a great number of little rivulets, which take their source at the foot of that vast ridge of mountains which separates the eastern from the western coast. Vigagora is the highest mountain in the north, and Botistmena in the south

These mountains contain in their bowels precious minerals and curious fossils. The traveller who perambulates for the first time and for the purpose of instruction, the mountainous wilds, intersected by valleys and declivities where nature, abandoned to genial fertility, displays the most singular and variegated productions, frequently cannot resist the surprise and terror that strike him at the sight of precipices, whose summits are crowned with lofty trees. His astonishment in-

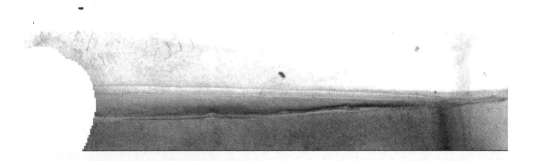

creases at the noise of those great cascades, whose borders are inaccessible. But those views truly picturesque vanish alternately before rural prospects, pleasant hills, plains, the vegetation of which is never troubled by the intemperateness, or vicissitude of the seasons. The eye contemplates with pleasure the spacious commons, which afford pasture to numerous droves of oxen and flocks of sheep. The rice and potatoe fields, exhibit likewise a new and most interesting spectacle. One beholds a flourishing agriculture raised almost at the sole expence of nature. The happy natives of Madagascar do not moisten the earth with their sweat, they hardly turn it with the spade, and this labour alone is sufficient. They dig little holes in the ground, at a small distance from each other, in which they drop a few grains of rice, and fill up these holes with earth, by a gentle motion of the foot; but what furnishes the most convincing proof of the extreme fertility of the soil is, that a field thus sown, yields an hundred for one.

(To be continued.)

No. III.

Copy of the Resolutions passed at the formation of the BATTICALOE BIBLE SOCIETY.

Resolved, That this Society be denominated the Twig of the Trincomalie Branch Bible Society; and that the design of forming the subscribers to the Trincomalie Bible Society into a distinct Society is, that their subscriptions may be duly collected and officially forwarded to the Society at Trincomalie; and that the books received may be properly distributed.

Resolved, That an Annual Report of the proceedings of this Society be forwarded in due time to the Trincomalie Society for insertion in their Report

Resolved, That a Committee be appointed, and to meet on the first Monday of every quarter. Two members of the Committee besides the Treasurer and Secretary shall be considered as able to transact any business

Resolved, That any person subscribing 12 Rds per annum be considered eligible to be chosen a member of the Committee.

Resolved. That Messrs Pennell, Bagnett, Ingham, and Osborne be appointed the Committee for the present year.

Resolved, That the Rev. T. Osborne be requested to take the joint office of Treasurer and Secretary.

Resolved. That the Treasurer and Secretary be furnished with suitable books for entering the receipts of subscriptions and donations; and also of receipt of books from Trincomalie, and an account of their distribution.

Resolved, That a copy of these Resolutions be forwarded to the Secretary at Trincomalie.

No. ix.　　　　　　　C

TO THE INHABITANTS OF BATTICALOE.

The above is a Copy of the Resolutions passed on Tuesday, January 18th, at the formation of the Batticaloe Bible Society; the object of which is to furnish the inhabitants of the Batticaloe District with the Sacred Scriptures in English, Dutch, and Tamul.

N. B. Subscriptions as low as one fanam per week, and the smallest donations will be thankfully received.

LIST OF SUBSCRIBERS.

	Quarterly.		Annual.		Donations.	
	Rds.	f.	Rds.	f.	Rds.	f.
H. Pennel, Esq.	15	0	....		25	0
J. Bagnett, Esq.	6	0	....		....	
G. Ingham, Esq.	6	0	....		15	0
Rev. T. Osborne, ...	6	0	....		15	0
H. H. Barbett, ...	3	0	....		....	
J. White,..............	1	6	....		....	
J. Leatherland, ...	3	0	....		....	
Head Modeliar,..........	3	0	....		....	
F. Hester, ...	1	6	....		....	
Serjeant of the 73d,......	....		....		5	0
Private of ditto,....	....		....		1	0
W. Petrus, ...	....		3	0	....	
W. Fernando.............	....		3	0	....	

Copy of the Resolutions passed at the formation of the BATTICALOE BENEVOLENT SOCIETY.

Resolved, That this Society be denominated the Batticaloa Benevolent Society, the object of which shall be to relieve the sick and infirm of the poor inhabitants of every denomination.

Resolved, That a Committee shall be formed at whose discretion the poor shall be relieved, and the Committee shall meet weekly.

Resolved, That suitable persons shall be appointed by the Committee to visit the poor weekly, giving them religious instructions; and to bring in their reports, stating the name, age, residence, income and circumstances of the poor visited.

Resolved, That no cases shall be relieved until the circumstances are laid before the Committee, except any particularly trying case should require immediate relief, when any one Member of the Committee may advance not exceeding 1 Rdr.

Resolved, That Messrs Pennell, Bagnett, Ingham, and Osborne be appointed the Committee for the present year.

Resolved, That the Rev. T. Osborne be requested to take the joint offices of Treasurer and Secretary.

Resolved, That the Treasurer and Secretary be furnished with suitable books to enter weekly the receipts and disbursements; and also to keep an account of the number and nature of the cases visited.

Resolved, That every subscriber of two dollars per month and upward be considered eligible to be chosen a member of the Committee.

Resolved, That the Secretary be requested to draw up an address in English, Portuguese, and Tamul, to be presented to the inhabitants of Batticaloe, stating the object of this Society, with a column to receive the names of subscribers weekly, monthly, quarterly, and annually, also to leave one column for donations.

To the Inhabitants of Batticaloe.

On Tuesday January 18th 1820, a Society was formed by the European inhabitants of Batticaloa called the Batticaloa Benevolent Society, the object of which is to relieve the sick and infirm poor of every denomination, and that proper persons shall be appointed by the Committee of this Society for visiting the poor, giving them religious instructions, and reporting their cases weekly to the committee, who shall impart relief according to the circumstances of the poor visited.

It was resolved, that a subscription should immediately be opened to receive the names of subscribers monthly, quarterly or annually. The books of receipts and disbursements will always be open to the inspection of such charitable persons as will favour this benevolent object with their subscription or donation, that they may see that their Charity is appropriated to a proper purpose.

LIST OF SUBSCRIBERS.

	Monthly. Rds. f.	Quartly. Rds. f.	Annly. Rds. f.	Donations. Rds. f.
H. Pennell, Esq.	5 0			
J. Bagnett, Esq.	10 0			
G. Hughes, Gent.	5 0			
G. Ingham, Esq.	2 0			
Rev. T. Osborne	2 0			
H. Bartlett,	1 0			
J. Leatherland,	1 0			
Head Modeliar,	5 0			
Subrian Modliar,	1 0			
P. Vincent,	1 0			
F. Hester,	0 6			
M. Ferdinando,	0 6			
P. Barbett,	0 6			
J. White,	0 6			
A. Sellesteen,	0 2			
Two Lascars,	0 2			
J. Kenny,		3 0		
D. Bartolomeus,		2 0		
J. Andrews,		3 0		
J. Doen,		2 0		
A. Schelra,		3 0		
Cutcherry Modeliar,			3 0	
Daniel Modliar,			3 0	
A Serjeant of the 73d,				2 0
A Private of ditto,				1 0

No. IV.

The 'Squire's Pew.

FROM A TRURO PAPER.

A slanting ray of evening light
　Shoots through the yellow pane;
It makes the faded crimson bright,
　And gilds the fringe again:
The window's gothic frame-work falls
In oblique shadows on the walls.

And since those trappings first were new,
　How many a cloudless day, [new,
To rob the velvet of its hue,
　Has come and pass'd away!
How many a setting sun hath made
That curious lattice-work of shade!

Crumbled beneath the hillock green,
　That curious hand must be,
That carved this fretted door, I ween,
　Acorn and fleur-de-lis:
And now the worm hath done her part,
In mimicking the chisel's art.

—In days of yore (as now we call)
　When the first JAMES was King;
The courtly Knight from yonder Hall,
　Hither her train did bring;
All seated round in order due,
With broider'd suit and buckled shoe.

On damask cushions, set with fringe,
　All reverently they knelt;
Prayer-books, with brazen hasp and
　In ancient English spelt, [hinge,
Each holding in a lily hand,
Responsive to the Priest's command.

Now, streaming down the vaulted aisle,
　The sun-beam, long and lone,
Illumes the characters awhile
　Of their inscription stone;
And there, in marble hard and cold,
The knight and all his train behold.

Outstretch'd together are express'd
　He and my lady fair,
With hands uplifted on the breast,
　In attitude of prayer;
Long visaged, clad in armour, he,
With ruffled arm and bodice, she.

Set forth in order as they died,
　The numerous offspring bend;
Devoutly kneeling side by side,
　As though they did intend
For past omissions to atone,
By saying endless prayers in stone.

Those mellow days are past and dim,
　But generations new,
In regular descent from him,
　Have fill'd the stately pew:
And in the same succession go,
To occupy the vault below.

And now, the polish'd modern 'Squire,
　And his gay train appear;
Who duly to the hall retire,
　A season, every year;
And fill the seats with belle and beau,
As 'twas so many years ago.

Behold, all thoughtless, how they tread
　The hollow-sounding floor,
Of that dark house of kindred dead,
　Which shall, as heretofore,
In turn receive to silent rest,
Another and another guest.

The feather'd hearse and sable train,
　In all its wonted state,
Shall wind along the village lane,
　And stand before the gate;
Brought many a distant county thro'
To join the final rendezvous.

And when the race is swept away,
　All to their dusty beds;
Still shall the mellow evening ray
　Shine gaily o'er their heads;
While other faces, fresh and new,
Shall occupy the 'Squire's pew.

END OF APRIL EXTRACTS.

Colombo: Printed at the Wesleyan Mission Press, for the Missionaries.

Extracts

FROM

QUARTERLY LETTERS, &c.

No. XII. JULY, 1820.

THE COLOMBO STATION.

Colombo, July 10, 1820.

VERY DEAR BRETHREN,

My worthy colleague has requested me to write our letter for the present quarter, as the completion of the School Report takes up most of the time he can spare from other duties. I shall cheerfully contribute what I am able to his assistance and your satisfaction.

The variable weather of the past quarter has been somewhat unfavourable to our work. The habits of the people will not allow them to be regular in their attendance on the means of grace when the earth is deluged, as it has frequently been, nor in such circumstances can we expect the Schools to be well attended. It is pleasing, however, to observe, that the fluctuation has been smaller than might have been expected; and that most of our appointments have been attended to. Fine weather seems to be now set in; and our work in its various departments assumes a pleasing and promising aspect.

Our Portuguese congregation at the Mission-House continues pretty large and very attentive. In the Pettah, our English congregations are much the same. In the Fort the place is indeed too strait for us: and few, I believe, attend, but who have conquered some difficulties for the sake of the truth; and many, we are well assured, are habitually devoted to God, and by their deportment adorn the doctrine of God our Saviour. Among our hearers, we have usually some respectable individuals; and some officers of the army occasionally attend.—It is a very gratifying reflection that our military members stand so high in the esteem of their superiors. They are readily supplied with passes and every facility they desire. Last week, seven of them were allowed a few days leave of absence to be present at the opening of the New Chapel at Negombo. This, they say, was a privilege not often granted. The Fort Society has been divided into three classes, in a way likely to secure their prosperity while under our care, and should they remove, will probably conduce to their permanence. Leaders are appointed from among their most approved members to meet them

No. XII. T

weekly, but as some are usually absent on duty at the time, we have arranged to meet the whole Society on Tuesday evenings by means of a fellowship-meeting. This arrangement promises to be beneficial on many accounts. It will especially unfold a greater variety of religious experience; and unite our friends in Christian love, who belonging to different regiments, and in consequence having little intercourse, would have always a tendency to disunion.

Our Singhalese preaching on Friday evenings at New-Bazar has been regularly continued. The spirit of the Gospel spreads there among the people in a gratifying way; and we should probably be more frequently encouraged in our work, were we made acquainted with the full extent of our efforts. Our friend Appleton has furnished me with two statements, the leading particulars of which I will transcribe.

"A Singhalese woman named *Baba Hamy*, aged about 50 years, lived in my neighbourhood. When preaching was begun in the New-Bazar School, she voluntarily attended. Afterwards she removed to live with her relatives at some little distance; but continued to attend the preaching as often as possible. Not observing her, as usual, for a time, I made enquiry, and understood that she was attacked with a disorder. This I was sorry to hear, and immediately called to see her. She appeared to be near death, but was able to understand me. I considered her a dying creature and gave her the best advice I was able. She gave me some very satisfactory answers, which led me to praise God immediately. I conversed and prayed with her, and left her with great joy in my spirit. She gradually recovered; and afterwards walked on her foot to my house to thank me, declaring that after my prayer she began to recover herself, and that no medicine had cured her She spoke of this to her neighbours and brought along with her all her family consisting of nine persons, and some of her neighbours who had never before heard the preaching of the Word of God."

The other account is as follows:

"In February last *Mattheus de Zoysa* a Singhalese compositor in the Mission-printing-office, suffered for 18 days a severe attack of illness. All the medical aid afforded him seemed in vain, and he began to be apprehensive of his end. Though a Catholic, he requested Mr. Gogerly might be sent for that he might have some Christian advice. Mr. Gogerly just then being unable to attend, requested I would call and see him. I immediately went to the young man's house, and found him in bed, apparently in a dying state. On speaking to him he was unable to utter a word. I remained with him about an hour. He seemed to regain a degree of strength as I spoke, and was able to converse a little, and his pious answers gave me much satisfaction. I wished to pray with him, and as the mother and sister were Catholics, previously asked their consent, which they readily granted. They kneeled down with me, and the young lad then observed he felt renewed strength and spirits in consequence of the conversation. On concluding, he said, while I was speaking to him of the love of God, in an extraordinary way he felt renewed strength. Instead of promising to make offerings to departed saints, I exhorted him to give glory to God, and put his whole trust in the merits of Christ. He was fully restored in a few days and came to thank me; and attributed his restoration under God to the visit I paid him."

On Whit-Monday the children from our Schools in this circuit were all assembled at the Mission-House, and seldom has a more interesting scene been witnessed. The day was fine, and all appeared in their gayest clothes. I preached with considerable freedom from Rom. 8. 15.

While it is pleasing to observe the progress of truth, it is lamentable to reflect on the multitudes who continue in ignorance. Some weeks ago, a man, apparently upwards of 30, was introduced to me as a candidate for baptism. The man shewed every evidence of sincerity, but his ignorance was remarkable. He spent his childhood in the neighbourhood of Kandy, but left that country, he said before he had a beard; which is grown as long as that of a Jew. His first notions of Christianity arose in his mind from attending a Romish Church on particular festivals. He understood nothing of what was said on those occasions, but it seemed to him very amusing, and supposing the religion taught by the Missionaries the very same, he applied for admission!

The business of the Printing office has proceeded without interruption during the Quarter. In addition to some minor productions, the Book of Exodus and the Book of Proverbs have been finished in Singhalese. The Book of Common Prayer in that language is nearly complete, but we have had to defer the finish of that work partly for want of paper, and partly because we are desirous of completing the second Edition of the Singhalese New Testament in time for the Anniversary Meeting. We are as far as the Epistle of James.—On a former occasion I mentioned a scheme I had drawn out for a Cingalese case. About two months ago I had one made or the new construction at my own expense, by way of experiment; and I am happy to say it answers the purpose remarkably well. It is exactly the length of the common English case, and about an inch and half wider. All the characters required are brought within one third of the former compass, and of course proportionate perplexity and loss of time is avoided.

We have done something by way of supplying the want of books complained of in the last Quarterly, by sending to the Brethren all that remained in the Book-room. We have also printed off a large edition of the second part of the Sunday-school spelling-book. That and the third part, are admirable elementary works for schools, and the reading lessons of the first part are judiciously drawn up; but the part comprehending the monosyllables seems not well calculated to lead foreigners to a correct pronunciation of our tongue. In this particular the scheme of Dyche appears to me unrivalled. Smith's edition of it is the best I have seen.—The last sheet of the Scripture Extracts in Portuguese is in the press.

I was gratified by reading in the last Ceylon Gazette, Resolutions of a School-Book-Society lately formed at Madras. If an association of the kind were set on foot here, it would probably give a powerful impulse to the progress of education, and be an era in the literary history of Ceylon. In no place are books more wanted, and though it cannot be said that ability to produce elementary works is altogether wanting, nobody will affirm that literature is on the most desirable

footing. My passion for writing is not strong. What little I have done
this way has been rather from a sense of duty. I should be glad for
every one to do what he may be able. The result of research is
sometimes the developement of first principles, though one may have
fan a barn full of chaff in order to get a grain of wheat.—A new edition
carefully revised and corrected of my Cingalese and English Vocabulary is in the press. I feel obliged to several Brethren who have
consented to undertake the sale of a number of copies sufficient
to enable me to bear the expence attending the work

I am scarcely recovered from the hurt I received by the horse falling
under me four weeks ago as I was going into the country to preach.
My right foot was so bruised that for a fortnight I could hardly suffer it to touch the ground, and though the pain from my right shoulder
is almost gone, yet when I move my arm in some oblique direction,
as in putting on my coat, I feel a sudden seizure resembling an elec-
tric shock. I consider the preservation from greater danger a signal
interposition of divine care. *To shew himself strong, the eyes of the
Lord run to and fro throughout the whole earth.*

Modern times have produced many Missionary portraits; and they
can hardly be examined without profit, but were the nature of our
work and our varied anxiety fully known, a few finishing strokes
would appear, which cannot be now expected. While the faithful Missionary in these regions is a teacher of the Gentiles and a Messenger of
the Churches;—in consequence of cares and duties which he dare
not transmit to the shoulders of others, he is in fact "a beast of burden, a slave of all work." If Mr Cecil justly wondered at the production of the Hymns for Children, by a writer of the metaphysical
talents of Dr. Watts, rather than at his Essay on Logic: and if Dr.
Johnson is right in observing in his life of that excellent character,
that every man, acquainted with the common principles of human action, will look with veneration on the writer, who is at one time
combating Locke, and at another making a Catechism for children in
their fourth year—that a voluntary descent from the dignity of science is perhaps the hardest lesson that humility can teach,—people of
reflection may imagine the difficulty of maintaining, in this enervating
climate, equability of temper, when studying, for example, the inflec-
tive parts of Indian Grammar, (on which the penetration of a Harris
might be well bestowed, in a language hitherto not registered on
paper;) to be summoned to manage the veriest trifles:—to

"suckle fools and chronicle small beer."——

It is from a wish to establish truth, not by way of complaining that I
advert to this topic, and of your concurrence in the sentiment, I have
little doubt We are emphatically workers, and in all things *are to
approve ourselves the Ministers of God, in much patience, in afflictions,
in necessities, in distress, by honour and dishonour, by evil report and
good report; as deceivers, and yet true; as unknown, and yet well known;
as dying, and behold we live; as chastened, and not killed; as sorrowful,
yet alway rejoicing; as poor, yet making many rich; as having nothing
and yet possessing all things.*—I remain, very affectionately yours,
                                    JOHN CALLAWAY.

THE NEGOMBO STATION.

Negombo., July 10. 1820.

Very Dear Brethren,

My quarterly communication has been delayed this time by an event so pleasing, that I persuade myself a relation of it in the commencement of my letter, will be my best apology.

Our new chapel was opened under very pleasing circumstances on the 6th instant; much preparation for which has, of course, occupied us fully: our dear Brethren from the Colombo and Caltura stations arrived the preceeding day, to lend me their very kind and efficient assistance on this interesting occasion, and as greatly heightened my joy by their presence, as they relieved my anxiety by their exertions.

From an early hour in the morning our friends began to assemble from the country. Our different Schools, attended by their teachers, and great numbers of their parents and relations, gave the little town the most animated appearance, while drawing on to the scene of general attraction. The morning service, which was in English, commenced by singing, to the beautiful music of *Eaton,* "Eternal power whose high abode, &c." and after solemn prayer had been offered up and Psalms 19, 103, and 145 read, the prayer of Solomon at the dedication of the temple, and the blessed 14th of St. John followed. Then after singing our own most appropriate hymn "*Except the Lord conduct the plan, &c.*" Brother Fox preached an excellent and profitable sermon from that noble text. Isaiah 52. 10 "*The Lord hath made bare his holy arm in the sight of the nations, and all the ends of the earth shall see the salvation of God;*" in which he traced the blessed progress of Divine truth, shewed its influence on the human heart, and directed us to the happy period when it shall have obtained its promised universal spread. We concluded with "*Jesus the word of mercy give,*" and after the collection our military friends (who had walked from Colombo to be present on the occasion) assisted us well in singing to its own delightful music "*Before Jehovah's awful throne. &c.*" On returning home, a most gratifying scene presented itself. The Singhalese children and their parents were all assembled under the trees in our garden for refreshment previous to *their* sermon. As soon as we came in, they seated themselves in ranks on the grass, and were served with coffee, biscuits, plantains and pines in abundance; for in *this* department we were largely assisted by the headmen around, who sent us many presents. After all were satisfied they marched two and two to the chapel, which however they found nearly filled to the doors already, and consequently great numbers were obliged to sit in ranks on the shady side of the building; it was intended to have had preaching on the outside also, but the venetians being thrown open they could all hear as well as inside, so general was the stillness and decorum which prevailed, and both outside and inside joined in the responses of the Singhalese liturgy and hymns, which the children sang delightfully. Brother Clough read the liturgy and the 72 Psalm most impressively, and delivered a very animated discourse from Isaiah 11. 9. "*They shall not hurt nor destroy in all my holy mountain, for the earth shall be full of the knowledge of the Lord as the waters cover the sea.*" It was heard with deep attention by all, for

U

although every window and door was lined outside, the front area of the chapel filled, and the vestry behind, no interruption took place, but every one seemed engaged. After this service a Singhalese marriage and several baptisms took place, which excited much interest among the people, some of whom I doubt not were pleased with us to see that there was no longer the lack of such a place as these holy rites can be performed in, for themselves and for their children. In the evening our congregation, as expected, was not so large, being chiefly confined to those in this place, and every person of a different profession being laboriously kept away by their vigilant pastors. We however had a favoured season while Brother M'Kenny after reading the 25th of St. Matthew delivered a very clear and practical sermon in Portuguese from Luke 4. 8. "*Thou shalt worship the Lord thy God and Him only shalt thou serve.*" Deep attention sat on all, nor did there seem any indication of fatigue or weariness in the people who had attended all day. The collection very far exceeded my calculation, knowing the exceeding poverty of the people. It amounted in all to 139 rix-dollars, but it was largely assisted by one very interesting circumstance. A Native Chief, the Modeliar of *Wellesere* sent me a subscription of 50 Rds. immediately after the Singhalese service, enclosed in a note, of which the following is a copy:

Negombo, 6th *July*, 1820.

To the *Wesleyan Mission House*, at *Negombo*.

" The enclosed fifty Rds. (50) in notes, is given by the undersigned Andries de Abrew Raja-paxie, Moodelar of the district of Wellesere, for the use of the above mentioned church."

(Signed)   A. DE ABREW.

This was as gratifying as it was unexpected, and a most liberal thing under all circumstances. Thus closed the deeply interesting services of the day, and thus we endeavoured to record the glorious Name of JEHOVAH in the house which is erected for his glory. A very gracious influence was felt, in answer to our earnest prayer, through the various devotions of the day; and I cannot but hope it will give a new impulse to the cause of our Redeemer in this place. I believe the Lord looked with approving mercy on our efforts and will bless the works of our hands. O may his glorious Name be perpetually adored here, and thousands of immortal souls be born for endless glory to the eternal honour of the Redeemer of the world, and to the ever-blessed Spirit, to whom be glory for ever!

I find, on finally arranging my accounts, that I shall scarcely be able to compass all the expences of the building within the sum of 5,500 rix-dollars including the purchase of the ground and every incidental expence, the furniture of the chapel and all its appendages; but I can never regret so large a sum having been laid out on so good a cause, even had it been much more; for when I look at the strength and beauty of the place, and consider that it will probably stand for ages as the HOUSE OF GOD, every expence and every trouble sinks in the estimate compared with the eternal good likely to result from it under the blessing of the Lord. A separate and sacred place in which to perform the holy solemnities and administer the Divine ordinances of our religion is assuredly a grand desideratum on all our stations; for our people, who are accustomed to see much changing among the Europeans ron the Island, will form no permanent attachment to us, and indee d epo-e no settled confidence in us, till they observe these solid and assured evidences that we are not mere birds of passage, or capricious visitors among them for a short time, but that we are come with an object in view which will be developed by a work of time and labour, by learning their language, by translating them the Scriptures, by building them chu. ches, by training up their children and preaching to them incessantly the Gospel of Christ. In a word to *live* among them; and, if heaven please, to die among them. A remarkable expression from the lips of a heathen man, who was present at the opening, from Kandy, is not inappropriate here. He is a very old man, and of course had never seen such a building before, having scarcely been out of the Interior but came down to see me on the occasion because my little Kandian School is in his garden... "Surely," he exclaimed, in admiration at the little place, "Surely this is the ඳේවාලය විමානය" literally, the *Palace or royal residence of the Gods!* Had I not been so remarkably favoured by his Excellency our late Governor in the gift of the stones and bricks of the old church (the whole of which is built into the new one) the building could not have been reared for less than 9 or 10,000 Rds. and even so, the materials could not have been purchased so *good* at any price now. A Catholic gentleman who came the other day to view the building said very pointedly, that the old Protestant church had had a complete *resurrection!* and not indeed far off from its former site, for it is just built on the other side of the church-yard! I am now having the church-yard neatly surrounded with a fence, gates, &c. so that we shall have a very decent accommodation just at hand for all the solemnities of our holy religion, from baptism to the grave.—And this is no slight consideration to a people accustomed to attach so much reverence to certain places. This evening, about 12 of our aged female members of Society drank tea on the green before the house, after all the workmen had been dining together, and it was truly pleasing to hear their expressions of gratitude that "*our church*" as they familiarly called it, had been so soon built in answer to their ardent prayers (it is just 11 months yesterday since the first stone was laid); and I cannot doubt but that it will tend to give a stability to our cause here unknown before. I am thankful to say that I have received 500 Rds. in aid of the building which I record with gratitude as follows:

	Rds.		Rds.
The Rev. W. Buckley Fox	50	The Rev. Alexander Hume	25
Benjamin Clough	50	James Sutherland	25
Thomas H. Squance	50	Mr. D. J. Gogerly	50
George Erskine	25	Schools &c.	36
John Callaway	25	Public Collection	139
Thomas Osborne	25		
		Total..Rds.	500

From other quarters I have derived no pecuniary assistance: I at first made an attempt to extend the subscriptions beyond the limits of our Brethren, but met with a repulse at the beginning which quite discouraged me, and I went no farther, but have no doubt of being carried through the whole by the good Providence of God without any claims on our Committee. I should however be ungrateful were I not to record with most sincere thankfulness the efficient aid of another kind which I have received from several of our dear Brethren, without which I do not hesitate to say I could not have proceeded with the work. Our Brethren on the Colombo station have ever been ready to assist me in any thing I wanted, but particularly I am obliged by the kind attention of our Financial Secretary, who on every emergency (and they have not been unfrequent) has promptly afforded me that temporary accommodation in a pecuniary way which was essential at the moment to the forwarding of the building. To our dear Brother Hume also, who was with me at the commencement of the work, I am much indebted. He lent me a ready assistance at that time, which took a world of anxiety off my mind; and added much by his judicious and friendly hints to the strength and elegance of the chapel..since then till now I have found a most efficient and ready help in my dear young friend and colleague, whom the Lord has raised up on the station, and who being always on the spot could enter into all my little plans, and second every effort in superintending the work, which he has done with so much cheerfulness and ability that it has at once given me pleasure and lessened my toil. Without his ever willing assistance the work must often have stopped when from excessive fatigue I have been obliged to lay by, or to be absent on the other concerns of the station. I mention this to the credit of our young friend and Brother, assured that it will afford real pleasure to all our dear Brethren, that their confidence has not been misplaced, nor their expectations disappointed, in calling him so early into the vineyard of the Lord. He is enabled now to conduct the public services in regular turn in either of the languages, and his diligence in study, and industry in redeeming his time, I have great happiness in saying, cannot fail to promote both his mental and spiritual improvement. I trust I shall have, as am aware I need, the indulgence of our dear Brethren for going into these long details, they will kindly remember that I am writing on a subject to me deeply interesting.

But I now hasten to other parts of my letter, and first with regard to the extension of our cause, I intimated last quarter, by the insertion of a note from our kind friend Mr. Walbeoff, the state of things at Chilaw. It is but a few weeks since he returned there, and calculating on the grand obstacle (the small pox) being now removed, he promised himself the pleasure of soon getting up our school-room, which I am very glad to say still occupies his attention, so that I continue to look forward to the pleasing circumstance of seeing our way opened there, with no small anxiety. The projected completion of the canal between this and Chilaw will greatly facilitate our future efforts, as the road by land would always be hindrance. Mr. and

Mrs. Walbeoff spent a night and a day at the Bungaloe, and at their particular request I baptized their little infant on the 21st of June, under circumstances truly interesting and affecting.

Relative to the interior, I also intimated in my last that our operations here were partially suspended by a local influence; which, however, now being removed, I have lately applied to the resident civil authority, Henry Wright, Esq. on the subject, and have received an answer favorable to our efforts provided the Lieut. Governor is pleased to sanction it, which I am now on the point of ascertaining. Part of Mr. Wright's letter I transcribe, in order to shew what a fine opening appears so far into the country as Kornagalle (which is 30 Miles within the Kandian limits) provided a Brother could be sent with the sanction of Government to reside there. Mr. W. says, referring to the situation of our present school, "I think a Mission school at this place would be more beneficial provided a Missionary was here to superintend it. There are several European children here, and rather a numerous garrison of officers and men of the 45th Regt. with whom a Missionary could perform divine service on Sundays, which now pass by without any meeting for public worship." The prospect here also is truly animating but there are many obstacles.

These frequent interruptions to our work, and its consequent slow progress, may prove a source of anxiety but need not discourage our efforts: the work *must* prevail, and seeming hindrances will ultimately help it forward. I have had much of this lesson to learn on this station and am yet but an unapt scholar, although I have often seen this truth demonstrated. We still suffer much from the persevering efforts of the Roman Catholic Priests to shut up every avenue of light from the people around, which however I should feel no pleasure in mentioning were it not to account for a declension in our schools, which must appear in our next report now soon to be written. Two flourishing schools in the town, which we have attended with no small assiduity for a long season, have been suddenly and totally destroyed by a single order of one of the Priests, who had taken offence at something our assistant Brother had said in preaching to the children. The people grieve, having been delighted with our attention to them and their children, but dare no more disobey their Priests than a conscientious man dares to commit sin, so complete is their bondage to the darkest ignorance and superstition. Surely they will be one day set free! their state is even more pitiable than that of the heathens.

I am thankful that we are not without encouragement in other quarters. Our little Society generally stands fast in the Lord. Our last love-feast was a memorable season, many declared with tears the goodness of God, and testified that Jesus hath power on earth to forgive sins. At the renewal of our tickets this quarter our numbers were 45, and 15 on trial. Last quarter we had 50 but that included the non-residents, our military friends, who, I regret to say have left us some time.

At a little village where we are just finishing a neat small chapel and have a large male and female school, a class of native women was formed *at their own request*; they are regularly admitted on trial, and

will I trust rejoice that ever their village heard the " joyful sound" of
redemption through the blood of the Lamb. I have often had occasion
to mention the very great kindness of Mr. Deane our respected Collector. He has been ever ready to any little suggestion communicated to
him for the good of the people, or to assist us in our various efforts in
Missionary work. Through the past quarter this kindness has been
largely experienced in the excellent arrangements which he made for
the accommodation of the poor sufferers with the small pox. As soon
as he received information from us that could be depended upon, he
caused a large temporary hospital to be erected, and when the wicked
malice of some unknown persons burned it down, he as promptly listened to our urgent request for its re-erection, and it has afforded a
comfortable asylum to many who were ready to perish, till that
awful scourge is now nearly passed by. For such kind and very
efficient assistance in our labour we cannot be too thankful, while yet
we rest our *dependance* on the Lord our God. Thanks to the Name of
the Lord I am still highly favored in every respect, and both in health
and experience have abundant cause to exclaim " *Bless the Lord
O my soul and forget not all his benefits.*"

I remain, very dear Brethren,
Your affectionate Brother,
ROBERT NEWSTEAD.

THE CALTURA STATION.

Caltura, July 23, 1820.

MY DEAR BRETHREN,

The expiration of another quarter reminds me of my call to communicate to you some information respecting the state of the work of
God in this circuit, and I am happy to say that the intelligence I have
to convey is of a pleasing nature. Since my last letter I have enjoyed
much of the presence and blessing of God, for though no three
months of my life have been more busily employed than the last, my
mind in general has been kept in much peace, and I trust my Christian
principles have been strengthened, and my faith and confidence in my
unchangeable FRIEND more established.

The principal tax upon my time and strength is the superintendence
of the erection of our house and little chapel; a work which involves
me in great anxiety and trial. However I know that the welfare of
the Mission here requires the sacrifice, therefore on this ground I
cheerfully make it. I have felt it my duty for several reasons to apply
to the Lieut. Governor for a licence to fell the timber required for
the house and chapel, &c. duty free, which I am happy to say he
readily granted; for this privilege I must acknowledge myself under
great obligations to J. Deane, Esq. by whom the subject was introduced to Sir Edward Barnes, with a recommendation from himself. To
accomplish this was an object of much importance, as it answers more

good purposes than merely saving the duty on the timber. The House
is now in a very forward state, and I hope it will be ready for our reception in two months more. The work of the chapel has been unavoidably delayed in consequence of the continued rains, which have
rendered it impossible to get the heavy timber required down the
river; however, as soon as the weather settles, I hope to lose no time
in forwarding the work.

I have opened my little subscription, having been kindly favored
with Mr. Deane's name at the top of my list: considering the nature
of the place, I am making considerable progress, and hope in the end
to make up 500 Rds. which will greatly assist me in building this
little temple for the worship of the *Lord Jehovah.*

Since my arrival in this country, greatly have I lamented that stu-
pidity, ignorance, and depravity which we are obliged daily to witness; and if those evils existed only among the natives it would be a
happy circumstance, but we also find them to a most distressing degree among those, commonly called country born, or who are of
European extraction, and as a kind of confirmation of this, I shall
relate an anecdote which I am sure you will read with surprise. There
is in this district a Portuguese man (at least a man entitled to the privilege of Burgher) who has had several children by a woman of his own
rank but to whom he was not married; about ten days ago this
woman became dangerously ill, and when he found there was no hope
of life he came to me and requested that I would go and marry them,
but I objected, saying that marriage was not for the sick and dying
but for those who were likely to live; however *he* could not be married
without a licence from the Governor; but supposing that he would
be able to get over my objections if he could obtain it in time,
he sent off a memorial by express to the Governor on the subject,
but before the licence came the miserable woman was dead. Notwithstanding he was not willing to be disappointed, but came to my
house with the paper in his hand, and asked me to go and perform
the ceremony, though the woman had been dead about *eighteen*
hours!!

On the 6th of this month I had the pleasure of seeing Br. Newstead
at his very interesting Station, having been invited to the opening of
his new chapel; and must say that the day I spent there must be
classed among those which have been the most pleasing of my life: the
little chapel is not only neat but beautiful, and it was charming indeed
to see so many of the *Natives* of the Island coming to the opening of
this House of God, not with their hands empty but filled with *Pice,*
which they gave with a cheerful countenance; however as the important
concerns of the day will no doubt be fully entered into by our good
Brother on the Station, I do not mean to enlarge, but merely wish to
gratify myself by noticing to you the pleasure I felt upon the occasion.

I remain, my dear Brethren,

very affectionately yours,

JOHN M'KENNY,

GALLE AND AMBLANGODDA STATION.

Galle and Amblangodda, June 22, 1820.

VERY DEAR BRETHREN,

The last quarter as usual has been marked with many of those unspeakable blessings which flow to mankind through the atonement and mediation of our only Lord and Saviour, for which we trust our gratitude will be lasting as eternity. Our congregations are large and continue to increase, and becoming attention and seriousness particularly manifest themselves in our hearers. These things are highly consolatory to us, and give us additional proofs that our *" labour is not in vain in the Lord."* Not unto us, O Lord! not unto us, but unto thy name *be* the glory.

Sabbath morning we have worship in our chapel at 10 o'clock, the liturgy read in Singhalese, and alternately a sermon in Portuguese and Singhalese. The children attend well, and some adults. After worship we examine and instruct candidates for baptism, &c. Wednesday we have worship in English, and on Thursday meet our increasingly promising class. Friday we preach in English, and Sunday evening in Portuguese to a numerous and respectable congregation. Tuesdays and Saturdays the members of our class, and others seriously disposed assemble in the chapel for prayer meeting, and on these occasions they sing lustily and pray like men who have endless light and glory in view! Our schools we pleasingly view, and mark their manifest improvement. They are commonly all visited once a week, and several of them oftener. There is worship in every school as usual on the return of Sabbath, and many of the boys may, for any thing we know, become *Divines, Philosophers &c.* from the stores of knowledge they are laying up in their memories. We have importunate applications to open 3 schools in addition to those already established. Thus dear Brethren have we given you a few hints of our work and proceedings during these last months. We are not without some inward and outward conflicts, but JESUS is the Conqueror's name, and we have humble confidence that ultimately we shall be more than conquerors through him who loved us, and

> " What are all our suffering here,
> If Lord thou count us meet
> With that enraptured host to appear*
> And worship at thy feet."

Sincerely and affectionately yours as ever,

GEORGE ERSKINE.
SAMUEL ALLEN.

* All the blood washed ; and will it not heighten our felicity to meet then the *sharers* of our *griefs* and joys, for *joy* we have!

JAFFNA AND POINT PEDRO STATIONS.

Jaffna, June 26, 1820.

My dear Brethren,

Nothing but our unsettled circumstances could have prevented me from contributing my pittance to the last quarterly. Brother Squance expressed a wish to spend some time at Point Pedro, in order that he might make arrangements for his journey to the continent, &c. and at the juncture when the letter ought to have been sent off we were changing our stations. I cannot help, in the first place, expressing the pleasure I derived from a perusal of the official letters from England, and particularly so when I read of the increase to our Sion. If our dear friends knew how much they strengthened our hands by their expressions of constant attachment I am inclined to think we should hear from them more frequently; their love binds us by ties that cannot be separated by time or place. What though old ocean roll his gloomy waves between us—what though we may no more see our friends, or the place which gave us birth—yet "we still are one in heart." I bless God that I am a Wesleyan Missionary, and under no fear of having my heart broken by unkindness—No, my Brethren, we are instructed by the counsels, cheered by the affection, and supported by the prayers and the property of thousands.

I think we have reason to take courage as it respects the work in Jaffna; our congregation is a little on the increase. Last Wednesday evening when I was preaching from "therefore being justified by faith, &c." a lady who joined us a few weeks ago, found peace through our Lord Jesus Christ: I doubt not but you will rejoice that another is added to the number of those who are witnesses of his power to save. Since I have been in Jaffna my time has been much occupied, but I will not complain, for I never was happier in my life. Brother Bott joins me in love to you.

I remain, dear Brethren,
your's affectionately,
JOS. ROBERTS.

Point Pedro, June 29, 1820.

My dear Brethren,

Since our general meeting I have been in so unsettled a state that I have had but little time to correspond with my Brethren. About the time my last quarterly should have been written, I was making arrangements to proceed to Madras, at the request of Br. Lynch, to assist at a Missionary meeting, and I believe it was his intention that I should remain there. In the mean time I received communications from the Committee instructing me to proceed to Negapatam as my future station. Brother Lynch however was still of opinion that I should go to Madras, but, after further consideration we are agreed that it is most proper to attend to the Committee's appointment. I feel all the importance of this arrangement, and

W

cannot anticipate entering on my new station without much fear and trembling; but that most gracious promise, left on record for the encouragement of all Missionaries, is more than sufficient to support me, " Lo I am with you always even unto the end of the world." I cannot retrace the dealings of Providence with me since the commencement of my missionary career, without feeling the most unshaken confidence in the faithfulness of God.

It is six years this day since the first Wesleyan Missionaries arrived in Ceylon; we landed under particularly trying circumstances, having but lately lost our venerable leader, and exercised with ten thousand fears as to the reception we might meet with, and the final issue of our Mission. But how soon were all our fears removed, and how pleasingly did our way open before us, and since then " what hath God wrought!"

With respect to myself I have repeatedly been brought to the border of the grave, but as often the hand of the Lord has been stretched out to heal.

> " Oft from the margin of the grave,
> Thou, Lord, hast lifted up my head;
> Sudden, I felt thee near to save,
> The fever own'd thy touch and fled."

But what I prize far more than health is usefulness, and though I have been in many things unfaithful, yet blessed be God he has not suffered me to labour in vain: he has given me some seals to my ministry who have often been my support in the hour of trial, and have caused me to rejoice when my hands would have hung down. I will therefore take courage and go forward.

I intend to go over to Negapatam immediately, in order to get a house, to look at the country around, and make arrangements, &c. that when I go to remain I may be able to enter upon my work without delay.

In this circuit the work of God is going on in the most pleasing manner, and from what we have already witnessed we are fully justified in expecting future success. Our English congregations in Jaffna have greatly increased, and a few have been added to our society. A few Sundays ago, while I was preaching, one of our members was enabled to believe for *full salvation*. And at a love feast in the evening (after the Sacrament) he modestly but boldly declared what God had done for his soul. On that occasion it would have been gratifying to any Missionary to see two or three rising up at once, eager to open their full hearts and make known what God had done for them. The most established Christian would have been delighted with their sound and deep experience.

A short time after, while Br. Roberts was preaching, another obtained mercy of God, her sorrow was turned into joy, and her language was "O Lord I will praise thee, though thou was angry with me thine angry is turned away and now thou comfortest me." These pleasing instances afford us encouragement to proceed in our work, and the promises of God insure to us ultimate complete success;

for "the word of God shall run to and fro, and knowledge shall increase till righteousness cover the earth as the waters cover the sea." Then "let us not be weary in well doing, for in due season we shall reap if we faint not."

For the last two months I have resided at Point Pedro, but have occasionally visited Jaffna. I have been particularly attentive to the school department, and am fully convinced that if we would have our schools prosper they should be visited at least once a week.

At preaching, I have generally had large congregations, and they have been as attentive as the natives commonly are. On Sunday last I had considerable liberty, but as I did not so fully enjoy the attention of the people as I wished, I changed my mode, and began to instruct them in the catechetical way. The whole congregation was immediately all eye and all ear. I am persuaded that this method of instruction will do more good to a native congregation in a quarter of an hour than the most eloquent harangue in the ordinary way of preaching.

I bless God that I have never had better health or been happier than I am present. My soul pants for a full uniformity to the Divine Image, and ardently prays for the prosperity of Zion.

I am, dear Brethren,
very affectionately yours,
T. H. SQUANCE.

THE TRINCOMALIE STATION.

Trincomalie, July, 10, 1820.

VERY DEAR BRETHREN,

Few occasions have found us more desirous, and less able, to set before you the labours of the last three months. Part of the time has been taken up by the visit paid to Batticaloa, by Brother Stead, to assist Brother Osborne in commencing schools, which doubtless will be mentioned in his communication of this quarter; and very much time has been spent among work people, by a considerable enlargement of the Mission House. To this description of toil and trouble several of you have had a painful introduction, which is always a grievous hindrance to more important pursuits, little noticed indeed at a distance but most distressing to those who have to undergo it. The satisfaction and convenience, however, which those must feel that follow us will be the greater, and may give to them other facilities to do good in more immediate Mission work. We have had so many difficulties to overcome, and have been so much confined at home by a multitude of most pressing engagements, and our people, employed in the different departments of our infant cause here, as teachers and visitors of schools, &c. have been so frequently interrupted by sickness, that several very necessary things unavoidably have been neglected. Our Bazar School and place of worship loudly demands attention, and we have been frequently solicited to put it into a decent state of repair for public worship, which we hope soon to be able to accomplish.

Little variation among our European Society has taken place, farther than the departure of some of our members to England, and the sudden and lamented death of Mr. Charles Norwood, the Admiral's steward. (vide miscellaneous page—) One also has drawn back to wordly company, but another has been given to supply the place, who is earnestly pressing toward the prize of our high calling of God in Christ Jesus.

Every thing in this country, accomplished for Christianity, we expect to be gained to her by patient labour, and that progressive success will crown her cause with a final victory. In all our statements we desire to keep within the limits of propriety, and at all times hope to repel captious enquiry by the stubborn evidence of facts: and although we cannot say that very many thousands flock round that particular standarb of Christianity which we have been called to lift up among the heathen, yet,—if we may be indulged in the figure,—on a general view over the contested field, we see numerous banners waving over each collected Christian troop; whilst *He* " who at sundry times, and in divers manners, spake in time past unto the fathers by the prophets, in those last days (speaketh.) unto us by *his* Son" whose animating language is "*Whatsoever ye shall ask in my name, that will I do, that the Father may be glorified in the Son.*"

We thankfully acknowledge the goodness of God that we labour not in vain, nor spend our strength for nought; already our eyes behold many signs of good among those to whom we are sent, while the pleasing satisfaction warms the benevolent heart and frequently discovers the gushing tear. And shall the sterility of part of the soil, the taunts of the wicked, the stubborness of ignorance, prevent our attempts to diffuse useful and religious knowledge? Far, far be the thought from every Missionary breast. That is what we do not anticipate and hope never to behold.

The month of June introduced our first anniversary of the Branch Bible Society. The pleasing and beneficial effects of this institution, we hope, will increase with the demands for its aid and support: several, we lament to say, cannot discern, as they affirm, any good effects from the influence of such societies, and God only can open their eyes to see better, yet many continue to support it, and to wish them generally success: and may this support be continued, until divine knowledge shed its cheering rays into the palace and the cottage, enlighten every mind, and beam upon every countenance!

The boys of our 1st school were informed, that the anniversary of the Branch Bible Society gave them another opportunity of shewing their juvenile zeal for the Lord of Hosts; this was enough, joy set every one upon his feet, and it sparkled in his eyes; which, if accepted in language, declared readiness to unite hand and heart, they appointed one of the first class as a little secretary,

who took down names and collected in that school only 37 Rds.
3 fanams, which at 12 ½ £ the rate of exchange, amounted to upwards of 3 pounds sterling. But the example spread farther; shortly
after the news reached the 2nd school, composed entirely of native
children, one of the boys came to know *if they might be permitted* to subscribe to the Branch Bible Society, which was immediately granted to them: their first attempt was 3 Rds. 6 fanams,
The nature of the Society was explained to the work people at
the Mission House, both Roman Catholic and heathen, who every
one subscribed more or less, making a total sum of 10 Rds. 6
fanams. Thus the energies of the natives themselves may be brought
to bear on the great object; and though the tributary streams
of a great river are often small when separately viewed, yet by
uniting they acquire rapidity and strength. This brings to our
mind a circumstance which happened last year. In explaining this
subject to the work people, one of the coolies who spoke first
said, he would give one fanam, about three half pence, or a fourth part
of his day's wages. It was said to him, well, you were created
by the good God that made heaven and earth. He has blessed
you with kind parents, who tenderly cared for your helpless infancy. He has given you health,—he provides you food day by
day; and now, in the cause of this blessed God, you give him back
one fanam. He was a little behind another boy when the last word
reached him, and pushing the boy hastily aside, he called out, I
will give *two* fanams Sir. It was replied no, no, we only want
you to understand how much you are favoured of heaven and that
it is your duty to do good.

We might mention many things of this kind which frequently
happen in our intercourse with the people; but, although the subject is pleasing, you are yourselves, dear brethren, constantly beholding the operations of divine grace upon the hearts of the heathen,
inclining them to hear and receive good; and it is therefore the
less necessary, in addressing you, to dwell upon them. During
Brother Stead's absence at Batticaloa, his Excellency Sir Richard
King embarked for Europe. Several of you were introduced to His
Excellency, and feel interested on the remembrance of the very
kind reception which you met with from him. His unaltered good
wishes for the welfare and success of the Mission, as expressed in
a letter, in reply to one addressed to him by Brother Carver, on
his departure, will also be gratifying to you all. The following
letter, referred to above, was addressed to his Excellency on his
leaving India

Mission House, Trincomalie, May 22, 1820.

SIR

Being informed by Captain Patterson of your Excellency's intention shortly to take your departure to England, I cannot deny
myself the pleasure of returning my sincere thanks for the un-
merited marks of attention which your Excellency has so many
times spontaneously paid me.

X

The condescension manifested to those of my brethren also, the Missionaries, who had the honour to be introduced to your Excellency, was deeply felt by them, and the impressions made by those acts of kindness will not be soon effaced.

Where necessary duties so widely separate us, we experience a satisfaction in acknowledging our obligations to those who step out of the way of their numerous engagements to shew us favours; allow me, therefore, the indulgence of my feelings in offering to your Excellency, all I have to offer, my most grateful thanks.

How much soever I may attempt it, yet I cannot disguise from you my deep regret at your Excellency's departure from this place. But, seeing every thing beneath is subject to change, where choice is not left us, we can manifest only our resignation by our willingness to submit.

That your Excellency may, on your return to that land which embosoms all we hold dear by the name of home, enjoy the protection of Him who rules the winds and seas, on whose blessing alone man's happiness depends, will be the prayer of

your Excellency's obliged servant,
ROBERT CARVER.

P. S. The last time poor Norwood was at the Mission House, I mentioned my design to send, before the Minden sailed, the couple of tame deer which accompany this; and I beg your Excellency will gratify my feelings by their acceptance. They are very tame creatures, and will easily be fed on board as they eat almost any thing of a grain kind.   R. C.

His Excellency the same day returned the following very condescending reply.

Admiralty House, Trincomalie, May 22, 1820.

MY DEAR SIR.

If it has been in my power to shew you any trifling marks of attention during my residence at Trincomalie, I am amply repaid by the gratification it has afforded to my own feelings, tho' I will not deny that that gratification is enhanced by the very handsome manner in which you have been pleased to offer your acknowledgments.

I shall at all times feel an anxiety for your welfare and happiness, as also of your brethren, in the praise-worthy undertaking in which you are engaged. May the termination of your labours prove alike satisfactory to yourself and beneficial to mankind.

Many thanks for the two deer you have been so kind as to send me, which I hope to be able to take safely to England.

and believe me, my dear Sir, faithfully yours,
RICHARD KING.

Thus, dear brethren, you are put in possession of the incidents which have taken place here. We have only to confirm to you

our tokens of affection, and our desire to hear of your personal
welfare and general success, where success marks your steps, and
of your christian firmness and patience where peculiar trials await
you. We are equally happy in performing the work appointed us
by the most high, as in partaking in the felicity of our brethren
who are particularly honoured by the Lord of Hosts: in health
or in sickness, in prosperity or in adversity, in life, in death,
may you, may we be the Lord's,

yours very affectionately,
ROBERT CARVER.
A. STEAD.

THE BATTICALOA STATION.

Batticaloa, June 29, 1820.

MY DEAR BRETHREN,

Our interest in the success of the great cause of missions is so closely
united, that we must share in the joy of each others prosperity and feel
alike in all the trials and disadvantages we may have to encounter.
Our particular object is one and the same, and so far as this is accomplished we rejoice together; and on the other hand when our plans are
frustrated, and for a moment something like discouragement appears,
we sympathize with each other and bear a part of the burthen; we
address the throne of grace with the same ardour as if the trial were
really our own, and cease not till our prayers and labours have prevailed. Having this union of soul in the most glorious of all works
in which man can be engaged, we must doubtless with similar feeling anticipate our quarterly communication, where we can at once
see the state of every circuit and the happiness or trials of every Brother. Hitherto we have been highly favoured, and the perusal of every
quarterly has had a tendency to excite us to thank God and take courage. I most cheerfully sit down to give a sketch of my labours during
the last quarter as they have been in general of a pleasing and encouraging nature. Many of those thing which I pursued with rather
doubtful steps last quarter have turned out successful this, and those
little buildings which I found so difficult to commence and more so to
persevere in, I have now the pleasure to see finished. The Bungalo
for the boys school in Batticaloa was opened on the 22d of May. The
service commenced at eleven o'clock. we sang in English, prayed in
Portuguese, and preached by interpretation in Tamul. The place
was well attended, the Collector and Sitting Magistrate with three Officers from the Fort were present and all the respectable Dutch and
Portuguese families attended, beside a goodly company of natives with
their children who stood in the veranda Immediately after service I
took down the names of the children, the number was small but has increased much since. There are now about 30 Tamul boys and 20 Europeans. The girls school was opened on the 12th of June which promises to do well. There are now about 20 girls that attend very
regularly. From 7 in the morning until 10 they read, and from 2 in

the afternoon until 5 they sew. This is quite a novel thing and excites much curiosity. Many think it a ridiculous thing and would be glad to see the school room empty, indeed one man sent a petition to the Collector to order to have it taken down, saying that it was a nuisance to him and his family as it was so near his house. Mrs. Osborne attends generally in the afternoon, when every one seems eager to shew her improvement in needle work. The school-mistress is very attentive to them and marches them to church every Sunday afternoon to the Portuguese preaching, which most of them understand.

The school at Wallerevoe was opened on the 13th of June. The Church service was read in Tamul and the responses made by four boys which I took with me from Batticaloa school. I then gave them an exhortation for about half an hour to which they were very attentive. The number of scholars at present is under twenty but will encrease I expect, as the village is very populous. The men promised if they could have service performed there on the sabbath-day they would attend, for this I have made some arrangement for the present, but cannot attend myself as I have service in Tamul at the new school at nine, in English at eleven in the morning, and Portuguese at five in the afternoon. I have employed the man who has officiated at the Government Church since the Proponent has been incapable of preaching; his work is to read the prayers, psalms, and lessons for the present, and I have a few sermons in Tamul which he shall read when the congregations become more regular. The school at Cottocclum I expect will be opened next week, which is about two miles distance from Wallerevoe, when the schoolmaster will go from the one to the other to perform service on the Sabbath-day. The places are well built and will seat about 100 people beside the school-boys The building a low wall and laying the floor with chunam must be my expence, all the other they have done themselves.

For the last two months we have had a larger class than usual, having had two pious soldiers here from Trincomalie who have returned this week. An Artillery man of Batticaloa has lately began to meet in class, he has for a long time had the character of a religious man by his comrades, chiefly I expect because he did not go with them to the same excess of riot. I believe he also *thought himself* religious for the same reason, but he does not appear quite so amiable in his own sght since he has read Alleine and Baxter on conversion. But still I fear he is not reduced to that godly sorrow that worketh repentance. During the time of preaching last Sunday I observed many of the soldiers in tears, but these impression last but for a short time, and many of them are ashamed that they were so ridiculous as to weep. These commotions in their feelings will however, I trust, ultimately lead them to him who alone can ca'm their guilty fear, and give them that peace which at present they feel they have not.

I am often much concerned for the descendants of Europeans who are in many respect much beneath the natives in poverty and indolence, and at the same time miserably puffed up with pride and vanity, a wretched mixture, and cannot fail to render these objects of pity to every considerate mind.

Their religion is a little of every thing which they think religious; they have the outward ceremony of the heathen, the rigid discipline of the catholic, a creed made up of Gentoo and Christian articles compounded, which they vary to their convenience and embrace and reject as is best unto their purpose. The Roman Catholic Priest, who has been here in his pastoral visit for a few months (and is now about to return) has been engaged for about 10 weeks in marrying, and many, *very many*, have turned Catholic for a wife of property and vice versâ. This I have found out from several circumstances lately, the following is one: a young man in company with several old men came to my house, requesting I would baptise him. Upon enquiry into his reason for wishing to be baptised he told me openly that he might be married, and inherit the property of a woman who was a Protestant. I found the man perfectly ignorant of Christianity, but promised if it was necessary he would learn any prayers or songs I wished him, and if he could not repeat them by the next Sunday, yet if I would marry him then he would get them the next week. I of course refused it altogether, for I found the woman and her money were all he wanted. The old man told me, if they went to the Catholic Church the Padre would baptise them immediately and marry them afterwards, but as his daughter was a Protestant (as ignorant I found as the man) he wished me to baptise him and marry them, and added that the Dutch Ministers would always do this. Thus it appears the Dutch baptismal register was filled with names, and on this sweeping plan of Christianizing the heathen they were able to publish to the world that there were so many thousands of Christians in the Island of Ceylon, when the fact is they are heathen still

During the last quarter I have been favoured by a visit from Br. Stead. This we found very profitable to us all. He was much encouraged by the prospect of this little circuit, and rejoiced with me in the probability of its becoming important. This short visit has left me to feel afresh that I am *alone*, but to this great privation I can reconcile myself for public good, hoping that before long this station will require one or two more labourers, and also that we shall be furnished with them from our land of Missionaries in due time. I have another little unpleasant thing here which I feel perhaps as much as any one would, in the length of time a letter is reaching this place from any part of the island. My letters from the south sometimes reach me in 15 days, but often in 20; from Trincomalie, a distance of about 75 miles, a letter is 6 and sometimes 7 days in coming, so that if a packet is opened for England I generally hear of it a few days after the vessel has sailed.

In my last I intended to have given you a slight sketch of this District but was not properly prepared with materials for the purpose. I will subjoin it now. I could have entered into many more interesting particulars, and enlarged considerably upon many of the following hints but have not time to write more than a letter on the subject. But if at any future time the brethren should be disposed to write the geography of their circuits or district, I will write more at length on this; and by the way, I think if materials were collected for this purpose at leisure, and afterwards all put together, it would perhaps furnish us with the best history of Cey-

Y.

bon extant, as far as it goes, and I am sure would be the most
interesting one to our friends at home, as they would be able to
form a tolerable idea of the field in which we labour.

       I am your ever affectionate Brother,

           THOMAS OSBORNE

THE MADRAS STATION.

MY DEAR BRETHREN.   *Madras, July* 7, 1829.

Since my last communications to you six months have elapsed,
six months are gone to Eternity; and seven years this day, since
I was on the leave of departing from my father and brother in
Europe.—and are seven years also gone into Eternity? I am
ready to exclaim, Where have I been? and what have I been doing?
for a moment I look back, and with a grateful heart acknowledge
that they have been years of mercy to me both from God and man,
and from a deep sense of my great unfaithfulness, I can with all my
heart render every mercy into the mercy of God in Christ Jesus. A
few circumstances cause to me to write this with more than usual
gratitude to God, I am no longer alone at Madras. Br. and Sister
Close so long expected are arrived, and I have now a fellow labourer,
who is both able and willing to work. He has commenced the study
of the native language, and I hope will get on very well. Our congregations are increasing.—The following is our weekly labour. Sunday morning at 7 service both in Town and Mission place, at 10 service in Tamul to the natives, at 7 in the evening service again both
in town and Mission place, Tuesday was one day for the soldiers in
the Fort, Wednesday our visiting day, and the native class, Thursday
preaching in English in town, and to the natives in St. Thome, Friday
to the natives in town, Saturday the class at the Mission house,—
and as we take the town week about our station is probably more
like an English or European circuit than any other station in India.
Theodorus is doing well, and I believe is one of the best interpreters
amongst us. Mr. —————— whom I have already mentioned to you
takes his turn with soldiers and the natives. On the 19th and 20th of
last month we held our first anniversary Missionary meeting, on
both nights our meeting was interesting, but would have been much
more so had not a good friend took it into his head to condemn
pretty severely such Missionaries as are turned their attention to
schools, and preached by interpreters. I believe the history of Missionary meetings does not afford a similar instance of a religious society being attacked in one of their own meetings by a Christian
Brother, who was kindly requested to assist on the occasion. To
all the other Missionary Brethren who so kindly assisted us, I feel
peculiar gratitude. Mr. Loveless in particular for his very essential
assistance on both nights. The collections amount to nearly 100
Pagodas. We printed and circulated 100 cards, and 500 copies
of Hymns The report is to be printed, and a few copies will be
sent to each station in Ceylon. Both Br. Close and myself, and
most of our friends are of the opinion, that we should purchase
a place for one new chapel in town, in a different place to
that which we now occupy, and a very eligible place could be purchased at 3500 Pagodas. But the sum is so large we are almost

frightened to think of it, and yet I am satisfied if our Fathers and Brethren in England only knew how we stand, and the situation and state of Madras, they would not hesitate to sanction the purchase. I most sincerely wish that Br. Fox would pay us a visit very soon, that he also might give his opinion, with fervent prayers for you all,

I remain in love, &c. &c

JAMES LYNCH.

VERY DEAR BRETHREN.   *Madras, July*, 1820

After a long voyage, during which goodness and mercy followed me and mine each day, I arrived here in safety on the 12th May, and set my foot on the shores of that country, which for the last three years I had desired to visit. This desire, I have good reason believe, came from God; and after removing obstacles which at first appeared insurmountable, He has given me the desire of my heart, viz. to preach to the heathen " the unsearchable riches of Christ."

I bless God for having conferred this greatest of all honours on me, and for having in the course of his providence directed me to labour in company with one, on whom I look as a Father in Christ.

From what your know of Brother Lynch, and from what you have heard of Mr. Durnford and other kind friends, you may judge of the reception I met with. The Lord reward them!

A few days after my arrival I had a fresh proof of the loving kindness and tender mercy of God, as manifested towards my dear wife. Having visited some friends one evening, or her return home she was taken suddenly and alarmingly ill; medical assistance was instantly called in, and we feared she was attacked by that disease which has lately proved so fatal to many in this country, the Cholera Morbus. What the disorder really was we know not, but it brought on premature labour, and she was at length safely delivered of twins, boys; one died almost immediately, but the other which we have named John Wesley, still lives, and with his mother is doing well " What shall I render unto the Lord for all his benefits?"

I find here an extensive field of labour, both among Europeans and natives; but I wish principally to direct my attention to the latter. For this purpose I have commenced learning the Tamul, and although I experience and anticipate many difficulties, yet the pleasing hope of soon acquiring it encourages me to go forward, and I trust ere long to be able to preach to the natives in their own tongue " The glad tidings of salvation."

I feel particularly obliged to those of my brethren in Ceylon who, by letter, have congratulated me on my arrival in India; and as I have not had an opportunity of reply to them all, I hope they will respectively consider this as an acknowledgment of their kindness

Hoping to hear good news from you soon, and praying that the Lord may revive his work among you and us, the ensuing quarter.   I am very dear Brethren,

Yours sincerely and affectionately,

TITUS CLOSE.

DONATION FROM THE BRITISH AND FOREIGN BIBLE SOCIETY.

We have the pleasure to inform the Brethren, that Br. Clough has received a letter from the Depositary of the B. & F. B. S. enclosing an invoice of books granted for the use of our Mission at the request of Sir Alexander Johnston. We now lay a copy before the Brethren. On the arrival of the books at the Custom House, Br. Clough addressed a letter to Government begging them to be allowed to pass free of Custom duties, and received immediately a very kind answer to say, the Honble the Lieutenant Governor had issued orders to the Comptroller General of Customs to pass them free of the accustomed duties. The Brethren on the out stations will please to say what they are in want of.

INVOICE.

London, January 13, 1820.

REV. SIR,

The Books specified on the annexed sheet have been granted to you on the application of Sir Alexander Johnston. Sir Alexander intends to write to you by the Columbo respecting their appropriation.

I am, Rev. Sir,
Your obedient Servant,
RICH. COCKLE.

Rev. Mr. Clough.

	£.	s.	d.
200 Minion Bible, Calf, each 6s. 2d.	61	13	4
300 Ediub. Pica Testament, Cloth, 1s. 9d.	26	5	0
25 Portuguese Bible, Calf, 9s.	11	5	0
275 ditto Testament, Sheep, Catholic version 2s. 2d.	29	15	10
50 De Saey's French Testament. Calf, 5s.	12	10	0
6 Italian Testament, Sheep, Martinus, 2s, 2d,	0	13	0
4 Cases	3	5	0
Bills of Lading and shipping expences	0	17	10
Freight £8, 11s, 9d, Insurance £6, 0s, 11d.....	12	12	8
	£151	17	8

Miscellaneous.

No. I.

DESCRIPTION OF MADAGASCAR.

Continued from No. XI.

The woods present a prodigious variety of trees, palm-trees of all kinds, woods used in dying, ebony, bamboos of an enormous thickness, orange and lemon trees.

Timber for building ships or houses is not less common here than other sorts of wood of a less serviceable nature. Flacourt says, that in the year 1650, he sent to France fifty-two thousand aloe-trees of the first quality. Physicians call this wood *agallochum*, and the Portuguese give it the name of *ragle wood*.

A maze of plants of the parasitic kind crowd this multitude of trees and bushes. The forests abound with agarics and mushrooms, of a pleasant and lively colour and an exquisite flavor. The natives call them *holas*, and very judiciously destroy those which are prejudicial to health.

Gums and useful resins are likewise gathered here. The lacteous juice which the islanders draw from the trees they call *finguiera*, yields by coagulation that singular substance known to naturalists by the name of *gum elastic*

The elasticity of this resinous gum, has of late been tried successfully for the benefit of the arts. Surgery has even derived some advantages from it, relative to the improvement of probing instruments and bandages. But it is also evident that this precious substance may be applied to many other uses.

The whole surface of the woods is covered with herbs unknown to the botanist, some are aromatic and medicinal, others of great service to dyers.

Flax, a kind of hemp which both in length and strength exceeds that of Europe, sugar canes, wax, different sorts of honey, tobacco, indigo, white-pepper, gumlack, amber, ambergris, several silky substances and cotton, would long since have become articles of trade which Madagascar might have furnished with profusion, had the Europeans, since their resort to this island taken pains to spread among the islanders those points of knowledge which are requisite to prepare and render valuable the divers articles I have just enumerated. The most indefatigable botanist could scarcely, in the course of a long life, glance on the natural history of the vegetation of the different parts of this island, whose extent in latitude comprises several climates.

There are few countries on earth which afford refreshments of all kinds more abundantly and at a cheaper rate to the navigator.

The inhabitants of Madagascar call themselves indifferently *Malegashes*, or *Madecasses*. They are in general well-shaped, and above the middling size. The colour of their skin is various, some tribes are of a deep black, others tawny; some have a coppery complexion, but the greatest number are of an olive colour.

All those that are black have woolly hair like the negroes of the coast of Africa. The hair of those who have the complexion of Indians or mulattoes, does not frizzle more than that of the Europeans, their nose is not flat; their forehead is broad and open, their lips not pouting, and every feature of their face is pleasant and regular. Their physiognomy bears in general the marks of a character replete with frankness and amenity. They never shew any eagerness of learning things, except such ones as relate to wants of the first necessity; and this desire is always tempered by moderation. They manifest even less than indifference to objects that require reflection. A natural supineness and general apathy renders insupportable to them every thing that rouses intellectual attention. Sober, nimble, agile, they waste the best part of their life in sleeping and diverting themselves.

The native of Madagascar only minds the present; he is void of all forecast, and does not even think that there are men on earth who trouble themselves about the future. These islanders are free beings, with an easy mind and a sound body.

The native of Madagascar is absolute master to do as he pleases; no obstacle, no constraint disturbs his freedom; he goes, exerts himself, does what he likes, except what may hurt his neighbour. No Malegash ever took it into his head to predominate over the thoughts or actions of any person. Every individual has a characteristic mode of being of his own, without his neighbour troubling or caring about him.

The island of Madagascar is divided in a great number of tribes. Its population many be reckoned at 4,000,000 of inhabitants, but this calculation is neither precise nor possible, according to the state the island is actually in, being divided into societies distinct from one another. Each society inhabits the canton it likes best, and is governed by its usages. A tribe consists of several villages, who all have a particular chief. This chief is sometimes elective, but more frequently hereditary. The land is never parcelled out, and belongs to those who take the trouble of cultivating it. These islanders have neither locks nor bolts, and live in a frugal manner. Want alone regulates the hour of their meals. It is however common to see them dine at ten in the morning, and sup at four in the afternoon. Their repast consists of rice beautifully white, very light, and well cooked; over it they pour a succulent broth of meat or fish, seasoned with pimento, ginger, saffron, and some aromatic herbs. These plain messes are served on the leaves of the plant raven; of these leaves they make spoons, plates and dishes. They are always clean, and never used twice.

The Malegashes know but two ways of dressing their meat; they either make it boil in pots of burnt clay, which they manufacture in a masterly manner, or let it broil on coals.

They are very dexterous in catching a number of birds unknown in

Europe, and as much sought after by naturalists for the beauty of their plumage, as by travellers who find them exquisitely palatable.

The pheasant, partridge, quail, wild duck, five or six different species of teals, the blue-hen, black-parrot, spoon-bill, turtle-dove, black-bird, green ring-dove, and a species of bat of an enormous size, afford a delicate and favourite subsistence to the people of Europe.

The Malegashes catch an immense quantity of fish, both in their rivers and in the sea.

Gold fish, thorn-backs of all sorts, soles, the largest pilchards, though rather inferior to our own; herrings, mackerel, oysters, muscles, lobsters, and turtles, furnish with plenty those islanders who inhabit the coast. The rivers procure them also excellent eels, and fresh water mullets, more luscious than those caught in the sea. On this coast of the island several kinds of fish are found, which people should not eat without having previously put a piece of silver under their tongue; if this silver loses its colour, and turns black, those that would taste such fish would find them fatal. The squadron of Admiral Boscawen sustained considerable loss of men at *Rodrigues*, for not having had recourse to this useful precaution.

(*To be continued.*)

No. II.

ISLE OF FRANCE.

[We have much pleasure in laying before our readers the following interesting Letter,—relating chiefly to Madagascar. It is communicated by Brother Carver, whose attention to this department of our publication merits our thankful acknowledgment.]

Port Louis, Mauritius, Nov. 1820.

MY DEAR SIR,

Since I last had the pleasure of writing to you I have been in Europe, and am but lately returned to this island. I am desirous of resuming a correspondence which I found so agreeable, and shall be glad to hear from you that Providence has favoured you in your arduous labours. I shall probably remain here for several years, and am endeavouring to be useful in my sphere, by introducing the Lancasterian system among my slaves. Although from the novelty and opposition to generally received ideas (which the attempt includes), it is looked upon with an evil eye by many. I trust experience will shew, that even in a temporal view the value of man, as an instrument of fortune, is increased by education. It is not until such conviction is established that I expect any imitators; and for this we require time, patience, and perseverance.

You have no doubt heard of the disastrous result of the mission to Madagascar. The only survivor, Mr. David Jones, who is a well instructed, religious, and zealous Missionary, now resides with me on my estate. He is the superintendant of the School, and is very successful in its establishment. The fever of Madagascar still returns upon him at times, and keeps him weak. He is studying all my Madagascar manuscripts, particularly with a view to the knowledge of the language and dialects of the country; and such parts of its history as relates to the repeated failures of former Missionaries of the Roman Catholic Church, who attempted to establish themselves in that great Island. The Portuguese and French both attempted in vain to convert the inhabitants to the Christian faith; and yet, to all human appearance, there could not be an easier task among any tribe or nation: for they have no creed to unlearn, no religion imbibed from earliest infancy.—In a religious point of view their minds may be considered as blanks ready to take any impression: and they are a people far above many of the black natives of the adjoining continent in civilization. The people of Madagascar have great intelligence naturally—here they are always chosen to be artisans, and seldom, if ever, sent to field-work: always desirous to learn something, whilst the Caffre, on the contrary, is unfit to learn a trade, is most contented whilst working under a burning sun, and when unemployed is most contented to sleep. The Madagascar man, when idle, loves to dance, and sits up half the night at his fire side telling stories. There is a marked opposition of character between the two races.

I should be glad to hear from you on the subject of your versions of the sacred Scriptures into the Singhalese or other languages; and am desirous of having copies of such as may be printed at Ceylon. I am forming a museum of natural history also, and should be glad to have a specimen of the different rocks and stones in your neighbourhood; they can be put up and forwarded to———— who will pay for me any expence. Any seeds of trees, roots, or plants also would be welcome to my garden, which you may recollect at Moka. I still preserve it, although I now reside at the opposite side of the island on a large sugar estate which I purchased, and where we have a population of above five hundred souls: forty five children form the school.

His Excellency, Governor Farquhar is not yet returned here, although we expect him shortly. He had an interview with some of the members of your Society in London on the subject of Missions to Madagascar, which may, I hope, be favorable to a more successful pursuit of that great object in that vast and interesting Island.

Pray write to me when your important avocations will allow you: I am most sincerely interested in the success of your labour. I hope you enjoy good health. Mr. Le Brun is doing very well at Port Louis: his school is very much increased—he has a little chapel—and he silently gets the better of the opposition which impeded his early progress.

　　　You have my best wishes for your success and happiness,
　　　　　　Ever very faithfully your servant.

To　R. Carver.　　　　　　　　　　　　　　T.

No. III.

No doubt several of the Brethren who are in the habit of reading the Ceylon Gazette, were a little surprised to see in the Gazette of July 8, the Circular Letter sent to our Societies in England, during the late spirit of discontent which unhappily prevailed among many of our countryman, by the *Committee for guarding the Religious Privileges* of the Methodists; the circumstance of its being published in such a way may require some explanation.

A few days after the letter arrived Brother Clough sent it to the Honorable and Venerable the Archdeacon, for his private perusal, without any idea that such an use of it would have been made by that gentleman; but on the day the Gazette was published Br. Clough received the following letter from the Archdeacon explanatory of his motives for giving it publicity.

Colombo, July 8, 1820,

DEAR SIR,

The Ceylon Gazette, just put into my hands, has reminded me of the liberty which I have taken with that excellent Wesleyan address by your Brethren in England, put kindly into my hands by you.

I am aware that I have probably done more than your delicacy had in contemplation, but my own feelings and concurrence in sentiment, impelled me to request the editor of the Ceylon Gazette to include in his publication this day. As I will yield to no man in feeling of loyalty to my king, or in abhorrence of those who would set at nought their God and Saviour, you will I trust, not require an apology from me, in having ventured without your permission, to make public in Ceylon the admirable production to which I now allude.

Believe me most faithfully, and with true esteem,
Your friend and Servant,
T. J. TWISLETON
Archdeacon.

Rev. B. Clough.

However novel this circumstance may appear, it must be acknowledged that the Archdeacon's conduct on this occasion was most handsome; especially when it is recollected that the excellent paragraph which preceded the letter was written by him As some of our Brethren may not have the Gazette alluded to, we beg to insert the paragraph:

"At the present anxious moment, when the minds of men are agitated with apprehension as to the termination of the great moral struggle now making within the bosom of our beloved country, every effort which tends to turn the scale in favor of loyalty and religion should be cherished and upheld.

It is most gratifying to all who take a pride in our antient constitution and feel content under laws, the purity and justice of which have never before been questioned, to know, that lost as many of our countrymen are to feelings of Englishmen, there is still a preponderating attachment remaining in favor of the legitimate government and the doctrines of the christian faith.

Many societies exist amongst us which by admonition and example fight the battles of our faith with a zealous and virtuous ardour. Amongst others, that society established by the late Revd. J. Wesley, stands amongst the the foremost in the holy ranks of our religious defenders and claims from an approving nation the just tribute of a grateful applause.—We have been favoured with the perusal of a series of resolutions passed unanimously at a full meeting of the Committee of that Christian community, expressing the concern with which they view the present alarming progress which infidelity and sedition have recently made in several parts of England, and uttering their abhorrence of the principles upon which they are spread and maintained.—As they breathe a purity of spirit, worthy of a people anxious to find favour in the sight of God, and to live well under the mildest Government on earth, we transcribe the sentiments of the Committee as they have appeared before us, feeling conscious that our readers will approve the manner in which the subject in question is treated."

It is a most gratifying reflection that after a trial of several years in this Island our principles are recognized as meriting this honorable mention through such a channel.

No. IV.

NEGOMBO NEW CHAPEL,

From the Ceylon Government Gazette.

On Thursday last the 6th instant, considerable interest was excited in the town of Negombo on the occasion of opening a new Wesleyan Mission Chapel, and publicly dedicating it to the worship of God. The services for the occasion were performed by several Ministers of the Wesleyan Mission. In the morning at 10 o'clock, the Revd. W. B. Fox from Colombo opened divine service by reading the Liturgy of the Church of England; after which he preached an appropriate Sermon in English from Isaiah 52 10. At two o'clock in the afternoon, divine service was again performed; when the Revd. B. Clough from Colpetty began by reading the Liturgy in Cingalese, after which he preached a suitable Sermon in that language from Isaiah 11. 9. In the evening at seven o'clock, the Revd John M'Kenny from Caltura preached an excellent Sermon in Portuguese from Luke 4. 8. After each of the services collections were made towards defraying the expenses which have been incurred by the erection of the building.

The novelty of the scene brought together a large company of people both of the town and from the neighbouring country, who appeared anxious to witness every part of the ceremony; and we doubt not the solemnity of the services, with the very neat appearance of the chapel must have struck the minds of *many*, not having witnessed any thing of the kind before.

Whatever good may ultimately result to the native and other inhabitants of Negombo from the erection of so elegant a place of worship, it ought to be recorded, with feelings of the sincerest gratitude, that this place principally owes its existence to the kindness and liberality of the Ceylon Government. The Revd. Robert Newstead under whose immediate superintendence and direction it has been built, was kindly furnished with a principal part of the building materials from Government in the most convenient manner. The stones and bricks are part of the ruins of the old Dutch Church in Negombo, and the whole of the wood required in building, was felled in the Chilaw District, by J. Walbeoff, Esq. by virtue of an order from Government.—Such instances of Christian liberality will endear the British Government in this Island to all classes of inhabitants; and will perpetuate the names of its Governors to posterity, as caring for the moral and religious improvement of the inhabitants of this important and interesting Colony.

No. V.

The following Extract is from a Letter translated into English from the Portuguese, which gives an Account of the design of the Schools established by those eminent and useful men the Rev. B. Ziegenbalgh and J. E. Grundler, and is dated Tranquebar, April 7, 1713. The design of those School corresponds so much with that which now appears greatly successful, that we may all adopt the prayer of those holy men, for the printing and distributing the word of life, which contributes so much to the manifestation of divine truth.

"*Grant O living God that the Christians here in India, and the multitude of Gentiles, may, with Hearts full of Gratitude, become sensible of this great benefit, and receive with joy that Word of Life which is, and shall be laid before them, printed in their own Languages; that the lively and spiritual knowledge of our Saviour Jesus Christ may enlighten their souls, in order to unspeakable and endless happiness.*"

R. CARVER.

To make it further known that our daily labour is not in vain, nor the expences thrown away with which we are so readily supplied, through the will of God, by charitable benefactors; but that they may hereafter bring a great blessing upon these *Eastern* countries; we shall add, to what has been above written, something concerning the *End* or *Design* of these *Charity-Schools*: which is briefly comprehended in these Three Points:

1. The laying a Foundation of true Christianity in tender souls.

2. The preparation of Disciples for the future Service of Christ's Church.

3. The bringing in the use of Books among Christians in the *East Indies.*

Concerning the first design, which is to *lay the foundation of true Christianity in tender souls:* We find, by daily experience, that such as are in years are not so well disposed, or able to apprehend the Christian Doctrines, and to attain to the knowledge of spiritual things, as younger minds are: besides, those that are grown up, being forced to work hard to get a poor livelihood, cannot spare time for frequent instruction: Wherefore it is our earnest care, that our scholars, of either sex, should, in the time of their childhood and youth, be fed, as it were, and nourished with Christian doctrines, so as that they may not attain to a bare *historical* knowledge, or even an outward practice of many christian truths, thereby *to become like tinkling cymbals;* but that their minds, by means of what they learn, may be sanctified, regenerated, and renewed, feeling within themselves the good and lively word of God, and knowing by their own experience, that true Christianity, and the *Kingdom of God* in the *soul,* doth not consist in words, but in a divine power, and a real taste of God's goodness in the heart: consequently that the holy doctrine of Jesus Christ, when learnt with such divine efficacy, must necessarily be accompanied with a pious life and a holy conversation.

This is the first and principal point, which, by the divine assistance, we are perpetually labouring to inculcate on our Children in the Schools, by continual precepts, admonitions, and prayer.

Touching the second *end* which is a worthy *preparation of Disciples* for the future service of the Church, and the schools in *India,* every days' experience gives us to understand, that, in order to have good and sufficient Masters, Catechists, Writers, and such others as may be useful on several occasions, it is necessary they should be brought up in good Schools; and that not only on account of their being well rooted and grounded in all good learning and piety, but of their being skilful in such methods of teaching as many be most for the advantage of others. For the Missionaries cannot do all themselves that is needful to be done in the Church and Schools, and therefore such Catechists and Masters as have been trained us in schools, from their youth, to a mature age, and fitted for such employments, will be a mighty help to them in their Ministry. And this hope, which we conceive of our Scholars, will not, we are sure, be in vain; since GOD gives the increase to such an education, for his own Glory, and the future happy enlargement of Christ's Church in the *East.*

As to the third and last *design,* which is, the bringing in a right *use of Books* among Christians in the *Indies;* We know it for a truth, that want and disuse of books is that which chiefly hinders true Christianity, and such a holy conversation as becomes the Gospel, from being introduced and propagated among Christians and Gentiles. How greatly the distribution of *religious books* tends to the advancement of true piety in *Europe*, is well known to those persons who have made it their business to promote religion and virtue.

Now this want of books in the *Indies* proceeds, in truth, from the want of well ordered Schools, for the good education of Children. Who can doubt but that the corruption of the *Portuguese Language* in the *East-Indies*, proceeds, in a great measure, from this want of good Schools and the scarcity of books? We say nothing of the Gentiles, and their neglect of so necessary a thing; but only speak of those who call themselves Christians, and profess to be converts from Heathenism, who by reason of their great neglect of this matter know very little of the Christian religion, either they or their children; and for the most part, cannot so much as write or read.

The care of procuring good Schools belongs in a special manner, to the Missionaries, and the *Padres*, who are set over the flock in *India*. But it is no small grief to us when we consider, that there are such in in the *Indies* as seek their own things, and not the things of Jesus Christ.

Wherefore, we earnestly beseech them, in the name of the Lord, that they will, for the future, lay this matter more to heart, and shew a more tender concern for the institution of good Schools, and a religious education of youth; this being the only way to raise a holy Church in *India* that shall be well-pleasing unto God, in his Son. For ours lves. though unworthy, we are very careful that such as are under our discipline, be they of either sex, whilst they are instructed in matters the most necessary to be learnt, shall at the same time be taught to read and write well; this being a means to promote the design and use of *books* in the *Indies* For in case those who shall hereafter become Christians, shall be able to search for the divine Truths in books; there is no doubt but such a search, accompanied with the operation of the Holy Spirit, will mightily conduce to the attaining the true knowledge of Jesus Christ, and his heavenly doctrine, and to a pious life, and holy conversation of Christians among the Gentiles.

No. VI.

It is our painful duty to record the premature and sudden death of Charles Norwood, steward to Admiral Sir Richard King, and a steady member of our society, during our acquaintance with him in India.

His mild disposition, and his cheerful readiness to convey any communications to the Brethren, when the vessel visited the different ports, commended him to most of them; but endeared him especially to the Brethren on this station.

It is but common justice to the dead to mention the high regard in which he was held by those, whose notice his station brought him under, and whose service he so faithfully performed. The arrangements to proceed to Europe, and the daily expectation of the Leander, bearing the flag of Sir P. Blackwood, to relieve them, led him to anticipate the happy termination of a correspondence faithfully kept up during his absence from his native land; but the disconsolate female may now behold the vessel return, but return without the object of her anxious expectations: he has descended to the grave, at noon, in this land of death.

It appears he caught cold by bathing immediately after using much exertion and being very much heated, which is a thing which certainly ought to be avoided. He was bled, but shortly afterwards the ship from England entered the harbour, when desire to see her, anxiety to receive intelligence, and expectation of a speedy departure, overcame prudence, and it was throught his cold was increased by going out of his room into the air to look at the vessel as she anchored. Soon after this circumstance he grew worse, and in a very few days was cut off before I heard of his attack of sickness, so that we had no opportunity so so much as to see him till the saint was fled.

He died May 10th 1820, and was interred the next day, aged 90 Years
R. C.

No. VII.

BOOKS OF THE MISSION LIBRARY AT TRINCOMALIE.

Asiatic Researches ...... 10 vols. Horne on the Psalms ... 2 vols
Clark's Paraphrase on the Leighton's Works .... 2 vols.
   4 Gospel   2 vols.   Several leaves cut out
Conybear's Sermons ...... 2 vols. Simpson's Sacred Literature 4 vols.

No. VIII.

SKETCH OF THE DISTRICT OF BATTICALOA.

The district of Batticaloa is situated about 50 miles south of Trincomalie, and extends from the river *Virgel* on the north to the *Kombockan river* on the south; a distance of 140 miles. extending from the sea westerly in an irregular line from 5 to 18 miles.

It is divided into eleven provinces known by the following names, *Corlepattoo, Erawoor, Manmoene, Erocwiel, Poretiroo, Samhantura, Karrewaw, Nandecuddo, Nindoor, Akkrepatto, Pannoea*. In each of these districts there are from twelve to twenty villages. Corlepattoo is the most northern, and Panoea the most southern province. On the borders of the province of Manmoene about 70 miles from Trincomalie, is the entrance of a fine lake, which extends southward for about 40 miles. At 4 miles distance from its mouth, a branch of it winds to the west about 5 miles, and reaches up to the north about 10 miles. The entrance is very narrow, but sufficiently deep for a vessel of 100 tons burthen to enter.

The lake is navigable by a vessel of this burthen for about 7 miles, but a boat which draws about 2 feet of water may proceed to Nanypattemone about 34 miles from the mouth of it.

At the distance of 4 miles up the lake is situated the Island of *Polcantivoe*, which signifies *Tamarind Island*, so called from the quantity of tamarinds it produces; but most commonly known by the name of *Batticaloa*. It is about 3 miles in circumference. On the east side of it is a small fort built by the Dutch, called the Fort of Batticaloa.

This Island is the seat of government for the whole district, and for its size is more populous than any other part of it. The number of burghers, men, women and children is upwards of 250; and of natives, upwards of 850. It contains four places of worship, 1 Protestant, called the Government Church, which is built on the esplanade; 2 Catholic, and 1 Gentoo. On the lake are situated about 53 villages, laying in the provinces of Erawoor, Manmoene, Eroewiel, and Sambantura, the population of which amounts to upwards 10,500 men, women and children. The population of the whole district is upwards of 30,000 of which nearly 9000 are Moormen who speak the Tamul and Moors language.

The inhabitants of Akkrepattoo and Pannoea are Veduhs; these speak either Tamul or Singhalese, profess no religion, have no priests, acknowledge no law or authority by their own consent, but are a sort of wild men, living in the jungle, cultivating no land. Their food is wild honey and the flesh of any animals they can catch; they generally daub it over with honey, and hang it up in the trees to dry, when they have more than is immediately wanted for their support.

Their employment is hunting, gathering honey and preparing wax for sale. This race of men are supposed to be the aborigines of the Island, and though outcasts, are of the highest cast in the district. The provinces they occupy are the most western and are mountainous. In every other part of the district the people are Gentoos, and speak the Tamul language, except in the small island of Polcantivoe, where the inhabitants are most of them Protestants, and Roman Catholics, and speak English, Dutch and Portuguese.

The climate, the greater part of the year, is remarkably healthy. From April to September the weather is excessively hot—the thermometer ranges between 82 and 90, the hot land-winds frequently prevail which are very unpleasant, and the most trying to the European constitution of any thing they meet with in this climate.

After the setting in of N. E. monsoon, in the month of November, the weather becomes very cold, with heavy rains, more or less, and this continues till the latter end of February, or the begining of March, during which time all the land near the lake with many of the villages are inundated. For many weeks during this season the inhabitants of Batticaloa have no communication with any other part of Ceylon either by land or water.

The soil, generally, is very good, and produces large quantities of rice, also a variety of fine fruit such as the pine-apple, mango, orange, lime, and a particular kind of lemon. The timber of this district is of a peculiar and valuable kind, and grows to an immense size. Among the principal are satin wood, ebony, halmonella (a fine light wood which is exported to Madras for building gigs, &c.) and grane which is used in ship building.

The animals are elephants, alligators, oxen, goats, hogs, panthers, commonly called cheetas or tiger-cats, bears, wild-boars, buffaloes, elk, hares and deer, with a great variety of others.

The birds are vultures, kites, cranes, storks, pelicans, peacocks, geese, ducks, teal, with a vast variety of birds of beautiful plumage, much resembling the birds of paradise.

The lake abounds with a great variety of fish, of fine flavour, which are sold by auction every morning in the fish bazar of Polian-tivoe. The people of the villages along the lake chiefly subsist on fish and fruit. The fish of the largest magnitude are the shark and pristis commonly called the saw-fish, from its having a long plane beak or snout with spines growing like teeth out of both edges This grows to an enormous size. The alligator also grows to a great size in this lake and are sometimes caught from 18 to 20 feet in length.

The insects are of almost an endless diversity and beauty, many of which are used as ornaments by the ladies, and thousands are sent to England for the same purpose.

The employment of most of the inhabitants of the lake is fishing, cloth-weaving, and boat building. The vessels built in this place are of a superior kind to those generally built in Ceylon, being square rigged, and some of them from 60 to 100 ton burthen, and are mostly employed in traffic with Trincomalie, Colombo, and Madras. In the other parts of the district, the people are generally employed in cul-tivating the land and hewing timber.

The natives are generally a quiet, harmless, and industrious people especially those who are at the greatest distance from Poliantivo, where the inhabitants differ much from any other part of the district, for having embraced the religion of Europeans they have also copied the vices of the lowest order of them, and can even swear in English tthough ignorant of that language. But not so the people of the country In many parts they enjoy domestic life. The father is often the priest of the family, having a small temple in his own compound where he officiates for himself and domestics, who all reside on his premises and are under his directions and law, at the head of which he appears as a patriarch. The rite of marriage is also performed by him Upon the subject of transferring property by marriage there is a curious tradition among them The property of the woman is not transfered to the man by marriage, nor can he bequeath it to his heirs, nor can the husband dispose of his property by will, in any respect whatever. But upon her death it returns to her family again. This refers only to inheritable property whatever thing may accumu-late after marriage belongs to them both, which descends to their children. But their own children are not heirs to the inheritable pro-

perty of either father or mother. the mother's going back into
her family again and the father's is inherited by the children of
his sister, and in case she has no children it goes to the slave children of the family. The origin of this singular usage is said to be
from the following circumstance. Many years ago, when these districts were governed by a native prince, a large alligator stopped
up the water-course of a large tank called Kandalie in Trincomalie,
so that the water overflowed, and inundated the whole of the lower
parts of the country. The priests reported to the prince that their
god was offended, and consequently had brought this evil upon them
to punish them, and that in order to have it removed the god must
be propitiated by the sacrifice of a child of blood royal. The
prince desirous that the sacrifice should be immediately offered requested his wife to give up one his children; she refused, upon this he
applied to his sister, stating the circumstance, who readily gave one of
hers at his request, saying she had many children, but only one brother. The prince immediately made it a law that the property of
every man should upon his death go to the children of his sister,
because his sister had sacrificed one of her children to appease an
incensed Deity and to save the country from ruin. However little
truth there may be in this relation, the custom prevails, which is
the course of endless disputes in families and incessant employ for
the Sitting Magistrate. Another bad tendency it has. The lands are
not properly cultivated and planted with trees, as the man naturally
says, why should I labour for that which my children after me cannot enjoy? The spread of the Gospel and introduction of English
laws will introduce peace and harmony, establish the present comfort and secure the eternal felicity of this plain, simple, but superstitious people.

** We should be glad to receive from our Brethren similar communica-
tions to the above, with any other interesting notice tending to render our
knowledge of the Island, and the state of the people among whom we are
called to labour more perfect, to secure the seasonable publication of such
communications, we have paged the Miscellany separately, and purpose to
put it in hand a month before the Quarterly Letters, that their publication
may in future be earlier, without interfering with the regular work of the
office : of course, such communications are required a month earlier than the
Quarterly Letters.

NO. IX.

ON INDIAN LITERATURE.

Whatever may be asserted on the brilliancy of fancy which sparkles through
many literary works in the East, few men will dispute the palm in favour of
the oriental writers, for that correct taste and sound judgment which are so
conspicuous on comparison in the classics of the West. Among many other instances of bad taste, the most prominent, in my estimation, is the pedantic
style which disfigures almost every prose production now extant in the Hindoostanee language, and which often renders it wholly unintelligible to every
reader, who is not as deep in Arabic and Persian lore, as the learned man

who composed the book itself. If excellence in a popular tongue consisted in writing any thing far above the conception of the people for whom it is intended, every body must allow, that the Hindoostanee authors and translators stand unrivalled in this species of composition. In fact, to say the least that can be observed on so absurd a perversion of talents and learning, most of the literary efforts of this description that I have seen, might be very good Arabic or Persian, for any thing I know to the contrary, were they not disjointed and disfigured by the occasional introduction of a Hindoostanee preposition or verb, which like a flash of lightning in a dreary night, serve but to render the surrounding darkness still more visible. This false taste is no where more discernible and preposterous than in the prefaces to oriental works, which are in general composed in an affected idiom, so much beyond the level of ordinary capacities and acquirements, that very few of the men who can comprehend the body of the publication itself, are qualified to wade through the wonderful display of erudition which announces its birth. ——— DR. GILCHRIST.

No. X.

Minutes of the Committee on reading the second Report of the Ceylon Wesleyan Mission Schools.

" The second report of the Mission Schools in Ceylon having been read, it was

Resolved, That the Committee after having heard this important document cannot separate without recording on their Minutes the feeling of satisfaction and delight with which they have listened to its interesting details; and do hereby express their unfeigned gratitude to Almighty God for the openings of usefulness among the rising generation of Ceylon, which are thus presented to the Mission in that Island; and their cordial approbation of the prudence, zeal and diligence which the Missionaries evince in this valuable department of their labours: the Committee being of opinion that Schools conducted as theirs appear to be on truly judicious, liberal and Christian principles, are likely to prove one of the most efficient methods of sowing the seed of eternal Life in the minds of a heathen people, and an excellent preparation for plans of ultimate usefulness, and a most powerful auxiliary to the preaching of the Gospel.

Resolved, That an abridgement consisting of three thousand copies of the 2nd Ceylon Mission School Report be printed for distribution.

Resolved, That the respectful thanks of the Committee be presented to Brigadier General Shouldham and to Mrs. Shouldham for the kind and condescending attention which they paid to the Mission School at Colpetty during their residence in Ceylon, and for their liberal subscription in aid of the School Fund"

No. XI.

Copy of a Letter from the Reverend George Burder, Secretary to the London Missionary Society, to Messrs. Fox, Erskine, Clough, and Newstead.

London, 24th December, 1819.

The Rev. Messrs. Fox, Erskine, Clough, and Newstead, Missionaries in Ceylon.

DEAR BRETHREN,

On the lamented return of our truly valuable Missionary Mr Knill, we received an affectionate letter written by you, expressive of your Christian love to him, and including a satisfactory testimony as to the absolute necessity of his return to England, on account of the alarming state of his health.

I am instructed by the Directors of the London Missionary Society, to express to you their sincere thanks for your truly Christian behaviour towards him, as a brother-labourer in the wide field of the heathen world; and for the candid and pious manner in which you express yourselves towards Missionary Societies not immediately connected with your own.

This is the genuine spirit of Christianity. We cannot all think and speak exactly alike, but we should put the best construction we can on our brother's sentiments, and seek the glory of Christ and the conversion of souls rather than the superiority of our own party: this is more especially necessary when we are called to labour among the heathen, that there may be no stumbling block occasioned by our differences, but rather that they may be constrained to say, as it was said in the primitive ages—" See how these Christians love".

With every sentiment of Christian esteem, and prayers for the continuance your lives and health, and for very great success,

I am, dear Brethren, for the Directors
Your affectionate Brother in the Lord,
GEO. BURDER,
Secretary.

Mr. Knill's health was much improved by his voyage, but yet he continues to be very weak; he is going to Devonshire to enjoy his native air—he has not lost, and I hope never will lose, the Missionary spirit. He wishes to go out again to a cooler climate.

No. XII.

SERPENTS OF CEYLON.

පිඹුරා Pimburā නාගයා nāgayā
දෙපත්නයා depat nayā බින්දෙපත්නයා bin de-
කොබෝනයා cobō nayā [pat nayā
පොලඟා polangā ලේපොලඟා ley polangā
නිදිපොලඟා nidipolangā තික්පොලඟා tik polangā
දුවණ පොලඟා duwana polangā පණිණ පොලඟා
අලු පොලඟා alu polangā [panina polangā
පොලොන්තෙලිස්සා polon telissā ලේමැඩිල්ලා ley
ඇස්ගුල්ලා æs gullā [medillā
කරවලා karawalā දුනුකරවලා dunu karawalā
වල්කරවලා mal karawalā තෙල්කරවලා tel ka-
හබරලියා habaraliyā [rawalā
මහපිලා maha pilā හාල්දඬා hāldandā
ගරඬියා garandiyā කහ ගරඬියා kaha garandiyā
වල්ගරඬියා wal garandiyā කුණකටුවා kunakatuwā
ආහරකුක්කා āharakukkā මගමරුවා magamaruwā
මම්මින්නා mamminnā දියනයා diya nayā
දියබරියා diya bariyā පලාබරියා palā bariyā
පත් නයා pat nayā පොලොල්උල්ලා polōullā
වාලකඩියා wālakadiyā ගැටපොලඟා getapolan-
වාපොලඟා wāpolangā හෙනකඬ henakandā [gā
දාරපොලඟා dāra polangā පිඹුරු පොලඟා pim-
කුණු පොලඟා kunu polangā [bura polangā
සුලු නයා sulu nayā මහ නයා maha nayā

₊ It is requested that the Brethren who have an opportunity of meeting with any of the above, or any other serpents
not named in this list, will kindly favour us with descriptions of
them, to which due attention will be paid.   EDIT.

Extracts

FROM

QUARTERLY LETTERS, &c.

No. XIII.   *OCTOBER*, 1820.

THE COLOMBO AND COLPETTY STATION.

COLOMBO.

Colombo, October 4th, 1820.

Very Dear Brethren,

If in some parts of our quarterly communications we enter into many particulars which are as well known to the Brethren labouring in stations contiguous to our own as to ourselves, we shall doubtless be excused, as such minute matters may be gratifying and instructive to Brethren who are distant from us, since they can know no more of our situation than we relate, for analogy, in a country where localities so materially differ, can lead but little to correct views of our station or labours.

One peculiarity of our station which we are in little danger of forgetting, is a great variety of duties which require all the strength we have to perform, which would nevertheless be accounted a welcome load if separated from the inconceivable anxieties with which they are generally attended. The numerous interruptions from visitors, to which Christian policy obliges us to attend, however trifling they may appear, seldom leave any time for personal improvement, except when people generally feel an inclination to go to rest.

To preach is the most pleasant and least laborious part of our duty, except on the Sabbath day, when, with the best arrangements we can make, our labour is fully equal to our strength. Neither myself nor my colleagues have enjoyed a very high degree of health this last quarter, a part of which I attribute to the weather, which has been more variable than I have known it in the same period since I came to Ceylon, and it has happened at that period of the year generally esteemed the least healthful.

We are thankful, however, that we have seldom been obliged to neglect any appointment, although it has sometimes been perhaps a stretch of duty to fulfil them. Whatever might have personally affected me has always been lightened by the affectionate and zealous co-operation of my beloved colleagues. In labours, joys, and sorrows,

No. xiii.   Z

we have been equal partakers, and in views of the importance of the
work, none, or all may claim the precedency.

We have mutually viewed the work as a present labour, and weighed
the most probable means to secure present success, and these have been
corrected by a more extended view in connection with such events as,
in all probability, will always in various modes and combinations have
influence on our labours.

The particular labours of our station have called forth all our wisdom, our patience, and our gratitude, and have left us little time to
theorize, except on the result of our labours. We have from the
beginning had cause to lament that thousands of Christians, so called,
both natives and European descendants are seldom or ever found in
a Christian place of worship. This rather excites our grief than our
wonder, for their general ignorance of the plainest religious principles defies all attempts at description. This difference between the
native Christians, so called, and those of European descent is however
often perceivable in what is, at least, a faint trace of what we have
seen in Europe. The most ignorant among them seem to have ideas
of the necessity of some preparation for dying, which I suppose
they have learned from the Roman Catholics, who have always had
teachers among them, and they seem to have borrowed the ideas
of that which is necessary from the same source, as in many cases
we have had reason to fear that the prayer of a minister formed
all the preparation deemed necessary in that important event.

When a person is declared to be near the grave, (seldom before)
we have often been sent for to pray with the sick, and we have
generally found them, not only in the extreme of weakness, but ignorant beyond all conception—we have seldom had much ground
for hope concerning the sick, but we have availed ourselves of these
opening doors to repeat our visits, in hope of profiting the living,
that they, when the same event shall happen, may be visited under
more favourable circumstances than that of their dying relatives.
For this opening, and I trust, not ineffectual door, we are indebted
to our acquirements in the Ceylon Portuguese, a language spoken
by thousands of natives as well as by those who consider their origin European. We have not always been discouraged with respect
to the dying, especially of those who could read a little Dutch,
as they have had some little acquaintance with the principle truths
of the word of God, and of some, where the slow progress of a
pulmonary affection has, without much pain, protracted life to an
unexpected period, we have had a pleasing hope of seeing them
at the right hand of God.

Our congregations in the Pettah vary little, they are still small,
a characteristic of all Christian congregations in Colombo. At 7
o'clock on the Sabbath morning we have English service at the Mission house which is attended by a few serious people who love the
truth and hear it with attention and profit. The number who
attend does not ordinarily exceed 20, but in Ceylon, and especially
in Colombo, this is a great number to attend at so early an hour. We
feel the highest satisfaction in preaching to this little company, be-

ing persuaded they are profited by all they are able to understand.
At 10 o'clock our Singhalese service commences, and most of the
children in the neighbouring schools are assembled at the Mission
house. Nearly all the children join in the responses of the abridgment of the Singhalese Liturgy, and manifest the most becoming attention to the plain discourses which are delivered. The attention
of some of the children is very striking, the emotions excited by
the different turns of the discourse being very distinctly marked on
their coloured countenances. A considerable number of the scholars
are truly serious, and about 20 are decidedly pious, and of the conversion of several of them in the most eminent sense of the word,
there is every satisfactory proof we could ask.

But all below these marked results of judicious and persevering labours cannot be deemed unimportant: we behold a generation rising up who are from childhood trained up in religious principles
and religious practices, who feel the sacredness of the holy Sabbath,
and who learn to bow their knees in secret before the father of the
Spirits of all flesh, and we have every reason to trust, concerning a
great part of them, that when grown up, they will not depart from
the path in which they have been accustomed to move. The importance of such a race rising up among a people who seem to have lost
all the common notions of right and wrong; where mental darkness
can admit of no additional shades, can scarcely be conceived of by
those who are not present in the work, nor fully appreciated by us
who are unceasingly engaged in the laborious but pleasing employ;
who sometimes are in danger of overlooking the *progress*, in attempting to see the *progression*. Little hesitation is necessary in saying
that the rising generation will form the most solid parts of a Christian Church in Ceylon. We always speak as we think and understand, and experience corrects and matures our knowledge. Whatever sentiment we may have hitherto recorded, which further experience has convinced us was a mistaken one, there remains one
which uniform experience confirms, that little is to be expected
from the present generation; that they will probably go down to the
grave in darkness, and leave the light of truth to shine on their
children. The almost total incapacity to comprehend the plainest
religious or moral truths, accompanied with any influencing sanctions,
is strikingly manifest in the adults of this country, and their apathy
and empty stare, though bright and clever in other things, is in this
respect astonishing almost beyond astonishment.

We are nevertheless not totally destitute of hope concerning them
all; we still labour with unabated vigour to do them good when
we can meet with them, and with respect to a few, God has blessed
the work of our hands, and glorified himself in their conversion.

The number of adults who attend the Singhalese service at the
Mission House is small, but the few that do attend are very hopeful
persons. A more considerable number would attend were it not for
a notion prevalent among them, which it is easier to reprove than
remove. They are poor people who are unable to purchase such

clothing as they believe proper and decorous to appear in among a
company of people, especially in the Maha Palliya, or Great Church,
as they call the Mission House. To accommodate such, and all others
we are able to collect together, we have week night preaching in
diff'rent places, in one of which the attendance of children and
adults is from 80 to 100, and sometimes a still greater number; in
this congregation every thing is gratifying. Our Evening service at
the Mission House is in English, and the congregation is fluctuating.
It is seldom large, except on particular occasions. The people are
however very attentive, and we trust do in some measure profit
by what they hear. The Portuguese congregation is about the same
as usual and seldom varies much except from local causes. In the
country places our progress in collecting regular adult congregations
is slow, but we do make progress. Some of our country congregations are very pleasing, especially that of Nagalgam about 3 miles
distant, which is remarkably uniform and, for a country congregation, large. Our Societies are a little on the increase and the classes
prosper. Several of our Members are in the interior and some of
them alone there; but we learn from them that, though deprived of
many of the means of grace, they find it good to draw near to
God. Others in public employments are scattered all over the
coast, so that there are but few places of any consequence where
none can be found who fear God and work righteousness. Some of
the boys formerly under the care of Br. Harvard are now grown
up, and retain their seriousness, and not a small number in these
parts acknowledge themselves under obligations to him which they
can never repay, but which they take all opportunities of remember-
ing. One of them lately brought a silver headed Kandyan walking
stick, desiring I would send it to Europe to Br. Harvard as a token
of grateful remembrance, which I felt little hesitation in comply-
ing with. I have scarcely met with any thing that has either affected or pleased me more than circumstances like these, for I have
been of opinion, and I believe I have not been alone in it, that as
in the two languages we use here, there is no proper word for
gratitude, that the existence of the thing is very doubtful.

The printing office has continued in active operation, though several of the hands have been laid up by sickness, or have been absent
from other causes. For several weeks we were obliged to employ
almost the whole strength of the office in the 2d Edition of the
Singhalese Testament, of 3500 copies, which we stood pledged to
complete before the anniversary Meeting, and with close attention
it was accomplished to the great satisfaction of the Colombo Auxiliary Bible Society. Most other works were therefore of necessity
suspended, for had we had double the number of compositors the
presses could have done no more. The quarto Book of Common
Prayer printed for the Bishop of Calcutta and the Archdeacon of Colombo, is nearly completed. Br. Clough's Singhalese translation of
a volume of short sermons for the use of schools will shortly be out
of the press, and, when finished, will be forwarded without delay, to
the stations where they are required. We hope in a few days to

receive the fount of Tamul types shipped at Trincomalie by Br. Carver, and should it be perfect, or but little defective, we shall be able to print for the Brethren labouring among the Malabars, any little work they may have prepared for the press.

I had lately the pleasure of visiting Br Newstead at Negombo, and witnessed with the most grateful feelings the establishment of an auxiliary Missionary Society under the most pleasing circumstances! I speak without hyperbole when I say, if I did not fancy myself among the simple honest hearted Christians which may be found in the North and other parts of England, the events of this day brought them to my grateful remembrance. The interest the people felt, and the attention they paid, rendered it through the whole meeting a labour to suppress the mingled tear of wonder and gratitude. I am no orator, I have no painter's pen, or I would convey the sensations I felt, and without lessening, impart to those who could not be present, the sublime pleasures of that interesting day. The people present, and perhaps their ancestors for ages past could never say ours in reference to any thing beyond their humble cottage; but now, they could say our Church, our Padri, our Society, our Cause and their countenances expressively said ours, throughout that interesting meeting. At a Love-feast which we attended at Negombo I was astonished beyond measure to find myself surrounded by about 50 coloured human immortal beings, many of whom spoke in their own tongues in a manner in which none can speak, who have not, in some degree, felt the powers of the world to come. The pleasing scene was continued with new variations—a new church was to be opened, the place was about 5¼ miles distant from Negombo, we were met by the people about 1½ from the place with all the demonstrations of joy and respect that the Singhalese people can shew, and they ushered us into a village where great numbers of people collected from many villages were assembled with countenances expressive of the highest interest and satisfaction. They reminded me of God's promise of the coming in of the fulness of the Gentiles. After having stopped to breakfast, about half a mile from the place designed to be consecrated to the true God, we sat out towards the place through a shady grove of trees, while the sound of the distant bell, sounding gradually more distinct as we advanced, announced to the neighbouring villages that the tribes of Zion were approaching to worship their God. About 200 yards before we reached the place an extensive lawn covered with trees, whose lower branches, were so elevated as to leave no part obscured, presented to our view, in the centre, a beautiful little church, ornamented with all that simple ingenuity for which the Singhalese stand unrivalled, and the walk leading to it ornamented with the filaments of young cocoanut leaves on each side, and *ornamented* without by great numbers of human beings, who as we approached made their respectful obeisance, while the feelings of joy and solemnity seemed to be equipoised on their countenances. The place, if twice the size, had been too small to contain the people, and those who were unable

No. xiii.   2 A

to enter surrounded the door and windows, and heard with the deepest attention all that was said. I am sure all heard Br Clough, whose zeal accompanied with a clear sonorous voice, I am sure, will never allow him to live many years within the tropics.

After the ordinary services were finished, there were several baptisms and marriages to perform, and, when ended, the children of different schools, and people of different villages, assembled about the house where we took refreshment, and in companies, similar as I suppose to those our LORD fed, made their respectful obeisance and departed.

With respect to myself I can truly say, my views and wishes have never changed since I left England. I have experienced sickness, weakness, fatigue, danger, and sometimes particular discouragement; but I have never feared the success of our labours—I have never suspected that our anticipations would be cut off. I see some of my Brethren sinking around me, and in secret often mingle my supplications with my tears. I attempt not to point out what GOD will do, but the prosperity of his work does not depend on our existence; though some fall in the battles of the Lord, GOD is still in the midst of his people. Br. Callaway joins me in love to you all.

I remain, very dear Brethren,
your's affectionately,
W. BUCKLEY FOX.

COLPETTY.

Colpetty, 10th October, 1820.

VERY DEAR BRETHREN,

At the time our last circular went to press I was so unwell and had so many things otherwise to occupy my attention and demand the little strength I had, that I was really prevented from writing you; and I must beg of you to consider this, and this only, as the cause of my silence at such a season. I always feel pleased and delighted at the sight of one of our periodical reports of the state of our Mission, and it is always peculiarly gratifying to my mind to contribute any little mite with which my very limited sphere of action may furnish me, and the searcher of hearts knows it would be a still more delightful task to perform, could I record in every paragraph more evident manifestations of his saving grace in the salvation of immortal souls. However I am not *repining* that I do not see more; perhaps were I in all respects more faithful, both with myself and in the work in which I am engaged, I might see more; still while I mourn before God on this account, I am thankful for what I do witness, and the assurance I have that our labour is not in vain.

I have, I am sorry to say, suffered a good deal lately from indisposition, arising chiefly from great weakness, and am frequently so borne down with this debility, that it appears, as though my work in Ceylon was nearly done. Yet I feel in a great measure resigned,

and can almost persuade myself, that in every suffering of this kind
I can trace the wisdom of God, and his goodness towards me.

On this side of our circuit we have had nothing marvellous in our
proceedings lately, either of a painful or a pleasing kind. I have
had some little things of rather an unpleasant nature to contend
with in two or three of the schools, but which I hope are nearly settled. I sometimes think that because Satan sees these schools are
our most important channels of usefulness, and bid finally to secure
permanant success to our cause and efforts, that his utmost energies are directed against them, and against us in them. I do not
know how it may be with others, but I may say that I seldom meet
with what I call a real vexation, but it comes from this quarter: yet
I bear it, because I feel conscious of how great importance it is to
support them in all respects. I am sure a great work of God is
going on in our Schools.

Our School in Colpetty is now doing better than it has done I
think for two years. The daily attendance is very considerable indeed, and the congregation on Sundays are increasing and a spirit
of devotion becomes more evident among them. The other morning on going into the school I met a number of the larger boys
coming out, it was about 10 o'clock in the forenoon, I asked them
where they were going, they replied with such apparent readiness
as showed a degree of delight, "We are going to the class meeting
Sir." There are in this School a number of fine steady youths,
whom I look upon with much pleasure, and cannot but hope, nay
I cannot but feel assured they will in the end be made great blessings in the country. I may say that from their infancy almost, their
minds have been stored with the most correct Christian instruction,
and as they rise up in life they appear to be imbibing and cultivating
a spirit of Christian piety; may the Lord bless them. Our School at
Wellewatta has tried me a good deal, and I am not quite sure what
I should do with it were it not for the little class of pious souls there.
I went a short time ago to preach at the place and before I had finished I was most grieved to see some things that I could not controul;
but after sermon I went and met the class, and what I saw and felt
while talking to these poor creatures of the things of God, people who
were once in heathen darkness and ignorance, had such an effect on
my mind that I determined to bear any thing rather than have re-
cource to decisive measures. I have had the headmen of the village
brought together again, and spoke seriously to them, one of whom
begged that if we would allow the School to remain he would bear
the whole expense himself—"For" said he "if the Church is forsaken
what shall we do?" I had them and the masters face to face yesterday, and all promised on a new plan to exert themselves afresh, and
the masters most willingly consented not to take any kind of remuneration or pay whatever until the school was brought into good order
again. The whole of the confusion occasioned in this village is by
the vile influence of Cappoas, they have entered into a league to
drive out the Missionaries and every thing like Christianity. The
headmen wanted me much to apply to Government to interfere, but

this I felt reluctant to do. The cause is God's, and here, after doing all I can, will I leave it.

Our little cause in Morrotto after some severe struggles is now gaining strength. And I think if we could only send a Native Assistant Missionary to reside in that place I hardly know where be could be more useful. I have not seen such a School in Ceylon take it in all respects. But it is at such a distance that I cannot get at them above once a fortnight. The last time I was there I found every boy and every girl in the School, with the exception of 3 or 4 little ones, could read both the English and Singhalese Testaments fluently! The other two schools, Ratmalany, and Kallebowella, are I believe doing very well. I have visited them both several times since I last wrote, and am much satisfied with the progress they are making, but especially the latter.

Our work in the Translating-room is making continual progress. I am thankful to say we have just finished the book of Numbers, and are now going on with Deuteronomy. It is most gratifying to see the united zeal which is displayed in this most important department of our work. Messrs. Armour and Chater continue to occupy their places in the room, and our native assistants are perseveringly firm in their part of the labour. Petrus Panditta becomes, in some respects a more interesting character than ever. In consequence of some suspicions which one of the principal native headmen expressed to me as to the reality of his conversion I have lately taken several opportunities of speaking closely to him, and the result of my examination has been truly satisfactory to my mind. I believe the man as sincere a convert as almost ever embraced the Gospel of Christ. I am not a little pleased to witness the steady attachment of George Nadoris to the good cause. His whole heart appears in the work, and I hope he is increasing in christian piety. He continues his place in the translating room.

I ought to inform you that a change has taken place in my plan of proceeding with the Dictionary, a change which, though it has retarded the work a little, will in the end prove advantageous. I had just completed my part in the first volume of this work about June last, and upwards of 300 pages were printed, with every prospect of seeing it completed the latter end of this, or the beginning of next month. I had so arranged my little plans, that if my life was spared, to return to England, at least for a season, when this work was done. But though I felt the greatest need of such a change of residence on account of the reduced state of my health, nevertheless, I felt perfectly willing to submit to any other arrangement divine Providence might point out at the time. About the time I have just mentioned, that is in June last, I happened to be at breakfast with the Collector, Mr. Deane, the Secretary of the Bible Society, when in the course of conversation concerning the printing of various works, I asked him if he knew whether or not it was the intention of Government to publish the Singhalese Dictionary, compiled by Samuel Tolfrey, Esq. I told Mr. Deane, that during our late excellent Governor's time I had often expressed a wish to see the work, but that notwithstanding the

Archdeacon and Mr. Bisset had interfered in the most pressing manner to procure me this favour, they had not succeeded. Yet I felt quite satisfied with the Governor's reason for declining the favour. Mr. Deane immediately wrote a note to Mr. Lusignan, Secretary for the Kandyan Provinces, and procured me the privilege I had so long wished. The next day, after communicating with Mr. Lusignan, I went to the Government house to see it, when I met several of the principal characters who severally interrogated me as to the propriety or impropriety of Government publishing it. And from what I could judge of it at the time I gave my opinion on the work, which I have since learned was exactly the same as was given by the late Mr. Tolfrey, and which had prevented Government from publishing before. However, without any of them saying any thing definitely on the subject, Mr. Lusignan begged me to take the whole work home with me (it is in 3 large manuscript folio volumes,) to devise some plan for its publication, and to submit my plan to the Honble the Lieutenant Governor. In the course of a day or two I wrote the following letter to Mr. Lusignan, on the subject.

To G. Lusignan, Esq. &c. &c. &c.

DEAR SIR,

Since you were so kind as to deliver into my care, on Saturday last, the manuscript work of Samuel Tolfrey, Esq. I have been looking it carefully over; and, according to your wishes, have been endeavouring to determine upon the best plan I could for its publication for the benefit of the colony. We are certainly in great need of some work of the kind, and it is remarkable that after Ceylon has been in the hands of European governments so many years, no work has yet been presented to the public to render immediate and effective help to those desirous of becoming acquainted with the language of the country. Hence, I think, there cannot be a divided sentiment either as to the necessity or propriety of such a publication. I beg therefore to repeat the proposal I had the pleasure to make to you last week, namely, if Government feel at all desirous of sending out this work in its present form, I will, with the utmost readiness and pleasure engage to go over and revise it, as well as I can, for the press; and with equal pleasure also will undertake the complete management of the proofs, and secure it coming correctly from the press, so that, if printed at the Government office, the principal expence will be the paper and binding materials, as I shall feel a pleasure in giving all the help in my power for the only remuneration that I may have, in some degree, promoted the prosperity of the colony.

At the same time I ought to mention to you my fears, that in the event of the work being published in its present form, it will be very far from affording those helps in the acquirement of Singhalese which are both desirable and necessary. And if I mention a few of its defects I beg to be understood as speaking with the utmost deference to the opinions of others; nor is it my intention, in the slightest degree to reflect upon the talents or great labour of the respected compiler of the work, for certainly it required a great exertion of both to produce such an attempt. However, the first defect, most obvious is, the want of a second part, *English and Singhalese*, which I should infer Mr. Tolfrey never attempted. Now, it appears to me that in general this is the first thing wanted, especially by the native headmen, who are in the constant habit of reading English books, and consulting an English Dictionary, but who would hardly ever think of refering to the Singhalese and English Dictionary. It is the same, in a great measure with Europeans: their first wish, in beginning the language of the country, is to see the English words paralleled with Singhalese, and on this account we began the publication of our work with this part of the Dictionary first. Another defect I would just take the liberty to point out, the present compilation does not contain one-third of the number of words which ought by all means to be included in the most condensed Singhalese Dictionary, we might wish to publish. The work appears voluminous, but this does not affect the question. The same number of primitive words under a different arrangement, and one which I should think an improvement, might have been put in half the compass. But the deficiency of words is so very great, that any person taking into his hand a Singhalese book on olas would find scarcely any help from this book. The present version of the Singhalese Scriptures is in a lower style of language than any Singhalese book on olas that was written previous to the arrival of Europeans in Ceylon, and, to try the experiment, I placed myself in the situation of a learner, and began to read a chapter in the New Testament, and on consulting this Dictionary I could scarcely find a single word in it, except the most common and familiar terms such as are found in the mouths of children.

The design of this work was to explain the spoken Singhalese, hence a great number of Dutch and Portuguese words are inserted, and although this must answer a certain end, still it is an exceedingly imperfect attempt. A Dictionary should be, what it proposes to be, an exhibition of the language in which it is written, but here is a defect large enough indeed: and this is not the worst, there is hardly any thing like etymological definition, concerning which the learner first enquires, and I fear, were this work published in its present form the expence incurred would not be advantageously laid out, and the student in Singhalese left almost unassisted. It would, therefore, be a most desirable thing, that if any publication of the kind be determined upon that it be made as perfect as possible, and such as will answer every end proposed and expectation held out. Yet if the Government should judge it right to print this Dictionary I will give it all the help in my power most cheerfully.

But while I have been looking over Mr. Tolfrey's work the following plan has suggested itself to my mind, which, in addition to what I have proposed, I take the liberty to mention to you, and if you approve, I shall feel exceedingly obliged to you to be so kind as mention it to the Honorable the Lieutenant Governor. I. Providing Government do not determine to publish this work in its present form, that if they will allow me the complete use of the copy I will engage to re-write the whole, according to a plan which I have long ago fixed upon for my own work, and of which I should feel a pleasure at a proper time to submit a specimen to the inspection of the Honble John D'Oyly, whom I conceive as the most capable of judging concerning a work of that kind. 2. That I would engage to add at least twice as many words more as are contained in Mr. Tolfrey's work, which are already compiled, and chiefly from the Singhalese ola books, and paralleled with words in the vernacular dialect, and finally with an English explanation. 3 That I would unite to this work the one I have already completed, which is now in the press, and which will be published in a few months, making about 570 pages, 300 of which are already printed. 4. I would humbly request that both volumes be published under the honorable sanction and patronage of the Ceylon Government, and that the Lieutenant Governor would condescendingly allow them to be dedicated to him. 5. I would propose that the name of the respected Samuel Tolfrey, Esq. be introduced in the work, in the most honorable manner, as the meritorious individual who laid the foundation of the work. 6 That the Ceylon Government be kindly pleased, as a remuneration for our trouble, to supply us with English printing paper and binding materials for both volumes. And that in return they receive 100 copies of each volume well bound and ready for the use of the servants of Government.

I must beg to add, that in order to make the work uniform, both volumes ought to be printed on Europe demy, for the volume we have been going on upon has been printed on China paper, so that a reprint be immediately begun, when I will engage to have the whole of the first volume out of press about Christmas next and the 100 copies for Government use bound and sent in about that time.

I hope Sir I have made my proposal quite plain to you, but if necessary will with pleasure give any further explanation, previous to your finally replying to my statement. I think it will be found on examination that this proposal which I have made is the fairest I could offer, though I shall readily attend to any other terms you may be so kind as point out. My chief reason for making the above was to furnish you with what strikes me as the outlines of an equitable arrangement, but wish to leave it entirely with yourself to make any change you may think proper. I will only add my opinion, that should the Honble the Lieutenant Governor kindly consent to this arrangement, the Government of Ceylon and the colony in general will be furnished with a standard work, which I think is likely to answer all the ends to be desired in such an undertaking, and that this work will be furnished to Government on the most economical plan possible. For providing Government agree to supply us with paper and binding materials for both volumes, it will not cost them so much by any means, as the publication of this single work of Mr. Tolfrey's printed at their own office. In addition to this, I fear that were this work printed in the Government office it would quite exhaust all patience. And this was one consideration which the late W. Tolfrey, Esq. particularly mentioned to me in a conversation I had with him on the subject a few days before his lamented affliction.

But I have need to request your kind excuse for troubling you with so long a note on the subject.

> I remain, your truly obliged and humble
> faithful servant,
>   B. CLOUGH.

N. B. It ought to have been mentioned in the above statement that if the work be printed on Europe Demy paper, about 75 Reams will be necessary for the two volumes, and if the Government should not be able to provide that quantity from their stores we shall feel a pleasure in supplying it at the island tarif rate.

In a short time Mr. Lusignan wrote me the following reply.

DEAR SIR,   *Colombo, Aug.* 14, 1820.

I have to apologize for not before answering your letter of the 3d containing proposals for completing a Singhalese and English, and English and Singhalese Dictionary, from the materials collected by Messrs. Tolfrey, Sen. and Jun and your own subsequent labours. The Lieutenant Governor acquiesces in the arrangement proposed by you to revise the Dictionary compiled by Mr. Tolfrey, on such a plan as Mr. D'Oyly may approve, to add the part you have in the press, and to print 500 copies of the whole, Government finding the paper and materials for binding, and receiving 100 copies for its own use. The mode of introducing Mr. Tolfrey's name, and the share he had in the compilation, can be adjusted in the preface. There is not a sufficient stock of demy paper in the Government store, Government will therefore purchase the whole from you at the price you mention, Rds. 30 per ream.   I remain, Dear Sir,
> your faithful and obedient servant,
>   GEO. LUSIGNAN.

This letter of course brought the matter to a close and I could not but immediately make up my mind to set about the whole work. I do sincerely hope it was providential. This I know, it is not a trifling sacrifice for me to make; for I am sure that my constitution requires to be recruited by some bracing climate. I often in my imagination gasp for an English Christmas breeze, but a fear of being out of my place or missing my providential way in any one instance makes me tremble. I have seen so much of the providence of God in the little history of my life, and especially with respect to this Mission, that I would much rather submit to any privation or even the loss of life itself than take one step I could not conscientiously expect the approbation of heaven upon. On this ground I have acted in this affair, I reasoned with myself thus: First, if it be the will of heaven I should continue in Ceylon, and not be absent from the Mission at all, he can easily give life, health, and every blessing I require. Secondly, I can truly say it is far more pleasing and gratifying to every feeling of my heart to remain in my work here, than to go to any other corner of the globe, yea to England itself, much as I love many of the dear people there, and much as I should like to see them. Thirdly, the prospect of continuing in the Mission and of being able to take some part in its concerns is far more satisfactory to my mind than the idea of leaving it. Fourthly, I must think it an advantage to a Mission, situated as ours is, to have any one of its departments connected with the local Government. Fifthly, the present arrangement is so much in our favour, that if divine Providence should spare my life to complete the work, the whole will be published with very little expence to the Mission, hence the number of copies sold will be clear gain. Lastly, the work coming out under such a sanction and patronage is likely to meet with a much more extensive sale. From such, and other considerations I hope the whole is providential. At all events it appears such to me at present, and I have endeavoured to follow the most advisable plan. I should feel my mind much more reconciled to my circumstances did such engagements allow me more time to attend to other departments of our work, which are dear to me. However, my maxim generally is not to fly from any undertaking which comes to me in the shape of a duty.

I feel truly thankful to God for the increased encouragement I feel in my work, and in the operations of the Mission generally. And though I have to labour under a complication of bodily weaknesses, which daily and hourly affect me in a greater or less degree, yet I have been mercifully enabled, during the last 6 months, regularly to go through every part of the circuit labours which in the order of things fall to my lot, as well as to my other engagements. Our principal success appears to me to be among the natives; the prospects of usefulness among them are the most promising; and I feel so confident that our efforts to carry the religion of Jesus Christ amongst this class of people are owned of God, that I do sincerely rejoice in what I now see, and what I can anticipate, even viewing the subject in the coolest manner possible.

Since my last letter I had the pleasure of witnessing two or three little scenes on the Negombo station which have greatly encouraged me: the opening of the new Chapel in Negombo was exceedingly interesting; though I hardly know at this time what ideas most affected my mind When I first went to Negombo on a School excursion, just after our Conference in 1816, the scene was certainly not the most cheering. If I except the Roman Catholic place of worship, I believe there was nothing in that large town even to remind the people of the existence of a God. A large town, containing thousands of inhabitants, surrounded with heathens and their temples. No Christian minister, no means of grace, no place in which the people could assemble for sacred purposes. The large Dutch church and the minister's house all in ruins, and trees growing even on the tops of the walls, and so surrounded on all sides with bushes, which enjoyed their uninterrupted growth, that it had the appearance of an elevated and romantic jungle. But now I saw a lovely little chapel which had sprung out of these very ruins, several of God's servants present, to hallow the spot, and assure the people that "*To them also was the word of Salvation sent.*" I saw more; I saw hundreds of people assembled from different parts of the town and country, who appeared astonished and delighted with what they saw, and not less thankful

No. xiii.   2 C

for the sacred Christian privileges which they now had the prospect of enjoying. In this instance our dear Br. Newstead has done, by the blessing of God, a great work. May heaven bless the labour of his hands! But a few weeks ago I went into the Negombo circuit to assist at the opening of another neat little chapel, so situated in the jungle that perhaps a white face will never be in it, unless it be the laborious Missionary who may go from time to time to carry the blessed news of salvation to those poor creatures, formerly bound in heathen darkness. The opening of this chapel was one of the most interesting scenes I have ever witnessed in Ceylon. The neat appearance of the chapel, its situation, the circumstances under which it has been raised, and the interest manifested by the crowds of people who attended on the occasion; and, I might add, the peculiarly happy state of my own soul while exhibiting to them the precious name of our blessed Saviour, all I say taken together made this one of the most happy days of my Missionary life. And what is still more pleasing, to find that in the whole of this part of the country, our pious school masters are labouring with all their powers to carry among the people the offers of salvation in the same spirit in which they themselves have received it. Little societies and little classes are springing up and uniting themselves together in the villages round about, and it is becoming quite common to hear the poor creatures tell the simple tale of their conversion to God, and relate the particulars in a clear and scriptural manner. And why should not this be the case in every station where we have publicly planted the Gospel standard?

I have been much struck lately with the increased demand there is on all hands for the word of God in all the languages in which it is published in this Island. The anxiety of the people, and especially the younger classes of them, to possess the Scriptures is really astonishing. The gift of Bibles mentioned in our last, from the British and Foreign Bible Society, though most handsome and most seasonable, have been found so inadequate to supply the demands on this station alone, that I have almost felt sometimes in refusing applications, as the Apostles felt with the loaves and fishes, "What are these among so many!" And I do hope the Christian world will never allow us to suffer the miseries of a famine of the word of life. It is plain that such a desire to possess it is a decided evidence that God is at work among the people, and only let these intimations of his gracious operations be followed up by active exertions on the part of the Christian church, and on the part of Christian Missionaries especially, and so sure as the promises of God have been given, so sure shall we have a blessed work in this country.

Our connection with the Bible Society, and through it with many respectable characters, is a very encouraging reflection, and it affords us facilities in our work which greatly assist us. The Honble the Lieutenant Governor has hitherto manifested nothing towards us but the most condescending and benevolent dispositions. He has been pleased on several occasions to express his decided approval of our plans of Missionary labour, and his sincere wishes that our exertions may be successful. He has most kindly and readily attended to all the applications which we have found it necessary to make to Government, and we have lately received both from himself, and through him, from several of our honoured countrymen in this island, many helps and assistances in our work, which will only be known to those absent from the scene of our labours, in the great day. Our honble and kind friend the Archdeacon, continues to favour us with all the countenance, support, and encouragement in his power, and which we have had from him since the commencement of our Mission. We have also met with many kind and condescending attentions from the Honble the Chief Justice, Sir Hardinge Giffard, since his arrival in Ceylon, and which we beg to mention with sentiment of the sincerest gratitude. We feel thankful also for the arrival of Sir Richard Ottley, as Puisne Justice in Ceylon, he arrived at Colombo on the 7th of this month, but I am concerned to say he has been confined to his bed by a severe fever, almost from the hour of his arrival. I am happy to say, however, he is much better, and hopes are entertained of his soon being out again, and we shall not cease to pray that his coming to this country may be made a blessing to thousands. Our worthy Secretary to the Bible Society, Mr. Deane, has been most kind to us in rendering us many, yea very many helps, not only as Secretary to the Society, but as Collector of this large district, without which several branches of our labour in these quarters must have suffered much loss. Such disinterested kindness and Christian benevolence I do hope will never be forgotten by us. For while we have our difficulties and hindrances to contend with, we have abundant cause of gratitude both to God and man. Our work is the Lord's and here is an unfailing source of encouragement and a ground of confidence which can never be shaken. May we be kept faithful.

Before I conclude I wish just to inform you, that our dear Brother Newstead is now with me in Colpetty. Poor fellow he is very unwell, and I am sure he has been overdoing himself with labour. I fear he will not be able to take his station again for some weeks. However, I feel the less concerned on this particular head from the great confidence I have in our dear young Missionary Mr. Sutherland. From the accounts which he daily transmits to Br. Newstead of the proceedings of the station it is gratifying to know that all things are going on as well as could ever be expected in the absence of Br. N. Thus our gracious Master provides for his work; bless the Lord for this young man.

I beg to conclude my present letter with renewed assurances of my sincere esteem and affection for you all, and how much it rejoices my heart to hear that you are prospering both in your own souls, and in your work, and also to beg a continued interest in all your prayers, a privilege which I ever estimate as next to grace itself May the Lord smile upon all our efforts to promote his glory, Amen and Amen.

B. CLOUGH.

THE NEGOMBO STATION

Negombo, September 29, 1820.

VERY DEAR BRETHREN,

Several pleasing circumstances in our work here having occurred through the past quarter, I rather think I shall have to engage your patience while I attempt to detail them as nearly as possible in the order in which they transpired; for, while on the one hand I am unwilling to be unnecessarily prolix, on the other I ever feel the necessity of not obscuring the progress of our blessed cause by too much brevity, and particularly as I am aware how essential it is for the information of our Committee, (even where it is not for our's on the Island,) to enter sometimes into a detail of circumstances.

I am truly thankful to the "*God of all grace,*" that I have been spared to witness the third anniversary of my Mission to Negombo, and though it has found me under circumstances of unprecedented weakness and debility, and a consequent suspension from my usual labours, yet under any circumstances such an event calls for the warmest gratitude to Him, who in a peculiar manner "*appointeth the bounds our habitation,*" and who hath caused "*goodness and mercy to follow* me *all the days of my life.*" The station and circuit around it, I am happy to say, assumes now an appearance of stability and permanence which promises, under God, to secure the continuance and spread of our sacred work: and the erection of our chapel with the regular administration of Christian ordinances has so greatly and rapidly promoted this desirable object that it is a source of continual gratitude to me. Our little altar is frequently encircled on the Sabbath days by those who bring their infants to present to the Lord in Christian baptism. Marriage is growing into far more honourable repute; and the holy sacrament is attended with the most scrupulous attention and becoming reverence, by about 15 regular communicants; these, with our usual love-feasts, and class-meetings, preaching in the different languages of the people, Missionary prayer meetings, &c. keep open the gates of our little Sion almost every day: and more than all, I rejoice to see not in vain, for our Sabbath day congregations have increased (chiefly from the country places round,) in a manner which I confess I never expected so soon to see here; and knowing, by long experience, the persevering opposition which exists to every thing which bears the unwelcome name of Protestants. I have just finished a careful examination of our little Society on renewing their tickets for the quarter, and am most thankful to say that I have not found a single instance of irregular conduct, which required particular censure, but many delightful proofs of a real work of God upon the heart; we have now seven regular little classes in different places, comprehending 79 persons of both sexes and various ages, met by six different leaders, 5 of whom were raised up on the Mission. Two of these classes are entirely of *females,* and in one of them there is so striking an instance of the power of divine grace, that, were it not too interesting a history to be short, I am sure the relation would delight the Brethren; it is sufficient to say that she was the proverb of the village for every kind of low and extreme wickedness (for it is not a little that excites their wonder here,) and she is now the wonder of the village for the remarkable change wrought in her life, by the power of the Gospel. I ought to add that 17 of the above are on trial, considered however as members, having been on trial 3 times the usual period, but I choose to keep them so on account of their youth, and from a desire to be more assured of their stability.

Our Schools do not so much encourage me by their numbers, as by their stability, and their growing importance as auxiliaries to preaching the Gospel and forming Christian societies. In addition to the destruction of two which I mentioned last quarter, our Negombo school has suffered considerable declension from the same cause there adverted to, and indeed all our schools are so sifted and opposed from two trying quarters, that every one who comes must make a decided choice, and hence I have more confidence in them now than I had at the first. Two of our school-rooms, one a most excellent and newly-built one, have been burned down this quarter, the best of them no doubt wilfully set on fire, the other (our Kandian school) we believe by accident, both are rebuilding, and our excellent Collector, J. Deane, Esq. is actively engaged in detecting and punishing the perpetrators of the other evil act. However, all these things do not and will not prevent their growing usefulness. I was wholly delighted to perceive at our last examination, the respectable advances which some of our elder scholars have made in general, but especially, in *Christian* knowledge. Our school villages are gradually becoming regular Methodist parishes as it were, among which we constantly itinerate, and of which we are recognized and respected as the accredited pastors and teachers; for we have only two schools which we cannot see every week, and one of those we do generally every fortnight; the Negombo original school is under our eye every day, for it is now taught in our own house, where we formerly held public worship, so that all we have to do with, young or old, come very often under pulpit instruction. The erection of little village chapels, where it is practicable will have the best effect in giving permanence to our labours. I had the unspeakable happiness a short time since to admit to Christian baptism 14 persons, in a school formerly purely heathen, five of whom immediately after the ordnance were received into our society with their newly acquired Christian names, having for a long time regularly met in classes as exemplary Catechumens, and of whose truly changed deportment and earnest desires no doubt could exist. It made a deep impression on the people present, who listened attentively to the address given on the occasion, and afterwards to a sermon, on the second Anniversary of the school,

I am happy to say my young Friend and colleague is a most efficient and willing helper in the work, and continues to give me and the Brethren who know him increasing satisfaction in every department of the important engagement to which he is called. Our assistant Brother also, I believe, finds his chief pleasure in being actively engaged among the heathen people, to whom he has a more ready access than ourselves from obvious reasons, and can carry on our Bazar preaching, &c. with fewer impediments whenever it is practicable.

Concerning the extension of our work. I have long been very anxious, about occupying Chilaw, but have in all my attempts been hitherto frustrated : the circumstances which have occasioned this delay are not however to be regarded as final hindrances but rather. I trust, as ultimate helps; for they have chiefly been the cutting of the canal to that place, and such other public works as have occasioned the frequent visit of the Lieutenant Governor, and so of course have too much occupied the Collector to allow of his attention being diverted besides. I must candidly say that I believe the Collector was chiefly desirous that a Missionary should *reside* on the spot, and has no confidence of much good being done, (though by a laborious and constant effort,) from any one so distant as Negombo, with that tremendous wilderness of sand between. But whenever it is occupied the canal will remove one half of the difficulty, and the place is open at any day when it can be efficiently occupied. I am now trying to *work my way* down by attempting the establishment of two new *Malabar schools* which enter into the *Chilaw District.* I have good hope of success, having been favoured with a spot of ground on which to build a school, by Mr. Deane, and having commenced our preparations rather quickly, for in one of the villages there is the marvellous sight of a *Roman Catholic church in ruins !* and I consider this a loud call to our exertions.

But on the whole I cannot forbear looking upon our detention from Chilaw hitherto as *Providential*, because our way is just now, after long exertion to go further in vain, so very favourably opening to the *Kandian provinces ;* the very great kindness, and readiness to enter into all our Missionary views, displayed by our excellent friend J. Deane, Esq. (to whose efficient help I have so often had occasion to advert,) has been particularly proved in this blessed opening. A reference to any former Negombo Quarterly letter since the Galle Conference, will shew the failure of many plans relative to this object and the alternate hopes and fears concerning it, although a brighter prospect now appears. I applied to Mr. Deane, kindly to *speak* to the Lieutenant Governor concerning it, as I feared to trouble him by writing any more, and the following extract from one of Mr. Deane's letters will shew how readily and efficiently he entered into the business, both with the Lieut. Governor and Mr. Wright, the Resident at Kornegalle, to whom I had written, and an extract from whose answer is also in my last Quarterly letter. Mr. Deane says, under date of 28th August, " I have since mentioned your wish of establishing a school at *Kornegalle*, to the Lieut. Governor, who appeared to approve of the plan, but thought that the application should be made through the accredited agent at that station ; I communicated this to Mr. Wright and would advise your writing again to him on the subject, when he kindly promises to forward the application to Government with his recommendation; so that I trust you will have no difficulties to contend with : Mr. Wright returns to the Interior this day."

I accordingly wrote immediately, and happened the next day to see his Honour the Lieut. Governor passing through Negombo, to whom I mentioned the circumstance again, when he again assured me that he approved of the plan, and would sanction any application which the Resident might make, I considered these events as very providential, and expected soon to have an answer from Mr. Wright, but as some time passed over, I began to be rather anxious, and wrote again, respectfully informing him of my interview with the Lieut. Governor, and begging permission to begin our operations. Before his answer arrived I was obliged a second time to leave my station from ill health, and seek a change of air with my very affectionate Br. Clough, at Colpetty, where I now am, finishing my letter on our delightful work, while almost wholly incapable of any greater exertion, and from this am often forced to rest. A frequent pain in the breast accompanied by excessive weakness, and other trying symptoms, in the opinion of the Brethren renders a present cessation from preaching and travelling necessary, and their kind, very kind attention and sympathy, with the change of air, rest and society, will do all that can be done to remove my present weakness; it is however, proper to say, that I feel at this time, a sort of internal weakness and general falling away, which, though I have often expected would follow from certain indications, I never felt before in this degree. I am at no loss to account for the cause, but am far from murmuring, knowing that I am in His gracious hands, *"who doeth all things well."* The day after my arrival here, I received the following letter from Mr. Wright, dated

Kornegalle, October 4, 1820.

SIR,

"My absence from home has delayed my reply to your last communication of Sept 25, and the cause of my previous silence was owing to an enquiry I was making to discover the feelings of the people on the subject of English instruction, should the opportunity be afforded them of obtaining it, before I mentioned the subject to Government, which would expect some information from me to form its opinion of the matter. The people at present manifest the greatest indifference, probably owing to their ignorance of its advantages; but as we have had no proof of their *reluctance*, I think they ought to be put to the test. It will be necessary first to built a school-room and a house for the residence of a Missionary, which I fear it will be difficult to do at this moment when so many other public works are carrying on to occupy the time and labours of the people, who are likewise just now very busy in reaping one crop and sowing for another. As I have not time to day, I shall tomorrow write to Government on the subject.

I remain, your's faithfully,
H. WRIGHT.

Much rejoiced to perceive so favourable a disposition towards our efforts in a gentleman invested with such high authority over the people, I felt it incumbent on me immediately to reply as follows:

Colpetty, October 6, 1820.

Sir,

"I beg to acknowledge the honour, of your obliging communication of the 4th October, which did not reach me till this morning, owing to my being here a short time for the recovery of my health which is somewhat impaired. I beg Sir, that you will favour me by accepting my best thanks not only for your handsome reply to my letters on the subject of the Christian instruction of the inhabitants of the Interior, but also for the very judicious remarks and liberal principles which it includes.

"My views (and I may venture to say, those also of our whole Mission) are so entirely in unison with those contained in your letter, that I shall feel the utmost pleasure in availing myself of the opening prospect of so much good, as soon as it shall please God a little to restore my health, and meanwhile, I beg to say, Sir, that your kind suggestions relative to any of our future operations so immediately under your own eye, as it respects times of the greatest convenience for the people, and when they are least (or not at all) required for the service of Government will always be my rule. The building of a School room and residence for a Missionary, are of primary importance, and shall be early attended to according to your very kind intimation,

"I infer that, in addition to those you have mentioned, the periodical rains also will soon be a *temporary* hindrance, but at all events, under the direction of Divine Providence, I will avail myself of the earliest possible opportunity to assure you personally how much I consider myself and our work obliged by your condescending information. I shall perhaps, (from an intimation at the close of your letter,) be favoured with yet further information from you when the answer is received from Government, and beg to have the honour to remain,

Sir, your much obliged and
obedient servant,
ROBERT NEWSTEAD.

H. *Wright, Esq.*
&c. &c. &c.

The expected answer is arrived, and while the Quarterly letter is in the press, I am most happy to be able to lay before our dear Brethren, copies of the encouraging documents, which in so full and honourable a manner opens our way completely into the heart of the Kandian country under the sanction of the highest authorities in the island.

Truly the hearts of all men are in the hands of the Lord, and how has he directed them in this instance for the advancement of His Cause! May the warmest feelings of our grateful adoration to His Holy Name be called into exercise on this interesting occasion!

The subjoined note from Mr. Wright, enclosed the official communication which follows from the Honorable John D'Oyly, the Resident in Kandy, and reached me this morning (Oct. 26th.) at the Mission House.

Kornegalle, October 23, 1820.

Sir,

The enclosed is a copy of the answer I received from Government to mine on the subject of establishing an English School at this place, and it has my cordial wishes for its prosperity.

I am, Sir, your obedient servant,

H. WRIGHT.

Kandy, October 14, 1820.

Sir,

I have the honor to acknowledge your letter of the 5th, stating a communication which you had received from the Wesleyan Missionary at Negombo relative to the establishment of an English School at Kornegalle, and your sentiments upon the advantages of it.

Having submitted the same to the consideration of the Lieutenant-Governor, I have the honor to inform you in reply, that he has no objections to the proposed measure, provided that the Government is put to no expence thereby.

I have the honor to be, Sir,

your most obedient servant,

H. Wright, Esq. Agent of   (Signed)   J. D'OYLY,
Government, Kornegalle,   *Resident,*

Since I have been here, the Rev. Mr. Browning of the Church Missionary Society, and Mrs. Browning, staid a night at our Bungaloe in Negombo, on their way to Kandy, where they have obtained permission from the Honble the Lieutenant Governor to reside; they are gone through Kornegalle, I should have been delighted to have accompanied them thither, had my health permitted it, but hope soon to follow them, if the Lord will. Thus, the blessed Gospel will probably shine forth in more places than one, in that region where hitherto impenetrable darkness has reigned alone, but it is still true that

> "Jesus shall reign where'er the sun,
> Doth his successive journies run.'
> His kingdom spread from shore to shore,
> Till moons shall wax and wane no more."

Thus, very dear Brethren you perceive what gracious encouragement the great Lord of the harvest is giving us in our labours, and what answers to all our united prayers in opening the door of faith to these Gentiles; surely the time is come when *their* ears so long accustomed only to the sounds of Devil worship or the songs of Budhu, shall hear the *"joyful sound"* of the *"Everlasting Gospel!"* And though it has occupied nearly 20 months to throw open the door on its hinges thus far, is it not worth the labours of 20 years, if one soul be instrumentally saved thereby?

Since writing my last letter I have been favoured with a second visit from several of our dear Brethren, who came to assist at the

No. xiii.   2 B

opening of a second little Mission Chapel in this circuit, at the village of *Seedua*: here, you are aware, we have long had a flourishing school of nearly 100 children, and within the last nine months we have also had a very encouraging class here; a chapel was wanted as a kind of centre to our growing cause in that very populous village, where we can go on a Saturday afternoon, and meet two country classes, and on the Sabbath preach at three places, which we constantly do, all within a few miles from each other, where regular though small congregations are accustomed to meet together with the school-children. The day of opening was indeed a day of jubilee to the over-joyed inhabitants. Every thing which ingenuity could furnish in the way of their elegant native ornaments, of olas, fruits, and flowers, was most tastefully displayed, and every avenue to the chapel, (which is a neat little walled and tiled building about 27 ft. by 22.) wore the appearance of a beautiful garden. The situation of the place, which is romantic and delightful in the extreme, greatly favoured these spontaneous efforts, and the whole excited the surprise and admiration of all present. I think the multitude was greater than at the opening of Negombo Chapel, and all listened, most attentively while Brother Fox read prayers, Brother Chater preached from Psalm cxxii. 1. "*I was glad when they said unto me let us go into the house of the Lord,*" and Br. Clough followed from Luke ii. 14. "*Glory to God in the highest,*" &c. all in the native language, and in a manner most animating and appropriate: we all breakfasted and dined in the village, and enjoyed the most lively satisfaction at beholding the contented and cheerful appearance of both parents and children, attend in all their best, and full of, I believe, truly grateful expressions. May the Lord Jehovah condescend there to record his glorious Name, and save immortal souls through Jesus our adorable Saviour! *

The visit of our dear Brethren gave me an opportunity I had long desired, of attempting to form *a little Auxiliary Missionary Society.* Only such efficient aid as our dear Brethren so very readily gave could have enabled me to accomplish the interesting object, but I rejoice to say it is established, under circumstances more promising than I could ever have anticipated. At a single day's notice given from the pulpit, our new chapel was filled on the morning of the 25th Sept. and expectation sat on every countenance; some of our Roman Catholic neighbours were present, and some are become subscribers, among whom is the Magistrate. Our Brethren severally addressed the Meeting in various languages, in a most animated manner, and an uncommon interest was excited. Our respected Friend and Brother Mr Chater entered much into the spirit of the engagement, as he had done the day before at our

---

* A third little village chapel is in progress with an encouraging prospect, the wood for which is cutting by an order from Mr. Deane, and also about an acre of Government ground set apart by that gentleman for that purpose, on an application being made to him. The circumstances of that transaction are likewise so truly honorable to Mr. Deane, and advantageous to us that a detail of them could only be prevented by the length I have already been obliged to go in this letter.

love-feast, where he rose up, after hearing several declare what God had done for their souls in a simple and affecting manner, and expressed his high satisfaction at what he had heard and witnessed, and then adverted to his own experience of the things of God, and the great work which God had wrought in the Island. A series of regulations were severally agreed to by the whole meeting unanimously,* and donations and subscriptions immediately entered in the books which gives us promise of at least 300 Rixdollars, and much more may be expected when we have got the system into exercise. But the trifling sum which can be raised by such an institution at present is a small consideration compared with the good which cannot fail to result under the blessing of the Lord, from the impulse which will be given to the minds of the people, from the diffusion of knowledge respecting the state of the Heathen, and Missions in general. For this infant institution, dear Brethren, I most earnestly entreat your united prayers. and so, "*God, even our own God, will give us his blessing.*"

Relative to my progress in the study of the native language, I have had such continued interruption that I feel on the whole discouraged, although I feel assured that could I give an undivided attention to it, I should have a very contrary feeling, for I like the language and long for a proficiency in it; the little I have attained is very useful to me so far as can go in our public services, and that little has been literally snatched at intervals, from the continually pressing and growing concerns of the station which could not have been neglected with a good conscience. I feel however the great importance of the acquirement so much, that I truly regret every thing that interrupts it, while yet I must say had I my time to go over again on this station I must in conscience pursue a similar path. I had hoped after getting these various engagements a little settled to sit down to a more continued effort at the language, and had made arrangements accordingly, but by the adorable Providence of God, I find myself again prevented. in a way I have not been before; it was from a close attention to that new arrangement of study that I was obliged suddenly to lay by, and come to Colpetty early in September, and ever since, all attempts at study have been out of the question. But the Lord will also over rule this for good.

A very providential circumstance has occurred within these few days, which will render my stay at Colpetty far from unprofitable or inactive, while yet it requires but a comparatively light exertion.

On a former visit to Colombo, I proposed to Mr Deane, as Secretary to the Colombo Bible Society, to engage the Committee to print an edition of the Book of Psalms in the Ceylon Portuguese, part of which I have had translated by me nearly two years, which would only need correction; he immediately, with his accustomed promptitude entered into it, received a specimen, and laid it before the Committee; on arriving here, I received the following note from him enclosing a Resolution of the Committee.

* See Miscellanea, No. I.

Colombo. October 4, 1820.

Dear Sir,

I have the pleasure to send a resolution passed by the Committee of the Auxiliary Bible Society at their Meeting, by which you will perceive they have agreed to print 1000 copies of your translation of the Book of Psalms into the common dialect of the Portuguese.

Believe me, dear Sir,

your faithful humble servant,

J. DEANE,

Sec. C. A. B. Society.

The Resolution states the wish of the Committee for the translation to be submitted to the inspection and correction of the Honble and Venerable the Archdeacon, and our friend Mr. Armour, from an acknowledged fear that we rather leaned towards an extreme in lowering the language to the vulgar taste in order to make it better understood. A short extract from the Archdeacon's letter on the subject will much explain their views, and define the chief of the improvements they wish to suggest; which, as I fully believe they will not much alter the standard, must of course be acceded to; because many advantages will attend their patronizing the work, independant of the spiritual good we may assuredly calculate upon from so large and blessed a portion of the word of God being made accessible to the numbers who are now wholly destitute of the privilege; as for instance, the pecuniary benefit which will arise to our printing concern should it lead to their also ultimately printing the whole New Testament, which we have so long had translated. The Archdeacon says, "In respect to your version of the Psalms, it was the opinion of the Gentlemen of the Committee, that however corrupt the Portuguese spoken here may be, it not necessary to shew total disregard to number and gender, and particularly in a printed work under their sanction and support. To me and Mr. Armour was consigned the task of acting as moderators between your Portuguese and the high Portuguese, and it is the medium adopted by me and Mr. Armour in our preaching, which is reported to me to be intelligible by our hearers. I wish certainly that number and gender should be adhered to, where the pronounciation or sound of the word is not so much altered as not to be understood. The addition of *s* in the plural cannot surely obscure the word, or *a* feminine, instead of *o* masculine &c. You will neither give me nor Mr. Armour much trouble if you will take care of these matters in the proof copies that you send us; we shall not probably differ much in other points, &c." I hope to be able so far to attend to it as to get it through the press in a short time, and rejoice exceedingly that I am thus favoured with the opportunity while I am here for a little while to relieve me from more laborious exertion. The Brethren of the Book Committee have also lately sanctioned the printing of the *Liturgy*, &c. in the same language, which I have likewise had by me some time, translated of necessity from time to time chiefly, for the use of my own congregation, and which will form with the Psalms, I cannot doubt, a very useful help to our people of that class, either in their public or private devotions. Both will be printed in the same size as Brother Clough's Singhalese Liturgy, for the convenience of binding together.

I feel one only wish,—to live entirely engaged in the blessed service of God, or to die to behold his glory; often I am at a loss to determine, when I silently meditate on the blessedness of both, which at the present to prefer; this however is happily not left to our choice, it is ours to believe and obey, to labour and to suffer in "Jesu's work below," assured that He will take care for the rest. Happy he who can attain to that degree of Christian elevation in which he can truly adopt the language of the blessed Apostle, *"For me to live is Christ and to die is gain."* I remain, very dear Brethren, with increasing regard and esteem,

most affectionately yours in our Lord Jesus,
ROBERT NEWSTEAD.

⁕ Although some of the preceding letters are long, and the difficulty of printing them is great, where the English work will not justify a large establishment in that department, every effort will be used to print the unabridged records of the labours of the Brethren communicated to the Editor; for as they are gratifying to us, they will doubtless be equally esteemed by the Committee, who are assured of our labours, and justly expect records of them.

But the Editor must be indulged if the Quarterly Extracts are a little delayed, as our general work, supposing we could always ensure the health of our workmen, may some times unavoidably delay their publication. Some of the numbers have contained about 140,000 letters which, if printed in the type and form of our 8vo Hymn book, would form a volume of the same size, and when it is added that they cost us 40 £. per annum the Editor will be justified in not making them the whole labour of the press.

EDITOR.

THE CALTURA STATION.

Caltura, October 12, 1820.

MY DEAR BRETHREN,

The arrival of this date reminds me of my engagement to contribute my mite as usual to our quarterly communications, and though I have nothing very particular to state respecting the work of the circuit, during the last three months, yet I should be sorry to deny myself the privilege of writing to you. I have to acknowledge the continuation of that divine goodness and mercy to myself and family which we have ever experienced: on the 23d of August my dear partner was safely delivered of a daughter, and has been blessed with a safe recovery, though it has been slow, and our dear little girl is doing well; now certainly in our circumstances on this station, these are mercies for which we cannot be sufficiently thankful, for if medical aid, *properly so called,* had been required, we could not have obtained it here, but our Heavenly Father knew our condition, and was pleased in great mercy to shew us his salvation. Since her confinement Mrs. M'Kenny's health has been very delicate; indeed, so much so that I thought it would be necessary to afford her the advantage of a change of air, but I am happy to witness in her these few weeks past a very considerable improvement, so as to render it unnecessary to leave the station. You will all I am sure kindly excuse my being so particular about these little domestic matters, as I know the affectionate concern which exists among us respecting every part of our Mission family.

For the last three months I have been perhaps more busily employed than is consistent with duty or good health in such a climate as this, but in fact at present I have no alternative; however I have the prospect of deliverance, and that at no distant period, as the new Mission House will be finished in a week or two, and the Chapel I hope to have completed about the end of December.

I have no reason to be discouraged respecting the work of God here, our congregations in English, Portuguese and Singhalese are tolerably regular, and very attentive, and latterly I have been greatly pleased to witness a considerable increase to our Singhalese hearers, and I trust this pleasure will be still more when we have our Chapel built.

My excellent pious and zealous assistant comes up in every respect to my wishes, and is a great comfort to me as well as a help in my labours. I shall notice one thing which you will be pleased to hear, which is his great improvement in the Singhalese language; when I took him up at Galle he did not know a letter of the alphabet, but now he not only reads fluently the Liturgy and such plain works, but also the New Translation of the Testament, so that now he goes through his work without any assistance. He has an excellent Singhalese scholar as his teacher, and I am greatly pleased to mark his industry in going forward towards a proper knowledge of the classic works in the language; in addition to this his English reading is considerable, and he is always ready to hold forth *the word of life.*

> I am, dear Brethren,
> affectionately yours,
> J. M'KENNY.

THE GALLE AND AMBLANGODDE STATION.

Galle, September 28, 1820.

VERY DEAR BRETHREN,

My beloved superintendent having just returned from Matura, and being much engaged with the accounts &c. relating to the stations under his care; has requested me to write the present quarterly.

Through the varying scenes of our Missionary labours and in all the events of our lives, we are comforted and protected by the love and power of God Almighty. Our class consists chiefly of pious soldiers, who attend regularly, and manifest much sincerity and earnestnes in their religious experience. Amongst them we recognise the genuine tokens of a spiritual work: and we thank God for the appearance and actual existence of real Methodism, in this region of darkness and desolation. Their disinterested love and attention to the means of grace, their habitual seriousness and upright conversation in the midst of many and great temptations are some of the fruits by which they are known. Many of these honest men *look on him whom they have pierced and mourn;* they feel how insupportable is a wounded spirit and their hearts are powerfully affected by that sorrow which worketh repentance unto life. Others, impelled by the dread of endless misery, and encouraged by the promise of the Gospel are agonizing to enter in at the strait gate, and some of them *have found him of whom Moses in the law and the Prophets did write.* We have also the happiness to state, that some of the officers at Galle are enquiring after religious truths, amongst these is Lieutenant Monck, a young gentleman from Ireland, of a respectable family. He came to Galle in a low state of mind, but through the blessing of God on the wise and tender treatment of Mr. Erskine, he is now truly pious, and such is the influence of grace in every heart, so constraining is the love of Christ, that Mr. Monck meets in class with private soldiers and rejoices that he was ever invited to that blessed means of grace. In all respects he merits our highest praise, and evinces how amiable and interesting a character is produced when religion influences the affections and meekness and firmness are united This pious officer has taken up his abode at our Mission House, intending to return home as soon as possible.

Every Sunday evening the Mission Chapel is well attended by a mixed congregation who come to hear a sermon in Portuguese. It is true we entertain doubts as to their religious sentiments and have but little evidence of their inward piety. The circumstance of their attendance is however encouraging, and proves that they reverence divine ordinances; for there is little in our Portuguese preaching calculated to gratify curiosity or to lull the awaking sinner to insensibility. Our school system continues in active operation and claims the best of our time and attention, and we do humbly hope that it is one of the means which God will employ in bringing in the *fulness of the gentiles.* Some of the boys have made surprising progress in various knowledge, this is especially the case with those schools which from their situation can be seen by one of us almost every day. Losing sight of the schools our [prospects of usefulness amongst the Singhalese, are still cheerless. The gross immorality and base ingratitude, the unparalleled deceitfulness and astonishing unconcern manifested daily by the natives deeply affect us in common with our Brethren, but we do not lose sight of the power of divine grace which can melt and pierce the hardest heart : we think of the universal compassion of him who gave his life a ransom for ALL. We anticipate with joy and encouragement, *the latter day glory*. From the sure word of prophecy we know that *Messiah's dominion will stretch from sea to sea and from the river unto the ends of the earth*. Our experience convinces us that God is love, and that Jesus is precious to them that believe, and we shall be

> Happy if with our latest breath,
> We may but gasp his name,
> Preach him to all, and cry in death
> Behold, behold the Lamb!

Yours affectionately,
SAMUEL ALLEN.

THE MATURA STATION.

Matura, September 30, 1820

DEAR BRETHREN,

The paucity of interesting occurrences in the sphere of our labour makes quarterly writing something like almanack writing. Yet I think I must once more tell you what you have often heard and in general know, that I am going on in my usual way. My Portuguese congregation still continues good, and I hope that their attention is not altogether in vain. The schools on this station are I think improving, but for all the rest we must still hope.

With feelings of sincerest regard for every one of you, I am as usual,

Your affectionate Brother,
A. HUME.

THE TRINCOMALIE STATION.

Trincomalie, October 12, 1820.

MY DEAR BRETHREN,

The unexpected circumstances into which we were plunged by the misfortunes of our dear shipwrecked Sister and Brethren, who were mercifully saved from the conflagration of the *Tanjore*, consumed by the lightning near this place, will more than apologize for the brevity of this letter. We have been unable to give you our small communication in the usual time for the same reasons as above mentioned.

Our Christian course of duty has been pursued in nearly the manner as our former letters have stated. Our religious services have, on many occasions become more beneficial and interesting, and our hopes of doing good have very much increased. Having completed, nearly, our late enlargement of the Mission House, our time which has been taken from us by very unprofitable duties, is returning into our hands, and we find no small pleasure in more regularly resuming our Mission work.

Since last we had the pleasure to address you, our station has been visited by Brother Squance, previous to going to the coast. His visit was beneficial to our people and to ourselves, and we hope his appointment to Negapatam, where he now is, will be made a blessing to many precious souls. He preached in one of our schools in the native language and expressed great satisfaction at the orderly and becoming behaviour of the scholars, as well as at the serious attention of the adult part of the congregation, which he observed, he had never at any school seen more numerous. It was very pleasing to observe several females, who sat a little hearing for themselves, go out suddenly and bring others in to hear also! Were we silent in offering praises to the Lord for his great mercies to us, when sudden calls into an eternal world strike pale the unthinking sinner, we might justly be ashamed before Almighty God, but for continual health to labour in the vineyard we can individually adopt the language of confidence, " *My mouth shall shew forth thy righteousness and thy salvation all the day, for I know not the numbers thereof.*" It is our melancholy duty to notice the premature death of another very worthy man, to whom we were under obligations of thankful respect for having rendered to our own Brethren and other Missionaries the most ready advice and help. In August last died suddenly Dr. Thomas Rodgers of the Naval Hospital. He fell a victim to the cholera. On Saturday evening he was in the best health, at the Mission House, kindly attending Br. Squance's little infant, which was indisposed, the attack of cholera commenced on Sunday and on Monday evening he was interred! So short, so futile is human life! M. Wellington, Esq. master-shipwright, of the Naval yard, died of the cholera the same day! Since these deaths, however, few others have taken place.

Another circumstance will close my letter. On Sept. 7, about 3 P. M. being both of us from home we were hastily informed of a ship being burnt between this place and Batticaloa, and that the passengers had escaped in open boats, among whom were three Missionaries: one a lady. We reached home with all expedition possible, but found the gentleman (J. Bellingall, Esq. Storekeeper to the Naval department, who had most kindly brought, in his carriage, our two Brethren and Sister from the boats in which they had made their escape) had taken them to his own house on not finding the Missionaries at home. To his house we quickly followed, and found to our inexpressible joy that all the passengers and crew were safely landed.

Our Brethren and others were dressing, in wearing apparel which the gentleman had provided, and soon afterwards they were able to recount to us their misfortunes. Their sun burnt appearance and tattered garments had given us some idea of the sufferings they had endured and their narrow escape. It was with no small trouble that I could persuade Mr. Bellingall to give up any of his guests, for he had got possession: but after dinner, we all met at the Mission House. Br. Hoole had gone before and Br. and Sister Mowat joined us in the evening, when we all united in solemn thanksgiving to Almighty God for his sparing mercies. Alexander, the Singhalese priest, came in also, and we made suitable preparation for all as far as our ability would permit. And it was very providential that our house was enlarged, for had such an accident taken place earlier we should have had no place of shelter for our Brethren. The gentlemen resident at Trincomalie displayed that kind and hospitable feeling which was highly honourable to themselves and thankfully acknowledged by the passengers in distress. And I would mention with the highest respect, the very great readiness with which Mrs O'Connell sent down dresses for the ladies, and her earnest desire to render them personal attendance had not indisposition prevented. Our sincere thanks are due to Commissioner Upton for that readiness with which he dispatched boats to bring in the passengers from their exposed situation, and afterwards condescending to call in his carriage, when passing the Mission House, and kindly offering every thing in his house that might be of service to us; and also, for causing to be provided with such expedition. H. M. Schooner to give a convenient and speedy passage to Madras.

To these kind and benevolent persons, and to many others, who manifested their anxious desires to render themselves in any way serviceable to the distressed passengers and sailors, grateful acknowledgements are due.

On the 15th September the passengers embarked at the Dock yard in H. M. Schooner Cochin, and stood off, with *three cheers* to Madras; thus quitting their friends at Trincomalie, where tenderness towards each other had been heightened by circumstances of distress.

My colleague Br. Stead unites with me in affectionate love to the Brethren.

ROBERT CARVER.

THE JAFFNA STATION.

Mission House, Jaffna, October 18, 1820.

MY DEAR BRETHREN,

It is now near eight months since I came to this station, various have been my fears, but the Lord has been faithful to his word. Since our last we have established a quarterly collection which is generally approved of. We have also commenced a Tamul service in the school every Sabbath morning, this is conducted by a young man who was converted under the ministry of the first Brethren that arrived in this place.

A few weeks ago I baptised a young man, he appears desirous of being a real Christian. Our Portuguese congregation is generally good and we have reason to hope that we do not labour in vain. Our English congregation is certainly very cheering; there is not a more regular reverential people; the glory be given to God. In the course of the last quarter some have been convinced of the folly of their ways, but alas! they have not obeyed these convictions. Not long ago a gentleman came to the preaching, (he was stranger) the text was "thou art weighed in the balances and found wanting." I observed him for a considerable time appear unsettled, at last he took up his hat and walked hastily out of the chapel; the reason he assigned for his conduct was this, Mr Roberts had weighed him so many times and he had so often been found wanting that he determined to be weighed no more. This is a strong proof of the depravity of human nature: we may convince the mind but God alone can change the heart. We have long felt great inconvenience for want of some thing to warn the congregation of the precise time of divine service; our kind friend Mr. Moovaart proposed a bell, to this we agreed: the friends have subscribed 170 Rds. towards the expence. Most of our members are truly alive to God; they have long had to bear the laugh and jest of their neighbours but these things have only strengthened them in their hope; they now begin to act a little on the offensive, their families and friends are warned to flee from the wrath to come, and I assure you the work is not done by halves, the people are told in plain terms what they are to expect if they die impenitent, that their lot must be amongst those whose business it is to weep and wail and gnash their teeth.

Our sacramental occasions are generally of the most solemn and affecting kind for Christ is never absent: "tears of joy our eyes o'er-flow." Last Monday the monthly prayer meeting was held at our house, there were ten Missionaries present including ourselves: it is truly gratifying to see those sent out by different societies unite in solemn prayer for each others prosperity, surely this is the spirit of the Gospel, may we ever continue to cherish these pleasing relations!

The last quarter many of our schools have been visited by affliction but they are now a little on the improve. The Point Pedro schools have been visited twice the last month but we cannot expect much good to result from them without a resident Missionary; there are seven parishes connected with Pt. Pedro, which according to the census of 1814 contain twenty-six thousand (26000) souls. In the Jaffna circuit where we have schools already established there are twenty thousand (20000) and to minister to these forty six thousand (46000) souls there are to two Missionaries who have each to compose an English sermon every week, to preach in Portuguese, to study languages, to superintend schools, and to perform many other duties connected with the sacred office. The whole district contains one hundred and three thousand eight hundred and forty nine (103349) and to explain to these the words of everlasting life there are ten Missionaries; seven sent out by the American society, one by the Church, and two by the Methodists: what can we do amongst so many? it is true we scatter here and there some good seed but for want of watering it becomes parched and dies. If we had two Missionaries stationed at Pt. Pedro, and one at Puttoor, there would be a probability of doing good; then we might easily communicate our thoughts, our hopes, our fears. I believe it is almost impossible for our friends in England rightly to appreciate the importance of this subject. I was nearly five months without seeing the face of a Brother or even a white face, (except a poor solitary Magistrate) and sometimes I was surrounded with water, scarcely a native would come

near our cottage as it is close upon the sea-beach numbers of them
were dying of the Cholera morbus, these circumstances have taught
me to value the advice and the consolations of a Brother. I am fully
persuaded that no one should be alone, and particularly in such a
place as Pt. Pedro. Puttoor would make a most delightful station,
it has good chuch which for little expence might be made fit for
public worship; the Brother stationed there might come to Jaffna
once a month which would serve to keep alive the energies of his
mind and warm the affections of his heart. But I must conclude,
Br. Bott joins yours most affectionately,

JOSEPH ROBERTS.

THE BATTICALOA STATION.

Batticolou, September 29, 1820,

MY DEAR BRETHREN,

The 29th of September is arrived before the printed extracts of
June the 29th, so that I am under the necessity for the sake of order
and regularity to write again before I have the pleasure of reading
your communications for the last quarter. I was not willing to put
off the time *appointed* for writing, for if there should be the same want
of punctuality in writing as in printing we can scarcely expect to be
favoured with more than two quarterlies in a year. But no doubt
some satisfactory reason, of which some of us are at present ignorant,
will be given by the *Brethren* who know the cause of this delay.*

I shall therefore proceed, hoping that the above remark may be con-
strued only as expressive of *that* peculiar pleasure I have in reading the
letters of my Brethren, which cannot quietly be disappointed for two
months.

The study of the Native character is certainly an important part of
a Missionary's work, and especially respecting their religious views and
prejudices, which they endeavour to hide from *us* as much as possible.
The more I am acquainted with the natives of this place the more
I am convinced of their deplorable ignorance and utter unwillingness
to be instructed; little as their minds seem capable of effort they are
watchful, ready and crafty in their defence of their religion. In this
they appear far above themselves, for when from their simplicity of
manners and total want of religious knowledge you begin to entertain
sanguine hopes of soon impressing their minds with the importance of
divine truth and of conducting them into the enjoyment of a pure
faith and divine morality, you soon discover that their ignorance and
superstition are invincible. Their regard for ancestry respecting religion as well as rank is such a principle of conscientious obligation that
were it not for the unfailing promises of God that this people shall be
subdued to the obedience of the Gospel through him who has power to
subdue all things to himself I should despair of the object of their
evangelization ever being accomplished. But within this last week I
have observed that upon every occasion of religious worship they are
careful that no part of their family is left behind, even the infants that

* For an explanation of this cause see Colombo letter.

are not able to walk are carried in the arms. The nature of their ceremonies are well calculated to attract the notice of the children; and
the noisy tomtoms and trumpets, with the gesticulations of the priests
and other performers on such occasions cannot fail to please and make
the children anxious for the return of such devotions: thus from the
least to the greatest they are taught to reverence the priest, to follow
the religion of their parents in adoring a wooden or a stone god, to
offer sacrifices to devils, and to be under the tyranny of a cruel and
absurd superstition, which teaches them to bow to various trees as they
pass them, or to put money into an ola bag (slung from one of the
branches for the purpose) to appease the devil who is supposed to
dwell in this tree that he may do them no injury.

Upon such occasions of festivity my schools are deserted, except a
few who are Catholics, these taking their turns in their various religious frolics, which are made so similar on many occasions to the
parade of the Gentoo's worship that a stranger would not be able to
distinguish between the one and the other.

I am often grieved to see so many new faces in my schools, the
number is generally kept up through the policy of the master whose wages
is regulated by it, but very few continue in the school long enough to
give me an opportunity of doing them much good. The object of
their parents appears to be only to have them capable of reading their
own books. But still I labour in hope. Many of the boys have transcribed the Catechism into their ola books, also the Lord's Prayer, the
Creed, and the Ten Commandments. These books are carried to their
houses and read there. These are far preferable to paper books which
last them but a short time, and are always considered *our* books, whereas those written an ola are more likely to be preserved and read.

Some of the boys have made large extracts from the Book of Common Prayer which they use in the School on Sunday mornings when
they attend public worship, which is but seldom and compulsion is out
of the question.

In one of the Tamul schools in the country I have service every
Sabbath morning at eleven o'clock, and generally a goodly number of
adults are present as well as most of the school boys; at another of
those places I expect next Sunday to commence divine service, the
same man who officiates in one will take the other in the afternoon.
I am sorry my engagements in Batticaloa will not allow me to attend
to this work sometimes myself.

The girls are getting on well with their sewing work, but very
slowly indeed with reading, for in the first place they have an objection *themselves* to learn to read, and their *parents* do not much wish
them to acquire knowledge of this kind, and in the next place there is
a great difficulty respecting the languages. The school sometimes
appears like the Tower of Babel when the confusion of languages took
place, I frequently hear nearly at the same time English, Dutch, Portuguese, Tamul and Malay spoken. I often need two interpreters in
order to be understood. The school mistress cannot teach Tamul
and does not understand English. The girls at present are spelling in
English but understand little or nothing of the language. If they study
the Ceylon Portuguese there are no books in that language, and those

who can write the low Portuguese always spell it after the Dutch form, using the k for the q &c. (i. e.) aquel (or aquelle) *that*, is spelt akkel, so that those who can read and write Portuguese cannot so much as read a chapter of the New Testament in low Portuguese. I intend to send a boy from the Tamul school to teach one part of them Tamul, and those of European descent shall be taught to read and write English.

I am not without hope that some of this seed cast into so many different soils will one day spring up and bear fruit.

On the evening of the 5th ult. about 7 o'clock the supercargo of the ship Tanjore came into my house, as it was the first in which he saw an European and being an entire stranger at Batticaloa (indeed did not know exactly that he had made Batticaloa) and informed me he had brought on shore Sir R. Otley and the Revd. T. Browning and wife : I hasted to the wharf and conducted all to my house. I was informed there were two Wesleyan Missionaries on board bound for Madras, but from the Captain's great haste to proceed were not allowed to come on shore. I intended going on board the next morning, but the vessel being anchored so far from land and having to procure vessels to bring Sir. R. O's baggage on shore I was not able to go.

I need say nothing of the melancholy accident which befel the Tanjore, as Br. Carver will doubtless give you the particulars as he received them from the mouth of the Brethren who were the painful witnesses of the terrific scene.

Brother and Sister Squance have lately paid us their farewell visit upon leaving Ceylon for Negapatam. I should have been very sorry to lose such a Br. from this side the Island were I not fully convinced that the climate of Jaffna will never agree with him, his life having been despaired of the two last rainy seasons, one of which I witnessed myself with no small degree of alarm. I have always had a particular regard for Brother Squance, and have been favoured by spending more than half my time I have been in India under his superintendence. The Lord has owned his labours in Jaffna and I have no doubt will also in Negapatam.

Our winter now begins to approach and my habitation is not at all in a state of repair to stand another such a season as last year was. The owner refuses to do any more repairs, but a little must be done or I expect it will fall about my ears. I have a great objection to expend any money on a premises which does not belong to the Mission, but as the rains are so tremendous I shall be under the necessity of doing a little. In dry weather the house is good and strong, but being built with unburnt bricks it melts away upon the touch of water. I am now under the necessity of thinking about what I must eat and what I must drink, &c. &c. as in a few weeks we shall all be shut up in the Island of Batticaloa for 4 months as Noah was in his Ark.

Mrs. Osborne and the children I am thankful to say are doing well : Batticaloa is the best climate we have experienced since we left home. But few people *who take care of themselves* are sickly here. But the best of all is " The Lord *is* with us" and thus our every blessing is blest and our every trial sanctified. Farewell.

I am Dear Brethren,
Yours ever affectionately,
T. OSBORNE.

THE MADRAS STATION.

Madras, October 19, 1820.

My DEAR BRETHREN,

Since my last to you God has very graciously brought two other Brethren and a Sister to Madras, of whose most providential and miraculous escape you no doubt have heard. I have no doubt but you will approve of their remaining at Madras until they acquire some knowledge of the native language, and their constitutions become a little seasoned to the climate. In all other respects our work goes on nearly as usual, our congregations are still increasing in town, and I believe the society is more alive to God than at any past period, our last sacrament and love-feast were crowned with the presence of the Lord. I rejoice to say that all the Brethren appear happy and truly engaged in their work. I have nearly finished two school houses one 1½ miles, and another 5 miles from the Mission house, and hope in these place to have opportunities of preaching the Gospel to the natives. A few days ago one of our native class died, and was the first interred in our Mission burying ground. On the 10th instant, Alexander, one of the Singhalese priests came here from Trincomalie, when I found that he could not read Tamul. The Brethren and I agreed that he should go to Ceylon, but as he evidenced great unwillingness to this we agreed to allow him to remain in case he would commence the study of the Tamul language, and also attend to our directions and instructions. On Monday 16th he requested a boy to go with him to town, and promised to return the same night. On Tuesday morning I received a note from him requesting me to send his box, as he found a Dhony just going. I wrote that as he did not let me know where he was going I would not send the box until he came to see me; he came in the evening but refused to let me know where he was going; I gave him his box, and so he left us. I have been greatly disappointed in him, and most sensibly feel for the public in England. I believe he is gone to Ceylon, but unless a change takes place in him for the better I fear he will do us and the cause of God little credit. But still he is in the hand of God, and as he is saved from idolatry, he may be brought to humble himself to God, and yet be useful. I remain in Gospel love, your's,

JAMES LYNCH.

Madras, October 19, 1820.

VERY DEAR BRETHREN,

The peculiar circumstances of our arrival in India lay us under the most pressing obligations to the exercise of the most lively gratitude to that God who has delivered us from most imminent danger and crowned our spared lives with loving kindness and tender mercies. The particulars of our shipwreck are generally known to you, and we have to acknowledge the receipt of letters from several of the Brethren evincing their sympathy and affection. The truly Christian love and hospitality manifested by our Brethren Messrs,

Carver and Stead, at our first arrival at land, and by the Brethren
at Madras, have certainly raised the confidence that we shall live
in the affection and prayers of all the Brethren and that God will
indeed bless us and make us a blessing. We do thank God sincerely
that the late dispensation of his providence has not been lost upon
us, and we trust that an increased love to Jesus and to the souls
of our fellow men are blessings not purchased at too dear a rate.
It is proposed that one of us, Br. Hoole, should proceed to Negapatam for a few months to assist Br. Squance, and that the other
remain at Madras till after the monsoon. We have commenced the
study of the Tamul and hope by the blessing of God at a future
period to preach to the people in their own language the Gospel
of God our Saviour, we rejoice in the work in which we are engaged. The work of God is prospering in Madras and we trust
that many will soon testify the power of the Saviour to forgive.

We are, dear Brethren,

yours affectionately,

JAMES MOWAT,

ELIJAH HOOLE.

Miscellaneous.

No. I.

PROCEEDINGS

OF A

MEETING HELD AT NEGOMBO, SEPTEMBER 25th 1820,

FOR THE PURPOSE OF FORMING

An Auxiliary Wesleyan Missionary Society.

ON the 25th September, 1820, a numerous and respectable meeting of the inhabitants of the town of Negombo was convened in the Wesleyan Mission Chapel of that place, for the purpose of considering the necessity and propriety of establishing an Auxiliary Wesleyan Missionary Society, to co-operate with the parent Society in London. The service commenced at half past 11 o'clock in the morning. In addition to the resident Missionaries and their Assistants, the Meeting was favoured with the presence of the Rev. J. Chater, Baptist Missionary, and the Rev. Messrs. Fox, and Clough, Wesleyan Missionaries. The following Resolutions were unanimously agreed upon, which were introduced to the Meeting by appropriate and animating speeches, and created unusual interest among the people, leaving on their minds the deepest impressions of the importance of Missionary exertions, and the necessity of vigorous individual assistance.

RESOLVED, I.—That this Meeting very highly approves of the spirit and object of Missionary Societies in general, in diffusing the religion of Jesus Christ throughout the world, and particularly most cordially rejoices in the labours and success of that Society in London called *The General Wesleyan Methodist Missionary Society.*

RESOLVED, II.—That many persons present having been much benefited by the Society's exertions are desirous of testifying their gratitude to God and the Society by forming themselves into an Association to be called, *The Negombo Auxiliary Wesleyan Methodist Missionary Society.*

RESOLVED, III.—That the sole object of this Society be to assist the parent Society in its great and increasing exertions throughout the world, but especially in *Ceylon,* by raising contributions to its funds, either by weekly, monthly, quarterly, or yearly subcriptions or donations, to be transmitted to the Committee, or appropriated as they shall direct in carrying on the work of God in this Island.

RESOLVED, IV.—That a Committee be chosen, and a Treasurer, Secretary and General Collector immediately appointed, to carry into effect the object of the Society.

RESOLVED, V.—That the Treasurer, Secretary, and General Collector, shall be the Missionaries on the Negombo Station for the time being.

RESOLVED, VI.—That the Committee shall meet on the first Monday of every month, in Negombo when the business of the Society shall be transacted, and the members attend the usual Missionary Prayer Meeting, held on those days in the Mission Chapel, on which occasions Missionary intelligence from all parts of the world shall be read in the intervals of prayer.

RESOLVED, VII.—That every person subcribing a Pice Weekly, a Fanam Monthly, or Rix Dollar Yearly, shall be considered Members of this Society, and entitled to attend its meetings.

RESOLVED, VIII.—That an Anniversary Meeting shall be held in the Wesleyan Mission Chapel in Negmobo, with a Report published of the Proceedings of the Society and a list of Subcribers.

RESOLVED, IX.—That the Schoolmasters of the Negombo Station shall be collectors for the Society in their different neighbourhoods, and that suitable books, &c. be furnished for their use.

No. II.

THE LOSS OF THE TANJORE.

Extract of a letter from Brother Carver to W. B. Fox.

Trincomalie September 9, 1820.

My dear Brother Fox,

Yesterday about 3 o'clock we were surprised to hear the rumour of a ship burnt by lightning on the outside of this harbour, some where between this place and Batticaloa, which proved lamentably true by the arrival of two of our Brethren and a Sister who had come passengers in her from England, who with most of the crew had escaped from her in open boats but without any provision or water, except a handful of biscuit and one bottle wine. It appears they left England May 20th, and made no call at any port. They lost sight of the Lizard point June 2d and saw Ceylon September 3d, could not make Pt. de Galle and steered for Trincomalie, anchored a few hours in the night at Batticaloa, Sept. 5th, and landed the Honble Sir Richard Ottley, his Secretary, and another, and *Adam*, one of the Budhuist priests, with all letters and packages for the Ceylon Mission; did not see Br. Osborne, and sailed on the 6th at one P. M. for Madras, Mr. and Mrs. Browning, C. M. were also safely landed at Batticaloa.

While yet in sight of land on the 6th, at 6 P. M. Saw a gathering storm; at 8½ tremendous thunder and lightning came on, which struck the vessel, tore out the bowels of one sailor and knocked another on the head, who fell dead half over the shipside and hung there till dragged on deck by another man. Suddenly smoke issued from the hold, and flames on the hatches being removed: the long boat was inveloped with flame and totally lost, and the other two boats with difficulty launched. Happily those who were undressed, with the rest of the passengers and crew, succeeded in gaining these two small barks, being nearly 50 people, and with but three oars only and one rudder they struggled hard to escape the range of the flames which awfully increased, and by the vessel drifting after them seemed to threaten a protracted fate. The burning ship illumined the whole hemisphere and gave awful proof of the power of the element which consigned all their effects to destruction, while yet another seemed ready to swallow them up in a watery grave. As their consuming ship diminished day-light approached and gladdened every heart with a sight of land; with great labour for 16 hours, crowded in small boats, they made a country vessel and all, with the two females were brought in safe to Trincomalie. The kindness of Commissioner Upton, and Mr. Bellingal and others were highly manifested, and deserve our warmest thanks. The Brethren and Sister are well, but have lost every thing they had, as also Alexander the priest who is with us, Excuse my haste. Accept of our love, and I know you will join us in grateful praise to Almighty God.

R. CARVER.

Extract from the Ceylon Government Gazette.

On the 15th instant the report of the arrival of the Free Trader *Tanjore*, and the landing of Sir Richard Ottley from her at Batticaloa, was received at Colombo,

Sir Richard we understand proceeded to Trincomalie for the purpose of setting off from thence through Kandy to the Seat of Government.

Soon after the report above mentioned was received in Colombo, an express arrived from the Collector of Trincomalie under date the 8th instant, announcing the unfortunate destruction of the *Tanjore* by lightning off Vandeloo's bay about 30 miles from the shore.— We regret to say that two seamen lost their lives.

The following are the particulars of this melancholy event as stated in the Collector of Trincomalie's dispatch.

The *Tanjore* left the Downs on the 23d May for Madras and Bengal, with Sir R. Ottley, Puisne Justice of Ceylon, on board—It was the master's intention to touch at Galle for the purpose of landing Sir Richard, but contrary winds and currents prevented him from doing so — They coasted along the S Eastern shore of the Island until the 5th instant, when off Batticaloa Sir Richard, and the other passengers for this island, were landed together with the mails for Ceylon.

On the 6th when standing on for Madras on the Trincomalie side of Vandeloo's Bay and about 30 miles from the shore, at ½ past 4 P. M. the Ship was struck by lightning and instantly took fire.—The people on board had hardly time to lower the boats, and secure their own safety by flight before she was in a state of general conflagration, and save the clothes they had on, and a chest of dollars that was in the after cabin, nothing was saved. They pulled all night towards the shore, and in the morning fell in with a Galle dhoney bound to Madras, which received, and landed them at Trincomalie on the evening of the 7th inst — On the morning of 7th, the wreck was still seen smoking from the boats.

Two seamen Thomas Phillips and John Williams were killed by the lightning.

No. III.

The following is a part of a letter I lately received from the Portuguese young man I brought from our little class in Jaffna who has been under the necessity of leaving me in consequence of severe affliction.

As it cannot but be gratifying to my Brethren to discover through his broken English such a strain of unfeigned piety, I submit it for insertion in the Miscellaneous part of our Quarterly correspondence.

THOMAS OSBORNE.

REVEREND AND DEAR SIR,

I arrived here on Sunday the 2d of April last, soon after, or on Monday the 3rd, the disease grew so severely hard that I was entirely out of my sense, talking all unmeaning languages, and in every thing

I was nothing but perfectly mad and the fits returned every little time with increasing severity, so that all who saw me entertained very few or no hope of my recovery, all these I have now from my friends who then saw me, but of myself I cannot recollect or don't know any thing at all what passed about three or four weeks before I was restored a little to health. My residence here, since I arrived, was at the house of my niece who is married to one Mr. J. Wambeek; it was the Lord that brought me under the care of these two, for their kindness and love which they shew, in their efforts for my recovery were no less different to that tender and affectionate loving endeavours which the tenderest of parents would bestow upon their children. By the grace of God the remedies used by a Tamul doctor for the cure of that grievous disorder, made their happy effect, and sometimes ago rescued me from the disorder, and now I am only weak in body, and hope very soon to be restored to my former state of perfectness.

The recollection of this peculiar goodness which the Lord in his tender compassion has shewn to me the vilest of his rational creatures, puts me into an awful silence before him, not knowing how or in what manner to express my gratitude for this kind benediction: but coming to the conclusion with which I satisfy myself, is this) to render unto him my whole soul and body a holy and acceptable sacrifice, being convinced that by no other means I can ever thank or please that God who for the sake of his beloved son our dear Saviour has (as it were) given me a new existence that I may live for his glory in future... Blessed be God, I have a sure trust that I will have my prayers answered, which are, that he may make me more and more thankful, yea, give me an entire thankful heart, that he will make me more like Jesus my Lord and Master, by giving me besides all a continual humble and loving disposition, that Christ may be formed in me the hope of glory, and as he has already given me to taste (even in a little degree) the pleasantness of religion, to make me perfect in holiness and in the end give me a place at his right hand.

Before I come to the conclusion of my letter, I wish not to be forgetful of all your goodness to me since the time I came under your care and direction, especially while I was at Batticaloa: Sir, I cannot be thankful enough to you for all that you have done to me; all the love and kindness which you have shewn to me are not like the dealings of many superiors towards those that are under them: indeed, Sir, you have not only been to me a worthy master but also a kind parent, so that it will be I judge an unpardonable fault on my side if I will ever attempt to charge you with any unkind dealing as done to me during the time of my stay with you: receive therefore I pray you my unfeigned and heartfelt gratitude, and be assured Sir, that if at any time there be any reciprocal service in which you will think that I can be obliged to you, I will as far as it lays in my power, endeavour to please you with such dutiful services: but after all let me not be thought by you that writing thus I do or intend to be flattering you, for to tell the truth, this is * not entirely the design of these my undissembled lines.

I have one thing more which I wish not to pass by uninforming, which is, that you will in addition to all that you have done to me

---

* Meaning not at all the design.

kindly to forgive me all the errors and misbehaviours which you have observed in me while with you, and not to hold all my failings behind unpardoned. so that they may not raise your displeasure towards me, for it regrets me to think that I have not been faithful and obliging enough to you as I should have been in return to all your goodness and love to me.

Wishing you all the blessings that a human heart can reasonably desire, and that the peculiar grace and favours of God may remain in your familly and on all what you do, I conclude with my best love and regard to you and Mrs. Osborne, as well as to Mr. Roelofsz, And remain with due regard and esteem,

Reverend and dear Sir,

your ever loving and truly humble servant,

FREDRICK HESLER.

No. IV.

ON THE LOVE OF GOD.

Communicated by Brother Osborne.

"Could ocean, rivers, springs, and lakes,

All that the name of water takes

Beneath the expanded skies,

Be turn'd to ink of blackest hue;

Add all the drops of falling dew

To make the wonder rise.

A Book as large could we suppose

As thinnest paper could compose,

As the whole earthly ball;

And every shrub and every tree,

And every blade of grass we see,

A pen to write withal.

Were all who ever lived on earth

Since nature first received her birth

Most skilful scribes, to place

In clearest light that wond'rous love

Found in the heart of God above

To Adam's sinful race;

Were each Methusalah in age

And every moment wrote a page

They'd all be tired and die,

The pens would every one wear out,

The book be fill'd with'n, without,

The ink be drain'd quite dry,

And then to tell that love, O then!!

Angels above as well as men,

Archangels e'en would fail;

Nay till eternity shall end

A whole eternity they'll spend

Nor then have told the tale.

Extracts

FROM

QUARTERLY LETTERS, &c.

No. XXV.   OCTOBER, 1824.

THE COLOMBO STATION.

Colombo, October 6th, 1824.

To the Rev. Messrs. BUNTING, TAYLOR, and WATSON.

REV. AND DEAR SIRS,

The work of our circuit during the past quarter has gone forward with much uniformity and regularity, not presenting many circumstances differing much from its general character, which has been too often described for you not distinctly to understand it. An account of the distressing sickness which has prevailed throughout the greater part of the Island formed an important feature in my last quarterly letter. I am now enabled, however, with feelings of inexpressible satisfaction and gratitude, to inform you that this painful visitation has been almost entirely removed; new cases of fever have been very rare for six weeks past; there are, it is true, many of the old ones still remaining, as it is exceedingly difficult for the natives to get the disease out of their constitutions when it has once got itself properly fixed.

The sickness was followed by so long a *drought* that a famine was calculated upon; and so formidable was the appearance of things that Government thought it necessary to adopt precautionary measures; but the rains have set in unusually early, and have continued to fall in sufficient quantity to renew the face of nature, and to cause the hearts of the afflicted natives to rejoice. The present state of things is favorable and promising; and all would be well, did the people but know and acknowledge the gracious hand from which their mercies flow.

I am sorry to say it becomes my duty now to record an event which will be deeply felt by all who have made themselves acquainted with the history of this mission. The Hon. and Ven. Doctor T. J. Twisleton, is no more! He died on the 15th

E

of August at Hambantotte, where he was with Mrs. Twisleton on a visit to his son in law William Gisborne Esq. His illness was short and his death very unexpected; the tidings produced in Colombo a sensation which I cannot attempt to describe! It is not an uncommon thing for persons of great consideration to quit the stage of time in these parts of the world
having little *said*, or *thought* about them, but how different the
case in question! quite a *depth* of feeling has manifested itself
amongst every class of inhabitants in the colony: and well there
might, for he was a constant and liberal friend of the poor,
he was kindness and condescension itself to his inferiors, and
his great urbanity of manners caused his society to be *court-
ed*, by those on a rank with himself. He took a lively interest in all the Christian and charitable institutions in the
colony, and was the ready and zealous promoter and suppor-
ter of every good work: and I am sorry to add, what indeed
you must be already aware of, that by Doctor Twisleton's
death, our mission has lost one of its best friends. By this
event the command is powerfully enforced *"cease ye from man."*
I have reason to believe from what I have lately heard, that
the late Archdeacon had something of a *Presentiment* of his
approaching death, and for several months was observed to
be unusually serious, alive, and zealous in the discharge of his
ministerial duties. Even when in the *country*, where he could
have few besides the members of the family to form his congregation, on the Sabbath he performed divine service and delivered a regular discourse. From the arrival of our Brethren on
the Island he discovered an evident predilection in favor of
our mode of preaching, and for *years* regularly attended our
chapel with his family, and although his appointment to the
Archdeaconry of Colombo required the observance of a line of
conduct somewhat different to that which he thought necessary
before the Introduction of an Ecclesiastical Establishment in
India, yet still he wished to hear us when he conveniently could,
and at our country stations laid aside the reserve he thought
proper to retain in Colombo and attended our Chapels: it is a
remarkable circumstance that the very last sermon he heard
preached was by Brother Callaway, at Galle!

On the 18th ultimo, I was called to sustain a very heavy
trial in being obliged to attend to the place of execution, (in
company with the Rev. Mr. Armour,) George Lawton, a private of H. M. 83d Regt. who was condemned for murdering
a native boy. Immediately after his condemnation he sent
for me, and however painful the summons, I could not but
obey; I continued to attend him till the mournful morning

on which he underwent the sentence of the law;* and, however great the tax might be which this duty laid upon my feelings, the satisfaction I derived from my intercourse with the unhappy convict, formed an ample compensation for the very acute sensations of distress which passed through my mind on witnessing a human being, and an *Englishman*, the subject of such sorrow, shame, and disgrace!

On first visiting him I found he had no disposition to say any thing by way of extenuation upon account of what he had done: he frankly confessed his guilt and acknowledged his sentence just. This I could not but regard as a favorable omen, a significant prognostic of what might be expected to take place, although I found him in a state of great ignorance as to religion, and without any expectation of the divine favor or hope of mercy; and although Messrs. Armour and Bridguell, with myself, laboured hard to give him a correct view of the plan of salvation by faith in Jesus Christ, the feeling of despair rather gained upon him than otherwise. However he attended to our counsel to use diligently the means of grace, and particularly to read the word of God and to give those parts especially to which we directed his attention, his serious consideration, which indeed he attended to with laborious assiduity, although for a considerable time without any comfort. However he did not seek in vain, for the Lord was pleased to give him sorrow after a godly sort; he was brought deeply to feel his sinfulness, and this feeling was of a very encouraging character as it was mingled with hope, and at times he could almost believe that there was mercy in the wounds of Jesus even for him; but again the enemy would come in like a torrent and fill his soul with the horrors of unbelief. Thus the contest went on until the last week of his confinement, when he began to find much more confidence and comfort in prayer, yet still his case was not fully satisfactory until the third day before his death, when he was entirely freed from every doubt and fear and was enabled to *rejoice* in the Lord. We looked on with much anxiety, trusting that this would continue, and we were not disappointed; his grand enemy was not suffered to come nigh him, and his peace and happiness continued uninterrupted. On the day preceding his death, he said, O this is the happiest day of my life, and by this time to-morrow I shall be in a glorious place! On the morning of his execution Mr. Armour and myself spent some time with him in conver-

---

* In this country a man under the sentence of death is always allowed about a *Month* to prepare for his end,

sation and prayer before he left the jail, and after we had
done he prayed himself aloud at some length with much life
and ardour. We left the prison about nine o'clock A. M. Lawton walked with a quick pace and much firmness to the fatal
spot, and read audibly from the general Hymn Book most of the
way: on coming to the place, we found him still in full possession of his confidence and breathing out his soul to God
in prayer and supplication. After we had commended him
to the mercy of an infinitely merciful God we took our leave; on
which he said, he wished for no delay; and added, stand near and
speak to me of Christ to the last! He ascended the ladder and
in a few seconds was launched into eternity; his last words
were, O Lord Jesus receive my soul!

It is a singular circumstance that this man was a *stranger* to
the boy he killed: he had only seen him a few times about
the barracks, and they had had no quarrel of any kind; but
Lawton was a notorious drunkard, and by the effects of his dissipation, and the punishments to which it subjected him, his
mind was worked into a state of desperation which made him
weary of life. First he thought of destroying *himself*, but afterwards came to the determination of killing some other person,
that in this way he might get out of the world! with this intention he loaded his musket, and the black boy whom he killed,
was the first person who afforded him an opportunity of carrying
into effect his cruel purpose!

It will give you pleasure to learn that this climate is likely to
agree remarkably well with Brother Bridgnell, my amiable and
worthy colleague. I only fear that the intensity of his application to the languages of the country, will in the end, affect his
health. The progress he has already made is very rare indeed:
he is quite efficient in Portuguese, and takes his regular appointments according to the circuit plan. He has also commenced to read publicly the Liturgy and Scriptures in Singhalese, and no doubt he will soon be prepared with Singhalese
Sermons enough, to make him independent of an interpreter.
Should his health continue as good as it is, he will have accomplished within a year, a work which twenty years ago was supposed out of the reach of any European to accomplish during
the period of his *natural life!*

Had we the number of Missionaries required and did our
means admit of it, there would exist no great difficulty in
extending our labours in the Kandian provinces, but at the
same time I conceive it only just to give it as my opinion that
the maritime provinces afford a much more inviting and encouraging prospect for successful Missionary exertions than

the interior of the country; however if both could enjoy the
benefit of Christian teaching it would be highly desirable, and
truly consoling to the benevolent mind. The following is an
extract from a letter I received a short time ago from our
particular friend, Major Audain, Commandant and Agent of
Government at Badula in the Kandian provinces, which I
transmit for the consideration of the Committee.

Badula, August 12, 1824.

My Dear Sir,

" I am more convinced every day of the very great advantages
this valley offers for a Missionary station. The Eastern provinces
which I command are extremely populous, and I have been applied
to by several of the Desaves and Headmen, who are very desirous
that their children should receive instruction. I am certain that
a Missionary here would meet with very great encouragement, and
that he would very shortly after his arrival have as large a school as
he could possibly attend to,—the Natives here are extremely ignorant
and would be happy to have the advantage of instruction; in short
I have known no situation so eligible for a Missionary as this On the
4th inst. I purpose writing to Government, inclosing a letter from Captain Mylius, Agent of Government at Alepota, offering a very excel-
cellent House that he has in Badula, newly built, for 650 Rixdollars:
there are two detached Houses within the distance of ten yards from
each other. One is a bungaloe containing a very large room with
virandas all around suitable for a School, the other is a dwelling house
consisting of two very good rooms and a sitting room, with excellent
offices attached to these, and nearly an acre of ground, the whole of
it a grant from Government. He has no use for it, and therefore wishes
to dispose of it for considerably less than it cost him. In my official
for the Governor's consideration, I purpose, strongly recommending
Badula as a Missionary Station, and shall state that the House is exceedingly well adapted for that purpose. I need not add that I shall
feel peculiar pleasure in giving every assistance, countenance and
support to whatever Missionary may come here."

We are all thank God quite well and I earnestly hope that my
Daughters and myself are growing in grace and in the knowledge
and love of our Saviour Jesus Christ. The late affliction has I
hope been blessed to us. Excuse this hasty scrawl as I am much
occupied; my Daughters wish, with me, our regards to Mrs. M'Kenny
and yourself, and believe me,

Very truly yours,

M. AUDAIN.

The Singhalese department of our printing concern still continues employed for the Society for Promoting Christian Knowledge, and the English is at present taken up in preparing
some books for our Schools, of which we have become almost
destitute. Brother Fox's Portuguese Testament and the En-

glish Hymn-book, have been completed, copies of which I
shall forward by the Ship Thames, which will sail for England in a few weeks.

On the 30th of last month, I had the pleasure of being present at the Fourth Aniversary of the Negombo Wesleyan Missionary Society, the meeting was well attended and very interesting indeed. Those little Societies, which are rising up in
the Island, will do much good.

                    With great respect and esteem I remain,
                              Reverend Sirs,
                                   very truly yours,
                                         J. M'KENNY.

                                   September 20th, 1824.

MY HONOURED FATHERS,

Distinguished as I am in being called to engage in the most
noble, the most important undertaking, that ever employed the
attention, or called forth the energies of man, I hope I shall
never, by any direlection of duty, or any deficiency of talent,
or zeal, produce in your minds a feeling of regret, that under
the influence of a misguided and too favourable judgment concerning me, you had appointed one to labour in a most important part of the Lord's Vineyard, who was unworthy of such
an honour, or incompetent to such a task. If I adhere to
the resolutions I have already ventured to state to you, and
by Divine help I shall, you will never have cause to regret my
appointment to the Ceylon Mission, on either of these grounds.

God, having formed the minds of men, as well their bodies,
upon the plan of universal variety, it can never be a matter
of surprise, that there should not be a *perfect uniformity* in
the *operations* of all Missionaries. Though they were all equally
holy, equally gifted, equally zealous, yet a diversity of *judgment*
in reference to the most efficient and successful mode of doing
good, must necessarily produce a corresponding variation in the
exertions of those honoured and happy men whom God has
chosen, and whom the church has sent out "to preach among
the gentiles the unsearchable riches of Christ." A variety of considerations arising out of peculiar circumstances, or local situation, must likewise tend to produce some difference, in the line
of conduct which the most matured judgment, and the most
sanctified heart, would deem adviseable or necessary. Pardon
me these observations: I presume not on such a subject to
throw any light into your minds, but I write them that you may
have a more perfect knowledge of mine. "Zeal without know-

ledge" I doubt not is useful, but zeal tempered, and regulated by Divine *knowledge*, and "the *wisdom* which cometh down from above," will be much more extensively, much more lastingly useful. However, I cannot conceal my fear, that I should be *too* calculating and wary in my exertions. It shall however be my care, to be equally zealous, and prudent; my study, to imitate the steady, unintermitted, unostentatious zeal of my Lord and Master; and my prayer, that I may be "full of Faith and of the Holy Ghost." As he who should attempt to take down a large edifice, by endeavouring *in the first place*, to root up the foundation, would most assuredly, either endanger his *life*, or his *reputation*, so on the contrary, I am careful not to *begin* wrong in the awfully great and difficult work before me: not indeed through any thing like a concern for my life or reputation (for if called upon, I would cheerfully sacrifice them both, to promote the interests of his cause, whose I am, and whom I serve,) but, I am fearful to commence my Missionary career, in any such way, as to cause the futility of my earliest efforts to breed discouragement, or check my subsequent and far more important exertions. However I sound no truce with the enemy, I contend *as I can* till I can do it *as I would*. My soul pants with real ambition, to be used as an instrument in the hand of "the Lord God Omnipotent," for accomplishing His gracious, and declared purposes, towards a world that, alas! even yet, "lieth in wickedness," and I labour constantly, in the exercise of a soul-elevating, soul-strenghtening Faith to realize the promises, of "the only true God, and Jesus Christ whom he has sent." In the moments of my deepest depression, and greatest suffering, since I left my native shores, I have not had the smallest regret that I had "LEFT ALL to follow Christ." I feel that "strong consolation," which the "two immutable things in which it is *impossible for God to lie*," are well calculated to afford. I might perhaps make more extensive progress in the learning of this world, had I remained at home, but this consideration weighs not with me, I esteem every thing on earth "less than nothing, and lighter than vanity," compared with Christ and his great salvation. The employment, and pleasures of those who "have their portion in this life," who live for themselves only, I account, the most striking, and awful contrast, to the noble exercises, and the refined enjoyments, of the thrice happy men, who are proclaiming in heathen nations, the name of the Saviour, through whose death and merits is preached unto us, "the forgiveness of sins," and the method of securing an inheritance, "incorruptible, undefiled, and that fadeth not away." I forward, through the medium of our quarterly publication of letters, these few observation connected with my feelings and experience, in the prospect of a long and I hope not the least successful service in the cause of Missions and of God. Other things I may well reserve for another occasion. I am happy to say that my health is uninterrupted, and that I have the *ability* as well as the *disposition* to apply closely to the languages of this country. I will speak of my *success* hereafter. The affectionate attentions of Brother and Sister M'Kenny are such as almost to make me forget, "I am a stranger in a strange land," and give me at once ample cause of gratitude to them, and to God.

Your obedient and devoted son in the Gospel,
WILLIAM BRIDGNELL.

THE NEGOMBO STATION.

Negombo, October 4, 1824.

REV. AND DEAR SIRS.

Since my last communication circumstances have occurred on this station which are highly calculated to excite grateful feelings towards Almighty God.

The pestilential fever, having visited almost every house, and crowded our burying-grounds with its victims, has almost disappeared; much rain has fallen; the fields and orchards, from which all *green grass was burnt up*, have resumed their former flourishing appearance; and though many persons are still lingering with tertians, and other diseases induced by fever, this part of the country is now, I believe, as healthful as it ever was.

I should be happy indeed, were it in my power to affirm, that these painful visitations of providence have been sanctified to the spiritual good of the afflicted; but whilst some have been brought to feel and acknowledge the necessity of regenerating grace, it is lamentable to reflect, that little religious feeling has been manifested, save in the observance of absurd and superstitious ceremonies. In the course of the quarter three persons have been admitted on trial, under circumstances which place their sincerity beyond suspicion. One of them is a convert from Roman Catholicism. He cannot have mere temporal good in view, for by uniting with us he has raised to himself a host of enemies without the most distant prospect of worldly advantage of any kind whatever. Surely conscience has much influence in such a change as this.

Four women belonging to the Sunday evening class have died

in the course of the year; two of them happy and triumphant
and the best hope are entertained respecting the two others.

Our Schools and congregations, which declined greatly, owing
to the sickness, are still far from being so prosperous as before;
and it is likely they will revive but slowly.

On the 30th ultimo we held the fourth Anniversary of the
Negombo Missionary Society; Br. M'Kenny took the Chair,
and the meeting was addressed by Mr. Chater, Baptist Missionary, and our Brethren Hume, Sutherland, and Gogerly,
all of whom are entitled to my best thanks; for notwithstanding the badness of the roads and the unsettled state of the
weather, they had the kindness to come from their different
stations to assist at the meeting, and their assistance was highly valuable. We had an interesting day,—a day which will be
long remembered by our people here. Though poor and despised, they saw themselves on this occasion indentified with
other societies, and numbered amongst the thousands of Israel.
The presence and the counsels of our excellent Brethren have
animated and encouraged us. May the impulse thus given to
our efforts continue to curge us onward, May success still more
abundant and glorious attend the preaching of the gospel in
every part of the world, until our blessed Saviour shall be universally known adored and loved:

> " Waft, waft ye winds his story
> " And you ye waters roll."

From the School report which will be submitted to the ensuing
district meeting, you will learn more particularly the state of
this circuit.

I remain, Rev. and Dear Sirs,

Respectfully yours,

SAMUEL ALLEN.

THE KORNEGALLE STATION.

Kornegalle, 8th October, 1824.

REV. AND DEAR SIRS,

Incessant engagements, of which the Brethren in general are
aware, rendered it impossible for me to prepare a letter last
quarter in time for publication. I had indeed but little information to communicate worthy of the perusal of those who interest themselves in the history and progress of Missions, for it
would be as painful to read as to relate the particulars of the

M

ravages that have been made in this part of the Interior by famine, disease and death.

Ever since my arrival in the beginning of the year, and indeed
from its commencement in November preceding, the fever has
continued to prevail without intermission; and until the middle
of August last, no sanguine hopes could be entertained of its
speedy removal. It is with extreme satisfaction however, that I
can now state that the pestilence has almost wholly subsided,
and that we have the prospect of its being succeeded by a long
period of general health.

During the interval to which I have just alluded every European, without exception, in this and the contiguous districts
were under the necessity of abandoning their stations, and of
availing themselves of the healthier climate of the Maritime
Provinces. It is melancholy to add, that to many of these
the change of air afforded no relief, and that several others on the
spot fell victims to the disorder before their removal could be
accomplished.

Among the latter I have the painful task of recording the
name of the lamented Mrs. Audain, a woman whose profound
piety, united with the most amiable disposition, could not fail to
render her respected and beloved by all who had the happiness
of knowing her. Throughout her severe affliction she manifested
the utmost submission to the dispensations of Providence, and
was frequently found engaged in prayer to the Giver of all grace
that her strength might be proportioned to her day. On one occasion particularly she fervently supplicated the Divine Blessing
on every member of her family, on Missionaries of all denominations, on heathen nations, and on all who were without hope
and without God in the world, and then turning round as if
composing herself to rest she concluded by saying, Now I commend myself into the hands of God.

The mortality among the natives has been such that had I
not been favored with the best opportunities of acquiring accurate information I could scarcely have credited the statements
that were made. On the most moderate calculation upwards
of 10,000 of the inhabitants of this district alone have been
numbered with the dead!

In some of the villages which I visited during the prevalence
of the fever, I found every individual without exception labouring under the disease; and in one, not a mile distant from
the Mission House, about 73 adults and 10 or 12 children died
in a few months. For a long time I was under the most serious apprehension that by the death and dispersion of the
children no traces would be left of our School establishment,

but on embracing the earliest opportunity of re-opening the Schools I was indeed gratified and thankful to find that only 4 had died out of 6 Schools containing 170 children!

The state of both the Bazar and Hospital was truly deplorable: to both I continued my visits daily until lately I was under the necessity of confining my attention to the latter. With the view of rendering some assistance to the people of the Bazar, I employed several native Doctors to visit the sick and to administer medicine, but I soon found them so averse to this arrangement that I had to abandon the attempt; and such is their disinclination to be visited at all, that frequently when called to attend the sick, although no time was lost in obeying the summons, I have found them dead before my arrival.

Those more immediately connected with our Mission did not escape the prevailing pestilence. For about three months I was deprived of every Schoolmaster and servant I had, during which time a man whom I had formerly employed as a cooly, rendered me what assistance, the intervals of an intermittent fever would admit of. I am happy to say that all who were ill have now recovered, and are returning to their duties.

From a sense of duty I remained here throughout the sickly season, and I feel myself called upon to render unfeigned thanks to Almighty God for his especial blessing in preserving me from every symptom of fever.

Since the pestilence subsided three Schools have been opened at the distance of 20 miles from this place, and 138 children have been thus added to the former number. Of these schools two were established in consequence of the written request of the inhabitants of the villages; we have now therefore on this station 9 schools, containing 308 children. The few Dutch inhabitants of the place lately made a request to have a service in the Portuguese dialect; their wishes I was happy to accede to, and appointed Tuesday evening for that purpose.

I have lately had the happiness of being favored with a visit from Brother Hume, which to me after my long solitude was extremely gratifying. Br. Hume had fewer opportunities of visiting the schools and preaching to the people than I could have wished, in consequence of the recent prevalence of the sickness. On his return I accompanied him to Negombo, where I had the opportunity of being present at Brother Allen's Missionary Meeting, I believe every one present was pleased and edified by what they saw and heard.

I remain, Rev. Sirs,

Yours sincerely,

J. SUTHERLAND.

CALTURA STATION.

Caltura, September 29th, 1824.

DEAR FATHERS AND BRETHREN,

The gratification which I feel in embracing the returning opportunity of addressing you through the official medium of our excellent Quarterly Extracts is surpassed by scarcely any thing except the gratification of seeing the particular blessing of God resting upon our work, and providentially following and resting upon myself personally. When I look back upon the mercies I have enjoyed since I last wrote to you officially; upon the opportunities with which I have been favoured of making known among the Gentiles the unsearchable riches of Christ—and upon the measure of success with which the Lord has graciously been pleased to own my imperfect and unworthy efforts, while I see enough to humble me under the mighty hand of God, I see at the same time abundance to excite the strongest confidence and the liveliest joy.

During the past quarter we have been daily employed in attending to our public or more private means of grace, and we hope that our class meetings and prayer meetings and preachings have been instrumental of good to some who but lately were wandering upon the dark mountains of vanity, like sheep without a shephard: and we have the consoling thought to support us under any little trial that may occasionally occur, that our work is with the Lord and our reward with our God. Our Schools go on, and confirm our expectation that they will be the means, through the blessing of the Most High, of raising up a seed to serve him in this moral wilderness while sun and moon shall endure. Though it requires great exertions to keep the Schools in such a state as to insure as far as by human means is possible the grand object of their establishment, yet the labour is a particulary holy labour which is my consolation in the greatest severity of it, but I never forget that to give ultimate and compleat success to all is the province of a holy and promise keeping God.

I have had the pleasure during the quarter of paying a visit to Brother Sutherland, and Brother Allen. Although the fever which the Almighty in his Providence has permitted, no doubt for some wise purpose to ravage Kornegalle and the country round it, has raged so long as scarcely to leave a trace of human existence all round for miles, yet by the blessing of the Father of all mercies, the place will I hope prosper, when the coutry is re-peopled by the springing up a new generation, and Brother Sutherland has mercifully been preserved that he may be a blessing among them. On my return he accompanied me to Negombo to see Brother Allen, where we were gratified by being present at the Anniversary of the Branch Society which is in Negombo. It was a season which I hope will be remembered by many who were present, and I hope the good they derived from it will appear after many days unto praise and honour and glory at the appearing of Jesus Christ, for we are sure that the least, and feeblest efforts of his faithful Servants, when made in him and for him can never be in vain.

Recommending myself and all my labours to an interest in your constant prayers. I am,

　　　　　Very dear Fathers and Brethren,

　　　　　Yours in the Gospel and love of Christ,

　　　　　　　　　　A. HUME.

THE GALLE STATION,

Galle, October 7, 1824.

DEAR BRETHREN,

It is with difficulty that I hold a pen, having scalded one of my fingers. I have never used an amanuensis, and as I write in pain. I hope this circumstance, along with punctuality, will sufficiently excuse brevity. This quarter I have unremittingly persevered in the work, but not without many painful exercises of mind. I have not however been without support; and on some occasions have felt unusual pleasure in public duty. To God who comforts the hearts of those that are cast down, be ascribed unceasing praise!

To speak of heat in a climate like this, is one of the most common place things imaginable. I have only to say, that our numerous journeys and consequent exposure to the sun have tended considerably to lower the tone of my health and spirit. Through mercy I am tolerably well at present—but I wish some arrangement to be made to lessen the labour and travelling consequent on conducting the concerns of two extensive stations. In the early part of the last month, Br. Stoup and I visited Matura. It gives me great satisfaction to say, that almost every place on the station is in a state of activity and improvement. The most remote school—that of Naorunna, is a very pleasing one. We were particularly pleased with the diligence of the girls, as well as the boys, in committing to memory portions of

the New Testament. Simon the School Visitor, keeps an account
of their progress, and that of others in committing paragraphs
to memory;—and I must add, that the selections are equally
simple in style and important in sentiment. The skill of the
good school-mistress there has been repeatedly noticed; and
on this occasion she shewed, as the Gospel of St. Matthew
versified. It appeared, from what I examined, to be close and
correct. The laws of Prosody in Cingalese seem not unlike
those of Hebrew—and the language being very harmonious,
there is the less necessity for rhyme. I don't wish to be understood as anticipating much usefulness from the woman's performance, but mention it as an instance of what even a Cingalese female can accomplish. Mr. Lalmon has made some alterations in the House and Chapel which are improvements to
both—and I am happy to say the expenses are nearly met by
the subscriptions of the people at Matura. The neat little Chapel was re-opened by a Discourse in the forenoon in English, and
one in the evening in Portuguese on Thursday the 16th.

Our work here proceeds much as usual. It is sometimes
hopeful and sometimes discouraging. At present ours is the
only preaching in English or Portuguese, as circumstances have
occasioned the removal of the Chaplain who had but just
arrived when I wrote last. We have changed our afternoon's
service to the forenoon as heretofore, so that our labours are
little affected by Mr. Garstin's removal. I am happy to say we
were treated by him with every civility; and that two of his
sons attend regularly at the Mission House to study the
country languages with Br. Stopp.

From sometime past I have been attempting to develope the
systems of demon and planet worship so general in this Country, and have succeeded in translating some Cingalese Books
that are used in this business. I hope when the undertaking
is complete to have a satisfactory account of the origin of the
terrors so general among the people. Every step of the investigation seems to shew the progress of man in folly and iniquity,
after losing the knowledge of God, till becoming vain in his
imaginations, he was abandoned to an undiscerning mind.—
The exertions of Missionaries are an undoubted dispensation
of mercy. May God give these people repentance to the acknowledging of the truth, that they may recover themselves out
of the snare of the devil, who are taken captive of him at his
will.

Sincerely yours,
JOHN CALLAWAY.

To *the* REV. MESSRS. BUNTING, TAYLOR, *and* WATSON,
Secretaries to the Wesleyan Missionary Society, London.

Galle, October 9, 1824.

REV. SIRS.

In due conformity to established order, I take up my pen
to transmit my regular quarterly communication, which, from
my present circumstances, must of course be circumscribed,
and I fear devoid of that information which renders the letters
of my Brethren so interesting. You are aware that little is to
be be done effectually in this Island, without an acquaintance
with the languages, at least among the native population, and as
I feel that my express call is to preach the Gospel to *them*, I
think I cannot serve the Mission better than by applying myself
to them. My progress is perhaps not so great as might be expected, but considering existing circumstances, I think it may
be said of me; "he hath done what he could." The climate, you
are aware, is very unfavourable to close application for those
who are newly arrived, and produces excessive lassitude and
enervation; but I hope I have now nearly got over these distressing feeling, as since the late rains I have felt my strength
much recruited, and I can now study more closely without feeling any ill effects from it; so that I am encouraged to hope
that the next quarter will be marked by more manifest improvement. My chief attention has hitherto been to the Portuguese
language, as it is more immediately connected with my present
sphere of labour; I now read sermons in it of my own translating, and hope in a short time to be a complete master of it.
The Singhalese is somewhat more formidable, and the ascent to
eminence, or indeed to competency, in a knowledge of it, more
steep and rugged, but I am not discouraged by these considerations; "Who art thou, O great mountain, before Zerubbabel
thou shalt become a plain," is the language of my heart, when
surveying its difficulties and complications. If I am negligent,
or indifferent in my work, I am sure it will not be without the
most acute feelings of guilt and remorse. I often feel more for
the deplorable state of those around me than I can express;
many a time is my soul bowed down within me, when I see the
thousands in this country who are given up to idolatry, and I
cannot speak a word that they understand, to direct them to the
"true God, and Jesus Christ whom he hath sent." But shall not
this tongue be speedily loosened, to set forth among them "my
great Redeemer's praise?" surely it shall.—"All power is given
to Jesus, in heaven and in earth, go ye *therefore*" said he "and
teach all nations;" my Mission then, as I trust I received it from

the great head of the church, is grounded upon the omnipotent power of him that sent me; and will not that power be exerted to qualify me for it? O for a portion of the Pentecostal effusion the gift of Tongues!

Since I last wrote, I have made some few excursions into the country. Brother Callaway and I have been to Matura, which to me was productive of great pleasure. I think the Schools in that circuit, taking them altogether, are the most flourishing of any I have visited, their examination gave me the highest satisfaction. Brother Lalmon appears to be truly alive to the importance of the great work in which he is employed, and to be making every exertion to spread the knowledge of Christ amongst perishing sinners; this, with his familiar acquaintance, with the languages must make him a very valuable and useful Missionary. Brother Callaway and myself visit Amblangoddy alternately once a month. I was there, in my regular turn, last week, and preached twice, by interpretation, in the Government School, which is very large and commodious. In the morning I had a large and attentive congregation which to me was a very gratifying sight, and excited some of my best feelings; in the evening but few attended. I think it a good plan to visit the people from house to house, or to preach by the road-side, when every one that passes generally stops to listen. I have sometimes adopted this method when I have had an interpreter with me; once in particular, when returning from one of our schools; on a Sunday, I stopped a few persons, whom I met on the road, and began to preach to them Jesus. Presently a great many others came up, and several of the inhabitants near the place, seeing a crowd, came together, until I suppose not less than fifty or sixty people, were collected round me; I continued to address them for about half an hour, and then requested them all to clasp their hands and close their eyes (which I think they did to an individual) while engaged in prayer, which appeared to have a very solemn effect, and I hope, the seed then sown, was not lost. I have since adopted another method with respect to prayer in little congregations of this kind, which I think calculated to be useful. I pray in short sentences, and request them all to repeat them after me, which they readily do. In this way their attention is kept alive, and the various petitions of the prayer must be more forcibly impressed upon their minds, which may lead them into the practise of praying for themselves.— At present I am only a learner, but I endeavour to do good, where, and as, and to whom I can; sometimes I feel a little discouraged and cast down, then again, I am cheered with some pleasing circumstance or gracious promise, but the "best of all is God is with us," and he will "be with us always even to the end of the world."   I have found no deficiency of spiritual comfort and enjoyment, from the loss of the society of my Christian friends in England. I prove the sweetness of communion with the Father of Spirits, though seperated from those with whom I once "took sweet counsel and walked to the House of God, in company," for he is

"One, in every time and place,"
"Full, for all, of Truth and Grace."

And now Rev. Sirs, commending myself again to your prayers, and to the prayers of all those who long for the prosperity of Zion, let me assure you that I remain,

Your obedient Son and Servant
In the Gospel of Christ,
RICHARD STOUP

THE JAFFNA STATION.

Mission House, Jaffna, October 4, 1824.

DEAR FATHERS AND BRETHREN,

When I reflect on the incidents which have occurred since I last wrote a quarterly letter from this place, sentiments of a very different nature alternately take possession of my breast: on the one hand I see great cause for self abasement, and on the other abundant reason for humble gratitude and fervent hope.   A merciful arm has been stretched out to guide, to strengthen and to bless.   "It is of the Lord's mercies that we are not consumed, because His compassion fail not."

The concerns of this station are very encouraging, and ought to excite our liveliest gratitude to God. On the 8th of August we changed one of our Sabbath English services for Portuguese, for which change the following reasons may be offered: 1st All those who attend English preaching understand Portuguese. 2nd The majority of the inhabitants understand Portuguese only. 3rd It was distinctly promised to those who subscribed to the New Chapel that on the Lord's day divine service should be performed in that language.   Thank God the trial has been made, and has exceeded our most sanguine expectations; the Chapel was literally crowded and still continues to be well filled every Sunday evening.   One circumstance which has increased our congregation must not be overlooked: Mrs. Schrader, a venerable old lady, who has preached in her

own house for upwards of twenty years, and who has translated nearly the whole of Mr. Wesley's sermons into Portuguese; began to feel herself incapable to attend to her public
duties; in commencing our new service, we felt ourselves at
a loss how to act, as she had preaching at the same time;
but the matter was no sooner mentioned, than she broke forth
in praises to God, that she had lived to see the day, when
she could give up her flock to the shepherds of Jesus; and expressed a wish that we should take her congregation under
our care; to this we acceded and the spirit of God has shewn
his approbation by granting great favors unto Zion. What is
rather remarkable, she did not begin to learn English until about
55 years of age, and now she regularly attends and understands
that service. We have also the pleasure to inform you that we
have established an adult Portuguese class consisting of ten
members; this is rendered the more interesting, as preaching
was first established in that house by our Assistant Brother
Mr. Hunter. The master of the house, who is Father-in law to
another of our Assistant Brethren, said with tears in his eyes at
the last class meeting, "I feel a desire to live very near to God,
I see He has given us this opportunity for the salvation of
our souls."

We have also commenced a Sunday service in Tamul in the
new chapel, and what will be equally gratifying to you, is, we
have formed a class of natives consisting ten members, (two of
them women). Brother Stead and myself were pleased, and
blessed with the experience of one of our native Schoolmasters;
he commenced by saying "The time would be too short to
relate all the Lord's dealings with his soul," and after giving us
some particulars of his childhood he observed, "Once I had a
great desire to learn English and thought the best way to acquire it would be to read the New Testament; this I did for
some time, but never thought of the meaning of what I read;
some time after this the Lord began to shine on my mind, and
gave me to see myself a great sinner: so that whether I put
on my clothes, or ate my food, whether I walked in the street
or slept on my couch, I was always sorrowful,—but at sl. I
had again recourse to the world and nearly lost all my desire
after good things, but the Lord again called me. I obeyed the
call, I sought and found his favour and was made to enjoy great
peace and great joy."——Have you that peace now?——
கேட்டதற்கு என் இருதயம் இளகிற்று; En irrithiyetfilen irruku
kuthu—"my heart is it" was the cheerful reply. I hope that
this man will ere long assist us to distribute amongst the families the unsearchable riches of Christ.

o

Some time ago we began an extensive system of visiting the people, but found we had not strength to continue as we commenced; this, however, still forms a considerable part of our duty and delight. The schools are in tolerable order, but we hope soon to see them improved.

That fine station Point Pedro is at preset supplied by John Philips, a native young man who was taken into the service of the Mission by Brother Squance: he is laborious in preaching the word and visiting the schools; but we hope you will soon let us have a married Brother from home for that station, and enable us to form a proper establishment amongst the people. I have already informed you, 0000 Rixdollars would build a good house, and the land was purchased in 1819. If this be done, it will unquestionably be the first native station in this district. Brother Stead who has just returned from a tour in that part, says "The schools are in excellent order, and a fair proportion of the boys read well in the Testament—they are also well acquainted with the catechisms, and answer questions on scriptural subjects with tolerable readiness and propriety. I found in nearly all the schools a few adults who listened with apparent interest to what I had to tell them about the religion of Jesus. I had also the pleasure to distribute some Tamul tracts among them, which were received with apparent eagerness. That a general impression in favor of the Mission has been made on the minds of the people is evident from their wish to have their children instructed by us: we have numerous requests to establish other schools, and in one village not more than a mile and a half from the Bungalow the people were so urgent that I paid them a visit and found upwards of 100 boys, together with some of their parents, waiting to receive me. I distributed tracts and conversed with them some time, and they promised to build a school at their own expence, after the pattern of the one at Point Pedro. It is to have a pulpit at one end; and they added "whenever you come to instruct us we will gladly attend."

Our weekly services in Jaffna may be classed as follows: Three in Tamul, one in Portuguese, and one in English, and which are made additionally heavy by having all the singing to conduct. Four classes, one of which is met by Mrs. Roberts the rest by ourselves. One public prayer-meeting to attend; these with the schools and other duties are almost too much for us: but we have the pleasure to inform you that help is at hand, a young man (who is the nephew to the old lady already mentioned in this letter and) who was with me at Point Pedro has begun to preach. I heard of him last Tuesday evening in Tamul, and was much gratified,

Our Benevolent Society in this time of scarcity (for we have not had rain for upwards of eight months) has been a peculiar blessing: the wretched matron and the solitary widow have been cheered with the soothings of friendship and the glad tidings of salvation. The orphan has been relieved with a monition and a smile, and the tear has been wiped from his eye.

And now, Dear Fathers and Brethren, "Lift up your eyes and look on the fields, for they are white already to the harvest." Send us an increase of faithful labourers, for the reaping time is come.

I remain, Your devoted and affectionate Servant,
in the Gospel of Christ,
J. ROBERTS.

The Brethren of the Mission are respectfully informed that the general School Report for the present year will be put to Press as early as possible after the first of January. The Superintendants of circuits will therefore have the goodness to forward their Reports of the different Schools on their Stations, as soon as convenient after Christmas.

Printed at the Wesleyan Mission Press.

Extracts

FROM

QUARTERLY LETTERS, &c.

ADDRESSED

To the Rev. Messrs. MORLEY, WATSON, *and* MASON;
Secretaries to the Wesleyan Methodist Missionary Society, London.

No. XXVII.   APRIL, 1825.

THE COLOMBO STATION.

Colombo, 15th April, 1825.

REV. AND DEAR SIRS,

Nothing can be more gratifying to our feelings than to have it in our power to communicate to you such facts as tend to give our prospects, as to extensive usefulness a cheering aspect. It sometimes happens, however, that we feel ourselves under the necessity of informing you of the existence of things rather discouraging in their nature. For some time past you have heard from us of the dreadful ravages of disease,—of thousands having been cut down and swept into eternity! But happy I am to inform you, that a gracious providence has been pleased to restore the Island generally to its usual healthful state. About two months since, the inhabitants of this settlement were thrown into consternation by the appearance again of the Spasmodic Cholera, but after continuing only a few weeks, its disappearance was as sudden as its commencement. Surely all these painful visitations are designed by the God of Mercy as loud calls to the people to "consider their ways, and be wise."—that when his judgments are abroad in the earth, they may learn righteousness.

On the subject of our work on this station for the past quarter, I have to notice the following particulars. Our congregation and society in the Fort have been much reduced by the removal of the 83d Regiment to Kandy and the 45th to Rangoon. We have still, however, on Sunday and Wednesday evenings an interesting attendance at preaching. The class consists at present of 12 members, which is met by ourselves in turn, the leader having been removed. We look however daily for a Regiment from England, which we hope will add both numbers and strength to our cause among the soldiers.

The good work begun in the hearts of so many of our Pettah congregation goes forward, and affords us much encouragement. We have formed a second class, or rather divided our large one into two, which promise to do well. Several of our new converts have manifested not only a deep interest for their own spiritual welfare, but have also discovered much concern for the salvation of others, and of their own relations and friends in particular; in consequence, they have in several instances evinced their willingness to open their houses for prayer meetings; which circumstance offers to us an opportunity of additional usefulness of which we are glad to avail ourselves, for nothing can be more desirable than to see applications coming from the people to come to their spiritual help, because we have so often seen our urgent invitations to them, to hear the Gospel imputed to any motive but to those influencing our hearts and directing our conduct. An exhibition of genuine christian philanthropy was in former years so rare a thing in this land of darkness, that it was but natural that the people should presume that the actuating principle, even of a MISSIONARY was *self-interest*; but now the purity of the motives, and the sacred character of the messengers of " *peace and good will towards men*," begin to to be better understood. The meetings which we have already conducted have been well attended, and we could not but notice the presence of many who never attend our chapels; by this means the knowledge of the Saviour's love will be extended, and we trust many may be brought to receive him with all their hearts.

It is with much satisfaction I inform you that Lady Barnes has expressed the decided wish of His Excellency the Governor and herself to encourage our schools; and a few weeks ago, when she had the kindness to call upon Mrs M'Kenny she fixed a day for visiting our school at Colpetty. Mrs. M'Kenny met her Ladyship at the appointed hour, when she was pleased to remain upwards of an hour hearing the children examined in English as well as in their own language. Her Ladyship appeared not a little pleased to see upwards of forty Singhalese girls learning to read and work. They were allowed the honor of coming forward one by one and presenting her Ladyship with the Europe work-bags, pincushions, housewives, thimbles, needles, thread, &c. with which the liberality of our friends at home has supplied them. Lady Barnes has been pleased to express her wish to visit all our schools, which distinguished attention cannot fail of having the most favorable influence upon them. From the increase of girls at Colpetty we have been under the necessity of adding to the school a separate room for their sole accommodation which makes the little establishment very complete, and secures to it an advantage which it had not before of having the girls separate from the boys.

I have just returned from a journey to Galle in which I was accompanied by Brother Bridgnell where we were invited to preach two of their Annual Sermons, and we were greatly rejoiced to find our dear Brother Allen in a state of rapid recovery after his most severe illness, which will be pleasing intelligence to you and all his friends at home. I trust the Lord will in mercy spare his life, that he may be long usefully employed in his work.

The *Alexander* has just arrived, and brought us the Documents of the last Conference, which, of course, although a little late, are full of interest to us.

Our Printing concern goes on briskly, and has lately produced several things highly important to our Mission Schools. Brother Callaway has completed a neat Edition of Doctor Clarkes *Clavis Biblica* in Singhalese, and an improved Spelling Book in Singhalese, and the same in Singhalese and English, which as it was much wanted, will be of vast utility in our Schools. Desiring a continued interest in your prayers.

I remain, very affectionately yours,

J. M'KENNY.

Colombo 19th April, 1825.

DEAR FATHERS AND BRETHREN,

Sometimes when I have considered the greatness of the work which I have undertaken to do, and the very small measure of wisdom and grace which I possess to qualify me for it, I have been tempted to charge myself with presumption. And though I feel it to be indispensably necessary that I should guard against every thing like despondency if I would be either useful or happy, I must at the same time, confess, I have no source of encouragement either in reference to happiness or success in this arduous undertaking, except in the conviction that the work is not mine, but His that sent me;—that to Him nothing is impossible, or unknown; and that every word of prophecy, and promise, which He has spoken shall be fulfilled in their sentest, "Heaven bids men run.—So I may strive with things impossible, yea get the better of them." If the gift of tongues might be hoped for in these times, how delightful then would be the task of a Christian Missionary. To be dailling for years, at words and grammar, and after all, to be in a very small measure conversant in the language of the people, among whom, we labour, whose very thoughts run in channels diverse from our own, and whose forms of expression are all new and uncouth; these difficulties and many others, arising from the native character and peculiar circumstances, together with, the comparatively small measure of success we realize, are enough to make the strongest and most stout-hearted feel a little dispirited at times. Nine months residence in India has corrected many of my mistakes respecting the great work of evangelizing the world. The difficulties of it I feel more forcibly than ever are such as to mock all mere human agency. And this persuasion leads me to pray more fervently for help from on high, and to encourage myself more constantly in the Lord, my God. We have not however to comfort ourselves only with the hope of what we see not; we have before our eyes, some causes of encouragement, and gratitude, and joy.

Among the natives I have not been so useful as I could have wished, but to have expected more than I have accomplished, in me, I think, would have been unreasonable. We must be furnished with weapons, and clad with armour, before we proceed to war, and considerable progress must be made in the language before any one is prepared to have much or close conversation with the natives on religious subjects. I feel thankful, however, that I am able, with the assistance of my native Teacher, to compose my own Sermons in Singhalese. The Portuguese is a remarkably simple language, and much more readily acquired than the other. But to obtain a knowledge of any language so as to be able to read and write it, I find is much less difficult than to acquire an ability to speak it with correctness, ease and fluency. I have not yet ventured to preach altogether extempore in Portuguese, but in our Prayer-meetings I have exhorted with some liberty.

Our visitations of the sick are among the number of our seasons and means of usefulness. On one occasion, I remember being peculiarly impressed. On my entering the chamber of the sick man, I found him, to all appearance, very near death. Having spoken faithfully to him and prayed with him, I addressed a word of exhortation to the Portuguese people as there were upwards of thirty in the house. These occasions are indeed *mollia tempora fandi,* and especially when the voice of advice or warning comes from the death bed. "The tongues of dying men enforce attention like deep harmony." The poor man, with an unusual degree of energy, seemed to lay hold on the only hope of a sinful and perishing world, the merits and the mercy of the almighty SAVIOUR. May all who heard him do likewise, and may every seed of divine truth which is sown, be seen after many days.

Two weeks ago, I set off in company with Br. M'Kenny, to Galle. We spent a night at Caltura, held a Prayer meeting there, and were encouraged by the evident piety, zeal and talents of some young men whom God is raising up, and whom doubtless he will use as instruments of great and lasting good to the inhabitants of that place. On Monday the 11th. instant, I visited Badigam, a Church Missionary Station, and the residence of the Rev. Messrs. Mayor and Ward, and was much gratified by all I saw and heard of their labours and plans of usefulness. On my journey thither I could not but reflect how forlorn would be the condition of Missionaries, and how mad their project, if they had not a divine COMMAND, as their authority for every exertion, and a divine PROMISE as a foundation for all their hopes. I was surrounded with the most beautiful scenery, and the gently flowing stream gave much additional beauty and liveliness to the whole. But I was alas! surrounded on every hand by men who are atheists both in sentiment and practice. The wisdom and power of the great Creator which are or may be so clearly understood from the things which are made, are unknown to them. How happy should I have been, could I have "preached unto them Jesus." A little before I reached Badigam, having to wait for a boat to cross the river, I entered into conversation with some native children who gathered round me, and was delighted to find that the Messengers of the Church of Christ had been there, and that some of them were instructed in the "the Holy Scriptures which are able to make them wise unto Salvation through Faith which is Christ Jesus." Beams of heavenly light are beginning to shine upon some of the most obscure heathen villages, and ere long, the glory of the Lord shall fully arise upon them. The operation of the little leaven is not seen—the progress is slow—but the process is going on, and eventually the whole shall be leavened.

While in Galle, I went with Br. Stoup to see the *Kandian* prisoners, and a Mahometan mosque. Was much struck with the zeal of the prisoners in support of their own religion. They have erected a small but very neat temple to Budhu in the prison yard, decorated with images, flowers, and drawings, according to the precepts and doctrines of their own superstition. The Moorman who had the care of the mosque was unwilling to admit us unless we would submit to take off our shoes, so after a little conversation (for he understood portuguese), we left him. The day is coming, O happy day! when the deluded followers of the bloody and lascivious impostor shall become the disciples of the meek and holy Jesus. I went in company with Brother M'Kenny to see the large establishment for the instruction of native children commenced and carried on under the superintendance of Mrs. Gibson, and on her sole responsibility. The school and dwelling-house are elegantly neat, and the premises are laid out with much judgment and taste. The perseverance, zeal and benevolence of this lady entitle her to a very distinguished place among the friends of the human race. Brother M'Kenny and I called upon Adam Sree Goona Munhi Rathana Vadheygay, in our way from Dodandoowa, his native village, where he is now a preacher of righteousness to his own countrymen, being a proponent or native preacher in the employ of government. Alexander Dherma Rama Apotantragay is made a Mohundium of the fisher caste, which is the office next in rank to that of a Modeliar, the highest held by native headmen.——I have seen him several times and conversed with him freely on religious subjects. Brother M'Kenny and myself have shown him much attention, and have pressed him to attend the preaching and join the class, but hitherto he has studiously kept aloof from us. Not one native in ten thousand will ever have half the pains taken for his salvation that he has had; but if we could suppose that one native in ten thousand who had received similar attentions would manifest half the ingratitude and indifference of this man, it would present the Singhalese character in a much more hopeless light than I have yet seen it. However, we are not answerable for the success or failure of our efforts. Our work is with the Lord.

I wish to "expect great things," and to "attempt great things." What degree of success may attend my labours, it is not for me at present to know. However, this I know, that so long as I remain in this Mission I shall continue to be what I now am,

Your faithful and devoted servant,
in the Gospel of Christ,
WILLIAM BRIDGNELL.

NEGOMBO, CHILAW, AND KORNEGALLE STATION.

Negombo, April 22d, 1825.

REV. AND DEAR SIRS,

The circumstances of the Negombo station have been so frequently and amply detailed in former communications, that little more is necessary than to state, that very few changes have taken place: yet there appears, especially in two villages, a gradually progressive work. I was much pleased a short time since, in giving tickets to the class at Seedua, to hear such simple and sincere expressions of warm attachment to the religion of the holy Jesus from the mouths of Singhalese females. May their number be abundantly increased! In Negombo the congregations continue small; and at present nothing else can be expected, the bulk of the population being Roman Catholics. Occasionally, however, some of these attend, although evidently in much fear of the spiritual censures which have been attached to hearing the Gospel. "I like much to hear the Gospel preached," observed one of the most respectable of that communion, "and I frequently come and stand outside by the window, where I can hear very well." The English service, at 11 o'clock on the Sabbath morning, is better attended than either the Singhalese or Portuguese; and the word is received with deep attention. In the villages, especially in the neighbourhood of Seedua, we are differently circumstanced: the majority of the people profess to be protestants; but, as the Government Schools have been withdrawn, they are generally as sheep having no shepherd. The distance from Negombo, and the unpleasantness of the road, render it difficult to visit it so frequently as is necessary. The preaching on the Sabbath-day, and occasional exhortations are insufficient to arouse the attention of the people to the vast importance of spiritual objects: they need to be visited from house to house; to have a teacher living in the midst of them, who will be able to avail himself of numerous opportunities of usefulness which cannot at present be improved. They now look upon us as their natural instructors, and receive with confidence the truths which are enforced upon them. The great advantage of their profession of protestantism in preparing the way for their reception of the truth as it is in Jesus, I have experienced in the difference of my feelings in proclaiming the Gospel to *them*, and preaching to the *Budhists* of the Seven Korles. These circumstances, in conjunction with the advice of the Brethren whom I consulted, have led me to determine on the erection of a small house at Seedua for the residence of the Assistant Missionary belonging to the station, Cornelius de Wijesingha, who is very desirous of labouring among them. I expect, through the sacred influences of the Holy Spirit accompanying his exertions, that this arrangement will be a great blessing to the populous villages in that direction. The preparation of the timbers for the building is in very considerable forwardness, and I hope to be able, in the course of the ensuing quarter, to complete the erection

The English school of Negombo is improving, as lately the Catholic priest, after several efforts which have proved fruitless, to establish a school, gave permission publicly to his flock to send their children wherever they pleased to obtain instruction. The Masters of this school are members of our society, and are active in the performance of their duty. The excessive poverty of the people in the villages prevents the daily attendance from being so good as is desirable in the country schools: the youngest of the children being compelled frequently to wander in the jungle in search of wild roots to satisfy the cravings of hunger. The females are in a great measure prevented from attending from a complete destitution of apparel: they move about in their huts nearly in a state of nudity, and the shame inherent in all females renders it impossible for them to come to school, however much they may be inclined. If any funds were at the disposal of the Missionary which he could appropriate to the supplying these destitute females with coarse apparel, our schools would be much better attended. Notwithstanding a few discouraging circumstances, the schools have been productive of much good, and still continue to spread a holy influence around them, and there is a sufficiency of success to animate to renewed exertions.

I am exceedingly sorry that Chilaw has necessarily received so small a share of my labors, as a very interesting congregation of European descendants, who are protestants may be constantly collected. Being altogether unacquainted with the Tamul language, I could have no intercourse with the natives when I visited them, but through the medium of an interpreter. The village of native protestants, situated in the neighbourhood of our school contains from 25 to 30 families, and it no other prospect of success attended the station than that arising from laboring among the European descendants, it appears sufficient to justify at least the stationing an assistant Missionary there, or even an European, if the strength of the Mission would allow it. Many very populous villages are in the neighbourhood, from several of which applications have been made through the School-master at Chilaw for the establishment of schools. These have of necessity been rejected for the present.

On the 24th of January, I left Negombo to visit the Seven Korles : at that time the fever which previously raged so furiously had partially subsided. The natives were busily engaged in reaping, and the crop which had failed during the two preceeding years, was very abundant: but both the judgments and mercies of God have hitherto failed to awaken feelings of gratitude in their hearts. I found them very conversible and willing to listen with attention to whatever was spoken, and in many instances to acknowledge the impropriety of their conduct, especially when it was shewn to be contrary, not only to Christianity, but to the moral precepts of Budhu. One of the principal vices to which they are addicted, (and which they do not attempt to defend, but only to palliate by the plea of poverty and general custom,) is a *plurality of husbands*; it being quite common for 4, or 5 brothers to have one joint wife. In some instances, if there be no brothers, friends or neighbours will associate themselves together to support the woman, who is to be equally the property of each. One instance was mentioned to me of one woman having seven husbands, who were brethren. In answer to an enquiry, if they had not frequent quarrels in consequence of this custom, it was acknowledged that it was the case sometimes. "But," exclaimed the man, (a petty head man of Billegalle,) "do you think that we, brothers, born of one mother, would quarrel on account of *a woman*: if she be not attentive to give satisfaction to each of us we will immediately send her back to her friends." Miserable females, I thought, you are treated with less kindness than the cattle that plough their fields. In truth, the state of the females is the most degraded possible, and it is only the introduction of pure religion which can remove this enormous evil.

Upon remonstrating with them on the sinfulness of their conduct, they replied "We now bear many things we were before ignorant of. How can we know what is right unless we have some one to instruct us?" This reply was impressive: I saw a people ignorant of the true God, and even from infancy taught to deny his existence, enslaved to vicious practices, and yet possessed of a quickness of thought for apprehending the truth when presented to them, promising to attend to instruction if it were afforded, and standing in the country

I

devoted to Budhu : the Pali verse ascribed to him came forcibly to my memory

සබ්දුනා. ධම්මදුනා. ජිනාති   සබරසං ධම්මරසා ජිනාති
සබ.රඃ. ධම්මරශි ජිනාති තණ්හක්බියො සබ්දුස්බ. ජිනාති

The most excellent* of all gifts is the gift of religious instruction, the most exquisite sensations are those of religious truth; the most exalted desire is that of religion: this desire overcomes all sorrow.

But the necessity of constant intercourse with them to lead them by degrees to understand *the truth*, is evident. I felt this particularly at *Kawdomoona*, where Brother Sutherland had established a school, about 5 months previous to my visit. He had only an opportunity of once (I believe,) visiting it, and perhaps my sermon was the first they had heard from a Christian teacher. Forty-seven Kandian men were present, and behaved with the utmost decency, while I endeavoured to enforce the being of God and the necessity of seeking his favor through Jesus Christ:—but the certainty that I should not see them again for several months, and that during that period they would never hear the name of Christ, except from the lips of the School-master, or a few of their children, caused a painful and chilling Sensation, and I could only recommend them to the mercy of that God with whom all things are possible.

The first place visited was Rillegalle: this is the first School Brother Newstead established in the Seven Korles. It was not flourishing—the number of scholars only 24 and the Master afflicted with fever. Several of the children read the New Testament fluently and repeat with correctness one or two Catechisms. In the vicinity of this place four other Schools are established, and it ought, if possible, to be occupied by a married Assistant Missionary. It is situated 26 miles from Negombo, and about 23 from Kornegalle ; but, as the bridges are broken down between it and Kornegalle, it could be more conveniently superintended by the Missionary residing at Negombo, than by the one in Kornegalle; the road also thro' Negombo is less infested with wild elephants than the other. *Dambadenia*, about two miles from Rillegalle has 24 children; this School has been much injured by the prevalence of fever. Kawdamoona, two miles from Rillegalle across the rice fields

* Although the common acceptation of the verb ජිනාති is, to *conquer* in this verse, excepting in the last instance it only marks, a decided superiority.

has a large School containing nearly 70 children and having at present a daily attendance of between 40 and 50. There was no School-room, the children being taught partly in the air and partly in a shed belonging to a neighbouring house. The Master is active and I believe lives in the fear of God. I directed an old shed to be erected sufficiently large to accommodate the children, many of whom come from a distance. About 4 miles from Rillegalle is situated *Kootogalle*, containing 35 children, who are taught in an Amlam by the road side. On my return two Budhuist priests seated themselves in it to dispute our possession; but their resolution failed them and they left us in quiet possession. The people were exceedingly attentive while I explained to the Priests the necessity of examining the doctrines of Christianity before they opposed them: assuring them that I had carefully examined, as far as it was in my power, those of Budhu:—they acknowledged the propriety of doing this, and thus publicly gave their assent to the admission of Christian books among the people.

About a mile from this place, at Hallayala, a School of 85 boys is taught by Joseph, the converted Kandian, of whom Brother Newstead has made frequent mention. The daily attendance is about 25. In the whole of these Schools the Scriptures are now read daily. Some fear at first existed, that opposition would be met with to this at the three last Schools, but none has been experienced.

We have no other Schools till we reach Kornegalle. This place and its vicinity suffered much more from fever than the places we have already noticed: the Schools at Nellawa and Tittewella were suspended; and those of Kornegalle and Gettowana barely had an existence. The first and two last are reviving, but Tittewella is for the present discontinued. I was much gratified at Gettowana (which has 24 boys) by the shrewd and correct answers they gave to several Scriptural interrogations, which proved that they had not been instructed in vain.

To disseminate Christianity among the Kandians a convenient digest, extracted from the Scriptures, and occasionally illustrated by short notes, is almost indispensably necessary. A complete copy of the Scriptures should be lodged in each School, but the volumes are two ponderous to be used with advantage as a School-book, and present an almost insuperable objection to the adult population. Such a work, had we the means of printing it, would be of great use also in the maritime provinces, and might be comprised in a duodecimo volume.

As I cannot personally visit the distant parts of the district mitted to my charge, more than once a quarter. They cannot derive much advantage from immediate instruction, but it is to be hoped that a vigilant superintendence, of the Schoolmasters, although exercised at a distance will not be in vain. The two assistant Superintendants of Schools have given me entire satisfaction. Commending myself, and the district in which I labor to your prayers,

I remain, Rev. and Dear Sirs,

Your obedient and faithful Servant,

D. J. GOGERLY.

THE CALTURA STATION.

Caltura, March, 1825.

DEAR FATHERS AND BRETHREN,

We have the pleasure of again offering you a short account of our labours, success and prospects. We have been steadily prosecuting our labours in the full hope that they will not be in vain ; and we have the gratification to know that our hopes have not been disappointed. We witness with feelings of lively gratitude to God who has in some degree crowned our labours with his blessing, the measure of success with which they have been accompanied and succeeded. Since our last meeting, one of the assistant Brethren appointed to this station has taken up his residence at Pantura, and the interest which seems to be generally felt in the residence there of a Christian Minister seems very considerable. The people attend at both the Pantura and Wekkedie Schools in far greater numbers than formerly. The Wekkedie School always interested us in consequence of the considerable number of adults who were in the habit of attending. We have frequently been much animated when spending a short time in that quarter to see the attendance upon week evenings for prayer-meetings of a considerable number of serious individuals of both sexes, and now we have every reason to hope that as they will have more frequent and regular opportunities of hearing the word of God and religious worship, that the hearts of some of them will be opened to receive the truth. The attendance at the Pantura school is also greatly improved. At this school our former congregations consisted chiefly of the children of the school and occasionally an adult or two, but now there is a tolerably good congregation of adults who we hope will not attend in vain. Thus this part of the station which has often caused us a good deal of pain begins at length to prosper. As the country inland from Pantura is very populous and altogether without religious instruction or instructors we think of opening a school in a very populous village which can easily be visited by our Assistant at Pantura.

In the vicinity of Caltura we are prosecuting our work in much our usual way; regularly attending to our schools, prayer-meetings, class-meetings, and preaching,—and we hope gradually inducing a regard for christianity and its ordinances. We have not a single week-day evening unemployed, and though we often feel our labour making very large demands upon our strength, we have no wish to lessen its quantity, but rejoice in so many opportunities of making known among the gentiles the unsearchable riches of Christ.

We returned from Galle a few days ago, whither we had gone to be with our dear Brother Allen who has had a very severe illness from which at one period it was not thought he would recover. But by the blessing of God on the means employed, he has once more been brought from the brink of the grave. His disease was of a very dangerous nature and required very copious bleeding to overcome it. He bore it however in the spirit of the christian, and proved the power of religion to support the mind in circumstances the most appaling. We have no doubt you will rejoice with us that he is again raised up to make known in a region where such knowledge is so much wanted, the love and grace of God in Christ Jesus. On the Sabbath before we left Galle viz. the 10th April, we had the pleasure of hearing Brother Bridgnell preach the annual Sermon for the Galle station from "Go ye unto all the world and preach the Gospel to every creature;" and had it not been for the rain which in the evening fell in torrents, we should have had the pleasure of hearing Brother M'Kenny in Portuguese. In the afternoon I had the privilege to address the Singhalese congregation from Isaiah lx. 11 and 12. The services of the day, though interrupted by rain, were interesting and profitable, and the congregations encouraging.

I am, Dear Fathers and Brethren,
Yours affectionately,
A. HUME.

THE GALLE STATION,

Galle, 16th April, 1835.

REV. AND DEAR SIRS,

Through divine providence, I am permitted to address you once more from the place where I first preached the Gospel among the heathen. Five years and nine months have soon elapsed, and when viewed in retrospect present a scene greatly chequered with trials and comforts, hopes and disappointments. Even with our present imperfect powers of intellect, many things we remember in our past lives, which have given rise to sorrow and regret, and many blessings which we are thankful for having experienced; how great and interesting then must be our discoveries amongst the forgotten incidents of past ages, when we shall know even as we are known, and when

"Each fainter trace that memory holds,
"So darkly of departed years,
"In one broad glance the soul beholds
"And all that was, at once appears!"

Since my arrival at Galle, I have seen more forcibly than ever the justness of an observation which the Brethren of the Mission have frequently had occasion to make, that the most important, and in many respects, the most encouraging department of our work, is the most trying to our minds, being attended with many anxious cares and painful disappointments.

The schools on this as on other stations, would not be worth retaining at the expence they create, did they not engage much of our time and attention, with a view to the improvement and diligence of the teachers, and also the prosperity of their respective charges. Our school-masters here, though all nominal christians, differ widely in character and attainments, and perhaps they are not inferior to the generality of their Brethren in other parts of the Island. A faithful schoolmaster is always a very valuable auxiliary to our work; it must however be confessed, the love of money and influence pervades so generally the minds of the persons whom we are obliged to employ, that a long course of good conduct and attentive regard to duty is necessary, in order to establish their characters, and render their motives unquestionable. The school-system on the Galle station has now been in operation several years, and it is pleasing to see evidence of advantages arising from it, which have already, in part, extended their blessed results beyond the grave.

The number in society is comparatively small, and were the Committee fully aware of the local obstacles which oppose the extension of this highly interesting branch of the mission, they would see to their entire satisfaction, that the Brethren who were employed here in former years acted conscientiously, and ever studied to promote, what, from their knowledge of the people, and long experience in the work, they conceived to be the best interests of the church of Christ. Young people in these parts are generally so circumstanced as to be almost under the necessity of adhering to customs and practices incompatible with the rules of our society, and the abandonment of these habitual improprieties of conduct, requires a strength of moral principle, rarely to be met with in a land peopled with the spiritually dead, or with those who consider themselves unaccountable and unattended creatures. It is true " there is only one condition previously required, of those who desire admission into these societies, namely, a desire to flee from the wrath to come, and to be saved from their sins," yet as this must be evidenced " by doing no harm—by avoiding evil of every kind," we cannot return those as members of our Society who are lovers of pleasure more than lovers of God. We have at present two classes which meet on Thursday evenings. Brother Stoup has several other persons under regular instruction of whom he entertains the best hopes, and the Committee may be assured, that although our classes are small, they consist, as far as man can judge, of steady christians, whose minds are under the influence of religion, and whose names, we hope, are in the book of life.

There being no Chaplain at present in Galle, we read prayers and preach in English in the Chapel at 11 o'clock on Sunday morning; and this, as well as the Portuguese service in the evening, is well attended; indeed we have the satisfaction and pleasure of preaching the everlasting gospel, in our own and in foreign languages, to what we consider in this country, large, respectable and attentive congregations. May the HOLY GHOST apply the word of salvation to the hearts of our hearers!

Amongst the natives the work prospers most at *Gindura,* a village four miles north of the Fort of Galle. Brother Stoup devotes much attention to this place, he speaks encouragingly respecting his prospects of usefulness, and his hopes of success appear well founded; but whether expectations be realized or disappointed, the prudent faithful labourer will not lose his reward.

Last Sunday, the 10th instant, the usual anniversary sermon was preached in English by Brother Bridgnell to a respectable company, who were much pleased with the discourse which Br. B. founded on, "Go ye into all the world and preach the gospel to every creature." In the afternoon Br. Hume preached in Singhalese from Isaiah lx. 11. *"Therefore thy gates shall be open continually, they shall not be shut day nor night that men may bring unto thee the forces of the gentiles, and that their Kings may be brought; for the nation and Kingdom that will not serve thee shall perish."* The congregation was not so large as might have been expected, partly owing we believe to the approach of the Singhalese new-year: when the natives of all ranks devote their time to amusement and festivity. Brother M'Kenny intended preaching in Portuguese in the evening, but heavy rain prevented the people from attending. Had not the weather proved unfavorable, I am persuaded the chapel could not have contained the congregation. The collections amounted to One hundred and nine Rix-dollars, eight fanams.

The signs of the times in Asia, as well as in Europe mark the commencement of a period more happy and glorious than the church has yet known: heathen nations are yielding to the sway of Christian conquerors. The way of the kings of the east is preparing: and converts to the religion of Jesus are increasing on every hand. All nations whom thou hast made shall come and worship before thee, O Lord! and shall glorify thy name, for thou art great and doest wondrous things, thou art God alone.

I remain, Reverend and Dear Sirs,
Respectfully and affectionately yours,
SAMUEL ALLEN.

THE MATURA STATION.

No communication from this Station has been received.

THE JAFFNA STATION.

Mission House, Jaffna, March 31st 1825.

DEAR FATHERS AND BRETHREN,

The sickness and distress of the last quarter (though now abated,) have greatly deranged our plans of usefulness, and placed us, as it respects our country work, considerably in the back ground. We are however in some degree recovering, and hope soon to acquire our former prosperity with a considerable increase.

In the begining of last month, I spent a fortnight on the Point Pedro part of the circuit, and was comforted amidst the discouragements arising from the strength of heathen preju-dices, in seeing that the Lord followed his word with a blessing. In the School-room erected by Brother Bott I had several interesting congregations of natives; and found real delight in publishing to them the glad tidings of salvation. In the house of the Magistrate also, I preached several times in Portuguese, and on one occasion, a young lady who had felt a godly sor-row for sin, but who could not believe, was enabled to say, my Lord and my God. I had also the pleasure of opening a fine school-room (built free of expence by the villagers) where there are one hundred native boys, and the people heard with great attention the words of everlasting life.

It was with considerable surprise and regret that I found the old Dutch church had been razed from the ground; and what is worse, that some of the stones were applied to the building of Verapeity temple வீரபத்திரா கொயில. I went into the area of that place, and found the desecrated mate-rials of the house of the Lord scattered over its surface: and amongst the rest, the fragments of a grave stone which when joined together, informed us that a gentleman had been buried there about 120 years ago, but this memorial of his death has not been spared; and his remains are now covered by the Plantain tree. I know it is very possible to attach too much importance to a matter of this kind, but it is quite clear that this once noble edifice was built for the service of the true and living God: and it accords with christian charity to hope that many sincere souls had there offered up prayers and praises to that Being who has declared himself to be jealous of his holy name. I also heard of the ruins of another large christian church at Varany (about ten miles from Point Pe-dro,) and, accompanied by the Magistrate, made a visit to that

place.   Through an inadvertence, we did not arrive there till
the evening: but the light of the new moon assisted us to inspect this once flourishing establishment, and seemed to give a
kind of melancholy interest to the sacred place, whose com-
partments are now covered with jungle and wild thorns and
occupied by a variety of poisonous reptiles.   It may appear
something like effeminacy of imagination and thought, but I
could not help saying, yes here once walked the priest in his
sombre attire giving his blessings or offerings up his prayers;
and there knelt the people confessing and adoring the "God
of the gentiles too."   But the priest has long since ceased to
chaunt and the people to pray: his house is now roofless: and
in the village the name of Christ is no more known.   I could
not help thinking also it would be a work of real mercy to
build up this waste place of Zion and if we could not do better, to appoint one of our native Assistants to preach and give
them the words of everlasting life ; a blessing of which in almost the best of times they were destitute.

The good work in Jaffna goes on steadily, and we hope in the
name of the Lord it will continue to prosper.   Some time ago a
gentleman sent 300 Rix-dollars which I distributed amongst
the poor: this with a sum of nearly 400 Rix-dollars collected
for a poor widow member of our congregation has done much
good.

The Portuguese class which was formed about seven months
ago became so large as to oblige us to divide it ; and we have
given one portion to a lady who was brought to God during
the ministrations of our first Brethren.

Thus, dear Fathers and Brethren, you see we have cause for
thankfulness and humility ; and we beg you will not forget us
in your prayers.

Brother Stead is well and happy in his work, and joins,
                                        Yours affectionately,
                                                J. ROBERTS.

THE TRINCOMALIE STATION.

Trincomalie, April 9th, 1825.

DEAR BRETHREN,

There are few conditions, in which it is possible for a person to be placed more replete with anxiety, than that of a Missionary to the Heathen: he feels that his responsibilities are
awful, and knows that the expectations of others very often
exceed the bounds of moderation,

For my own part, I almost blush when I calmly reflect on some of my first letters and observations on missionary subjects. Every step I took proved the ardour of my mind; but after having laboured so many years, with what success God only knows, but certainly not correspondent either with my wishes or expectations, I have learned that much patience and persevering industry are requisite, and after all we may possibly not have the gratification of much real fruit.

At the commencement of the quarter, the work of God on this station had a promising appearance, and I can have no doubt but many were sincerely inquiring " What must we do to be saved?" Some of these hold fast their confidence—many have fallen away,—one has been removed by death and his soul, has I trust, entered the paradise of God.

For myself, I am sorry to add, that continued affliction for nearly the last three months obliges me to leave my station for a short time.

> I remain, dear Brethren,
> yours truly,
> J. BOTT.

THE NEGAPATAM STATION.

Negapatam, March 17, 1825.

DEAR BRETHREN,

In contributing my share of information, it may not be unacceptable briefly to state the labour of the station I occupy. On Sunday morning English service is performed in the Dutch Church, and in the evening Portuguese service in the chapel which has been lately erected. On Tuesday evening is the Tamul service, and on Thursday evening the Portuguese meets. These are three schools on the station containing 140 children.

The chapel has to a great degree answered every purpose we had in view in its erection. The congregations are larger; and under my present circumstances, it affords a common ground on which I can with the greatest propriety meet those who might hesitate to come to the Mission-House.

About the middle of last month, I made a visit to Trichinopoly where we have a small society of Soldiers in the 48th Regiment. I spent a very happy and profitable time with them. There are 14 in society and 6 on trial, and I believe most if not all of them are desirous to be Christians indeed.

My Superintendent of schools has been very active in distributing Tracts and speaking to the people on religious subjects, and I most sincerely hope we may see good done among the Heathen here.

I need scarcely intimate that I have at various times severely felt the loss I have lately sustained. But God has been my help and consolation. The last quarter has abounded with mercies for which I ought to be grateful.

I am, Dear Brethren,

yours affectionately,

JAMES MOWAT.

THE MADRAS STATION.

Conjeveram, January 25, 1825.

DEAR BRETHREN,

From this Heathen place, I drop a few lines for your information, to explain the reasons for my present journey. My last from Madras stated, that Brother Hoole was sick at Negapatam. He arrived however better than I anticipated; and I was the more glad, of his ability to take the work for eight or ten days, because it liberated me, and afforded an opportunity for this present trip, which has been long so very necessary, but which we could not perform before. Immediately therefore on Brother Hoole's arrival, preparation was made to carry into effect the establishment of a native school at Wallajahbad, where we have not had any person to take care of the premises, and which the people began to think we had forsaken. Our assistant Missionary Mr. Kats was going to Negapatam, and I wished him to go by way of Wallajahbad, and I would follow, the day after he set out from Madras. On Saturday we arrived, and the Commandant Lieutenant Colonel Pereira, sent out notice to the Military (which are now few in number) that divine service would be held on Sunday January 23d "at the Wallajahbad chapel." I dined at the Commandant's on Saturday, and the next day all the military not necessarily engaged, including the Commandant himself, were present. The Liturgy was read and a sermon delivered, to a very attentive congregation. Mr. Kats addressed a congregation in the Tamul language in the afternoon. In the evening I had conversation with an excellent Lady and Gentleman lately from England; and closed the day with reading to the family, and prayer. From this amiable couple I received many expressions of kindness and attention. A few periodical papers or notices were distributed to great advantage; and I had no room for regret except when reflections broke in upon me of *what good we were not doing* by being prevented from taking excursions much more frequently than we (in our weak state) can now perform. A person kindly undertook to look after the erection of the native school; and I left the master and another christian man to remain to manage the business, until we can make another visit, because I durst not stay long lest Brother Hoole should be injuring himself by taking all the work of the station, Native and English: a labour which has been described to you in a former letter. Having made some necessary observations concerning the state, population, and circumstances of the place, which all ended in one expression of sorrow that we could pay so little attention to places where apparently the door stands wide open to enter in and do good, I took leave of the people, and this morning found myself among the Bramins at the Temple of Conjeveram. Several of them knew me, and put me in mind that I had been there at the discovery of the god, and that we had rain in consequence soon afterwards; and as a proof, they shewed me the tank (about 100 yards square and very deep) which had in it more water than would take a man overhead. This brought on a long conversation, maintained with great animation on their part. I pointed out the folly of attempting, to impose upon any but very ignorant people, with such a stupid matter as an evident log of wood; and noticed the cringing credulity of the poor women and children, who waded through the mud to see this dumb idol; and appealed to their consciences and their common sense if they were not guilty of a gross imposition. They replied to the whole by a hearty laugh when I referred to the poor people being so grossly imposed upon! A number of Brahmins followed me to the Choultry, and sat down conversing on various topics of a general nature, their principal object was to receive some present for shewing the temple. I turned the scale upon themselves by observing that I was now promoting charitable gifts to support schools, and I should be very happy to have their names on the list with any subscription which they might be disposed to bestow. They declined my proposal and did not succeed with their own.

Great Conjeveram. We reached this early in the afternoon: I walked round the principal temple, and through several parts which appear going fast to decay. The banyan-trees have got into parts of the buildings, and they are growing, and shaking down the upper works. The whole range of buildings at this place, the numerous choultries, or rest-houses, and stone works of this assemblage of heathen temples, have cost prodigious labour to bring them up to the extensive size which they now are.

Here I found so great a call for tracts and Tamul books that my stock was soon exhausted, and I could not fill half the number of hands which were stretched out to receive them. The Brahmins came into the choultry and sat down to converse with me, and every one of them requested tracts and took them away to read, with an apparent disposition with which I could not but feel pleased. Another person came to ask whether another school was not to be established, and he had brought a person with him to recommend as a master. He requested a part of the scriptures, but I could not meet his wishes, and many poor boys were obliged to go away very unwillingly with a promise that when I came, or one of us came, next month, we would be mindful to supply their wants.

They lingered about, hardly believing me, or thinking a month a very long time to anticipate what they now wished, putting into their hands. At length one man came and pleaded so much with me, that I went to look if a copy of the gospel might not be left, and I found the gospel by St. John. On remonstrating with my servant, why he had kept back this copy, he said, he could not think master would give away the *last book* but keep one for himself, especially as the journey was not *half* done. However after holding the gospel in my hand some time, I thought, the man asks so earnestly I cannot refuse him, and he bore it away expressing great thankfulness. Many persons hearing others had got books, came also, and I felt all the disappointment of a person not having faith, when I set out, to believe, that God would open a way for his own word to be distributed. I am now therefore without a tract, without a single gospel or testament, and have not travelled over half the ground intended. I hope my faith will be enlarged in future, that I may not suffer again the condemnation which I now feel on finding myself destitute of the scriptures and tracts, that I may not have another opportunity (perhaps) of distributing.

Surrounded by the noise of heathen worship,

I am, affectionately yours,

R. CARVER.

Poonamalee, January 27th, 1825.

DEAR BRETHREN,

Two days ago I addressed a letter to you from Conjeveram. In order that you may have a connected view of this short journey, I beg leave to send a few remarks concerning the places and people which I visited on my way back to Madras. Having given directions concerning the enclosure of the ground of the Chapel at Wallajahbad, and employed a person to take measures to erect in it a suitable Native School, the place being at an angle of the native village and bazar, and therefore very favourable for the attendance of the Children: all my Stock of Tamul Tracts exhausted at the lesser and greater Conjeveram, I rose early to set out to a part of the Country I had not visited before. Perhaps the best and easiest way for myself will be to hand you the remarks contained in my Journal; which are copied for your information,

Wednesday January 26th, 1825, Left Great Conjeveram about 3 o'clock in the morning, and stumbled over bad ground in the dark till we had nearly lost ourselves, not being able to discern the way. A rough old fellow resisted my servant, and would not shew him the road. I called the man and spoke a few kind words to him, and his lion-like disposition was pacified, and he trudged on till day-light, shewed us how to do for ourselves. We met with little interesting on our way. As we receded from Conjeveram, the trees began to disappear, and the Country was naked and little cultivated. About mid-way we came to some ruined Choultries of massy stone-work, but which could not resist the destructive force of the expanding banyan-tree, that seemed to mock and cast to the ground the labours of man, with derision and contempt. Near them a very large vaulted brick-house shared the same fate: it appeared of Moorish origin and had been like an impregnable castle to its owner. In some parts cultivation was pretty vigorously conducted, and the fields had a green and pleasant appearance. Though it was mid-day and the sun was very hot, yet the people were singing and drawing water * upon the simplest of all principles, the very balance power of our steam engine beam. The expedition with which two men can draw water supplies a constant stream which is directed to all parts of the field. At one of these stone Choultries we were obliged to remain during the heat of the day:

---

* Therefore with joy shall ye draw water out of the wells of Salvation. Sing unto the Lord, &c. &c. Isaiah XII. We are frequently led to passages of Scripture, when observing the customs of the East.

the distance between the place we had left and Tripassoor being about 30 Miles was more than we could accomplish without some refreshment. A Moor's burying ground was on our right and a deserted heathen temple on our left. One of our people had a very singular stroke (as we supposed) of the sun. He was taken suddenly with a shaking of the hands and turned round rapidly on his heels. On recovering a little he said that he felt affected with giddiness in the head, which no doubt was caused by the heat of the sun. Being obliged to remain and endure the heat and glare of the sun and little to engage myself I began a conversation with an old man, who attended to wait on passengers, about the villages and people which we could perceive at some distance from us.—He proved quite conversant and acquainted with all the events of the Country, and especially with the troubles in Hyder Allay's and Tippoo's wars. Monsr. Lally's name was quite familiar to him and indeed it is so yet to many natives who remember his severities. The old man's father was in the British service in the fatal action near the place, where these remarks are made, when Colonel Baillie's† detachment was nearly all destroyed and himself made prisoner, this boy was there also but escaped and now recounted the barbarities of that unhappy day as if it had been but an event of yesterday. He named several officers who were either killed or taken. You may judge how much interested I was in a circumstance, where so many of my countrymen a few years ago had shed their blood, to burst the Shackles of that tyranny which oppressed this people and to open a way for Missionaries to approach with the sacred Scriptures, the very last recesses of idolatry. Could any of us pass through the places where these things happened and perhaps tread upon the very dust of our countrymen, without a sigh for their sufferings or gratitude to God for the present open door which he has given us, we should be unworthy of the name of Briton or of Christian.

Tripassoor. We had dispatched a messenger to inform the pensioners stationed here that I would preach to them on passing through, and not having named the hour, they were assembled when I reached the place. Conversation occupied the company a short time, and I went to prepare for the evening service. A large number of the people assembled to hear the word of God, and they paid very great attention indeed to

† See an interesting account of this Engagement in the Encyclopedia Perthensis Vol. xii, p. 111, 112. A pensioner told me that he passed over the ground in 1800 and then it was strewed with bones and sculls.

what was delivered. Many children were present to whom I gave a few minters which a kind Lady had entrusted to me to bestow upon any deserving them. They were received with great thankfulness by the girls, descendants of Europeans. Several periodicals were distributed to the pensioners, but our stock was not half sufficient to supply those who were desirous of receiving them. I therefore promised to send them some religious works by the first opportunity. If any people deserve our sympathy, such persons as these are, ought to be of the number; laid aside after many years of service for their country, and many of them slaves to bad habits, they are stationed at this inland heathen place, without any one to watch over them, no Minister resident near them; every man is left to follow his own way, without any check or moral restraints. It can be no wonder that intemperance and gross evils exist, or that indifference to the Sabbath and divine things should become manifest. Without knowing much of the extent to which vice may reign in a place where I remained a few hours only, I can bear testimony to the decency and solemnity with which these poor people listened to the word of God that was read and explained to them. May the Lord follow it with his gracious blessings, and fasten the truth upon their minds; and may his sparing mercy lead them every one to unfeigned repentance!

The station of Tripassoor appears greatly reduced from its original importance. It has a rather extensive brick Fort but it is in ruins, and, as a place of defence abandoned. The cadets who were sent here to study the language and prepare themselves for the service, were removed to Cuddalore, and since that period the pensioners have been placed here, they occupy the buildings which remain, but many of them are scarcely tenable. Several heathen temples are enclosed within the walls of the fort, but they are partly falling into a ruinous state. The native population does not appear large.

Trivaloor is a short distance from Tripassoor, and much more famed for its heathen temples. I went into the principal one, which has a large tank of water near it, faced with cut granite, and apparently upwards of three hundred yards square. At this place the people hold the Monkeys belonging to the temple in great veneration and the tribes of them which infest the place are exceedingly mischievous, pulling the tiles from the roofs of houses, and stealing and destroying every thing within their reach, and no person dares to molest them, or throw a stone at them, so that they walk about one, and grin and snarl with impunity. The Bramin of the temple refused entrance into it, and I therefore left the place with a slight inspection.

At a place called *Trioor* some little distance we came to a number of ruined temples I walked through parts of them. Sent for the Bramins who complained loudly that most of the temples were going to decay, and that they could not get money sufficient to keep them in repair, much less build new ones. The large ribs of granite had been thrown down on every side, and one part of the temple only was in any tolerable state of repair, the Bramins had become poor, and were reduced in number, and that they had been declining nearly one hundred years. Indeed the place bore evident marks of poverty and ruin: a respectable person pleaded very much to have a school here, and said 100 children would be collected. *Poonamalee* : we reached this place about noon. I called upon One of the pensioners to inform him of my arrival, and that I would preach that evening to the people: of this he gave notice during the day. The minister at this station, the Rev. Mr. Wetherherd kindly offered me the rites of hospitality and after taking some refreshment with him I walked round the garden and premises. He is superintendant of the Poonamalee male and female Asylums. About one hundred and fifty children are in each. These children chiefly belong to the soldiers of different Regiments stationed in the presidency. Divine service was held in a school of the Church Mission, where a very interesting company assembled Afterwards I went to the residence of one of our Members, and upon enquiry I was able to collect eight persons who resolved to meet in class, which several of them had long neglected to do. I exhorted them not to forsake the assembling of themselves together pointed out the good effects of union, put their names upon a class paper, and resolved to visit them again soon. I then prayed with them and commended them to the care of our gracious and heavenly Father who can supply the place of Ministers and preserve the faithful soul that trusts in him.

A little after midnight I reached the Mission House Madras.

Yours affectionately,

R. CARVER.

Madras, February 24, 1825.

DEAR BRETHREN,

To give a connected view of the work on this station it will be necessary to notice a few particulars subsequent to the month of August 1824. In the communications from us in October last we were unable to give any information of the general state of the society. It was needful that I should become acquainted with the station before any remarks could be expected from me. During the latter part of the year our situation became so peculiar, and the labours so multiform and oppressive that this opportunity is the first afforded us to turn our attention to these subjects. Soon after my arrival at Madras, I experienced some indisposition, and had one smart attack of a spasmodic nature, but through mercy, and by a timely application of suitable medicine, nothing serious, beyond a few days confinement ensued: another person however who had a similar attack on the same night, expired about seven o'clock next morning.

About the latter end of August Brother Hoole accompanied me to Wallajahbad and Conjeveram, which has been noticed in the Report of the Auxiliary Society for Madras. The celebrated temples of the latter place exhibit a considerable knowledge of masonry and sculpture, and they are built on a large and magnificent scale, chiefly of granite. At little Conjeveram, one Mandabam (a place open on all sides, composed of pillars of granite covered with ribs of rock cemented together with lime) of one hundred pillars, is a very remarkable specimen of labour. The sculptures are so numerous, men, horses, and animals intermixed (cut with much spirit in a bold projecting design) that it takes a considerable time to look over them. The principal figures are representations of the actions of their gods, and consequently several are of a description subversive of all decency. Great is the repute in which these temples are held, and every thing that could be done has been attempted by the Brahmins to establish the opinion that these places and all near and around them is sacred ground. The Brahmins generally, are civil, but some times persons of their class, carry their cringing attentions to meanness. I was much struck on one occasion lately, with reflections on the great change which must have taken place in India, since the British power appeared in it. Once, every approach to heathen temples was debarred, or difficult, but now a person may generally inspect them at his leisure with the exception of one place where the idol is deposited. The temples and choultries are astonishing monuments, of patient labour and persevering industry exercised in the prosecution of a wrong cause. Were christians to use in India a proportionate measure of zeal in the cause of their Divine Master we should soon hear it said "The Lord had made bare his holy arm in the eyes of all the nations, and all the ends of the earth, shall see the salvation of our God. Confounded be all they that serve graven images, that boast themselves of idols." Concerning a second visit to these places and other parts you have had information by letters from Conjeveram and from Poonamalie.

The melancholy intelligence of the death of Sister Mowatt at Negapatam, reached us in October. Our bereaved Brother's case demanded immediate attention, and Brother Hoole kindly offered to proceed without delay to render him every help and consolation in our power which this unexpected stroke had made necessary.

In November the anniversary of the Auxiliary Society for Madras was held, and very respectably attended. Brother Hoole's absence on this occasion was severely felt by me, because much local information was necessary, which his residence on the station would have given him an opportunity of affording. The Brethren of the London Society, the Rev. Messrs. Crisp, Marsie, Taylor and Traveller laid us under great obligations by their kind and ready assistance at the Anniversary. About this period and afterwards when Brother England became sick the work fell unusually heavy upon me: but being graciously favoured with health, the places of worship were supplied, with but very little interruption. The Lovefeast was held in December, although I had no one to assist me, and the watchnight was observed at the close of the year, having to conduct the whole service alone.

At the end of the year the schools were examined. This branch of our work has not been so much cultivated in Madras as we wish to see it. The schools at Royapettah, St. Thome and at St. Thomas's Mount might be greatly improved (and others might be established) could due attention be paid to them. What little has been done however may form a basis upon which a superstructure may be raised, and we hope that when help from Europe shall enable us to give attendance to these things that a very satisfactory improvement in the school department will soon be experienced. Access to the people is becoming easier every day. The cause conducted upon christian principles will be attended by the blessing of the most High; though it may be sometimes apparently slow in its progress, yet it will be certain in its growth, and it will take deeper root among the people, until it becomes established.

At Wallajahbad a Schoolmaster was placed in January last, and we are informed by his first report, that he has been successful in collecting several Children. We are erecting a School at this place distinct from the Chapel, which will make that establishment complete.

The Congregations in the Circuit had been regular and serious from my knowledge of them, till our entrance upon a new year, when a spirit of zeal and deligence was particularly manifested. Several arrangements were made to render our labours more effectual. The accounts of the Auxiliary Society for Madras were ordered to be closed annually on December 31.—A Branch Society for Royapettah and St. Thome dated its origin from the 1st. January. At Royapettah a Native Association took its rise at the same time. Many of the members of the Society at Madras expressed a strong desire to have some means of cultivating a more intimate acquaintance with each other in the pursuit of useful knowledge, and to improve themselves in every way within their power. A meeting was therefore convened, when it was resolved unanimously that a library should be established on liberal principles, for the use of the Society chiefly, not excluding others proper to be associated with them, to be denominated, *The Wesleyan Mission Library for Madras.* More particulars concerning it will be given afterwards. Seral handsome Donations of Books have been made to it already, and other donations which may be made will be thankfully acknowledged.

Another circumstance, noticed in our communications of October, we have much pleasure in referring to again. Brother Hoole then stated our intention of commencing divine service in the Portuguese language, and to call into action the abilities of the converted Catholic Priest. Brother Hoole began by preaching the first sermon himself, and the Sunday following Mr. Martins made his first attempt in St. Thome, in the very midst of the people from whose errors he has so lately emerged. Perhaps a short extract from my journal of that day may be admitted.

"Sunday, February 6, 1825. In the evening at seven o'clock Mr. Martin the converted priest delivered his first sermon, in our chapel at St. Thome, from Luke xviii. 13. "O Deus tem misericordia de me pecador." God be merciful to me a sinner. The people had been duly informed by a public notice, sent

o

round, in English and Portuguese. The little chapel was filled, and many persons crowded round the doors and windows to hear the word. A good deal of interest appeared to be excited by this circumstance; and especially among the Roman Catholics. One poor woman exclaimed, as the Priest and I approached the chapel, Lord Jesus what shall happen next! meaning it is supposed, how strange a thing had happened that a Romish priest should preach in a protestant, a Methodist chapel! His language was rather higher than that commonly used at Madras; but the people assured me they understood him very well. He appeared a little embarrassed for a few minutes at the commencement; but he overcame that soon, and then spoke in a free and easy manner. May the Lord, who chooses his own instruments for the conversion of men, be graciously pleased to direct us, to assist and encourage those with whom we may, in this land be favoured and entrusted.

In my letter from Poonamale, I named having formed a class of eight persons who had for some time forsaken the assembling of themselves together. Brother Hoole visited them this month from whence he addressed a note to me, the following is an extract: I arrived at Poonamalle in good time, and by about half past six o'clock had a full house, I suppose from 60 to 80. After preaching in English, I desired those who understood Tamil to remain, and I gave them a short address and prayed; poor people, they complain of much of want of instruction. After this I met the class, which has increased to eleven; in doing this I was obliged to use three languages. There seems to be an earnest spirit of enquiry among them, and I think if we could give a little attention to this quarter we should see a little more fruit of our labours than in some places.

Regular services have been conducted among the military in Fort St. George which have been very well attended and very encouraging. Our correspondence with the societies in different parts of India has been rather extensive. Several numbers have been communicated, and others remain to be copied and forwarded. Three hundred copies of the edition of our Hymn Book, printed at Colombo, has at length arrived in Madras, where they had been a long time much wanted. We are obliged to defer observations on many other things till another opportunity.

Dear Brethren, yours Affectionately,

R. CARVER.

Madras, March 9th, 1825.

DEAR BRETHREN,

It has been a matter of considerable satisfaction to myself, and no doubt to you, that we have had so much pleasing information to communicate from this part of mission labours. Although we have had to pass through deep waters, yet our Heavenly Father has not left us without the consolations of his Holy Spirit, nor suffered us to labour in vain among the people. That we cannot attend to the calls made upon us, nor administer to the spiritual wants of a people willing to hear the words of life and salvation, and in many cases begging, nay imploring help, is to small concern and grief to us. But what are we among so many? Indeed what proportion is there between the entire company of teachers and the mass of population to be taught?

On Sunday March 6th, I preached to St. Thomé to a most encouraging and attentive congregation. The Roman priest accompanied me, and afterwards preached therein Portuguese. In the evening, English and Tamul services at Royapettah were conducted by Brother Hoole; I also attended to assist in introducing our own Hymns and tunes among the people. They begin to sing some of them pretty well, and it appears to give spirit to the services, which have frequently been dull and cold by low and lifeless singing. In the evening I preached in the new chapel Royapettah Graemigua, and then administered the Holy Sacrament to about forty people. On my return home at ten o'clock in the night I found Br. Hoole equally fatigued as myself with the labours of the day. He had been among the natives in the streets and lanes distributing tracts and conversing with the Heathen; when it became dark he told them that he must go to the chapel, he had to assist the priest; one of the people observed, "O! he need not do that, they would bring a light and he could stay and make a sermon to them, they would hear!"

Our communications with different parts of India, and our labours around Madras, will not permit us to give so much attention to the recording of things which you may wish to hear, yet you may depend upon receiving whatever strength and time will admit of. Yesterday I was among the people at St. Thomas's Mount; and to day we have received very pleasing letters from our society at Rangoon. We have been for some time very anxious to hear concerning them.

To preserve a little order in my remarks, I may notice a few things concerning St. Thomas's mount in the first place,

For several months we have given all the attention we could to the mount. The place is occupied as a cantonment for the Artillery. Many widows of officers and men who have fallen in the Birmese war reside in it: and of course a population of natives. The Native school is well conducted, and we hope to see fruits in due time. With the people of the army and the residents there we have endeavoured to cultivate an acquaintance; and in order to render religious instruction by preaching, more beneficial, we have followed it up with pastoral visitation. We generally contrive to go early and even remain late that we may have a better opportunity to converse on religious subjects, though it be sometimes midnight when we get home: having to travel 7 or 8 miles. Our situation is such that we cannot visit this place more frequently than once a fortnight but lately one of our leaders in H. M. 69th Regt. now stationed at Fort St. George has felt himself so much interested in the work as to visit it and preach to the Soldiers on the Sabbath-day. The congregations have increased, and many persons of the Army have held prayer meetings in the school Chapel every day, and some wish to meet in Class. These sent a request by this Leader, who gave us the names of as many as were desirous, to be thus united in a Christian body that they might improve the opportunities afforded them for spiritual instruction, to be formed into a Class. They requested a special visit, to be made immediately, but to this our only reply was, " We really have not one day to spare, being engaged every day in the week, you must wait, till the usual day to visit the Mount shall give us an opportunity to see you. We will however come earlier and meet you in the middle of the day." Accordingly I went up in the morning (of the 8th of March) and after waiting upon the Chaplain, who is of liberal sentiments and lately from England, and dining with him and his amiable Lady, I met the people in the school chapel and formed them into a class consisting of eight members. The rules of the society were read and given to each and after speaking to all of them, and praying, we commended each other to God. May He keep them from evil and prosper them. In the evening I preached to a larger congregation than usual. We expect to form a female class but want a leader.

The protracted war in Burmah has been fatal to many of the troops and several of our society have died through the fatigues consequent upon so much exposure and so many privations. Accounts concerning the christian experience of some of them in their last hours have been sent to us, and they have afforded fresh proof, if proof were wanting, that God is faithful.

A few words below extracted from a letter from one of our Leaders in the Army may be acceptable. It was written on February 12, 1825, and enclosed Rupees 150: the next day they embarked on the River to proceed towards the Capital of the Birmese Empire.

To Revd. R Carver,

DEAR SIR,

I suppose you have heard of the death of the late Sergt. Major Thompson, of the 3rd Regt. He died at Martaban 28th November 1824 about seven o'clock on Sunday evening, I often called to see him during his illness at Rangoon. Although his affliction was severe and of a painful nature, I always found him resigned to the will of his Heavenly Father. I one day asked him if he did not wish to be restored to health; he answered, I have no choice nor will of my own; let the Lord do what seemeth him good.— I observed I often felt it difficult to suffer the will of God. He said I thought so once, but at present feel it perfectly easy and pleasant; I have Strength according to my day: these afflictions will work out for me a far more and eternal weight of Glory.

He spoke after, of that glorious rest that remaineth for the people of God. The Devil (he said) endeavours to persuade me that I have no part nor lot in the matter, yet I apply to my loving Saviour; he is the chiefest among ten thousand, and to me altogether lovely : I shall soon see him as he is, and where he is I shall be also. On another occasion when I called to see him, he told me that he hated Sin in every shape, and said, "*What should I do now if I had religion to seek! What a blessing when heart and flesh fail, to have Christ for my Portion!* Like David I often enquire, *When* I shall appear before God. I long for an opportunity to meet with the people of God."—I desired Br. Coleman to meet me at his house :—as soon as he saw us, he said I am glad to see you *both*, but wish you would come *One* at a time. I profit more by your *separate* conversation. When we were speaking of the society in our different regiments, and the happiness we experienced since we had an opportunity to meet for public worship at the great Dagan pagoda, and the advantages we expected to derive from these blessed means, he said "I will come up to the pagoda and conduct the means, I desire nothing so much as to speak for Him who has done so much for me (at that time he was too weak to walk one hundred yards, yet I could scarcely persuade him to stay at home.) He said, on another occasion, I expect to leave my bones among the Birmans, I am as near heaven in this country as in any other. Jesus is Omnipresent and will by and by find my body, should it mingle among ten thousand Birmans. If this earthly tabernacle is soon disolved (and I think it soon will) I have a building of God, not made with hands eternal in the heavens. Conversing with him another day, we observed a heathen worshiping the sun: before he had performed his devotions a cloud with rain covered the object of his adoration——he continued on his knees and refused to rise until the shower and cloud had passed away; when he felt the beams of a meridian sun he concluded his devotion and retired. Brother Thompson made some remarks and asked me if I ever rose from my knees before I was warmed and comforted by the beams of the sun of righteousness. I felt this a severe reproof and said, I had often retired cold and careless, and that this heathen had taught me an important and necessary lesson. I visited Br. Thompson every day when not on duty and always found him in the same heavenly frame. The society have lost a worthy member and a decided and exemplary christian. W. S.

> Yours, affectionately,
> R. CARVER.

This letter came too late for insertion in its proper place.

THE MATURA STATION.

Matura, April 15th, 1823.

REV. AND DEAR SIRS,

The encouraging prospects of usefulness on this part of the circuit during the past quarter call for our sincere gratitude to God. Our schools, with one or two exceptions give us as much satisfaction as on the whole can be reasonably expected, and we have been happy to perceive that by the public reading of the scriptures several have been seriously impressed with the importance of divine things. Such have always been taken notice of and added to the number of those who receive private and more particular instruction. In this way about 13 have been admitted since the beginning of the year.

Our congregations continue undiminished both at the schools and at the Mission House, and an English service has been regularly held since my arrival, with the view of impressing the inhabitants with a proper sense of the obligation of the Sabbath. At Kaddawidda we have an interesting congregation every Lord's day; a very respectable family with a few of their neighbours are always found waiting to hear the word of God at the appointed hour; eight adults have at this place, after the usual term of trial, received tickets of admission into society.

Lately the establishment of prayer-meetings in the town has been attempted with great hopes and some success; in 14 houses of the Dutch inhabitants they have been received with much thankfulness and even joy: on concluding them I have from some received notes expressive of the interest they take in them, and their anxiety that they should be continued. They are always well attended. At Wirigam prayer-meetings of the same nature among the Singhalese have been commenced, and from the encouraging appearances at the begining, I have every hope that they will be generally received by the people.

During the last three months Brother Lalman at Belligam has had to pass through many severe afflictions; the intervals however in which himself or his family have enjoyed good health, he has carefully employed for the improvement of the part of the circuit where he resides. A Portuguese congregation with several prayer meetings in Singhalese have been established, and the regular attendance of as many as can be looked for at the place fully justifies their continuance.

We have in view various plans, which with the blessing of God appear calculated to promote the prosperity of the work, but until they assume some degree of maturity, we decline mentioning them lest our expectation might be disappointed? For what has been already done, to God be all the praise.

                    I am, Rev. and Dear Sirs,
                              Yours sincerely,
                         J. SUTHERLAND.

. The Brethren of the Tamul district are respectfully informed that, the next District Meeting will be held in Jaffnapatam, and will commence on the last Monday in July, 1825, according to the Minutes.

                              R. CARVER.

Extracts

FROM

QUARTERLY LETTERS, &c.

No. XXIV.   JULY, 1824.

THE COLOMBO STATION.

Colombo, 30th July, 1824.

To the REV. MESSRS. BUNTING, TAYLOR, *and* WATSON; *Secretaries to the* Wesleyan Missionary Society, London.

REV. AND DEAR SIRS,

IT was with peculiar pleasure that I learned from Mr. Watson's letter of the 28th January, that it is the wish of our Committee, that the Publication of our Quarterly Letters and School Reports should be continued, of which pleasing intelligence I have given due notice to all the Brethren of the Districts; at the same time, recommending, that all letters should be addressed to the Secretaries for the time being, and viewed in the light of official communications, which will answer the ends of securing to our Committee, regular and important information relative to each station, and of gratifying the Brethren of the Mission with all the local intelligence desirable to be known respecting the labours of each other. Our Periodical Publication, called "Extracts of Quarterly Letters" having now your full sanction, I am persuaded the Brethren will feel encouraged to make it, if possible, more interesting than it has yet been.

I feel happy, yea rejoiced, at being enabled to assure you, that the work of God continues to prosper on this Station. Since our last Meeting, we have had the consolation of witnessing the power and saving efficacy of Divine Truth on the minds of several young men, members of our Pettah congregation, who have joined the Society, and as they know comparatively little of English, we must conclude they have principally received their religious impressions through the medium of the discourses they have heard in Portuguese, that being their vernacular language, and in which they relate their experience in Class Meeting. The Preacher's Class, which meets every Thursday evening in the Mission Chapel, is now so large, that we think we shall be obliged to divide it at no distant period, Oh! that these young converts may be kept faithful unto death.—There is one thing which inspires us with confidence in their *sincerity*;—they have no *temporal* advantage in view by making a Christian profession.

....r work among the Soldiers in the Fort is at present, perhaps, m......raging than it ever has been. Since we rented Mr. Chater's pl.......rship, our congregation has greatly improved; in fact, on the .....ay evening, it is seldom that a spare seat is to be found; the military class prospers, and its members are much united among themselves—several of whom have suffered greatly during the late sickness, but none of the Society have died in Colombo. When visiting them in the hospital I have had many opportunities of witnessing, in their experience, the glorious triumph of grace over extreme suffering, and the fear of death. The experience of the apostle appeared to be common to most of them; " *For me to live is Christ, but to die is gain,*" I think I can only remember one case in which there was any thing expressive of a decided wish to live, if consistent with the divine will; and this arose out of a feeling worthy of Christianity: the poor man, worn to a skeleton with continued fever, and sinking under extreme weakness, turned his eyes to his wife, (who stood weeping, and disconsolate by his bed,) and said, for the sake of this poor woman and my child I should like to live a little longer, if it were the will of God. The scene was too *touching* not to be sensibly felt: I was led out much in prayer for his restoration, and in a few weeks afterwards, he was perfectly convalescent. The hospital of this small Garrison has exhibited, for some months past, one of the most dismal scenes I ever witnessed; for some time there were not less than one hundred individuals in it, principally laid up with fever, to which about fifty have fallen a sacrifice. With the exception of the military, we have not had in Colombo many European cases of fever, and none have been fatal, with one exception. This dreadful disease has raged principally among the country-born and natives. The Mahometans, who are considered the most healthy and robust class of natives, have been great sufferers; hundreds of them in and about this populous town have been carried off, and the mournful aspect of things has been increased, by their barbarous and chilling processions in the night, crowds of them parading the streets, and calling out with *all their might* to their false prophet for relief; and the pitiable Singhalese, who have not yet been brought under the influence of the Gospel, have had recourse to their Devil's ceremonies, thinking in that way to procure assistance. Under these circumstances of course we could not look on with indifference; we have felt it our duty to hold prayer meetings every Monday evening to supplicate the throne of grace in behalf of the people of the country; we have found these to be seasons of much profit to our souls, and this painful dispensation has tended greatly to quicken us, and to increase our faith and confidence in God. Our meeting for supplication is held in Mr. Chater's

Chapel, in the Pettah, and in our own, alternately; and now I rejoice to say, we feel ourselves called upon to unite *praises* with our prayers, upon account of the very favorable change which has taken place already: the weather is cooler, rains have fallen throughout the country, and there is a cheering prospect of the entire removal of the malady with which the country has been so long afflicted.

Our Schools are as promising as formerly, but they have been much interrupted by the general sickness, and several of our scholars have died. However, now that the country is improving, they will return to their usual state of prosperity.—we have been able to keep up our Friday night service, at Colpetty, since the re-opening of the School in April last year. I have already written to you on the subject of the excellent New School-room we have obtained in the New Bazar, and of the increasing prosperity of that interesting Institution: the building may be with as much propriety designated a Chapel as a School, as it contains a pulpit, and has two sermons a week, one on Sunday morning, at 11 o'clock, and the other on Wednesday evening, at seven, with lamp light, which services are well attended. The Catechisms we lately received from you, we esteem very valuable, and with as little delay as possible we shall have an edition of them printed in Singhalese for the instruction of our scholars, who do not know English; a series of Catechisms such as those sent us, was just what was required in our Schools, and we feel particularly thankful for them.

Our sacramental services are in general times of much profit: we have always from 25 to 30 communicants present, and it affords a pleasing evidence of the *uniting* power of the Gospel, to see people of so many different nations, joining to yield a ready obedience to their Lord's command, " *Do this in remembrance of me.*" Here we see English, Dutch, Portuguese, and Singhalese, surrounding the Redeemer's Table, waiting to receive *the Bread of Life!*

Long ere now you will have received the proceedings of the Meeting which was held in our Pettah Chapel, on the 26th of March, for the purpose of the Colombo Circuit. It was long my wish missionary Society, for the Colombo Circuit. It was long my wish to attempt something of this kind, not that I was unaware of the difficulties which stood in the way: however, the arrival of Sir R. Ottley from the Cape, and the readiness with which he entered into our views, with the very friendly disposition of the Hon. Sir James and Lady Dorothea Campbell towards the measure, convinced us that it was our duty to proceed, and the manner in which the proposal was received by many of the most respectable persons of the settlement, inspired us with confidence as to the final result. We were, however, rather unhappy as to the time of holding the Meeting, for unexpectedly two of our most distinguished friends, Sir James Campbell, and G. Lusignan, Esq. were obliged at the same hour to attend a meeting of council, which was suddenly called; and the duties of many of our friends who hold situations in various Government offices, prevented their favouring us with their presence on the occasion: however, it is but justice to ourselves to remark, that the appointment of the hour which proved so unfavorable, was not altogether controulable by us; but should we be spared to hold our first Anniversary, our past experience will naturally dictate a better arrangement. However notwithstanding, we had not so many present as we expected, we have been enabled to establish the Society on such a foundation, that it is likely to stand, and prove a help and blessing to the Mission. Since the commencement of the Colombo Auxiliary Society, I have had the pleasure of attending the formation of a Branch to it on the Caltura station, under very pleasing circumstances; but for the particulars of which I must refer you to Brother Hume's own account. Happy am I to say, that the present aspect of the Work throughout the district is very encouraging. In the commencement of the year we could not but feel in some degree cast down, from the great reduction which took place in our number; but this very circumstance operated as a spur to greater diligence, and to more complete dependance on God; and surely we may say that he who comforteth those who are cast down, comforted us by sending to our help our dear Brethren Bridgnell, and Stoup: by them, and their affectionate and interesting communications, our spirits were greatly refreshed; we were enabled to thank God, and take courage. We have reason to be thankful that notwithstanding all our fears, the Mission Press has been kept to the present, in active operation. The Singhalese department has been employed on the Christian Institutes, translated by the Rev. Mr. Armour, for the Society for Promoting Christian Knowledge; the Portuguese, on Brother Fox's Testament, and the English, on an Edition of the large Hymn Book, for which we have very pressing demands, and the expence of which we are prepared fully to meet; when the work shall have been completed, a few copies shall be forwarded to the Committee. As Brother Gogerly's salary is now taken off this Establishment, it is likely to go on without farther end with the revision of the Singhalese Scriptures, which their very matured experience will enable them to make much more perfect, but when the C. A. B. Society may find it convenient to put the Second Edition to Press, according to the benevolent wish of the Parent Society, is it not easy to say, as our funds are very low, nor do I see (without some great exertions be made,) any prospect of their being in a more prosperous state. We know, however, when the nature of things is known, that the Parent Society will readily afford relief.

I remain Rev. and Dear Sirs,

Yours Affectionately,

J. M'KENNY.

To *the* REV. MESSRS. BUNTING, TAYLOR, *and* WATSON,
77 *Hatton Garden, London,*

HONOURED FATHERS,

The great and constant interest that you feel in the labours and successes of every Missionary must be my apology (if an apology be needed,) for addressing you through this medium, so soon after my formed communication. The conviction that " I cannot go where universal Love breathes not around," is that which has often cheered me, since I became the " messenger of the Churches " in England to those who are " ignorant, and out of the way " in Ceylon. That conviction still encourages, still supports me. To see the selfsame loving spirit manifested by those who bear the Name and proclaim the Truth, of "the God and Father of all," with that which he Himself has displayed in all his ways, and words, and works, is after the enjoyment of " fellowship with the Father and with his Son Jesus Christ," the highest, purest, most prolific source of human delight. This happiness is mine. In the truly affectionate manner in which I was received by Br. and Sister M'Kenny—in the promptitude and kindness of the congratulations presented by the Brethren in the District—in the wisdom, zeal, piety, labours, perseverance, and success of those, with whom I am appointed to serve as a Son in the Gospel—in the Christian fellowship which I have with a few who are at once " poor in spirit " and " rich in Faith "—I see so many calls for gratitude and joy. The sense, however, which I have of my insufficiency for the great and good work in which I am engaged, though not painful, yet deep and humbling tends, not indeed to lessen, but to moderate my joy.

The devout and fixed attention manifested by the soldiers in the Fort and the truly Christian spirit, consistent conduct, and decided piety of many of them are often brought to grateful remembrance. May they ever remain the faithful soldiers and servants of Christ. On hearing Mr. McK. preach in Portuguese (the first time I had heard the language distinctly spoken) I felt much—much my own insignificancy among a people of strange language from the consideration that my *only* business in this Island is to teach and impress the people with the solemn realities of Death, Judgment, Eternity, and to offer to all Salvation, and Eternal Life, in the Name of Jesus Christ our Lord—much I felt the need of " giving all diligence" that I may indeed be a *Labourer* in the cause of Christ—much did I " covet, and earnestly, the best gifts, " and much did I pray that the arm of the Lord might be revealed; that the world might see that the Only true God, and Jesus Christ whom He has sent are the same yesterday, to day, and for ever. As to my studies, I find that the same measure, and intensity of application in this country with that which we might safely use at home, cannot be allowed, but at the certain loss of health, and the very great hazard of life.

a greatest :

Missionary, before his acquirement of the native languages, is to abstain from excessive study. The zeal an imprudent Missionary may possess, may be comfortable and cheering to himself and beneficial to others; but I am fully persuaded that no one can extensively serve the interests of this mission, but he who has an equal share of wisdom and zeal. I am well aware of the many and very great difficulties which attend a work so honourable and so arduous as that in which under your auspices, and by your appointment I am now engaged, and shall carefully endeavour to keep that charge which was given to me in the presence of many witnesses. To please God, and to save souls, shall be the grand principles of all my conduct. By these will I be taught when to act,—when to forbear from acting; when to go forward, when to stand still, when to be resigned and when to be laborious. To my uninterrupted and persevering exertions as your servant and the servant of Christ, I shall never fail to add my fervent prayers for the rapid and universal spread of the Gospel—till my work is done,—or, till,—

> "One song employs all nations, and all cry
> *Worthy the Lamb for He was slain for us!*
> The dwellers in the vales, and on the rocks—
> Shout to each other, and the mountain tops—
> From distant mountains catch the flying joy!
> And nation after nation taught the strain
> *Earth rolls the rapturous Hosanna round!*

Such are the purposes—such the prayers—

       My Honoured and Revered Fathers,
         of your Devoted Son in the Gospel.

Colombo 27th July 1824.   WILLIAM BRIDGNELL.

NEGOMBO STATION

To the General Secretaries of the Wesleyan Missionary Society.

       Negombo, 30 July, 1824.

REVEREND SIRS,

Since I last wrote, many parts of this Island have been awfully visited with affliction. Fevers and agues have raged in this circuit to an unprecedented degree. In Negombo, Chilaw, and the adjacent villages, scarcely a family has escaped; and many have died in the public roads, and others, forsaken by their unfeeling relatives, have miserably expired in the jungles.

On the 10th of June I was taken very ill with severe head-ache, and fever; which continued, with only symptomatic abatements, until the 2d inst. I do sincerely thank God for every thing relating to thither to assist at the formation of a Missionary Society for that Station. Br. Hume shewed me every attention, and lost no time in accompanying me to Colombo, where I had not only the best medical advice in the Island, but also the happiness of residing in Dr. M'Kenny's family; and I feel it my duty to state, that I never can forget the kind solicitude with which they watched over me. I could not have been more tenderly taken care of in my father's house. I am thankful, that although I suffered a great deal from various causes during the paroxysms; the fever being intermittent, I enjoyed intervals of ease which I could calmly devote to self examination and prayer.

This merciful visitation has given me clearer views of the mercy of God—of the solemnity of eternal things—of the value of time, and the importance of the work in which I am engaged. Oh! that I may ever feel the necessity of working, while it is called to day; with that force of conviction which the thoughts of it inspired, when I believed that my spirit was about to enter the eternal world.

During my absence, Cornelius has conducted the affairs of the circuit with faithfulness, zeal, and prudence; he has visited the sick and relieved the distressed, with great resolution and generosity; he has laboured beyond his strength, and assisted the needy beyond his means—I insert the following extract from one of his letters, because it contains some interesting particulars.

" I am sorry to inform you that the fever is still by no means diminished, both in the town and the country; the day before yesterday twenty-eight persons died, yesterday twenty-two, and to day twenty-seven. And while I was preparing to go to the country this morning, I heard of the sudden death of Mitcho Hamy, (a steady female member of our Society,) who was now some time ago sick with fever, and lately recovered from the same; during her indisposition I always found her happy, and quite resigned to the will of God; and when she was very ill, she assured me that the Holy Spirit did comfort and reconcile her mind and soul, and also asked me to solemnize the Lord's Supper, but I told her that I would do it with great pleasure, but I cannot attend to it as I am not authorized for the same: then she burst into tears; and since she has rapidly recovered, only she had a little swelling, to which she took medicine yesterday; and she went to bed as other days, and this morning found her dead. The cholera also has made its appearance since late in this place, but it has not prevailed much. The inhabitants of this place now hardly get coffins for their dead, consequently they do bury the dead after it is wrapped with mats. With much trouble I got a coffin for Mitcho Hamy, and I committed her remains this evening, having solemnized the service both in the church and grave-yard."

The fever proved fatal to another member of our Society; Mrs. Perera, who lived and died in the Lord. Some accounts of her I will send by an early opportunity.

I remain,

Faithfully and Obediently Yours,

THE CALTURA STATION.

Caltura, 30th July, 1824.

DEAR BRETHREN,

I am sure you cannot expect any information in quarterlies, but of a desultory and general kind—our Missionary Meeting is the principal thing, that the last three months have had to boast of out of the ordinary track, which has had justice done to it in the printed proceedings. Our Schools continue to exercise us in the usual way, sometimes with hopes, and sometimes with fears; and our labours are fully as abundant, and equally successful as ever they were. The arrival of new help is another thing of which the past quarter can boast, and which I am sure could not but greatly gratify every one of us. I hope our Heavenly Father will long preserve our dear Brethren, and abundantly bless them in their great and good work. As I am tired after preaching, I will say no more, but that I am

Your affectionate Brother,

A. HUME.

THE GALLE STATION.

Galle, 31st July, 1824.

DEAR BRETHREN,

In addition to my ordinary engagements on this and the Matura Station, I had to attend to the Garrison duty on Sundays till lately, when I was relieved by the arrival of a Chaplain. I am happy and thankful to say I have good reason to think my labours were attended with spiritual good.

Another Missionary having been most kindly sent out by the Committee, we have thought it advisable to commence preaching in English on Sundays in the afternoon, at 3 o'clock. This appears to be the most convenient hour; as it does not interfere with any of the services already established. We are now able likewise to pay more attention to the country parts of the circuit than has been possible for some time past. Our assistants meantime have been very attentive to their duty; and I am happy to observe, that our work altogether has seldom had a more pleasing appearance.

This year I have had much to do in repairs and alterations. The roof of the Mission House has been taken off, and perfectly set to rights at a moderate expence; and the workmen are now finishing two windows put up in the end of the Chapel uniform with the rest. This is a manifest improvement, as it renders the Chapel as cool as need be wished. Some friends having offered to contribute towards the expense, I dont mean to make any charge of it in the Station accounts.

The little Chapel at Matura is now enlarging, and will be in every respect improved. Brother Lalman has sent me a list of subscriptions towards the undertaking; and I believe most of the expenses will be met. It is expected to be finished in the course of a fortnight, when I purpose accompanying Brother Stoup to Matura, in order to open the place and to shew him the station.

The Anniversary of the Branch Bible Society of Galle was held lately. The weather was unfavourable, and the company rather small, but the advantages accruing to the public from the Institution are sensibly felt, and the subscriptions equal those of the foregoing year.

An Association has lately been formed here for the benefit of the aged and helpless poor, which promises well. The public had been long shocked by the weekly spectacle of 40 or 50 beggars in every stage of misery and disease. They have all had their respective circumstances investigated, and now receive weekly a small allowance without entering the fort. When these poor creatures have come a begging, I have repeatedly addressed them, and conversed with them about their souls; but at the same time I have taken care to relieve them. Their acuteness has sometimes surprised me, yet extreme circumstances are generally unfavorable to the cultivation of piety, and the ascertainment of truth. Give me neither poverty nor riches, said a wise petitioner.

Sincerely yours,
J. CALLAWAY.

THE GALLE STATION.

Galle, 1st *August,* 1824.

HON. FATHERS AND BRETHREN,

Having arrived at my station in safety and peace, you will of course expect from me some short notice of the same, which I gladly send you. With heartfelt gratitude do I recount the many mercies which the Lord hath bestowed upon me since that memorable period when I received your parting counsel and blessing; and I do not place amongst the least of them that gracious support and consolation which I experienced under that otherwise painful circumstance, the leaving (perhaps for ever) my native shore. I am persuaded that no other motive would have ever induced me to take such a step but that alone of " preaching among the Heathen the unsearchable riches of Christ;" but with such a motive, far from feeling any thing like sorrow or regret at the period to which I allude, I then rather exclaimed with wonder and self-abasement, " Unto *me,* who am less than the least of all saints is this *grace* given!" Our passage, which occupied twenty weeks, from the time of our embarkation to that of our landing at Colombo, though rather a long one, yet many circumstances conspired to make it pleasant. We had remarkably *fine weather* during the whole of it, which enabled us to spend our time pleasantly and profitably. Our fellow passengers were very agreeable; their behaviour towards us was ever marked with politeness and respect, which tended greatly to mitigate the wearisomeness of so long a voyage. We had anticipated some little inconvenience and interruption of our comforts, from having so many troops on board, but in this also we were agreeably disappointed, as it afforded us an opportunity, which we gladly embraced, of preaching to them the Gospel of Christ; the little meetings which we held amongst them, were in some measure a substitute for those abundant means of grace which we had left with our country; they were often attended with the Divine Presence, and proved " seasons of refreshing" to our souls. It was truly gratifying to hear Soldiers and Sailors uniting with us in singing " our great Redeemer's praise," and to see them bow the knee with silent reverence while we addressed the throne of grace, or sit in motionless attention to hear the word of life expounded and enforced; and we are encouraged to hope, that the seed thus sown, though sown in *weakness*, will not perish, but that it will hereafter spring up and bring forth much fruit; however, we have the testimony of our consciences, that with " simplicity and godly sincerity we had our conversation" among them. On our arrival in this Island we were received with the most cordial affection by our dear Brethren, especially by Brother and Sister McKenny, with whom after spending a few days, I proceeded to my appointment at Galle. On my journey to this place I had an opportunity of seeing a part of the labours of our Brethren, and also of the fruits of them, which I do assure you was highly gratifying! I chiefly allude to the Schools which I visited, and which I found in the greatest order. I examined several of the Scholars in reading both Singhalese and English, in which they acquitted themselves, especially in reading English, in a manner which far exceeded my expectations; they also repeated the Catechisms and the Lord's Prayer with great correctness. I was not less pleased with the *Masters* than with the Scholars: most of them appeared to be very intelligent men, and well acquainted with the principles of the Christian Religion, and some of them gave me a very consistent and scriptural account of their experience. When I had thus, like Barnabas, " seen the Grace of God, I was glad, and exhorted them all, that with purpose of heart they should cleave unto the Lord." Since my arrival at my station I have begun to apply myself to the languages, in which arduous task I am encouraged to expect divine assistance, for without Jesus I am convinced " I can do nothing." I never felt my weakness more than at present, but I know where my strength lieth; " thou O Lord, art a shield for me, my glory and the lifter up of my head." And now honoured Fathers and Brethren, entreating a continued interest in your

prayers, and assuring you of my increasing attachment and devotedness to that great and glorious work in which I am engaged, allow
me to subscribe myself.

Your Son, and junior Brother,

In the Gospel,

RICHARD STOUP.

To the Rev. Messrs. Bunting, Taylor,
and Watson, Secretaries to the Wes-
leyan Missionary Society.

Colombo:—Printed at the Wesleyan Mission-Press.

Extracts

FROM

QUARTERLY LETTERS, &c.

ADDRESSED

To the Rev. Messrs. MORLEY, WATSON, *and* MASON,
Secretaries to the Wesleyan Methodist Missionary Society, London.

NO. XXX.   *JANUARY,* 1826.

THE COLOMBO STATION.

Colombo, 10th January, 1826.

REV. AND DEAR SIRS,

We can assure you that our anxiety to supply you with faithful communications respecting the state of our highly interesting mission continues unabated, being well aware of the great importance of attending to this duty; and should we be led to introduce any matters which may appear to you not to possess much interest, our solicitude on this subject will form our apology.

It is a pleasing reflection to our minds that notwithstanding the necessary sameness of our work, yet every succeeding quarter presents us with some interesting facts, which you no doubt regard as worthy of notice.

Since my last communication, the garrison of Colombo has been strengthened by the arrival of H. M. 97th Regiment, and we have been no little rejoiced to see most of the late vacant seats in the Fort Chapel occupied by our newly arrived countrymen, several of whom have already expressed a desire to flee from the wrath to come. In connection with our good work among the military, we have to notice a very interesting event, which is the death of William Brewington, the leader of the Society in the 83d Regt. He went up with his company to Kandy, when they were removed from Colombo, and there continued with great zeal and diligence to watch over the little flock: occasionally letting us have simple but interesting accounts of the state of his class, and the progress of the work of God among the soldiers in the

4   A

Interior. However it has pleased the Lord to call this eminently pious man to his eternal reward; he died at Kandy on
the 13th ultimo, and we have been much comforted, by the
accounts we have received of the blessed state of his mind to
the very last. The Rev. T. Browning, Church Missionary, paid
our dear friend much attention at all times, but particularly
during his illness; and the following is an extract of a letter
from this Gentleman to me on the subject.

Kandy, December 14, 1825.

MY DEAR SIR,

    I understand from John McGowan of the 83d, that it was
the wish of William Brewington, who died in Hospital yesterday, that I should write a line to you to inform you of his
death. He has had rather delicate health ever since he came
to Kandy; but has been able to attend his duty till within
the last two months, during which time he has been very ill of
dysentery. About a month ago he was getting much better and
had some hope of recovery ; but after a relapse he became
so weak that he gave up all expectation of returning health,
and when the Medical officer intimated to him the necessity of beginning to look out for another world, he answered with great confidence that he had not to begin that work,
but wished rather to die than to live. During the remainder
of his life he continued to enjoy an almost uninterrupted
peace of mind. There was nothing rapturous or transporting,
but a steady confidence in the merits of Christ Jesus, which
enabled him to look forward to death with satisfaction and
delight. He told me he sometimes felt that he was a great
sinner, but he recollected that he had a great Saviour. Since
he has been very ill he has had McGowan constantly to attend him, who says that he continued to the end to enjoy
the same degree of peace and consolation. The night before
he died, on waking from a doze he asked McGowan if that
was the right time, and when McGowan asked him what time,
he said did you not hear me sing? and then repeated with great
emphasis, all the Hymn beginning " My God the spring of all
my joys &c." saying that was very expressive of his feelings.
    Thus, my dear Sir, I have given you a brief account of this
good man, which I have no doubt you will be happy to receive.
I have always been much pleased with Brewington since I have
known him, and have, I think, witnessed in him a gradual
progress in grace and christian experience, and I have no
doubt he is now praising and glorifying that Saviour whom
he loved and served in sincerity.

The death of truly pious and useful men is felt by the church of Christ in every part where the Redeemer's Kingdom is established, but it is more powerfully felt in a country like this, where the holy man is perhaps one in ten thousand; but *the Lord is righteous in all his ways.*

The Prayer-Meetings in the houses of several of our friends, which were first noticed in my letter of last April, are continued and well attended, and are much calculated to increase and extend the work of God among us.

We have lately formed another class at the Mission house, consisting of Females only; at present the number is only four, but we must expect an increase, particularly as it is under the care of so zealous and excellent a Leader as Mr Mooyaart. We have also got a new juvenile Class formed at the New Bazar School, which consists of 24 promising boys, which is met by Mr. Chinner the English Master of the school.

The religious state of Colombo altogether, is very encouraging at present; the union that exists between Christians of all denominations is most remarkable: we often meet together at each other's houses for the express purpose of holding Religious intercourse, and on these occasions, all distinctions are lost in the firm conviction, that we are all the lovers and followers of the same Master, and that the object of our ambition is to see who will be most like him in *humility, deadness to the world, resignation to the divine will,* and *extensive usefulness.* Indeed it may be said with truth of the little Flock of Christ in this place that *great grace rests upon them all*   O! that the little leaven may continue its influence until the whole Lump be leavened.

The concerns of the Bible Society have from various causes gone on but slowly for some time past, however in this department also our prospects brighten. At a late Meeting our active and excellent friend Mr. Mooyaart was chosen Secretary, an event which is to be regarded in a very important light in relation to the future success of this valuable institution. Several plans are already under consideration and arrangement, in order to further its interests, and I doubt not but we shall soon be able to communicate some pleasing information on this subject. I have now to notice our late District Meeting held in Colombo last month; this was a time of deep interest to us all, and I know not that I have ever witnessed greater faithfulness among Brethren. The ordination of our five Brethren, Sutherland, Gogerly, Lalman, Anthoniesz, and Cornelius, commanded an uncommon degree of interest. The several services were performed in English, Portuguese and Singhalese; upon each occasion, our chapel was well filled: a great degree of solemnity pervaded the assembly; and much feeling was excited by the relation of the *conversion* and *experience* of the Brethren who were set apart for the work of God. May the effect produced by these services long remain, and the fruit be found after many days

From the plan of stations sent home you will perceive that I am appointed to Caltura, a place where I have been made useful and where I still hope to be so. I think I may say I have done much to promote the welfare of the Colombo station, and of the district in general for the past three years; and retiring from office, I do so with abundant evidence that I have in my official capacities secured the confidence and affectionate respect of my Brethren: this with a good conscience towards God and Man, is to me an abundant reward for all my past labours. My present Missionary prospects coincide fully with my views and feelings. I entered upon my past engagements from necessity, and now that I am relieved from them in the way of Providence, I feel happy and thankful, and ardently desire an interest in your prayers, that my success in labouring to bring the natives to "*Behold the Lamb of God that taketh away the sin of the world,*" may be very abundant.

I am, Rev. and Dear Sirs,
very affectionately yours,
J. M'KENNY.

THE CALTURA STATION.

Caltura, 30th December, 1825.

REV. AND DEAR SIRS,

Well aware that few things are more gratifying to you or more desired than good news from a far country, we shall feel a high satisfaction, if what we have to mention in reference to the state of our blessed work on this station afford you any pleasure. Our recent letters have put you in possession of the plans of labour we have adopted and of the hopes we entertained of very great success attending our efforts; our hopes are now in a very pleasing manner being realised. We seem to have not only gained the confidence of the people but to have in a very considerable degree excited a lively interest about the things of religion: this is principally to be attributed to the extensive introduction of Prayer-meetings among the natives. Scores who never would have come to us or to the house of God, are thus reached by the Gospel, and though as a whole they be not capable of appreciating christianity, the morality of its precepts never fails to recommend it to the good will of the little companies who attend our meetings. Their nods of assent, their fixed attention, and the frequent remarks they make on scripture subjects, prove to us not only that our words are understood, but that a deep interest is felt in the important truths advanced. Among numberless other remarks that have been made, and questions which have been proposed, the following was a few days ago put by a sensible shrewd native. Coming with the Bible in his hand he read several verses in the 11th chapter of Leviticus, to the seventh verse, when he stopped and enquired what was the meaning. There was in the enquiry more implied than at first meets the eye. We read in the 6th and 7th verses a positive command, and he knew that not only the English Civilians but even Missionaries made no scruple to eat either the hare or the swine; and it was evident he wished to see how I would solve the apparent inconsistency of violating a positive law of my own book. Of course a considerable explanation was necessary to make him see how a certain class of laws in the Bible became annulled by the introduction of christianity, while another class being of a moral character were binding at all times and on all men. He smiled, and seemed to think the solution rather ingenious than satisfactory. A similar question was some time prior put by another man. He had been reading the Testament, and came to the passage in the 6th of Matthew "Thou shall not kill." He came to me, and enquired if *killing* and *murdering* were not the same. I did not at first see his drift, and without referring to the use of the words when used in reference to animals, I explained the difference of meaning when applied to the taking away of human life. He however kept his own idea in view, and when I had explained he enquired how we could violate our own laws in *murdering* animals. My explanation seemed to him as the explanation of the Mahomedans for violating the laws of Mahomed about eating swine seems to us. One says it is the head only that is forbidden, another says it is the tail, one says it is this leg, another says it is that, and thus among them the whole hog is devoured. However these little matters show us that the Bible is read, and that our religion has so much interest as to be worthy of attention in its influence upon our lives. Those of the natives who have become acquainted with the Missionaries generally cease to take the gauge of Christianity from the conduct of Europeans generally, for they easily perceive a marked difference; but when they perceive such apparently violent departures from the laws of that book we profess to love, they scarcely know how to think of our conduct. They read the law, they see the conduct, they mark the difference, but it is time only, and increased knowledge of the holy Scriptures, that can enable them fully to appreciate the reconciliation of such apparent discrepancies. In a few instances, I have of late heard the voice of prayer ascending from native huts, as the family within were surrounding the family altar; and in one case in particular, the service was conducted by a little boy. The becoming manner in which he was reading a chapter of the New Testament, with an audible voice, collected a number of the people round the door of the hut, who, as I was passing, were listening attentively to the little worshipper within: the circumstance seemed to surprise very much. I have several times in walking out in the evening heard the same boy singing his evening hymn. From the mouth of babes and sucklings God will perfect praise.

Our Schools continue to prepare with a good degree of effect a generation that will praise the Lord. They are forming the character of the future race of christians. They are infusing precepts of morality, sowing seeds of truth which under the divine blessing will shoot forth in the practice, and be matured into habits, in after life. Every one of our Schools is not only a nursery of moral but of religious principles. The children are taught not only knowledge but the knowledge of God, the knowledge of his son Jesus Christ, and the way of salvation by him; and every school contains a few plants which we have every reason to hope will in time be trees of righteousness, the right hand planting of the Lord. We have particular expectations in reference to the schools in and about Pantura, and indeed of the work generally in that part. The Lord has evidently in a very uncommon degree given a hearing ear, and we hope he will not withold the understanding heart, from the population of that part of the station. I am happy to think that in future it is likely to have a fuller share of attention paid than it has yet received. The work will have the advantage of Br. M'Kenny's unceasing activity, and as he is well acquainted with not only the station generally, but the importance of Pantura in particular, there is no doubt it will continue to prosper. As after this year it is to be a separate station, I indulge the hope that next year I shall be appointed to it to labour again where God has already blessed our labours.

Our Class-meetings are still kept up, and are in general seasons of refreshing, at least to myself, and I hope too to others. Our Sacramental occasions have of late been particularly interesting, the presence of God has been with us in a very gracious manner, and we have rejoiced with glad hearts in the full confidence that we shall feast together in the kingdom of our God. Our congregations continue steady, and are I hope profiting by the numerous sermons which they hear in the different languages. On Christmas day the chapel was well filled, and the power of God seemed to rest upon us, and again on New year's day, when they seemed to feel as well hear "how frail they are." On a review of the last twelve months I cannot but rejoice, for though I have suffered a good deal from indisposition, and particularly at the beginning of the year, and my exertions had necessarily to be reduced proportionally to my strength; yet prosperity has crowned the efforts I have been able to make, and I am about to leave the station not less flourishing than I found it. It has been, as every other station will more or less be in this vale of tears, a scene of some trials and many mercies. But out of all the Lord hath brought me by his grace, and to him I desire to ascribe all the praise and glory, intreating a continued interest in your prayers.

I am, Rev and Dear Sirs,
Yours very Affectionately,
A. HUME.

~~~~~~~~~~~~~~~~~~~~~

THE GALLE STATION.

Galle, January 20th, 1826.

REVD. SIRS,

Although but few circumstances have transpired during the last quarter of a very interesting nature, yet we trust that the good work is upon the whole going on well on this Station.

You are partially acquainted with the disadvantages under which we labour in this Country, but you cannot fully enter into all those circumstances which tend to counteract our efforts in the Cause of our Redeemer; they are many and various, and in surveying them in connexion with our own weaknesses and imperfections, we are often led to exclaim "who is sufficient for these things?" We think however we may in a qualified sense say with the Apostle Paul, " Now thanks be unto God which causeth us always to triumph in Christ, and maketh manifest the savour of his knowledge by us in every place." It is true that we do not see those frequent instances of clear and decided conversion to God that attend the Ministry of the word in England, yet we are confident that good, and great good, in various ways is resulting from our labours. *The tone of moral feeling has been greatly raised* amongst the various classes of inhabitants in the island, both European and Native, since the residence of Christian Missionaries amongst them. This I have often heard remarked by persons long resident in the country, and well qualified from their extensive acquaintance with its society, to make such an observation. *The knowledge of Christian Doctrine is gradually spreading amongst the Natives,* and especially those of the higher classes, and though it may be said of many of them that " they fear the Lord and serve their own gods," yet we doubt not but this knowledge will eventually clear away the darkness of superstition and Paganism from their minds, and "shine more and more unto the perfect day." *The Sabbath is more reverenced than formerly,* though there is still room to wish that it were strictly observed: yet we are happy to see that in and near the towns where Europeans reside there is generally a partial cessation of worldly business, and more of those who are nominally Christians attend some place of worship. I think it may be said with respect to Galle, that there is as little business going forward in it on a Sunday, as in the generality of country towns in England.

Our English Congregations in Galle have undergone a considerable declension in consequence of the change of the Troops stationed here, and also of the removal of several of the European residents belonging both to the Civil and Military Departments, some of whom were constant, and others occasional hearers. However, we hope that as the new ones arrive and become settled, we shall have an increase of attendants, and an ingathering of souls to the fold of Christ.

On the 2nd Inst. I had all the children of the neighbouring Schools assembled in the Galle Chapel, when I preached to them from John iii, 16. "God so loved the world that he gave his only begotten Son, that whosoever believeth in him should not perish, but have everlasting Life." It was a most interesting occasion; the Children were all remarkably neat and cleanly dressed, and behaved very orderly; the Chapel was quite filled, and they read aloud the reponses of the Liturgy, very distinctly. How delightful to hear from the lips of Heathen children, "We praise thee, O God, we acknowledge *thee to be the Lord.* All the earth doth worship *thee, the Father everlasting.*" Surely amongst this assembly one might contemplate the members of a future church, which "shall stand as pillars in the Temple of our God, to go no more out."

Since my return from the District Meeting I have felt much the responsibility of being appointed to this Station alone, and it has led me to enquire and to consider how I may more lay myself out for the glory of God, and for the advancement of that great work in which I am engaged; and I do feel determined, by divine grace assisting me, to give myself wholly to these things. My health, I am happy to say, is much improved, and as I am in consequence more capable of labouring in the good cause, I feel an increasing delight in it; I can say with sincerity that the longer I am engaged in Mission work the more I love it, and rejoice that I am "a chosen vessel to bear the name of the Redeemer before the Heathen." May I prove faithful, "and walk worthy of that high vocation wherewith I am called."

Commending myself and my work to your prayers, and to the prayers of all who love our Lord Jesus Christ in sincerity, I have the happiness to remain,

Faithfully and Affectionately yours,
RICHARD STOUP.

THE MATURA STATION.

Matura, January 10th, 1826.

Rev. and Dear Sirs,

As I have resided chiefly at Galle during the last quarter, my labours at Matura have been necessarily limited to monthly visits. It will not therefore be expected that I can enter much into detail respecting the several departments of the work; I am happy however, to be able to state that the affairs of the circuit have been successfully carried on by Brother Lalmon, who has unremittingly continued his labours, in preaching to crowds assembled on the high ways, and in the public markets. He has expressed himself highly gratified by the marked attention manifested on such occasions, as well as by enquiries on the part of some, strongly indicating that his statements of religious truth had not been heard by them altogether in vain.

A recent visit to Matura, afforded me the gratification of finding all the schools in a very prosperous state, in consequence, I am happy to say, of greater attention on the part of the Schoolmasters, and the increased assiduity of the school-visitors in the discharge of their duty. Among the latter I feel myself called upon particularly to mention the name of Don Simon de Silva, our assistant superintendent of schools at Wirigam, without whose active assistance the schools must suffer much; his piety and exertions must always recommend him to the notice of every Missionary, under whose direction he is appointed to act.

On the 5th instant, the Christmas vacation having expired, public teaching was resumed in all the schools in the circuit. A visitor was appointed to attend at each place for the purpose of ascertaining the numbers of children who had returned to their instruction. From the Reports which have been transmitted to me, I am most happy to learn, that in addition to a much larger attendance than was expected, 29 boys and 3 girls were, on that occasion, admitted in the several schools. The business of the day was opened with singing, and prayer, and reading a portion of scripture, followed by a suitable address to the children.

Those whom we consider members of our society continue to walk worthy of their profession. Of 3 classes containing 29 adult members, 18 are communicants, who I have every reason to think, to the extent of their ability and information, perform the duties, respect the institutions, and value the privileges of Christianity.

Our congregations have in no instance decreased since our last communication; those assembling at our schools in the country, although not large, continue to animate us in our Missionary excursions, and we have the satisfaction of adding, that at Belligam particularly, an increase has lately been observed in the attendance of Singhalese females at our places of worship. The one attending our Portuguese service on Sunday evening, is however liable to considerable fluctuation, in respect of numbers, in consequence of the occasional removal and return of the individuals connected with the Cutcherry of the district.

To this circumstance also, must be attributed the irregularity which has necessarily occurred in conducting the Prayer Meetings mentioned in a former letter from this Station; as the houses in which they were held, were chiefly those of persons employed in the public offices, when they were required by the local authorities to transfer their residence to another and distant part of the country, the discontinuance of these services became unavoidable. In the families of those however, who are not affected by such changes, the Prayer. Meetings have been regularly and uniformly held. We soon expect to increase their number among the Singhalese, as well as Dutch inhabitants, but forbear expressing any confident anticipations of success. Those already established have, we trust, been the means of impressing the most invaluable truths on the minds of many, who otherwise must have continued destitute of every means of religious instruction; and in the hope that those we intend to establish, will be similarly and singularly useful, we find our encouragement to persevere.

On the whole, in reviewing the history of the Circuit for the past quarter, while we retain a feeling conviction of our own deficiencies and imperfections, we see every reason to *thank God and take courage, forasmuch as we know that our labour is not in vain in the Lord.*

I remain, Rev. and Dear Sirs,
Sincerely and respectfully yours,
JAMES SUTHERLAND,

THE NEGOMBO AND CHILAW STATION.

Negombo, January 23, 1826.

REV. AND DEAR SIRS,

A review of the circumstances of this Station during the past year, affords many reasons for gratitude to the great Head of the Church, mingled with many for humility and encreasing diligence. The congregations in every place, excepting the town of Negombo, have been considerably increased. In 3 villages the preaching of the Gospel has been introduced: and the word of God has been received with attention and apparent profit. Twenty-two adults have been admitted on trial, and give evidence of their desire to flee from the wrath to come, by forsaking all outward sin, and by a careful and devout attendance upon the means of grace. Even since the commencement of this year nine additional Members have been admitted on trial in two of the Villages where preaching has been recently established. It must not however be disguised, that the work is but in its infancy; that these young converts need constantly to be watched over with the most tender solicitude, and fed with the *Milk* of the Word. The work of Grace appears to be deepening in some of those who have been longer Members of Society, and they have all continued so far as we have had opportunities of observing them, to walk worthy of their high calling.

It is with peculiar pleasure that I observe the females beginning to occupy their proper place, and become among the foremost to dedicate themselves to the service of God. They generally form the larger part of our congregations; in many instances accompanied by their husbands and children. I feel much pleasure in holding forth the word of Life in these villages, among a simple people, removed in a great measure from European influence, and scarcely ever visited by a white man except the Missionary. Brother Wijesingha labours among them with zeal, prudence, and success.

Our small number in the town of Negombo has been reduced by death. One of the first of those who attended the preaching of Br. Newstead, has been removed to the Church triumphant. She died a few days after I left Negombo to attend the District Meeting, with a sure trust and confidence in the mercy of God through Christ, and was conveyed to her grave chiefly by the young men who met in the same class with her. Our assistant Superintendent of Schools, Mr. Lutersz, assisted in carrying her to the grave, and then read the funeral service over her remains.

The low state of the cause of Christ in the town of Negombo is cause of great humiliation, and I feel altogether at a loss what steps to take. May it please the Lord to open doors of usefulness, and to remove the hindrances which keep back the people from hearing the glad tidings of salvation through faith in Jesus Christ.

Yours very affectionately,
D. J. GOGERLY.

THE JAFFNA STATION.

Jaffna, January 11th, 1826.

DEAR FATHERS AND BRETHREN,

From a review of the past quarter we may truly say, "Hitherto hath the Lord helped us." Through indisposition I have found it difficult to attend to the duties of my station, but the arrival of Mr Hunter, and an increased degree of strength, have enabled me to go forward. In the beginning of the quarter we had a pleasing instance of the propriety of being instant in season and out of season, in the conversion of a Roman

Catholic woman: she fearing to come into the house where we had preaching, stood at the outside, but the word reached her heart; she went home, and resolved never to leave her house until she felt herself to be a new creature. The Lord had mercy upon her, and blessed her with confidence and peace through believing on Jesus: shortly after she was taken ill and died, witnessing to those around her that death had no sting for her, and that the grave had no victory.

The Lord has also visited our Society, and taken three of our members to himself. The 1st a respectable Tamul woman, called Justina, who was carried off by the Cholera in the short space of 12 hours: this modest unassuming woman was seldom absent from her class, and she gave full satisfaction as to her devotedness to God. During the progress of the disease she frequently spoke of her Saviour, and told her friends it was no use to trouble themselves. At one time she said நீங்கள் ஏன் வருத்தப்படுகிறீர்கள் என் யேசு இங்கேவந்து நிற்கிறார் நான் அவரிடத்தில் போறேன். Neeakle ean varattappadukereeŕkle en yeasu ingevanthunittkeraar, nan avarredattil poraih, i e. "Why do you trouble yourselves? My Jesus has come here—I am going to him." She almost immediately expired, and I doubt not has joined many of her sisters from the West, the North, and the South, and is now sitting down with the patriarchs in the kingdom of heaven. Blessed and heart cheering consideration, we have not labored in vain.

The 2nd, Katherina Livertsz, was also very regular at her class, and spoke with great simplicity of the comforts of religion. She died of the same disease as Justina. When Katherina's leader went to visit her during her illness, she said, "Meu Jesus te da força par mi," My Jesus gives me strength. She has left a widowed mother and sister, who are both members of of our Society.

The 3rd, George Garvin, of the Royal Artillery. He had been for a long time more or less indisposed, and about a year ago became seriously concerned for his soul. Garvin continued a long time in a very gloomy state, but about two months ago the Lord had mercy upon him, and gave him to feel he was his child; he was no longer reserved, but told to all what a Saviour he had found. When I called upon him I found him very happy: he seemed to feel pleasure in nothing so much as talking about Jesus. Two days before his death he rejoiced exceedingly, and seemed "quite in the verge of Heaven."—"There, said he, the chariots have come for me—I hear musick—I am going to the new Jerusalem:" he then called for his children, and said, your

Father is going to die, he has been a bad man, but he is going to heaven On the next day however he had a severe conflict with the enemy: his wife was in a great agony to see the change, she fell on her knees, and attempted to pray in English, but not being able to proceed she began in Portuguese, and a poor C. ffre who was attending Garvin also began to pray. Garvin continued to struggle, but said I am not left. His daughter, a child * of 11 years of age, seeing the distress of her father, fetched her Testament, and read, "resist the devil and he will flee from you. Satan had desired to have you, that he may sift you as wheat, but I have prayed for thee, that thy faith fail not." The God of peace shall bruise satan under your feet. He was soon after delivered, and said now I can praise my God; and as he departed lifted up his hands in token of victory.

The Schools (with the exception of the girls) have been greatly injured by the Cholera, but the disease having abated it is hoped they will soon rise again.

> I remain, dear Father's and Brethren,
> affectionately,
>   J. ROBERTS,

THE MADRAS STATION.

Madras, December, 1825.

DEAR BRETHREN,

From a number of interesting matters which we wish to bring to your notice, we must be contented to select a few things for this communication.

We stated in our last letter that Br. Hoole was left in charge of this circuit, whilst the Brethren attended the district meeting in Ceylon; and in his letter from this station he has detailed some of his labours in our absence. Previous to leaving Madras I had arranged with Brother Mowatt, of Nagapatam, to meet me at Trichinopoly, and we reached the house of the Chaplain, the Rev. Mr. Wright, on the 9th of July, nearly at the same time. We remained with him five days, and were treated with the utmost attention and kindness. We visited our people in the Army, met the class, and preached in the chapel raised by our people in His Majesty's Royal Regiment, before their departure to Burmah,

---

* This little girl had learnt the second part of the Conference Catechism. See Paragraph, What is the present state of the fallen Angels?

My journey from Madras to Trichinopoly was through an interesting country, upwards of two hundred miles in extent, wherein are situated some of the most famed and ancient heathen temples, the residence of revered Brahmins, and a very numerous population. The route from Madras, through the seven Pagodas (which exhibit so many and superior marks of ancient sculpture,) Sadras, and Pondicherry, presented nothing but what has been frequently described. At the French settlement I attended the Cathedral, which is undergoing a thorough repair. An aged European Priest was catechising the children in Tamul, in the Lord's prayer, and he spoke the language with great fluency. From Pondicherry to Macavaram, near Tranquebar, nothing beyond the usual circumstances of travelling took place. Macavaram is situated in a fine part of the country, refreshed by the waters of the rivers Cavery and Coleroon, and very populous. I examined the temples, and remained during the day in the ruins of a once splendid choultry, on the banks of the river; which I recognized having slept in seven years before, when on a journey from Jaffna to Trichinopoly. In the evening I was preparing to take my departure, when John Devasagayam came to me, and expressed much regret that he did not know of my arrival. He accompanied me to a place where he is superintending the building of a house and school, for the residence of the Reverend Mr. Barenbruck; it being the intention of his society to occupy Macavaram as a Mission station. The weather, which had been excessively dry, and the wind parching, assumed all at once a different appearance, by the rivers flowing down from the high country. The water distributed through a thousand channels was conveyed to the trees and fields of corn in every quarter. It seemed to be the object of every ones attention, and the people washing and bathing on every side as we travelled, sufficiently testified how welcome and how grateful the waters are, to a thirsty land. Some rain also fell, and by sleeping out in a wet night, I caught a severe cold, which was followed by a hot burning fever. After leaving Combaconum, where I had the pleasure to see a Brother Missionary, the Reverend Mr. Mead, we were stopped at midnight by the people of a small village, who came clamorously to request medicine for a young man (about 25) who had been bit by a serpent. He was sleeping in an open verandah; the beast had crept near, and inflicted a wound in his right shoulder, and he died in three hours after being bitten. The wound was about three inches in length, as the fang of the animal had made a long scratch before it fixed in the principal incision, which appeared very black with the poisonous matter. He could not swallow any thing, and remained in a state of heavy stupor till life was extinct.

On approaching Trichinopoly, my way was through the celebrated Island of Seringam, but as it was dark when I crossed the river, my desires to see these famed temples were restrained, till a more suitable occasion. We were requested, on Sunday the 10th July, to read prayers and preach in the Mission Church in the Fort, which I did. On Monday, I met the class of our people among the Military; several spoke their experience with clearness, and gave satisfactory testimony that they had been taught by the spirit of God, the the things belonging to their peace. Great simplicity and devotion marked the Meeting. In the evening I preached to them, with much liberty. Bro. Mowat accompanied me on the 12th, to see the temples of Seringam. The Collector, G. W. Saunders, Esq. most kindly favoured us with attendants to shew us what is usually seen. We crossed the river at sun rise, and found five Elephants in waiting, which preceeded us with music to the sacred place. The great space of ground occupied by this mass of temples, renders the first sight of them very imposing; but notwithstanding all I had heard of these celebrated structures, they are not equal to many other temples, either for the beauty of workmanship or the height of the towers. Here the Traveller sees nothing equal to the temples of Conjeveram, except some massy unfinished gateways or towers. The riches of the temple were spread before us, consisting of gold vessels and precious stones to a considerable value, but which I have not time to describe.

We remained at Tanjore but a few hours, and after reaching Negapatam, were joined by Bro. England. After preaching in the Church at Negapatam I was seized with a burning fever, which was checked by a timely application of medicine, and we proceeded to Point Calymere. Here we suffered a very painful detention of many days, after being driven back from the Coast of Ceylon, but in a second attempt we reached it in safety.

The minutes of the district Meeting will have given what information is necessary concerning it, and I may therefore confine my remarks to continental India. Brother and Sister Williamson had arived at Madras, in our absence, and Bro. Bott had taken his departure for Europe. Our first business on my return was to arange things for the sixth anniversary of the Auxiliary Society for Madras, which was held on September 20th. The Sermons on the occasion were preached by the Reverend W. Taylor, of the London Missionary Society, and the Reverend J. T. Williamson, lately from England. The general meeting was numerously attended, and the receipts of the Auxiliary Society for Madras, from its commencement in 1819 to December 31st, 1824, amounted to Rupees 10,346, and the subscriptions &c. from January to December 1825, are upwards of 4000 Madras Rupees. The sixth Report has been printed, accompanied by the first Tamul report, read to the Native Society in the chapel at Royapettah, on the 9th of October 1825.

Respecting the society in this Circuit, we can observe generally that a work of grace is evidently seen with many, whilst others need seeking after and stirring up to diligence. Brother Hoole in our absence was indefatigable, and he had little rest till relieved by his brethren from some part of the extensive labour of so wide a station. In some places a spirit of hearing has been awakened, and at others an encrease in the Society has taken place. There is one part of our work in Black Town, which has hitherto greatly perplexed the brethren, and they have made repeated efforts to remedy the evil, but without success The large new Chapel there ought to have one Minister resident near it, in order that he might more effectually watch over the flock, and promote the work in general. As we are at present situated, by having a Mission upwards of four miles from the Chapel in Black Town, the Missionary is involved in a journey of nine miles to preach and to visit the people. That pastoral visitations must be very superficially made will be evident to all who know the engagements of a Missionary. Were a Minister resident among the people, and to devote his leisure hours to a vigorous enquiry after them, and diligently to seek out and invite others to the means of grace, we have no doubt of the pleasing results to be expected. New classes might be formed, and through the blessing of God, some extensive improvements respecting visiting and preaching to the Natives in a very populous neighbourhood might also be accomplished. In consequence of not having any house on the Chapel premises we shall have to take a convenient house for the purpose, till a representation can be made to the Committee for the purchasing or building one. Indeed this station requires some very effective exertions, which would no doubt be crowned with corresponding success, were the attempts prudently made. Not less than three new Chapels, a more convenient Mission house, a superior English and Tamul school, and a printing establishment, are necessary to give effective energies for so numerous and so extensive a population as that to which we have access. Other societies are making great exertions, and may the Lord make them a blessing to the people. We also have a work to perform, loud calls sounding in our ears, and deep obligations, to discharge which we trust will not be neglected. It is not merely with regard to the establishment of our cause in Madras and its neighbourhood, that the situation of the brethren is one of the greatest importance, but the relation which they bear to other societies, and the part which they are called to take in directing and assisting their operations, will commend Madras to the Committee's most serious attention. These circumstances place the brethren under great responsibilities, and give them a considerable influence in promoting the evangelization of a vast heathen population. In addition to the translation into Tamul of the *Rules* of our society, which have been in the hands of our Native converts at least three years; of "*Ward's Facts*," the *first and second Catechisms*, and a selection of *Hymns* from our large Hymn book, Bro. Hoole, for upwards of two years has discharged the office of Secretary to the * Sub-committee for the Revision of the Holy scriptures in the Tamul language. He has also translated several Tracts into Tamul and Portuguese for the Tract association, of which he is likewise Depositary. The Revd. Dr. Rottler has requested brother Hoole to assist him in revising his Dictionary of the Tamul language, designed to embrace every word therein, high or low, and which the Venerable and aged Missionary is anxious to have published before his death, being upwards of 75 years of age. By the distribution monthly from the Mission House in Royapettah, of upwards of Sixty Rupees among the poor of our immediate neighbourhood, in behalf of the Friend in Need society, some influence is gained among the people, chiefly Roman catholic, and many opportunities are offered in this work of mercy to direct poor needy souls to Christ, beseeching them by the mercies of God to present themselves a living sacrifice, holy acceptable in his sight.

---

* The Sub-Committee for the revision of the Tamul Scriptures.
The Revd. Dr. Rottler, President ⎫ of the Society for promoting
    „   L. P. Haubroe   ⎬   Christian knowledge.
    „   E. Crisp   ⎭ of the London Missionary
                                            Society.
    „   W. Sawyer   of the Church Missionary
                                            Society.
    „   E. Hoole, Secretary, of the Wesleyan Society.
The third Report of the Madras A. B. S. states, that "Mr. Rhenius's revision forms the ground work of their labours;" He has advanced to the Book of Revelations, and the Sub-Committee to John.

It may be considered my duty in this part of my communication to notice more particularly the exertions of the brethren on Continental India, but the subject *of establishing and erecting places for Divine Worship, and Schools,* with their relative condition and importance, must be left for a future letter, and I must confine myself to *the languages,* in which, it will be seen, some of the brethren have not been the least assiduous.

The following statement details part of their labours.

Tracts translated into Portuguese by Mr. Hoole:—

The history of James Byrne or the advantage of reading the Scriptures. A avantagem de ler as Escrituras.

The history of Mary. Religiao verdadeira exemplificada em a Historia de Maria, hum caracter Vivente.

Tamul Tracts for publication, translated by Mr. Hoole:—

Dialogue on Salvation.

ரட்சணியத்தின பேரில் சம்பா ஷேண.

The nominal Christian.

நல்லபெயர்போரா த குண மே வேனு மென்று காட் டியது.

Investigation of the Shasters.

சாஸ்திரங் கனின ஆராயசி.

Cause of Sin.

பாவத் திக்குக் காரண பின்ன தென்று காட்டியது.

Two years ago Bro. Hoole paid some attention to the Teloogoo language, but was interrupted by his severe illness, and has not since had strength and opportunity to resume it. He has however done a little work for the Tract Society in that language, and is now engaged in comparing the two translations of the Holy Scriptures into that language, by the late Revd. Mr. Pritchett and by the Revd. Mr. Gordon, at the request of the Secretary of the Madras Auxiliary Bible Society, in order to ascertain their comparative merits.

Sermons in Portuguese, by Mr. Martins, the converted Roman Catholic Priest, printed and circulated by the Madras Tract association:—

No. 13. The faithful saying. Esta he huma Palavra Fiel.

No. 14. The direction and promise of the Gospel. Cre em Jesus Christo e tu seras Salvador,

No. 18. The foolish bargain. Que approveita, a home, se grangrear todo o Mundo, e perder sua Alma.

Besides these Sermons Mr. Martins has written many others in Portuguese, on some of the principal subjects of the Holy Scriptures; and it his intention, if time will permit, to send Copies to the Committee of a few of them, with an English translation.

A journey to Wallajahbad being necessary, brother Hoole undertook it, and as we have not any Tamul Assistant, after preaching in English in Black Town at 7 o'Clock, I read the Liturgy at Royapettah at 10 o'Clock, on the Sabbath day, and conducted the Native services in Royapettah Chapel every Morning, till his return. I would not trespass willingly beyond the limits allowed these communications, and therefore I shall conclude by an extract or two with which brother Hoole has kindly favoured me from his journal at my request. The work at Poonamallee has been named in former letters, and it is gratifying to know by the following extract that this good work is improving.

Monday, 21st November, 1825. After making the arrangements necessary for my proposed journey of ten or twelve days, I left the Mission house with the prayers of my brethren for the divine blessing and direction. I proceeded immediately to St. Thomas's mount, to give directions about the repairs of our School and preaching-room there, which has suffered considerable damage from the late heavy rains: from thence I went to Poonamallee where I found the Congregation assembling in the Court yard of the house of one of the Pensioners. It was a clear and beautiful evening, the air was so calm as to allow us to hang lamps in the trees, which formed extensive and convenient chandeliers; the chairs and benches brought from various quarters were soon well filled; I took my station in the Veranda, raised two or three steps from the ground, and preached with great satisfaction to a congregation in which religion is making almost daily advances. Here also we have much need of a place of worship: the prayer meetings held almost daily are so numerously attended, that none of own Soceity have a house large enough to accommodate them; but when a Missionary visits them, we are obliged to assemble in the open air. Seven persons have been admitted on trial since our last visit; one of them a young man lately from Ireland, who has been obliged to leave home and all, in consequence of becoming a Protestant.

"An account of a venerable Roman Catholic Padre will be interesting, because of the very different opinion he expressed to the sentiments of the Abbe Dubois, with whom he was well acquainted.

"About noon (*November 29th*) we arrived at Keelcheri, a village (between Wallajahbad and Tripsoor) inhabited chiefly by Teloogoo Roman Catholics: it is the residence also of a Romish Priest, Padre Austrey. My people stopped at his house, and he came out to welcome me; his appearance was venerable, for